Lecture Notes in Computer Science 8011

Commenced Publication in 1973
Founding and Former Series Editors:
Gerhard Goos, Juris Hartmanis, and Jan van Leeuwen

Constantine Stephanidis
Margherita Antona (Eds.)

Universal Access in Human-Computer Interaction

Applications and Services
for Quality of Life

7th International Conference, UAHCI 2013
Held as Part of HCI International 2013
Las Vegas, NV, USA, July 21-26, 2013
Proceedings, Part III

 Springer

Volume Editors

Constantine Stephanidis
Foundation for Research and Technology - Hellas (FORTH)
Institute of Computer Science (ICS)
N. Plastira 100, Vassilika Vouton, 70013 Heraklion, Crete, Greece
and University of Crete, Department of Computer Science
Heraklion, Crete, Greece
E-mail: cs@ics.forth.gr

Margherita Antona
Foundation for Research and Technology - Hellas (FORTH)
Institute of Computer Science (ICS)
N. Plastira 100, Vassilika Vouton, 70013 Heraklion, Crete, Greece
E-mail: antona@ics.forth.gr

ISSN 0302-9743   e-ISSN 1611-3349
ISBN 978-3-642-39193-4   e-ISBN 978-3-642-39194-1
DOI 10.1007/978-3-642-39194-1
Springer Heidelberg Dordrecht London New York

Library of Congress Control Number: 2013941140

CR Subject Classification (1998): H.5, K.4, J.3, H.4, H.3

LNCS Sublibrary: SL 3 – Information Systems and Application, incl. Internet/Web
and HCI

Typesetting: Camera-ready by author, data conversion by Scientific Publishing Services, Chennai, India

Printed on acid-free paper

Springer is part of Springer Science+Business Media (www.springer.com)

Foreword

The 15th International Conference on Human–Computer Interaction, HCI International 2013, was held in Las Vegas, Nevada, USA, 21–26 July 2013, incorporating 12 conferences / thematic areas:

Thematic areas:

- Human–Computer Interaction
- Human Interface and the Management of Information

Affiliated conferences:

- 10th International Conference on Engineering Psychology and Cognitive Ergonomics
- 7th International Conference on Universal Access in Human–Computer Interaction
- 5th International Conference on Virtual, Augmented and Mixed Reality
- 5th International Conference on Cross-Cultural Design
- 5th International Conference on Online Communities and Social Computing
- 7th International Conference on Augmented Cognition
- 4th International Conference on Digital Human Modeling and Applications in Health, Safety, Ergonomics and Risk Management
- 2nd International Conference on Design, User Experience and Usability
- 1st International Conference on Distributed, Ambient and Pervasive Interactions
- 1st International Conference on Human Aspects of Information Security, Privacy and Trust

A total of 5210 individuals from academia, research institutes, industry and governmental agencies from 70 countries submitted contributions, and 1666 papers and 303 posters were included in the program. These papers address the latest research and development efforts and highlight the human aspects of design and use of computing systems. The papers accepted for presentation thoroughly cover the entire field of Human–Computer Interaction, addressing major advances in knowledge and effective use of computers in a variety of application areas.

This volume, edited by Constantine Stephanidis and Margherita Antona, contains papers focusing on the thematic area of Universal Access in Human–Computer Interaction, and addressing the following major topics:

- Universal Access to Smart Environments and Ambient Assisted Living
- Universal Access to Learning and Education
- Universal Access to Text, Books, eBooks and Digital Libraries
- Health, Well-Being, Rehabilitation and Medical Applications
- Access to Mobile Interaction

The remaining volumes of the HCI International 2013 proceedings are:

- Volume 1, LNCS 8004, Human–Computer Interaction: Human-Centred Design Approaches, Methods, Tools and Environments (Part I), edited by Masaaki Kurosu
- Volume 2, LNCS 8005, Human–Computer Interaction: Applications and Services (Part II), edited by Masaaki Kurosu
- Volume 3, LNCS 8006, Human–Computer Interaction: Users and Contexts of Use (Part III), edited by Masaaki Kurosu
- Volume 4, LNCS 8007, Human–Computer Interaction: Interaction Modalities and Techniques (Part IV), edited by Masaaki Kurosu
- Volume 5, LNCS 8008, Human–Computer Interaction: Towards Intelligent and Implicit Interaction (Part V), edited by Masaaki Kurosu
- Volume 6, LNCS 8009, Universal Access in Human–Computer Interaction: Design Methods, Tools and Interaction Techniques for eInclusion (Part I), edited by Constantine Stephanidis and Margherita Antona
- Volume 7, LNCS 8010, Universal Access in Human–Computer Interaction: User and Context Diversity (Part II), edited by Constantine Stephanidis and Margherita Antona
- Volume 9, LNCS 8012, Design, User Experience, and Usability: Design Philosophy, Methods and Tools (Part I), edited by Aaron Marcus
- Volume 10, LNCS 8013, Design, User Experience, and Usability: Health, Learning, Playing, Cultural, and Cross-Cultural User Experience (Part II), edited by Aaron Marcus
- Volume 11, LNCS 8014, Design, User Experience, and Usability: User Experience in Novel Technological Environments (Part III), edited by Aaron Marcus
- Volume 12, LNCS 8015, Design, User Experience, and Usability: Web, Mobile and Product Design (Part IV), edited by Aaron Marcus
- Volume 13, LNCS 8016, Human Interface and the Management of Information: Information and Interaction Design (Part I), edited by Sakae Yamamoto
- Volume 14, LNCS 8017, Human Interface and the Management of Information: Information and Interaction for Health, Safety, Mobility and Complex Environments (Part II), edited by Sakae Yamamoto
- Volume 15, LNCS 8018, Human Interface and the Management of Information: Information and Interaction for Learning, Culture, Collaboration and Business (Part III), edited by Sakae Yamamoto
- Volume 16, LNAI 8019, Engineering Psychology and Cognitive Ergonomics: Understanding Human Cognition (Part I), edited by Don Harris
- Volume 17, LNAI 8020, Engineering Psychology and Cognitive Ergonomics: Applications and Services (Part II), edited by Don Harris
- Volume 18, LNCS 8021, Virtual, Augmented and Mixed Reality: Designing and Developing Augmented and Virtual Environments (Part I), edited by Randall Shumaker
- Volume 19, LNCS 8022, Virtual, Augmented and Mixed Reality: Systems and Applications (Part II), edited by Randall Shumaker

I would like to thank the Program Chairs and the members of the Program Boards of all affiliated conferences and thematic areas, listed below, for their contribution to the highest scientific quality and the overall success of the HCI International 2013 conference.

This conference could not have been possible without the continuous support and advice of the Founding Chair and Conference Scientific Advisor, Prof. Gavriel Salvendy, as well as the dedicated work and outstanding efforts of the Communications Chair and Editor of HCI International News, Abbas Moallem.

I would also like to thank for their contribution towards the smooth organization of the HCI International 2013 Conference the members of the Human–Computer Interaction Laboratory of ICS-FORTH, and in particular George Paparoulis, Maria Pitsoulaki, Stavroula Ntoa, Maria Bouhli and George Kapnas.

May 2013

Constantine Stephanidis
General Chair, HCI International 2013

Organization

Human–Computer Interaction

Program Chair: Masaaki Kurosu, Japan

Jose Abdelnour-Nocera, UK
Sebastiano Bagnara, Italy
Simone Barbosa, Brazil
Tomas Berns, Sweden
Nigel Bevan, UK
Simone Borsci, UK
Apala Lahiri Chavan, India
Sherry Chen, Taiwan
Kevin Clark, USA
Torkil Clemmensen, Denmark
Xiaowen Fang, USA
Shin'ichi Fukuzumi, Japan
Vicki Hanson, UK
Ayako Hashizume, Japan
Anzai Hiroyuki, Italy
Sheue-Ling Hwang, Taiwan
Wonil Hwang, South Korea
Minna Isomursu, Finland
Yong Gu Ji, South Korea
Esther Jun, USA
Mitsuhiko Karashima, Japan

Kyungdoh Kim, South Korea
Heidi Krömker, Germany
Chen Ling, USA
Yan Liu, USA
Zhengjie Liu, P.R. China
Loïc Martínez Normand, Spain
Chang S. Nam, USA
Naoko Okuizumi, Japan
Noriko Osaka, Japan
Philippe Palanque, France
Hans Persson, Sweden
Ling Rothrock, USA
Naoki Sakakibara, Japan
Dominique Scapin, France
Guangfeng Song, USA
Sanjay Tripathi, India
Chui Yin Wong, Malaysia
Toshiki Yamaoka, Japan
Kazuhiko Yamazaki, Japan
Ryoji Yoshitake, Japan
Silvia Zimmermann, Switzerland

Human Interface and the Management of Information

Program Chair: Sakae Yamamoto, Japan

Hans-Jorg Bullinger, Germany
Alan Chan, Hong Kong
Gilsoo Cho, South Korea
Jon R. Gunderson, USA
Shin'ichi Fukuzumi, Japan
Michitaka Hirose, Japan
Jhilmil Jain, USA
Yasufumi Kume, Japan

Mark Lehto, USA
Hiroyuki Miki, Japan
Hirohiko Mori, Japan
Fiona Fui-Hoon Nah, USA
Shogo Nishida, Japan
Robert Proctor, USA
Youngho Rhee, South Korea
Katsunori Shimohara, Japan

Engineering Psychology and Cognitive Ergonomics

Program Chair: Don Harris, UK

Universal Access in Human–Computer Interaction

Program Chairs: Constantine Stephanidis, Greece, and Margherita Antona, Greece

Virtual, Augmented and Mixed Reality

Program Chair: Randall Shumaker, USA

Waymon Armstrong, USA
Juan Cendan, USA
Rudy Darken, USA
Cali M. Fidopiastis, USA
Charles Hughes, USA
David Kaber, USA
Hirokazu Kato, Japan
Denis Laurendeau, Canada
Fotis Liarokapis, UK

Mark Livingston, USA
Michael Macedonia, USA
Gordon Mair, UK
Jose San Martin, Spain
Jacquelyn Morie, USA
Albert "Skip" Rizzo, USA
Kay Stanney, USA
Christopher Stapleton, USA
Gregory Welch, USA

Cross-Cultural Design

Program Chair: P.L. Patrick Rau, P.R. China

Pilsung Choe, P.R. China
Henry Been-Lirn Duh, Singapore
Vanessa Evers, The Netherlands
Paul Fu, USA
Zhiyong Fu, P.R. China
Fu Guo, P.R. China
Sung H. Han, Korea
Toshikazu Kato, Japan
Dyi-Yih Michael Lin, Taiwan
Rungtai Lin, Taiwan

Sheau-Farn Max Liang, Taiwan
Liang Ma, P.R. China
Alexander Mädche, Germany
Katsuhiko Ogawa, Japan
Tom Plocher, USA
Kerstin Röse, Germany
Supriya Singh, Australia
Hsiu-Ping Yueh, Taiwan
Liang (Leon) Zeng, USA
Chen Zhao, USA

Online Communities and Social Computing

Program Chairs: A. Ant Ozok, USA, and Panayiotis Zaphiris, Cyprus

Areej Al-Wabil, Saudi Arabia
Leonelo Almeida, Brazil
Bjørn Andersen, Norway
Chee Siang Ang, UK
Aneesha Bakharia, Australia
Ania Bobrowicz, UK
Paul Cairns, UK
Farzin Deravi, UK
Andri Ioannou, Cyprus
Slava Kisilevich, Germany

Niki Lambropoulos, Greece
Effie Law, Switzerland
Soo Ling Lim, UK
Fernando Loizides, Cyprus
Gabriele Meiselwitz, USA
Anthony Norcio, USA
Elaine Raybourn, USA
Panote Siriaraya, UK
David Stuart, UK
June Wei, USA

Augmented Cognition

Program Chairs: Dylan D. Schmorrow, USA, and Cali M. Fidopiastis, USA

Robert Arrabito, Canada
Richard Backs, USA
Chris Berka, USA
Joseph Cohn, USA
Martha E. Crosby, USA
Julie Drexler, USA
Ivy Estabrooke, USA
Chris Forsythe, USA
Wai Tat Fu, USA
Rodolphe Gentili, USA
Marc Grootjen, The Netherlands
Jefferson Grubb, USA
Ming Hou, Canada

Santosh Mathan, USA
Rob Matthews, Australia
Dennis McBride, USA
Jeff Morrison, USA
Mark A. Neerincx, The Netherlands
Denise Nicholson, USA
Banu Onaral, USA
Lee Sciarini, USA
Kay Stanney, USA
Roy Stripling, USA
Rob Taylor, UK
Karl van Orden, USA

Digital Human Modeling and Applications in Health, Safety, Ergonomics and Risk Management

Program Chair: Vincent G. Duffy, USA and Russia

Karim Abdel-Malek, USA
Giuseppe Andreoni, Italy
Daniel Carruth, USA
Eliza Yingzi Du, USA
Enda Fallon, Ireland
Afzal Godil, USA
Ravindra Goonetilleke, Hong Kong
Bo Hoege, Germany
Waldemar Karwowski, USA
Zhizhong Li, P.R. China

Kang Li, USA
Tim Marler, USA
Michelle Robertson, USA
Matthias Rötting, Germany
Peter Vink, The Netherlands
Mao-Jiun Wang, Taiwan
Xuguang Wang, France
Jingzhou (James) Yang, USA
Xiugan Yuan, P.R. China
Gülcin Yücel Hoge, Germany

Design, User Experience, and Usability

Program Chair: Aaron Marcus, USA

Sisira Adikari, Australia
Ronald Baecker, Canada
Arne Berger, Germany
Jamie Blustein, Canada

Ana Boa-Ventura, USA
Jan Brejcha, Czech Republic
Lorenzo Cantoni, Switzerland
Maximilian Eibl, Germany

Anthony Faiola, USA
Emilie Gould, USA
Zelda Harrison, USA
Rüdiger Heimgärtner, Germany
Brigitte Herrmann, Germany
Steffen Hess, Germany
Kaleem Khan, Canada

Jennifer McGinn, USA
Francisco Rebelo, Portugal
Michael Renner, Switzerland
Kerem Rızvanoğlu, Turkey
Marcelo Soares, Brazil
Christian Sturm, Germany
Michele Visciola, Italy

Distributed, Ambient and Pervasive Interactions

Program Chairs: Norbert Streitz, Germany, and Constantine Stephanidis, Greece

Emile Aarts, The Netherlands
Adnan Abu-Dayya, Qatar
Juan Carlos Augusto, UK
Boris de Ruyter, The Netherlands
Anind Dey, USA
Dimitris Grammenos, Greece
Nuno M. Guimaraes, Portugal
Shin'ichi Konomi, Japan
Carsten Magerkurth, Switzerland

Christian Müller-Tomfelde, Australia
Fabio Paternó, Italy
Gilles Privat, France
Harald Reiterer, Germany
Carsten Röcker, Germany
Reiner Wichert, Germany
Woontack Woo, South Korea
Xenophon Zabulis, Greece

Human Aspects of Information Security, Privacy and Trust

Program Chairs: Louis Marinos, ENISA EU, and Ioannis Askoxylakis, Greece

Claudio Agostino Ardagna, Italy
Zinaida Benenson, Germany
Daniele Catteddu, Italy
Raoul Chiesa, Italy
Bryan Cline, USA
Sadie Creese, UK
Jorge Cuellar, Germany
Marc Dacier, USA
Dieter Gollmann, Germany
Kirstie Hawkey, Canada
Jaap-Henk Hoepman, The Netherlands
Cagatay Karabat, Turkey
Angelos Keromytis, USA
Ayako Komatsu, Japan

Ronald Leenes, The Netherlands
Javier Lopez, Spain
Steve Marsh, Canada
Gregorio Martinez, Spain
Emilio Mordini, Italy
Yuko Murayama, Japan
Masakatsu Nishigaki, Japan
Aljosa Pasic, Spain
Milan Petković, The Netherlands
Joachim Posegga, Germany
Jean-Jacques Quisquater, Belgium
Damien Sauveron, France
George Spanoudakis, UK
Kerry-Lynn Thomson, South Africa

Julien Touzeau, France
Theo Tryfonas, UK
João Vilela, Portugal

Claire Vishik, UK
Melanie Volkamer, Germany

External Reviewers

Maysoon Abulkhair, Saudi Arabia
Ilia Adami, Greece
Vishal Barot, UK
Stephan Böhm, Germany
Vassilis Charissis, UK
Francisco Cipolla-Ficarra, Spain
Maria De Marsico, Italy
Marc Fabri, UK
David Fonseca, Spain
Linda Harley, USA
Yasushi Ikei, Japan
Wei Ji, USA
Nouf Khashman, Canada
John Killilea, USA
Iosif Klironomos, Greece
Ute Klotz, Switzerland
Maria Korozi, Greece
Kentaro Kotani, Japan

Vassilis Kouroumalis, Greece
Stephanie Lackey, USA
Janelle LaMarche, USA
Asterios Leonidis, Greece
Nickolas Macchiarella, USA
George Margetis, Greece
Matthew Marraffino, USA
Joseph Mercado, USA
Claudia Mont'Alvão, Brazil
Yoichi Motomura, Japan
Karsten Nebe, Germany
Stavroula Ntoa, Greece
Martin Osen, Austria
Stephen Prior, UK
Farid Shirazi, Canada
Jan Stelovsky, USA
Sarah Swierenga, USA

HCI International 2014

The 16th International Conference on Human–Computer Interaction, HCI International 2014, will be held jointly with the affiliated conferences in the summer of 2014. It will cover a broad spectrum of themes related to Human–Computer Interaction, including theoretical issues, methods, tools, processes and case studies in HCI design, as well as novel interaction techniques, interfaces and applications. The proceedings will be published by Springer. More information about the topics, as well as the venue and dates of the conference, will be announced through the HCI International Conference series website: http://www.hci-international.org/

General Chair
Professor Constantine Stephanidis
University of Crete and ICS-FORTH
Heraklion, Crete, Greece
Email: cs@ics.forth.gr

Table of Contents – Part III

Universal Access to Smart Environments and Ambient Assisted Living

Universal Access to Learning and Education

Universal Access to Text, Books, eBooks and Digital Libraries

Health, Well-Being, Rehabilitation and Medical Applications

Access to Mobile Interaction

Part I

Universal Access to Smart Environments and Ambient Assisted Living

Design for Adapted Devices: An Evaluation Tool of Smart Things for Seniors

Javier Barcenilla[1], Charles Tijus[2], Djamel Aissaoui[1], and Eric Brangier[1]

[1] Université de Lorraine - Metz, PErSEUs, Ux Lab. Île du Saulcy, 57045 Metz, France
[2] CHArt-LUTIN, Cité des Sciences et de l'Industrie - 30 Avenue Corentin Cariou,
75019 Paris, France
{Javier.Barcenilla,Djamel.Aissaoui,
Eric.Brangier}@univ-lorraine.fr,
tijus@lutin-userlab.fr

Abstract. In addition to usual Information and Communication Technology (ICT) devices, things such as clothes and homes are becoming smart and can be used for specific aging needs. However, because there is a diversity of senior impairments, one must diagnose needs, expectations or skills of seniors in order to provide the best adapted functions and usages. This study is about how to choose the best care method for seniors by providing a diagnosis based on a tool called "Design for Adapted Devices" (DAD). DAD tries to develop adaptable systems based on the comprehensive diagnosis of human deficits and needs of future users, taking into account the aspects of the individual's activity. DAD takes into account several dimensions of user diversity like skills and abilities (motor, cognitive skills, etc.) and measures deficits that modulate users' performances (social support, experience, etc.). Applied to seniors, DAD gives prospective data to define future smart things.

Keywords: Universal design, senior needs, smart things, impairments diagnosis.

1 Introduction

As pointed by O'Connel [1], the range of issues that impact design for an aging population is broad-ranging. The scope of this paper includes the first phase of conception: knowing seniors as possible end-users, how to diagnose deficits, impairments, and needs, as well as abilities and skills, in order to establish the corresponding profiles that might help design the adapted ICT devices and services. "Design for Adapted Devices" (DAD) is a proposed method, which provides a set of possible ergonomic and technological solutions depending on needs and diagnosed deficits. "Seniors" includes active people, retired people, seniors with disabilities, seniors living alone or with their family, seniors living in a retirement home; all of them having specific abilities, capacities and needs.

The ICT industry has ignored in most cases requirements of groups like elderly or disabled people (usability of perceptual and motor skills, cognitive stimulation,

C. Stephanidis and M. Antona (Eds.): UAHCI/HCII 2013, Part III, LNCS 8011, pp. 3–11, 2013.
© Springer-Verlag Berlin Heidelberg 2013

cognitive remediation...). Reasons for this are diverse: economic issues, lack of knowledge about human center design, stereotypes concerning older people, and especially lack of information about the special needs of the elderly and disabled users [2].

In 2000, roughly 600 million citizens were over the age of 60. By 2050, that number will rise to over 2 billion. In addition to the growing proportion of seniors, there will be more and more devices and technology in demand to meet the needs of the elderly in terms of habitat management, ergonomics objects, use of services, etc. All of these devices will have to be properly adapted to the progressive decline of physical, perceptive, and cognitive capacities of aging people in order to be what we call "smart things for seniors."

Thus, the rapid development of ICT is a problem in terms of inability to access new devices for people with sensory or cognitive deficits, which is often the case with the elderly. As a primary solution, many ICT innovations, not specifically designed for the elderly, are marketed as such, with the further subsequent evaluation of how much they are appropriate to elderly: identifying usability difficulties in order to make recommendations for design in the future. This is, for instance, the method used by Vandi, Rico-Duarte, Thibault, Rougeaux, and Tijus [3] to provide design recommendations for interactive tablets intended for seniors.

Conversely, some researchers [4] have pointed out shortcomings and limits of the first (reactive) approach to conception for seniors and promote for more proactive approaches: "*it is important that the needs of the broadest possible end-users population are taken into account in the early design phases of new products and services*" (p. 2-7). Others authors advocates also on designing for people with specific needs: accessible design [5], assistive technology [6], barrier-free design [7] transgenerational design [8], universal design, etc. All of them agree to include people with physical or cognitive deficits in the first step of the design process, a method that can be applied within Living Labs for seniors [9]. A Living Lab is an open innovation laboratory where the users are placed in a context of technologies to imagine, develop and create innovative products and services that satisfy their capacities, expectations and needs. Living Labs are involved in the design of innovative systems where people, in our case seniors, are no longer simple users but become actors of the design process.

Given the importance of the first step in the proactive design process, taken into account users' needs, the purpose of this study is to present the "Design for Adapted Devices" method and its corresponding tool, for the diagnosis of deficits and needs of a particular category of users, allowing the choice of aid to provide and specify how devices and services must be adapted (fig. 1).

DAD is a software tool, the object of the tool is to facilitate and standardize procedures for deficit diagnosis of people with some kinds of disabilities. To do this, it proposes available psychometrics tools and an interview guide to refine the evaluation.

DAD was first developed to provide ergonomics solutions for users with different disabilities in work places, to permit them having a professional activity, and it is presently used to support the decision-making on the type of technologies that should equip Smart Homes for seniors. Inputs and outputs of DAD are provided in figure 1.

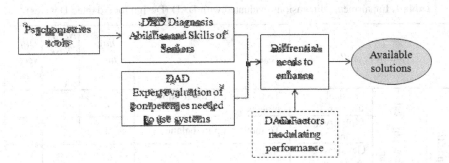

Fig. 1. Design for Adapted Devices method for evaluating deficits and needs of seniors and for providing adapted solutions

2   The Diagnosis of Deficits and Needs

The research on person-system interaction generally focuses on a single aspect of interaction (either sensory deficits, motor, or cognitive), without considering the cumulative and interactive effects of different deficits. In a prospective ergonomic approach, as that proposed by Robert and Brangier [10], DAD is to develop adaptable systems based on the comprehensive diagnosis of human deficits and needs of future users, taking into account the aspects of the individual's activity.

To proceed with DAD, several dimensions of user diversity were taken in account and more precisely those found in the literature [11], [12], keeping in mind that these dimensions could be specified in different ways (e.g., more precisely or more widely). Effects of some of these factors in using and adapting technology are well documented in literature [13], [14], although interpretation differs among researchers.

Seniors' deficits may be classified as disabilities when they are not modulated by skills and abilities (motor, cognitive skills, etc.). The DAD diagnosis grid is made of 10 dimensions. Six dimensions measure deficits, while four dimensions evaluate those factors that modulate performances (social support, experience, strategies, etc.). Each of these dimensions comprehends sub-dimensions for further specifications (Table 1 and Table 2).

While making a diagnosis of a person's abilities, "modulating factors" must be evaluated because they could influence in a positive or negative way a person's performance:

- Effects of medication on the ICT supported activity: drugs may play a role in the task realization. For instance, chronic treatments must be taken into account because they may have an important role in the activity (memory, attention, etc.),
- Interpersonal skills and social support: ability to be in relationship with others as a function of intrinsic qualities such as self-control, communication, social network, being in an environment facilitating social support and exchanges, etc.,
- Expertise and experience with ICT may facilitate adoption of proposed solutions,
- Interest for solutions proposed that might induce positive or negative attitude.

Table 1. Impairments dimensions evaluated with DAD (Design for Adapted Devices)

Abilities / skills			Tasks / Needs	Diagnos. Grade	Need / Task Grade	Diff. Needs Grade
Physical and sensory capacities	D1. Motor skills and physical resistance	Physical strength	To take, to lift and to move objects	2	4	- 2
		Mobility and balance	To move kipping balance	4	1	+3
		Gestures precision, Manual and digital dexterity	Adapting movements to goals	1	4	-3
		Fatigability / stamina	Having a steady performance with time and effort	2	1	+1
	D2. Perceptual abilities	Vision (close / distant)	Perceiving visual close and distant stimuli	2	3	- 1
		Hearing	Thresholds for perceiving auditory stimuli	5	3	+2
		Skin sensitivity	Perceiving tactile and thermic stimuli	3	3	0
Cognitive Capacities	D3. Memory and attention	Attention (selective / divided / steady)	Being able to focus on a task / to select relevant stimuli / to carry out several tasks	5	5	0
		Working memory	Retaining, recovering and processing information for a short period	5	5	0
		Long-term memory	Retaining, recovering and processing information for a long period (episodic / semantic / procedural)	5	5	0
	D4. Language	Oral comprehension	Ability to understand oral language	5	3	+2
		Written comprehension	Ability to understand written language	5	5	0
		Oral Expression	Ability to use words and grammar in oral conversations	5	3	+2
		Written Expression	Ability to use words and grammar to produce written discourse	5	3	+2
	D5. Temporo - spatial orientation	Temporal orientation	Ability to locate him (her) self in the course of time	5	1	+4
		Visuo-spatial orientation	Ability to analyze, represent and to locate him (her) self in the space	5	5	0

Table 1. (*continued*)

D6. Planning and problem solving	Reasoning	Ability to combine different sources of information in order to formulate rules and conclusions	4	5	-1
	Problem identification	Ability to identify that something is going wrong and find solution	5	3	-2
	Planning	Being able to anticipate and foresee actions and results	5	3	-2

Table 2. Performance modulating factors evaluated with DAD (Design for Adapted Devices)

Factors modulating activity	D7. Social / inter-personal skills	Environment and social support	Being in a environment facilitating social support and exchanges	5
		Extent of social network	Extent of social network and exchanges	4
	D8. Expertise and experience with ICT	Novice	Having reduced skills in using technical systems	5
		Intermediate	Having intermediate skills using technical systems	1
		Expert	Having excellent skills in using technical systems	1
	D9. Interest for ICT and acceptability	Support	Taking an interest in technical support	1
		Functionalities	Taking an interest in technical functionalities	3
		Goals	Taking an interest in goal system	5
	D10. Effects of medication on the ICT supported activity	Psycholeptics	Reduction of psychological activity (sedatives)	5
		Psychoanaleptics	Stimulating action on activity	5
		Psychodyslectics	Disrupting effects on activity	5

In addition, and to establish which deficit should be compensated or rehabilitated for seniors, experts with the system or with the technical domain are submitted to the same grid, in order to evaluate the skills required to use the ICT device or service. Each ability or skill is evaluated on a Likert scale from 1 to 5. Expert grade for each sub-dimension is the mean of all evaluations. The differential between a given person evaluation and the expert evaluation provides what is to make up.

To illustrate how to use DAD, let us to examine the case of Mrs. Jeanne Jones, a fictitious character described by the persona (Brangier and Bornet [20]) represented in figure 2.

This persona profile was derived from structured interviews carried out among different populations of seniors (retirement homes, pensioners' clubs, elderly people associations, etc.). The object of this complementary work was to obtain different profiles of seniors with specific needs in different contexts, and to confront our analysis grid to different cases in order to dress senior profiles in terms of disabilities to be compensated.

In this Persona profile, diagnosis (see table 1 and figure 2) shows two main deficits (manual and digital dexterity and close visual acuity) carried out by two main pathologies that many elderly people suffer from: polyarthritis and macula degeneration. However, as she was a literature professor and she adores reading and writing, she would like to continue these activities. She does not take medication; she is socially supported, but doesn't like technology. Even though, technology can most likely give her a better life... Facilitating access to writing, helping with orientation, and increasing perceptual abilities are activities that could be supported by adapted technology. In fact, differential analysis between deficits of Mrs. Jones and expert evaluation shows that e-books and programs for writing are not adapted for Mrs. Jones and that ICT technologies should provide ways to compensate her weaknesses (see tab. 1).

Jeanne Jones Widow, 2 children and 3 grandsons		Slogan: If you want something done right, do it yourself

	Personal informations:
Since few years ago Mrs. Jones suffers from a chronic polyarthritis. The advance of the pathology prevents her from making properly use of her hands. Furthermore, she has also a diagnostic of macular degeneration that has as a consequence a considerable weakening of her visual abilities. Nevertheless, Mrs. Jones makes it a point of honor to keep her autonomy! She lives along and has every day the visit of an auxiliary nurse as well as the visit of her children and her grandsons more	Job: Retired literature professor Location: Alsace Influences and values: - The simplicity of use - The respect of difference - The renaissance and classical literature - The technical assistance

| Scenario for use:
She wishes to get back to her passions, which are reading and writing, although her defects. | Objectives:
To provide a diagnosis and an adaptation for a system to allow Mrs. Jones to compensate the motor defects of her | Potential resistances and frustrations:
- Inaccessible places for persons with impairments |

Fig. 2. Persona profile of a senior used to take into account her needs

Data obtained from DAD can be presented also in a radar chart format, which permits to visualize directly the deficits to be compensated (see figure 3). In this graphic we can see the gap between the individual abilities and skills and the abilities and skills, as evaluated by experts, required to meet the need and to maintain the person's independence and activity. As we can see in this person's profile, cognitive skills as memory and attention are well preserved, although the person may have some difficulty in planning and problem solving. Similarly, we notice a decrease of some motor and perceptual abilities, which should be made up for the intended purpose.

Although the issues addressed here concern research in ICT devices and services, this tool may also be useful for other practitioners working with senior impairments (occupational therapists, physical therapists, public health nurses, psychologists, etc.) for envisioning solutions with respect to age or disability. On the other hand, many practitioners and researches in the ICT field (computer science, engineers, etc.) have not been made aware of issues related to disabilities, or have not been trained in the theory and practice of evaluating users with specific needs. This tool may help them improve their practical skills.

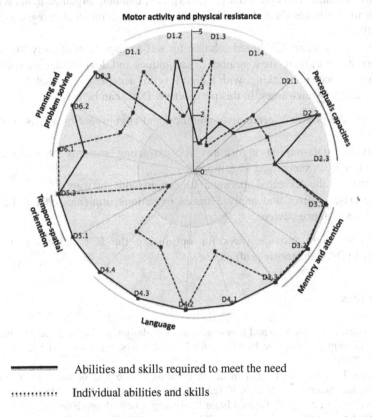

Abilities and skills required to meet the need

Individual abilities and skills

Fig. 3. Diagram showing the profile of impairments to be compensate resulting of the differential evaluation of needs and abilities required, as evaluated by experts

3   Providing Solutions

Providing solutions is figuring out how to adapt ICT technologies to the seniors' profiles. In terms of innovative solutions, since DAD was defining the users' requirement profile, a module configuration that you can enable / disable can optimize the adaptation of the interface of the ICT technology to each senior.

For example, Fitts's Law [15], which is associated with affordance principles [16], can be used to configure interactive tablet interface in a way that is adapted to the "visual perception - finger" loop for each senior. Fitts's Law predicts the time required to reach a target, according to the distance of the target and the size of the target. Based on data obtained from a senior (time taken to reach a target icon interface), Fitts's Law should help find the right size to give activated areas of the touch interface to optimize the senior's interaction with the tablet. To visually distinguish the target from its distractors in order to visually guide the senior's touch, the work of Treisman about how to make icons pops out [17], [18], [19] can help organize icons within the interface to maximize their discriminability based on contextual categorization that create affordance.

In Smart Homes, an ICT-based solution for self-management of daily life activities of seniors at home, there are a number of techniques and devices that are useful, easily interactive, decision-making, with a high level of acceptance, learnability, usability and satisfaction by end-users. In this perspective, DAD can be used

- to assess the physical, perceptive, attention and cognitive dimensions of their use by seniors;
- to develop data-mining algorithms for extracting patterns of human-devices interaction from supervised learning,
- to implement the dedicated apartment for seniors with software;
- to supervise, collect and analyze traces of actions implemented on the seniors in-home assistance devices.

All of these might provide ways for optimizing the ICT devices and services according to DAD diagnosis profiles.

References

1. O'Connel, T.A.: The why and how of senior-focus design. In: Lazar, J. (ed.) Universal Design: Designing Computer Interfaces for Diverse Users, pp. 43–92. Halsted Press, New York (2008)
2. Haddon, L., Paul, G.: Design in the ICT Industry: The role of users. In: Coombs, R., Green, K., Richards, A., Walsh, V. (eds.) Technology and the Market: Demand, Users and Innovation, pp. 201–215. Edward Elgar Publishing, Cheltenham (2001)
3. Vandi, C., Rico-Duarte, L., Thibault, T., Rougeaux, M., Tijus, C.: Seniors et Tablettes Interactives. Livre Blanc de la Délégation aux Usages de l'Internet (2011)
4. Emiliani, L.: Perspectives on accessibility: from assistive technologies to universal access and design for all. In: Stephanidis, C. (ed.) The Universal Access Handbook, ch. 2, CRC Press (2009)
5. Erlandson, M.F.: Universal and accessible design for products, services and processes. CRC Press, Boca Raton (2008)
6. Jacko, J.A., Leonard, V.K., Scott, I.U.: Perceptual impairments: New advancements promoting technological access. In: Sears, A., Jacko, J.A. (eds.) Human Computer Interaction: Designing for Diverse Users and Domains. Taylor & Francis, Basel (2009) .

7. Lazar, J.: Universal design: Designing computer interfaces for diverse users. Halsted Press, New York (2008)
8. Pirkl, J.J.: Transgenerational design: products for an aging population. Van Nostrand Reinhold, New York (1994)
9. Tijus, C., Barcenilla, J., Vandi, C.: Challenges and Ethical Issues in Living Labs for Open Innovation. In: Proceeding of the Challenges e-2012 Conference, Lisbon, Portugal (2012)
10. Robert, J.-M., Brangier, E.: Prospective Ergonomics: Origin, Goal, and Prospects. Work (Reading, Mass.) 41, 5235–5242 (2012)
11. Ashok, M., Jacko, J.: Dimensions of user diversity. In: Stephanidis, C. (ed.) The Universal Access Handbook, ch. 4, CRC Press (2009)
12. Lewis, C.: Cognitive disabilities. In: Stephanidis, C. (ed.) The Universal Access Handbook, ch. 7. CRC Press (2009)
13. Czaja, S.J., Charness, N., Fisk, A.D., Hertzog, C., Nair, S.N., Rogers, W.A., Sharit, J.: Factors predicting the use of technology: Findings from the center for research and education on aging and technology enhancement. Psychology and Aging 21(2), 333–352 (2006)
14. Hirsch, T., Forlizzi, J., Hyder, E., Goetz, J., Stroback, J., Kurtz, C.: The ELDer project: Social, emotional, and environmental factors in the design of eldercare technologies. In: Proceedings of the Conference on Universal Usability, pp. 72–79. ACM Press (2000)
15. Fitts, P.M.: The information capacity of the human motor system in controlling the amplitude of movement. Journal of Experimental Psychology 47(6), 381–391 (1954)
16. Gibson, J.J.: The ecological approach to visual perception. Lawrence Erlbaum Associates, Hillsdale (1986)
17. Treisman, A., Sato, S.: Conjunction search revisited. Journal of Experimental Psychology: Human Perception and Performance 16, 459–478 (1990)
18. Tijus, C.: Résoudre des tâches en contexte: l'affordance comme phénomène de pop out. In: Bastien, J.M.C. (ed.) Actes Des Deuxièmes Journées D'étude En Psychologie Ergonomique, EPIQUE 2003, Boulogne Billancourt, Octobre 2-3, pp. 295–302. INRIA, Rocquencourt (2003)
19. Léger, L., Tijus, C.: L'effet de l'hétérogénéité sémantique dans la détection de mots. Psychologie Française 52, 367–385 (2007)
20. Brangier, E., Bornet, C.: Persona: A method to produce representations focused on consumers' needs. In: Karwowski, W., Soares, M., Stanton, N. (eds.) Human Factors and Ergonomics in Consumer Product Design, pp. 38–61. Taylor and Francis (2011)

Shaping an Integrating Kitchen Space with Gesture-Based Control System

Agata Bonenberg

Faculty of Architecture, Poznan University of Technology,
Nieszawska 13 C, 60-021 Poznan, Poland
agata.bonenberg@put.poznan.pl

Abstract. This article provides a summary of research into the integrating kitchen design: a kitchen designed for simultaneous use by people with mobility problems, including wheelchair bound persons as well as able-bodied people. By introducing mobile gesture controlled modules into kitchen furniture it is possible to dynamically adjust furniture for use in seating or standing positions. An important aspect of research problem is such location of elements which would optimize the simultaneous use of kitchen by two persons: able-bodied and disabled.

Keywords: Integrating kitchen, gesture control system, accessibility, degree of integration, spatial conflict, disabilities.

1 Introduction

This article is devoted to issues related with the integrating kitchen design: a kitchen designed for a simultaneous use by people with mobility problems, including wheelchair bound persons as well as able-bodied people. Ability to dynamically adjust elements of kitchen furnishings to the requirements of all space users (able-bodied and disabled) is a condition which determines whether common activities and everyday interactions will be undertaken – behaviours that are crucial in post-traumatic therapy, therapy for people with disabilities, and prolonging the independence of the elderly. An important aspect of this problem is the ability to use an electric drive to support mobility of structure elements and gesture-based remote control for moving individual furniture modules. This results in a digitally expanded spatial environment which supports its user.

The article focuses on spatial and compositional solutions which result from the use of complex technologies, new functional requirements, and safety requirements within "mobile" environment. Other elements taken into consideration include important aspects related to culture and customs in spatial design, which are linked with social perception of disability. The topic was analysed as part of a project: "New lines of mobility support products and accessibility of the environment for the elderly and disabled people".

C. Stephanidis and M. Antona (Eds.): UAHCI/HCII 2013, Part III, LNCS 8011, pp. 12–21, 2013.
© Springer-Verlag Berlin Heidelberg 2013

2   Methodology

The methodology accepted for research purposes included a combination of design ideas, as well as conclusions and theoretical research carried out according to the *research by design* method, i.e. *practice-based research*. *Research by design* is a recognized method which makes it possible to draw conclusions and expand knowledge in disciplines related to creative activities: architecture, industry design and art [1]. The designs presented herein constitute a creative input in spatial problem solution and play a role of an occasional experiment.

Research analysis stages:

- Developing a research thesis
- Thesis verification in the form of design simulation of the integrating kitchen:
  -analysis of design proposals for various types of layout: single row of furniture, two rows, U- or L-shaped, and kitchens with an island.
  -analysis of design proposals for mobile furniture modules.
  -analysis of kitchen's visual quality and style.
- Comparison of data related to the area of the room, layout of furniture, obtained accessibility, and degree of residents' integration, degree of modularisation and visual quality according to the *research by design* methodology.
- Conclusions.

3   Theses

Research and simulation related to the problems of kitchen space architectural arrangement and kitchen furniture designs shall verify three main assumptions:

- The use of mobile elements supported by gesture control system in kitchen makes it easier to undertake common, simultaneous activities by able-bodied people and people with disabilities; therefore it increases integration of the users of the space.
- Appropriate arrangement of kitchen space helps to optimize the number of jobs and functions that can be carried out by at least two persons.
- The presence of fixed and mobile modules in the furniture affects furniture forms and it can bring it closer to the visual effect of world's leading kitchen designs.

4   Concept Verification in the Form of Design Solutions Analysis

4.1   Spatial Arrangement Requirement

Concepts related to the flexible and multi-functional modelling of the space have been repeatedly brought up by the author both in theory [2] and design realisations[1]. This experience constitutes a basis for reflections and experiments related to dynamic changes of the functions of the space by using mobile elements in interiors. Kitchen realizations have also become a place where behaviours and habits inspired by the particular spatial solution could be observed.

Examples developed by the author, which constitute a starting point of the integrating kitchen design feature:

- an effective use of the space
- combination of several functions in one space
- the use of fixed and mobile partitions optimizing functional zones in the flat
- the use of contemporary style in harmony with modern architectural trends

Spatial conflicts occur in every kitchen used by more than one person and in the case of designing a place that will be simultaneously used by able-bodied and disabled persons conflicts are also caused by:

- differences in abilities and physical condition
- restricted or impossible access to kitchen elements, blocked access for walking people and wheelchair users.
- significant diversification of the ergonomic adjustment of furniture for able-bodied people and people with disabilities.

The purpose of the integrating kitchen design is to reduce the two latter conflicts, the access-related one and the ergonomic adjustment of furniture.

4.2   Integrating Kitchen – The Use of Fixed and Mobile Modules

Flexible integrating kitchen space, where the most important elements used in the food preparation process can be simultaneously used by an abled-bodied person and a disabled one, comprises of fixed and mobile modules. Such solution benefits from lower electricity costs of actuators and their control [3]. It is important to situate individual modules in a way that facilitates simultaneous cooperation. Chapter 4.4 includes a comparison of mobile furniture modules designs, while Table 1. shows an example of an assessment of the accessibility of individual kitchen appliances.

---

[1] Author's design realisations: Interior design of a 110 m2 flat at ul. Modra in Poznań, design of a 40 m2   studio flat at ul Morawskiego in Poznań, design of an apartment at ul. Wielicka in Warsaw.

4.3   Design Simulations of Integrating Kitchen Solutions with Fixed and Mobile Modules, Types of Layout, and Legal Regulations

According to Polish technical and construction regulations [4] (as of 01.01.2012) the clear width of a kitchen in a multi-family building should equal at least 2.4 m in a flat and at least 1.8 m in a studio flat. These measurements determine the shape and type of kitchen arrangements and considerable restrictions when designing a kitchen for disabled people.

The arrangement of the integrating kitchen furniture in a studio flat with the minimum kitchen width is impossible in the case of closed rooms because after putting 60 cm-wide furniture there will be no room for the wheelchair to be turned around. However, a kitchenette opening into a hall can be used, which enables an arrangement of a kitchen with a single row of furniture. Also, extra lighting is not required for a studio flat, which worsens visual conditions in the case of a design prepared for an elderly person.

The minimum 2.4 m clear width of a kitchen in flats makes it possible to arrange an integrating kitchen with a single row of furniture or an L-shaped kitchen due to the fact that there must be room for a wheelchair to be turned around. Here, technical conditions also allow the kitchen to be joined with a living room. Based on the kitchen arrangement simulations it might be concluded that using an "open plan" and joining kitchen with the living room makes moving around the flat easier and provides more opportunities for verbal and visual communication.

The clear width of a kitchen that enables free arrangement using two rows of furniture, U- and L-shaped, must be 2.75 m. These layouts provide the greatest comfort when using a kitchen.

Design simulations of 10 kitchens were carried out for the purpose of the research, which illustrate:

- an arrangement of fixed and mobile modules,
- ability to ensure small distances between basic appliances (distance triangle: cooker, fridge, and sink)
-and make it possible to assess an accessibility of various functions by two people working simultaneously: an able-bodied person and a disabled one.

An example below shows one of the 10 simulations, and illustrates research principles. The arrangements were made based on real kitchens proposed by developers in single- and multi-family buildings in Poznan and Warsaw. Issues taken into consideration included various shape, kitchen areas, the location of gas connection and ventilation. In some cases kitchen was arranged in several ways. Diagram (Table 1.) prepared for each solution shows potential spatial conflicts in a sample kitchen with an assumption that it will be used by two persons: one with a disability and one able-bodied. The designs include an open-plan kitchen with a single row of furniture, a closed kitchen with a single row of furniture, a closed kitchen with two rows of furniture, an open-plan L-shaped kitchen, an L-shaped kitchenette, a closed L-shaped kitchen, a U-shaped kitchenette, a closed U-shaped kitchen, two kitchens with islands.

Symbol "N" indicates which actions cannot be simultaneously performed in the kitchen, "T" indicates ability to safely perform two actions, and "O" indicates small restrictions in activities.

Table 1. An example of the simulation of accessibility of six main functions in the integrating kitchen

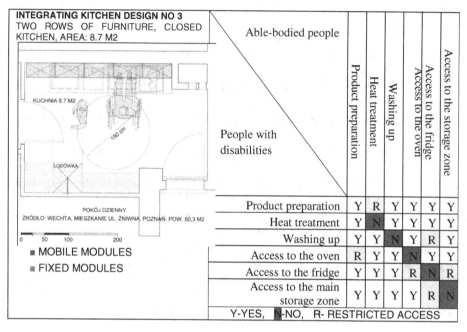

INTEGRATING KITCHEN DESIGN NO 3 TWO ROWS OF FURNITURE, CLOSED KITCHEN, AREA: 8.7 M2 / Able-bodied people / People with disabilities	Product preparation	Heat treatment	Washing up	Access to the oven	Access to the fridge	Access to the storage zone
Product preparation	Y	R	Y	Y	Y	Y
Heat treatment	Y	N	Y	Y	Y	Y
Washing up	Y	Y	N	Y	R	Y
Access to the oven	R	Y	Y	N	Y	Y
Access to the fridge	Y	Y	Y	R	N	R
Access to the main storage zone	Y	Y	Y	Y	R	N
Y-YES, N-NO, R- RESTRICTED ACCESS						

(Floorplan labels: KUCHNIA 8.7 M2; 150 cm; LODÓWKA; POKÓJ DZIENNY; ŹRÓDŁO: WECHTA, MIESZKANIE UL. ŻNIWNA, POZNAŃ. POW. 50,3 M2; 0 50 100 200; ■ MOBILE MODULES; ■ FIXED MODULES)

Based on an analogical analysis of 10 examples it can be concluded that:

- the largest amount of spatial conflicts occurs in L- and U-shaped kitchens and the smallest amount in kitchens with a single row or two rows of furniture.
- when it comes to ensuring shortest distances between basic kitchen appliances (the fridge, sink, and cooker triangle), U-and L-shaped kitchens come first. However, the scopes referred to in literature have been modified: distance from the fridge to the sink measures usually between 120 and 210 cm for normal kitchen, and in the integrating kitchen it should measure between 152 and 210 cm, distance from the sink to the cooker between 120 and 210 for normal kitchen, and in the integrating kitchen between 152 and 210, distance from the fridge to the cooker between 120 and 270 cm, and between 152 and 270 cm for the integrating kitchen.

To sum up, kitchens with two rows of furniture turned out to be the most useful for two reasons. They cause the lowest amount of spatial conflicts resulting from the simultaneous use by two people: a wheelchair bound disabled person and an abled-bodied one. At the same time, the distances between basic kitchen appliances (the fridge, sink, and cooker triangle) remain small.

4.4 Solutions Used When Designing Mobile Modules of the Integrating Kitchen

A collection of kitchen furniture was created for the purpose of the integrating kitchen. Mobile modules designs feature kitchens that are comfortable to use both for wheelchair bound and able-bodied people.

4.4.1 A Set of Mobile Worktops

Worktops in integrating kitchen move upwards and can be regulated vertically by up to 20 cm. Individual modules can be moved independently which enables one person to work at a lowered module (person with disability) and the other at a raised worktop. Worktop position can be changed while working. Concave worktops facilitate drainage in one direction and prevent dripping to the sides.

Mobile worktops can contain an electric cooker or sink. The sink and cooker modules have been fitted with a top covering panel, which increases usable area of a given module. The worktop control mechanism can be moved manually; optionally, it can be powered electrically.

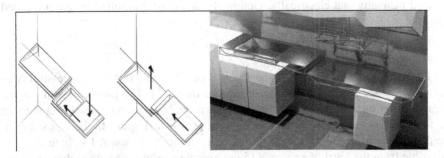

Fig. 1. Mobile kitchen worktops. Rendering by A. Bonenberg.

4.4.2 Mobile Lower Cabinets

Two sets of double drawers have been placed under the worktop level, and they move horizontally on a double rail fixed to the wall. By sliding the drawers apart it is possible to push the wheelchair under the worktop. While moving them together makes the kitchen look similar to the ones designed for able-bodied persons. Apart from two drawers (deep at the bottom and shallow on the top) each module is fitted with an additional pull-out worktop.

4.4.3 Upper Cabinets with a Pull-Out Internal Basket

The upper cabinets can be opened from a standing position - one of the front planes can be tilted, it can also be used from a seating position thanks to a drop openwork basket. The upper cabinet fronts have been designed as asymmetric, flat pyramids. The division into planes camouflages brackets of the openwork pull-down shelves.

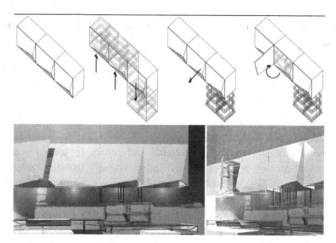

Fig. 2. Upper kitchen cabinets. Rendering by A. Bonenberg.

The capacity of one pull-down module is approx. 30 kg. Cabinet mechanism can be operated manually and electrically. Optionally, it can be controlled by gesture-based system.

4.4.4   Kitchen Cabinet

In a kitchen a major problem for wheel-bound people is the restricted accessibility to the storage space located in the upper parts of the room. The proposed solution enables all upper modules to be slid down to a comfortable position in the lower parts of the furniture in accordance with the diagram shown in Figure 2. It is possible to simultaneously use the furniture in sitting or standing positions. All storage space is accessible from the level of approx. 115 cm, mobile module capacity includes: 40 kg. Cubic volume of the cabinet is 1.25 m3 and useable capacity is 1.04 m3. It can be electrically powered.

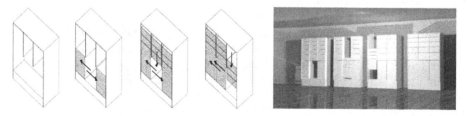

Fig. 3. Cabinet operation diagram. Rendering by A. Bonenberg.

4.4.5   Cabinet for Household Appliances with a Turn-Around Top

The problem related to the limited accessibility of upper storage space can also be solved by fitting a top above a piece of furniture that can be accessed by a wheelchair bound person. The idea of the top is for its body to revolve around an axle fitted to the wall. It can be turned by 90 °. After placing it at a right angle to the wall an openwork basket for crockery and products storage can be pulled down. The advantage of the top is that household appliances that cannot be moved can be placed in the lower piece of furniture: a cooker, microwave oven, under-counter fridge, and dishwasher. Two such appliances can be fitted into the cabinet. The maximum pull-out module capacity is: 25 kg, cabinet cubic volume: 1.7 m3, and it can be electrically powered.

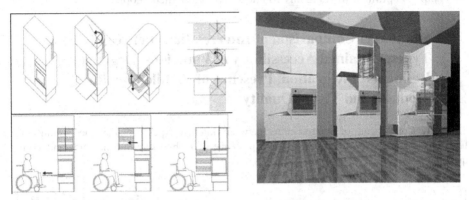

Fig. 4. The rotary top cross-section; lower cabinet contains an oven. Rendering by A. Bonenberg.

4.5 Visual and Compositional Qualities, and Style of Furniture Based on an Example of the *Integrating Kitchen* by a bonenberg

Research indicates that cultural aspect is very important when it comes to preferences related to the composition of a kitchen for disabled people [5]. Although the style and colours of kitchen furniture depend on individual preferences of a customer, when designing furniture for disabled people one basic preference can be observed: minimizing obvious compositional differences between kitchens designed for able-bodied and disabled people. Thus, either traditional or contemporary styles can be applied, but it is important to minimize the visibility of features which indicate that the space is used by disabled people. A particularly visible characteristic of a kitchen designed for disabled people is void space under the worktop which enables the wheelchair to be moved freely. In the *integrating kitchen* the "void space effect" is reduced to the minimum due to the use of under-counter mobile cabinets which can be moved horizontally. And although this solution creates a gap that enables a person to work at the worktop, this gap is significantly smaller than in other known solutions.

In the *integrating kitchen* design the author followed contemporary trends in architecture and interior design. A priority was to build kitchen furniture in a style that can be successfully used in closed rooms and as an addition to the living room decor (an open-plan kitchen) which results from the research presented in chapter 4.3. Characteristic forms of facets proposed in the design are on the one hand present in the mainstream structural solutions of contemporary architecture, and on the other hand they are used here to cover and camouflage functions typical for solutions designed for disabled people. Systems used to open cabinets, and brackets which enable worktops to be moved are treated as an ornament of the front part of the worktop.

The appearance of kitchen furniture is also important when selling a property and it can have an impact on the transaction - typical kitchens designed only for people with disabilities are seen by a new buyer as having little use. It must be emphasised that the integrating kitchen can be used in many different ways. The group of users can include people who want to perfectly adjust worktop height to their own height, so it also helps to optimize working environment for able-bodied people.

5   Summary: Comparison of Interrelations between Kitchen Types, Obtained Accessibility of Functions, Degree of Residents' Integration, Presence of Mobile Furniture Modules and Visual Quality

Table 1. Comparison of interrelations between kitchen types, obtained accessibility of functions, degree of residents' integration, presence of mobile furniture modules and visual quality

	Kitchen type	Vicinity and accessibility of three main functions[2]	Degree of residents' integration	Presence of mobile modules in the furniture	Compositional consistency[3]
1.	Kitchen with a single row of furniture, open-plan, 8.7 m2	1	80%	80%	5
2.	Kitchen with a single row of furniture, closed, 6.7 m2	1	80%	80%	5
3.	Kitchen with two rows of furniture, closed, 8.7 m2	3	86%	60%	4
4.	Kitchen with two rows of furniture, closed	3	86%	60%	5
5.	L-shaped, open-plan kitchen, 8.7 m2	4	73%	66%	4
6.	L-shaped kitchenette, 7.9 m2	5	75%	75%	4
7.	U-shaped kitchen, open-plan	4	70%	61%	3
8.	U-shaped kitchen, closed	5	73%	54%	3
9.	Kitchen with an island	5	72%	62%	5
10	Kitchen with an island	4	78%	64%	5

Based on the analysed kitchen designs and the above comparison it is clear that the presence of mobile modules makes simultaneous work possible which enhances residents' integration. Accessibility of individual functions depends mainly on the layout of the kitchen; compositional consistency seems to be unrelated to the above factors.

---

[2] In order to assess vicinity and accessibility of three main functions, the distances between basic appliances (triangle: cooker, fridge, and sink) has bee taken under consideration.

[3] Evaluation based on 3D model simulations expert assessment.

6   Conclusions

Based on the prepared arrangements of responsive spaces in ten integrating kitchens and the presented five furniture solutions with gesture control system, it can be concluded that:

- Positive assessment of the degree of residents' integration depends on the useable area of the kitchen and type of layout. Layout helps to optimise the amount of work and functions that can be carried out in there.
- From the perspective of collision-free functioning, kitchens with two rows of furniture turned out to be most useful. The L- and U-shaped layouts are useful only if kitchen area exceeds 9 m2. The use of mobile elements supported by gesture control system in kitchen makes it easier and quicker to undertake common, simultaneous activities by able-bodied people and people with disabilities; therefore it increases integration of the users of the space.
- Visual and compositional qualities and style of the furniture are important assets of the *integrating kitchen* design which takes into consideration the cultural aspect related to disability. Furniture forms are close to the visual effect of world's leading kitchen designs.

References

1. Büchler, D., Biggs, M., Perrone, R.: Academic Research in areas of Design Practice w International Conference on Design Research, Brasil, Rio de Janeiro (2010),
   http://www.academia.edu/948665/
   Academic_Research_in_areas_of_Design_Practice
2. Bonenberg, A.: Media, Przestrzeń, Architektura, Transformacje przestrzeni społeczeństwa informacyjnego, Wyd. Wydział Architektury Politechniki Poznańskiej, Poznań (2013)
3. Branowski, B., Rychlik, M., Sydor, M., Zabłocki, M.: 3D graphic database containing ergonomics data used when assessing virtual designs /kitchen adaptations for disabled people, "Wicnik" National University of Leopolis Polytechnic. Printing House of Leopolis Polytechnic (2011)
4. Wąchocki, R.: Przepisy Techniczno-budowlane dla budynków, ujednolicone teksty rozporządzeń, Polcen, Warszawa, p. 52, s.93 and 94 (2012)
5. Ko, Y., Kudo, T.: Development of Kitchen Models for Wheelchair Users – Focused on the Development and Evaluation of a System Kitchen Model Chich Reflects Conditions of Korea and Universal Design Concepts,
   http://www.idemployee.id.tue.nl/g.w.m.rauterberg/
   conferences/cd_donotopen/adc/final_paper/031.pdf (access February 10, 2013)

Universal Access: A Concept to Be Adapted to Technological Development and Societal Change

Laura Burzagli and Pier Luigi Emiliani

National Research Council of Italy, Institute of Applied Physics, Florence, Italy
{l.burzagli,p.l.emiliani}@ifac.cnr.it

Abstract. Society is undergoing a transition toward an information society, due to the very fast development of ICT technology. This transition is creating a new complex social environment that requires new ways of looking at universal accessibility and methodologies to guarantee it. After an analysis of the present situation and possible developments, the main conclusion of the paper is that not only the information society (equipment and services) must be designed for all, but also that it must be designed by all. This means that users must be integrated not only in the phase of requirement analysis, but as actors in designing and implementing solutions.

Keywords: Universal design, Design for All, Ambient intelligence.

1 Introduction

Universal access implies the accessibility and usability of information and communication technologies by anyone, at any place and at any time, regardless of social class, ethnicity, background or lack of physical, sensory, cognitive abilities. Universal access aims to enable equitable access and active participation of potentially all people in existing and emerging ICT mediated human activities, by developing universally accessible and usable equipment and services. These equipment and services must be capable of accommodating individual user requirements in different contexts of use, independent of location, target machine and run time environment [1] [2].

This paper aims to show how the application of this general principle is changing in accordance with the development of technology and its impact on users.

Therefore, a short outline of the main technological developments is offered, with some general comments about their impact on society.

Then, the complexity of the new emerging situation is outlined, which requires changes in the way the problem of accessibility has been tackled so far.

Finally, it is maintained that the situation requires non only that the information society must be designed for all, but that it must also be designed by all, meaning that users must be introduced not only in the phase of requirement analysis but also in the design and implementation of possible accessible solutions.

C. Stephanidis and M. Antona (Eds.): UAHCI/HCII 2013, Part III, LNCS 8011, pp. 22–29, 2013.
© Springer-Verlag Berlin Heidelberg 2013

2   Ongoing Developments

Society is undergoing a transition toward an information society. This is caused by many different factors, two of which are considered here for their direct impact on universal access: (i) the very fast development of information and telecommunication technology itself and (ii) the new approaches to its use for producing equipment and applications, which have impact on the way people carry out activities related to access to information and interpersonal communication. A correct analysis of the changing living environment cannot be limited to the description of new protocols of access to information and communication and new applications, but must also include the impact of technology in people's daily life. On different levels, this impact concerns every citizen, regardless age, economic condition, or geographic location.

2.1   Technological Developments

From a basic technology perspective, the available computational power is ever increasing while the size, power consumption and cost of the corresponding components are decreasing, with a corresponding impact on many equipment of general use, as, for example, cell phones, which incorporate additional intelligence and offer new advanced functionalities. Nanotechnology is also developing very fast, with foreseen impact e.g. in the sector of sensors, which will become not only wearable but also implantable and able to navigate through the human body. Finally, computing power is being made available in the network.

From an interaction perspective, wherever a person is, she is supposed to be able to use whatever display is convenient, for example on a wall using a projector that project keyboards, displays and control panels on it, to access any information, carry out computing activities, view movies, listen to music, communicate etc. Alternatively, it is possible to project an image, which floats in space in front of a person and is seen only by the person using glasses or goggle-based systems. It is also possible to project the image directly onto the retina. A gesture recognition system can be used to operate the controls that float along the display. Voice technology is developing hands-free operation and voice control. The cost to build speech output into products has reduced to the point where speech can be provided on almost anything. External electrodes in the form of a band or cap are available as commercial products for elementary control of equipment directly by the brain.

From the network perspective, the World Wide Web, originally used as a document repository, is rapidly transforming (Web 2.0) into a fully-fledged virtual collaborative environment, facilitating media services, interaction and communication. The future network is seen as a space where services are made available and can also be implemented and/or modified by end users. Moreover, Internet it is developing toward an Internet of Things, where everyday objects, rooms, and machines are connected to one another and to the wider digital world.

However, the integrated use of the above technology is creating a more general evolution and the society is in transition toward an information society, caused by its reorganisation as an interconnected intelligent environment (Ambient Intelligence – AMI [3]).

From a conceptual perspective, there is a change from a model based on products (computers, terminals) and activities (tasks) to be carried out through them to a model in which functionalities are made available to people, irrespective of their real technical implementation, by intelligent objects available in the environment. From the perspective of users, including users with activity limitations, there is a fundamental change from an approach based on adaptations of products to be accessible in order to give the possibility of carrying out necessary activities, to a situation where emphasis is placed on the goals of people that the environment should be able to infer and support with functionalities adapted to the capability of any single user.

Following the originators of the AmI vision [4], Ambient Intelligence is defined according to its properties. Technology is supposed to be: (i) Embedded in the physical and social environment of people; (ii) Context Aware - employing machine perception, a model of activities of people and their social and physical context can be obtained; (iii) Personalized - addressing each user as an individual person; (iv) Adaptive to context and activities of the person; (v) Anticipatory - predicting user's needs and taking action to support them.

It is clear that some concepts and methodologies used so far in the field of accessibility (for example, personalisation and adaptivity) are supposed to become integrated in the very fabric of the emerging technological environment.

2.2   Changes in the Use of Technology

Even if society is far from a complete implementation of the Ambient Intelligence paradigm, ICT is becoming more and more pervasive and is changing the life of people, at work, at home and during leisure time. For example, many home appliances and cars have often processors on board and people are increasingly supported by or have to cope with the intelligent components that offer them functionalities.

This starts to have some visible consequences. For example, people are becoming less interested in accurate knowledge of devices (hardware) and the way they are controlled (software), but more interested in the functions provided by them. The main question is not: how is an equipment implemented, but how can I use its functionalities. For example, with a mobile phone, people starts to be more interested in how to send an SMS than in the hardware and software characteristics of the specific equipment.

This in turn has an impact on how people interact and use the technology. Different relationships between users and technology are emerging. For example, it is becoming common that people, before starting the engine of their car, get information about the state of the system and its previous patterns of usage on the screen of the onboard computer. A cooperation is established in order to take care of the car maintenance and data about the usage are made available, as the amount of gasoline used for a particular trip. During the travel, the car can offer advices on how to drive in order to reduce consumption or to adapt to the road characteristics.

Another interesting aspect is related to access to information. In the past, this was possible only in specific places, such as at home or at work. Now, people start to give for granted that they can browse the World Wide Web in any place and at any time, even if with different devices or terminals. This has an important impact on how information is collected, organised and presented (for example, in a way that is adapted to the size of the available display).

3   Complexity of the Emerging Situation

If one would like to characterise the new emerging situation with a single words, this could be: complexity.

Starting from the most important perspective, i.e. the user, so far information technology and telecommunications (apart from plain telephony and television) was a business for specialists. Even if some of them had difficulties in using available equipment and applications due to the lack of necessary abilities, they were part of the literate part of the society and ready to learn alternative ways of using the technology. Now, users are all citizens and difficulties can be expected not only due to lack of physical, sensory, cognitive abilities, but also from the fact of being part of a specific social class, ethnicity, educational background. The number of ICT users is increasing and, correspondingly, also the number of people who may need support for accessibility.

Another element of complexity is connected to the differences of age. Young people, the so-called digital natives, consider the interaction with digital devices as natural and are eager to get and test new equipment and interactions. At the moment, the market is essentially addressing this user group. Adults have often followed the technology evolution. They have been educated to take into account the design and the characteristics of the technology, i.e. what it could do rather than the available functions. Many of them are not interested in most of the available functionalities. Finally, elderly people often realize that some new technology can give them important services in term of safety, health and leisure (such as mobile device), but address their interest to a limited set of functions and for each of them to a limited and well defined number of usage steps.

From a technological perspective, so far reference could be made to a Personal Computer with a keyboard, a monitor, a microphone and loudspeaker as a standard configuration. Now different devices are available: Personal Computers in the offices or at home, but also laptops, tablets, and smart phones. Then, environmental control systems are also becoming available. All these equipment have different characteristics (e.g. dimensions of screen) and software configurations (e.g. the operating system).

Finally, the variety of available equipment and functionalities made available by them has also an important impact from the interaction perspective. Interaction with ICT applications is no more limited to the manipulation of objects in windows on a screen with a pointer and the input of text. New forms of interaction are emerging, as voice interaction, gesture recognition, and tactile interaction. Even if from a perspective this can be considered positive for universal access, because different modalities of interaction can be accommodated, however it is also introducing additional complexity in the ICT environment.

In addition to new technological opportunities and, sometimes, novel inclusion problems, the ongoing transition toward an information society is creating interesting conceptual changes. From a situation in which the emphasis was in the access to information and point-to-point interpersonal communication, now it is necessary to guarantee people the possibility of taking part in a knowledge process, in which information is produced in cooperative activities and communication is inside groups of cooperating participants [5]. This in turn increases the number and therefore the different characteristics of people in the different user communities. While accessibility has been traditionally a concern of people with activity limitations, now all the citizens must be considered among people who can potentially need support for accessibility. Therefore, forms of presentation of information and necessary interactions need to evolve toward an, in principle, unlimited number of configurations, with continuous adaptations to match the characteristics of user changing, for example, for modifications in the context of use.

Finally, applications are no more limited to specific usage contexts (as work, home, leisure) in specific places, but most of them are supposed to migrate across different usage contexts and/or spaces (work, home, public spaces). This may create problems not only from the perspective of availability of necessary resources (e.g. network connection and bandwidth) everywhere and suitable interactions in different contexts of use, but have an impact on more general levels, as privacy, security and trust.

Obviously, the above short description is far for complete, but it is sufficient to give an idea of the new opportunities offered by the developments in ICT and of the complexity of the situation that could emerge. Many experts, for example the members of the ISTAG panel, think that the technology under development has the potentiality to hide this complexity from the user, as clearly expressed in the specifications of the AmI environment above reported. One of the purpose of activity in universal accessibility is to help in guaranteeing that this will really happen.

4   From Design for All to Design for and by All

As previously stated, universal access implies customisation of equipment, their interfaces and services and applications to the abilities of potential users. Even if the principle of universal design is unique, different approaches can be adopted to apply it.

Traditionally, this customisation has been obtained with the use of assistive technology, i.e. technology to be connected to a system designed for the "average" user addressing the requirements of specific groups of users (for example, a Braille display or a voice synthesizer for people who are not able to see the screen or a mouse emulator for people who do not have enough motor control to use a mouse). More recently, the concept of design for all has been developed. The idea in the paper is that design for all must be generalised to take into account the emerging situation [6].

4.1   Design for All

When the number and rate of development of new systems and applications started to increase, adaptation of products on an ad hoc basis became less viable and new approaches to guarantee universal accessibility were looked for.

One of them is the so called Universal design (or Design for All in Europe), whose generally accepted definition is "The design of products and environments to be usable by all people, to the greatest extent possible, without the need for adaptation or specialized design" (http://www.trace.wisc.edu). Recently a detailed discussion of this approach was carried out in the framework of the European project "Design for all @ eInclusion", whose results are reported in [7].

A valid implementation methodology for Design for All is based on the concept of automatic adaptation (adaptability at run time according to the user profile and real time adaptivity to the current activities of the user). A demonstration of the viability of this technical approach, whose results are reported in [8], were developed in the framework of several EU funded projects, even if some results appears now limited by the level of available technology.

4.2   Generalisation of the Design for All Approach

The need of a generalization of the design for all approach and its implementation methodologies is essentially caused by two concurring circumstances: (1) the technological development; (2) the way technology is used.

Design for all is based on customisation. Since the initial phases of development, the artefacts are designed in order to produce automatically different features and interactions according to the user profile (adaptability) and the utilisation (adaptivity). Even if this process has already given important and useful results, the need of generalisation is due to the fact that the concept of artefact itself (e.g. a telecommunication application) tends to become blurred. Features and functionalities of applications tend to vary in order to meet the varying activities of people and the ways to carry out them. Moreover, the modifications tend to be decided by the users themselves and often are implemented by them as part of a user community. Therefore, with the proliferation of modified applications and ways of using them, it become very complex to satisfy all request at design time or to be able to introduce a sufficiently flexible adaptivity. The abilities of people are no more the only design data to take into account, but it is necessary to consider that the way of using the system and application may vary because in time people change their behaviour patterns.

The situation is becoming more complex and potentially interesting, if the social aspect of present developments are considered. Up to now, the focus was put on the accessibility as such, i.e. on the possibility of accessing information or point-to-point interpersonal communication through a suitable interface. Now, the very concept of accessibility is changing, because the goal of people's activities with a processing or communication device is also changing. Becoming members of a knowledge society, people are not only interested in receiving information and communicating, but also in giving a personal contribution to the common knowledge. The problem is no more to grant a person access to an equipment to look for information or to communicate, but to empower a community who deals with different problems and tries to achieve a solution cooperatively. Therefore, a modification of universal accessibility from static concept to a dynamic process is necessary. Accessibility means being able to carry out the tasks, developing in time, necessary to be part of the knowledge society.

Therefore, in addition to guarantee adaptability and adaptivity of equipment and applications to the user characteristics, it is necessary to make available a direct link with the intelligence embedded in them, through which the single user can consciously modify the features of the application or its interface. This is in accord with the emerging paradigm whereby users themselves become actors in producing, even cooperatively, information and applications. The crowdsourcing concept, defined by Wikipedia as "the practice of obtaining needed services, ideas, or content by soliciting contributions from a large group of people, and especially from an online community, rather than from traditional employees or suppliers", becomes important. People are no more considered active only in accessing information and communicating, but also in the production of information and in the implementation of solutions of interest for the society.

Therefore, end users must be introduced in the design for all procedure so that products can be designed in order to cope with available knowledge about user requirements and behaviour through automatic adaptability and adaptivity, but also open to modification by users themselves (design for and by all).

Moreover, if a social dimension is considered as included in the universal accessibility concept, some of the problems of people in accessing information and communication can be solved with the help of other people instead of by technological adaptations. A social network can represent a different option to solve some user's problems in being part of the knowledge society, not due to a perfect design of the artefacts in it, but to the cooperation with other users. In this scenario, a community is made aware of the problems of one of the members and a solution may arise from the support by other members [9].

5   Conclusions

Universal accessibility is a very important concept and it must be pursued in order to implement an information society that does not run the risk of discriminating a (large) part of the population. Methodologies for the implementation of ICT products (equipment and applications) must change to cope with the change of behaviour of users.

The main idea presented in the paper is that universal access is not a static concept, but a dynamic process that must adapt to changes in technology and the way people use it.

This implies the need of involving users not only during the phase of requirement elicitation, but also in the design and development of possible solutions of accessibility problems.

References

1. Emiliani, P.L., Stephanidis, C.: Universal access to ambient intelligence environments: opportunities and challenges for people with disabilities. IBM Systems Journal 44(3), 605–619 (2005)
2. Stephanidis, C. (ed.): The Universal Access Handbook. CRC Press - Taylor and Francis Group (2009)
3. Information Society Technology Advisory Group (ISTAG): Ambient Intelligence: from vision to reality. Information Society Technologies Programme of the European Union Commission (IST) (2003),
   ftp://ftp.cordis.europa.eu/pub/ist/docs/
   istag-ist2003_consolidated_report.pdf
4. Aarts, E., Marzano, S.: The New Everyday views on Ambient Intelligence. OIO Publishers, Rotterdam (2003)
5. Project WeKnowIt: D9.4.2 - Final white paper on Collective Intelligence (2011),
   http://www.weknowit.eu/sites/default/files/D9.4.2.pdf
6. Emiliani, P.L.: Perspectives in Accessibility: From Assistive Technology to Universal Access and Design for All. In: Stephanidis, C. (ed.) The Universal Access Handbook, pp. 2.1–2.18. CRC Press - Taylor and Francis Group (2009)
7. Emiliani, P.L, Burzagli, L., Billi, M., Gabbanini, F., Palchetti, E.: D2.1 - Report on the impact of technological developments on eAccessibility. DfA@eInclusion Project (2008),
   http://www.dfaei.org/deliverables/D2.1.pdf
8. Stephanidis, C. (ed.): User Interfaces for All. Laurence Erlbaum Associates, Mahwah (2001)
9. Karampelas, P.: Techniques and Tools for Designing an Online Social Network Platform. Lecture Notes in Social Networks, vol. 3. Springer (2013)

Collective Intelligence for Einclusion

Laura Burzagli and Pier Luigi Emiliani

National Research Council of Italy, Institute of Applied Physics, Florence, Italy
{l.burzagli,p.l.emiliani}@ifac.cnr.it

Abstract. Collective intelligence is a concept under development that could have an important impact on eInclusion, adding a social component to the actions in favour of disadvantaged people. Even if some interesting applications of the concept have been presented, their description so far mainly deals with the technical aspects of their implementation. The main message of the paper, based on preliminary work in the laboratory and experiments in the field under preparation as an activity in the AAL (Ambiente Assisted Living) project FOOD, is that a careful analysis of the features of the problem to be addressed and of the community potentially active in the support cooperative network can lead to a more efficient set up and running of applications based on the collective intelligent concept.

Keywords: Universal design, Collective intelligence, Ambient Intelligence.

1   Introduction

The term intelligence is used with different meanings according to the field of application and addressed problems. Recently, this term has often been used in ICT, specified by two different adjectives. Ambient intelligence mainly identifies environments where intelligence embedded in objects unobtrusively supports people in specific activities, for example at home, at work, and in open spaces. A different meaning is assumed by the term, when it is connected with the adjective collective. In this case it characterizes a phenomenon that involves a group of people who communicate through a network sharing their knowledge in order to solve common problems. The concept of collective intelligence can be considered as a new emerging feature of communities of connected human beings and a new contribution to the acquisition and production of knowledge. This paper deals with networking of people carrying out a specific set of activities dealing with feeding. Its main objective is to set up and test a method to identify necessary services and applications in this environment and the crucial aspects where collective intelligence can have a significant impact, with main emphasis on eInclusion.

2   Examples of Applications

Collective intelligence is being used in many applications and is defined in several different ways [1]. Some authors hypothesize that good results can be reached with a

C. Stephanidis and M. Antona (Eds.): UAHCI/HCII 2013, Part III, LNCS 8011, pp. 30–37, 2013.
© Springer-Verlag Berlin Heidelberg 2013

form of collective intelligence arising from the merging of web 2.0 with the semantic web [2]. As an example of this approach, a multilayer infrastructure can be considered where information without a defined structure originated in a social forum is filtered and organised, starting from a natural language interpreter which enrich and populate an ontology. This can allow new users of an application (for example a recommender system) to have increasingly accurate answers from the system.

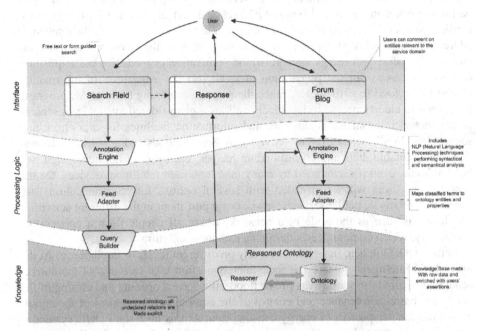

Fig. 1. – Block diagram of the collective intelligence system

In Figure 1 the block diagram of a collective intelligence system set up in our laboratory [3] is shown. It has been applied to a tourism information system, where people with activity limitations can have information about the accessibility of hotels. A general ontology and information produced in the European project C.A.R.E. [4] are enriched extracting data from natural language comments available in recommender systems used as a repository of common knowledge.

Another interesting application in the field of eInclusion has been set up by IBM [5]. It addresses the problem of non-accessible Web pages. On request by a user, a network community takes care of modifying Web pages to make them accessible, e.g. when a screen reader is used.

However, so far most of research in the field has been devoted to understand if and how a collective intelligence system could be implemented. An additional interesting question is whether a sufficient knowledge can be extracted from the application field and the characteristics of the community potentially available to start a targeted design of applications based on a collective intelligent approach. The context of the

FOOD project, in which the laboratory is presently involved, offers an interesting application environment to carry out this investigation.

3   The FOOD Project

FOOD (Framework for Optimizing the prOcess of feeding) [6] is a three years project part of the Ambient Assistive Living (AAL) scheme. It deals with the feeding process, considered as an activity to be carried out in an intelligent environment: the kitchen. It addresses all the relevant aspects: (i) the management of the environment itself, including e.g. safety and energy saving; (ii) the preparation of food; (iii) the acquisition of goods necessary for the preparation of food; (iv) the acquisition of information related to the food (e.g. recipes). Since the project, belonging to the AAL program, is devoted to elderly people, other functionalities are considered available as sensors of parameters relevant for health care and information facilities for diet check and suggestions. In all these different activities, as getting goods and acquiring information about suitable diets and corresponding recipes, each user is not considered isolated at home, even if surrounded by many interconnected intelligent devices. On the contrary, the users will be provided with several options for communication with caregivers, relatives, public services, who can support them in the different activities. The house is seen as the node of a network, where all people form a cooperative community, which communicates through a technological infrastructure.

In the FOOD kitchen, inhabitants can rely on different levels of intelligence. At the lower level intelligent objects and their interconnection take care e.g. of the correct behaviour of all alarm sensors (as fire or flood), the correct opening and closing of the doors, the basic maintenance and control of the equipment, the control of the equipment from the perspective of energy consumption. At this level the FOOD system, if correctly implemented, provides users with the sort of unobtrusive intelligence that facilitates the daily life activities without being too invasive and therefore probably not appreciate by them. Then, all networked and centrally controlled equipment of the kitchen are supposed to support the person in tasks connected to the preparation of food, from reminding them that they have to prepare it to controlling that all activities are compatible with security standards and coherent with the task people are carrying out. At an higher level, intelligent agents have the responsibility of supporting people in activities relevant for acquisition of food that can be automatized, at least partially, as: inventory and control of the goods that people have at home, automatic acquisition, if authorized, or support to the acquisition of food for shops in the neighbourhood, suggestion of diets compatible with the health situation. On top of it, the collective intelligence of the people in the network of caregivers, relatives, neighbours and Internet users in general is supposed to be active. This is the intelligence that is the main interest in this paper. It can be instrumental in favouring many of the above considered activities, introducing a social component that could be invaluable for the well-being of people, particularly of older people, many of whom suffer from some form of segregation from the society.

Other aspects that must be considered in the design and implementation of applications based on collective intelligence to support older people in their independent living at home are the investigation of factors that could concur to limit the interest of end users in being part of a cooperative network and the possibility of modelling the possible behaviour of the network, aiming at an efficient implementation.

4   The FOOD Community

As described above, the FOOD project is not limited to some sort of advanced house automation, but also includes a specific system layer where the use of technologies is supposed to facilitate social interaction with relatives, neighbours, caregivers, Internet users in general and access to network services.

Therefore, in order to study the possible impact of networking itself and of collective intelligence on increasing the quality of life of people at home, it is necessary to identify carefully the characteristics of the network community considered potentially available and contributing to the pilots carried out in the project. Obviously, not only the people directly involved in the pilot (about ten families each pilot) must be considered, but all groups of people involved.   The list includes:

- End users;
- Relatives;
- Neighbours;
- Caregivers;
- Experts in field related to the feeding process such as doctor, chefs, etc.;
- Personnel of shops or markets.

Contributions by each of them, even if with different roles, are needed in order to provide efficient services, pooling their knowledge about a specific application sector. Obviously, if all previous competences are included, the system increases in complexity, being the network made up of people with different knowledge, expertise, and language.

Being part of the AAL scheme, FOOD is supposed to carry out three pilot demonstrations of the proposed and implemented applications. They will be carried out in the Netherland, Rumania, and Italy. This introduces further complexity, since the communities on which the foreseen collective intelligence support will be based belong to different cultures, with significant differences, for example, in social habits, economic situations, penetration and availability of technology and technology-based applications.

Finally, an additional level of complexity of the analysis comes from the fact that the FOOD system is being set up in different steps, starting from the displacement of the basic technology for the control of the environment and growing to be a node of an open network. Therefore, the services and applications and all components of the social network are not available at the same time. A community with all members considered above, who contribute with their knowledge to the intelligence in the system, is not available from the start. The network is supposed to grow in time and, therefore, the development of its characteristics needs to be carefully modelled and guided, in order to avoid frustration due to an incomplete deployment of the expected functionalities. On the other side, a real richness of different expertise is available, including also partners in the project made up of researchers, industry, end user organisations, and design institutions.

To cope with the above described complexity, instead of setting up the network and running experiments with it, a different approach has been adopted. First, the network is modelled and its main characteristics as a social network are identified, in order to help developers to identify the main modules of the entire system. One of the main objectives of this analysis is to allow an easy integration of this level of collective intelligence with the other intelligence levels active in the kitchen.

5   Modelling of the Collective Intelligence Network

In order to apply concepts of collective intelligence in a specific application field (FOOD), the system under development and its functionalities are examined taking into account a model of collective intelligence available in literature [7]. Other interesting models are offered by the MIT Centre for collective intelligence [8]. The same problem is schematised with a small number of parameters, according to the metaphor of the human genome. Starting from four basic question, which are: Goal (what), Incentive (why), Structure/process (how), Staffing (who), a complete model can be constructed. A comparison between the two approaches is, however, outside the scope of the discussion here.

In the used model, first a classification in active and passive systems is introduced. If users do not realize its presence, the system is defined as passive. Some passive systems are used for infomobility, where the controller of the car can detect dangerous situations and introduce modifications in driving. In active collective intelligence systems a crowd behaviour is created and coordinated through specific system requests. For this last category an additional classification is introduced, considering competitive and collaborative systems. FOOD system is an example of active collaborative system, because users are supposed to cooperate with other members of the community in order to reach individual targets. In the modelling exercise, the analysis towards the implementation of a collective intelligence system is facilitated by the discussion of the following list of elements:

- Type: difference between passive and active systems;
- Set of user actions: it includes all the actions, influencing the results, that an individual user can perform;
- System state: it includes the minimum set of variables that can identify the system. In the FOOD environment examples are the quality of the recipes in connection to health problems, as a compromise between quality of ingredients and cost, and the quality of social contacts developed in the network;
- Community and individual objectives. This is very important, since it stresses that technological knowledge is not sufficient to build an effective collective

intelligence system, if the objectives for every user and for the community are not carefully identified and met;

- Critical mass of participants in the network that can sustain it;
- Motivation of participants.

These two last elements refer to an aspect which merits a lot of attention. There are indeed too many applications with an excellent implementation, which do not provide the expected results, due to an insufficient number and motivation of involved members.

The developed modelling procedure can be utilised to organise the work, hopefully leading to a correct set up and running of applications based on a collective intelligence approach in the FOOD system. The first step is the identification of objectives. The global objectives can be stated as: (i) increasing of general awareness about the food cycle; (ii) facilitation of the diffusion of the information to the end users; (iii) support in the identified necessary steps (from acquisition of food, to the control of cooking) for correct feeding. The individual objectives correspond to the list of services identified as necessary in the needs elicitation phase of the project. The list of services includes three main clusters:

- Environmental control;
- Food management;
- Shopping.

In the first cluster the control of several sensors for fire, gas, open doors, connected to an alarm system, is foreseen. These services are private and not interesting for the cooperative network. A second group is dealing with food management. This includes a food inventory, a recipe database and a food box. At this level the FOOD network is active and needs the cooperation with different actors, such as medical doctors, nutritionists, and relatives in order to identify the correct nutrient values of ingredients in the suggested recipes. At the third level related to shopping, the network involves still more people and adequate motivation for participation must be elicited. Relationships with shops or markets are introduced. This level includes a virtual market (a list of ingredients among which the user can choose) , the shopping list, payments.

Table 1 compares two contexts, the first is the open software development community that is very well known and the second is the FOOD system. This comparison is under analysis in order to provide designers an additional instrument to set up a useful system.

The critical mass is a parameter, whose influence in design of collective intelligence applications is of particular importance. This parameter can be defined only in an approximate way at the beginning of the application set up and is supposed to become more accurate after a first phase of test. This is why an indication of this parameter is not included in the previous table.

Table 1. Parameter of CI systems

CI system	Open Software Development Community	FOOD system
Type	Active, collaborative	Active, collaborative
Set of users actions	Contribute source code	Contribute food knowledge
System state	Software quality	Quality of information about the food process
Community Objective	Increase quality of produced software	Increase awareness of food cycle and facilitation of the process
Individual objective	Personal goals (adding no existing functionalities , fix bugs, customize to own needs)	Personal goals (see previous list of services)
Critical mass		
Motivation	Enjoyment, socialize	Enjoyment, socialize

After this first categorization, the most critical points of the FOOD system have been identified more carefully. One of them is motivation. If users do not find immediately a substantial utility from the system, they will limit their interaction only to a small group of standard and trivial activities, without trying to construct a personal way to take full advantage of the intelligent environment.

6   Conclusions

The paper considers the problems in setting up collective intelligence systems not only from a technological point of view, but also from the perspective of the possible compliance with a number of parameters which describe the system. Using this analysis, the designer identifies aspects of the system related to the possible impact of a collective intelligence system, before considering the most appropriate software tools for the implementation of the system.

This procedure has been adopted in the AAL FOOD project, which includes a limited number of end-users, but is supported by several different support groups with different expertise, with the objective of showing that older people can benefit from the development of a collective intelligence system.

References

1. WeKnowIt project: Final white paper on Collective Intelligence D9.4.2 (2011)
2. Burzagli, L., Gabbanini, F., Emiliani, P.L.: Adaptations Based on Ontology Evolution as a Mean to Exploit Collective Intelligence. In: Stephanidis, C. (ed.) Universal Access in HCI, Part I, HCII 2011. LNCS, vol. 6765, pp. 327–336. Springer, Heidelberg (2011)
3. Burzagli, L., Como, A., Gabbanini, F.: Towards the convergence of Web 2.0 and Semantic Web for e-Inclusion. In: Miesenberger, K., Klaus, J., Zagler, W., Karshmer, A. (eds.) ICCHP 2010, Part 1. LNCS, vol. 6179, pp. 343–350. Springer, Heidelberg (2010)
4. C.A.R.E. project website, http://www.interreg-care.org/site/
5. IBM The social Accessibility Project,
   http://www.research.ibm.com/social/projects_sap.shtml
6. FOOD project website, http://www.food-aal.eu/
7. Lykourentzou, I., Vergados, D.J., Kapetanios, E., Loumos, V.: Collective Intelligence Systems: Classification and Modeling. J. of Emerging Technologies in Web Intelligence 3(3) (August 2011)
8. Malone, T.W., Laubacher, R., Dellarocas, C.: Harnessing Crowds: Mapping the Genome of Collective Intelligence, MIT Centre for Collective Intelligence, WP n.2009-001

Ambient Assistive Technology Considered Harmful

Yngve Dahl[1], Babak Farshchian[1], Anders Kofod-Petersen[1],
Silje Bøthun[2], Kristine Holbø[2], and Jarl Kåre Reitan[2]

[1] SINTEF ICT, Strindveien 4, 7465 Trondheim, Norway
[2] SINTEF Technology and Society, Klæbuveien 153, 7465 Trondheim, Norway
{Yngve.Dahl,Babak.Farshchian,Anders.Kofod-Petersen,
Silje.Bothun,Kristine.Holbo,Jarl.Reitan}@sintef.no

Abstract. Ambient assistive technology (AAT) is envisioned as a powerful tool for facing the growing demands the demographic change toward an aging society puts on care. While AAT is often expected to increase the quality of life of older people, this paper holds that relevant interventions often embody values that can contradict such visions, and in some cases even be harmful to care receivers. We argue that the strong focus AAT puts on illness and risk management reflects a medical model of care, which often disregards the psychosocial challenges that impairments and disabilities associated with old age can rise. We suggest that design of AAT could benefit from using the social model of care as design inspiration and value foundation. Such an approach puts focus on the *person* rather than the *illness*. The paper ends by providing a short description of work in which the social model of care is adopted as a basis for design of AAT.

Keywords: Ambient assistive technology, Disability, Elderly care, Ethics, Human values, User-centered design, Value sensitive design.

1   Introduction

The population of the world is aging [1]. As a result, there is an expected increase in the prevalence of chronic illnesses and disability associated with old age [2]. This situation puts extra pressure on elderly care in many countries. Ambient assistive technology (AAT) is often envisioned as a powerful tool for facing the growing demands the demographic change toward an aging society puts on professional and family care. AAT is expected not only to reduce care costs and remedy the anticipated lack of adequate care providers for the elderly, but is also envisioned to support aging at home and increase quality of life among people of old age [3]. Most available AATs, however, tend to focus on risk management. Typically, such applications involve the use of sensors to detect events that may be critical to a care receiver's health or safety, and to inform caregivers of such incidents so that timely interventions may take place. Examples of such systems applied in the context of elderly care with chronic illnesses include GPS tracking systems, fall detection systems, and systems that monitor biometric data (e.g., heart rate and respiration). The strong emphasis these solutions put on management and control of symptoms echo in many ways what

C. Stephanidis and M. Antona (Eds.): UAHCI/HCII 2013, Part III, LNCS 8011, pp. 38–47, 2013.

is often referred to as a *medical model* of care [4]. The medical model of care has been criticized for constraining care to focusing on declines, negative issues, and physical care, rather than quality of life issues for the elderly and the psychosocial challenges that a person with a disability may face [4]. The alleged shortcomings of the medical model have given raise to what is known as the *social model* of care, or *salutogenesis* [5]. Rather than focusing on the disease, social models of care tend to put focus on the individual needs and disabling environmental barriers. In elderly care there has been a gradual shift over the last decades from a medical model to a social model of care.

With respect to the vision of increasing quality of life, the social critique of the medical model of care implicitly questions the appropriateness of the conceptual model that forms the basis of most AATs. This has motivated us to take a critical look at the extent to which AAT can be considered beneficial for elderly people in need of care, and if such interventions might even be considered harmful. The goal of this paper is to outline a position on the ethical foundation of AAT with a view to motivate work toward value-driven design of this type of technology. We also illustrate how social models of care may serve as a basis for design of AAT by describing work toward a safe walking technology for elderly people with dementia, and a system intended to promote social interaction for elderly within a local community.

2   Motivation

As computer technology is pervading more and more aspects of our lives, the implications of technology on human values are becoming an increasingly important aspect of HCI research [6]. The emergence of the Value Sensitive Design framework [7, 8] during the 1990s, and more recent attempts to alter or develop the framework further in order to address various issues (e.g., [9]), can be seen as recognition of this. Designing technology for ethically sensitive areas, such as elderly care, has raised the need for reinvention with regard to what the field looks at and the lenses that are used. In particular, we see a need for establishing a theoretical and ethical foundation that can help guide design of computer technology aiming to serve assistive purposes in care. Such a foundation (or lens) can help give designers a morally justified basis for taking design-related decisions in situations where conflicting perspectives and value trade-offs exist.

3   Background

The medical and social model of care represent in many ways two distinct value sets, which in turn have had different implications on provision of care. The different perspectives the two models have on the concept of disability are central in this context. Below, we will present a brief overview of the two models of care, and how they are shaped by different understandings of what disability constitutes.

3.1   Disability and Care within the Medical Model

The medical model of disability holds that illness or disability results from a physical condition, which is intrinsic to, or part of the individual [4]. The model holds that the illness or disability reduces a person's quality of life and is the source of disadvantages to that person. From the perspective of the medical model, managing or curing illness or disability put emphasis on identifying the illness or disability and understanding how to control or alter its trajectory.

The medical model regards disability as a problem of the person. The problem is the result of disease or other health condition, which consequently requires medical care provided by professionals. In the medical model, medical care is viewed as the central issue. Management of the disability aims to "cure" the individual or to cause behavior change in the individual that would lead to reduce the problem.

3.2   Disability and Care within the Social Model

The social model of disability explicitly distinguishes between *impairment* and *disability*. Impairment refers to some bodily defect and usually corresponds to a medically classified condition. Impairment, however, does not constitute a disability in itself. Within the social model, disability is understood as a function of the interaction between the person and the environment [4]. As such the social model considers disability to be external rather than being a part of the person. The extent to which a person experiences disability is intimately dependent on the degree of which the person lives in a supportive physical and social environment. As such, a disability is understood as contextually dependent variable, i.e., a result of the gap between the capabilities of an individual and the demands of the environment.

Setting out from this principle, disability studies have typically put emphasis on external barriers that contribute to disable a person. Within the social model, disability is often considered a socially created problem. Hence, management of the problem requires social action. An example of this type of action could be to make required environmental modifications in order to promote full participation of people with disabilities in all areas of social life.

One variant of the social model of care, which over the last two decades have been particularly influential in professional dementia care, but also in elderly care in general, is the person-centered care model that emerged from the work of the English social psychologist Thomas Kitwood [10]. Kitwood re-conceptualized dementia and raised attention toward human values in care. From a medical model which considered dementia strictly as a biomedical phenomenon (and implied a strong focus on management of disease symptoms), Kitwood [10] encouraged a shift toward recognizing the psychosocial aspects of the dementia and the need to preserve *personhood*, or "the self", in dementia patients by means of positive interaction techniques. According to Kitwood, personhood is the standing or status bestowed upon one human being, by other in the context of relationship and social being. Accordingly, to maintain personhood in the wake of cognitive deterioration (or other impairments) a person depends on those around him. Identity, attachment, inclusions, occupation and comfort are basic psychological needs, which are essential for maintaining personhood status.

3.3   A Conceptual Comparison of the Medical and the Social Model of Care

Table 1 summarizes the conceptual differences between the medical and the social model of care with respect to key aspects.

Table 1. The medical versus the social model of care

	Medical model of care	Social model of care
Objective	Eliminate impairment and disability.	Challenge social exclusion.
Focus	Diagnosis through medical insight.	The person; not the disability.
Cause of disability	Physical or mental impairment is the cause of disability.	Focus on environmental and social barriers that exclude people with a disability from mainstream society.
Authority	Health care providers.	People with disabilities.

4   Understanding Ambient Assistive Technology as Value-Laden

As elderly care is gradually turning toward AAT to address the challenges that arise as a consequence of demographic changes, the question of which care values the technology promotes increasingly becomes central. To understand how AAT can be considered to "reflect" a medical model of care requires that we first account for the non-neutral perspective of technology in relation to ethical and social issues.

The principles about the non-neutrality technology of where developed by 20th-century media theorists, such as Ellul [11], Mowshowitz [12], and Postman [13]. A central idea in the non-neutral perspective on technology is that that technology harbor values, which come into play regardless of the intentions of the user [14]. This can include values held by technology designers or values held by society. Technology, again, shapes individual behavior and social systems [15].

The non-neutral perspective on technology claims that when we use technology, the technology to some degree "uses" (or influences) us. The way a specific technology is designed sets premises for use. A revolver has been designed to fire bullets. While one might also use a revolver to hammer nails into an object, it has not been designed for such purposes and its usability with respect to this activity will accordingly be limited. In this sense, technology "insists" on being applied in certain ways. From the non-neutral perspective, then, technology acts as an autonomous force on users.

Applying the principle of the non-neutrality of technology in ethical and social issues, technology used for provision of elderly care is not merely instrumental – to a certain extent the technology also carries with it its own effects. Technology usage can give positive and negative consequences no matter how the technology is used.

Social models of care have had increasing influence on elderly care over the last decades [16]. It has helped and promoted a more holistic approach to care, which put

focus on individual needs as experienced by care receiver. In spite of this development, we find that digital assistive technology targeting elderly care often contain
value biases that arguably align with the old care culture. Similar to the medical model of care, most AATs put emphasis on risk management and disease symptoms and a
person a care receiver's "weaknesses". In this sense, there is a potential tension between newer care culture and the care ideology harbored in AAT. The non-neutral
perspective on technology reminds us that identifying value-biases can be challenging
as biases may be imbedded in design details [17]. Identifying the value-biases of
technology targeting elderly care is nevertheless important in order to take measures
that may prevent harmful side effects of use.

5   Ambient Assistive Technology Considered Harmful

Above we explained the theoretical background for how technology can be considered value-laden tools, and how most AATs can be considered to harbor a care ideology that aligns with the medical model of care. In the following, we discuss three
aspects relevant for understanding in what way AAT can be considered to have
potentially harmful or negative effects on the wellbeing of people in need of care. The
aspects that we will discuss include (1) negative effects on the interaction between
caregiver and care receiver); (2) loss of agency on the part of care receivers; and (3)
obtrusive effects on care receivers' everyday life.

5.1   Effects on Interaction between Caregiver and Care Receiver

According to the non-neutral perspective on technology, information and communication technologies do not simply convey information; they also present their specific
perspective on the world. They are in other words metaphors through which we can
understand reality. One of the potential dangers of AAT and particularly remote
monitoring applications in the context of care, then, is linked the "image" they convey
of the care receivers. There is a risk that caregivers understanding of a care receiver
becomes biased when the person in need of care is primarily seen through the "lens"
of monitoring technology [18]. By putting emphasis on disease or symptoms of the
disease, there is a chance that caregivers learn to know care receivers by their disease
rather than what characterizes them as persons, and understanding their subjectively
defined experiences and needs. For example, literature which questions the application of GPS to track persons with dementia who shows wandering behavior argue that
the technology can create blindness to the underlying reasons for why a person with
dementia might show such behavior [18]. Understanding a care receivers subjectively
defined experiences and needs is essential in a holistic approach to care.

5.2   Loss of Agency

The second danger of AAT applied in elderly care we will address is related to the
potential loss of agency, and what can be considered the under-utilized possibility to
build on the retained strengths and abilities of the care receiver. Implicit in many

AATs is the conceptualization of the care receiver as a passive stakeholder. Often AATs offer none or very limited interactive possibilities to the care receiver. The conceptual model on which many AATs are based do not appear to acknowledge care receivers as potential active user of technology. Conventional tracking technology applied in dementia care, for example, offer no means for the persons carrying a position tag to try and help themselves. Instead, caregivers appear as the intended user group of most AATs, and functionalities typically reflect their work needs.

For example, a system that monitors aspects of physical activity without providing feedback to the elderly person in a manner that makes sense to the users can also be considered to prevent care receivers from taking a more active part in their own well-being. Such a system can be viewed to increase elderly peoples' dependency on caregivers. In this sense, AAT may also be considered to disempower the care receiver.

5.3   Effects on Care Receivers' Everyday Life

The third concern we will raise with respect to AAT applied in elderly care, relates to the potential obtrusive effects such interventions may have on a person's life and living environment. Many interventions arguably require the person in need of care to adapt to the technology in some way. This may include adapting new routines in order to allow the technology to work according to its purpose (e.g., remembering to put on a sensor device), asserting that the technology is operative (e.g., that a device has been recharged), and reorganizing one living environment (and thereby changing ones relationship to it [19]). While the need for adapting oneself or ones environment to AAT might be considered "justifiable" from a strict safety perspective, and that acquiring an illness requires one to adapt ones way of living in any case, technology can also be a source of excess disability. Excess disability refers to deficits that arise from factors that do not relate to a disorder or illness, as such. Examples of such factors can be a person's physical and the social environment. As AAT increasingly is becoming a part of these environments, interventions can also form a contributing factor to excess disability. With respect to design, then, the concept excess disability calls attention to the importance of developing technology that seamlessly integrate with care receivers lives and routines.

6   Using the Social Model of Care as Design Inspiration

In this section we will describe work towards two AAT solutions that take their motivation from the social model of care.

6.1   Designing Safe Walking Technology with and for Elderly People with Dementia

People with dementia form a vulnerable group, as symptoms associated with the condition (e.g., memory loss and communication problems), make it difficult for them to stand up for their rights [20]. The group is often subject to excess disability as a result of prejudice and social stigma associated with the condition (ibid.). Technological interventions that target dementia care stand a particular risk of causing excess disability for the group. One reason for this is that very few technologies available have been particularly designed for people with dementia, but rather appropriated from other domains [18].

Taking inspiration from Kitwood's person-centered care philosophy [10], and particularly the fundamental ethical principle that people with dementia have a right to participate in decisions that can influence their lives, we have worked closely with people with mild dementia and their families on designing technology supporting safe walking for the group. The activity has been part of the Norwegian research project *Trygge spor* ("Safe tracks").

Our main motivation has been to form an understanding of what people with dementia want from technology aimed to support safe walking. Through a set of participatory design workshops we have identified the following factors to influence the views of the participants with dementia on how safe walking technology can fit their needs and life situation:

- *Desire for control and self-management*: Having a technology that can offer the person with dementia direct assistance in challenging situations, via a user interface he or she can master, was central for the participants with dementia. Receiving assistance from others (e.g., family members) was considered a less favorable option, and was regarded as a back-up solution reserved for safety-critical situations.
- *The subjective experience of symptoms*: The participants gave different accounts of how they experienced disease symptoms, and to what degree they experienced that their condition affected their safety when they performed outdoor activities on their own. Personal experiences from episodes the participants had experienced as difficult or challenging tended to influence their vision of safe walking technology.
- *Routines and skills*: We found that the knowledge and skills of people with dementia can act as an inspiration source for user interface design. Providing people with dementia user interfaces that build on familiar concepts enables the group to build on such abilities as they have retained.
- *Empathy for caregivers*: From the perspective of the persons with dementia who participated, freedom of movement was not only reserved to being able to go for outdoor walks whenever and wherever they wanted. Being able to perform outdoor activities without raising concerns among close family members was also important for the group. For some participants, the concerns raised by family members was a central factor for accepting remote monitoring of outdoor activities. Technologies that supported self-management for the person with dementia was seen as a means for relieving close family members of the burden of caring, and possibly saving them from having to intervene.
- *Local environment*: The participants' familiarity with their local environment and their confidence that people living there would assist them in difficult situations also played a central role with respect to how they perceived their own safety situation. The participants' perceptions of the local environment also influenced the extent to which they considered remote monitoring technology (e.g., GPS) beneficent for their own safety.

We plan to use the needs, desires and preferences described above to inform the design of future functional prototypes, which can be tested in real-life situations.

6.2 Supporting Social Interaction among Elderly within the Local Community

Medical conditions, or lack of the same, are not the main parameter ensuring a happy senior life. Living alone and isolated is a prevailing problem among the elderly population; in particular in the western world [21, 22]. Addressing isolation and loneliness is increasingly being recognized as an important aspect of improving elderlies' living conditions. Loneliness is commonly associated with disconnections from society, lacking social relations and not being appreciated [23].

Tackling loneliness and isolation is the main concern of the ongoing Ambient Assisted Living project *Co-Living*. Encouraging elderly to participate in social activities is done through a personalized mobile social recommender system encouraging active living [24].

The co-living system is based around the idea of offering relevant activities to elderly through a recommender system. Events are currently supplied by the municipality and described along relevant dimensions, such as physical and dancing or social and café [25]. Users' interests are also modeled and the combination of events and user interests are used as the foundation of recommendations. Yet, a traditional event recommender does not necessarily satisfy the socialization issue. Thus, co-living includes three features that are specifically designed to encourage socialization. First, group recommendations in the form of, e.g., "You should attend the polka class this Monday with Mr. Johnson who also enjoys dancing", which should promote attending social events. Secondly, users can invite others to join them at activities. Finally, users have the possibility to publish their own events, which will be published and recommender just like the official events supplied by the municipality.

The system is currently being tested and evaluated in two different sites. In the Netherlands elderly in a retirement home are using the system as an integrated part of their services. The second installation is running in Norway, where elderly living at home is using the system on a daily basis. Preliminary reports suggest that the system is well received by both people living in an institution and at home. The project is currently in its final stage and more thorough results will be available during the second half of 2013.

7   Summary and Concluding Remarks

In this paper we have argued that, with respect to the envisioned benefits AAT can give elderly people in need of care, there appears to be a fallacy between equating the increased possibility for detection of health or safety critical events with empowerment of and improved life quality for elderly. Drawing on non-neutral perspective of technology in relation to ethical and social issues, we have argued that AAT tend to reflect a medical model of care. We have discussed how the emphasis this model places on illness and risk management also can have potentially negative effects on a care receiver's quality of life. In particular, we discussed how AAT may (1) alter caregiver-care receiver interaction and reduce opportunities for face-to-face contact; (2) lead to loss of agency on part of care receivers; and (3) have an obtrusive effect on care receivers' life and possibly contribute to excess disability. We have also provided examples of how an alternative social model, which forms a more holistic approach to care, can be used as design inspiration for AAT.

This paper has highlighted that the extent to which technological interventions in elderly care are beneficial (or even harmful) to care receivers is intimately dependent on how we conceptualize disability, and how we understand the needs of people living with chronic conditions. The understanding of AAT as value-laden tools strengthens the argument that ethics and human values need to be paid explicit attention as part of their process of design.

Acknowledgements: This paper has been written in the context of the Co-Living project (Ambient Assisted Living (AAL) Joint Programme, contract no. AAL-2009-2-097), and the Norwegian research projects *Trygge Spor* (contract no. RFFOFJOR 208820) and *KupA* (contract no. NFR219842).

References

1. Muenz, R.: Aging and Demographic Change in European Societies: Main Trends and Alternative Policy Options. Number 0703 in SP Discussion Paper. Social Protection Advisory Service – The World Bank, Washington, DC, USA (2007)
2. World Health Organization. Global Health and Aging (2011)
3. Nehmer, J., Becker, M., Karshmer, A., Lamm, R.: Living assistance systems: an ambient intelligence approach. In: Proceedings of the 28th International Conference on Software Engineering (ICSE 2006), pp. 43–50. ACM, New York (2006)
4. Brandt, E., Pope, A.: Models of disability and rehabilitation. Enabling America: Assessing the Role of Rehabilitation Science and Engineering, 62–80 (1997)
5. Antonovsky, A.: Health, Stress and Coping. Jossey-Bass Publishers, San Francisco (1979)
6. Bannon, L.: Reimagining HCI: toward a more human-centered perspective. Interactions 18 (2011)
7. Friedman, B., Kahn, P.H., Borning, A.: Value sensitive design: Theory and methods. Technical Report 02-12-01, Dept. of Computer Science & Engineering, University of Washington, Washington, Seattle, WA (2002)
8. Friedman, B., Kahn, P.H., Borning, A.: Value sensitive design and information systems. In: Himma, K.E., Tavani, H.T. (eds.) The Handbook of Information and Computer Ethics. John Wiley and Sons, Inc., Hoboken (2008)
9. Borning, A., Muller, M.: Next steps for value sensitive design. In: Proceedings of the 2012 ACM Annual Conference on Human Factors in Computing Systems (CHI 2012), pp. 1125–1134. ACM, New York (2012)
10. Kitwood, T.: Dementia reconsidered: the person comes first. Open University Press, Buckingham (1997)
11. Ellul, J.: The technological society (Trans. Wilkinson, J.). Vintage Books, New York (1964)

12. Mowshowitz, A.: The Conquest of Will: Information Processing in Human Affairs. Addison-Wesley, Reading (1976)
13. Postman, N.: Technopoly: The Surrender of Culture to Technology. Vintage Books, New York (1993)
14. Ellul, J.: The Technological Bluff. Grand Rapids. Eerdmans Publishing Co., MI (1990)
15. Freier, N.G., Consolvo, S., Kahn, P., Smith, I., Friedman, B.: A Value Sensitive Design Investigation of Privacy for Location-Enhanced Computing. In: CHI 2005 Workshop on Quality. Exploring Wider Implications of HCI in Practice, Value(s), and Choice (2005)
16. Epp, T.D.: Person-centred dementia care: A vision to be refined. The Canadian Alzheimer Disease Review 5 (2003)
17. Dahl, Y., Holbø, K.: Value biases of sensor-based assistive technology: case study of a GPS tracking system used in dementia care. In: Proceedings of the Designing Interactive Systems Conference (DIS 2012), pp. 572–581. ACM, New York (2012)
18. Astell, A.: Technology and personhood in dementia care. Quality in Ageing 7, 15–25 (2006)
19. Baldwin, C.: Technology, dementia, and ethics: Rethinking the issues. Disability Studies Quarterly 25 (2005)
20. Astell, A., Alm, N., Gowans, G., Ellis, M., Dye, R., Vaughan, P.: Involving older peo-ple with dementia and their carers in designing computer based support systems: some methodological considerations. Univ. Access. Inf. Soc. 8, 49–58 (2008)
21. Donaldsom, J.M., Watson, R.: Loneliness in elderly people: an important area for nursing research. Journal of Advanced Nursing 25(5), 952–959 (1996)
22. Routasalo, P., Pitkala, K.H.: Loneliness among older people. Reviews in Clinical Gerontology 13, 303–311 (2003)
23. Hauge, S., Kirkevold, M.: Older Norwegians' understanding of loneliness. International Journal Qualitative Studies on Health and Well-being 5 (2010)
24. Mathisen, B.M., Olalde, I., Kofod-Petersen, A.: Co-Living social community for elderly. In: Proceedings of the 12th International Conference on Innovative Internet Community Systems (2012)
25. Gulbrandsen, S.K., Fikkan, E., Grunt, E., Mehl, K., Shamsolketabi, S., Singh, J., Vrucinic, M., Mathisen, B.M., Kofod-Petersen, A.: Social Network for Elderly. In: Proceedings of the 12th International Conference on Innovative Internet Community Systems (2012)

Home Robots, Learn by Themselves

Osamu Hasegawa and Daiki Kimura

Tokyo Institute of Technology, Japan
{hasegawa.o.aa,kimura.d.aa}@m.titech.ac.jp

Abstract. To build an intelligent robot, we must develop an autonomous mental development system that incrementally and speedily learns from humans, its environments, and electronic data. This paper presents an ultra-fast, multimodal, and online incremental transfer learning method using the STAR-SOINN. We conducted two experiments to evaluate our method. The results suggest that recognition accuracy is higher than the system that simply adds modalities. The proposed method can work very quickly (approximately 1.5 [s] to learn one object, and 30 [ms] for a single estimation). We implemented this method on an actual robot that could estimate attributes of "unknown" objects by transferring attribute information of known objects. We believe this method can become a base technology for future robots.

SOINN is an unsupervised online-learning method capable of incremental learning. By approximating the distribution of input data and the number of classes, a self-organized network is formed. SOINN offers the following advantages: network formation is not required to be predetermined beforehand, high robustness to noise, and reduced computational cost. In the near future, a SOINN device will accompany an individual from birth; this will allow the agent to share personal histories with its owner. In this occasion, a person's SOINN will know "everything" about its owner, lending assistance at any time and place throughout one's lifetime. Besides having a personal SOINN, an individual can install this self-enhanced agent into human-made products - making use of learned preferences to make the system more efficient. If deemed non-confidential, an individual's SOINN could also autonomously communicate another SOINN to share information.

Keywords: SOINN (Self-organizing Incremental Neural Network), Home robots, Machine learning.

1   Introduction

To compensate for a shortage of labor in the near future, it is vital to develop an intelligent robot that works for human beings in real living environments. To build such a robot, we require a system that can autonomously learn from real world interactions with humans, its environment, and electronic data. Therefore, we proposed an ultra-fast and online incremental transfer learning method [1]. This method uses the STAtistical Recognition on Self-Organizing and Incremental Neural Network (STAR-SOINN), which is an extension of the original SOINN [2]. We performed a

C. Stephanidis and M. Antona (Eds.): UAHCI/HCII 2013, Part III, LNCS 8011, pp. 48–53, 2013.
© Springer-Verlag Berlin Heidelberg 2013

comparative experiment with previous offline [3] and online [4] methods using "Animals with attributes" dataset [3]. In this experiment, we attempted to estimate attributes of the unseen animal's image by transferring attribute information of learned animals. On the basis of experimental results, our method can maintain recognition rate equivalent to the online method. Table I shows the learning and test times and the features of these methods. The results show that our method is an ultra-fast transfer learning method, and can have potential practical applications.

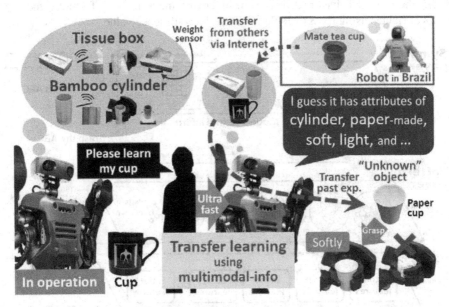

Fig. 1. Framework of our research

The online incremental transfer learning method that we propose did not use or focus on certain modalities (e.g., sound, touch, and weight) because comprehensive combining of such modalities is difficult. For example, a "heavy" attribute can only be understood by a weight sensor. This implies the system cannot understand such an attribute from an image even if the system collects a huge amount of image. Therefore, the system requires a confidence value that represents the relationship between an attribute and a modality. In this paper, we propose multimodal transfer learning using the STAR-SOINN[1]. Figure 1 shows an overview of our research. This system can estimate attributes of an "unknown" object by transferring a robot's prior experimental learning of other objects. This implies that the robot can understand conceptual categories of any object in front of the robot, and can use this knowledge to act accordingly. This feature is required an intelligent robot that can work in real environments, because there is a wide variety of objects in such environments.

2   Proposed Method

Figure 2 shows a system overview of the proposed method. In the learning phase, the robot receives real data from its environment, interactions with humans, and electronic data, e.g. Internet. It then extracts features and trains each STAR-SOINN to remember the features for each attribute. After a short training, the system also uses the learning data to update the confidence value using attribute estimation. In the test phase, the robot receives real data from its environment, extracts features, and estimates attributes using the STAR-SOINN and the confidence value.

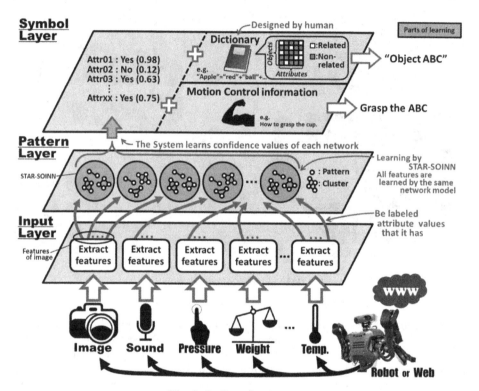

Fig. 2. Outline of our system

Table 1. Comparison of previous research

Method	Proposed[1]	[4]	[3]
Online learning	○	○	×
Learning time	7 mins	6 hours	70 days
Test time	1.5 mins	4 hours	2 days
Use real-valued attr.	○	×	×
Easy to update attr.	○	×	×

Fig. 3. A multi-modal robot used in our experiment

3   Experiment and Result

We conducted two experiments to evaluate the proposed method. One experiment was to verify the effects of the confidence value, and the other was to estimate the "unknown" object using a humanoid robot. In these experiments, we defined 23 attributes for each object used.

1. Verify the effects of the confidence value

We developed two systems; the proposed system, and a system that simply added modalities (i.e. it did not use the confidence value). We used these objects shown in Figure 3, and 3 modalities (image, sound, and depth). Table II shows the accuracy of these methods. The proposed method is more accurate than the method that simply added these modalities.

2. Estimate "unknown" objects using the robot

Figure 3 shows the robot, sensors, and learning objects used in this experiment. The robot learned these 20 objects from the 5 modalities using the proposed method. The system took approximately 1.5 [s] to learn one object. We then gave the robot four unknown objects, and checked the results of the attribute estimation for these objects. Figure 4 shows the result for the "mate tea cup"(=unknown object). The system correctly determined the attributes such as cylinder and wooden-made. Approximately 90% of estimations succeeded in determining the correct attributes. The system took approximately 30 [ms] for a single estimation, excluding action time.

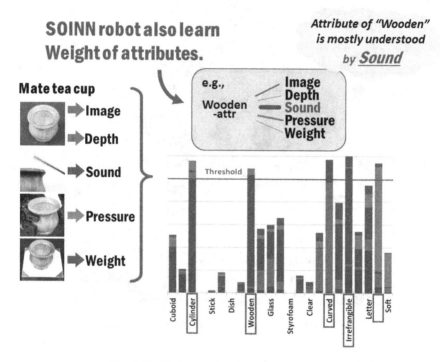

Fig. 4. Prediction results of "unknown" object

Table 2. Accuracy of these methods

Methods and modalities	Accuracy
Proposed method (Image, Sound, and Depth)	**94.3%**
Simply added modalities (Image, Sound, and Depth)	80.2%
Using only Image sensor	40.7%
Using only Sound sensor	62.3%
Using only Depth sensor	67.6%

4 Future Work

In the future, we think the Internet has a huge amount of information about many objects by such modalities using robots all over the world. Therefore, the robot will ask to other robots when it get information. We hope this system has the potential to become as the base technology for future robots.

Acknowledgment. This work was sponsored by the Japan Science and Technology Agency's CREST project.

References

1. Kimura, D., Pichai, K., Kawewong, A., Hasegawa, O.: Ultra-fast and online incremental transfer learning. In: The 17th Symposium on Sensing via Image Information, Kanagawa, Japan (June 2011) (in Japanese)
2. Shen, F., Hasegawa, O.: A fast nearest neighbor classifier based on self-organizing incremental neural network. Neural Netw. 21(10), 1537–1547 (2006)
3. Lampert, C.H., Nickisch, H., Harmeling, S.: Learning to detect unseen object classes by between-class attribute transfer. In: IEEE Conference on Computer Vision and Pattern Recognition (2009)
4. Kawewong, A., Hasegawa, O.: Fast and incremental attribute transferring and classifying system for detecting unseen object classes. In: Diamantaras, K., Duch, W., Iliadis, L.S. (eds.) ICANN 2010, Part III. LNCS, vol. 6354, pp. 563–568. Springer, Heidelberg (2010)
5. Araki, T., Nakamura, T., Nagai, T., Funakoshi, K., Nakano, M., Iwahashi, N.: Autonomous acquisition of multimodal information for online object concept formation by robots. In: 2011 IEEE/RSJ International Conference on Intelligent Robots and Systems (IROS), pp. 1540–1547 (September 2011)
6. Bosch, A., Zisserman, A., Munoz, X.: Representing shape with a spatial pyramid kernel. In: Proceedings of the 6th ACM International Conference on Image and Video Retrieval, CIVR 2007, pp. 401–408. ACM, New York (2007)
7. Dalal, N., Triggs, B.: Histograms of oriented gradients for human detection. In: IEEE Conference on Computer Vision and Pattern Recognition, vol. 1, pp. 886–893 (June 2005)
8. Haasch, A., Hofemann, N., Fritsch, J., Sagerer, G.: A multi-modal object attention system for a mobile robot. In: Proc. IEEE/RSJ International Conference on Intelligent Robots and Systems, Edmonton, Alberta, Canada, pp. 1499–1504. IEEE (August 2005)
9. Kimura, D., Pichai, K., Hasegawa, O.: Ultra-fast and online incremental transfer learning with the internet. In: The 18th Symposium on Sensing via Image Information, Kanagawa, Japan (June 2012) (in Japanese)
10. Kimura, D., Pichai, K., Hasegawa, O.: Unknown object recognition by images on the internet using ultra-fast and online incremental transfer learning. In: Meeting on Image Recognition and Understanding, Fukuoka, Japan (August 2012) (in Japanese)
11. Kumar, N., Berg, A.C., Belhumeur, P.N.: Shree K. Nayar. Attribute and simile classifiers for face verification. In: IEEE International Conference on Computer Vision (ICCV) (October 2009)
12. Nakamura, T., Nagai, T., Iwahashi, N.: Multimodal object categoriza-tion by a robot. In: Proc. IEEE/RSJ International Conference on Intelligent Robots and Systems, pp. 2415–2420 (2007)
13. Ozasa, Y., Iwahashi, N., Takiguchi, T., Ariki, Y., Nakano, M.: Integrated multimodal information for detection of unknown objects and unknown names. In: 2012 RISP International Workshop on Nonlinear Circuits, Communications and Signal Processing (March 2012)
14. Pan, S.J., Yang, Q.: A survey on transfer learning. IEEE Trans. on Knowl. And Data Eng. 22(10), 1345–1359 (2010)
15. Rohrbach, M., Stark, M., Szarvas, G., Gurevych, I., Schiele, B.: What helps where – and why? semantic relatedness for knowledge transfer. In: CVPR (2010)

The Future of Universal Access?
Merging Computing, Design and Engineering

Simeon Keates, David Bradley, and Andrew Sapeluk

School of Engineering, Computing and Applied Mathematics, University of Abertay Dundee,
Dundee, Scotland, UK
{s.keates,d.bradley,a.sapeluk}@abertay.ac.uk

Abstract. Technology is advancing at a fast pace while the shape and nature of computers continues to evolve, with tablets and smartphones illustrating the move away from the traditional notion of a laptop or desktop computer. Similarly, networking and sensing technologies are also developing rapidly and innovatively. All of these technologies have the potential to enfranchise users with severe functional impairments to be better able to control and interact with other people and their surroundings. However, this is only possible if those designing the novel systems based upon these new technologies consider such users' needs explicitly. This paper examines how these technological advances can be employed to support these users in the near future. The paper further discusses issues such as the need for security as systems evolve from control of specific environments to a potential model for interaction in any location.

Keywords: Universal access, mechatronics, accessibility, environmental control systems, alternative and augmentative communication (AAC), tablets.

1   Introduction

Advances in technology have the power to enfranchise users, for example to help them interact with and control their environment. However, technology also has the power to disenfranchise users. If one section of the general population is able to utilize technological developments to perform tasks more efficiently or to access novel services and another section of that same population is not able to do so, then the technology can be considered to have contributed to their individual and collective disability. The power of technology to divide potential users into those who can and those who cannot access a new technology has often been referred to as the "digital divide" [1]. The concept of "universal access" arose from the need to consider the needs of all sections of the population to be able to access new products and services, and thus render the notion of a "divide" as obsolete.

It is worth noting that designers do not begin with the intention of deliberately excluding potential users. Excluded users are excluded customers and, consequently, represent lost potential profit opportunities. Put simply, excluded users will not buy your products and services. So, it is worth exploring the origins of design exclusion.

C. Stephanidis and M. Antona (Eds.): UAHCI/HCII 2013, Part III, LNCS 8011, pp. 54–63, 2013.
© Springer-Verlag Berlin Heidelberg 2013

1.1   Universal Access and the Design of New Technologies

New technologies are often driven by an idea for innovative functionality or features. Once the idea has taken shape, design and development can begin and the race is on to be the first vendor in the marketplace to offer the new product. Being the first to the market is still widely seen as gaining a competitive advantage that can persist for a substantial period of time until other factors, such as lower price or enhanced usability, help other products eat into the market share [2].

In the rush to be first to the market, the overriding imperative is to produce a product that works. It does not necessarily have to work well nor be particularly usable. Consequently, the focus is usually on meeting the engineering challenges first and foremost. However, this is not always the case, for example, the development of the experimental IBM Watson system. Watson was developed to see whether Q&A technologies had advanced to the stage where such a system could feasibly compete against people in a fairly unrestricted challenge. This culminated in the Jeopardy!^{TM} challenge [3]. However, while this was a significant engineering achievement in its own right, there was still a strong recognition of the importance of meeting the needs of the end users and this is central to the development of commercial versions of the system [4].

There are other causes of exclusion. For example, sometimes the designers are simply not aware that the products or services that they are developing may be deployed by users who have different functional capabilities. It has been said before that, unless otherwise instructed, designers will often design for themselves [5]. In other words, they will typically envisage the user as possessing the same capabilities, knowledge and experience as themselves. This is only human nature – we know ourselves better than anyone else. The full range of reasons for design exclusion and methods for countering that exclusion are considered elsewhere [6]. However, they can be summarized as recognizing the need to explicitly consider the needs of all users through the whole product lifecycle – from initial design to final decommissioning [2] – and how advances in technology offer both potential opportunities for, and challenges to, access to new products and services.

With this perspective firmly in mind it is timely to consider how recent advances in mobile, sensor and communications technologies can offer increased opportunities for universal access. One area where these technologies can combine to offer new opportunities is that of environmental control systems.

2   Environmental Control / Home Automation Systems

Environmental control systems (ECS) and home automation systems (HAS) allow users with severe functional impairments to carry out tasks such as switching on lights or changing the temperature in their house [7]. For the purposes of this paper, we will use ECS to describe both types of systems.

Users of such systems might typically be wheelchair users and experience limitations such as restricted range of motion, spasms, tremor and reduced strength. They may have conditions such as cerebral palsy or muscular dystrophy. As such, they typically find using many domestic devices, such as light switches and heating controls, almost impossible to use unless they have been especially adapted to their personal needs. Environmental control systems remove the need for the users to reach light switches on a wall, by allowing remote control of these devices from their wheelchair.

Early systems typically used infrared technology – such as found in the typical television remote control – to control transducers embedded in each device intended to be controlled and had a very simple architecture [8]:

1. The central processing unit (CPU) – the core of the system that processes the user commands and transmits the control signals, typically from switches, to the corresponding peripheral devices
2. The visual display – to show the user the environmental functions and peripheral devices that are available
3. The transducer – the control switch used to register the user's input action and convert it to a control signal that is sent to the CPU
4. The peripherals – the devices embedded in the environment that are to be controlled through the environmental control system via automated actuators

The basic underlying architecture of environmental control systems has not changed substantially since the mid 1980s when these systems began to appear commercially. However, the enabling technologies available have changed substantially. Rather than viewing components such as the CPU, visual display and transducers as separate entities, the advent of more powerful environmental control systems in recent years has allowed these features to be co-located in a single unit. Similarly, trends are moving towards viewing the context of use as not simply a house with a few automated devices, but, increasingly, a smart environment offering ambient intelligence [9].

Furthermore, developments in mainstream computing now raises the interesting prospect of such systems being controlled by a simple app on an off-the-shelf device such as an Appe iPad or Samsung Galaxy. Similarly, other communication technologies than simple infrared beams mean that it is possible to control devices in the home from ever increasing distances. The remainder of this paper will look at those technologies and the implications for the design of the environmental control systems of the near future.

3   Communication, Location and Control Technologies

There are several communications and location technologies available that can be potentially used for controlling an ECS.

3.1   Communication Technologies

The following is an indicative list of the range of communication technologies that can be used:

1. Infrared (IR) beams. These are the traditional communication technology of choice for controlling devices in the home. They have low power consumption, meaning excellent battery life. However, they only offer strictly "line-of-sight" control and have limited range (<10 m), meaning that their range is limited to devices within the user's immediate proximity. They also offer very little security as there is no command authentication required, i.e. there is no requirement for a password nor for the device sending the command codes to be recognized or identified. As long as the correct command codes are received, then the environmental control system will respond to the command, regardless of the source of origin of the command.

2. Radio Frequency (RF) controllers. These work on the same principles as IR ones, but with the difference that radio waves are capable of penetrating through some solid matter. The greater the power used, the greater the penetration. Consequently, RF controllers offer more flexibility in use, through a longer range and relaxing the line-of-sight requirement. However, security is still comparatively weak.

3. Bluetooth. Extending the control range a little further, Bluetooth can be used to transmit control commands up to 100 metres. Bluetooth has a major advantage in being widely available through many devices, especially mobile and smartphones. It also has good security potential if set up correctly. However, if left unprotected, the ubiquity of Bluetooth controllers is a potential disadvantage, as it would become quite straightforward to penetrate an open network. Bluetooth also suffers from more substantially power requirements, and thus decreased battery life, than many of the alternative technologies.

4. Low-rate wireless personal area networks (LR-WPANs). The IEEE 802.15.4 standard [10] offers digital radio control of devices up to 1 mile apart, which is a significant step in increasing the potential control range of an ECS. LR-WPANs also offer a substantial increase in security, supporting the use of cryptographic methods to ensure point-to-point communications. However, such networks are designed to support only small, infrequent packets of data rather than more substantial volumes. Consequently, while they could be used to switch lights on, for example, they would most likely struggle to support a live video feed.

5. Global System for Mobile Communications (GSM). The next increase in the distance over which an ECS can be controlled is to move from point-to-point personal network connection to using established networks and submitting the control commands securely via those. One example of this is sending SMS control messages via the GSM mobile phone networks. Use of the GSM networks allows an ECS to be controlled from anywhere in the world where there is a usable phone signal. However, such messages can suffer from significant delays in their delivery and sometimes even non-delivery. This question mark over the reliability of delivery of the commands is a significant problem with GSM-based control. Security is typically achieved by requiring authentication codes in the SMS messages sent. These codes, or keys, can be of any length and so offer a reasonable amount of security.

6. Internet. An alternative solution that also offers global reach is to control the ECS via Internet technologies. Wi-Fi connections are available in many buildings and mobile phone networks typically support 3G or 4G Internet connectivity in many

metropolitan areas. While such connectivity is not as geographically widespread as, say, GSM coverage, Internet connections offer a far greater bandwidth for communication, potentially supporting live video feeds with comparative ease and also offering access to typical Internet security protocols. Arguably the biggest disadvantages are the power requirements to maintain such a connection leading to short battery life compared with, for example, an IR remote control and also that network coverage, while growing continually, is still far from universal.

With the potential increase in range of the new communication technologies from line-of-sight, where the user would have to be within the house, to potentially global, it is helpful to be able to identify where the user is. This knowledge can be used to tailor the functions available to the user – effectively there can be a set of "remote" functions and a set of "at home" functions. There are different technologies that can be used to establish the location of the user.

3.2   Location Technologies

There are two principal location technologies of interest here:

1. Radio Frequency Identification (RFID) tags - RFID tags act more as a proximity detection system rather than a location detection one. Effectively, they can be used to establish that a tagged object is within a particular distance of the sensor or reader. That distance can be up to 200 metres, depending on the output power of the tags. The advantage of RFID tags is that an independent local proximity detection network can be established.
2. Global Positioning System (GPS) - GPS is the system used in many navigation aids. It uses the triangulation of signals from a network of satellites to establish in objects location and even its velocity. As its name suggests, a GPS-enabled device is capable of establishing its location anywhere in the world. However, it does have substantial power demands and can deplete batteries in a matter of hours. Essentially an outdoor technology requiring a line-of-sight to satellites, it can be confused by geographical features, such as tall buildings and mountains, thus limiting the data resolution that can be obtained.

There is in addition a third possible approach:

3. Local sensor network - Significant research has been performed towards developing ambient intelligent environments [9]. This research facilitates the development of more ad hoc networks of sensors that can also locate the position of a user within a space. These sensors could range from simple passive infrared (PIR) sensors to sophisticated computer vision systems, where a camera is used to find the user within the living space. Such sensor networks, especially those based on vision techniques, can be very powerful offering the ability to detect whether a user has fallen down, has been inactive for an extended period of time or is showing

signs of emotional distress. However, they are still somewhat experimental, expensive to install and only work within the limited distance range of the sensors.

With an understanding of these technologies, it is possible to begin to see how new environmental control systems could be designed and how their functionality can be extended from simply switching lights and domestic appliances on and off to offering a more comprehensive ability for a user to control his or her environment.

3.3   Control Technologies

Typically, environmental control systems are operated via a special purpose control unit designed specifically to interact with control actuators on each of the domestic appliances that are to be controlled. The advantage of this approach is that the risk of incompatibilities between all of the components is virtually eliminated. It also facilitates the development of custom interfaces to meet the specific needs of an individual user as the transducers can be selected to meet the movements that are easiest and most reliable for that user. For example, these could include binary switches, electromyogram (EMG) sensors, etc.

However, such customized controllers are often expensive and do not always support any functionality beyond control of the identified peripherals. So, they do what they are designed to do and do it well, but if the user wants to add new functionality or to interact with another environment, then those controllers are most likely not going to be suitable for that.

This is where the rise of the new generation of ultra-mobile computing technology raises intriguing possibilities. Tablet computers, such as the Apple iPad and the Samsung Galaxy, are increasing in raw computational power and capability. They are small and lightweight and could fit easily onto a wheelchair in the same way that many special purpose alternative and augmentative communication (AAC) devices have done for a number of years.

These new tablet computers are already designed to interact with domestic appliances, such as televisions, and can even replace devices such as the telephone by using Voice over Internet Protocol (VoIP) calling services. They are straightforward to connect to the Internet and many also offer access to cellular data networks.

The new tablets offer a new model for software development and deployment. The ability to download and install small, agile applications (apps) quickly and easily allows the tablets to deliver highly customizable interaction opportunities to the users. A number of commercial home automation apps are already available for tablets, typically based on the Universal Powerline Bus (UPB) standard, where control signals are sent over a building's existing electricity cables [11] or where the intended peripheral is independently TCP/IP enabled, i.e. is capable of being connected to the Internet.

It is not difficult to envisage how using such a device to control an ECS could lead to interesting possibilities for improving a user's ability to not only interact with and control their local domestic environment, but also provide a more generalized and universal ability to interact with a wider range of environments and systems from an increased spread of geographical locations. Such systems go beyond the concept of traditional environmental control systems. For our purposes here, we will refer to these new, more powerful systems as unified control systems (UCS).

4   A New Model of Unified Control Systems

As discussed in the preceding section, apps already exist for using a tablet to control home automation / environmental control systems. Similarly, AAC apps have been developed to allow the use of tablets to be used for interpersonal communication for users with difficult speaking[1]. Many tablets are already GPS-enabled, providing location detection and they all provide access to the Internet, either through Wi-Fi connectivity or mobile phone data networks.

Thus it can be seen that the elements for a single, combined "unified control system" are largely in place. It could be argued that what is needed now is a framework for bringing this disparate functionality into a cohesive structure. Rather than simply focusing on getting the existing apps to "talk to each other," it is worth examining a variety of possible use-case scenarios to see how a unified control system might be structured.

4.1   Example Use-Cases

The following are a few example use cases for unified control systems, These illustrate how an appropriately designed control system, based on general standards, can significantly improve the independence of a user with a severe motor impairment:

1. Remote control of the house. This is perhaps the most obvious use case. Most environmental control systems are designed to support control of the domestic appliances within a home when the user is physically located there. Home automation systems are intended to support remote control of those systems. The unified control system should support both of these options and offer the ability to autonomously control the functions of the house (such as turning on the heating if the temperature falls too low) and to allow the user to customize all of the automated features of the house at will.

2. House access control. A fully automated house should include a capability to "centrally lock" the house, not unlike how remote central locking is available on most cars. A simple extension of this model, though, is to offer central or selective unlocking. A suitable enabled unified control system should be able to identify when the user is approaching the house and automatically unlock and/or open the front door to allow the person to enter the house without having to issue an explicit command. One possible method for achieving this would be to use GPS location to

---

[1] Examples of some of the AAC products available can be found at:
http://www.friendshipcircle.org/blog/2011/02/07/
7-assistive-communication-apps-in-the-ipad-app-store/

establish when the user is within the grounds of the house. Additionally, the users should be able to use the cameras within the house to securely grant access to repair personnel and the like. Such permission may require explicit confirmation commands by the user – i.e. "Should this person be granted access to the house?"

3. Access to other smart environments. If the unified control system uses widely accepted standards, then it should be possible to allow the user to interact with and control any other smart environment that they enter. Such functionality would offer a significant increase in their level of independence as they would be offered the same level of personalized control of their general environment as they would have in their own home.

4. Inter-personal communication. If a tablet computer is used as the controller, it would be straightforward to add AAC functionality to allow it to operate as a text-to-speech device. It is also possible to couple that to VoIP services, say, to provide a fully accessible telephone capability within the one device.

5. Areas of life endeavour. Keates et al. [12] proposed 5 areas of life endeavour for users with severe functional impairments that computer systems should focus on supporting. These included: lifelong learning and education; workplace; real world (extended activities of daily living); entertainment; and, socializing. Looking at the first of these, it is straightforward to envisage how a unified control system should be able to control the user's workplace as well as their domestic environment.

6. General computer use. A tablet computer is capable of supporting Internet access, personal entertainment and many other functions. These could be embedded in and supported by a general user interface (UI) structured to meet the functional capabilities of the user.

4.2   Examples of the Technology in Practice

The School of Engineering, Computing and Applied Mathematics (SECAM) at the University of Abertay has been researching methods of developing smarter environments and enabling users to interact with and control those environments. There are 2 example systems that are of particular interest here. Both systems were exhibits in the "Robotics" exhibition hosted by "Sensations", the Dundee Science Centre, in the summer of 2012:

1. The GSM-enabled doll's house. A custom-built doll's house has been installed with a GMS receiver and actuators on the doors, lights and windows (see Figure 1). Visitors to the "Robotics" exhibition were invited to send SMS control messages, consisting of 10 different hexadecimal commands codes, to the house to see the effects of the actions. The house has since been enhanced to include Wi-Fi and support commands from a graphical user interface. The next stage of development is to add additional features to the house, including embedded sensors and webcams to support more typical domestic operations. A smart meter will be added, so users can monitor the power consumption of the house remotely, including the effects of running different domestic appliances on the house's overall energy consumption.

Fig. 1. The GSM controlled doll's house. This photograph was taken at the Robotics exhibition hosted by the Dundee Science Centre in the summer of 2012.

2. A mobile personal communication device. A remote chat-bot was installed in a model robot dog (see Figure 2). The chat-bot was controlled via a regular touch-screen, which would be straightforward to substitute with a tablet. The system demonstrated how easy it is to operate a complex chat-bot on a device with limited local capability, but with an Internet connection. The chat-bot processing was performed on remote servers, minimizing the need for local processing power. The next stage of development is to make the dog autonomously mobile, allowing it to follow the user to provide more mobile communication functionality.

Fig. 2. A chat-bot in a robotic dog. The next stage of development is to add more functionality to make an autonomous mobile communication device.

5   Conclusions

This paper has examined possible developments for supporting users with severe motor function impairments by examining how existing technologies can be brought together in innovative ways to support the interaction with and control of a wider set of environments and contexts of use. The technologies required to facilitate the development of such a system largely already exist. What is required is a suitable framework for bringing these capabilities together into a cohesive user experience, ideally through a single user interface. The next steps for this research team will be to develop the existing prototypes further to examine how such a framework could be developed.

References

1. Pieper, M.: Digital divide and learning disabilities: counteracting educational exclusion in information society. ACM SIGACCESS Accessible Computing 83, 37–41 (2005)
2. Keates, S.: Designing for accessibility – a business guide to countering design exclusion. CRC Press (2006)
3. Keates, S., Varker, P., Spowart, F.: Human-machine design considerations in advanced machine-learning systems. IEEE/IBM Journal of Research and Development 55(5), 4:1-4:10 (2011)
4. Keates, S., Varker, P.: The game is afoot, Watson: DeepQA systems and the future of HCI. In: Rebelo, F., Soares, M.M. (eds.) Advances in Usability Evaluation Part II, pp. 341–348. CRC Press, Boca Raton (2012)
5. Cooper, A.: The inmates are running the asylum: why high tech products drive us crazy and how to restore the sanity. SAMS Publishing, Indianapolis (1999)
6. Keates, S., Clarkson, P.J.: Countering design exclusion – an introduction to inclusive design. Springer, Heidelberg (2003)
7. Dickey, R.: Electronic technical aids for persons with high level spinal cord injury. Central Nervous Systems Trauma 3(1), 93–110 (1986)
8. Dickey, R., Shealey, S.H.: Using technology to control the environment. American J of Occupational Therapy 41(11), 717–721 (1987)
9. Emiliani, P.L., Stephanidis, C.: Universal access to ambient intelligence environments: Opportunities and challenges for people with disabilities. IBM Systems Journal 44(3), 605–619 (2005)
10. IEEE: IEEE Standard P802.15.4/D18, Low Rate Wireless Personal Area Networks (2003)
11. Powerline Control Systems: Universal Powerline Bus - The UPB System Description (2003),
    http://www.smarthomeusa.com/Common/UPB/UPBdescription.pdf
12. Keates, S., Kozloski, J., Varker, P.: Cognitive impairments, HCI and daily living. In: Stephanidis, C. (ed.) Universal Access in HCI, Part I, HCII 2009. LNCS, vol. 5614, pp. 366–374. Springer, Heidelberg (2009)

WorkSense: An Interactive Space Design for Future Workplace

Hsuan-Cheng Lin and Taysheng Jeng

Department of Architecture, National Cheng Kung University, Tainan, Taiwan
shiuanlin@gmail.com, tsjeng@mail.ncku.edu.tw

Abstract. Technological advances have initiated obvious changes in types of work so that the traditional cube office layout cannot meet current users' needs. This paper aims to develop an experimental platform for the workplace which is centered on satisfying users' demands. Living lab studies are examined in order to evaluate the uses of the place, with different interactive installations of furniture in the space, and a back-end BIM platform, to present a humane smart workplace of the future.

Keywords: interactive design, living space, smart space, future workplace.

1   Introduction

The development of technological devices and applications, such as laptops, handheld devices, tablet PCs, cloud computing, and wireless network systems, have all become more advanced during the last few years. With the evolution of office tools and the popularity of various technological products, people can handle official business anytime and anywhere; some people even proposed that we should abandon the office space altogether.

However, in order to maintain personal growth and organizational skills, face-to-face communication is absolutely indispensable. The source of creativity in the workplace is still human-based, so that the human-centered design of the future workplace should not be denied. The workplace should contain business resources, which means human beings and their creativity. Office space converted into the workplace not only can handle office requirements, but also serve as a social place that can stimulate creativity. Because of the importance of sensibility and creativity, the office should focus more on the human component to create a workplace which is full of activity, yet charming so that everyone wants to stay inside.

2   A Shift towards a New Age of Workplace Design

The studies on future workspace mostly follow two directions, one is from the perspective of the hardware in determining the design of the space, with the focus on multifunctional furniture and the use of flexible space [1][4]; the other direction is

C. Stephanidis and M. Antona (Eds.): UAHCI/HCII 2013, Part III, LNCS 8011, pp. 64–69, 2013.
© Springer-Verlag Berlin Heidelberg 2013

from the software perspective, with the focus on the system that can support seamless tasks, team work communication and coordination [2][3][5].

Due to space limitations and changing requirements of the workplace, the office desks' layout no longer dominates the office space. The workplace is gradually being transformed into a social activities platform. Because people can hand official business everywhere thanks to the technological support, the main purpose of the future office will be to serve as a social place for, meetings and discussions with people face to face.

This paper proposes two hypotheses regarding the future workplace:

1. Efficient work will no longer constitute the main purpose of the office space; it will be replaced by the need to enhance creativity and human perception.
2. Smart space should be sustainable and humane, which means space should enhance energy efficiency, the 3Rs (Reduce, Reuse and Recycle), and augment human capabilities, such as health, mobility and memory.

3   The Design of Future Workplace

We converted a stairwell space into a design studio space, as a platform for future workplace experiments, as shown in Figure 1 (floor plan) and Figure 2 (actual space). The users are the design graduate students who will carry out the living lab experiments to evaluate the space potential. We designed the space according to the constraints of the existing space and restrictions into different types of work space:

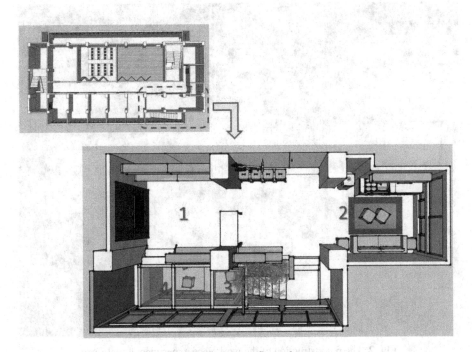

Fig. 1. Workspace floor plan

1. Standing office area with high tables and large display equipment for public use, which can easily accommodate discussions with other people.
2. Lounge space for casual discussions.
3. Public work station area with seats for long time use.
4. Experimental interactive space with sensors and actuators where permit meditation and rest, with the layout of the workplace shown in Figure 3.

Fig. 2. The reconstruction of the workplace experimental platform

We tried to use the different gaps in space to create space diversity; we derived a steel and glass platform, staircase landing for work station, and a small ladder classroom space for group lectures. We also used the ladder drain place to create an indoor large-scale planting space to improve indoor air quality and relax users' stress in the workplace.

Fig. 3. Different types of workspace: the upper row is the office work area; lower row from left to right are: Lounge space, Work station area, and Experimental interactive space

4   Interaction Design in the Future Workplace

4.1   Interactive Devices

We are going to install several interactive devices in different areas in the workplace, such as the bicycles with sensors on them; the sensors can monitor the use of the bikes and send the data to cloud. People who are using this system can do more exercises with this social interactive design, and compete with colleagues; the moving interactive units with LEDs and speakers can change the indoor microclimate. With each interactive device, sensor and the equipment, it is as if you installed an APP in the smart phone, the hardware and its software in the physical space and also in the back-end system. For example, if you need to install an air quality sensor, it would provide not only the sensor, but also the "drivers" for the workplace, by which you can monitor the air quality data and access the data on the system platform.

4.2   Sensing Technologies

We also put different kind of sensors into the workplace, such as air quality sensor, electric power meter, light sensor and infrared sensor to monitor the equipment and users' activities in the workplace. The collected data are sent to a real-time Autodesk Revit model via a Revit API program, which can provide back-end management of workplace and users' workplace usage pattern analysis; the system architecture is shown as Figure 4.

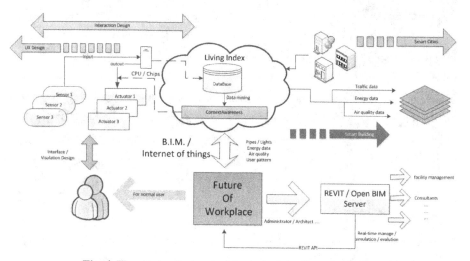

Fig. 4. The sensing system architecture of the future workplace

We call this integration of interactive devices and space usage patterns "WorkSense", and look forward to proposing social innovation designs of future workplaces. We collect all the data and upload to the cloud; then the normal users can access their own data from designed interface. The administrators can use REVIT as a BIM (Building Information Modeling) platform to manage the equipment and other facilities. The BIM information can also be provided to consultants, such as building structural consultant, property management, and other technicians to maintain the workplace.

5   Conclusions

A future workplace should not only focus on a place which is "Green" and "Humane" with interactive technologies, but also a space which can monitor the physical data and the usage pattern in the BIM platform for more advanced applications in a humane smart workplace of the future. With the workplace BIM platform, users can install their own devices in both the physical and virtual systems. The future workplace can augment human capabilities and provide an efficient, sociable, and creative platform. Then all the user activities and environment data can be collected in a data base for different analyses.

The "WorkSense" is a long term ongoing project that includes the user experience workplace design, the interior design, the interactive device design, and the BIM platform which can provide useful data, from a signal smart space which can be extended to a smart campus and even to a smart city [7][8].

References

1. Probst, K., Perteneder, F., Leitner, J., Haller, M., Schrempf, A., Glöckl, J.: Active office: towards an activity-promoting office workplace design. In: Proceedings of the 2012 ACM Annual Conference Extended Abstracts on Human Factors in Computing Systems Extended Abstracts, pp. 2165–2170 (2012)
2. Tennis, J.: Designing the Future of Collaborative Workplace Systems: Lessons Learned from a Comparison with Alternate Reality Games, pp. 1–7 (2011)
3. Sun, T., Doubleday, N., Smith, A.: Designing experiential prototypes for the future workplace. In: Proceedings of the 2012 ACM Annual Conference Extended Abstracts on Human Factors in Computing Systems Extended Abstracts, pp. 331–334 (2012)
4. Raskar, R., Welch, G., Cutts, M., Lake, A., Stesin, L., Fuchs, H.: The office of the future: A unified approach to image-based modeling and spatially immersive displays. In: Proceedings of the 25th Annual Conference on Computer Graphics and Interactive Techniques, pp. 179–188 (1998)
5. Russell, D.M.: Ubiquitous search for smart workspaces. Universal Access in the Information Society 11(3), 337–344 (2011)
6. Jeng, T., Ma, Y.-P., Shen, Y.-T.: iAWN: Designing Smart Artifacts for Sustainable A wareness. In: Stephanidis, C. (ed.) Universal Access in HCI, Part III, HCII 2011. LNCS, vol. 6767, pp. 193–202. Springer, Heidelberg (2011)
7. Lee, J., Baik, S., Lee, C.: Building an integrated service management platform for ubiquitous cities. Computer 44(6), 56–63 (2011)
8. Gil-Castineira, F., Costa-Montenegro, E., Gonzalez-Castano, F.J., Lopez-Bravo, C., Ojala, T., Bose, R.: Experiences inside the ubiquitous oulu smart city. Computer 44(6), 48–55 (2011)

Building Up Virtual Environments Using Gestures

Alexander Marinc, Carsten Stocklöw, and Andreas Braun

Fraunhofer Institute for Computer Graphics Research IGD, Darmstadt, Germany
{alexander.marinc,carsten.stockloew,
andreas.braun}@igd.fraunhofer.de

Abstract. When realizing human-machine-interaction in smart environments it is required to create a virtual representation of the environment that encompasses not only location of the different devices supported but may also contain meta-information such as technical and logical communication layers or a description of supported functionalities, e.g. by using semantics. Creating this representation typically requires technical knowledge and manipulation of object representation files. Therefor it is a major challenge to enable this set-up for regular users, by providing an easy way to establish the virtual environment and the respective position and orientation of integrated devices. In this work we present a novel user-centered approach to create these physical parameters in the virtual representation. Based on intuitive gestural interaction we are able to define the boundaries of appliances and select their capabilities. We have evaluated this method with various users, in order to investigate if such a gestural modification of virtual representations provides an easy way for regular users to create their own smart environment.

Keywords: Smart Environments, 3D modeling, distributed computing.

1   Introduction

Considering the increasing amount of technical devices in modern households, new possibilities are desired to enable natural (in terms of intuitive usage) interaction with them. The very base of such modern forms of interaction like pointing-gestures, voice recognition and digital navigation is a virtual representation of the real environment. This model should at least contain information about the physical properties (shape, dimensions, orientation, position) of elements (devices, furniture, walls, ...) and their technical properties (network-address, controllable properties / provided services, type of the device).

In the past months we have created a concept to build-up all named properties. The basic idea is here to use a virtual 3D reconstruction of the environment to support the user in configuring all parameters, as shown in **Fig.1**. This virtual reality can support End-User programming, as already has been shown by Kelleher et al. [11]. Big steps in 3D reconstruction with consumer devices for the mass-market has recently been done by Izadi et al.[4] and "KinectFusion". But also other researchers like Du et al. [5] made   progress here and allow using such techniques more easily.

C. Stephanidis and M. Antona (Eds.): UAHCI/HCII 2013, Part III, LNCS 8011, pp. 70–78, 2013.
© Springer-Verlag Berlin Heidelberg 2013

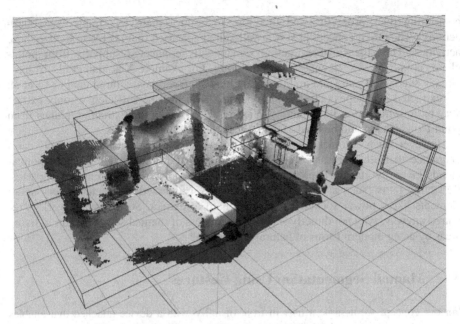

Fig. 1. Concept for modeling whole virtual environment

Here we want to set focus at creation of the physical parameters of devices in the environment. Current approaches like complex CAD applications (e.g. Autodesk AutoCAD[1], Blender[2] or CATIA[3]), more easy-t-use solutions like Trimble Sketch-Up [9] or approaches from science, like presented by Stahl et al. [1] are using a computer mouse as input-device. Consider the needed experience to modeling a 3D-Space using a 2D input-device this is not very well suited for common users.

Therefor we present here a new user-oriented approach to create the physical parameters of a virtual representation of living areas using gestures. Here we currently are focusing on the positioning of bounding boxes, but the general concept can be easily extended to place also other bounding volumes and maybe even create freeform volumes. We can benefit here from the fact that we do not need to create exact matches, but boundaries that are sufficient to get a clear expression about the environments geometry.

2   Related Works

In previous work [2] we have already shown how modeling environments based on OWL ontologies [12] can improve pointing gesture recognition in smart spaces. What we need is a platform supporting the concepts of a service-oriented architecture. A good overview about different possibilities in this domain is given by Papazoglou et al. [3] and Bodhuin et al. [10]. This allows us to associate devices with services

---

[1] http://usa.autodesk.com/autocad/, 24.02.2013.

[2] http://www.blender.org/, 24.02.2013.

[3] http://www.3ds.com/products/catia/, 24.02.2013.

controlling their properties and therefore to control them by simple "one-click-actions". The OSGi concept [13] is a well-suited approach that is able to realize these activities. The process of extracting semantically connected subparts from point-clouds is known as segmentation or clustering. For example Xiaojuan et al. [6] have already successful extracted architectural elements from unstructured data or Li et al. [7] extracted 3D shapes out of point-clouds. Also it may be sufficient to only extract very basic information like done by Wahl et al. [8]. They are extracting planes from point-clouds that could be used to determine whole bounding boxes.

However, such automatic approaches always have the drawback that they can't guarantee that all necessary elements are found. Additionally the gathered points-clouds given by current approaches are often very noisy and can contain big gaps. Reflecting parts (such as the TV in **Fig.1.**) may be missed completely. Very small elements like a power socket will be very hard to extract. So if manual work is required anyway, why not directly support the process of manual segmentation in living areas by using modern forms of natural interaction?

3   Manual Segmentation Using Gestures

For our concept we assume a user in front of a TV with a device attached that enables basic tracking of the user's skeleton data. Making an initial gesture the user can start the process of adding a new bounding box to the scene. The first challenge is now to determine the initial starting-point for the bounding box. As the easiest approach we could take a standard position in the (virtual) front of the user. The problem in this case is that this is not the best-suited base for the next steps, as it is hard to move the box over larger distances using gestures. Therefore we introduce the concept of defining a starting point in 3D space as shown in **Fig.2.** The idea here is to extract several pointing vectors from the tracked skeleton data and determine an approximating intersection point of all of them.

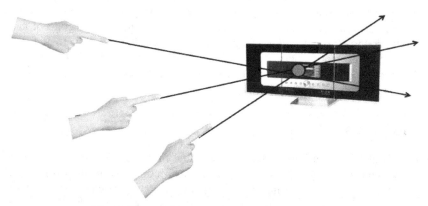

Fig. 2. Determining a spot in 3D by using gestures

Using such a point as the center of a new bounding box we can continue with the next step. Here **Fig.3.** gives a first impression of the basic idea.

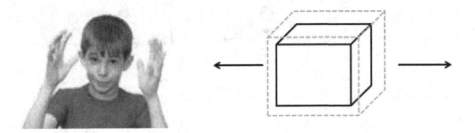

Fig. 3. Setting position, size and orientation of a box by using gestures

The distance between the hands and their orientation will be used as initial values to create more detailed configurations. By changing the distance between both hands the size of the box can be modified; by rotating them in a spherical manner it can be rotated and by moving the hands in some directions in parallel, its position can be translated. Once the user lets both hands fall down to the legs the editing is finished and the new bounding box created. By repeating all these steps a basic representation of the real environment can be created also by end-users that are not familiar with 3D interfaces and modeling.

3.1 Gathering the Initial Position

First we want to have a more detailed view into the details of the process to find an initial point p as a center for a new bounding-box. Therefore we extract a pointing-ray out of the tracked skeleton-data of a user. Here we are using the joints at the shoulder and the hand to determine a ray $\vec{v} = p_{shoulder} - r * (p_{hand} - p_{shoulder})$. In a first attempt we take several rays $\vec{v}_1, ..., \vec{v}_n$ over time and determine the point with the lowest distance to all of the lines given by $\vec{v}_i$. In practice this turned out to not be well suited, since the process takes a lot of time and does not lead to more exact results if we increase n above three. Finally we settled with an approach that is only using two lines to determine a point in 3D space.

Here the idea is to give the user a first pointing ray $\vec{v}$ in the direction of the object or a place where he wants to create a bounding box. After this is fixed he can point along this line to fix a final position. The resulting line we denote as $\vec{u}$. In both cases a time of two seconds (nearly) not moving the arm indicates to proceed to the next step.

Once $\vec{v}$ is fixed and the user pointing to fix $\vec{u}$ we continuously display the current-ly approximated position of p, whereas p is determined by the middle of the two points where the distance between the lines given by $\vec{v}$ and $\vec{u}$ is minimal, as shown in **Fig.4.**

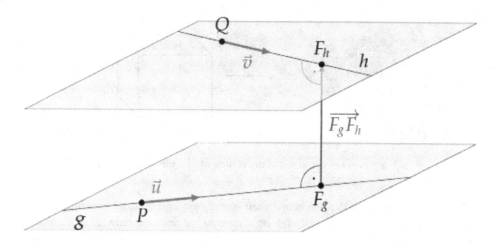

Fig. 4. Compute point of nearest contact from two vectors in $\mathbb{R}^3$ (figure by http://www.ina-de-brabandt.de[4])

In addition to this approach we also tested to get $\vec{v}$ and $\vec{u}$ in parallel by using both arms (one arm for one vector). But in particular for distances that are further away as four meters we received bad results using this approach. This can be attributed to the fact that it is hard to hold both hands fix to a single direction over a longer period of time. In the realized approach we also had troubles with points that are far away., The bigger the distance from p to the user's position, the smaller the angle between $\vec{v}$ and $\vec{u}$ and in consequence small changes have a larger effect. But this is simplified by the user only moving the point along a fixed line. In a next step we can consider smoothing those gestures by using also angles between $\vec{v}$ and $\vec{u}$, where p is normally behind the user to enable more exact operations in distances that are far away.

3.2   Setting Volume Parameters

The problem of setting (exact) position, size and orientation of a bounding box is in a first way separated from the issues handled in section 3.1. We initialize a bounding box with one size in every dimension (1 meter in real space) and the center in the origin of an affine space in $\mathbb{R}^{3\times3}$. To describe all transformations we use a transformation matrix in $\mathbb{R}^{4\times4}$ for each box.

Our first attempt was to gather all parameters in parallel. This means to initialize an identity box by using an initial gesture like given in **Fig.3**. Now the distance between the hands influence the size of the box in all dimensions, the angle is given by rotating the hands around an imaginary sphere and the position can be determined by "carrying" the virtual box through space.

It quickly became apparent that this approach is not suited if we assume that there is only one tracking device in front of the user (instead of many around to cover him

---

[4] http://www.ina-de-brabandt.de/vektoren/a/
abstand-gerade-ws-lot-1fd-punkt.html, 24.02.1013.

in 360 degree). Here in to many situations parts of the user are covered in a way that not both arms can be tracked. In this case it is not possible to determine all three dimensions concurrently (even if this is needed for most of the objects). Therefore we split the process in several parts. We first ask to give the position by moving hands or the whole body, then to give the size in three steps (width, height, depth) by modifying the distance of the hands and finally the orientation in two steps (first rotation around the y-axis and then   around x-axis) by rotating the hands relative to each other. For each step a time of two seconds with constant hand position (we used values from about 5 centimeters for transformation respective 5 degree for rotation) is used to indicate that this value should be fixed.

Even as this approach works quite well there was the need for one additional change. To simplify the interaction the changes are linearly increased. This means the further away the hands are from the initial position the more influence this change has on the transformation of the virtual object. This allows both applying more severe changes in a parameter, but also allows detailed operations.

4   Prototype Application

We combine the single approaches given in sections 3.1 and 3.2 to an overall process. Similar to what we have already done in previous work   we used ontological descriptions as data-model to save the geometry to be created [2]. This can be easily created out of files specified in X3D, e.g. created by the same program that realizes user interaction. As input-device to evaluate the gestures we have used the Microsoft's Kinect[5] that is interfaced using the OpenNI[6] SDK.

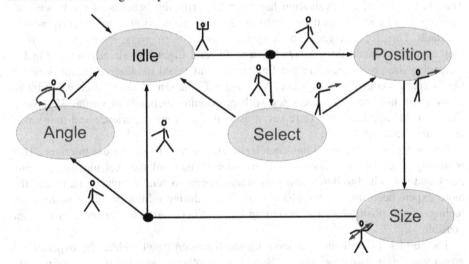

Fig. 5. The whole process of setting bounding boxes

[5] http://www.microsoft.com/en-us/kinectforwindows/, 26.02.2013.
[6] http://www.openni.org/, 26.02.2013.

The whole process of setting one or many bounding boxes into a virtual surrounding is given in **Fig.5**. It is realized as a state-machine that guides a user through the different steps of gathering the required parameters. We are starting at the "idle" state. Here the Psi-pose can be used to indicate the intention to create a new box or changing an existing one. Several users can be in front of the camera, but once a user started the creation process he need to finish or cancel it before another user can interact with the system.

If the user wants to select an existing box he just needs to hold the left arm straight in an angle of about 45° relative to the body. To create a new box he needs to use the right arm in the same way. In first case the positioning process like given in section 3.1 needs to be performed by the user and the box next to the determined point is selected. In both cases the next step is to determine the position of the box. This can either be done using the methods described in section 3.1 or by moving the box like shown in section 3.2. Here a straight arm (indicated by the three joints between shoulder, elbow and hand are in line, having no angle larger than 5° in between) is used as an indicator of what is currently desired by the user.

Now the size and angle can be also given like described in 3.2. Since manipulation and further processing are easier if a bounding box is axis-aligned the setting of the angle is only optional. Here again the arms can be used to indicate if this is desired or not. After this final step we are in the idle-state again.

5   Evaluation

The main focus of the evaluation has been to verify the benefits of the process to build up your environment using gestures vs. using the previous implemented mouse-interface. Therefore we tested both systems with eleven users, measuring the time they needed to create three boxes (Couch, TV and Light like already set in **Fig.1.**), measuring the errors found in the final result and asked qualitative feedback about their experience using the system. As basic information of every user we want to know about his previous experience with positioning elements in virtual 3D spaces (by e.g. CAD applications). Here seven users had a strong experience and four never used such a concept before.

For both groups the result has been less exact then using the mouse interface. This is mainly given by two reasons. First the measurement of the skeleton-data is quite noisy and not suited to determine parameters in centimeters. Second in particular the more experienced users often changed the view during editing to get a more exact feeling of the position of the bounding-box. When using the gestures this is not possible.

The results differed most concerning the time-constraints. Here the experienced group was faster using the mouse. However the other group was quicker using gestures. Accordingly the feedback of the first group regarding the system was very reserved, whereas the second group enjoyed the experience to influence the virtual 3D spaces easily.

In conclusion the results indicate that the system even in its prototypical form is well suited to allow common users to build up a virtual environment. Given the drawbacks above it seems not to be suited for the requirements of experts, or at least will require strong modifcations. Even if this result is not surprising, it shows that with respect to End-User-Programming the general approach seems to be a step in the right direction.

6   Conclusions and Further Work

We introduced an approach that allows common users to build up a virtual space that can be used as a base for modern forms of interaction, like pointing-gestures. Where fully automatic algorithms may easily fail in segmenting specific parts of reconstructed environments, our approach is using the abilities of the user to specify the system according to his needs. Bounding boxes for relevant devices can be placed simply by using different forms of arm gestures. As our evaluation has shown this approach has drawbacks concerning exactness and interaction time for experts, but allows untrained users a much quicker access to the system.

Regarding future work the most important issue is to extend the approach. Currently it is only used to gather the physical parameters, but with respect to the usage in real living areas all parameter(type, device specific inputs, …) need to be given only using gestures or at least a concept is needed to combine them with more traditional inputs. Also more detailed evaluations are needed to get a better impression how quick the learning process of influencing 3D space with a computer mouse is and therefore if there is a discernible advantages for beginners. Also it is desirable to implement alternatives for the used gestures and compare the results with the current approach. It may be possible that an alternative allow also experts to interact quicker with the system than they would using a mouse.

References

1. Stahl, C., et al.: Synchronized realities. Journal of Ambient Intelligence and Smart Environments 1, 13–25 (2011)
2. Marinc, A., Stocklöw, C., Tazari, S.: 3D Interaction in AAL Environments Based on Ontologies. In: Ambient Assisted Living, pp. 289–302 (2012)
3. Papazoglou, M.P., Van Den Heuvel, W.J.: Service oriented architectures: approaches, technologies and research issues. The VLDB Journal 16 16(3), 389–415 (2007)
4. Izadi, S., et al.: KinectFusion: real-time 3D reconstruction and interaction using a moving depth camera. In: Proceedings of the 24th Annual ACM Symposium on User Interface Software and Technology. ACM (2011)
5. Du, H., et al.: Interactive 3D modeling of indoor environments with a consumer depth camera. In: Proceedings of the 13th International Conference on Ubiquitous Computing. ACM (2011)
6. Xiaojuan, N., et al.: Segmentation of Architecture Shape Information from 3D Point Cloud (2009)

7. Li, X., Godil, A., Wagan, A.: 3D part identification based on local shape descriptors. In: Proceedings of the 8th Workshop on Performance Metrics for Intelligent Systems. ACM (2008)

8. Wahl, R., Guthe, M., Klein, R.: Identifying planes in point-clouds for efficient hybrid rendering. In: The 13th Pacific Conference on Computer Graphics and Applications (2005)

9. Murdock, K.L.: Google SketchUp and SketchUp Pro 7 Bible, vol. 606. Wiley (2009)

10. Bodhuin, T., et al.: Hiding complexity and heterogeneity of the physical world in smart living environments. In: Proceedings of the 2006 ACM Symposium on Applied Computing. ACM (2006)

11. Kelleher, C., Pausch, R.: Lowering the barriers to programming: A taxonomy of programming environments and languages for novice programmers. ACM Computing Surveys (CSUR) 37(2), 83–137 (2005)

12. McGuinness, D.L., Van Harmelen, F.: OWL web ontology language overview. W3C Recommendation, 10 (March 10, 2004)

13. Alliance, OSGi. Osgi service platform, release 3. IOS Press, Inc. (2003)

Gathering the Users' Needs in the Development of Assistive Technology: A Blind Navigation System Use Case

Hugo Paredes, Hugo Fernandes, Paulo Martins, and João Barroso

INESC TEC (formerly INESC Porto) and University of Trás-os-Montes e Alto Douro,
Quinta de Prados, Apartado 1013, Vila Real, Portugal
{hparedes,hugof,pmartins,jbarroso}@utad.pt

Abstract. Assistive technology enables people to achieve independence in the accomplishment of their daily tasks and enhance their quality of life. However, the development os assistive technology does not always follow user needs and expectations, comprising their usability and effectiveness. This paper discusses the design and evaluation strategies for assistive technologies applied to a blind navigation system case study. The research carried out focused on the gathering of user requirements for ensuring enhanced autonomy of blind people in their daily life. The picked requirements were used in an architecture that unifies the benefits of a redundant blind navigation system with a set of services that are provided by daily used information and communication technologies. The system combines guidance, navigation and information gathering, extending traditional aids with realtime knowledge of the surrounding environment to provide an enhanced assistive tool for autonomy of the blinds. Moreover, the developed solution fills the gap of existing solutions that require the users to carry a wide range of devices and, mostly, do not include mechanisms to ensure the autonomy of users in the event of system failure.

Keywords: usability evaluation, interviews, blindness, assistive technology, navigation, autonomy.

1 Introduction

"Assistive Technology is any object or system that increases or maintains the capabilities of people with disabilities" [7][1]. However, little proof exists to support the real benefits of assistive technology both for the researchers and the users, and the contention that users are satisfied with relevant aspects of these assistive technologies [21]. Moreover, there are well known problems associated with the design and development of assistive technologies that have been widely discussed by the community. Authors explore the agenda, development and value of assistive technology from different perspectives, from its development to the users' satisfaction [7,21,16].

---

[1] According to the Assistive Technology Act of 1998, S.2432.

C. Stephanidis and M. Antona (Eds.): UAHCI/HCII 2013, Part III, LNCS 8011, pp. 79–88, 2013.
© Springer-Verlag Berlin Heidelberg 2013

Following the development of a core blind navigation system in the SmartVision project, the evaluation of the prototype revealed that further requirement analysis was needed [9]. Some of those requirements were introduced in the nav4b prototype that preceded the Blavigator project [10]. However, the technological solutions introduced required a shift in the research strategy and the usage of new methodologies to enhance the gathering of user requirement and their real needs. The major research questions that arise at those stages concern: (1) the context where blind or visual impaired users need to use a navigation system; (2) how the users interact with the system; (3) the availability of the system; and (4) how and why the application helps the users to enhance their autonomy. In order to address these questions a study with visually impaired users was developed, which sought the evaluation of their daily habits in order to examine how assistive technology might be an aid in their autonomy. This approach follows the principles of User-Centred Design [22], where *"technology related policies and services need to emphasise consumer involvement and their long-term needs to reduce device abandonment and enhance their satisfaction"* [16].

This paper presents the exploratory study of user requirements in the Blavigator project for blind navigation. The methodology used for the study is analyzed and discussed, followed by an explanation of the work developed. The core of the study is a semi-structured interview that was conducted with users with different levels of blindness. The analysis methodology used to gather data from the interviews [23,2,25] allowed reevaluating the system requirements and weaving new directives on the real needs of users for a blind navigation system. The process of analysis and development of accessible applications is discussed taking into account the experience gained from this use case and the analysis of reference bibliography in the domain. The discussion follows with the lessons learned and the needs to be addressed. The presented study reveals that, as in similar studies [4], users' input is an important component to help guide designers in producing assistive technologies. Moreover, the choice of the evaluation methodology follows the HCI research patterns and *"must arise from and be appropriate for the actual problem or research question under consideration"* [11]. A final lesson regards the presence of the users in every phase of the development of assistive technologies, in order to ensure that the system actually behaves as we expect and meets their requirements [6].

The structure of the remaining paper is as follows: Section 2 describes background and related work. In section 3, the Blavigator project is presented highlighting its features and major requirements. The fourth section focuses on the research methods applied in this study. Section 5 gives an overview of the empirical findings gathered from the field work. A discussion of the empirical results is presented in Section 6. The last section provides some final remarks.

2   Background

Assistive technologies play an important role in the lives of many people by providing the means to perform their daily living activities and helping people with disabilities to achieve greater independence and enhance their quality of life. From the various assistive technologies available nowadays, a special focus was put on those related with mobility. Mobility is a fundamental part of life for every human and heavily depends on sight for orientation and navigation. However, blind and visually impaired people need to rely on other senses, such as touch and hearing, to ensure their mobility [17].

Current technology enabled the creation of systems that assist people with special needs to navigate, eliminating many of their mobility restrictions [14,24]. The development of such systems has been discussed by several authors [26]. Most of these studies evaluate the needs and requirements of electronic travel aids. Sanchez '[19] argues that this systems should not focus on the replacement of traditional assistive tools, as the white cane, since it is "very unlikely to redesign such a device that is cheap, portable and useful". According to the author, efforts should be made in order to detect and inform users about obstacles and provide more accurate information about the environment. In a user centric perspective, Pressl and Wieser [18] worked in a project with the collaboration of blind people in order to develop "a prototype of a navigation system which covers the overall spectrum of navigational components". Polacek et al. [17] follow the same perspective, conducting an in-depth evaluation with blind users in order to evaluate the relevant aspects of navigation for the blind. In their study, the authors also focus the integration of "sensors for position and rotation acquisition, algorithm for route computation and an interface allowing the user to control the navigation system".

In the last decade several projects have emerged aiming to enhance indoor navigation [8]. The BIGS System, proposed Na[15], includes an infrastructure, the smart floor, and a portable terminal unit. A more complex system was presented by Ding [5] consisting of RFID tags, a portable reader which can be integrated into the white cane, a mobile phone, a Call Center and a central information server. Jacquet et al. [13] developed a system based on a white cane with a laser telemeter and GPS, that provides guidance information as well as descriptive details about places based on semantic descriptions. Recently, Chen [3] proposed the inclusion of pre-built RFID tags in blind pathways. Moreover, the SmartVision project aims to develop a system for assisting the blind navigate autonomously, integrating GPS, Wi-Fi, RFID and computer vision technology [1]. In a complementary perspective, the TANIA system, which was originally developed to provide the blind with a navigation device, was extended with an RFID reader or the recognition of tagged objects [20]. The integration of navigation and object recognition was previously explored by Hub et. al[12].

3   The Blavigator Project

The navigation for the blind has been shown as an area of interest in the scientific community across the last few decades. Some of the issues associated with these systems are generic assistive technologies, and other related to the specific context of the case study. For the last years, our team has developed prototypes of navigation systems for the blind in order to solve some of the problems associated with these systems. On the genesis of the current Blavigator project, which integrates the study presented herein, is the Smartvision project.

The main goal of the SmartVision project was to develop and integrate technology for aiding blind users and those with severe visual impairments into a small portable device that is cheap and easy to assemble using off-the-shelf components. This device should be extremely easy to carry and use, yet providing all necessary help for autonomous navigation. It should be stressed out that the device was designed to be an extension of the white cane, not a replacement, and to be "non-invasive", issuing warning signals when approaching a possible obstacle, a point-of-interest or when the footpath in front is curved and the heading direction should be adapted. In this sense, the SmartVision prototype addressed three main applications: (1) local navigation for centring on footpaths etc. and obstacle avoidance, in the immediate surroundings, but just beyond the reach of the white cane; (2) global navigation for finding one's way; and (3) object/obstacle recognition, not only on the shelves in a pantry or supermarket, but also outdoor: bus stops, taxi stands, cash machines (ATM) and telephone booths.

Based on one of the technologies of the infrastructure of the SmartVIsion, the Radio Frequency IDentification (RFID), used to create electronic trails and tags, the Nav4B system [10] , proposed the integration of blind navigation with day-to-day life supporting information systems, as traffic lights and public transportations. Moreover, the system focus on the ergonomics and ubiquity go the solution, using typical blind aids: a white cane; a smartphone; and bone- conduction headphones.

The Blavigator project extends the main goals of the SmartVision project with the concept of the Nav4B architecture. In other words, the Blavigator prototype intends to be an integrated navigation system which increases the autonomy of daily life significantly while being, at the same time, cheap, reliable, small and easy to use. Therefore the hardware platform chosen for the Blavigator prototype was a smartphone. This platform embeds all the sensors required, like stereo vision, digital compass and a GPS antenna, and also provides all the data connections needed, like Internet connection and Bluetooth for interfacing with the instrumented white cane. Moreover, in the development of the Blavigator project an extensive study of user requirements was performed as detailed described in the next sections.

4   Research Methods

The experience acquired in the development of navigation systems for the blind demonstrated the importance of assessing user needs. However, as in the bulk of computer systems, users do not know their needs accurately, the study and requirements gathering goes through the analysis of their habits and how the technology shall be embedded in their everyday life. Research methodologies for conducting such studies are diverse, using, among others, ethnographic techniques, interviews and surveys.

In this sense, the research method used was a semi-structured interview that provides a closer interaction with the existing sample. This methodology ensures greater richness and quality of information collected, to allow direct contact and interaction with the sample during the interview, contrasting with other methodologies based on surveys. Moreover, the use of ethnographic techniques required special conditions which could hardly be guaranteed (such as the ethnographer be blind so be able to experience the same experiments and thus report).

A semi-structured interview is characterised by the existence of a previously prepared script that serves shaft guiding the development of the interview, ensuring that the various participants answer the same questions without following a strict order to adapt the interview development to the interviewee.

The selection of the users for the sample group should ensure that they represent a subset of the study universe, to guarantee the scope of the study, the search universe and the data sources in conjunction with the time and funds available. Thus, a sample set of five individuals male and female, from different age ranges and visual impaired or legally blind were selected.

In order to characterise the sample group in detail, the interview guide began by gathering the age, sex, origin of visual impairment or legally blind interviewee. The script also contained indications to the interviewer to ask for the permission of the interviewee to perform the audio recording of the interview for later analysis of more reliable data collection ensuring his/her privacy rights. Following the set of objectives for the study, the interview guidelines included questions about the use of devices and assistive technologies for enhancing the mobility and independence of blind users, as other everyday use objects. To measure the degree of autonomy of the individual, the interview also focused on urban obstacles and barriers, whether fixed or mobile. Additionally, and when possible, individuals were questioned in relation to the degree of nuisance caused by those barriers to their daily lives and the environments in which they arose (known / unknown, interior / exterior). Therefore it was ensured that a perspective of the wider difficulties experienced by each individual was gathered. For a better characterisation of the individuals' knowledge about the assistive technologies for describing the environment, stakeholders were asked about their experience in usage of tactile flooring, traffic lights with sound and subtitles in braille (for example at bus stops). This nuclear base of information helps to understand the level of independence, autonomy and knowledge of each individual in this domain. Finally, the script contained questions guidelines that aim to find the ideal solution to provide autonomy to users. However, the questions should not be directly asked to the user, but presented with various types of answers and without limitation. That strategy allows the individual the opportunity to express themselves by using situations they experienced.

5   Empirical Findings

The interviews were conducted in an informal and familiar environment to the interviewee. This methodology promotes the interview to arise as an informal conversation, having some points on which the interviewer should conduct the interview, but always ensuring freedom of the interviewee to express their opinions. Consequently, and depending on the individual interviewed, the duration of the interviews ranged between 105 and 15 minutes.

The characterisation of the interviewed individuals revealed that two intervenients were legally blind and the remaining three were visual impaired. The legally blind individuals lost their vision during their life, one at 24 and the other at 20 years of age, and are currently 32 and 38 years old respectively. As the blind individuals were not born blind, they had to adapt to a new reality. In the general context, they seem well adapted to this reality and are very independent individuals without any shame to ask and answer any question about any subject. Moreover they pursue an active life, personal and professionally, and are very curious about new technologies which can increase their autonomy, saying that "I really like being autonomous and I am volunteer for new experiences." Meanwhile, visual impaired individuals have been losing their vision gradually throughout their life. All individuals consider living in quiet towns. Some of them often use public urban transportation. One of the individuals reported that she only uses public transport when travelling to large cities, because she needs to.

The usage of mobile phone is transversal to all the surveyed users. The choice of all of them fell on the same brand as it was one of the first to provide a screen reader for these devices. Among the various functions available the interviewees make calls, store phone numbers and events on the agenda. In everyday life all of the interviewed blind individuals use the white cane, although one of them was waiting for a seeing eye dog to ensure increased mobility and autonomy. The usage of white cane was not as common among the partially sighted surveyed, thus their mobility was more conditioned. The clock is also an object of everyday use, in its various versions: audio, tactile, etc..

The opinion of respondents is unanimous concerning the amount of existing barriers, as there are numerous urban barriers, particularly poles, dustbins, letterbox, public telephones, terraces and products displayed on the sidewalk in traditional stores. The barriers are not only found in external areas, but also inside buildings, where often information is scarce, particularly regarding the location of services and identification of stairs and elevators. Despite the barriers faced, individuals are also unanimous in considering that in already known paths of their daily life, obstacles and their liable locations are easily detected, even if they are just temporary obstacles.

Regarding the existing aid individuals are skeptical and rely more on their senses than on the information provided by electronic devices. For example, in the case of traffic lights with audio information one of the users stated: *"who can assure me that the traffic lights are working well and when I cross the street I will not be hit by a vehicle?"* However there are situations in which Assistive technology may be useful as one of the users remarked by saying: *"I like the automatic doors more because the recognise us when we arrive"*. The nonexistence of information is another problem mentioned: *"public transports lack indications about the destinations, I often have to ask the driver"*.

As for navigation in familiar surroundings blind individuals report that since reference points are not changed, they feel completely free to walk without a cane. The situation turns out to be not much different on the outside, showing that they rediscovered the cities where they live just with the help of their white cane. One adds: *"I travel alone on buses, usually recognize the path by the movement of the bus and easily know my location"*. Still on his autonomy the other individual states: *"I can go anywhere, I quite manage my autonomy and mobility"*. The independence / autonomy of partially sighted individuals is different, having been noted that, for example, one of the individuals has a higher dependence mainly from her mother who carries and accompanies her everywhere. A revealing fact was to find that in unknown areas, outside her hometown, she does not have any problem in using her white cane. However in her hometown she is a bit more retracted *"when I go into another town, like Oporto, I use a cane but here I do not use it. I am ashamed."*

6   Discussion

In general, all individuals surveyed are accompanied by the same objects, just like any other person without any special need. The objects are the personal mobile phone, laptop computer, watch, keys, and obviously in the case of the blind, the white cane. Therefore, mobility and autonomy assistive technologies must be integrated in objects that are common in the everyday life of their users.

User requirements also include information about architectural barriers and movable obstacles that should be communicated to users so that they can choose alternative paths / routes. The lack of information about the surrounding environment is a key problem described by users, also requiring information on specific locations, particularly inside the buildings. The needs are extensible to services, one of the key problems identified being the lack of information in the public transports.

It is also worth mentioning that the study carried out is not conclusive about how the indications and information can be delivered to the users. None of the respondents were explicit in their preferences, and the results were conditioned by the hypotheses they were given during the interview. The interviewees are nonetheless broadly in agreement on this point: the indications should be clear and concise and more ancillary information should be available optionally, although it would relay more security to the individual if the path was done along a wall in order to always have feedback for orientation, instead of traversing the space without reference points.

Finally, one of the most prominent aspects of the study relates to the need for usage of a system to support mobility and navigation for the blind. In everyday life users use the same pathways, the same schedules, knowing the environment that surrounds them very well, so there is no need for any information other than that relating to urban temporary barriers and obstacles that may arise. Consequently, the usage of a navigation system for the blind will be equal to their usage for a normal person, that is, when moving to an unknown location.

Some of the problems highlighted in this study are common to previous studies, in which we studied the habits and daily life of users [19,17]. Despite the variety and richness of the information gathered, the need to perform functional tests with prototypes is clear, in order to evaluate the adaptation of the system used and its usage.

7 Final Remarks

The improvement of the functional capabilities of people with special needs is often achieved through the use of assistive technologies. These technologies ensure an improvement of the general welfare of the people, enhancing their capabilities. However, their design is sometimes limited. Some of the solutions are too specific and therefore have very high costs. Other solutions are designed to ensure universal access, with features that allow its usage by a broad population. Nevertheless, and particularly in this last case, some of the solutions are designed in the laboratory without examining the real needs of individuals.

In the work presented in this paper we highlight the need for interaction with users to gather the system requirements for assistive technologies. In order to illustrate this need a navigation system for the blind is presented as a case study. The system has evolved in order to narrow down its requirements according to the users needs.

In the last iteration of the system development semi-structured interviews were conducted with potential users in order to understand their daily habits and thereby assess the requirements of a system that supports them in their mobility. The research methodology used proved suitable to the study, particularly by creating an informal atmosphere with the interviewees and not target their responses to the objective of the ongoing work. Therefore the problems and the real needs of users in their day to day life were perceived and the requirements for the enhancement of the system were gauged, in order to increase their autonomy and mobility.

The work carried out showed some limitations, namely at the level of obtaining information from users concerning what they would expect in a system to support their mobility.

Furthermore, the need for the evaluation of the development process as a whole, ie, a complete development cycle, from the requirements elicitation until the prototype testing, is also evident,. Therefore the main purpose of future work is to understand if the whole process of development was actually adjusted to the user needs, performing applicational tests with the same sample group using a prototype navigation system that reflects the needs evidenced in the study.

Acknowledgements. The Portuguese Foundation for Science and Technology (FCT) supported this research through the project RIPD/ADA/109690/2009 – BLAVIGATOR: a cheap and reliable navigation aid for the blind. We would also like to thanks the undergraduate and graduate students of the University of Trás-os-Montes e Alto Douro, which were involved in this process, for their support.

References

1. du Buf, J.H., Barroso, J., Rodrigues, J.M., Paredes, H., Farrajota, M., Fernandes, H., ao José, J., Teixeira, V., Saleiro, M.: The smartvision navigation prototype for blind users. JDCTA 5(5), 351–361 (2011)
2. Burnard, P.: A method of analysing interview transcripts in qualitative research. Nurse Education Today 11(6), 461–466 (1991)
3. Chen, J., Li, Z., Dong, M., Wang, X.: Blind path identification system design base on rfid. In: 2010 International Conference on Electrical and Control Engineering (ICECE), pp. 548–551 (June 2010)
4. Choi, Y.M., Sprigle, S.H.: Approaches for Evaluating the Usability of Assistive Technology Product Prototypes. Assistive Technology 23, 36–41 (2011)
5. Ding, B., Yuan, H., Zang, X., Jiang, L.: The research on blind navigation system based on rfid. In: International Conference on Wireless Communications, Networking and Mobile Computing, WiCom 2007, pp. 2058–2061 (2007)
6. Dix, A., Finlay, J.E., Abowd, G.D., Beale, R.: Human-Computer Interaction, 3rd edn. Prentice-Hall, Inc., Upper Saddle River (2003)
7. Edyburn, D.: Rethinking assistive technology. Special Education Technology Practice 5(4), 16–23 (2004)
8. Faria, J., Lopes, S., Fernandes, H., Martins, P., Barroso, J.: Electronic white cane for blind people navigation assistance. In: World Automation Congress (WAC), pp. 1–7 (September 2010)
9. Fernandes, H., Conceição, N., Paredes, H., Pereira, A., Araújo, P., Barroso, J.: Providing accessibility to blind people using gis. Universal Access in the Information Society 11(4), 399–407 (2012)
10. Fernandes, H., Faria, J., Paredes, H., Barroso, J.A.: An integrated system for blind day-to-day life autonomy. In: The Proceedings of the 13th International ACM SIGACCESS Conference on Computers and Accessibility, ASSETS 2011, pp. 225–226. ACM, New York (2011)
11. Greenberg, S., Buxton, B.: Usability evaluation considered harmful (some of the time). In: Proceedings of the SIGCHI Conference on Human Factors in Computing Systems, CHI 2008, pp. 111–120. ACM, New York (2008)
12. Hub, A., Diepstraten, J., Ertl, T.: Design and development of an indoor navigation and object identification system for the blind. In: Proceedings of the 6th International ACM SIGACCESS Conference on Computers and Accessibility, ASSETS 2004, pp. 147–152. ACM, New York (2004)
13. Jacquet, C., Bellik, Y., Bourda, Y.: Electronic locomotion aids for the blind: Towards more assistive systems. In: Ichalkaranje, N., Ichalkaranje, A., Jain, L.C. (eds.) Intelligent Paradigms for Assistive and Preventive Healthcare. SCI, vol. 19, pp. 133–163. Springer, Heidelberg (2006)
14. Kitsas, I.K., Panoulas, K.J., Kosmidou, V.E., Taplidou, S.A., Saragiotis, C.D., Hadjileontiadis, L.J., Panas, S.M.: Smarteyes: An efficient mobile phone/navigator for blind or visually impaired people. In: Proceedings of the Forum for the ICT Professionals Congress, FITCE 2006 (2006)
15. Na, J.: The blind interactive guide system using rfid-based indoor positioning system. In: Miesenberger, K., Klaus, J., Zagler, W.L., Karshmer, A.I. (eds.) ICCHP 2006. LNCS, vol. 4061, pp. 1298–1305. Springer, Heidelberg (2006)
16. Phillips, B., Zhao, H.: Predictors of assistive technology abandonment. Assistive Technology: the Official Journal of Resna 5(1), 36–45 (1993)

17. Poláček, O., Grill, T., Tscheligi, M.: Towards a navigation system for blind people: a wizard of oz study. SIGACCESS Access. Comput. 104, 12–29 (2012)

18. Pressl, B., Wieser, M.: A computer-based navigation system tailored to the needs of blind people. In: Miesenberger, K., Klaus, J., Zagler, W.L., Karshmer, A.I. (eds.) ICCHP 2006. LNCS, vol. 4061, pp. 1280–1286. Springer, Heidelberg (2006)

19. Sánchez, J., Elías, M.: Guidelines for designing mobility and orientation software for blind children. In: Baranauskas, C., Abascal, J., Barbosa, S.D.J. (eds.) INTERACT 2007. LNCS, vol. 4662, pp. 375–388. Springer, Heidelberg (2007)

20. Schmitz, B., Hub, A.: Combination of the Navigation System TANIA with RFID-Based Initialization and Object Recognition, p. 2 (2009), http://www.icevi-europe.org/dublin2009/index.html

21. Stickel, M.S., Ryan, S., Rigby, P.J., Jutai, J.W.: Toward a comprehensive evaluation of the impact of electronic aids to daily living: Evaluation of consumer satisfaction. Disability and Rehabilitation: An International, Multidisciplinary Journal 24(1-3), 115–125 (2002)

22. Vredenburg, K., Mao, J.Y., Smith, P.W., Carey, T.: A survey of user-centered design practice. In: Proceedings of the SIGCHI Conference on Human Factors in Computing Systems, CHI 2002, pp. 471–478. ACM, New York (2002)

23. Wengraf, T.: Qualitative research interviewing: biographic narrative and semi-structured methods. Sage, London (2001)

24. Willis, S., Helal, S.: Rfid information grid for blind navigation and wayfinding. In: Proceedings of the Ninth IEEE International Symposium on Wearable Computers, ISWC 2005. IEEE Computer Society, Washington, DC (2005)

25. Witzel, A.: The problem-centered interview. Forum Qualitative Sozialforschung / Forum: Qualitative Social Research 1(1) (2000)

26. Zhang, J., Ong, S.K., Nee, A.Y.C.: Navigation systems for individuals with visual impairment: a survey. In: Proceedings of the 2nd International Convention on Rehabilitation Engineering & Assistive Technology, iCREATe 2008, Singapore Therapeutic, Assistive & Rehabilitative Technologies (START) Centre, Kaki Bukit TechPark II, Singapore, pp. 159–162 (2008)

Ambient Assisted Living Development in East Slovakia

Dušan Šimšík[1], Alena Galajdová[1], Daniel Siman[1], and Daniela Onofrejová[2]

[1] Department of Automation, Control and Human Machine Interactions, Technical University of Košice, Letná 9, 042 00 Košice, Slovakia
{dusan.simsik,alena.galajdova,daniel.siman}@tuke.sk
www.tuke.sk
[2] Pontech spol. s r.o., Kisdyho 19, 040 01 Košice, Slovakia
onofrejova@gmail.com
www.pontech.sk

Abstract. Authors describe preliminary results and some new plans in the development project of the new social service in Kosice city in East Slovakia. On 20 users group of Kosice citizens it is shown how applied research has been translated into practical innovation of regional social service based on ICT technology. Results were obtained in frame of the International European project MonAMI – Mainstreaming on Ambient Intelligence, supported by the 6-th framework program of the European Commission. It shows how ambient technology platform MonAMI and related ICT services were adapted into society in a city and rural area too in Slovakia. MonAMI is European project focusing on ambient assisted living concept to increase autonomy, enhance ICT services for monitoring purposes for carers and support safety of vulnerable people living alone. Current plans for further development and implementation in praxis in cooperation with the SME are described.

Keywords: seniors, ambient assistive living, sensor networks, open architecture, tele-health.

1 Introduction

The main goal of the MonAMI project was to develop a technological platform based on mainstream technologies and services [1]. The developed social services were focused on the scenarios for the Ambient Assisted Living of seniors and/or persons with disabilities [2]. MonAMI technology platform hasthree levels architecture, and it consists of sensors, logical and external services and interfaces [3]. The main interconnecting abstraction of the system is a set of interfaces OSGi4AMI currently accessible as an open source project [4]. They define precisely functions and operations of all devices, actuators on various platforms as well as services – OSGi components [5]. Therefore new devices, either wired or wireless, may be easily added to the system. Central component of the installation in household is a Residential Gateway (RG), where 1-Wire and ZigBee sensors or actuators are connected. The front-end of RG can be represented by a touch screen computer, or any mobile technology as smart phone, tablet or a TV [9].

C. Stephanidis and M. Antona (Eds.): UAHCI/HCII 2013, Part III, LNCS 8011, pp. 89–96, 2013.
© Springer-Verlag Berlin Heidelberg 2013

MonAMI system is build from three pre-defined packages. The first package is devoted to monitoring of temperature, luminance, connected electrical appliances, etc. The second package is a remote control of various actuators/switchers to activate a motorized device or any electrical appliance, which run automatically activating when a situation is recognized by the control system or when a person gives an appropriate command. The third package is about sending messages and warnings for notification of risky situations, related to household or personal senior's situations (gas - smoke detection, social alarm, and presence on risky place in an inappropriate time).

2   Development of Socialict Services for Seniors in Slovakia

Situation in Slovakia can be described by the following main features.

1. Legislation support of the social services using communication technology in Slovakia is defined in the law since 2008 in act "Social law" Nb. 448/2008. It defines two types of social services that use a communication technology:

    a. Monitoring and signalization of help needed. This social service is supplied to a physical person who has a risky health status to prevent or eventually solve an emergency situation.It is provided for 24-hours as a distance, voice, written (SMS) or electronic communication with user based on signaling or audiovisual device linked to an emergency center.

    b. Emergency help using a communication technology. Emergency help provided mainly as social advisory to a physical person using telecommunication service to person who is in a critical social situation or in other risky life situation, which is not able to solve by own.

2. Local small centers have been built in the last few years by the charitable or nongovernmental organizations. They use a kind of telephone with emergency button and a special bracelet. Telephone has a sensitive microphone and user can communicate with emergency 24-hour available center, link to Red Cross emergency service, or with a carer/relatives. The second model is more frequent.

3. Centralized approaches are used for systems implemented by the regional nongovernmental offices. Only 3 of total 8 self governmental offices have built a social calling centre and offer social emergency service to seniors. They work independently, and don't cooperate mutually. Experienced centers try to initiate one common system in Slovakia.

4. Mainstream ICT services enlargement. Providers of telecommunication services in Slovakia don't offer yet mainstream services that might be used by seniors and persons with disabilities for the social service as defined by the law. There are some first attempts, which will be described later.

3   MonAMI Services Implementation Plans

3.1   MonAMI Services Architecture

The idea of MonAMI platform creation was to construct technology platform derived from subsistent standard technologies. The platform is assigned to deliver services, which integrate reliable wireless (ZigBee) SON networks, wired networks, user friendly interaction technology, wearable devices and components for health monitoring [3]. The MonAMI platform basically consistsof five main subsystems:

1. Set of wired (1-wire technology) and wireless (ZigBee technology) sensors and actuators.
2. Server of the user interface (Universal Control Hub).
3. Dynamic service platform based on OSGi.
4. Touch screen as main user interface.
5. Telco web platform to manage alarm, services and services update.

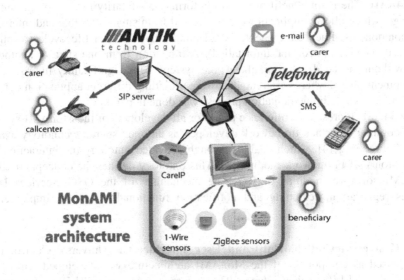

Fig. 1. MonAMI social service and home automation platform

The MonAMI platform is centralized on the Residential Gateway (RG). The role of RG is to centralize the MonAMI services in one point, which enables to share the same resources by all services and afford opportunity to create even extended individually formulated services.

Residential Gateway. The Residential Gateway (RG) is any computer where the main logic of the system is running. It could be a small computer with x86 architecture and Java technology support. In the project we have used a touch screen computer – ASUS Eee Top. However, the screen is not a requirement, since the UI may run remotely on another computer, TV, PDA or a smart phone and communicate with the

RG through a predefined protocol. We have used UCH which is based on http and socket communication. All the sensors and actuators are connected directly to RG, where the hardware layer is due to the usage of OSGi4AMI interfaces hidden to remaining system.

Therefore, hardware implementation of the sensors and actuators is transparent to the services and they appear in the system as software objects with predefined methods and functionality, which is expected to be implemented by all drivers' vendors.

The Residential Gateway (RG) used in MonAMI platform consists of 4 main parts:

- Felix Framework (OSGi)
- Communication to external entities: COM
- Technical services
- Functional services

Each of this main part is divided into elements representing services, drivers, libraries, external components etc.

OSGi4AMI. The main benefit of OSGi platform is modularity in Java programming language, which allows applications to be created from small, reusable and interoperable components. Each component, called bundle has its own life cycle (installed, started, updated, stopped, and uninstalled). A transition from one state to another is done without the need to restart the whole system. This significantly improved the development phase, where different sites were providing different application components and the whole implementation process was done in parallel.

OSGi4AMI represents a reference point for all developers of the MonAMI system. It is a common interface framework developed as an open source technology available at SourceForge[4], which enables through provided ontology the interaction between MonAMI Framework modules[5]. This ontology defines the concepts used by MonAMI software modules of RG. The mechanism of the OSGi services layer enables registration, searching and notification functionality of new implemented services.

UCH (Universal Control Hub) and User Interface. The Universal Control Hub (UCH) used as component of the MonAMI architecture was developed within the scope of the EU FP6 project *i2home*. The architecture of this UCH is conforming to the Universal Control Hub Specification [UCH] as provided by the Universal Remote Console Consortium (URCC). Conceptually, the UCH implements a profiling of the Universal Remote Console (URC) technology as specified by ISO/IEC 24752 [6] and acts as a middleware between controllers and targets. The UCH server acts as a gateway between applications running the RG and the User Interfaces (UI).The HTML-based User Interface the front-end of MonAMI platform consists of 3 different UI parts with specific dedications to Beneficiary UI, Carer UI, and finally Developer UI, which is auto generated standard Webclientdedicated to developers and testers.All three UIs are using a set of API functions provided by the Webclient JavaScript Library (WJSL) for communicating with the UCH. The WJSL provides the HTML – based binding to sockets provided by UCH.

Telco and Tele-Management System. Tele-Management system is a web tool that allows installing and uninstalling OSGi4AMI software bundles remotely to RGs.The Telco system provides SMS and e-mail service using the service-provider infrastructure.

Devices and Services in MonAMI Platform. The devices are the common representations of the physical devices virtually connected to the RG. They encapsulate the real device operation, and expose members related to its functionalities. Devices in MonAMI platform are basically organized into:

- Sensors – devices able to sense physical magnitudes (temperature, presence, humidity, etc.)
- Actuators – devices able to change status of physical simple apparatus (switching on/off, open binds, etc.)

The services used in MonAMI platform can be modified and upgraded easily because of OSGi4AMI modularity so they are fully adaptable. They operate above devices' layer, recruit existing ones, combine each other and provide high level information to the RG. Services can use other services to offer enlarged functionalities. MonAMI offers an alternative for common and open platform for AAL solutions looking in large scale implementation of new social services. It is a part of AALOI open initiative sources [10].

The scalability of MonAMI platform and OSGi4AMI interfaces allows to develop own services adjusted for particular user needs. For example, there were developed components as: new user interface highly oriented on a touch screen with big sized buttons, using intuitive PCS symbols and/or pictures.

Services provided in MonAMI platform are focused on three categories - monitoring where beneficiaries and carers are able to monitor different values locally and remotely by UIs; remote control used mainly by beneficiaries to turn lights or appliances on/off; an alarm notification covering services of various types of alarms which are triggered by disallowed situations.

3.2   MonAMI Services Trials in Kosice city

Developed services in MonAMI project were tested for four months in 20 households of seniors (65+) living alone in Kosice city. Two of the participants hired formal carers; other 18 were linked to relatives, mostly their children. Four of them lived with the working relatives.Main tested services were:

- Gas and Smoke SURE services– monitoring level of gas or smoke; if it has been detected, alert is sent,
- App SURE – if the user has forgotten to switch off an electric device and this device is in usage for more than a predefined time or energy spent, device is switched off,
- Temp SURE – sends an alert if temperature is lower or higher than a predefined threshold for a longer time,

- Zone SURE – if the system recognizes (or do not recognizes) a user activity during a predefined time in predefined area and it should not be (should be) recognized, responsible person is informed about situation.

During 3 months period, the data about house status and users activities from each household were receiving automatically by service logs flow.Users were contacting 3 times for giving requested feedback. Results were positive regarding technology reliability and service quality[8, 9]. Majority of users is still using installed technology 2 yearssince testing was finished. New installations of the social system in Košice city are connected to the City emergency center and run by the Municipality since 2012.

We used questionnaires to evaluate users and their carers' satisfaction with tested services. They provided useful and effective feedback to researchers and developers in the content of user acceptance, service accessibility and usability. Among the most positively evaluated services belongs Zone SURE, which recognizes that people enter a room/area in improper time or that people haven't entered a room/area when they are expected to. Another highly appreciated service was Connect SURE, which connects the user to carer through CareIP to be able to evaluate and recognize a critical situation.

Seniors'self-confidence aroundpossible risks of falling or insecurityraisedafterMonAMI system was installed. Tested services weredeclared very helpful in increasing the confidence by14 out of 20 participants (70%);4 of themassigned services moderately helpful and only 2as unhelpful. As an example, there was a case when a user with very low mobility was courageous enough to go out on the balcony and work again on seeding and maintaining flowers even when being alone at home due to herself-confidence increased by the MonAMI system[8].

Municipality of Kosice city accepted our basic model of the social service as a part of city social services development. Based on our ideas and activities, they established 24-hours working call center for social service and they offer also some financial support for those users who fulfill criteria to get it.

3.3   Some Rural Developments of Social Services for Seniors

As there is no centralizedor local mainstream system in Slovakia so far, there were several attempts to transfer ICT technology from other countries systems to Slovak rural conditions. Mostly they were based on initiative of the charitable and NGO organizations. Local small communities use technology like Caretech, Medcare, NEO based on simple service using special communication units and wearable alarm device (bracelet, necklace) for communication with their carers.

Number of seniors using any social ICT service in Slovakia in May 2011,when testing of MonAMI services was running, counted in total 161 users in 8 centres; BanskaBystrica – 20, Nitra – 30, StaraLubovna – 35, Poprad – 30, Presov – 10, Kosice municipality – 21, MonAMI Kosice – 20.Numbers are increasing due to the involvement of municipalities from more cities.

3.4   Discussion and Further Development Plans

Following the qualitative data obtained during the trials and interviews we collected new ideasfor the further development of the MonAMIplatform. Services should be provided with the voice outputs signalization on the user interface for user's notification about alarm situation.Increase the quality of social games available on the user interface.Provide adjustable accessto the web sites dedicated to elderly directly from the user interface.Add remote door control and video door-keeper,enable using nomad ICT technologies as a user interface, tele-health services, fall detectionand support of seniors outside of their home.

One critical argument of users and companies on market dealing with home automation and social ICT based services is acceptable price. This was our main goal in cooperation with anSME company that is developing, producing and installing their products for domotic automation in Slovak households. The goal is to integrate MonAMI services platform within PontechE-con technology to be able to offer an acceptable, modern and innovative system.

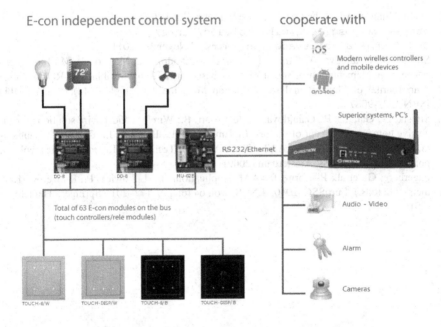

Fig. 2. E-con architecture

Acknowledgements. The research leading to these results has received funding from the European Community's 6th Framework Program (FP7/2007-2013) under grant agreement IST-5-0535147 MonAMI - „Mainstreaming on Ambient Intelligence "and Slovak grant agency VEGA „1/1162/11 – "Theoretical principles, methods and tools for diagnostics and rehabilitation of seniors mobility".

References

1. Fagerberg, G.: Mainstream Services for Elderly and Disabled People at Home. In: Emiliani, P.L., Burzagli, L., Como, A., Gabbanini, F., Salminen, A.L. (eds.) AAATE 2009. Assistive Technology Research Series, vol. 25, pp. 287–291. IOS Press, Amsterdam (2009)
2. Marco, A., Casas, R., Bauer, G., Blasco, R., Asensio, A., Jean-Bart, B., Ibane, M.: Common OSGi Interface for Ambient Assisted Living Scenarios. In: Gottfried, B., Aghajan, H. (eds.) Ebook series: Ambient Intelligence and Smart Environments, vol. 3, pp. 336–357. IOS Press, Amsterdam (2009)
3. Kung, A., Jean-Bart, B.: Making AAL Platforms a Reality. In: de Ruyter, B., Wichert, R., Keyson, D.V., Markopoulos, P., Streitz, N., Divitini, M., Georgantas, N., Mana Gomez, A. (eds.) AmI 2010. LNCS, vol. 6439, pp. 187–196. Springer, Heidelberg (2010)
4. OSGi4AMI, Source Forge, http://sourceforge.net/projects/osgi4ami/
5. OSGi Service Platform Core Specification, rel.4,
http://www.osgi.org/download/r4v41/r4.core.pdf
6. URC Consortium: Universal Remote Console Standard,
http://myurc.org/publications/2004-CHI-URC.php (accessed November 2011)
7. OSGi Alliance: About the OSGi Service Platform (June 2007)
http://www.osgi.org/wiki/uploads/Links/
OSGiTechnicalWhitePaper.pdf (accessed November 2011)
8. Simsik, D., Galajdova, A., Siman, D., Bujnak, J., Andrasova, M., Novak, M.: First experience of implementation of social services based on ICT in Slovakia (CD-ROM). European Journal of Physical and Rehabilitation Medicine 47 (suppl. 1) (2), 33–34 (2011) ISBN 1973-9087
9. Simsik, D., Galajda, P., Galajdova, A., Jean-Bart, B.: Wireless and 1-wire solutions for inclusive home environment of seniors. In: Emiliani, P.L., Burzagli, L., Como, A., Gabbanini, F., Salminen, A.L. (eds.) AAATE 2009. Assistive Technology Research Series, vol. 25, pp. 303–308. IOS Press, Amsterdam (2009)
10. Fagerberg, G., et al.: Platforms for AAL Applications. In: Lukowicz, P., Kunze, K., Kortuem, G. (eds.) EuroSSC 2010. LNCS, vol. 6446, pp. 177–201. Springer, Heidelberg (2010)

Resource Management for Multimodal and Multilingual Adaptation of User Interfaces in Ambient Assisted Living Environments

Carsten Stocklöw[1], Andrej Grguric[2], Tim Dutz[1], Tjark Vandommele,
and Arjan Kuijper[1]

[1] Fraunhofer Institute for Computer Graphics Research,
Fraunhoferstr. 5, 64283 Darmstadt, Germany
[2] Research and Innovations Unit, Ericsson Nikola Tesla d.d.,
Krapinska 45, 10002 Zagreb, Croatia
{carsten.stockloew,tim.dutz,arjan.kuijper}@igd.fraunhofer.de,
andrej.grguric@ericsson.com, tjark_vandommele@gmx.de

Abstract. Providing multimodal user interfaces in Ambient Assisted Living scenarios is a challenging task due to large variety of modalities and languages that can be used as well as impairments and preferences of end users. Creating an application that can cope with this multitude of presentation possibilities is highly complex. However, by separating the application from the presentation layer and representing the dialog in an abstract form, it is possible to perform adaptations according to the output parameters. In this work, we present the concept for a Resource Server for multimodal and distributed systems which is capable of storing different kinds of resources and associated metadata, and adapting abstract dialogs. We propose the introduction of a presentation identifier as placeholder for a set of concrete resources, a two-stage mapping between identifiers, and a selection algorithm to cope with the problem of multiple matching resources.

Keywords: Ambient Assisted Living, User Interaction, Resource Server.

1 Introduction

Ambient Assisted Living (AAL) comprises methods, technologies, products, and attendances applied to improve the quality of life for people of all ages. Considering predictions of the demographic changes in western societies, AAL particularly focuses on elderly and differently abled people. These user groups often suffer from a large variety of impairments, which makes it necessary to provide highly adaptive user interfaces [1]. By separating the application from the presentation layer and describing the user dialogs in an abstract and modality-independent way, it is possible to perform adaptations in accordance with a user's needs and preferences. By allowing descriptions of user interfaces in declarative and abstract terms much flexibility is gained, which especially becomes useful in multimodal systems. In such a scenario, the modality with which a dialog is

C. Stephanidis and M. Antona (Eds.): UAHCI/HCII 2013, Part III, LNCS 8011, pp. 97–106, 2013.
© Springer-Verlag Berlin Heidelberg 2013

presented is not chosen by a specific application, but by an underlying system that has access to information about the user's profile and about the system's contextual state. A presentation of this dialog is then created by the system according to the selected modality. Thus, the developer of an application can entirely focus on the application's functionality and does not need to devote energy to the problem of how to handle different modalities.

However, this approach has one major drawback. The resources (such as images, texts, audio files, etc.) needed to create a presentation of an abstract dialog have to be provided by the application. As a software developer for the AAL domain, it is almost impossible to predict the available devices and the required modalities upfront. Therefore, the developer has two options. Firstly, he could offer large amounts of different resources and try to cover each modality, device, and language. Or secondly, he could focus on covering only a few, specific use cases and only provide the necessary resources for those; thereby reducing the addressed group of end users that can use the application. Both options are not suited for AAL environments, because they either require too much work on the developer's site, or might render the application practically useless.

As a consequence, we propose the introduction of a *Resource Server* for managing the individual resources of user interfaces in AAL systems. This new component is capable of storing different kinds of resources and associated metadata, integrating additional resources, and providing resources to components of the system. Furthermore, we propose the idea of using unique identifiers (*Uniform Resource Identifiers*, URIs) for elements in the abstract dialog description for referencing a set of resources independently of specific modalities. This identifier (*presentation-URI*) is used to adapt the dialog according to the concrete modality, possible access restrictions and preferences of the end user. A two-stage mapping is used to map the identifier to a set of concrete resources to provide the possibility to map the identifiers themselves in case that two or more different identifiers are used by different applications to describe the exact same resource. This way, our approach also provides the option to reuse resources of other applications easily in order to further simplify the development of new products. The mapping can be changed and extended at any time even while the system is running - the changes applied will then be taken into account for all subsequent dialogs.

Furthermore, we incorporate a selection algorithm to cope with the problem of more than one matching resource. This algorithm uses different classes of restrictions to compare them to the available resources for each presentation identifier and selects the most suitable of them. With those restrictions, it is possible to map the situation in which a dialog will be presented. Specifically the user's preferences, the chosen modality, the features of the selected output device and the capabilities of the component that creates the dialog's presentation can be modelled by those restrictions.

2   Related Work

The idea of a resource server for intelligent, multimodal and distributed systems
was also proposed by Zimmermann and Wassermann and was implemented by
the *URC-Consortium*[1][2]. They define a resource server as *"a platform for the
storage, processing and retrieval of information related to user interfaces for
service environments"*[3]. To access the resources the software developer can
either use a web front-end or a HTTP-Protocol, which was specifically created
for this system [4]. However, this system is focused on the provision of complete
user interfaces which limits the re-usability of individual resources.

Ponnekanti et al. [5] propose a system called *iCrafter* to automate the creation
of user interfaces for distributed systems. For that purpose they use specialized
Interface-Generators, that are capable of creating an interface for a previously
defined functionality. In order to select which generators are used, the user has
to specify the funtionalities that will be used. This is done with the help of
a designated device that runs an *Interface-Manager*, which has knowledge of
the available functionalities. Therefore, this Interface-Manager is the link between the hardware the user wants to use and the functionalities of the system.
When the user has chosen the desired services, suitable Interface-Generators
are selected and the corresponding interfaces are created. In that process a
Generator-Database is used by the generators to obtain information about the
functionalities, like the positions of the respective hardware.

The *Personal Home Server*, discussed by Nakajima et al. [6], is another concept for creating personalized user interfaces autonomously. This approach uses
a beacon, such as a mobile phone or a special watch, to store information about
user interaction related preferences. The user has to carry this beacon so that it
can send information about the user's preferences to any device in the vicinity
that might use a user interface. This way, the interface can be personalized for
the user. Using this system as a resource server, however, is not feasible. As this
system is decentralized, it is costly to integrate new resources into the system.
Furthermore, because of the use of wireless technology, bandwidth shortages
might occur. This can slow the system down if it is used in an environment that
contains many output devices, such as an AAL-system.

3   Concepts

3.1   Architecture

Figure 1 shows the overall architecture of the system. By separating the application layer from the presentation layer and representing the dialog in an abstract
form it is possible to provide adaptions to the dialog. The idea for such a separation is not new, the most prominent example is the World Wide Web which uses
a webserver as UI Provider, a browser as a UI Handler, and HTML as format

---

[1] http://www.myurc.org

for dialogs. The Resource Server can then be integrated in this system as a component that can be called from the UI Handler because only the UI Handler has knowledge about the concrete capabilities of the output device. In the following sections we will describe the different components of this architecture and section 4 will detail the integration of the Resource Server in an AAL platform.

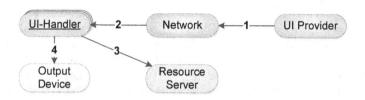

Fig. 1. Architecture

3.2 Presentation-URI

In a system without a Resource Server, the resources needed for a user dialog are being provided by its corresponding application. When developing such an application the programmer specifies which resource to use for which element of the dialog in the abstract description of that dialog. As these resources are not abstract but concrete, the dialog description is not truly abstract itself. As a consequence, such a dialog can only be used for output devices that support all the used resources, which greatly reduces its flexibility. Moreover, in a distributed system the software developer has no information about the location of the resources once they are managed by the Resource Server.

For these reasons we propose the usage of a **presentation-URI**. Such a presentation-URI is the abstract description of a resource which is associated with a set of concrete resources. This set contains resources that all represent the same data in different ways. For example there could be an audio file in which a person says 'sunny', several text files with the word 'sunny' in different languages or multiple image files of different resolutions with a sun and even images containing text in different languages.

When developing an application for a system with a Resource Server the developer uses the presentation-URIs in the abstract dialog description instead of concrete resources. As no concrete elements are left in the dialog description it is truly abstract and can be used for any output device. Which concrete resource is used to present a dialog has to be determined by the Resource Server, which uses information about the user, the chosen output device and the current context to find the most suitable resource for each presentation-URI.

In order to provide for an easy reuse of resources provided by other applications, the presentation-URIs can also be associated to one another. This way multiple applications that use the exact same resources but address them with different presentation-URIs can access the same resources. Therefore, it is sufficient to store each resource once and maintenance of the resources is simplified.

The mapping of resources to presentation-URIs as well as the mapping of presentation-URIs to each other can be changed and extended at any time while the system is running. These changes will then be taken into account for all subsequent use of the resources.

3.3   Server Component

The core of the Resource Server is its **Server Component**. It stores and manages the resources of all applications and distributes them to the elements of the system that intends to use them. For that purpose it receives requests by the system which it answers by sending either information about resources or the resources themselves. The requirements for the server component are:

Storing Resources: This is the core functionality of the server component. As it is not possible to predict which kind of resources will be used by the applications, the Resource Server must be able to store resources in all common formats as well as newly defined file types. Furthermore, the Resource Server has to prevent resources from accidentally being altered by other components of the system.

Storing Metadata: In addition to the resources themselves, the Resource Server also needs to store metadata that describe the contents of the resources. This metadata is important for determining which resource to use if there are multiple resources from the same file type for one presentation-URI. Due to the fact that it is not known which property distinguishes two resources of the same set, the system has to be designed in a way that allows the developer to define new metadata categories. However, for compatibility reasons some common categories like 'lang' for language should be defined by default.

Searching for Resources: In order to provide a maximum flexibility in the usage of the resources, the server component has to be able to search for resources. In other words it has to be possible to find a resource not by addressing it with its presentation-URI, but by defining a set of properties and filtering the metadata of all resources for those properties.

Aggregating Resources: For the purpose of reducing the delay caused by transmitting the resources to the different elements of the system, the Resource Server should be able to aggregate multiple resources before they are sent. Especially when many small resources like text snippets for buttons, labels etc. are requested, it is inefficient to deliver each resource separately. Preferably, the system would request all those resources at once and the resource component would aggregate them either in one file or with the help of an archive file. While combining several resources in a single file is simple and intuitive, it only works if all resources are of the same type and if that file type can be aggregated at all. More flexible is the use of an archive file, which may contain all kinds of resources. On the other hand, that approach needs some additional computing of the server component as well as the component that requests the resources. Therefore, there can be cases in which aggregating resources cannot reduce the transmission delay.

There are several server technologies that can be used to fulfill the requirements mentioned above. The easiest way would be to use the **file system** of the underlying operating system. The resources would be stored in a specific folder and for each resource a text file would be created which would contain the metadata of that resource. However, when searching resources by their properties, each of those text files would have to be opened and analyzed which is very inefficient. A better approach would be to use a **relational database** to store the metadata. In that case, a database with three tables would be created to provide a maximum of efficiency when searching for resources.

The first table, called *resources*, contains mandatory information about every resource stored on the server component. The primary key, which is needed in every table of a relational database, would be an automatically generated resource ID (*R_ID*). Furthermore, there are fields that save which application stored the resource (*bundle*), its file name (*filename*), the corresponding file extension (*fileextension*), the path in the file system where the resource is stored (*path*) and its presentation-URI (*uri*).

The second table contains the metadata of all resources and therefore is called *metadata*. In this case the primary key is a combination of the field's resource ID (*R_ID*) to specify which resource this property belongs to, the category of the property (*category*) and a field called (*value_no*). The third component of the key is necessary because it is possible that a category of metadata has several values simultaneously. The last field of this table is called *value* and contains the actual information about the resource.

If any resource is used by more than one application the different presentation-URIs for that resource are associated with each other, as mentioned above. The presentation-URI which is already connected to the resource will become the 'master'-URI while the other will be called 'slave'-URI. This information will then be stored in a table called *URI-mapping*, which consists only of the fields *slave* (primary key) and *master*.

Figure 2 shows an example of a resource and its metadata stored on the server component.

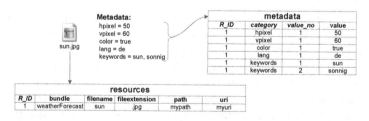

Metadata:
hpixel = 50
vpixel = 60
color = true
lang = de
keywords = sun, sonnig

sun.jpg

metadata

R_ID	category	value_no	value
1	hpixel	1	50
1	vpixel	1	60
1	color	1	true
1	lang	1	de
1	keywords	1	sun
1	keywords	2	sonnig

resources

R_ID	bundle	filename	fileextension	path	uri
1	weatherForecast	sun	.jpg	mypath	myuri

Fig. 2. Storing metadata of a resource in a relational database

3.4   Client Component

Although multiple servers are possible, the typical realization of this scenario contains only one server in an intelligent environment. If this environment is designed as an open distributed system then potentially multiple nodes can access the functionalities of the server. To simplify the integration of different UI Handlers with the Resource Server, a client component can be integrated into the system which takes care of mapping the presentation-URIs to concrete URLs used by the UI Handler. It ensures the connection between the system and the server component and mediates the requests and responses between them. Thus, only little changes to the UI Handler have to be performed to include functionalities of the Resource Server.

Another benefit of this approach is that it is possible to use specialized client components. For example, if a component of the system is written in a different programming language, a client component that is capable of processing requests from this component can be used. This way access to the Resource Server is flexible and it can be used by every component in the system.

3.5   Selection Mechanism

In most cases each presentation-URI will be associated with more than one resource, which yields the necessity of a selection mechanism. Although other approaches are possible, this selection will take place in the client component, as mentioned above. This is due to the flexibility in the usage of specialized client components, which can be exploited to implement different selection strategies.

We propose a universal selection mechanism to select resources for a user dialog, which can be altered to meet the needs of different scenarios. This mechanism uses information about the current context, the capabilities of the UI-Handler and the output device to create restrictions. Additional restrictions may be supplied by the application that wants to display the dialog. Those restrictions are then compared with the metadata of each resource to determine if it is suitable for the dialog.

The most important information is which types of resources can be processed by the UI-Handler and its output device. This constraint is heavily dependent on the modality that was chosen for the dialog but can also be influenced by the UI-Handler and the output device. For example, if the dialog shall be presented visually, all acoustic resources can be ignored. In addition to that the UI-Handler might not be able to render HTML files, thus those can be omitted as well. Therefore, the UI-Handler has to submit information about which MIME-types can be processed (*whitelisted*) and which cannot (*blacklisted*). Due to the importance of this information, the server component uses the file extension of each resource to determine its *MIME-type* automatically and saves it as a property in the metadata table. This ensures that the MIME-Type is set for every resource and can be used for the selection.

To ensure an efficient comparison of the resources and the restrictions, the latter should be divided into three classes:

1. **Must have:** Those restrictions define properties that a resource has to contain in order to be selected. Otherwise, the resource will be ignored.
2. **Must not have:** Properties that are described in this class are not allowed to be present in the metadata of a resource.

3. **Nice to have:** Restrictions in this class do not reduce the number of candidates for a presentation-URI. Instead, they are used to rate the remaining resources if more than one meets the restrictions of the other classes. In that case a resource is awarded one point for each nice-to-have-restriction it fulfills. Afterwards the resource with the highest score is chosen unless there is more than one resource with a top rating, in which case one of those is randomly picked.

Although it is possible to select a resource with those three classes of restrictions, this system is very inflexible and cannot cope with the variety of properties that can be stored in the metadata of the resources. Therefore, an additional attribute that describes the type of a restriction has to be applied. Possible attributes are:

- **if set:** This attribute states that the restriction shall only be evaluated for resources that contain a value for the corresponding property. For example, a resource might not contain any information regarding its language, because it is an image that does not contain words in any language. Naturally, such a resource should still be selectable even if a restriction is given that requires the language to be English.
- **in range:** By using this attribute it is possible to define a restriction that does not expect a specific value of a property, but allows the value to be in an interval. This can be used to select images with a resolution in an acceptable range. In addition to the interval boundaries, information whether those boundaries are inside or outside the interval have to be given.
- **x of:** This attribute can be used if a set of properties is given and it does not matter which of those are met, as long as a certain amount is. For example, it is possible to ask for resources that contain three of five keywords.
- **no attribute:** Restrictions that do not contain an attribute are still possible and are evaluated as discussed above.

Further attributes can be defined and are particularly useful for more specialized selection mechanisms. Consequently those mechanisms can adopt to the diversity of different resources.

4   Implementation

The concepts described in this work have been applied to the open AAL platform *universAAL* [7] which is supposed to become a standardized general-purpose platform for AAL environments. The universAAL platform is a consolidated combination of prior work, not following a completely new approach but rather integrating approved concepts from a variety of projects in this area. By default, this platform uses an OSGi container (although different containers are possible), making it easy to integrate additional modules such as the resource client.

Figure 3 illustrates how the Resource Server is, in general, used to provide resources for an output dialog sent by an application.

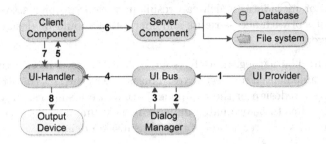

Fig. 3. Transmission of a dialog from application to output device

1. The application forwards an abstract dialog to the UI-Bus. Since the system contains a Resource Server, no concrete resource is used in this dialog. Instead, the corresponding presentation-URIs are used.
2. The UI-Bus transmits the dialog to the Dialog Manager. This component adds information about the current context to the dialog and assures that no other dialog has higher priority.
3. As soon as the Dialog Manager releases the dialog for presentation, it is returned to the UI-Bus. Using the attached context information, the UI-Bus decides which UI-Handler will create the output.
4. The UI-Bus sends the dialog including the context to the chosen UI-Handler.
5. The UI-Handler realizes that the dialog contains one or more presentation-URIs and thus forwards it and the context to the client component. Additionally the UI-Handler sends information about the capabilities of itself and its associated output device to the client component.
6. The client component needs four steps to process the request from the UI-Handler:
   (a) First it extracts the presentation-URIs contained in the dialog.
   (b) Then it requests the available information about all resources associated with those presentation-URIs from the server component, using a HTTP-request.
   (c) Afterwards, if any of the presentation-URIs is associated with more than one resource, the client component uses the information about the context and the UI-Handler to choose the most suitable resource.
   (d) Lastly it integrates the path of each selected resource into the dialog.
7. The client component submits the altered dialog to the UI-Handler, which creates a presentation of the dialog.
8. This dialog is sent to the output device, where it is presented to the user.

5   Future Work

Security: While the operating system can provide some security against attacks from outside of the system, no protection is provided against malicous applications that run inside the system itself. These applications can access or alter any resources or metadata, which can result in various problems. Accordingly, a security protocol with access rights and encryption should be designed for the Resource Server.

Compression: The aggregation of resources, as discussed in chapter 3.3, has neither been implemented nor tested yet. This is due to the fact that this concept requires a major redesign of the components that use resources. In addition to those changes it has to be evaluated under which circumstances the compression of resources results in a reduction of the transmission delay.

Web-Frontend: For easy administration of the resources and their metadata a web-frontend for the server component should be developed. As the nature of such a component enables it to influence many aspects of a system, special attention should be paid to its security and privacy features.

Acknowledgements. This work is partially financed by the European Commission under the FP7 IST Project *universAAL* (grant agreement FP7-247950).

References

1. Hawthorn, D.: Possible implications of aging for interface designers. Interacting with Computers 12(5), 507–528 (2000)
2. Zimmermann, G.: URC Technical Primer 1.0 (DRAFT). Technical report, Universal Remote Console Consortium (2008)
3. Zimmermann, G., Wassermann, B.: Why We Need a User Interface Resource Server for Intelligent Environments. In: Schneider, M., Kröner, A., Alvarado, J.C.E., Higuera, A.G., Augusto, J.C. (eds.) Workshops Proceedings of the 5th International Conference on Intelligent Environments, pp. 209–216. IOS Press (2009)
4. Zimmermann, G.: Resource Server HTTP Interface 1.0 (DRAFT). Technical report, Universal Remote Console Consortium (2009)
5. Ponnekanti, S.R., Lee, B., Fox, A., Hanrahan, P., Winograd, T.: ICrafter: A Service Framework for Ubiquitous Computing Environments. In: Abowd, G., Brumitt, B., Shafer, S. (eds.) UbiComp 2001. LNCS, vol. 2201, pp. 56–75. Springer, Heidelberg (2001)
6. Nakajima, T., Satoh, I.: A software infrastructure for supporting spontaneous and personalized interaction in home computing environments. Personal and Ubiquitous Computing 10(6), 379–391 (2005)
7. Furfari, F., Tazari, M.R., Eisemberg, V.: universaal: an open platform and reference specification for building aal systems. ERCIM News (2011)

An Integration Framework for Motion
and Visually Impaired Virtual Humans
in Interactive Immersive Environments

Frank Sulzmann[1], Roland Blach[2], and Manfred Dangelmaier[2]

[1] University of Stuttgart, Stuttgart, Germany
frank.sulzmann@iat.uni-stuttgart.de
[2] Fraunhofer IAO, Stuttgart, Germany
{roland.blach,Manfred.dangelmaier}@iao.fraunhofer.de

Abstract. A flexible framework has been created to test products taking into account different impairments. This system offers new opportunities to check products and design products as accessible as possible. The modular approach allows the integration of further models and analysis tools.

Keywords: framework, service orientated software architecture, modular approach, digital human model, virtual human, visual impairment, immersive environment, virtual reality.

1   Introduction

In the European Union about 16% of the population are over 65 [1] and around 20% of people over 50 experience severe physical disabilities. Furthermore up to 15% of the populations across the European Union have visual, hearing, speech, cognitive, or motor impairments [2]. This shows that people with disabilities are not a tiny minority and new products have to be designed taking into account the needs of impaired persons. With increasing life expectancy, visual and hearing impairments also increase [3].

Often designers are not fully aware of this situation and do not have the adequate knowledge to assess accessibility of their products. Furthermore existing development tools (e.g., several CAD tools or simulation environments) give little out-of-the-box assistance [4]. To improve the situation, a promising approach is to give designers the experience of accessibility issues by simulating impaired digital humans in immersive virtual environments or by using the first person view to place the designer into the body of an impaired user. This enables engineers and developers to test their products interactively from the perspective of people with special needs, increasing their awareness of the accessibility issues. This is expected to lead to better adapted products.

1.1   Application Scenarios

The simulation of impairment is done by a simulation engine introduced in [5]. The focus of this work is the visualization of vision and motor impairments in Virtual

C. Stephanidis and M. Antona (Eds.): UAHCI/HCII 2013, Part III, LNCS 8011, pp. 107–115, 2013.
© Springer-Verlag Berlin Heidelberg 2013

Reality. A framework has been developed to integrate simulation engines and digital human models into virtual reality. Furthermore the framework allows the combination of different approaches and provides multimodal interfaces for the end users beginning from two-dimensional graphical user interfaces such as web frontends up to 3D user interaction based on motion capturing techniques.

Since there is a lot of significance of virtual reality in architecture and automotive, the focus lies on these domains taking in account the special needs of elderly people and handicapped person with limitations in mobility and vision.

Considering the great variety of potential existing impairments requiring very specific simulation components, different digital humans and simulation environments do exist; it is obvious that a single tool cannot provide all solutions. Therefore it is desirable to combine various individual simulation components in a single virtual environment which can be seamlessly experienced by the product developer.

Our contribution is the description of a system architecture for the flexible coupling of virtual human simulation components including visual and motion impairments and an immersive visualization/auralization platform. To do this, existing integration schemes have to be extended. This facilitates the usage for the designer such that he can combine and switch between different simulation models deliberately and therefore experience various impairments. In the following we are describing our technical approach which is used in two application scenarios. The evaluation and thorough discussion of the usefulness of such simulations to comprehend the needs of impaired people is beyond the scope of this paper.

2   Related Work

2.1   Immersive Interfaces for Virtual Humans

Virtual reality allows a user to step through the computer screen into a three-dimensional (3D) world. The user can look at, move around, and interact with these worlds as if they were real. It is also a new media for information and knowledge acquisition, and representing concepts of ideas in ways not previously possible. VR can be a powerful tool for testing and evaluating new products and ideas, decreasing the time to market and reducing product cost. [6] One of these ideas is to simulate and visualize motion and vision impairments.

The digital human model "RAMSIS" [7] in its original state addressed demands on ergonomics, comfort and safety. It is a well-accepted tool in the automotive industry and one of the most used digital human models [8]. With the enhancements from VERITAS, ergonomists are enabled to use virtual user models with parameterized disabilities. Therefore ergonomists are able to evaluate products taking in account the special needs of elderly and impaired without using an additional tool. The detailed statistical knowledge about body dimensions is given by RAMSIS and the degrees of various disabilities are given by the knowledge of VERITAS.

In the original desktop version of RAMSIS it is a demanding task to control the manikin and use it correctly [4]. In our work integrated RAMSIS in virtual reality and used mocap-techniques to control the manikin. We evaluated if this approach helps to facilitate the handling of virtual humans and reduce the amount of time.

2.2   Virtual Human and Impairment Simulation

In [5] a framework for impairment simulation has been introduced. It is based on an innovative virtual user modeling technique describing in detail all the physical parameters of the user with disability. The proposed user modeling methodology generates a dynamic and parameterizable virtual user model that is used in a simulation framework to assess the accessibility of the designs. The framework consists of Virtual User Model, Task Model and Simulation model, all expressed in UsiXML format. The universal description of User, Task and Simulation Models with the extensible UsiXML language increases the interoperability and allows the practical implementation of embedded accessible product solutions.

Our contribution is the enhancement and the integration of this simulation technology in virtual reality and to enable the users to interact in real-time with the simulated manikins.

3   Approach

We follow a service oriented concept, where the human model simulation acts as a simulation server and the virtual environment engine configures the services and integrates the data streams of the simulation server with a 3D-scene. The system provides then real time interaction capabilities concerning view and navigation as well as simulation control.

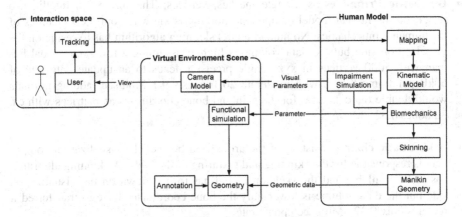

Fig. 1. Virtual Human Framework Overview

Two principal modes control the experience:

- **Third person view:** The user interacts with the virtual environment and can navigate freely in the 3D-scene observing the virtual human performing a prescribed task. Furthermore the user is able to use tracking of body parts to define target points for the virtual human to teach a specific pose, if the digital human model is capable to be controlled via external target points. This allows for intuitive teaching of the digital human model on the spot.

- **First person view:** The users' view is controlled by the virtual human experiencing a virtual impaired body based on the task description. Also visual impairments can be simulated by overlaid dynamic view filters which are provided by the human model if it is capable to so. This is the closest the designer can experience the situation of an impaired person.

We have implemented a first prototype of this architecture, embedded in a design evaluation application. It is capable to operate with two human model modules, the RAMSIS virtual human and the VERITAS core engine human model which provides also visual impairment simulations. It is coupled to the immersive virtual reality engine LIGHTNING [9] which provides also a front end to the user. Technically the system is fully functional and serves as a test bed for the application in real world design tasks.

3.1   Geometry Updates

Two levels of data exchange for the geometry data have been considered:

- **Geometric Primitives** as triangle meshes, vertices: The simulation intelligence resides in the human model component, nothing is known about the semantics of the human biomechanics. No human model skinning algorithm has to reside on the visualization side but the data volume is higher: assuming a low poly virtual human with 5000 vertices in xyz, single precision leads to an update data rate of 60kB per frame that is with moderate 20 frames/s 9.1 Mbit/sec (adding normals would double the data rate) for the skin and bone coordinates as matrices with ca. 30 bones 0,32 Mbit/sec.

- **A kinematic chain** consisting of the articulated bones: The visualization component is responsible for the skinning and texturing of the body. A skinning algorithm has to be available and the skeleton model has to be known on the visualization side but the data volume is lower only the bone coordinates have to transferred it remains only 0,32 Mbit/sec update rate.

The time of the initial data exchange has not been considered here as critical. The update data rates are plain needed dada rates no protocol overhead or network collisions are considered. The first case is technically challenging if the visualization is carried out on a cluster where the mesh data has been spread over several machines. In our implementation we have realized the first approach as only little information of the underlying human model should be required. The system can be used in a single machine but also in a cluster mode. To minimize the data exchange, multicast networking protocols have been used with the known problems of package loss using the UDP protocol. As long as all machines are connected to a single ethernet switch the losses are neglectable. If larger network infrastructures should be used reliable multicast techniques could be added easily.

3.2 Vision Updates

For the vision updates two approaches are feasible:

- **Impairment Parameter Exchange** where the filter algorithms are available on the visualization side and the image distortions will be computed locally.

- **Distorted image transfer** where the impairment simulation will be carried out on the human model server. If the filter have to be applied on the actual clear image as e.g. blurring in case of low vision the actual undistorted images has to be transferred to the simulation.

In our implementation we have realized the first approach as the read back and transfer of the camera image is not feasible for real time visualization for a direct filter approach as it is not only time consuming but also induces latency in the rendering pipeline. For some specific visual impairments, it could nevertheless be interesting to reconsider the approach if the impairment could be modeled as an operation where the actual camera image can be modulated with a generic image as it would be possible with color distortions or blind spots.

4   Implementations

4.1   Interactive Assessment of Architectural "Smart Living Spaces"

The above described architecture has been used to in the context of the evaluation of architectural spaces, specifically smart living spaces. Automated environments have been used to alleviate the life of impaired and elderly people in the context of so called "smart homes". As these environments require IT infrastructure to sense, compute and operate these environments it is evident that these components are an integral part of the interior planning for future homes. We have implemented an evaluation application which connects the VERITAS Simulation Core and a domotic simulation for home automation with an immersive virtual environment to provide a digital experience space for developer and designer. The overall system architecture is shown below.

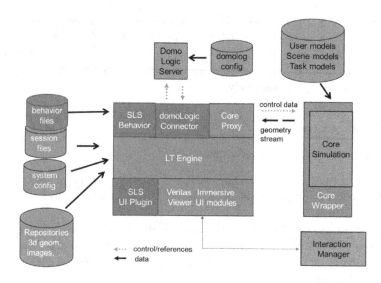

Fig. 2. Interior design domain: System overview including Smart Living Space (SLS) modules and the immersive interactive 3D engine Lightning (LT Engine)

Designers can model the interior of a home and its components e.g. sliding doors and are able to simulate the sensing technology with the domotic simulator and can immediately evaluate the geometrical design including the functions. This could be used to plan the sensor layout for motion sensors and experience the environment form the perspective of a wheel chair user or a vision impaired person.

4.2   Interactive Assessment Process in Immersive Automotive Scenarios

In the automotive area commercial tools like RAMSIS have been used since years to evaluate new designs. Therefore users and engineers in the industry have experience using these tools. Furthermore these tools have been integrated into the engineering workflows.

It can be assumed that these users neither intend to replace their existing evaluation tools completely nor they intend to re-implement their engineering workflows. Studies showed that the handling of virtual manikin is still a demanding, time consuming task and that ergonomic evaluation tools need more simulation functions. [4]

So it is a promising approach to use virtual reality with motion-capture techniques in combination with existing commercial tools and the VERITAS simulation core. Furthermore a concept and workflow has been developed to show how these tools can be used in praxis. The assessment process is shown in figure.

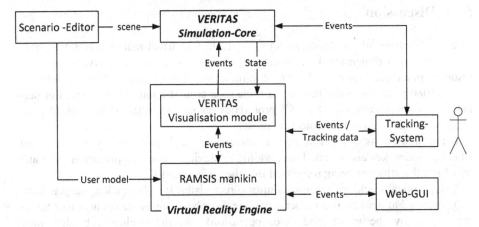

Fig. 3. Automotive domain: Workflow and interactive assessment process

Vision parameters and motor disorders can be defined using the VERITAS scenario editor to create the appropriate user models. The acuity parameters are extracted and transferred to the corresponding opening angles of view cones and the parameters of the impairment vision module. Motor disorders and reduced mobility are transferred into restrictions of the manikin's skeleton joints. When loading the VERITAS user models into the virtual scene, the according reach zones are calculated by the RAMSIS manikin taking in account the limitations of the joints. These generated reach zones are the basis for the reach assessment. Additionally an interactive reach assessment can be done using motion capture and inverse kinematics to control the manikin like a virtual puppet in real-time. If the user model is not able to achieve the provided postures and movements, it will stop the movement and a warning is displayed in a form of red warning spheres surrounding the according joints.

To reduce the time of preparation of assessment sessions, a minimum set of tracking targets in combination with inverse kinematics is used to track the user's movements. Targets for head, hands and the pelvis are the minimum setup, which can be extended by targets for feet. During the assessment in virtual reality user can switch between the manikins' view (first person's view) and the view of an external observer (third person's view).

In both cases the user can interactively evaluate the manikin's view. The view cones and the eye point are moving along with the user's head movements in real-time. The vision cone indicates which area of the scene is visible for the manikin. In third person's view the user is able to navigate freely through the scene. But the tracking and the interaction is working in the same manner as in the first person's view mode.

In addition to these view cones a vision impairment module has been developed to visualize eye disabilities such as cataract.

5   Discussion

Due to limitations of projection systems available for virtual reality it is not feasible to evaluate two dimensional graphical user interfaces in an immersive setup. The resulting pixel size is about 1.5 up to 2 millimeters, if projectors with a resolution of 1920 x1080 pixels are used to cover a projection area of about 3.0 x 2.0 m. Furthermore the representation of the GUI prototypes embedded in the virtual world is limited to a small area of the projection plane.

Other limitations are given by the integration of haptic devices like steering wheels, handbrakes and so on. These additional devices cover the projection area and may limit the effect of being immersed into the virtual reality.

Using optical tracking systems requires direct visibility. The tracking targets have to be detected at least by two cameras at once. So a big issue is the occlusion of tracking targets by the user's body (self-occlusion) and the occlusion by hardware mock-ups.

Apart from technical issues and limitations virtual reality is an appropriate media to represent concepts of ideas in ways not previously possible. Virtual reality lets the user to experience disabilities to a certain degree experience the effects of being visually impaired respectively having limited mobility using the first person's view. In third person's view the user is able to observe the manikin and the effects of its disabilities.

Conceptually the service oriented approach shows promising properties as the components can be decoupled and use their own computer hardware. There are of course limitations: Most human models need a geometric and functional representation of the scene and also proprietary task descriptions. So a careful handling of data consistency between all components is necessary. E.g. in our current implementation the scene description for the virtual scene for the immersive engine is completely taken from the digital human component at runtime. Additionally the architecture would allow for coupling several independent virtual humans which can interact with the virtual scene and each other.

This would be beneficial as it provides a high flexibility of choice. In current implementations the API for bringing in dynamic geometry in the simulations is limited. The ideal solution would be that any virtual human can be placed in arbitrary dynamic environments and interact with it plausibly. This needs probably to standardize functional API between different physical simulation engines such that the effects of one simulation can easily be imported in the other engines world. Although worthwhile from the application developers' point of view, it is not clear if tool and engine provider are interested in sharing.

6   Conclusion

A flexible framework has been created to test products taking into account different impairments. This system offers new opportunities to check products and design products as accessible as possible. The modular approach allows the integration of further models and analysis tools.

We could show that commercial toolkits such as the digital human model "RAMSIS" can be integrated in the simulation framework and virtual reality successfully. The VERITAS simulation models allow describing limited human functionalities for elderly and people with disabilities. As an added value virtual reality enables the users to experience the effects of being visually impaired respectively having limited mobility.

However an open question remains: How close can we get to experience a different functional body with mainly visual cues and does that lead to better product design?

This will be part of our future user evaluations.

References

1. Eurostat regional yearbook 2008. Luxembourg: Office for Official Publications of the European Communities (2008)
2. Report of the Inclusive Communications (INCOM) subgroup of the Communications Committee (COCOM) COCOM04-08
3. WHO World Health Organisation, The world is fast ageing – have we noticed? (March 1, 2013), http://www.who.int/ageing/en/
4. Digitale Menschmodelle als Werkzeuge virtueller Ergonomie: Universitätsbibliothek Chemnitz (2010)
5. Kaklanis, N., Moschonas, P., Moustakas, K., Tzovaras, D.: Virtual user models for the elderly and disabled for automatic simulated accessibility and ergonomy evaluation of designs. Universal Access in the Information Society, 1–23 (2012), http://dx.doi.org/10.1007/s10209-012-0281-0 (English)
6. Mujber, T.S., Szecsi, T., Hashmi, M.S.: Virtual reality applications in manufacturing process simulation. Journal of Materials Processing Technology 155, 1834–1838 (2004)
7. Geuss, H., Seidl, A., Krist, R.: RAMSIS: ein System zur Erhebung und Vermessung dreidimensionaler Koerperhaltungen von Menschen zur ergonomischen Auslegung von Bedien- und Sitzplaetzen im Auto (1995)
8. van der Meulen, P., Seidl, A.: Ramsis – The Leading Cad Tool for Ergonomic Analysis of Vehicles. In: Duffy, V.G. (ed.) HCII 2007 and DHM 2007. LNCS, vol. 4561, pp. 1008–1017. Springer, Heidelberg (2007)
9. Blach, R., Landauer, J., Rösch, A., Simon, A.: A Highly Flexible Virtual Reality System, Future Generation Computer Systems Special Issue on Virtual Environments. Future Generation Computer Systems Special Issue on Virtual Environments. Elsevier, Amsterdam (1998)

BioCyberUrban parQ: An Ubiquitous and Pervasive Computing System for Environmental Integration

Suzete Venturelli, Francisco de Paula Barretto, and André Bassani de Freitas

Computer Art Research Lab,
University of Brasilia, Brasilia, Federal District, Brazil
{suzeteventurelli,kikobarretto,dedebf}@gmail.com
http://midialab.unb.br

Abstract. The goal of BioCyberUrban parQ project is to connect the living things, objects and environment in order to enable their cybernetic communication/coexistence in Sarah Kubitschek Park (Brasilia's city park). Art and society context aim the processes of physical, intellectual and moral users consciousness development, along with all living beings in the City Park. Therefore we seek for a better ecosystem coexistence, integration and communication through the crowd-collected data as the foundation of this cyber community.

Keywords: cyber objects, computer art, art and technology, pervasive computing.

1 Theoretical Framework

The BioCyberUrban parQ project was developed at the Computer Art Research Laboratory (Midialab) in collaboration with laboratories from the Faculty of Technology and the Scientific Technology Development Center (CDTC), both from the University of Brasilia. It started in 2011 and was designed to be developed in stages, as raising funds for its development. Undergraduate, graduate and post-graduate students from the University of Brasilia and the Community College of Brasilia (IESB) are involved[1].

This proposal has been inspired particularly by science and biology - especially the autopoietic mechanisms of life and the reflection of how living things are organized, developed, evolved and adapted to the environment. The concept of autopoiesis, as the organization of the living, originated in the Chilean biologists Humberto Maturana and Francisco Varela work in 1970s [1]. This idea was developed in the theoretical biology context and was early associated with artificial life simulation long before the term artificial life was introduced in the

---

[1] The main students involved are Guilherme Shimabuko, Marcelo Rios, Juliana Hilário, Ana Lemos, Bruno Braga, Sidney Medeiros, Camille Venturelli Pic, Claudia Loch, Roni Ribeiro, Fábio Fonseca, Hudson Bomfim and Eber Felipe Oliveira.

C. Stephanidis and M. Antona (Eds.): UAHCI/HCII 2013, Part III, LNCS 8011, pp. 116–124, 2013.
© Springer-Verlag Berlin Heidelberg 2013

late 1980s in [2]. Pier Luisi presents a good concept review in [3]. Besides we are influenced by the work of Garnet Hertz[4] and Stocker and Schöpf [5].

BioCyberUrban parQ fits into the computer art and technology context. Therefore is based on its post-human philosophical perspectives, which provides new concepts and contemporary challenges to the art and technology traditions with innovative programs that challenge the technologies use for military purposes and others exploitation, proposing alternative human-machine interaction.

Post-human manifesto was first published by Steve Nichols [6] and is a concept discussed in contemporary art, science fiction, futurology and philosophy fields, about the possibility of non-humans forms responding like human thought [7].

This project demonstrates a possible technology application to stimulate sensitivity and sensuousness. We've seen the rise, in past decades, imaginary and nonconformists creations, whose aesthetic results criticizes the major enterprises, which seek only financial resources, giving a minimum return to community development. BioCyberUrban parQ brings the possibility of users participation in this digital ecosystem formation, currently feasible in terms of computational and cybernetic technologies of communication.

In parQ's theoretical context Art, Computer Science and Engineering fields are involved in order to develop objects whose characteristics are derived from ubiquitous and pervasive computing. Giving continuous communication and computer technical progresses, it seems that we're riding in complete computing activities integration into human everyday.

Ubiquitous computing will let the user visit the park without paying too much attention to the fact that there is a computer system allowing a more natural and transparent human-computer interaction. On the other hand, pervasive computing enables this natural interaction since the gathering and interaction data been made through everyday objects, embedded with computing devices. This mix of ubiquity and pervasiveness enable a cybernetic communication fluid among living beings, environment and cyber objects [8]. Mark Weiser in 1988 proposed this new idea with the phrase ubiquitous computing, when he was Xerox Palo Alto Research Center (PARC) Chief Technologist.

In a few words, the main idea is the ubiquitous and pervasive information system implementation that connects living beings, objects and environment at Sara Kubitschek Park. The main goal is to build a new collaborative cyber ecosystem, self-sustained by the appropriation of these elements by the public of the park, like modified benches and mobile phones. In this sense, parQ is also a pacific-activist action that suggests solutions to social problems, like access and appropriation of public spaces by the local population in order to valorize and take good care of the environment as a whole.

2   The parQ Project

ParQ will be implemented in Sarah Kubitschek Park, which is the largest urban park in the world, with 1.62 square miles, overcoming the Central Park in New York. This park allows on foot or cycling activities for both amateurs and professional athletes. There is a 2.5 miles route for beginners and two longer routes for more experienced athletes, with 3.7 and 5 miles. Besides sport practices, there are several restaurants, a large woodland with picnic tables, an amphitheater, a kart track, playgrounds, an amusement park and an equestrian center. It is signed by three important people in the art, architecture and urbanism fields: the architectural design is by Oscar Niemeyer, the landscaping work was done by Roberto Burle Marx and urban area was developed by Lúcio Costa (all of them have participated on the concept and construction of Brasilia).

The system parQ is composed by a social network (parQ.unb.br), an android app to explore the park (parQ), another android app for counting footsteps (pedParQ), a cyber-object bench with a scale for measuring weight (bench-scale) and an ambient sound for plants and humans composed by sensors (plantaParQ). All these components aim to encourage coexistence among living things, objects and environment, to enable the coexistence and cybernetic communication in the City Park of Brasilia.

The main part of the system is composed by a social network/community, as seen in figure 1, which converges all the gathered information, including mobile devices data. Furthermore, it aims to develop cyber objects that are installed in the park, with a function to communicate and feed the social network and mobile devices by sending different types of information. That is, while being used by the public, these objects are build up according to their interests.

Fig. 1. ParQ social network interface (2013)

The social network, parQ.unb.br, can be considered itself a complex autopoietic living system since it is able to self regulate through human interaction, reflecting the changes in it's inside configuration and database, according to these interactions and data gathering.

This online social network, which is a subnet of Wikinarua , has all basic features of a regular social network but presents some innovations, since the information is presented in a collaborative cartography in which each user has it's own personal blogmap. Information is, then, presented as a collective web-cartography that is basically a confluence of all existing blog maps. Nevertheless, this autonomous community is connected with other social networks like Facebook and Twitter, sharing and disseminating the information.

The system consists of sub-systems set and these elements provide connection/communication and delivery real-time information between/to phones and databases. We consider Augmented Reality as the interval between the real and the virtual, a mixed reality that merges reality and virtuality.

The system has three main principles: the first one is knowledge about the operating environment, the second is reproduction quality and the third is presence metaphor. By definition, it is a social network as a social entities set, such as individuals or social organizations connected by relationships built from their social interactions. With the advent of Web2.0, new possibilities and paradigms have emerged. Between these newborn paradigms the most relevant for this social network is the content and modeling construction of its final shape been made through users interactions. With this new user provided content there might be the rise and formation of new social groups.

The main features of parQ are:

– Computational open platform;
– Collaborative Mapping/Data crowdsourcing;
– Interaction between members;
– Data Sharing;
– Construction of Identities;
– Augmented Reality Application (figure 2);
– Distribution and communication of applications, games, cyber objects and widgets;

3   Cyber Objects: Expert Systems Embedded in the Cybernetics Field

At this point of the work we are designing some objects to be placed in the City Park. We call these objects cyber objects. They form a kind of expert system according to the classic definition derived from the cybernetic. Cybernetics is a science control systems, living or non-living, founded in 1948 by the north-American mathematician Norbert Wiener. Based on this definition, our world is full of overlaid systems that interact with each other. Therefore we can consider society, economy, computer network, machines, enterprises, cells, organisms, brains and everything else like a system.

All computers and intelligent machines as we know today are cybernetic applications. Cybernetics has also provided powerful methods to control two main systems: society and economy. A cybernetic system may be identified as an elements set, which interact with each other. These interactions set might be based

(a) Menu

(b) Augumented Reality

Fig. 2. ParQ augumented reality application running in an android phone (2013)

on substance information or energy exchanges. The elements of this compound system react and change according to these exchanges, changing itself or the possible interactions set with other compounds. Communication, signal, information and feedback are main concepts of the cybernetic field, fitting all criteria to also be an autopoietic system.

When items are organized in a system, the interactions between components cause a qualities set, which is not owned by any isolated component. For example, a given capacity of a living being, like running cannot be expressed by any of its isolated organs. In the same way a machine like a computer has higher qualities levels than the sum of its parts. Some the objects we're developing aim to use living being knowledge to solve problems. They represent knowledge, data gather or rules like any other computer. These rules and data might be triggered when necessary by digital devices. These objects possess a software layer that allows them to execute some tasks which might involve a decision making process. This knowledge is some times incorporated by some snippet code in order to reflect a knowledge change in the code itself.

We are working with knowledge based systems in order to manage different levels of interactivity between machines and other living beings without direct human interference as additional resource non-supported by orthodox programming technics. There has already been developed a street signpost cyber object, based on QRCodes, which leads the user to the social network uniform resource locator (URL) through his mobile device, figure 3. There is also a secondary cyber object which is a trash can, attached to the signposts and connected to the social network, whose function is to monitor the environmental education level of passersby and allow a remote visualization through a preinstalled web camera.

The ParQ project presents a systemic approach, since it's being developed in the context of pervasive and ubiquitous computing, which thus is required. We recur to Weiser and Brown's concept of calm technology in order to project information systems able to perform in the outskirt of our attention, based on cognitive psychology studies about attention mechanisms [8]. The second cyber object is a scale-bench, which verifies the health of sport practitioners and sends the collected data to the social network and mobile devices. This cyber object, figure 4, collaborates with relevant data related to the users average health. The creative process in this project involves clear notions of pervasive computing where computers are within the objects. Moreover, the project uses the ubiquitous computing in which computers are scattered and hidden in the environment of the Brasilia's City Park, an ubiquitous art inclusion into everyday

Fig. 3. 3D simulation of QRCode signpost and smart trash can final design (2013)

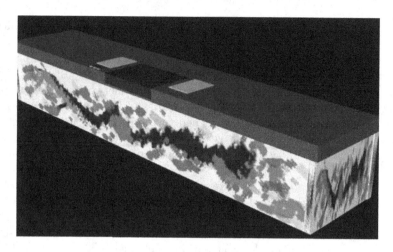

Fig. 4. Exact 3D model of the implemented bench-scale (2013)

life. According to Luigi Carro and Flávio Rech Wagner [9], there are currently great demand for mobile computing, ubiquitous and high computational power. They quote as classic examples the entertainment and telecommunication area where mobile devices and set-top-boxes increasingly demand more CPU operation per seconds and huge amounts of available memory. To 4G telecommunication equipment, they say, it is foreseen the computer processing need on the order of Teraflops and memory capacity on the order of Terabytes.

There are also appearing significant examples for mobile computing new markets especially in healthcare. In this area, with computer technology, there is a possibility of remote population health monitoring, using large databases. It is interesting especially to populations with access difficulty to the necessary means in large centers such as Brazil.

At the same time one aim to dilute the devices medley that surrounds computer technologies, parQ seeks to make unnecessary too much cognitive effort from the users to perceive the motivation behind the artistic proposal, using ubiquitous computing. By adopting unexceptional objects and expanding some of their original functions with computing devices that can process information and communication with other systems, like our social network.

One example of artistic work that involves ubiquitous computing is the installation of Live Wire, projected by Natalie Jeremijenko. The installation presents an electric engine in a room's roof connected to the internal Xerox research center network. In this art work, the information flow interferes directly on the electric engine's rotation speed. The larger information flow, faster the motor turns, causing a loud noise.

Finally this proposal involves an environment information system, containing the data visualization gathered from animals and environment. In order to achieve it we will recur to biosensors which are sensorial devices used to determine the concentration of substances and other parameters that might be interesting from the biological point of view. These biosensors might communicate wirelessly, like smart sensors to enable the digitalization of such environmental data. The correspondence between the system and the real world considers that the information is truly relevant also from an aesthetic point of view.

3.1   PedparQ: An Anti-sedentarism Gameart

The development of a gameart is part of this project and aims to connect the park users with our parQ network through the use of mobile devices in order to think about technology as an extension of your body. The proposal entitled PedparQ (ped stands for feet in Portuguese) seeks not to let the user became sedentary. Therefore, when activated, PedparQ counts the footsteps and if it doesn't reach a minimum, will consider the user as sedentary and in this case an alert sound is played on the mobile device. This game art will be connected to parQ social network and will send automatically this data.

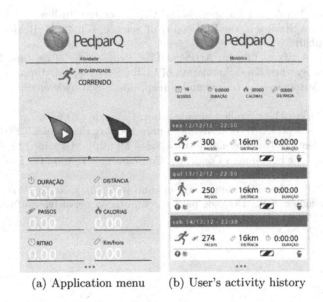

(a) Application menu   (b) User's activity history

Fig. 5. ParQ augumented reality application running in an android phone (2013)

4   Conclusion

The social network parQ.unb.br was implemented in 2011, adapting functions such as the graphical user interface and the database server itself from Wikinarua, integrating the parks security cameras with the social network, a cyberradio implementation, network communication implementation and data interaction visualization between living beings, objects and the environment.

Next we expanded the functions of database and software parQ for Android phones. The software parQ passes or streams information from the server database to mobile devices, as well as information from other social networks shared with parQ. We are now developing and implementing items like the interactive biocybernetic communication between the park and the parQ social network, the mobile augmented reality application that will be able to recognize nature, objects and environment shapes.

We emphasize that the concepts presented here, such as pervasive or ubiquitous computing or ubiquitous provoke from the methodological point of view, a strongly integrative work from many areas such as computer science, art and engineering. It is on this synergic development that we aim to bring on discussion about which are the impacts that the result of this research will provoke in the structures and competences of other research groups in Brazil.

References

1. Maturana, H., Varela, F.: Autopoiesis and Cognition: the Realization of the Living, 1st edn. Boston Studies in the Philosophy of Science, vol. 42. D. Reidel Publishing Company (1980)
2. Langton, C.: Artificial life. In: Artificial Life: Proceedings of an Interdisciplinary Workshop on Synthesis and Simulation of Living Systems, vol. 4, pp. 1–47 (1989)
3. Luisi, P.L.: Autopoiesis: a review and a reappraisal. Naturwissenschaften 1, 49–59 (2003)
4. Hertz, G.: Cockroach controlled mobile robot. Gizmodo (2008)
5. Stocker, G., Schöpf, C.: Hybrid: living in paradox. Ars Electronica (2005)
6. Nichols, S.: The post-human manifesto. Games Monthly Magazine (1988)
7. Pepperell, R.: The Posthuman Condition: Consciousness Beyond the Brain. Intellect Ltd. (2009)
8. Brown, M.W.R., The, J.S.: coming age of calm technology. Xerox PARC (1996)
9. Carro, L., Wagner, F.R.: Desafios para a computação pervasiva no futuro cenário tecnológico. PPGC - UFRGS (2012)

Part II

Universal Access to Learning and Education

Approaches to E-Learning

Susanne Akrawi Hartvig[1] and Eva Petersson Brooks[2]

[1] Centre for Design, Learning and Innovation, Department of Learning and Philosophy,
Aalborg University Esbjerg, Niels Bohrs Vej 8,
6700 Esbjerg, Denmark
sah@learning.aau.dk
[2] Centre for Design, Learning and Innovation, Department of Architecture and Media
Technology, Aalborg University Esbjerg, Niels Bohrs Vej 8,
6700 Esbjerg, Denmark
ep@create.aau.dk

Abstract. E-learning has made its entrance into educational institutions. Compared to traditional learning methods, e-learning has the benefit of enabling educational institutions to attract more students. E-learning not only opens up for an increased enrollment, it also gives students who would otherwise not be able to take the education to now get the possibility to do so. This paper introduces Axel Honneth's theory on the need for recognition as a framework to understand the role and function of interaction in relation to e-learning. The paper argues that an increased focus on the dialectic relationship between recognition and learning will enable an optimization of the learning conditions and the interactive affordances targeting students under e-learning programs. The paper concludes that the engagement and motivation to learn are not only influenced by but depending on recognition.

Keywords: e-learning, interaction, dialectic relationship, recognition.

1 Introduction

The information and computing technology plays an increasing role in the society today and challenges the traditional understanding of teaching and learning [1]. With the use of information and computing technology the learning environment has changed. Traditionally, the learning environment was associated with auditoriums, classrooms and textbooks. Today, the Internet and the wireless network make it possible for learning to take place at any place and at any time [1, 2]. This opens up for new ways of teaching where e-learning can play a smaller or bigger role.

The main reasons for implementing e-learning are economic, geographical and technological circumstances [3]. E-learning has the benefit of enabling educational institutions to reach more students. Compared to traditional learning methods where time and space confine the enrollment of students, e-learning does not have these limits. Therefore e-learning gives students who would otherwise not be able to take the education to now get the possibility to do so [4]. Due to the opportunities created

C. Stephanidis and M. Antona (Eds.): UAHCI/HCII 2013, Part III, LNCS 8011, pp. 127–132, 2013.

by e-learning, many people are now attracted to training and education who would not have before considered it possible or even relevant to their lives [1].

Looking at the disadvantage on the other hand, e-learning moves the teaching and learning from the classroom to online interaction and thereby removes the possibilities that physical presence - the face-to-face interaction between the teacher and the students – offer. Especially when it comes to social and healthcare education this can be seen as a challenge. Traditionally these schools have developed the students' personal qualities developed in dealings with other people. Therefore, with the change from traditional classroom teaching to distance learning new challenges and questions arise.

Wertsch [5, 6] emphasises the mediating role of tools as communication resources, shaping social interaction and influencing the knowledge being conveyed. Hence, e-learning can be considered as a mediating process. Petersson [7] defines this process as a semiotic interplay bridging guided interaction and individual actions.

This semiotic interplay illustrates a holistic overview of a complex situation focused upon qualities integral to the design of e-learning experiences leading to desired learning process and outcome. The learning within and the design of e-learning situations constitute a situated activity with inherent actions and interventions [7, 8].

According to Monty et al. [9] e-learning should not be seen as a new tool but as a new context of learning. It is not necessarily meaningful to use traditional teaching materials or methods and apply them to e-learning. There is a need of a rethinking of the learning design based on the new context. Only in this way, it is possible to take advantage of the new possibilities e-learning that gives [9]. The new context demands a rethinking of how to teach online. There are several reasons for that. Studies show that it is not possible to achieve successful teaching online by using teaching methods that we normally use. The teaching must be based on the possibilities for active interaction and dialogue between the students and the educators where learning is something students engage in creating. By e-learning technology it is possible to learn by creating contacts and seek network (connectivity) and enter into these communities. But it demands that online education is organized in such a way that the students can use the possibilities. Secondly there are changes in the society which demands that the students develop new methods concerning how to deal/act [9]. But when dealing with the challenges of using e-learning it must be relevant to investigate how we learn as individuals. What is central for us as humans if we should be able to learn? What are the preconditions that need to be met to be able to achieve learning and development? The theory of recognition by Axel Honneth [10, 11] offers a realm of understanding that brings new perspective to the context of learning and e-learning. His basic assumption is that recognition is a precondition that must be met to be able to learn and develop as individuals. Based on the theory of recognition this article sets forth a new focus on the emergence of recognition as fundamental in e-learning contexts. By focusing on recognition it becomes decisive how it is experienced and achieved.

This paper presents a new approach to e-learning by presenting the theory of recognition by Axel Honneth [10, 11] focusing on aspects that appear relevant for e-learning design. This will demonstrate the firm basis of the theory and also point out its views on different kinds of recognition and spheres and how these play an important role when dealing with (e-)learning. Finally the article will suggest central research questions and topics for future work with the theory of recognition as basis.

2   Axel Honneth's Theory: The Struggle for Recognition

With the theory of recognition Axel Honneth outlines an approach that is both highly original and firmly rooted in the history of modern social theory. Honneth situates his project within the tradition that emphasizes not the struggle for self-preservation but rather the struggle for establishment of relations of mutual recognition as a precondition for self-realization [12].

Inspired by Hegel and his model of the struggle for recognition and George Herbert Mead and his naturalistic pragmatism, Honneth builds his theory on social relationships as central to the development and maintenance of our identity as human beings. The connection between social patterns of recognition and individual prerequisites for self-realization is the ground on which Honneth develops his framework for interpreting social struggles. Well-established, ethical relations are essential for humans in order to be able to flourish.

2.1   An Overview

Relationships of mutual recognition are essential because they are crucial for our development as individuals – and our ability for sensing, interpreting, and realizing our needs and desires. We develop three modes of relating practically to one self: Self-confidence, self-respect, and self-esteem. Honneth argues that to be able to relate to one in these ways involves recognition from others.

Honneth distinguish between three different kinds of relationships where recognition is needed:

- Close relations of love and friendship
- Legally institutionalized relations of universal respect for the autonomy and dignity of persons
- Networks of solidarity and shared values within which the particular worth of members of a community can be acknowledged [10, 11]

These relationships must be established through social struggles for recognition since they are not historically given. It is in these relationships that self-confidence, self-respect and self-esteem are being developed.

2.2   Love and Self-confidence

Self-confidence is the basic relation to oneself that is developed in relationships of love and friendship. Our first relationships to others are decisive for our development of the capacity to express needs and desires without fear of being abandoned as a result. Honneth uses the object-relations theory of early childhood experience in which interactive relationships are necessary for the development of children [10, 11, 12].

2.3   Rights and Self-respect

Honneth connects the development of self-respect with the recognition of being a morally responsible agent. Honneth draws on Immanuel Kant's view that every person has the right to be recognized and respected as capable of acting on the basis of reasons and therefore also capable of participating in public deliberation [10, 11].

When it comes to self-respect being accorded legal rights are crucial. Rights give the opportunity to assert claims, and defend the rights you have been given. If the fullest form of self-respecting should be realized, one needs to be recognized as possessing the capacities of being a legal person and morally responsible agent [10, 11].

2.4   Solidarity and Self-esteem

With self-esteem one has the sense of being irreplaceable and having something of value to offer. Honneth agrees with Mead claiming that one needs to know that one does better than others to be able to distinguish oneself from others.

Honneth, however, does not agree with the view that the division of labour in modern industrial societies allows all individuals to find their roles in which to excel. His argument is that cultural aspects play an important role when it comes to self-esteem [9]. The values of a particular culture determine what is and what is not considered as a significant contribution to the common good and what is not. This will determine which job functions, educations etc. that will convey a sense of personal accomplishment. Therefore, what is counted as a contribution in a culture is decisive for individuals' opportunities for self-esteem. With this view it is possible to conceive the conditions for self-esteem as a field of cultural struggle for the recognition of previously denigrated contributors to the common good.

Honneth connects self-esteem with solidarity, which should be understood as the cultural climate in which it is possible to acquire self-esteem. According to Honneth we can only use the term solidarity when some shared concern, value or interest are present [13].

The term 'solidarity' is contingent since the values of a society vary. Which particular values that are approved depend on the social and cultural struggles. Struggles for recognition can be seen as attempts to change social patterns that denigrate individuals to a condition where individuals have real opportunities to acquire esteem. Not simply for being a member of a group but for being an individual contributing to a shared project.

The three dimensions of recognition, which have now been described, are the fundament of Honneth's normative theory of an ideal society where individuals have real opportunities to acquire self-confidence, self-respect and self-esteem. These dimensions of recognition are necessary for the full development of the identity of an individual. It is important to add that recognition in Honneths' perception must go both ways – meaning that recognition must come from someone whom one recognizes [10, 11].

3   Recognition and Learning

Based on the theory of recognition we achieve a new approach to learning where recognition goes ahead of learning and development. The dialectic relationship between recognition and learning makes it essential to focus not only on learning methods and styles but also on recognition as the foundation in any learning environment.

First, Honneths theoretical distinction between three spheres where recognition is needed contributes with a general focus not only on the student in a formal learning situation but on the student as a social individual with experiences of recognition and a way of relating to one self that influence her preconditions of learning.

Recognition in the sphere of solidarity including experiences in educational institutions becomes important since the recognition offered here influences the students learning and development. The student must be given opportunities to achieve recognition because of his or her particular qualities; to sense that (s)he has something of value to offer the community.

In order to be able to offer students an experience of recognition in learning environments it is important to investigate what the experience of recognition requires. Both in relation to the society in general to assert which values are approved today and in relation to the specific learning context. The concept of recognition gives a deeper understanding of, and focus on, the individual as unique and thereby a recognition of their diverse qualities, competences and ways of learning.

Just as the movement of learning from traditional classroom teaching to distance learning demands new learning methods that are based on the new learning context, there is a need to focus on recognition in relation to this new context as well. In other words, how can recognition be taken from the classroom – the physical presence - into an unlimited room independent of time and place?

4   Future Work

What Honneth offers is a realm of understanding to study how we learn and develop as individuals. Focusing on the dialectic relationship between recognition and learning offer possibilities for enabling an optimization of learning conditions targeting students under e-learning programs. Consequently, in conclusion, the engagement, interest and motivation to learn are not only influenced by, but depending on, recognition. To understand and address these dependencies in the context of e-learning, a study will be implemented including students from a Danish distance education within the social and health sector (high school level). The study will apply a micro-development and process-oriented approach to identify possible links between recognition and learning.

References

1. Slevin, J.: Etivities and the Connecting of E-Learning Experiences through Deliverative Feedback. Tidskrift for Universiteternes efter- og Videreuddannelse 9 (2006)
2. Steinmüller, L.M.: Pædagogik og E-Læring. In: J.A.K. bladet, 3f (2001)
3. Christensen, G.: Anvendelse af E-Læringsmaterialer til særlige målgrupper. In: Det Nationale Videncenter for e-læring (2010)

4. Fredskild, U.T.: Optimizing the Learning Potential for the Distance Learning Students. In: University College Syd, Sygeplejerskeuddannelsen (2012)
5. Wertsch, J.V.: Voices of the Mind: A Sociocultural Approach to Mediated Action. Harvard University Press, Cambridge (1993)
6. Wertsch, J.V.: Mind as Action. Oxford University Press, New York (1998)
7. Petersson, E.: Non-formal Learning through Ludic Engagement within Interactive Environments. Doctoral dissertation, Malmoe University, School of Teacher Education, Studies in Educational Sciences (2006)
8. Petersson, E.: Editorial: Ludic Engagement Designs for All. In: Digital Creativity, vol. 19(3), pp. 141–144. Routledge, London (2008)
9. Olsen, C.S., Monty, A.: Hvordan bliver studerende aktive i fjernundervisning? In: Almeborg, S., Nyvang, T. (eds.) Tilrettelæggelse af efter- og videreuddannelse på universitet, vol. 4(8), UNEV (2006)
10. Honneth, A.: Behovet for anerkendelse. Hans Reitzels Forlag, Copenhagen (2003)
11. Honneth, A.: Kamp om anerkendelse. Hans Reitzels Forlag, Copenhagen (2006)
12. Anderson, J.: Translator's Introduction to Axel Honneth. In: Anderson, J. (ed.) The Struggle for Recognition. The Moral Grammar of Social Conflict. MIT Press, Cambridge (1996)
13. Nørgaard, B.: Axel Honneth og en Teori om anerkendelse. Tidskrift for Socialpædagogik 16 (2005)

Deaf Students and Comic Hypermedia: Proposal of Accessible Learning Object

Raul Inácio Busarello[1], Vania Ribas Ulbricht[2], Patricia Bieging[3],
and Vilma Villarouco[4]

[1] Universidade Federal de Santa Catarina, Brazil
raulbusarello@gmail.com
[2] Universidade Federal de Santa Catarina e Universidade Federal do Paraná, Brazil
vrulbricht@gmail.com
[3] Universidade de São Paulo, Brazil
pbieging@gmail.com
[4] Universidade Federal de Pernambuco, Brazil
villarouco@hotmail.com

Abstract. This article presents the perceptions of deaf users that had participated in an experiment about the use of comics as hypermedia learning object
of descriptive geometry. The methodology used was exploratory research,
applied based on qualitative method. From that the prototype was created and
subsequently tested with the sample of the public. This article presents: an
approach to the profile of the public searched; the structure of the prototype
created; and the results of applying through perspective of deaf students. As a
result it was observed that: the comic's structure and adapted to the hypermedia
presentations facilitate the content's assimilation by the deaf student. The participants had been adapting quickly to form navigation proposed in learning object. Moreover, the media creates an emotional appeal to the audience, which
contributes to their learning.

Keywords: deaf, comics, hypermedia, accessible, learning object.

1 Introduction

This experiment has as theoretical foundation a studies series that shows the difficulty
in learning deaf students because difficulty of them reading written texts. The ideal
for learning deaf students is the emphasis on graphics and visual learning environments [7] [15]. Hypermedia environments contribute to the education of the deaf students as they allow access to multimedia that make easy learning various content [19].
Similarly researchers who advocate the use of storytelling as a tool for knowledge
generation in hypermedia environments shows that the nonlinearity of the medium
allows the student to define and control the browsing process and reading of data. It
enabling the user knows the story through comfortable and convenient way [5] [16]
[18] [20] [21]. Comics are a storytelling form formed by text and image that facilitating the process of representation of reality by students [6] [10]. Comics structure

C. Stephanidis and M. Antona (Eds.): UAHCI/HCII 2013, Part III, LNCS 8011, pp. 133–142, 2013.

consists of interconnected images in sequential frames enable greater integration of content with the imagination of the reader. It making possible to reader impose the same pace of reading and therefore learning [9]. Besides comics are being readily adapted to environments hypermedia [13].

In that context the aim of this paper is to present the perceptions of deaf users who participated in the experiment on the generation of knowledge through the use of learning objects in comic hypermedia [4]. This learning object has focus on learning the concept of Orthogonal Cylindrical Projection.

The methodology is exploratory based on qualitative research. The implementation took place from the use of the prototype with the target audience where it was possible to collect the student's opinions. Data were collected from: 1. Questionnaire completed by the volunteers before they have contact with the prototype; 2. The activities results while the volunteers using the prototype; 3. Researcher written notes while the volunteers were using the prototype and activities; and 4. Focus group data obtained by researcher from the transcript of video record. The target audience was research volunteers members of two educational organizations for deaf people in Florianopolis city, SC, Brazil.

This paper is restricted to present the profile of the research public. It presents too the structure of the comics hypermedia prototype learning object. In the end the paper presents the results of prototype applying search through the perspective of users.

2   The Research's Deaf Students

Volunteers from two educational organizations for the deaf people of Grande Florianopolis City, SC states, Brazil, had participated to the research. One of these organizations is *Institute for Hearing and Language Therapy*: it is a non-governmental organization. It have a goal of developing the potential of deaf communication and educational focus in oralism and the need to recognize the use of – Brazilian Sign Language – LIBRAS [11]. Another one was *Deaf Association of Grande Florianopolis*: "is a civil organization focused in areas as an socio cultural, educational, vocational, recreational and healthcare nonprofit that attending the deaf and their families" [1]. The association acts as though assisting together with an official bodies and public power, public, whose goal is to promote education, professionalization and the inclusion of the deaf in the labor market. All it through agreements and contracts with public and private sector. Among its objectives this organization offers several levels of LIBRAS course, orientation and support to parents of deaf people. Additionally, the organization offers events about deaf culture and lectures in the areas of health, education, justice, work and psychology to society.

The research was conducted in the beginning of September 2011. As a requirement volunteers should: 1. Being over age 15, because the content of graphical representation of a learning object is usually taught in high school or higher and requiring certain instructional luggage; 2. They could be men or women, of any race, belief, social class, provided they had some kind of hearing disability; 3. The students needed had minimal familiarity with computer. That because the prototype's construction purpose is to develop a tool for online learning.

In the first *Institute for Hearing and Language Therapy* nine people were willing to be research volunteers. In *Deaf Association of Grande Florianopolis* three people were willing to be volunteers. In total the survey was conducted with twelve volunteers. To ensure anonymity, they were being identified from the naming, such as: Volunteer 1, Volunteer 2 to Volunteer 12 [4].

At both institutions was requested the interpreter assistance to make communication between researcher and volunteers. By the number of participants in the first organization two interpreters assisted in communication and in the second one just one. The surveys were recorded on video and made on different days.

2.1   Profile of Volunteers Search

As the profile of research volunteers through a structured questionnaire [4] it can be seen:

- Five of the volunteers were aged between 15 to 20 years; one between 21 a 24; two between 26 to 30; two between 31 to 35 and two between 36 to 40;
- Seven volunteers are female and five male;
- About the deafness degree: four volunteers are partially deaf and eight completely deaf. Two of the partially deaf volunteers declare that are completely deaf in one ear and partially deaf in the other one;
- About the period in which lost hearing, six were born deaf. Three said they lost their hearing before learning the Portuguese language oral and written. Three lost their hearing after learning the Portuguese language oral and written;
- All volunteers communicate using LIBRAS;
- Five stated that they use and communicate through writing. However, all twelve volunteers filled out a written questionnaire. It suggests that all volunteers read and write though some with more difficulty than others;
- One of the volunteers told not to use the internet. Of the other volunteers that use the Internet: eight access content related to sports and leisure and five seek journalistic information;
- Nine of the volunteers declare use Facebook or Orkut, social networks where communication is through text. Seven said they use MSN, tool that beyond the text can add the video too. Only one volunteer said using the tool OOVOO. It also enables communication throygh video. However to communicate in social networks eleven of the volunteers said using text for do this. Eight said they also use the webcam to communicate on the Internet;
- Nine of the volunteers using the internet as a study tool, where the biggest practice is research for school work and access to University's ambient course or others who have disciplines in On-line learning;
- About comics contact: two of the volunteers said they did not enjoy reading this media. However ten of them like it;
- All volunteers said they had never have contact with the contents of Orthogonal Cylindrical Projection.

3   The Prototype Learning Object in Comic Hypermedia

To the storytelling building first the researcher crossed data gender and age of audience with research data of the readers profiles comics [22] [23]. From this data it was establish that the comic book created as learning object, must have as style references the work of Brazilian comics designers. It must be emphasis on a light storytelling flow and a subtle humor.

The second topic to be considered before the design and development of the comic screenplay is that any media object to be considered learning object should be added to other learning objects. It must approaches two basic requirements: learning and reuse [12]. That means this object must have the ability to be reusable by different developers and different instructional contexts. Furthermore, this object should allow greater interactivity-with the student. It must encouraging the student reflection and culminated in the formation of new concepts by the individual.

The object built stresses the nonlinear character. It organized on small learning objects put in a coherent and logical context according the storytelling. It contributes to forming a learning object larger. The comic is based on a nonlinear storytelling where the students should have a single entry and exit of the object, but with several links possibilities within the story [17]. The output successfully depends of the student's answer into the system with positive return during the final evaluation.

It is necessary that the story has a logical storytelling with a defined beginning middle, and end. In this way was used as the basis for the dramatic structure of the storytelling paradigm that divides the story into three acts [8]: Act I is the character and story presentation; Act II corresponds to the character's confrontation and obstacles to character arrive on him/her goal; and the Act III is the resolution of the story. Turnpoint is the situation that changes a Act to another. It could be incident requiring a certain character's action.

The entire storytelling consists of individual pieces that are arranged and unified story. It enables that in the story designing could be structured nonlinear form despite it needs complies with the consistent storytelling development. A hypertext storytelling can be structured both linearly and non-linear [3]. However how the screenwriter will work the language structure elements it gives the storytelling pace. Moreover, a comic series embedded in other comic series creates a sense of depth in story [14]. Links can be a resource that encourages the reader to know aspects that complement the main storytelling. It contributes to greater student interaction and possibility to he/she reviews the content presented by another way [16].

Accordingly it the researchers structured the comics through a linear main storytelling. It presents a fictional storytelling content Orthogonal Cylindrical Projection and ends in a student evaluation. Depending on the student answers he/she is able to advance in content where he/she will accessing another learning module or continue with the same story reviewing the educational content in other ways.

The second part of the storytelling has the same learning content but with different story. It is accessed after the assessment if the student had incorrect answer. The content of the storytelling links also has a linear character. Its nonlinearity in fact may or may not be accessed from a particular time in the story. These little side stories are returned to the point where the student accesses it.

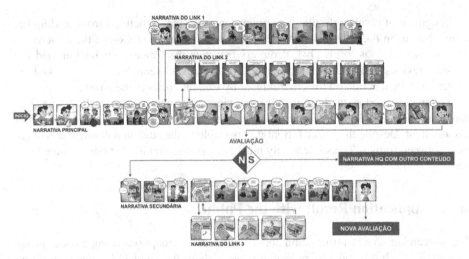

Fig. 1. Nonlinear comics structure - theme cylindrical projection orthogonal [4] (based on [17])

3.1   Browsing in the Comic

From the building of the story the researchers created an interface designed where deaf student could navigate by storytelling. Thus the prototype is structured: on a neutral background; it has an identification in the storytelling upper left corner with the content of the learning object; the text and design of the characters action is centered on the screen into a frame; browsers to access the frames before and after; and a map at the bottom with the structure of storytelling.

Fig. 2. Layout of the interface navigation of the learning object prototype [4]

Based on guidelines for the adaptive web interface design [2] the aspects of the prototype structure which help user navigation are: use of arrows; description links; map navigation; and use arrangement of elements on screen to prevent the student distraction.

Lodgment of comics: despite the comics language was structured from reading between frames in the digital environment the manner of presentation of these elements may include various forms [14]. Browsers facilitate the frame visualization and between previous frame and later frame. The space between frames is marked by effective student action on the environment by student clicks at the arrow.

The map is used as medium to full story view. This map shows all the frames that make up the storytelling in linear order. It indicating which frame is being shown at the moment. Despite the linear format it is possible to the student a non-linear navigation between frames. The student only must click on the picture that he/she want to be see.

4   Application Result with the Public

The researcher sought information about volunteers' perceptions using a focus group tool to do it. Those students' perceptions were about the comics' language as a way viewing way the content and the proposed use this storytelling in learning. This discussion took place in an open where participants were free to do comments and questions. The researcher's role was to lead the discussion into the theme. But he did it without neglecting any other issues that might arise.

4.1   The Comics Language

The learning proposed presented through the use of the comics language was well accepted by the study volunteers. The images contributed to the deaf volunteers could better understand what content should be taught. The volunteers stressed that it is important to use pictures to help the deaf people in text comprehension.

The Volunteer 12 stated that until the application had not seen a learning tool with a focus on deaf that uses the comics' language. It stressed that experience is valid and that the use of image helps them in understanding the subject. The volunteer reports that at the beginning of the content found reading a little difficult, but then managed to assimilate. Moreover the Volunteer 12 surprised about the presentation of the content.

Likewise the Volunteer 10 also was surprised by the proposal. He had some difficulty in understanding the content, but just on beginning.

For Volunteers 3 and 6 the images helped them in understanding the text because this feature prevents often get asked what the meaning of a particular word is. They said that in this context the picture was very important because if the content was presented only by text survey participants could not understand. The Volunteer 11 identifies that there are many word meanings that deaf people do not know. In addition the volunteer understands that some words have more than one meaning, so understanding of reading may be impaired. However the image contributes to understanding the text.

In this context the Volunteers 10, 11 and 12 believe that through the use of the comics language was easy to understand the proposed content. Likewise, the

Volunteers 1, 5 and 9 said the picture helped them to understanding the picture. However, the Volunteer 1 in some moments the text reading harmed the content understanding.

The Volunteers 1, 3, 5, 6 report that failed to understand some words written in Portuguese, but in this case the image helped them the content. Beyond it helped in the actual understanding of unfamiliar terms. To the Volunteers 10 and 11 was not very easy to understand a few phrases because terms were unknown. But they said the comics language facilitated the understanding of the story context of the story.

The Volunteers 1, 2, 3, 4, 5, 6, 7, 8 and 9 said had been certain difficulties in understanding written words. But it not detracted the meanings of the history contents.

For instance: the Volunteer 9 explained that when she reads a book , not understands many words and it confuses the story meaning. However through the comics' language it was easy to understand. To this volunteer is easy to understand when a context is presented by some writing text and it is illustrated by a picture. The Volunteer 5 adds that when writing in Portuguese language is simplified, and still accompanied by a picture it turns easy to understand the meaning.

The Volunteer 3 understands that the Orthogonal Cylindrical Projection concept was understood easily because the comics present a little text, pictures and contents used together. This volunteer stresses that just reading the comics was able to understand the learning content. This opinion was divided among all study volunteers. To the Volunteers 10, 11 and 12 the picture and words enabled the complete understanding of the message even when certain words were not understood.

4.2   Learning Particularities

The storytelling in comics proposed has facilitated the visualization of the Graphic Representation specific concepts. Also it provides that this content was shown through a playful storytelling.

The volunteers identified themselves with the drama of the story and the characters. It contributed to the understanding of educational content. The Volunteer 5 liked the story because it was about the character's life. She said feel good read. The Volunteer 12 was surprise by the story and the character's reaction. Volunteer 6 was eager to see the end of story because he twisted by character. Volunteers 1, 3 and 9 were identified with the story because they had lived a similar situation that the character lived. The Volunteer 11 liked reading because it was the love story between boy and girl.

For volunteers the plot and the characters were not displaced didactic content in the storytelling. Both contents were work so that was easy to understand by volunteers. They agreed after interacting with the comics learning object they could understand a little about the concept of Orthogonal Cylindrical Projection. The Volunteer 12 identifies that the comics' prototype helped introduce the discipline. However he emphasizes that needs to do more research on the subject to understand deeply the content.

The Volunteer 10 reported that he had done drawing classes and that what he did was similar to that seen in content of learning object. The volunteer understood the contents, but he said it is difficult. Volunteer can not tell if the difficult is in relation to how content is organized in comic learning object. However he identifies which also had difficulty in drawing classes in the past too. The participant said that comics helped him better understand the content, but he still identifies that need exercising more the content.

5   Final Thoughts

This article presented a part of the perceptions of deaf users. They participated in the experiment on the generation of knowledge through experience of the student by the learning object hypermedia [4].

As a result it was observed that: the peculiar structure of comics in a hypermedia enviroment is facilitators for the assimilation of the content by the student. All volunteers adapted quickly to the shape of the proposed navigation of learning object. The volunteers agreed that they could understand the educational content through the comics.

Moreover, the presentation of the learning object proposal creates an emotional appeal to the deaf audience. It contributes to the transmission of educational content. First: the presentation of content through sequential images helped the assimilation of concepts by the survey participants. It is constitutes as an important communication tool for these people. Second: the emotional relationship between story and students deepened story helping the learning context. The emotional relationship that story presented the concepts tied to the plot was well accepted by the volunteers. It favored that the volunteers understand the concepts learned from the characters' actions.

During the research the researchers noticed that the written text remains an obstacle to the deaf person communication. However the redundantly between text and image in comics facilitated understanding by the volunteers and that they even learning possible terms - in written form - unknown.

References

1. ASGF, Associação de Surdos da Grande Florianópolis. Quem somos, http://www.asgfsurdos.org.br/?page_id=3 (accessed in September 19, 2001)
2. BATISTA, Claudia Regina. Modelo e Diretrizes para o Processo de Design de Interface Web Adaptativa. Tese para obtenção do título de Doutor no programa Pós Graduação em Engenharia e Gestão do Conhecimento da Universidade Federal de Santa Catarina, área de concentração Mídia e Conhecimento. Florianópolis (2008)
3. Braga, M.C.G., Pereira, A.T.C., Ulbricht, V.R., Vanzin, T.: Hipermídia: uma jornada entre narrativas e roteiros. Congresso Nacional de Ambientes Hipermídia para Aprendizagem – CONAHPA. Florianópolis de 09 a 13 de abril de (2006)
4. Busarello, R.I.: Geração de conhecimento para usuário surdo baseada em histórias em quadrinhos hipermidiáticas. Dissertação apresentada para a obtenção ao título de Mestre no Programa de Pós-graduação em Engenharia e Gestão do Conhecimento, área Mídia e Conhecimento, da Universidade Federal de Santa Catarina. Florianópolis, SC (2011)

5. Castro, C., Freitas, C.: Narrativa Audiovisual para Multiplataforma – Um Estudo Preliminar. Sociedade Brasileira de Estudos Interdisciplinares da Comunicação – Intercom. Ano 2 | # 07 | edição bimestral | janeiro a abril de (2010)
6. Cirne, M.: Quadrinhos, sedução e paixão. – Petrópolis. Vozes, RJ (2000)
7. Corradi, J.A.M., Vidotti, S.A.B.: Ambientes Infor-macionais Digitais Acessíveis a Minorias Lingüísticas Surdas: cidadania e/ou responsa-bilidade social, http://dci2.ccsa.ufpb.br:8080/jspui/bitstream/123456789/412/1/GT%208%20Txt%203-%20CORRADI.pdf (accessed in July 5, 2010)
8. Field, S.: Manual do roteiro: os fundamento do texto cinematográfico. Objetiva, Rio de Janeiro (2001)
9. Gerde, V.W., Spencer Foster, R.: X-Men Ethics: Using Comic Books to Teach Business Ethics. Journal of Business Ethics 77, 245–258 (2008), doi:10.1007/s10551-006-9347-3
10. Hughes, J., King, A.E.: Dual Pathways to Expression and Understanding: Canadian Coming-of-Age Graphic Novels. Children's Literature in Education 41, 64–84 (2010), doi:10.1007/s10583-009-9098-8.
11. IATEL, Instituto de Audição e Terapia da Linguagem. Quem Somos, http://iatel.org.br/home/?page_id=11 (accessed in September 19, 2011)
12. Macedo, C.M.S.: Diretrizes para criação de objetos de aprendizagem acessíveis. Tese para obtenção do título de Doutor no programa Pós Graduação em Engenharia e Gestão do Conhecimento – PPEGC, da Universidade Federal de Santa Catarina. Florianópolis (2010)
13. Mcloud, S.: Desenhando Quadrinhos: os segredos das narrativas de quadrinhos, mangás e graphic novels. M. Books do Brasil Editora Ltda. São Paulo (2008)
14. Mcloud, S.: Reinventando os Quadrinhos: como a imaginação e a tecnologia vêm revolucionando essa forma de arte. M. Books do Brail Editora Ltda, São Paulo (2006)
15. Menezes, D.B., et al.: Mitos sobre a língua de sinais e o surdo: percepção de professores da Universidade Federal de Goiás. Relatório das atividades realizadas para a Prática como Componente Curricular, Goiânia (2009)
16. Murray, J.H.: Hamlet no holodeck: o futuro da narrativa no ciberespaço. Itaú Cultural, Unesp, São Paulo (2003)
17. Nunes, E.V., Busarello, R.I., Dandolini, G., Souza, J.A., Ulbricht, V.R., Vanzin, T.: Construção de objetos de aprendizagem acessível: foco na aprendizagem significativa. Cadernos de Informática, Número 1. In: Anais do VI Congresso Ibero-americano de Telemática (CITA 2011), Gramado RS, Brasil, Maio 16-18, vol. 6 (2011)
18. Rodríguez, J.A.: El relato Digital: Hacia um nuevo arte narrativo, http://www.scribd.com/doc/23242364/El-relato-digital-hacia-un-nuevo-arte-narrativo (accessed in June 3, 2010)
19. Skourlas, C., et al.: A wireless distributed framework for supporting Assistive Learning Environments (2010), http://delivery.acm.org/10.1145/1580000/1579167/a53-skourlas.pdf?key1=1579167&key2=9745821821&coll=GUIDE&dl=GUIDE&CFID=97473285&CFTOKEN=70764351 (accessed in August 8, 2010)
20. Sobral, H., Bellicieri, F.N.: Influências dos meios digitais na narrativa (2010), http://www.mackenzie.com.br/fileadmin/Pos_Graduacao/Mestrado/Educacao_Arte_e_Historia_da_Cultura/Publicacoes/Volume5/Influencias_dos_meios_digitais_na_narrativa.pdf (accessed in April 14, 2010)

21. Steiner, K.E., Tomkins, J.: Narrative Event Adaptation in Virtual Environments, http://delivery.acm.org/10.1145/970000/964453/p46-stein-er.pdf?key1=964453&key2=8654055721&coll=GUIDE&dl=GUIDE&CFID=92527425&CFTOKEN=74453275
22. Vergueiro, W.: A atualidade das histórias em quadrinhos no Brasil: a busca de um no-vo público. História, imagem e narrativas. No 5, ano 3 (setembro 2007) ISSN 1808-9895
23. Vergueiro, W., Bari, V.A.: Perfil da leitora brasileira de quadrinhos: uma pesquisa partici-pativa. Trabalho apresentado XXV Congresso Anual em Ciência da Comunicação, Salva-dor/BA, 1 a 5 Set (2002)

Developing Story Performing System for Children

Chien-Hsu Chen, Shao-Yu Wang, and Yi-Chai Nina Lee

Department of Industrial Design, National Cheng Kung University, Tainan 70101, Taiwan
chenhsu@mail.ncku.edu.tw, {wasami89,jellynina}@gmail.com

Abstract. Storytelling activity is an effective method to enhance children's presentation ability, logical thinking and imagination in elementary education. In this paper, researchers observed elementary school children in the course of Performing Art and discovered the difficulty for them to operate the puppets. Hence, the purpose of this paper is to take advantages from both technology and storytelling activities to solve this kind of problems. A real-time chromakey technique system which is able to composites the actors and the scenes in real-time is conducted for children to create plays intuitively as well as record their performance for sharing, therefore reduce the frustration and increase the motivation of children in creating stories.

Keywords: storytelling, elementary education, performing system, collaboration.

1 Introduction

Children express themselves with storytelling and learn to deal with the social issue through storytelling. Also, storytelling can improve children behavior such as presentation ability, linguistics skills, logical thinking, communication skills, and imagination [1-4]. Hence, the method of storytelling becomes an efficient educational tool, and being widely applied in the elementary education [5].

Drama is a popular topic in the field of performing art while storytelling activities are mainly being taught in the course of performing art in Taiwan. Storytelling in drama is the combination of conversation, narrative, and dramatic discourse which are intentional planned [6]. It is benefit to children by producing a play. However, parents believe that general subjects such as Mathematics, Chinese and Science courses are much more valuable than the performing art course, and it also costs a lot of time to complete a play for the performing art course. Therefore, parents usually request school to reduce the activities in performing art course. As the result, children might lose the opportunities to develop multiple capabilities in conversation, narrative, and dramatic discourse. In order to increase the learning efficiency of performing art course, researchers expect to develop a system that can support the storytelling activities in performing art course.

Anderson [7] indicated that experts in drama education discuss about the possible effect in collaboration preforming with technology. As for experts in interaction design have implemented digital storytelling systems for children while drama

C. Stephanidis and M. Antona (Eds.): UAHCI/HCII 2013, Part III, LNCS 8011, pp. 143–152, 2013.

educators seldom use those design in formal course. Also, Di Blas [8] indicated that there are few cases had successfully implemented the digital storytelling systems in the field of schools. The technologies for supporting cooperative storytelling did not approach the practical level in school environment. Most of tools and systems that support to the collaboration in story creation [9, 10] are applied in experimental or informal learning settings. In Taiwan, digital tools such as e-books or interactive textbooks are used in the general subjects in order to increase the efficiency and encourage the interest in learning.

However, there are few technologies which could benefit to storytelling activities in performing art course. Therefore, this study expects to design a system which supports performing art course with interactive technology. The design will be based on the observation in the formal learning settings, and encourages the children's performing motivation.

2   Related Work

Research about storytelling is very popular in the field of education and interaction design. Variety of tools or interaction environment such as KidPad [11], JabberStamp [12], and StoryRooms [13] have been developed.

Danae and Victor [14] designed "Magic Carpet", a classroom collaboration system which uses the tangible interfaces for storytelling for 5-7 year-old children. Children are able to deploy the brainstorming activity with traditional tools such as pen, paper and puppets, each group will learn to work together to create a story. The evaluation of Magic Carpet was held in classroom environment, finding the best way of interaction with an intensive iterative design process.

In the "Picture this!" [15] tool, children can play games and making video at the same time. Children play the dolls naturally and intuitively, and operate different record functions through gesture. The children's play will be feed on a screen in real-time. The video process benefits children in practicing social interrelationships and visual perspective taking.

Providing a real-time feedback to user will benefit to story and video creation [13, 16]. Children are more familiar with the effect they performed in the system, and make the story perfect. However, those systems are not applied in the formal education environments, nor are planned to focus on the learning purpose of school. It's difficult to reach the aim that technologies support education. Due to the specific devices such as handheld projector, mobile PC and sensors are expensive, and the environment will be limited to achieve the high technology systems, so storytelling activities become not easy to implement.

Therefore, low-cost solution is used in this study for children creating their own story. Real-time chromakey technology is applied, and it only needs a camera and a computer to construct the system. This system is not only limited with specific hardware, but also combined with the existing classroom environment and integrated within the regular curricular activities at school. Improve the willing of teachers to use this system.

3   Method

3.1   Contextual Inquiry

In this study, "Contextual Inquiry" [17] is used to develop the system. In this method, field interviews are conducted with users in their workplaces while they work, observing and inquiring into the structure of the users' own work practice. Work models capture the real practice and daily activities of the people [18]. Contextual Inquiry design is based on user's context such as physical space, the work, task, sequence, the behavior or intentions, tools used, other people, and how they collaborate together and so on.

The first step of Contextual Inquiry is "identification of needs" (Fig.1a) which is to learn about what is the problem user dealing with. Researchers can find out the identification of needs with interview and observation in the field. The design guidelines and principles can be analyzed by the data collected from previous steps. According to the guideline, the prototype will be designed and evaluated to approach the needs. Finally, the ultimate design will come out and be implemented and deployed to a production.

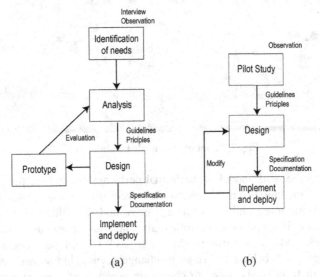

Fig. 1. (a) Redraw of Research Process of Contextual Inquiry. (b) The research process of this study.

In this study, researchers observed the performing art course in elementary school per hour a week during 14 weeks, and the observation was recorded by camera. The process of the research is modified to be appropriate for the performing art course (Fig.1b). The problems children face to in performing art course would be found by observation in the pilot study, and then the researchers would found solutions to the problems. The design would base on the knowledge gathered in the pilot study, and be completed and tested by the children, so that flaw in the design would be found and improved.

3.2   Pilot Study

In the pilot study, researchers expect to explore the design guideline of the system. At the beginning of the semester, the teacher would introduce the purpose and topic of the performing art course. Children were grouped into five teams, and there were 5-6 children in each team. The first task is to complete the scrip of play, shown as Fig.2. The script template teacher provided includes: abstract of the story, the design of all characters and played by which children. The background music also need to be considered in the script. After the script was finished, children started to make the tangible puppets and scenes. When all of the props were done, children were going to the rehearsal step with the script. At the final of the semester, children brought out the formal performance in school.

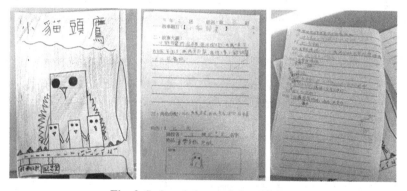

Fig. 2. Script of play made by children

Fig. 3a shows the work model of the formal performance, and the performing area is in the front of the classroom. The performers were usually four children, but there were still need one more child to change scenes, and the other one to control the background music. If soundtrack controllers also have to perform as performers, they should go back and forth between the stage and CD player. For the scenery controllers, they stood behind the stage to change scenes, but sometimes they also need to move in front of the stage to check the progress of story at any time. The audiences' seats faced to the stage. The teacher stood behind the classroom to control the camera and record video. Because children may occur some unexpected events such as the scene stuck in stage that may interrupt the play, the teacher has to remind them through her body language to avoid those problems.

During the observation, the problems were identified as following: 1) The story was chosen from a storybook children adored. However, transferring the storybook into drama script is difficult for them. Usually, storybook was a third-person narrative written, but a script is composed with conversations. As the result, some of the groups were over relay on that book, it caused that in the scripts they wrote were full of the aside, not the conversation between the performers. The teacher needed to spend a lot of time teaching children how to transfer into the conversation style. 2) For drawing the scene, it need to takes a lot of time and effort to finish because the paper size is as big as 54cm * 39cm in each scene. 3) Due to the stage is too small, children's bodies will block some part of puppets and they cannot manipulate smoothly during the performance. In additions, it is hard to change the scenes by the children (Fig. 3b) 4) During the performance, the teacher stood behind the audience to remind the children with her body language in order to adjust the play, but children always miss it because they have too many work to do in the play. 5) The scenery and soundtrack controllers sometimes needed to be a performer at the same time, that result they forget to change the role between the performer and scenery or soundtrack controller. Therefore the performance would be interrupted and be replayed.

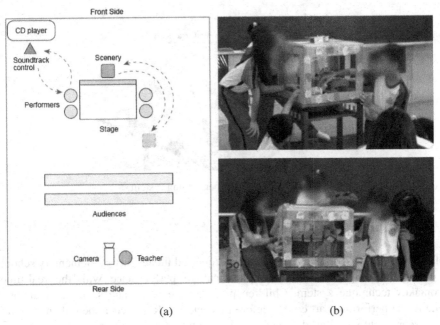

(a)   (b)

Fig. 3. (a) Work model for original performing art course. (b) The performing states in class.

3.3   Design and Implementation

According the problems discussed in the observation, we propose a design solution with the real-time chromakey [19] story performing system, so that children can see their own performance in play.

The design guideline principles are indicated as following: 1) For reducing the waste time in making props and changing scene, the chromakey technology will be used in the system. With this technology, the scene drawn in the small size can be scanned into computer and enlarged through the projector. Also, the scenes can be changed easily through computer. 2) Due to the stage made by paper box is too small, the green screen performance area will be used to provide an open space that the performers can perform smoothly. 3) The real-time composite effect can provide the performers to perform and see their video synchronously. 4) Because it is difficult for children to transfer the storybook into drama script, the "story elements matrix" [20] developed by this research group will be used to guide the children to create their story step by step.

In the story performing system, the green screen stage was set up to replace the paper box stage used in performing art course. The camera of computer was used to capture and record children's performance. The video which is capture by camera with mirror effect conducted by Photo Booth [21] was used to execute the scene composite effect. The distance between the camera and green screen is approximately 50 cm that the camera can capture the whole performance area (Fig 4).

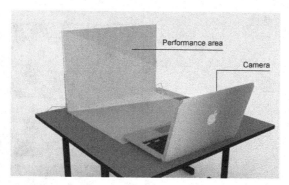

Fig. 4. Deploy of the performing system

4   Testing and Modification

Before the performing process, researchers requested the teacher of elementary school to choose a group of children to participate a performance with the real-time chromakey technique system. Children prepared the props and sceneries that they made in the performing art course before this activity. Researchers help them to scan those scenes into digital data, which was inputted to computer and prepare to composite. Researchers set up the devices include green screen and computers, and explained the whole performing process include chromakey composite and screen recording. Children only have to concentrate on performing their story in front of the green screen. Before recording video, children tried to familiar the environment and the relative position of green screen and computer screen. During the performing process, the video captured by the camera was shown on the screen for children to see their performance synchronously. In the test, the size of green screen was determined according to the size of the performing art course: 54 cm * 39 cm. Children can see their puppets and scenes merging on the computer screen in real-time. The prototype is shown in Fig 5.

Fig. 5. The prototype of performing system

The researchers observed that the multi-light source in the environment cause shadow on the green screen, which affected the quality of chromakey. The white balance function of camera made the green screen difficult to be identified. Also, the green screen was too small so that the camera had to very close to the performing area. Therefore, the system was modified to solve those problems.

In the modification version, green screen was enlarged to 109 cm * 78 cm. The distant between performing area and green screen became longer so that shadow interference can be avoided. In the hardware aspect, an external camera was set on the tripod. The real-time video was projecting on the big screen in the front of the classroom (Fig. 6). Children can inspect their action more clearly.

Fig. 6. The modification version of performing system

The researchers observed that children adjust their position through observing their video projected on the big screen in real-time. The teacher can also guide characters' correct position in front of the big screen. Those benefits cannot be applied in the traditional course.

5   Discussion and Conclusion

The performing system in this study solved problems in the traditional performing art course. In the original class, children hold the puppets into the stage made by a paper box that caused them difficult to move, or block each other (Fig. 3b). Instead of using the scene and the space of paper box, the green screen provided larger performance space for children. The scenes were changing by children but might be stuck in the box. Also, children standing behind the box could not find the correct scene immediately. In the performing system, the scenes are changed in digital way, and it can reduce the waste of time to pull out the stuck scene during the changing process.

The work model and deploy were modified as shown in Fig. 7. The performing stage was move to the behind of classroom for merging the system into the original classroom orientation. The performing video was projected on the screen in the front of classroom. Children played the story in digital way and the video was real-time composited with the chromakey program. The computer can be a workstation that execute scenery and soundtrack change. Therefore, children can saw their play projected on the big screen in front of them immediately. Children can see the teacher guiding near by the big screen. The distance between stage and workstation was decreased, and only one person is needed to control scene and soundtrack. Therefore, actors don't have to go back and forth between stage and workstation, also can saw the progress of story that may reduce the error during the acting. Audiences can view both the live performance and the composited video at the same time.

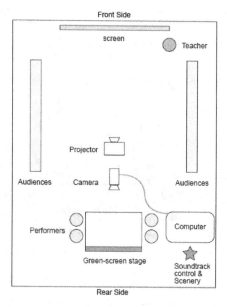

Fig. 7. Work model for performing system

In this research, we used the Contextual Inquiry method to discover some problems of performing art course in elementary school that can be solved by technical support. Through twice examinations, researchers noticed the change of children's performing behavior. Children play the puppets in front of the green screen was smoother than in the original performing art course because they can see their performance intuitively and change the scenes easier. With the real-time chromakey technology, children can make scenes and props in a smaller size. The props can be enlarged through the digital projecting. Besides the classroom environment, this system can also be used in the larger space, such as performance hall. Enlarging the size of green screen to apply in the drama or body training course can provide benefits in children's physical and mental development.

References

1. Bruner, J.S.: The culture of education. Harvard University Press (1996)
2. Loizou, E., Kyriakides, E., Hadjicharalambous, M.: Constructing stories in kindergarten: Children's knowledge of genre. European Early Childhood Education Research Journal 19(1), 63–77 (2011)
3. Wright, A.: Creating stories with children. Oxford University Press, USA (1997)
4. St. Amour, M.J.: Connecting children's stories to children's literature: Meeting diversity needs. Early Childhood Education Journal 31(1), 47–51 (2003)
5. Sugimoto, M.: A Mobile Mixed-Reality Environment for Children's Storytelling Using a Handheld Projector and a Robot. IEEE Transactions on Learning Technologies 4(3), 249–260 (2011)
6. Segal, E.: Storytelling and Drama: Exploring Narrative Episodes in Plays. Poetics Today 33(1), 127–130 (2012)
7. Anderson, M., Cameron, D., Carroll, J.: Drama Education with Digital Technology. Continuum International Publishing (2011)
8. Di Blas, N., Paolini, P., Sabiescu, A.: Collective digital storytelling at school as a whole-class interaction. In: Proceedings of the 9th International Conference on Interaction Design and Children. ACM (2010)
9. Alborzi, H., et al.: Designing StoryRooms: interactive storytelling spaces for children. In: Proceedings of the 3rd Conference on Designing Interactive Systems: Processes, Practices, Methods, and Techniques, pp. 95–104. ACM, New York City (2000)
10. Antle, A.: Case study: the design of CBC4Kids' StoryBuilder. In: Proceedings of the 2003 Conference on Interaction Design and Children. ACM (2003)
11. Benford, S., et al.: Designing storytelling technologies to encouraging collaboration between young children. In: Proceedings of the SIGCHI Conference on Human Factors in Computing Systems. ACM (2000)
12. Raffle, H., et al.: Jabberstamp: embedding sound and voice in traditional drawings. In: Proceedings of the 6th International Conference on Interaction Design and Children. ACM (2007)
13. Decortis, F., Rizzo, A.: New active tools for supporting narrative structures. Personal and Ubiquitous Computing 6(5-6), 416–429 (2002)
14. Stanton, D., et al.: Classroom collaboration in the design of tangible interfaces for storytelling. In: Proceedings of the SIGCHI Conference on Human Factors in Computing Systems. ACM (2001)
15. Vaucelle, C., Ishii, H.: Play-it-by-eye! Collect movies and improvise perspectives with tangible video objects. Artificial Intelligence for Engineering Design, Analysis and Manufacturing 23(3), 305–316 (2009)
16. Scott, S.D., Mandryk, R.L., Inkpen, K.M.: Understanding children's interactions in synchronous shared environments. In: Proceedings of the Conference on Computer Support for Collaborative Learning: Foundations for a CSCL Community. International Society of the Learning Sciences (2002)

17. Goodwin, K., Cooper, A.: Designing for the Digital Age: How to Create Human-Centered Products and Services. John Wiley & Sons (2009)
18. Holtzblatt, K., Wendell, J.B., Wood, S.: Rapid Contextual Design. Elsevier Science (2005)
19. Online, O.D. chromakey (2013),
    http://oxforddictionaries.com/definition/english/
    chromakey?q=chromakey
20. Yi-Chia Nina Lee, S.-Y.W., Chen, C.H.: Developing a Guided Storytelling System: Dream Stage. In: International Conference on Graphic and Image Processing, Singapore (2012)
21. Inc, A. Photo Booth (2013), http://www.apple.com/ca/osx/apps/#photo-booth

Introducing an Information System
for Successful Support of Selective Attention
in Online Courses

Martin Ebner, Josef Wachtler, and Andreas Holzinger

Institute for Information System and Computer Media
Graz, University of Technology
martin.ebner@tugraz.at

Abstract. Human learning processes are strongly depending on attention of each single learner. Due to this fact any measurement helping to increase students' attention is from high importance. Till now there are some developments called Audience-Response-Systems only available for face-to-face education even for masses. In this publication we introduce a web-based information system which is also usable for online-systems. Students' attention will be conserved based on different interaction forms during the live stream of a lecture. The evaluation pointed out that the system helps to enlarge the attention of each single participant.

1   Introduction

Students are confronted with an increasing quantity of information: masses of shapes, colors, and text. However, they can process only a limited amount of this information at one moment [1]. Most of the perceived information is filtered out centrally [2]. It has been shown that a mechanism known as selective attention is the most crucial resource for human learning [3]. Consequently, to manage this attention enhances both behavioral and neuronal performance [4]. Further very important parts of a high-quality learning process especially of an online course are the interaction and the communication between all groups of participants [5]. This means that all sorts and directions of communication are key features for an increased attention and a valuable base to reach the course-goals.

Due to the mentioned facts attention is perhaps the scarest resource within a teaching process, it is of vital importance to think about possibilities on how to control the attention of the students. One possibility in the field of enlargement of the attention with synchronous communication includes so-called Audience-Response-Systems (ARS), which are systems enabling the lecturer to present questions to students during the lecture in a standard classroom situation [6]. These questions could be answered by the students with a special handset and finally the answers are shown to the lecturer so that he can adapt the rest of the lecture according to these results. Many studies reported that an ARS has the power to enhance the attention and the participation of the students [7]. So for instance [8] compared an ARS with other classroom communication methods

C. Stephanidis and M. Antona (Eds.): UAHCI/HCII 2013, Part III, LNCS 8011, pp. 153–162, 2013.
© Springer-Verlag Berlin Heidelberg 2013

(e.g. answering questions by hand-raising). They noticed that questions presented by an ARS reached the highest formal participation (100%). In addition a further study regarding the advantages and disadvantages of the usage of an ARS performed by [9] claims that an ARS makes a long lecture more interesting and improves the students retention. Furthermore the provided feedback and analysis enhance the learning process for both students and lecturers. However an ARS should not be overused because it could unnecessary slow down the lecture. These facts are also confirmed by [10]. Due to the mentioned studies and facts we like to bring the idea to a complete on-line courses.

2   Theoretical Background

Let us first explain why we think our work is important. When we recognize a physical object (e.g. color, shape, etc.), or when we listen to a speech: it is a measurable information process [11]; yet, this process is heavily influenced by what is called selective attention [2]. Originally, this term goes back to [12] as he proposes a model of the human information processing system [13] and has been further developed and adopted by the three-memory system by [14]: The environmental information is processed by sensory processing registers (STSS in Figure 1) in the various physical modalities (visual, auditory, haptic, gustatoric, olfactoric) and further entered into the so called short-term store (working memory in Figure 1). The information remains temporarily in this working memory, the length of stay depending heavily on control processes (attentional resources in Figure 1). While the information remaining within the working memory, it may be transferred into the long-term memory, heavily dependent on the attentional resources. The model is one of the most used models and very important for the explanation of human learning processes [15], [16], [17] and is still in use today, consequently serves also as the theoretical basis and model for our work (see Figure 1):

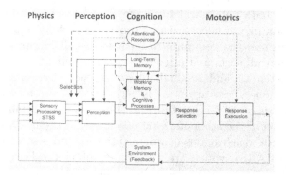

Fig. 1. This model, based on the famous three-storage model by [14] and described by [18] is still the most used and shows the powerful influence of attention to all human information processing [Image taken from [19]]

3   Study

The developed web-application (see Section 4) is used to sustain and enlarge the attention of the attendees of the live broadcasting of the lecture *Cleanroom Technology*[1] which is offered by the *Life Long Learning* department at Graz, University of Technology. This lecture presents the cleanroom technology as a core technology with its influencing factors and the basics of the most important production technologies from a scientific point of view to offer a specialist training to the attendees. This is done due to the fact that cleanroom technology is required in many fields of the economy nowadays.

The broadcasting on the web of this lecture is provided by the *E-Presence Server*[2] and the developed web-application supports this live-stream. Until now five units of the lecture took place and each unit had a length of two hours. It was observed that every session was followed by seven to twelve attendees.

The first unit of the lecture showed that the calculated degree of attention (see Section 4.2) was very low (less than 40%). A reason for that might be that the content of the lecture is very difficult and that the event was not paused. Furthermore most of the asked questions were also very difficult so that the attendees needed a long time to answer them and so the degree of attention decreased.

Due to the problems of the first unit the lecturer was advised to present the contents a little bit slower and in addition he stopped his presentation when a question was asked. With this improvements the degree of attention became better during the second and third unit of the lecture.

Finally the calculation of the degree of attention of the fourth and fifth session of the lecture delivered a high and stable value. This means that every attendee reached a degree of attention of at least 75%.

4   Implementation

This Section explains the main functionalities and shows some details of the implementation of the developed web-application. As mentioned above it provides different methods of synchronous interaction and communication to support any kind of web-content (e.g. the broadcasting of lectures on the web) during events at fixed time. This is done to sustain and enlarge the attention of the attendees [10,5].

Figure 2 presents the basic architecture of the application on a high level of abstraction. So it should be possible to obtain an overview of the different components.

It can be seen that a web-server (e.g. the *Apache HTTP-Server*) and a database-server such as *MySQL* are forming the base. These two servers are

---

[1] http://portal.tugraz.at/portal/page/portal/TU_Graz/Studium_Lehre/
Life_Long_Learning/ULG%20Reinraumtechnik

[2] http://curry.tugraz.at/

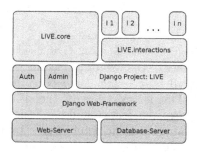

Fig. 2. Basic Architecture of the Web-Application

responsible for making the application accessible over the web and for storing all pieces of data.

To provide a consistent abstraction for the implementation the mentioned servers are encapsulated by the *Django-Web-Framework*. This popular framework for web-development uses the programming-language *Python* and follows the *model-view-controller* architectural pattern. Furthermore it offers a wide range of useful components, for example, a mighty database-API, a template-system, or some basic security mechanisms. In addition the *Auth*-package of *Django* supports the implementation of the user-management and the package named *Admin* offers an interface to build an administration-tool. [20,21]

The definition of the Django-project called *LIVE*[3] forms together with the mentioned packages the base for the actual implementation of the web-application. So the package named *LIVE.core* contains the basic components such as the management of the users or the program-logic to control an event in all phases of its life cycle (see Section 4.1).

Furthermore there exists a package called *LIVE.interactions* which offers a consistent interface for the implementation of the different methods of interaction and a mechanism to control their correct run during an event (see Section 4.2). Finally Section 4.3 describes the interaction-methods which implementations are based on the mentioned interface.

4.1 The Core-Package

As mentioned above this package contains the implementation of all basic functionalities of the web-application. So it provides the management of the user-accounts and of the events. In addition it offers an administration interface.

Due to the fact that only registered and authenticated users should be allowed to use *LIVE* a powerful user-management is implemented with the help of the *Auth*-package of *Django*. This implementation defines three types of users:

1. **Normal users** are allowed to edit their personal data and to join events. During an event they are also able to use the offered interaction-methods.

---

[3] Short for *LIVE Interaction in Virtual learning Environments*.

2. **Users with lecturer-privileges** are additionally allowed to create, edit, start, and stop events.
3. **Administrators** have also the possibility to access the administration-tool.

The probably most important part of the package *LIVE.core* is the event-management. It offers the possibility to control an event in all phases of its life cycle.

At the beginning a user with lecturer-privileges has to create the event. So a suitable dialog asks for the title, for the scheduled begin and end, and for the URL pointing to the web-content which should be supported with interactions. Furthermore the offered interaction-methods could be selected. The dialog stores the collected data in the database with appropriate models.

Now the user who created the event can start it to enable the interaction and communication. For that the real begin is set in the model of the event. After starting it a user-interface for the lecturer is build dynamically (see Figure 3). It shows (1) some information about the event and offers the possibility to stop it on the top left side and on the right (2) the calculated degree of attention of all attendees is presented. Below there is a area for occurring interactions (3) and some control-elements to invoke interactions (4).

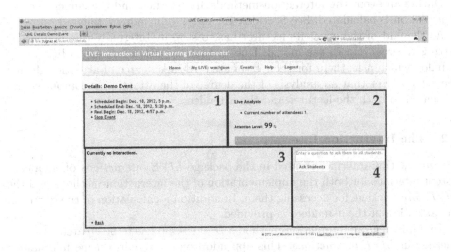

Fig. 3. The User-Interface for the Lecturer during an Event

After the start of an event users are able to join it. Internally a model is used to connect a user to an event. A joined user is immediately redirected to a special user-interface which is shown in Figure 4. It can be seen that the supported web-content fills the most space of the user-interface (1). The sidebar of *LIVE* on the left shows some general information about the event with an ample which represents the current degree of attention (2). Below there is some free space for occurring interactions (3) and there are some control-elements to leave the event or to start different interactions (4).

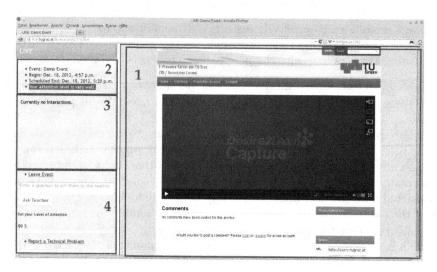

Fig. 4. The User-Interface for the Students during an Event

During an event the interaction-methods are handled and the current degree of attention is calculated. See Sections 4.2 and 4.3 for more details.

At the end of the event its lecturer has to stop it. Internally this is done by setting the real end in the model. Due to that the attendees are redirected to a dialog which asks them for their estimated average degree of attention during the event. After that an analysis of the degree of the attention is computed and presented to both the lecturer and the attendees.

4.2   The Interaction-Interface

The interaction-interface located in the package *LIVE.interactions* offers a consistent interface for both the implementation of the interaction-methods and the *LIVE.core*-package for accessing them. In addition a calculation of the degree of the attention of the attendees is provided.

To implement an interaction-method a *Django*-app has to be created as a sub-package in *LIVE.interactions*. This app additionally requires a module named *settings* which should contain at least the name and a short description of the interaction-method. Furthermore it should define its type by choosing one of the following:

1. **Automatically started**
   The interactions of an interaction-method of this type are automatically presented to the attendees in a random way. For that the *settings*-module has to provide a number which defines how often the interactions should appear per hour.

2. **Started by the attendees**
   This type allows the implementation of interaction-methods which could be started by the attendees. Due to that the *settings*-module should contain the path to a template to include the necessary control-elements in the user-interface.

3. **Invoked by the lecturer**
   With interaction-methods of this type the lecturer is able to invoke them. Again it is required that the *settings*-module offers a template containing the corresponding control-elements.

In addition to these possibilities of invocation there are three different so called interaction-models to display an interaction on the screen of an user. The first one is responsible for presenting an interaction to an attendee. In contrast to that there exists also a model to show an interaction to the lecturer. Finally a further model is present to pop up an alert on the top of the user-interface of the lecturer. All mentioned interaction-models contains the date and time of both the start and the response.

The package *LIVE.core* asks every five seconds through an interface of *LIVE. interactions* if an interaction-model has reached its start-time. If yes a special view of the interaction-method which provides the content of its interaction is called to display them. Within this view everything which is possible with current web-technologies is allowed.

The package *LIVE.interactions* offers a further major functionality of the web-application namely the calculation of the degree of the attention during an event. As mentioned above the calculation is invoked by *LIVE.core* and for that a class is provided. This class asks every interaction-method to compute the degree of attention within its context as a value between 0 and 100 percent. For that every interaction-method has to implement an interface to provide its way of computation. Finally the complete degree of attention is computed by forming the mean over the results of the interaction-methods.

Generally every interaction-method is allowed to compute its degree of attention in its own way but due to fact that most of the interaction-methods are evaluating the reaction-time of its interactions given by the interaction-models a corresponding function is provided. Figure 5 shows this way of computing. It can be seen that two parameters are required. The first one (*SUCCESS_UNTIL*) defines how many seconds after the start an attention of 100% could be reached and the other one (*FAILED_AFTER*) states after which period only 0% of attention are reachable. Between this two points the degree of attention is decreasing in a linear way. This means that the degree of attention is decreasing if the attendees are reacting slower. To find meaningful values for these parameters several test-runs under real conditions (e.g. as a support of the live-streaming of the lecture *Societal Aspects of Information Technology* at Graz, University of Technology) were performed. After each run the parameters were adopted to the observed reaction-times and with the fourth run the values became stable.

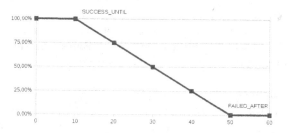

Fig. 5. The calculation of the degree of attention based on the reaction-time of its interaction

4.3   The Interaction-Methods

Based on the interface presented in the previous section six different interaction-methods were implemented. At first there are two automatically invoked methods.

So one method of interaction asks some very simple and general questions to the attendees which should be answered by clicking a button. This happens in a random and automatic way ten times per hour. Furthermore the degree of attention is computed with the described reaction-based method.

In comparison to that the second automatic interaction-method works very similar. The only difference is the usage of a captcha[4] instead of the questions.

Additionally there is an interaction-method which could be invoked by the lecturer to ask a question to the attendees. For that a template which is integrated in the user-interface of the lecturer provides a text-box and a button to submit the question. With the help of the interaction-model the question plus a dialog to answer it is presented to the attendees. If the question is answered the lecturer receives them through an interaction-model. Finally the lecturer could also answer his question as a reference. Again the calculation of the degree of attention is done by evaluating the reaction timespan of the asked attendees.

Similar to that the first attendee-started interaction-method offers the opposite asking-direction. This means that the attendees could ask a question to the lecturer.

A further attendee-invoked method offers the possibility to set the degree of attention by hand through a slider. A template includes them in the user-interface and if it is moved the new value is saved with a suitable model. In contrast to the previous presented interaction-methods the calculation of the degree of attention is based on the values set by the attendees.

Finally there exists a dialog to report a technical problem to the lecturer through an attendee-started interaction-method. So a template embeds a link to the dialog in the user-interface. After a problem-report is submitted the alert-interaction-model is used to present the report to the lecturer. Due to the fact that this interaction-method is not used regularly it is not part of the computation of the degree of the attention.

---

[4]   Short for *Completely Automated Public Turing Test to Tell Computers and Humans Apart*.

5   Discussion

To gain more information how the observed degrees of attention were generated (see Section 3) the attendees were asked to provide a feedback. Most of this feedback addresses two main points. The first one claims that questions which covers the content of the lecture are more useful for the attention than other general questions. Furthermore the second issue which was reported by the attendees states that they feel very uncomfortable with their computed degree of attention because it was very low.

Due to the reported point that content-related questions are more favored than other sorts of questions the interaction-method which presents a captcha to the attendees was deactivated after the first unit of the lecture. In addition more questions which addresses the content of the lecture were asked and the lecturer paused the presentation to give the attendees a better possibility to answer the questions more concentrated. So the questions looks better integrated in the lecture and due to that the attendees feel much more satisfied.

The second reported point claims that the computed degree of attention was much lower than the estimation of the attendees. So this leads to a high disaffection about this value. Based on this feedback the mentioned pauses around the content-related questions were introduced. Furthermore the lecturer was advised to present his lecture a little bit slower. As a consequence the computed degree of attention grows and becomes stable on a high level during the following units of the lecture (see Section 3).

6   Conclusion

This document presents a web-application which provides different methods of interaction in real-time to support any kind of web-content and which offers a calculation of the degree of attention of the attendees. This is done to reach a sustainment and enlargement of the attention (see Section 4).

In addition some observations of the usage of the developed web-application as a support for the broadcasting of a lecture on the web are shown in Section 3. The feedback of the attendees of this lecture is discussed in Section 5.

Based on that it is planed as further work to do more research to better understand in which form the interactions disturb or support the lecture so that a higher enlargement of the attention could be reached. Furthermore the web-application should receive the functionalities to support static web-content (e.g. the recording of a lecture) too.

References

1. Shiffrin, R.M., Gardner, G.T.: Visual processing capacity and attentional control. Journal of Experimental Psychology 93(1), 72–82 (1972)
2. Moran, J., Desimone, R.: Selective attention gates visual processing in the extrastriate cortex. Science 229, 782–784 (1985)

3. Heinze, H.J., Mangun, G.R., Burchert, W., Hinrichs, H., Scholz, M., Münte, T.F., Gös, A., Scherg, M., Johannes, S., Hundeshagen, H., Gazzaniga, M.S., Hillyard, S.A.: Combined spatial and temporal imaging of brain activity during visual selective attention in humans. Nature 372, 543–546 (1994)
4. Spitzer, H., Desimone, R., Moran, J.: Increased attention enhances both behavioral and neuronal performance. Science 240, 338–340 (1988)
5. Carr-Chellman, A., Duchastel, P.: The ideal online course. British Journal of Educational Technology 31(3), 229–241 (2000)
6. Tobin, B.: Audience response systems, stanford university school of medicine (2005),
   http://med.stanford.edu/irt/edtech/contacts/documents/
   2005-11_AAMC_tobin_audience_response_systems.pdf
   (accessed October 9, 2012)
7. Ebner, M.: Introducing live microblogging: how single presentations can be enhanced by the mass. Journal of Research in Innovative Teaching 2(1), 91–100 (2009)
8. Stowell, J.R., Nelson, J.M.: Benefits of electronic audience response systems on student participation, learning, and emotion. Teaching of Psychology 34(4), 253–258 (2007)
9. Silliman, S.E., Mcwilliams, L.: Observations on benefits/limitations of an audience response system. In: Proceedings of the American Society for Engineering Education Annual Conference, Salt Lake City, Utah, June 20-23 (2004)
10. Latessa, R., Mouw, D.: Use of an audience response system to augment interactive learning. Family Medicine 37(1), 12–14 (2005)
11. Yu, Y., Crumiller, M., Knight, B., Kaplan, E.: Estimating the amount of information carried by a neuronal population. Frontiers in Computational Neuroscience 4(10) (2010)
12. Broadbent, D.E.: A mechanical model for human attention and immediate memory. Psychological Review 64(3), 205–215 (1957)
13. Broadbent, D.E.: Perception and communication (1958)
14. Atkinson, R.C., Shiffrin, R.M.: The control processes of short-term memory. Institute for Mathematical Studies in the Social Sciences, Stanford University (1971)
15. Moreno, R., Mayer, R.E.: Cognitive principles of multimedia learning: The role of modality and contiguity. Journal of Educational Psychology 91(2), 358 (1999)
16. Holzinger, A.: Multimedia basics. Learning, cognitive fundamentals of multimedial information systems, vol. 2. Laxmi, New Delhi (2002)
17. Holzinger, A., Kickmeier-Rust, M., Albert, D.: Dynamic media in computer science education; content complexity and learning performance: Is less more. Educational Technology & Society 11(1), 279–290 (2008)
18. Wickens, C., Lee, J., Liu, Y., Gordon-Becker, S.: Introduction to Human Factors Engineering, 2nd edn. Prentice-Hall, Upper Saddle River (2004)
19. Holzinger, A.: Biomedical Informatics: Computational Sciences meets Life Sciences. BoD, Norderstedt (2012)
20. Django Team: Django documentation, https://docs.djangoproject.com/en/1.4/
21. Holovaty, A., Kaplan-Moss, J.: The django book, http://www.djangobook.com/

Development of the Hearing Communication System in an Individual and the Classroom

Manabu Ishihara[1], Shin-nosukei Suzuki[1], and Jun Shirataki[2]

[1] Oyama National College of Technology, Oyama-City, Tochigi, 323-0806 Japan
[2] Kanagawa Institute of Technology, Atsugi-City, Atsugi, 243-0292 Japan
ishihara@m.ieice.org

Abstract. Sign language interpretation and PC captioning are used as means of assisting hearing impaired people to get information. A noise in classroom is bigger than expected, so it became a problem for hearing impairments who need concentrate listen. And children and students can't listen teachers speech is easy to imagine which become a factor of interfere. In classrooms, speech is infrequently transmitted to a child without interference from background noise. Background noise refers to any undesired auditory stimuli that interferes with what a child wants, or needs, to hear and understand. Therefore, a product are sold which use FM wireless transmission. We have developed a supporting system of nursing care for the hearing disabled people, using a tablet PC. This proposed system devices a system which the LAN invented in the school. And it also use speech transmission on wireless LAN then they consider to use a smartphone and mobile games device. In the system, we choose a interface of GUI which is a few operation for beginner. Results of monosyllabic intelligibility test calculate 86% average. We can judge the system is utility.

Keywords: Wi-Hi, LAN, hearing impaired people, tablet PC, intelligibility.

1 Introduction

The problems of children who require hearing support in school have been indicated. Currently, students having hearing impairment levels that range from mild to severe are studying at schools. Standards for classroom architectural planning and environmental management exist, but the classroom noise standards prescribed in the school environmental hygiene standards assume usage by non-disabled students[1-3]. To assess the compliance of those standards, an investigation of the classroom environments of hearing-impaired students has been reported[4,5]. Children who had previously attended special needs schools have become able to attend regular classrooms, but their academic performance may deteriorate when they are unable to hear the voices of their teachers. In classrooms, speech is infrequently transmitted to a child without interference from background noise. Background noise refers to any undesired auditory stimuli that interfere with what a child wants, or needs, to hear and understand. Background noise sources in the classroom include external noise (noise that is generated from outside of the building, such as airplane traffic, local

C. Stephanidis and M. Antona (Eds.): UAHCI/HCII 2013, Part III, LNCS 8011, pp. 163–171, 2013.
© Springer-Verlag Berlin Heidelberg 2013

construction, automobile traffic, and playgrounds), internal noise (noise that originates from within the building, but outside of the classroom, such as rooms adjacent to cafeterias, lecture rooms, gymnasiums, and/or busy hallways), and room noise (noise that is generated within the classroom). Sources of room noise include individuals talking, sliding of chairs or tables, and shuffling of hard-soled shoes on non-carpeted floors. Heating, ventilating, and air-conditioning (HVAC) systems usually also significantly contribute to classroom noise levels. Due to the myriad of potential sources of noise, classrooms often exhibit excessive levels of background noise. Systems are available that use existing technology to implement speech transmission via FM radio waves and deliver those transmissions to pupils and students[6,7]. Although such systems are commercially available, they have not become popular due to such issues as ease of use, problems of radio wave utilization, and pricing issues. The present paper reports on a developed hearing support system using a LAN-based voice communication system.

2   System Overview

The noise levels generated in classrooms has been reported as ranging from 55 to 95 dB, which indicates a wide distribution of levels[4]. The approximate numbers of students having different degrees of hearing impairment are listed in Table 1, and those of students attending schools or classrooms specifically for hearing-impaired persons are listed in Table 2[8].

Table 1. Approximate numbers of hearing-impaired students

Conductive deafness	Mild sensorineural deafness	Sensorineural deafness	Total number
0.35%	0.54%	0.25%	1.13%
70,000	110,000	50,000	230,000

Table 2. Numbers students enrolled in special classes

No. of students at schools for the deaf	6719
No. of students in classes for the hearing-impaired	2199
Total	8918

As can be seen from Tables 1 and 2, most students are enrolled in regular classes. Representative noise levels in classrooms are shown in Fig. 1. At these noise levels, hearing-impaired students have difficulty in hearing speech in a regular classroom, and as a result, their academic performance may deteriorate. As one solution to this problem, a system that uses FM wireless transmission has been used, and its effectiveness has been verified. The system reported in the present paper realizes two-way communication between a teacher and a student, rather than the one-way communication from teacher to student of the aforementioned FM wireless system, and has also been designed so as not to be overly expensive.

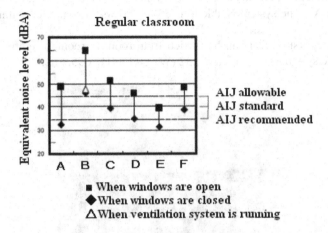

■ When windows are open
◆When windows are closed
△When ventilation system is running

Fig. 1. Equivalent noise levels in regular classrooms

The newly developed hearing support system using a LAN environment is configured with a Linux OS Web server. Figure 2 shows an overview of the system.

System functions include transmission and reception of voice packets, automatic acquisition and management of IP addresses of reception nodes, and a user interface.

The user interface that has been designed such that calls can be initiated or stopped and reception nodes can be managed by clicking a button located on a Web page. Accordingly, calls can be made in a familiar Web environment with simple operations.

When a reception node attempts to use this system, it first accesses the Web server and then the system is operated from the Web page that opens. At this time, information such as the IP address of the accessing reception node is stored at the server.

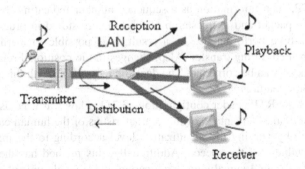

Fig. 2. Overview of the system

2.1   Hardware

This developed system is configured with a Web server, but is not necessarily intended for use only within a single LAN. By incorporating a Web server and a hearing support system into a small PC, such as that shown in Fig. 3, and then connecting the PC to a LAN, the system is able to use Web browsers connected within the same domain.

To realize a system that can be carried from room to room, a lightweight, palm-sized portable system is constructed: 132 (W) x 47.5 (H) x 95.4 mm (D); 0.6 kg.

Fig. 3. Photograph of the hardware

2.2   Software

The developed system uses Apache as the Web server software. Figure 4 shows the operational flow and the data flow within the system.

The RTP (Real-time Transport Protocol) transmission and RTP reception components shown in Fig. 4 are the components that carry out the voice communication. Because the user interface is provided on the Web, an applet with wide usability has been prepared. For this purpose, the applet was created in the JAVA language and uses the Java Sound API, which is a sound-related API.

The utilized protocol, RTP, is a protocol used with IP telephony and similar technology. With RTP, such information as a sequence number indicating the positional relationship of the packet and a timestamp of the time are stored in order to support transfers and real-time performance. As a result, it is possible to learn whether a packet has disappeared during transfer. Also, changes in the positional relationship of the arrival of a packet can be corrected. The decision to use RTP with this system was made based on these features.

Figure 5 shows the RTP header configuration. G.711 μ-law was used as the speech codec. This method takes advantage of the characteristics of the human ear and compresses the speech by varying the quantization level according to the magnitude of changes in the loudness of the speech. Additionally, this method has the advantage that a single unit of digital signal data is converted into a single unit of compressed data. Consequently, speech data can be efficiently compressed and transferred to a communication circuit. This method has a sampling frequency of 8 kHz and a transfer rate of 64 kbps.

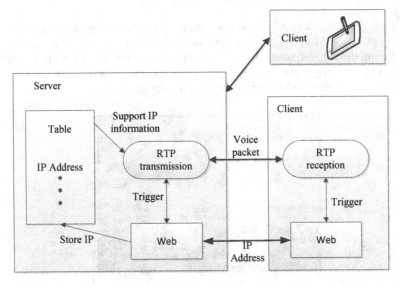

Fig. 4. Signal flow

V	P	X	CC	M	PT	Sequence number
Timestamp						
SSRC (Synchronization source)						
CSRC (Contributing Source identifier)						
Extension header						

V: version, P: padding, X: extension, CC: CSRC count,
M: marker, PT: payload type

Fig. 5. RTP header configuration

Figure 5 shows the RTP header configuration. G.711 μ-law was used as the speech codec. This method takes advantage of the characteristics of the human ear and compresses the speech by varying the quantization level according to the magnitude of changes in the loudness of the speech. Additionally, this method has the advantage that a single unit of digital signal data is converted into a single unit of compressed data. Consequently, speech data can be efficiently compressed and transferred to a communication circuit. This method has a sampling frequency of 8 kHz and a transfer rate of 64 kbps.

To use this system, the applet is run in a Web browser. The applet is a Java program that is downloaded to the Web browser, embedded in the page of the browser, and then run. Since the applet can be run in an environment in which Java has been installed in the device to be used, as long as that task can be carried out, the program can be run in any environment. Additionally, since the applet can be run in the Web browser of the user interface, it is easier to use than programs written in other languages.

Since many users utilize a Web browser on a regular basis, operation is considered not to be a problem. Moreover, calls can be initiated and stopped using a mouse or the other pointing device (for smart phones and portable game devices.), simply by clicking upon a button. In general, no other operations are needed other than clicking on a button. Figure 6 shows an example of web display design.

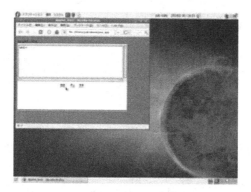

Fig. 6. Wed Design

The connect button is clicked to initiate a call. When this button is pressed, sound begins to be captured via a microphone and transmitted to a LAN. This button is also pressed when responding to a voice packet that has been received.

The update button is basically used by the transmission side (server side) that is performing 1: N communication. A list next to the update button displays information about the reception nodes. This information contains the IP addresses of the reception nodes currently being accessed. Clicking this button updates the information being displayed. Figure 7 shows an example of transmission node operation.

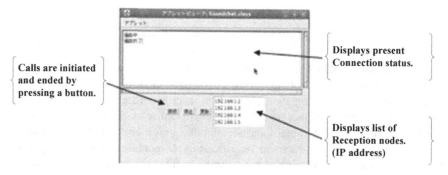

Fig. 7. Example of transmission node operation

2.3   How Long Is Channel Usable?

The traditional sample-based encoder G.711 uses Pulse Code Modulation(PCM) to generate 8-bit samples every 0.125ms, leading to a data rate of 64 kbps. The packetizer follows the encoder and encapsulates a certain number of speech samples into packets and adds the RTP(real-time transport protocol), UDP(user datagram protocol), IP, and Ethernet headers. The voice packets travel through the data network. An important component at the receiving end, is the playback buffer whose purpose is to absorb variations or jitter in delay and provide a smooth playout. Then packets are delivered to the depacketizer and eventually to the decoder which reconstructs the original voice signal.

The required bandwidth for a single call, one direction, is 64 kbps. G.711 codec samples 20ms of voice per packet. Therefore, 50 such packets need to be transmitted per second. Each packet contains 160 voice samples in order to give 8000 samples per second. Each packet is sent in one Ethernet frame. With every packet of size 160 bytes, headers of additional protocol layers are added.

These headers include RTP + UDP + IP + Ethernet 6 with preamble of sizes 12 + 8 + 20 + 26, respectively. Therefore, a total of 226 bytes, or 1808 bits, needs to be transmitted 50 times per second, or 90.4 kbps, in one direction.

A simple example can illustrate the basic methodology used in determining network requirements for voice traffic.

The voice constitutes the IP packet of this 200 bytes length by one every 20msec and transmits to LAN. We send out 50 packets for one second. The voice packet of the IP telephone is stored by a frame of the LAN. In the ethernet, 14 bytes and FCS for error checks are 4 bytes a header. We calculate length of 218 bytes in total.

At time to transmit a voice frame, it is time for 218+8+12 = 238 bytes (1,904 bits). In the 10Mbps ethernet, it is the length of approximately 0.19msec at communication time. The length of the IP packet is 200 bytes same in the case of ethernet in the wireless LAN. It gets the information such as headers of the wireless LAN. By this system, we are comprised of a pre-amble and wireless LAN header. This total time is 215.3msec (192msec + time for 32 byte).

The data constitution is constructed in data of 200 bytes and FSC of 4 bytes. Furthermore, this transmit data and exchange ACK frames every uniformity time(10msec). The length of ACK frame is approximately 203msec.

Finally the average of the random waiting time of frame length in front and the bit wide is approximately $360\,\mu$ sec. It is the sum total at time to use it to transmit one voice packet in wireless LAN.

$215.3 + 148.4 + 10 + 203 + 360 \fallingdotseq 937$ (μ sec)

A single course of the IP telephone is realized by transmitting every this frame 50 every second. It is 46.9msec/s at time to occupy wireless LAN.

Furthermore, the wireless LAN is LAN of the media joint ownership type. Therefore, we use the same band by an interactive call. We will occupy the time of 937msec/s to realize 1 call of the IP telephone in the wireless LAN of 802.11b.

We calculate in the same way as ethernet. In the wireless LAN environment of 802.11b, we get the IP telephone channel of approximately 10 channels.

3   Communication Test

A monosyllabic intelligibility test was carried out with the developed communication system. The monosyllabic intelligibility test used a random number of 100 Japanese-language monosyllables. The monosyllabic intelligibility was scored as follows.

$$Monosyllabic\ intelligibility = (No.\ of\ sounds\ correctly\ answered/No.\ of\ test\ sounds) \times 100 \tag{1}$$

The sequence of monosyllables was randomized so that the test participants could not anticipate their order. The test participants were five men in their twenties having normal hearing. It is thought that the characteristics of normal-hearing persons can be used to correct digital hearing aids. The monosyllabic intelligibility test results for the five participants are shown in Fig. 8.

As shown, monosyllabic intelligibility ranged from 82% to 90% (mean: 86%). Because a sentence intelligibility of 90% or greater can be expected, the speech transmission capacity is deemed to be sufficient for practical applications.

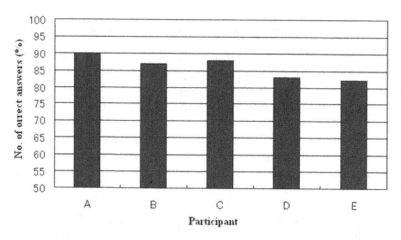

Fig. 8. Monosyllable intelligibility test results

4   Conclusion

The surprisingly loud noise environment found in classrooms is a problem for hearing-impaired persons and others who require concentration to listen. Moreover, it is not difficult to imagine that learning would be adversely affected if a teacher's voice were to be difficult for students to hear. For this purpose, products that use FM wireless transmission are commercially available. The system proposed in the present paper instead uses an existing LAN at a school. Because speech transmission is implemented via a wireless LAN, smart phones and portable game devices can also be used with this system. Use of these mobile devices enables the expense to be reduced. Of course, this system also supports the use of slate PC and notebook PCs.

For the system, a GUI that is easy to use for beginners and that requires few operations was adopted for the interface. A monosyllabic intelligibility test yielded a mean result of 86%, which is considered to be sufficient for practical applications.

References

1. Ministry of Education, Culture, Sports, Science and Technology-(Letters: Departmental order BUN-HATU-TOKU-No278) (1997) (in Japanese)
2. Ministry of Education, Culture, Sports, Science and Technology-(Letters: Departmental order Syougainoaru Jidouseitono Syuugaku ni tuite: BUNKA-SYO -No291) (1997) (in Japanese)
3. Ministry of Education, Culture, Sports, Science and Technology minister's secretariat education institution part, Facilities rule (2003) (in Japanese)
4. Nishizawa, K., Munakata, J., Sakuma, T.: Architectural Acoustic Performance and Teachers' Awareness on Hearing Impaired Classrooms -Survey on classroom acoustics for hearing impaired students Part 1. J. of Architectural Institute of Japan 598, 9–14 (2005) (in Japanese)
5. http://www.edu.city.kyoto.jp/hp/
   kita-y/kitashien/kenkyu&kensyu/kenkyu&kensyu.htm (in Japanese)
6. http://www.rion.co.jp/products/communication/pdf/
   fm-system.pdf (in Japanese)
7. Tachiiri, H., Yoshino, T., Takahashi, N., Itami, E., Naitou, H.: The Development of Hearing Aid Frequency Response Simulator Program using Articulation Index. Report of IEICE 92(455) (ET92 99-118), 29–36 (1993) (in Japanese)
8. Tachiiri, H.: OnkyoHoshoga Hituyouna Kodomotati. In: Proc. of Autumn Meeting ASJ, No. 2-7-10 (September 2008) (in Japanese)

Design and Development of Accessible Educational and Teaching Material for Deaf Students in Greece

Vassilis Kourbetis

Institute of Educational Policy, 36 Tsoha St., 1521 Athens, Greece
vk@iep.edu.gr

Abstract. The project of the Institute of Educational Policy: "Design and Development of Accessible Educational & Instructional Material for Students with Disabilities" in part aims at developing accessible educational material with Greek Sign Language (GSL) as the main access mode. Material for GSL teaching as a first language to Deaf children is also under development. Part of the project is the development of best practices and standards to be followed in the process of designing, developing and documenting GSL material. The study and the project results, as well as the proper use of the material will be the main focus of an in-service training course for professionals working with deaf children.

Keywords: Deaf children, Greek Sign Language, accessible educational material.

1 Introduction

In the last decade, since the official recognition of Greek Sign Language (GSL) as the first language of Deaf children (Public Law 2817/2000), there has been an expansive development of various types of educational material for teaching content subjects, including GSL, in the primary and secondary education of the Deaf in Greece.

Recently (April, 2012) Greece adopted the UN Convention on the Rights of Persons with Disabilities as a public Law (N.4074/12). In Article 24, on Education, the convention clearly states: "*States Parties shall take appropriate measures, including: Facilitating the learning of sign language and the promotion of the linguistic identity of the deaf community;... and ... to employ teachers, who are qualified in sign language* [1].

Universal Design for Learning ("Universal Design" or "Design for All") foregrounds educational practices by creating diverse educational environments, tools, educational materials and support services [2].

The rapid increase in numbers of Deaf students with different and diverse educational needs in the general school system is a reality requiring new educational practices. Ensuring equal opportunities and encouraging equal access to knowledge for all students, no matter what type of school they attend, is considered a basic and non-negotiable principle in any democratic society, in order for the education system to

C. Stephanidis and M. Antona (Eds.): UAHCI/HCII 2013, Part III, LNCS 8011, pp. 172–178, 2013.
© Springer-Verlag Berlin Heidelberg 2013

play a significant role in mitigating social inequalities [3]. The communicative environment for most deaf children in Greece and many other countries, is restricted since they are not exposed to quality adult models of sign language communication [4].

In the above context, the need of extensive electronic language resources for Greek Sign Language (GSL) has increased. Moreover, the necessity of educational applications together with their implementation in educational platforms has been made clear [5]. Besides, in recent years there has been an increasing interest in multimodal interfaces regarding human-computer interaction (HCI), [6, 7].

The curricula development supported by the Hellenic Pedagogical Institute (2004) for Deaf students, raise a number of requirements regarding the content, the use and the accessibility of educational materials by Deaf students[8].

Educational software is an excellent tool for both the student and the teacher, not only for learning purposes but also for teaching sign language and teaching with sign language. The introduction of such software in the educational process of Deaf children has been evaluated by the educational community and has proved to be an enjoyable and interesting supplement to standard studying practices [7, 10, 14, 12].

Furthermore, video recording of a translated printed text into sign language in either a digital document with a synchronized multimedia content, or books read on DVD co-occurring with sign language, are developed in many countries [13, 9]. Sign language on the web is becoming a much greater possibility and web-based video is more practical for educational purposes. Video web services, such as YouTube, are becoming more and more widespread because information presented through sign language video increases its accessibility and its usefulness by deaf people [15, 16]. In this work we present the methodological approach as well as the relative standards for the development of educational and teaching documents for deaf students in Greece.

2   Method

For the implementation of this project we have developed a methodology and guides for adapting textbooks of all curricular subjects with a concentration on the first two grades of primary school level, so that to be fully accessible by deaf students and other students with different types of disabilities.

There is an increasing need to develop educational material both in printed and digital form in GSL. The use of suitable digital technology will make school materials fully accessible.

We are developing a dedicated web-based information system to be used for adaptation and integration of the educational content in digital environments accessible to deaf students as a major implementation tool that complies with all published standards of accessibility (See Web Content Accessibility Guidelines WCAG 2.0).

We have chosen to develop the material in both DVD and web designed format that have been proven to enhance mental imagery, may be an enjoyable and interesting supplement to standard educational or teaching practices and work well with deaf students. We avoided the use of signing avatar technologies based on the quality of the natural signing representations they offer. We have followed reported best practices for the production and development, such as: filming strategies, choosing signers, sign selections and associations, the process of inventing signs, natural variations in signs and teacher education and in-service professional development [13, 3, 15, 17, 18].

2.1   Development of Bilingual Applications

The multimedia electronic form (either in the form of a single DVD copy or a web application) combines the presentation of the original printed book in GSL, the text in subtitles underneath the presentation of the GSL in the video, as well as the voicing of the text by a native speaker. The data in multimedia PDF, video and audio files will be available in independent files for multiple uses.

Major attention has been paid to the relationship between the spoken and the sign language text, so that end-products will be used effectively in bilingual educational practices.

The signed text is in accordance with the Greek text at a word, phrase or period level. The quality of the text in GSL is the most important aspect of accessibility and will also play a key role in the evaluation of the end-product. The translation of a text in GSL can be either very close to the original structure or a free translation. Within the same textbooks, the authors sometimes either seek for content comprehension or put emphasis on learning vocabulary, Modern Greek grammar or on the development of phonological awareness. If the objective is to understand the text, then the signers - interpreters will follow a more liberal approach. If the objective is grammatical, syntactic or phonological awareness, then interpretation mostly follows the original source.

It is made evident from all the previous productions that signing Greek texts is an extremely demanding and difficult task. The signing of the texts was done in cooperation with experienced native signers, deaf tutors or consultants (all fluent in Greek) on the one hand and professional interpreters of GSL on the other. These two categories of professionals worked collaboratively as a team of bilingual translators. The subject knowledge, knowledge of the target group and experience in educational interpreting are also important factors and has been taken into account.

As far as the process of signing Greek texts to GSL is concerned, we have proposed the following methodology. Firstly, the text is divided into smaller sections, so that they can be easily memorized and explained in front of the camera. Secondly, the interpreter who is a native speaker of Greek translates the text into GSL. Finally, the native signer and the interpreter watch the signed text twice or three times and compare the signed text with the Greek text. It is emphasized that, during the conversion of textbooks in accessible educational materials, signed text is crucial because the efficiency of GSL is the core of the project.

2.2   Development of Applications for Teaching GSL

A large part of the program is aiming at designing and developing two new applications for both the Kindergarten and for the two first grades of the primary school. The first one involves educational materials for teaching Greek Sign Language (A and B grade) and the second learning materials for Greek Sign Language (GSL) readiness (Table 1).

The contents of these applications will be developed in accordance with the objectives of the Greek Sign Language Curriculum for the Kindergarten and the first grades of the primary school. Moreover, the organization and structure of the content will follow a language acquisition sequence. Besides, the presentation of the application contents will be accomplished in a way to facilitate learning of complex concepts and generalizations, which are usually difficult for students that do not possess GSL as a first language. It will also include illustrations for visual recognition and understanding of concepts, as well as diagrams needed for overall comprehension.

Another parameter defining the content is that of the lexicon and grammatical structures used for the development of multimedia applications. The lexicon and grammatical structures should be rich, homogeneous and consistent with that of the language textbooks for grades A and B. The objective is to facilitate the learning process through comparative teaching practices in the two languages. In this context, the creators of the material document the correlations and the potential deviations (when required for educational reasons) in the vocabulary and the grammatical structures between the GSL and Modern Greek language.

Another factor related to the content of the materials is that they will include additional references from the Internet in order to raise the students' interests in applications contributing to maximizing the educational effect. In addition, all material will be in a format that can be used by the proposed web based platform for teaching GSL.

3   Results

3.1   Educational Material

The digital educational material is either a bilingual application or an application for teaching GSL. We had to cover the communicative needs of young deaf children in the nursery and primary school and that of their hearing teachers and parents. The materials address all levels from the Kindergarten to the Second Grade of the primary school (K-2) (see Table 1).

3.2   Teacher Training

Teacher training is a part of any new innovation in the educational practice. Teachers have expressed the need of in-service training as an integral part of their daily educational practice and their career development [19]. We have designed an in-service training program that will be implemented for more than 1500 teachers, in the thirteen administrative Regions of Greece. Teachers selected for in service training will be working with disabled students in either general or special needs schools. The training will be initiated when all material is developed and will focus mainly on the use of the material.

Table 1. Digital educational materials development for deaf students 2011-2013

	Title of the support materials	Target Group	Content	Means of recording	GSL learning
1	Mathematics Primary	Grade A Grade B	Bilingual (Greek - GSL) application (Math)	DVD	First, second
2	Language	Grade A Grade B	Bilingual (Greek - GSL) application (Language)	DVD	First, second
3	Study of the Environment	Grade A Grade B	Bilingual (Greek - GSL) application (Social studies)	DVD	First, second
4	Literacy Anthology	Grade A & B	Bilingual (Greek - GSL) Literacy	DVD	First, second
5	Greek Sign Language readiness	K-1	GSL application (Language)	DVD	First
6	Greek Sign Language	Grade A Grade B	GSL application (Language)	DVD	First
7	Purchase of software (platform) for GSL digital content	1-6	All the above	Web based platform	First, second

4   Conclusions

The Project "Design and Development of Accessible Educational & Instructional Material for Students with Disabilities" is fully compatible with the Convention on the Rights of Persons with Disabilities. The deliverables of the Project enable students with disabilities to be included in the general education system, where they can access an inclusive, high quality and free primary education and receive the support required in order to maximize academic and social development. Furthermore, it facilitates the learning of sign language and the promotion of the linguistic identity of the deaf community. The training of professionals incorporates the use of appropriate modes, means and formats of communication, educational techniques and materials to support deaf students effectively.

Acknowledgments. This research has been co-financed by the European Union (European Social Fund – ESF) and Greek national funds through the Operational Program "Education and Lifelong Learning" of the National Strategic Reference

Framework (NSRF) under the project: "Design and Development of Accessible Educational & Instructional Material for Students with Disabilities".

References

1. Convention on the Rights of Persons with Disabilities,
   http://www.un.org/disabilities/convention/
   conventionfull.shtml
2. Mace, R.L., Hardie, G.J., Place, J.P.: Accessible Environments: Toward Universal Design, North Carolina State University, The Center for Universal Design, Raleig, NC (1996)
3. Kourbetis, V., Hatzopoulou, M.: With my Eyes: Educational Perspectives and Practices for Dead Children. Kastaniotis, Athens, Greece (2010) (in Greek)
4. Kourbetis, V., Adamopoulou, A., Ferentinos, S.: From Disabling to Enriching the Deaf World: Forms of Discrimination Deaf People Encounter in Europe. OMKE, Athens, Greece (2001) (in English and Greek)
5. Sapountzaki, G., Efthimiou, E., Karpouzis, C., Kourbetis, V.: Open-ended resources in Greek Sign Language: Development of an e-learning platform. In: Proceedings of the Workshop on the Representation and Processing of Sign Languages, LREC 2004, Lisbon, pp. 13–19 (2004)
6. Elhadj, Y.O.M.: Multimedia educational content for Saudi deaf. In: Huang, T., Zeng, Z., Li, C., Leung, C.S. (eds.) ICONIP 2012, Part IV. LNCS, vol. 7666, pp. 164–171. Springer, Heidelberg (2012)
7. Karpouzis, K., Caridakis, G., Fotinea, E., Efthimiou, E.: Educational resources and implementation of a Greek sign language synthesis architecture. Computers and Education 49(1), 54–74 (2007)
8. Arampatzi, K., Gɪrtis, K., H.M., Kourbetis, V., Zografou, E.: Design and Development of Accessible Educational and Teaching Aids for Students with Disability. In: Tseles, D., Malafantis, K., Pamouktsoglou, A. (eds.) Education and Society: Research and innovation in new technologies, pp. 22–27. Sychroni Ekdotiki, Athens (2012)
9. Cannon, J.E., Fredrick, L.D., Easterbrooks, S.R.: Vocabulary instruction through books read in American Sign Language for English-language learners with hearing loss. Communication Disorders Quarterly 31(2), 98–112 (2010)
10. Gentry, M.M., Chinn, K.M., Moulton, R.D.: Effectiveness of multimedia reading materials when used with children who are deaf. American Annals of the Deaf 149(5), 394–403 (2004)
11. Johnston, T.: Language standardization and signed language dictionaries. Sign Language Studies 3(4), 431–468 (2003)
12. Andrews, F., Winograd, P., DeVille, G.: Deaf children reading fables: Using ASL summaries to improve reading comprehension. American Annals of the Deaf 139(3), 378–386 (1994)
13. Hladík, P., Gůra, T.: The hybrid book - one document for all in the latest development. In: Miesenberger, K., Karshmer, A., Penaz, P., Zagler, W. (eds.) ICCHP 2012, Part I. LNCS, vol. 7382, pp. 18–24. Springer, Heidelberg (2012)
14. Gentry, M., Chinn, M., Moulton, D.: Effectiveness of multimedia reading materials when used with children who are deaf. Am. Ann. Deaf. 149(5), 394–403 (2004)
15. Fels, D.I., Gerdzhev, M., Hibbard, E., Goodrum, A., Richards, J., Hardman, J., Thompson, N.: Sign language online with signlink studio 2.0. In: Stephanidis, C. (ed.) UAHCI 2009, Part III. LNCS, vol. 5616, pp. 492–501. Springer, Heidelberg (2009)

16. Debevc, M., Kosec, P., Holzinger, A.: Improving multimodal web accessibility for deaf people: Sign language interpreter module. Multimedia Tools and Appl. 54(1), 181–199 (2011)
17. Lang, H.G., Hupper, M.L.P., Monte, D.A., Brown, S.W., Babb, I., Scheifele, P.M.: A study of technical signs in science: Implications for lexical database development. Journal of Deaf Studies and Deaf Education 12(1), 65–79 (2007)
18. Signing Books Website,
    http://www.sign-lang.uni-hamburg.de/signingbooks/
19. Major Training Program Website, Training Needs Study – Results,
    http://www.epimorfosi.edu.gr/

Universal Design and Accessibility Standards in Online Learning Objects

Cláudia Mara Scudelari de Macedo[1] and Vania Ribas Ulbricht[2]

[1] Universidade Federal do Paraná, PPGDesign, Curitiba, Paraná, Brazil
Pontifícia Universidade Católica do Paraná, EAD, Curitiba, Paraná, Brazil
Universidade Federal de Santa Catarina, EGC, Florianópolis, Santa Catarina, Brazil
[2] Universidade Federal de Santa Catarina, EGC, Florianópolis, Santa Catarina, Brazil
Universidade Federal do Paraná, PPGDesign, Curitiba, Paraná, Brazil
claudia.scudelari@gmail.com, ulbricht@floripa.com

Abstract. This article notes that the media used in distance learning mode can create barriers to access such content for people who have some form of disabilities. Introduces the principles of universal design, aggregates the standards, guidelines and recommendations for creating accessible web content, developing a set of guidelines for creating accessible learning objects, aiming to support content-developing teachers in creating learning objects accessible to people with disabilities.

Keywords: Distance Education, Learning Objects, accessibility.

1 Introduction

The computerized environments that foment distance learning have become tools of great potential in formalized educational institutions, in organizations and even more in self-regulated learning.

Digital content that power the web-based education in the form of learning objects are present at all levels of teaching and learning educational segments. These resources can provide new learning opportunities closer to the learning objectives for a population previously exposed to the difficulties of access to formal education. However, the creation of these resources while favoring the answers to the heterogeneity of the students; may represent an exclusion factor for individuals who do not possess access to technological resources or who are unable to access them due to possible disabilities.

2 Media in Distance Learning

The main basis for a program of Distance Education (DE) is to take learning anywhere, anytime, to anyone, which makes this method suitable to the demands of the current individual by means of conveniences such as flexibility of time, use of varied resources and independence of the local study. Currently in Brazil, in classroom

C. Stephanidis and M. Antona (Eds.): UAHCI/HCII 2013, Part III, LNCS 8011, pp. 179–186, 2013.
© Springer-Verlag Berlin Heidelberg 2013

teaching, educational institutions admit hybrid programs, in which a portion of the content is taught completely through DE, using mainly computational media.

The DE is a planned education system that requires deepening of the methods and special strategies for creating courses, educational content, using various media and technologies appropriate to the circumstances of teaching and learning. [1].

Several factors influence the selection and mix of media, and according to [2], [3] and [4], the most important item of influence is the adequacy of the media to the profile of the student and the needs of the content.

According to [3], p. 102, "One of the key steps in the selection process of media and technology is to identify the attributes of media required by the instruction objects or by the learning activities, as well as the characteristics of the students and the environment, reliability and simplicity of serving systems, which suggest or eliminate certain media and economic factors or organizational that may affect its viability."

The contents used in Web-based distance learning, are developed by content-developing teachers, supported by instructional designers or media producers, and are rendered available in digital libraries, repositories of learning objects, virtual learning environments, blogs, etc. ., according to the established educational strategies and goals. However, they are created in formats, presentation styles and contexts not always suitable to the needs of the users.

In this paper, we present accessibility issues that should be considered in the preparation of the materials that compose the web based distance-learning.

3   Accessibility in Web Content

The current DE favors the use of assistive technologies and enhances the process of inclusive education and continuing education, despite the possible accessibility barriers; it is today the most suitable means of disseminating knowledge to the group of people with some form of disability.

The number of people in the world recognized as having some form of disability exceeds 750 million, and in Brazil, this number approaches 45.6 million people representing 23.9% of the population. The care of these individuals without discrimination and support their participation in society is a worldwide concern, especially in the countries members of the Organization of the United Nations, (UN).

The web accessibility envelops access for all individuals regardless of their characteristics, disabilities or special needs, situation or preferred tools; it notes the deficiencies inherent to the individual's age, cognitive handicap, social and cultural issues, along with the use of alternative browsers, outdated devices, use of assistive technology and critical environmental access situations.

The inclusive education focuses on the participation of people with disabilities and with special needs at all levels and learning situations, along with digital inclusion, which relates to the elimination of any barrier to access, even if temporary. In the area of educational technology, it represents the use of appropriate equipment and programs, content and presentation of information in accessible formats or alternative capable of the learning outcomes equivalent to any individual. [1].

According to the World Wide Web Consortium (W3C) web accessibility means that people with disabilities can use the web, or can perceive, understand, navigate and interact with the environment and contribute. The accessibility of the web content is the main goal of the W3C, which provides recommendations of communications accessibility, likewise, the Institute Management Systems - Accessibility (IMS-ACC), aims to find solutions to make learning accessible online. [5], [6].

3.1   Deficiencies on the Access of Digital Media

The most common deficiencies found in web access, according to [7] and [8]; are visual, auditory, motor, mental and cognitive deficiencies. This does not exclude the gifted people, people in different conditions in the social, emotional and intellectual level, the hyperactive, the marginalized, and other atypical situations of access to information.

Among the visually impaired are the blind, those with low vision, color blindness, the nearsighted, elderly, and those exposed to environments with low luminosity, those using very small screens; the main difficulties of such users is viewing maps, links, animations, colors, font size, navigation, tables, forms, and images in general. As access resources, they use Braille displays, alternative text, screen readers, special monitors, magnifiers, different contrast settings, monochrome monitors, and narration about the images.

As hearing impaired are considered the deaf, or with low hearing, people who work in noisy environments, those with speech disabilities, and those who use different languagesç they have difficulties understanding of audio clips, beeps, or any transcript textual. They are usually aided by subtitles on videos or presentation by interpreters.

The cognitive deficiencies relate to individuals with limited perception of information by means of using a different language, to computer beginners, people lacking motivation, the individual's age, the gifted, the autistic or hyperactive. These people have difficulty reading, interpreting the used language, disorientation in navigation or in the response time when answering question and filling out forms. Content developers using clear and simple language, orientation of information, mechanisms facilitating navigation, flexibility of interaction time or repeated presentations, assist them.

Among the mentally or motion impaired are dyslexic individuals, those with memory or attention deficit, those with intellectual disabilities, mental retardation, Down syndrome, cerebral palsy and epilepsy. These users have difficulties in navigation, links access, interaction, in the use of keyboard or mouse; they use special keyboards and mouse, physical supports, voice synthesizers, special screens, and software adapted for human-machine interaction.

Some difficulties in viewing pictures or download files may also be due to equipment or used device, such as connection speed, outdated equipment, and screen size, the use of unusual devices or operating systems. [1].

4   Digital Learning Objects

Learning objects were created based on the object-oriented paradigm of computer science. Its main goal is the reuse in different contexts and interchangeability. The most used definition for learning objects is given by the Institute of Electrical and Electronics Engineers - Learning Technology Standards Committee (IEEE - LTSC): "Any digital or not entity, that can be used, reused and referenced during learning supported by technology ". [9] Under this definition may be included media content, instructional content, instructional software and software tools. These resources in digital format can be: electronic texts, multimedia content, images, animations, video clips, simulations, readings, presentations, educational games, web sites, digital movies, Java applets, online tutorials, courses, tests, questions, projects, study guides, study case, exercises, glossaries, or anything otherwise used for educational purposes.

The main characteristics of these materials are flexibility, customization, and interoperability, ease of search, update and management. These features are described by metadata and content. The metadata allows its localization and reuse from repositories or external links, but also allow one to obtain information about the context of use, quality, characteristics or conditions of use of the learning object. The content, regardless of granularity, is complete and modular, platform-independent, non-sequential, attends a single established learning objective, and is unique in its metadata description.

5   DE Accessibility – Principles and Recommendations

The development of accessible distance learning courses must consider the participation of students and instructors with visual impairment, difficulty in learning, mobility impairments or hearing. If an individual teacher, tutor or student with disabilities enters into a distance-learning course, all the material in this course must be accessible to that individual. [1].

The accommodation of individuals with disabilities in distance courses via the Web is consistent with web accessibility in general and provides a greater degree of independence to the individual.

In this research, a set of guidelines was developed which derived from the following general recommendations of accessibility from international organizations: IMS GLC-and W3C-WCAG 1.0 and 2.0, and the principles of Universal Design applied to the creation of content for the web. From the recommendations, we selected those that are, if observed by teachers authors of learning objects in the act of creation, should extend the use of this object to learners with possible disabilities. [1].

5.1   Universal Design

In the eyes of universal design, a product is universally accessible if perceptible to all individuals without the need for adaptation. One way to allow access pages and digital materials for a distance course is the application of these principles, which are more sensitive to individual preferences and abilities, in the creation of the content, without the need for adaptation or special design for people with disabilities. CUD – NCSU, apud [10].

The CUD defines universal design as "Designing spaces, artifacts and products that aim to meet simultaneously people with different characteristics [...] based on the elements or solutions that make up accessibility."

In inclusive education, all individuals should have access to the same educational and pedagogical content have the same perception about everything that is presented without information loss or detriment of content relevant to the understanding of a topic. This approach complies with the Universal Design principles of multiple media: the representation to allow access to information and knowledge, action and expression so that the student can demonstrate his knowledge, to assess the student`s interests, to offer appropriate challenges and extend motivation.

The universal design principles established by the Center for Universal Design (CUD) at North Caroline State University (NCSU) apply to all study materials without the need for adaptation or special design for disabled students, and products designed according to these principles facilitate the work of all individuals, with or without disabilities. [8].

The universal design incorporates accessibility requirements in the design instead of giving an alternative design to meet specific needs. This is not about developing other content specific and targeted to meet deficiencies, but to enable the individual with disabilities the access to the same information.

5.2   W3C

The recommendations of the W3C web accessibility standards are the most widely used worldwide. Its recommendations and accessibility guidelines are introduced in Essential Components of Web Accessibility 2.0 of the WCAG (Web Content Accessibility Guidelines), published in December 2008. These patterns describe how to make accessible Web sites and Web-based content, applicable to any learning material based on electronic resources. [1]

In policies for accessibility of Web content, the W3C is explicit when it says that although there is a multitude of situations, every page design, in order to enhance accessibility, must assess several groups of disabilities or deficiencies simultaneously, and by extension the universe of Web users.

The WCAG 2.0 accessibility features four principles: Noticeable, Operable, Understandable and Robust. To meet these principles, it has twelve recommendations, with the basic goals that authors should fulfill to make a content accessible. For each recommendation, it is presents a list of success criteria classified into three levels that must be met to be in accordance with these recommendations [5]. The WCAG 2.0 covers the largest number of Web technology, and is testable by automatic or human evaluators.

5.3   IMS

IMS GLC - Accessibility Project Group - provides specifications for the development of learning technology. The IMS-ACCGuide, vol. 1.0 classifies the various shortcomings and difficulties that may be presented by users of online educational materials, related to the resources and assistive technologies used by these individuals, and recommends procedures to developers so that their contents are accessible, whether accessed directly or supported by assistive technologies. [6].

In these recommendations are offered six principles of accessibility for persons with mobility disabilities or cognitive impairment: 1- Customization based on user preferences, 2- Equivalent access to audio or visual content, 3- Compatibility with assistive technologies, 4-Context information and navigation guidance, 5-IMS specifications or other relevant specifications, 6-Use the XML language.

6   Directives for the Creation on Accessible Learning Objects

The accessibility in digital media is connected to the media presentation, so, in order to render these materials are accessible, its creators should consider the possible shortcomings of potential users who interact with the content, during the selection and customization of media since the first moment of its creation.

The definition of media used in creating a learning object originates from the analysis of the objectives of the learning resource and instructional and adopted instructional strategies. Thus, it is understood that while the author-teacher sets the content, sequence, segregation, approaches, and media presentation, can expand the accessibility of his learning object.

The research of applied and qualitative nature, developed with the goal to orient content-creating teachers during the construction of accessible learning objects, demonstrated the integration of the principles of universal design, with the recommendations of accessibility in web content, to determine a set of guidelines for creating accessible learning objects. These guidelines are sufficient and synthesized set of recommendations, structured in topics aimed at each type of media that can be used to make a learning object.

The created guidelines, combined with the educational objectives of an instructional event, form the basis of the knowledge of authors, reducing the need to create versions tailored for each possible disability of the individual users. These guidelines were tested by a group of university professors, experienced in the development of digital educational content.

The research instruments in this verification were a basic guide to creating learning object following pedagogic approaches and accessibility guidelines that subjects should follow to develop their educational content. This first test showed satisfactory results; learning objects from different areas of knowledge were created, accessible to individuals with disabilities.

The digital learning objects are displayed and distributed through one or more media elements, for having a measurable learning objective, any content or interaction contained in a learning object should be perceivable through used media and translated into knowledge by all users.

The guidelines provide recommendations designed to make media elements accessible through the provision of alternative media, since the main point of researched recommendations is connected to the provision of alternative or equivalent content. The W3C recommends that equivalent text be provided to all non-textual content, so the content should not be associated with textual equivalent text, images have alt-text, audio and video have transcription, and animations have descriptions.

The IMS features two types of accessible content: alternative and equivalent [6]. A content is defined as equivalent when it is identical to another, but supplied in a different mode, for example, a text available in audio and even associated with a file for printing in Braille. However, an alternative content is an extension of equivalents content and are provided in different ways, but with the same ultimate goal of learning. According to W3C, the equivalent text responds to the same functions and covers the same information as the non-text content.

The first recommendation of the universal design sets that it must be provided the same means of use for all users, identical or equivalent when possible, and when not, alternative, and that any segregation or exclusion of individuals in general be avoided. It also recommends that the user may be capable of choosing between different content presentation options with ease.

In the generated guidelines, it is recommended that alternate access the contents be created only when the use of equivalent content is not sufficient. This position assesses the principles of universal design and the recommendations of the IMS, and are suited to the characteristics of reusability of learning objects, since they have identical content in another modality.

7   Conclusions

The educational inclusion also constitutes the provision of necessary resources to overcome any barriers identified by individuals during the access to information and educational content. The accessibility of learning objects used in distance education must be seen as an integral aspect of the design process; it must consider all media and teaching strategies used to make the courses accessible. This approach ensures the use of these resources by anyone, anywhere, regardless of physical, technical, or environmental limitations; and they facilitate the personalized teaching learning. The possible deficiencies presented by an individual cease to be a factor of exclusion and are seen as special features that characterize the differences between all subjects.

The use of the accessibility guidelines in web content described by the W3C WCAG 2.0, along with the indications of IMS, support the developers and authors of web content in the use of techniques that enhance accessibility. They relate to alternatives likely to be included in the creation of content, conditioned to individual characteristics, equipment of access, user agents, and the use of assistive technologies.

Learning objects built considering the factors of accessibility and universal design can be used by people with disabilities just as effectively as if used by any other user.

References

1. Macedo, C.M.S.: Diretrizes para criação de objetos de aprendizagem acessíveis. 271f. Tese (Doutorado em Engenharia e Gestão do Conhecimento) – UFSC, Florianópolis, Brazil (2010)
2. Tarouco, L.M.R., Cunha, S.L.S.: Aplicação de teorias cognitivas ao projeto de objetos de aprendizagem. RENOTE – Revista Novas Tecnologias na Educação - Cinted - UFRGS, Porto Alegre 4(2) (2006)
3. Moore, M., Kearsley, G.: Educação a Distância: uma visão integrada. Thomson Learning, São Paulo (2007)
4. Alessi, S.M., Trollip, S.R.: Multimedia for Learning - Methods and Development - 3a.Ed. Allyn & Bacon, A. Pearson Education Company, Massachusetts, USA (2001)
5. W3C – Escritório Brasil, http://www.w3.org/WAI/intro/w3c-process (access August 2008)
6. Barstow, C., Rothberg, M.: IMS Guidelines for Developing Accessible Learning Applications. IMS Global Learning Consortium, http://ncam.wgbh.org/salt/guidelines/index.html (access February 2008)
7. Nielsen, J.: Designing Web usability – The Practice of Simplicity, pp. 296–311. New Riders Publishing, USA (2000)
8. Chisholm, W., May, M.: Universal Design for Web Applications, 1st edn. O'Reilly Media, Inc., Sebastopol (2009)
9. IEEE-LTSC-LOM. The Learning Object Metadata standard. In: IEEE Learning Technology Standards Committee Web site: http://www.ieeeltsc.org/working-groups/wg12LOM/lomDescription (retrieved March 20, 2005) (access Auguest 2008)
10. Burgstahler, S.: Access to Internet-Based instruction for People with Disabilities (2000). In: Hricko, M. (ed.) Design and Implementation of Web-Enabled Teaching Tools. Idea Group Inc., Hershey (2002)

Effective Usage of Stereoscopic Visualization for the Learning of a Motional Mechanism

Shu Matsuura

Tokyo Gakugei University, Faculty of Education, Fundamental Natural Sciences,
4-1-1 Nukuikita, Koganei, Tokyo 184-8501, Japan
shumats0@gmail.com

Abstract. 3D stereoscopic display is expected to be an advantageous interface of the learning materials to facilitate viewer's spatial recognition. To reduce the visual fatigue in viewing rotational motions, and to make use of the effect of stereoscopic display, an intermittent exposure method was considered and compared with continuous exposure method. Further, the effect of one-second exposure supplemented with the projected rotational motion was examined. It was suggested that even such a short-time exposure was effective for improving spatial recognition, reducing the visual fatigue remarkably.

Keywords: 3D stereoscopic display, rotational motion, spatial perception.

1 Introduction

Stereoscopic 3D (S3D) display is one of a popular technological trend for the interface of the machines such as Nintendo 3DS[1]. S3D graphics is also advantageous for educational purposes on account of following reasons: (1) depth recognition stabilizes the perception of the 3D structure; (2) the 3D image of the moving object is easily recognizable; and (3) real-time manipulation of the virtual camera enhances intuitive exploration [2].

However, visual discomfort and fatigue from viewing the stereoscopic presentation has become an issue for the introduction of 3D stereoscopic materials into classrooms [3]. Therefore, an appropriate instruction method must be developed in order to effectively use such stereoscopic displays.

Many students have difficulties in understanding physical phenomena that is occurring on the moving objects. Commonly, it is more difficult to understand when the motion of substance in question changes on the moving object [4]. Typical example of this is the commutator, the slip rings, of a simple DC motor. For an easy-to-understand presentation, the stereoscopic visualization is expected effective.

In this study, we compare the effects of two scenarios of showing S3D materials in the learning of DC motor, i.e., continuous and intermittent exposure of S3D, on the understanding of the role of commutator and the onset of visual fatigue. Then, in order to clarify the effect of short time exposure of S3D on the recognition of a three dimensional structure, we carry out a simple test on the three dimensional perception

C. Stephanidis and M. Antona (Eds.): UAHCI/HCII 2013, Part III, LNCS 8011, pp. 187–194, 2013.

induced by a rotational motion projected onto a 2D plane, and by the addition of short time and continuous exposure of S3D images.

2   Method

2.1   A DC Motor Model

A model of a DC electric motor, created by using Adobe Flash CS5 with Papervision3D library, rendered a side-by-side S3D image with a resolution of 1000 × 600 pixels for each viewport, and a maximum of six types of vectors were exhibited in the model space. The vectors exhibiting electric current and magnetic force were drawn on the wire in rotational motion. In addition, the moving elements along the wires and a commutator expressed the flow of electrons (Fig. 1).

In order to display the motor model, a dual projector with linear polarization (portable 3D projector 3DP-TX04, T&TS CO., Ltd.) was used to project superimposed side-by-side images (1024 × 768 pixels) onto an 80-inch polarization-preserving screen. The students viewed the images through polarized glasses, and they were asked to move to appropriate positions in front of the screen.

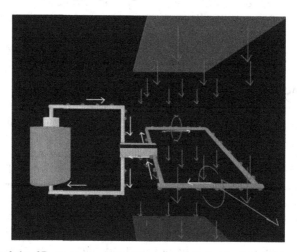

Fig. 1. A view of the 3D motor model with vectors of physical quantities. A commutator, colored pink and sky blue, is shown at the center with the yellow current vectors and small red discs exhibiting the electrons.

2.2   Classroom Demonstration

Lectures using a S3D model were conducted in three different classes in the Faculty of Education at Tokyo Gakugei University. For the first two classes, majorly consisted of second-year students, the stereoscopic images were continuously exposed to the students during the lectures. This type of exposure to the students is hereafter referred to as "continuous exposure."

For the third class, which consisted of 30 third-year students, S3D images were shown during the explanation of the first scene and just before the transition to the following scene. This type of exposure is hereafter referred to as "intermittent exposure."

All three classes began with a demonstration of an experiment based on Fleming's left-hand rule. After a demonstration of the experiment, motor model viewings were conducted in the following manner. First, the entire motor model was shown in non-stereoscopic display. After an explanation of the model, S3D viewing was commenced from the entire view, then, close-up views of rotating wire from multiple points, and it ended with the close-up and explanation of the commutator. Finally, a questionnaire regarding experiences of visual fatigue was presented to the students.

2.3   A Perception Test on Rotating Lines

Two lines with randomly chosen lengths and directions were generated inside a fixed cubic frame, and were rotated along an axis that was set at a randomly chosen position inside the cube space (Fig. 2). The angle of rotation was chosen at random, while the direction of rotation was fixed. The rotating motion was animated, and the duration time of rotation was approximately three seconds at longest. For presentation, the generated lines, which were shown fixed for one second ("rest phase"), were rotated ("rotation phase"), and were again fixed to let the examinee choose a line of which center position was seen closer the examinee. The following three types of display were tested. 1) Non-stereoscopic display, in which only the projected rotation images played a role of pictorial clues for 3D recognition. 2) Pre-exposure of S3D images for one second, in which the lines and cubic frame were shown in S3D in the rest phase. After the rest phase, the images and animation were shown in non-stereoscopic display. 3) Continuous exposure of S3D, in which images were shown in S3D from the beginning to the end. The examinee sat at approximately 2m from the screen and viewed the images. They chose lines by the mouse-over on line. Each examinee carried out choosing more than 100 times successively for each display type.

Fig. 2. A view of the rotating lines test. Gray lines of fixed cube show 1000 arbitrary unit length. Two lines in sky blue show test lines and are rotated along a randomly chosen axis.

3   Results and Discussion

3.1   A Comparison between Continuous and Intermittent Exposure Method

Figure 3 shows the results of students' responses in regard to the effectiveness of non-stereoscopic 3D display (white bars) and to the improvement of effectiveness in S3D (gray bars). Students were asked whether the non-stereoscopic 3D image was effective to figure out the structure and mechanisms of the elements of the motor. 74% of students agreed or strongly agreed with the statement. Then, students were asked whether the S3D display improves their recognition of structures. 87% of students agreed or strongly agreed the improvement of effectiveness on understanding the structure by changing the display from non-stereoscopic to stereoscopic.

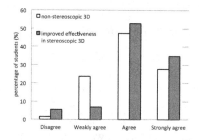

Fig. 3. Results of questionnaire on the effectiveness of 3D and S3D display on understanding the motor model under a continuous exposure instruction

In the questionnaire, while 63% of the students remarked that S3D helped understanding the structure, 3 students commented that they were too much attracted by the visual components rather than they could concentrate on the consideration of the physical mechanisms of motor. This implies that S3D helps to understand a complex spatial structure easily, but it might not always beneficial to let the learner consider the content in depth.

Table 1. Crosstabs of students' responses with regard to the effectiveness of S3D on understanding spatial structure and visual discomfort under continuous and intermittent S3D images

			Visual discomfort [%]			
		Exposure method	Disagree	Weakly agree	Agree	Strongly agree
Effectiveness to understand [%]	Disagree	continuous		2.9		1.4
		intermittent	3.3			
	Weakly agree	continuous		1.4	1.4	4.3
		intermittent		13.3	10.0	3.3
	Agree	continuous		10.0	20.0	22.9
		intermittent	10.0	10.0	6.7	23.3
	Strongly agree	continuous	1.4	4.3	11.4	18.6
		intermittent	3.3	10.0	3.3	3.3

Table 1 shows the results of students' responses on the effectiveness of S3D and the visual fatigue after watching rotational motion carefully, compared under continuous and intermittent exposure. Also, fig. 4 shows the bar charts of the table 1 for two exposure methods. Nearly all the students under continuous S3D exposure more or less got visual fatigue or visual discomfort to the S3D animation of rotational motions, although they admitted the effectiveness of it on learning. Under the intermittent exposure method, rate of those who disagree and weakly agree with the onset of visual discomfort was raised remarkably. 33.3% of the students did not feel strong discomfort, but felt sufficient effect on spatial recognition. However, 13.3% of the students responded as "weakly agree" to both of the questions. They have a capacity to watch more S3D to establish understanding.

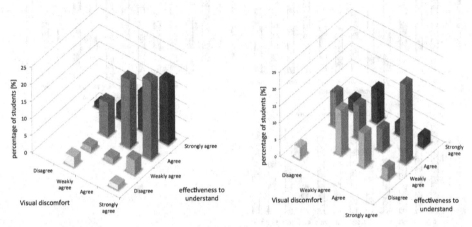

Fig. 4. Students' responses on the visual discomfort and effectiveness of S3D display. Left: students under continuous exposure of S3D images. Right: students under intermittent exposure of S3D images.

3.2   Effect of Short-Time Exposure of S3D on the Recognition of 3D Structure

In order to consider a proper way of S3D utilization to stimulate students' interest and facilitate spatial recognition, avoiding visual discomfort, detailed examinations on S3D rotational motion images are required.

Besides the stereopsis, the rotational motion of object stimulates the recognition of spatial structure even when one has only the projected images of a motion. Table 2 shows the average scores of the two-lines rotation test. The test was carried out for 11 university students around age 20, and a male of age 53. A noticeable person-to-person diversity in the scores were found.

Table 2. Crosstabs of students' responses with regard to the effectiveness of S3D on understanding spatial structure and visual discomfort under continuous and intermittent S3D images

	non-stereoscopic display	pre (1 sec) - exposure of S3D	S3D continuous exposure
average (% rate of correct answers)	67	67	73
standard deviation	11	8	11

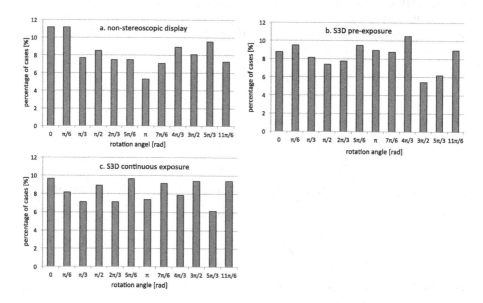

Fig. 5. Histograms of the percentage rates of incorrect choice cases in the 3D recognition test at various rotation angles for non-stereoscopic display, pre-exposure of S3D and continuous exposure of S3D

As seen in table 2, the average rates of choosing collect lines in non-stereoscopic display and 1 sec exposure of S3D before rotation were almost the same. This result indicates that the animated rotational motion helps to build the recognition of spatial structure. At first sight, this effect is strong enough to establish spatial recognition that the supplemental pre-exposure of S3D images did not affect when the exposure is short-time. The rate increased for continuous S3D exposure.

Here we proceed to more details. Figure 5 shows the histogram of the rates of incorrect choices at various rotation angles. The rate of choosing incorrect line was higher at small angle of rotation since less information was provided from small angle rotation. However, this tendency decreased in the pre-exposure of S3D. This is because that spatial structure is recognized before rotation. The failure histogram looks nearly flat for the rotation angles under the continuous exposure of S3D.

Figure 6 shows the rate of incorrect choices at various distances between lines. The distance was defined as the difference of center positions of lines along with the depth direction. The difference of depths of two lines is difficult to distinguish when the distance between them is small both for the rotating images and the S3D images. As seen in the figure, profiles of histograms in the non-stereoscopic and the short-time S3D exposure cases were nearly equivalent. However, in the cases of S3D continuous exposure, the range of the distances in which the failure frequently occurred was seen restricted within 1/10 of the length of the side of fixed cubic frame.

These results imply that we may find an appropriate effect on the spatial recognition even by a second of S3D exposure, avoiding visual fatigue due to long exposure. Detailed study on the duration of S3D effect after exposure is required. Use of S3D image has possibility to leverage the learning contents if the contents creators are more aware of the spatial recognition.

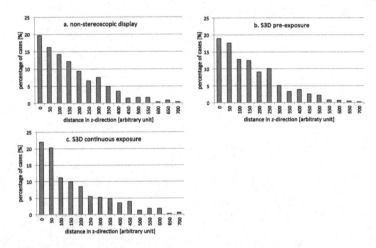

Fig. 6. Histograms of the percentage rates of incorrect choice cases in the 3D recognition test at various distances of two lines for non-stereoscopic display, pre-exposure of S3D images and continuous exposure of S3D display

4   Concluding Remarks

It was suggested that a control of S3D exposure was required in the sense of the spatial recognition, concentration to the content, and visual discomfort. It was also suggested that even a very short-time exposure of S3D helped a viewer's spatial recognition. More accumulation of knowledge is expected for the valuable application of S3D as an interface of the learning materials.

Acknowledgments. This study has been funded by a Grant-in-Aid for Scientific Research (C) 21500842 from the Ministry of Education, Culture, Sports, Science and Technology, Japan.

References

1. Schild, J., Masuch, M.: Fundamentals of Stereoscopic 3D Game Design. In: Anacleto, J.C., Fels, S., Graham, N., Kapralos, B., Saif El-Nasr, M., Stanley, K. (eds.) ICEC 2011. LNCS, vol. 6972, pp. 155–160. Springer, Heidelberg (2011)
2. Matsuura, S.: Use of camera drive in stereoscopic display of learning contents of introductory physics. In: Proc. SPIE 7863, pp. 7863: 786324-1–796324-7 (2011)
3. Lambooij, M., Ijsselsteijn, M., Fortuin, M., Heynderickx, I.: Visual Discomfort and Visual Fatigue of Stereoscopic Displays: A Review. J. Imaging Science and Technology 53(3), 030201–030201-14 (2009)
4. Yoshii, T., Matsuura, S.: Educational Benefits of Stereoscopic Visualization from Multiple Viewpoints, Illustrated with an Electrical Motor Model. In: International Conference on 3D Imaging 2011 Proceedings (CD-ROM) (2011)

Educational Inclusiveness through Ludic Engagement and Digital Creativity

Rachel McCrindle

School of Systems Engineering, University of Reading, Reading, UK
r.j.mccrindle@reading.ac.uk

Abstract. This paper describes an approach to teaching and learning that combines elements of ludic engagement, gamification and digital creativity in order to make the learning of a serious subject a fun, interactive and inclusive experience for students regardless of their gender, age, culture, experience or any disabilities that they may have. This approach has been successfully used to teach software engineering to first year students but could in principle be transferred to any subject or discipline.

Keywords: Ludic engagement, games, digital creativity, group work, soft skills, subject knowledge.

1 Introduction

Ludic engagement may be considered as a way of blurring the distinctions between work and play [1] such that participants are motivated by curiosity, exploration, and reflection rather than the externally-defined tasks [2]. Although frequently associated with computer interfaces ludic engagement can also be more generally focused on the development of artistic prototypes and projects that bring together the disciplines of art, design, entertainment and product development, creating products that combine artistic expression with science and technology principles [3]. Additionally, by taking concepts from computer games, art, interactive media, social networks and modding cultures, ludic interfaces and approaches can create environments which are sensitive to cultural, gender-related, age-related and ethnic specificities [4] and which can be made more inclusive for people with special learning needs or physical disabilities [5].

Within an educational context, ludic interfaces and engagement can be used to blur the traditionally separate academic theories of learning and theories of play into creative, immersive and engaging environments for learning [6]. In the extreme, Quest to Learn, a public school in New York City is offering a ludic model for student engagement whereby their approach to learning mimics the action and design principles of games in the classroom. In this model students encounter a series of increasingly complex, narrative challenges, games or quests, as they move through the curriculum such that learning, knowledge sharing, feedback, reflection and next steps emerge as a natural function of play [7].

C. Stephanidis and M. Antona (Eds.): UAHCI/HCII 2013, Part III, LNCS 8011, pp. 195–202, 2013.
© Springer-Verlag Berlin Heidelberg 2013

In this paper we describe how concepts of gamification and ludic engagement [8] have been combined with more traditional teaching practices of experiential learning [9] and activity led learning [10] and application to real world considerations, in order to engage students in the learning process of a subject discipline. In doing so, this approach to learning shares concepts with the problem and project based-learning model adopted by Aalborg University [11].

2   Approach to Learning

Game design and digital creativity have been used for the past eight years as an innovative way of teaching software engineering to a large class (100-200 students) of first year undergraduate students taking degrees ranging from Management and IT to Computer Science to Electronics and Cybernetics. As well as differences between degrees studied, variability due to gender, culture, age, internationalization, physical and social disabilities, is evident amongst each cohort, alongside many preferred learning styles. Added to this, students frequently find it difficult to comprehend and appreciate this subject at the point where it is taught, that is, prior to utilising it in the real world either on placement or in graduate employment. In order to increase engagement and understanding of the subject matter, transgress different learning styles and encourage team based working, gamification and ludic approaches are superimposed upon a structured engineering development process.

In this 20 week long assignment students work in teams to design and develop a 'physical' board game that will teach novice software engineers or 1st year students 'software engineering'.

In order to realize deeper learning and understanding of the technical and managerial processes involved in the development, delivery and support of software-based systems, students go through an engineering process themselves in order to develop board games that incorporate the principles of software engineering such that if someone else plays their game, they too learn about software engineering – thereby reinforcing learning on several levels. Deliberately, they do not program the game because programming skills are taught in a different module, they should concentrate on the whole lifecycle rather than just the programming aspect, and the level of programming required to produce a comprehensive game is far too complex for a first year module assignment. They do however use digital media tools to help them create their artwork and presentations and to encourage creativity.

The intention of the assignment is to embed the activities of the software engineering lifecycle into the students learning process and encourage deeper learning of the material presented in the lectures. Working in teams, students consider how to develop the rule-based system that drives the nature of their game, create worlds in which they actively participate, use strategic thinking to make choices, seek content knowledge, enhance understanding of complex concepts, and consider how to transfer their knowledge across to others.

In addition to learning software engineering concepts (e.g. software lifecycle stages, management of projects, risks and contingency, resources, application to industry, consequences of failure), students develop their creative skills (e.g. through team branding, novel ideas and application of concepts, 2-D and 3-D design skills, graphic design, presentation of information and software/tools to delivery creativity). The students also develop 'softer' skills so valued by today's employers such as the ability to work as a team, time management skills, communication skills, design and development skills, problem solving, leadership, problem resolution, responsibility and consequence of actions.

One key intention of the work is that it is 'fun' and achieved via an interactive process rather than a more conventional type of assignment with a key aim being that the learning process of the student becomes embedded in the 'play' aspects of the game. Although some structure is imposed on the process (a series of 11 staged deliverables are created over the 20 week period) the students are encouraged to unleash their creativity and develop their own style and genre of games as evidenced by titles such as the Llamageddon, Killer Programmers and the Quest for the Governmental Contract, the IT Crown, Software Jungle and Alex's Adventures in Software Engineering, to name just five of the 170+ games developed over the past eight years. Some of these games are illustrated in Figure 1.

Fig. 1. Examples of games developed to teach software engineering

Although the students are given identical initial specifications, the work that they produce encompasses many different designs and approaches to game play – just as in the 'real' world where different software engineering teams would produce distinct architectural designs, use different algorithms and produce different graphical interfaces to their designs. Further ludic engagement is evident through the posters and presentations produced by the students to promote their games, with almost all of the work being of a high standard and some of it exceptional. Examples of several posters are shown in Figure 2.

Fig. 2. Posters advertising four different games

3   Making Learning Inclusive

One of the key aims for using games and ludic engagement as a focus for teaching and learning is to encourage students to work together to complete a significant piece of work. Whilst one key goal of this approach is for the students to develop a deeper knowledge and understanding of the subject being taught, an equally important goal is for the students to develop their softer skills, and in particular those related to communication and team work. A cohort of students typically has a mix of degree disciplines, gender, culture, age, special education needs and physical disabilities. Whilst some students naturally find group work and communication easy and intuitive, others find it a highly challenging and uncomfortable process.

In order to ensure that the learning experience for this module is as inclusive as possible we have incorporated a number of ways to encourage and facilitate team formation, bonding and working, that involves preparation prior to the module, monitoring during the module, and reflection after the module. These include:

- Liaising with the disability officer for our School so that we are aware of any students with particular learning needs or disabilities.
- Ensuring that we have rooms booked that facilitate group work rather than traditional classroom style activity.
- Gradually introducing students to group work through a developing series of team tasks in the first few weeks of the module and prior to the start of the main assignment – enhanced by sweets and chocolate!
- Observing the behavior of the trial teams to look for poorly functioning teams, students who appear uncomfortable in their teams, and teams lacking any form of self-direction.

- Having students assess their skills and background experience against the range of activities in the project specification and promoting an ethos that everyone is good at something and has a team role to play.
- Including in the 11 deliverables a wide range of activities and learning outcomes encompassing ideas creation, planning and management, report writing, development activities and creative presentations such that everyone is likely to 'shine' in one or more activities.
- Administering a light touch Belbin test [12, 13] to the students backed-up by a discussion session to make them consider the type of team player they are, as well as their likely strengths and weaknesses when working in a team.
- Logging attendance at all group sessions and following up absenteeism before teams become too fragmented.
- Appointing a project manager for the team and encouraging self-management of the team, but working closely with a team and its individuals if relationships start to break down.
- Including lectures on group dynamics and having industry promote the benefits of working in diverse and global teams, thereby encouraging students to embrace and celebrate diversity rather than trying to avoid it.
- Allowing the students to choose their team name, game genre, presentation style etc. in order to facilitate the blending of the serious side of the assignment with the game dynamics and thereby blurring the distinctions between work, play and learning.

4   Engagement in the Learning Process

Some excellent and highly creative work has been produced and of the 1200+ students that have participated in this activity only one student has been unable to be placed in a team. At the end of the 20 week process students have to critically review their approach to the assignment, assess what they have personally learnt from working in a team and suggest improvements for how it might run even more effectively in subsequent years. Several comments from students are given below:

"...many lessons were learnt about working in a team that would not have been acquired if I just had to write an essay on 'group work' or 'management', this experience will certainly be helpful in the future, as in this field, team work is essential."

"...another enjoyable aspect of the project was overcoming the challenge we had set ourselves by coming up with a complicated design. Once it was finished I felt a great sense of accomplishment because we had met our own specifications"

"...at first I was skeptical about undertaking a non-computer related project for software engineering, and about the same for the usefulness of working in a group. I can proudly say that the idea of getting us used to group work by this method is a good one, the idea that we are to produce a non technically involved project made it easier for us to establish how to work in a team before also having to learn more on top of that. I found that working in a team was less stressful than having to go through a project on my own and it was better in terms of productivity and efficiency and shared expertise." (Aspergers Student).

Fig. 3. Awards Day

In addition to the more formal assessment of the work and in order to celebrate the successes of the students as well as adding another fun, yet competitive, edge to the work, the Annual Software Engineering Brilliance Awards or SEBAs are organized whereby the students present their work to a panel of judges from industry and academia, competing for prizes in categories related to their game design and pedagogy, posters, presentations and documentation in order to win monetary or technology related prizes as well as the coveted SEBA. See Figures 3, 4 and 5.

Fig. 4. and **Fig. 5.** Anticipation prior to the SEBA announcements and a SEBA

5 Summary

This approach to teaching software engineering can be measured by various parameters ranging from the visual and pedagogic quality of the work produced; overall performance of students taking the module; positive comments by the students about how fun and engaging the learning process of a subject like software engineering can be; the amount of use of the processes, knowledge and soft skills learnt in subsequent modules, on placement, and upon graduation; winning the UK's Higher Education Academy Engineering Subject Centre's Teaching Award; and by the activity being recognized as an example of best teaching practice by our professional accrediting institutions and the global corporations with which we interact.

This is not to say however that the process is an easy one, there are challenges for both staff and students and the activity requires a significant time investment for it to run smoothly as well some resource for games production. The activity has been running for eight years now with 1200+ students taking part. Although the overall premise of the assignment has remained consistent, tweaks have been made to the process each year based on staff experience and student comments.

Additionally, although these games are focused on teaching software engineering, the ways in which subject knowledge can be embedded into the games, the development processes undertaken, the digital creativity activities, soft skills elements and the overall ludic nature of the games based activity are relevant to, and easily transferrable to, all disciplines whether science or humanities based.

Acknowledgements. Thanks are due to all the students who have participated in this activity and the demonstrators/staff who have helped me run it over the past 8 years.

References

1. Lindley, C.A.: Ludic Engagement and Immersion as a Generic Paradigm for Human-Computer Interaction Design. In: Rauterberg, M. (ed.) ICEC 2004. LNCS, vol. 3166, pp. 3–13. Springer, Heidelberg (2004)
2. Gaver, W., Bowers, J., Boucher, A., Gellerson, H., Pennington, S., Schmidt, A., Steed, A., Villars, N., Walker, B.: The Drift Table: Designing for Ludic Engagement. In: CHI 21004, Design Expo. ACM Press, New York (2004)
3. Sommerer, C., King, D., Mignonneau, L.: Interface Cultures: Artistic Aspects of Interaction. Transcript Verlag (2008)
4. Fuchs, M.: Ludic Interfaces. Driver and Product of Gamification. GAME Italian Journal of Game Studies (2012), http://www.gamejournal.it/ludic-interfaces-driver-and-product-of-gamification/
5. Peterson Brooks, E., Brooks, A.L.: Ludic Engagement Designs for All (LEDA): Non-formal Learning and Rehabilitation. In: Designs for Learning, 3rd International Conference Exploring Learning Environments, pp. 78–80 (2012)
6. Selander, S.: Designs for Learning and Ludic Engagement. Digital Creativity 19(3), 145–152 (2008)

7. Quest to Learn, Institute of Play (2012),
   http://www.instituteofplay.org/work/projects/
   quest-schools/quest-to-learn/
8. Deterding, S., Dixon, D., Khaled, R., Nacke, L.: From Game Design Elements to Gamefulness: Defining "Gamification". In: MindTrex 2011. Tampere, Finland (2011)
9. Kolb, A.Y., Kolb, D.A.: The Kolb Learning Style Inventory - Version 3.1 Technical Specifications, Experience Based Learning Systems (2005), http://www.whitewater-rescue.com/support/pagepics/lsitechmanual.pdf
10. Wilson-Medhurst, S., Dunn, I., White, P., Farmer, R., Lawson, D.: Developing Activity Led Learning in the Faculty of Engineering and Computing at Coventry University through a Continuous Improvement Change Process. In: Research Symposium on Problem Based Learning in Engineering and Science Education, Aalborg, Denmark (2008)
11. Aalborg University, Principles of Problem and Project Based Learning, the Aalborg PBL Model (2010),
    http://www.pbl.aau.dk/digitalAssets/33/33124_pbl_aalborg_modellen.pdf
12. Belbin, Belbin Team Role Summary Descriptions,
    http://www.belbin.com/content/page/5002/
    BELBIN(uk)-2012-TeamRoleSummaryDescriptions.pdf
13. Belbin, Team Roles in a Nutshell,
    http://www.belbin.com/content/page/5664/
    Belbin(uk)-2011-TeamRolesInANutshell.pdf

Can Accessible Digital Formats Improve Reading Skills, Habits and Educational Level for Dyslectic Youngsters?

Simon Moe and Michael Wright

Nota, Danish National Library for Persons with Print Disabilities, Copenhagen, Denmark
{sme,mwr}@nota.nu

Abstract. Dyslexic children face significant barriers when reading printed text. It has been well documented that subsequent lower reading frequency impacts the ability to read, vocabulary and the desire to go to school, causing a negative spiral. Finally, poor reading skills contribute to a significantly lower level of education than for the rest of the population. In 2010 Nota conducted a national study of dyslexic children's reading frequency, the use of hybrid audio and welfare. 500 children were interviewed in a telephone survey for half an hour. Further interviews were also conducted with 200 randomly selected children. The study supports a positive correlation between dyslexic children's access to and use of accessible digital formats and their reading habits, satisfaction with school and ambitions for further education.

Keywords: Audiobooks, Dyslexia, Print Disabilities, Daisy.

1 Introduction

According to the PISA investigations from 2009, 15% of a year group in Denmark are functionally weak readers and just under 5% are really good readers (Læsning i PISA, 2009). The effort to raise the very weakest readers' learning environment and reading skills is a key challenge if changes are to be made in these conditions. However, the opportunities to compensate for finding it difficult to read – alternative access to literacy – are equally as important.

In order to be registered with Nota, one must produce written documentation signed by a professional or institution, which documents dyslexia or a similar level of severe reading difficulties. At Nota we are currently seeing a surprisingly large increase in registration of children and adolescents with dyslexia. Supposedly this development is due to a combined effect of stronger political focus on the subject, recent streamlining of the municipal handling of the issue and improvement in the services delivered by Nota as well as stronger communication efforts. In 2013 there are 6,565 dyslexic users in the age group 12-16 years old. In a few years it has thus become one of Nota's largest isolated user groups and at the same time a number, which is expected to correspond to about 50 % of the total dyslexic population for that age group (Cf. table 1, chapter 3).

In order to better meet the wishes of this group and to better support and guide these children and adolescents in joint efforts to acquire knowledge and contribute to society; Nota took the initiative to investigate this group more closely.

C. Stephanidis and M. Antona (Eds.): UAHCI/HCII 2013, Part III, LNCS 8011, pp. 203–212, 2013.

This report focuses on the part of the investigation's results, which concern the relationship between using audio books on a daily basis, and how one perceives being happy and manages at school. Here the investigation pointed out a statistically significant correlation. With more certain knowledge about impact and applicability, hybrid accessible media can ease the way and strengthen resolve through the education system.

2   Review of Literature

There are several areas where hybrid audio books are thought to have a beneficial effect on poor readers. Within reading research a distinction is usually made between two equally crucial processes, which together constitute the basis for reading, namely decoding and speech perception (i.e. Elbro, 2007). Decoding is the unique process of recognising words and letters; speech perception is a part of the ordinary linguistic generation of meaning. It thus makes sense to investigate a research-related justification of whether hybrid audio books can support these processes separately or as a whole.

In addition to these two processes it is necessarily a prerequisite that one is motivated to read and practises reading intensively. Therefore well being and reading frequency as well as how often the individual is engaged in reading are also important parameters for the student's success.

2.1   Speech Perception

Earlier studies suggest that audio books as compensation and as a supplement to printed text have a positive effect on speech perception for challenged readers.

A research project undertaken at J. Hopkins University in 2003, compared 67 challenged readers in two experimental groups and a control group and showed an increase of 38% in reading score for speech perception, for those students who use audio books accompanied by text. The study concludes that "it is noteworthy that the use of audio text had a significant effect on secondary level content acquisition" (Boyle et. Al., 2003).

2.2   Decoding

The hybrid audio books, which this project is about, are characterised by the text and audio being presented synchronously to the reader. The reader also sees the words whilst they are being reading out loud. It is conceivable that this hybrid form of reading could have a positive impact in relation to improving the reader's decoding of words as well.

According to an American study from 2000 reading in combination with text and computer-assisted recitation has an effect on the later unaided word reading, non-word reading and phonological awareness.

In the study several different forms of recitation are to be compared – both when the computer reads out segments of words and whole words for the reader. In both cases the study concludes that there is a significant positive effect on the reader's ability to decode, concluding "Computer-speech support for whole words appears as helpful as segmented support in the speech- supported reading in context." (Wise et al., 2000).

There is a basic difference in the form of reading that was investigated in this study and the way Nota's readers follow the text whilst they are listening. For one thing Nota's books are read aloud by a human being – not a computer – and for another the words are only marked out at sentence level. Therefore closer studies of this form of reading will be needed in order to be able to conclude whether it has a significant impact on the reader's decoding competence.

In addition the frequency of reading – and particularly reading which gives rise to understanding and learning – is crucial to the student's automation "There is only one route to automation of a skill: practice". (Elbro, 2008) A significantly higher reading frequency will in itself, strengthen the student's decoding.

2.3   Well-Being

By lowering the threshold in order to reach the textual content, audio books can have a great bearing on the student's well-being and reading frequency. In a research project from 2009 Italian researchers investigated the combination of the audio books' effect on reading abilities with the impact on psycho-social factors and well-being. They conclude that audio books in lessons for 11-16 year old teenagers who had been tested for dyslexia had a significantly positive effect on the students' results, motivation and involvement.

"After 5 months of experimental training, the experimental group showed a significant improvement in reading accuracy, with reduced unease and emotional– behavioural disorders, as well as an improvement in school performance and a greater motivation and involvement in school activities." Anna Milani Et al. (2009)

3   Method

This report has been prepared on the basis of an investigation that Nota have carried out in collaboration with the analysis company Epinion. The most important results take as their starting point a telephone survey undertaken by 497 of Nota's members in the age group 12 to 16 years old. For comparison 200 randomly chosen children and adolescents in the same age group have answered the same questions. In the report the two groups are differentiated by calling Nota's user group "the user group" and the 200 randomly chosen are called "the comparison group".

3.1   About the Random Sample of Nota's Users and the Population with Dyslexia

According to Videnscenter for handicap, hjælpemidler and socialpsykiatri (VIHS) (the Danish research centre for the disabled, assistive technology and social psychiatry) 5-7% of the population is dyslexic, whilst foreign investigations estimate that 2-5% of the population are dyslexic according to where one sets the limit for dyslexia (VIHS, 2013). If one assumes that 4% of the Danish population suffers from dyslexia, this figure corresponds to the registered number of 47% of the dyslexic population in the age group.

It is against Danish legislation to take registers of a disability such as dyslexia. Therefore there is no access to representative random samples of the total population of dyslexic. Nationally, representative investigations of this population have not been undertaken either.

Table 1. 6,565 adolescents with dyslexia are today registered with Nota, corresponding to 47% of the assumed total population of dyslexic in the age group 12-16 years old

DK Youth between 12 and 16	Est. Dyslectics	Enrolled at Nota
344.103	13.764 (4%)	6.565

This investigation is representative with regard to Nota's members and consequently therefore representative of approximately 47% of the 12-16 year old dyslexics in Denmark. Some initial assumptions about the user group's divergence from the total may, however, be made:

The dyslexic youngsters in Nota's user group are both discovered and diagnosed as such and thus - presumably - better aided than dyslexic youngsters in general who may or may not have been identified as having severe reading difficulties.

Regardless of whether it is the individual themselves, parents or a teacher who has registered them – enrolment is an indication of an active movement in the direction of better learning environment support etc. than for the average population.

There is reason to surmise that *the degree* of dyslexia is the same for Nota's users as for other dyslexics in the population, but overall it is assessed that the learning environment as well as support and well-being in a school and family context etc. is stronger. This particularly applies to the most active percentage (with regard to the use of Nota's products) the 12-16 year old users.

4   Results

4.1   Hybrid Reading

66% of the respondents always use text to assist the audio books. Either in an ordinary book or on a computer screen.

Table 2. Do you use text to assist reading, when you listen to audiobooks from Nota?

User group	Total
Yes, in an ordinary book	37%
Yes, on a computer screen	18%
Yes, either in an ordinary book or on a computer screen	11%
No	33%

4.2   Positive Effect of Audio Books

Just under a third of the user group listen to audio books daily or weekly; every third person never listens to an audio book. Thus audio books are for a large percentage of these children and adolescents an absolutely central way of reading – and thus gaining knowledge and experiences. By comparison only 3% of the comparison group listen to audio books weekly or more often. The comparison group is a representative random sample, so the 3% is presumably comprised of dyslexic/children and adolescents with dyslexia (c.f. Introduction).

Table 3. Do you ever listen to an audio book?

	Comparison group	User group
Daily	1%	11%
Weekly	2%	21%
Monthly	3%	22%
Rarer than once a month	10%	18%
No	82%	28%
I don't know what it is	1%	0%
Total	100%	100%

Every other person in the user group uses or has used schoolbooks in the form of audio books. It is primarily a remedial teacher or another teacher who is responsible for purchasing them when this happens. There is no legislation or other scheme which ensures students access to audio books or other alternative school materials in secondary schools in Denmark.

Table 4. Do you have or have you had any of your school books in the form of audio books?

User group	12	13	14	15	16	Total
Yes	47%	51%	61%	57%	41%	51%
No	53%	49%	39%	40%	56%	48%
Don't know	0%	0%	0%	3%	2%	1%
Total	100%	100%	100%	100%	100%	100%

The investigation documents that there is a positive correlation between the use of audio books, homework habits, reading habits and well being in school.

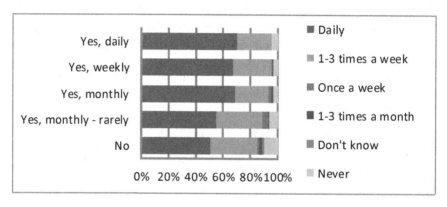

Fig. 1. Use of audio books I "How often do you do homework?" No":n=137. "Yes, but less than once a month":n=89. "Yes, every month":n=89. "Yes, every week":n=106. "Yes, every day":n=55. Total:n=497. Statistically significant with a level of significance of 5%.

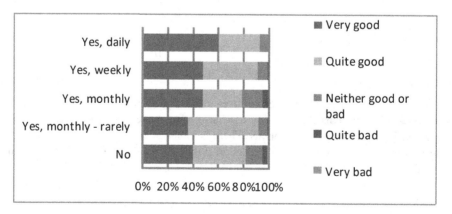

Fig. 2. Use of audio books I "On the whole how do you feel about going to school?" Same number as in figure 1. Statistically significant with a level of significance of 1%.

4.3   Reading and Homework

On the whole 2% of the members consider that they read better than the average for 12-16 year olds. 80% responded that they would like to use their holidays or spare time to become better readers.

The user group resemble the comparison group with regard to time spent on homework and time spent reading. 90% of the user group does homework daily or two to three times a week, the corresponding figure for the comparison group is 92%. 77% of the user group spend half an hour or more reading each day, this applies to 85% of the comparison group. Also in relation to media habits and consumption the two groups resemble each other, even though there are several places where the adolescents in the user group stand out positively in relation to a more comprehensive use of media and technology.

4.4   Technology and Assistive Technology

99 % of Nota's users have access to a PC that they can use. Only 1% has neither an IT rucksack (An IT rucksack is a support computer handed out by the school) nor PC. It is significantly more common for the dyslexic adolescents to have a computer with them daily at school (46%) than in the comparison group (17%).

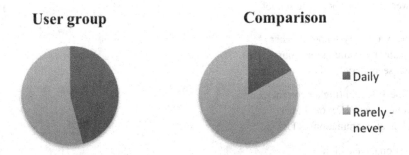

Fig. 3. Estimated percentages of those who have either a computer or/and IT rucksack with them daily at school. Every other person from the user group has a portable computer or IT rucksack with them daily at school. This only applies to a fifth of the comparison group.

4.5   Schooling and Well-Being

60% have changed school one or more times, which is 20% more than the comparison group. The most frequent reason for a change of school is dyslexia. Thus a fifth of the user group have experienced changing school as a consequence of reading difficulties.

When asked about well-being Nota's members, however, generally indicate that they feel good at school and in the lessons, despite reading difficulties and the change in school. 98% reply that they always receive the reading help from home or elsewhere, when needed. 94% also indicate that they receive help and instructions for the assistive technology that they need. Conversely the adolescents in the user group do not generally know a lot about what help and offers they have a right to (46%).

4.6   Education Plans

15% of the user group plans to go on to an upper secondary education after secondary school. In addition 7% plan on an upper secondary education after a stay at a lower secondary boarding school. 28% plan to continue straight away with a vocational education, whilst a further 12% will plan such things after a stay at a lower secondary boarding school.

By comparison 46% of the comparison group are planning to continue with an upper secondary education after secondary school, whilst only 8% plan on a vocational education. The reading difficulties also have an apparent and crucial effect on the adolescents' plans for the future.

Table 5. Overall – answers to the question: Have you plans to go on to one of the following courses when you have finished at secondary school/primary school

Educations plans	User group	Comparison group
Lower secondary boarding school	31%	14%
Upper secondary school, Higher Preparatory Examination Course (HF), upper secondary level evening school	9%	40%
Business School (higher commercial examination (HHX) or Higher Technical Examination (HTX))	6%	6%
Vocational education	28%	8%
Don't know	19%	23%
Other/possibly study a subject in more detail	7%	10%
Total	100%	100%

5   Discussion and Future Steps

Before Nota's investigation we did not anticipate that adolescents with dyslexia used audio books to support their schooling and reading skills to the great extent shown. Follow up qualitative investigations suggest that the audio books are regarded more as "homework" than "experiences" amongst the adolescents – and this function is supported by both the teachers and parents around them (Jensen, 2012). Many parents ensure that the adolescents have a printed copy of the book and keep up with it all the time.

66% of the respondents always use text to assist listening to audiobooks. This substantiates that the dyslexics themselves *regard* the reading as reading training rather than fun. The positive correlation between use of audiobooks, well-being in school, reading frequency and time spent on homework combined with the high amount of hybrid reading, suggest that hybrid audio books are in many ways an obvious candidate for a standard format for accessible schoolbooks for people with reading difficulties. The technology presents many new opportunities to support such a generalisation and new opportunities within, among other things, speech synthesis and synchronisation make it less costly than previously.

However, there is still qualitative didactic research missing in precisely how the formats shall be constructed. In what situations is speech synthesis adequate? What significance has typography, formatting and media for the various end users and contexts? What significance has marking out at the word and sentence level etc.?

We hope that this and other reports which show a positive effect of digital hybrid formats, will lead to increased knowledge and exploration about the formats' significance and potential for people with reading difficulties. We will then move in the direction of parity between availability to literacy and experiences in the future.

References

1. Aller, E.: Læsning i PISA, UVM.dk (2009), http://uvm.dk/Uddannelser-og-dagtilbud/Folkeskolen/De-nationale-test-og-evaluering/Internationale-evalueringer/PISA/PISA-2009/PISA-2009-laesning (accessed February 27, 2013)
2. Boyle, E.A., Rosenberg, M.S., Connelly, V.J., Washburn, S.G., Brinckerhoff, L.C., Banerjee, M.: Effects of audio texts on the acquisition of secondary-level content by students with mild disabilities. Learning Disability Quarterly 26(3), 203–214 (2003)
3. Elbro, C.: Læsevanskeligheder, 2.imp, 1st edn., p. 39. Gyldendalske Boghandel, Nordisk Forlag A/S, København (2007, 2008)
4. Elbro, C.: Læsning og Læseundervisning, 2.imp, 2nd edn., p. 164. Gyldendalske Boghandel, Nordisk Forlag A/S, København (2001, 2008)
5. Jensen, B.W.: p. 14. Nota (2012) http://www.nota.nu/kvalitativt-studie-af-sammenhaenge-i-uddannelsessystemet (accessed March 1, 2013)
6. Lyytinen & Erskine.: Early Identification and Prevention of Reading Problems,Child Research Centre & Department of Psychology, University of Jyväskylä, Finland (2006), http://www.child-encyclopedia.com/documents/Lyytinen-ErskineANGxp.pdf (accessed February 27, 2013)
7. Milani, A., Lorusso, M.L., Molteni, M.: The Effects of Audiobooks on the Psychosocial Adjustment of Pre-adolescents and Adolescents with Dyslexia, p. 87. John Wiley & Sons, Ltd. (2009)

8. Nota, Epinion.: Auxiliary aids and access to learning for children and young people with dyslexia/severe reading difficulties, Nota, pp. 18, 19, 29, 30, 31, 32, 39, 54, 56, 90 (2010), `http://www.nota.nu/sites/default/files/` `English_version_of_survey.pdf` (English translation)

9. VIHS, Om Ordblindhed, `http://socialstyrelsen.dk/handicap/ordblindhed/` `om-ordblindhed` (accessed March 1, 2013)

10. Wise, B.W., Ring, J., Olson, R.K., et al.: Individual Differences in Gains from Computer-Assisted Remedial Reading. Journal of Experimental Child Psychology 77, 197–235 (2000)

Using Mediated Communication
to Teach Vocational Concepts to Deaf Users

Ingrid Teixeira Monteiro, Aline da Silva Alves, and Clarisse Sieckenius de Souza

Departamento de Informática, PUC-Rio
Rua Marquês de São Vicente 225 – 22453-900 Rio de Janeiro, RJ - Brazil
{imonteiro,clarisse}@inf.puc-rio.br, aline@icict.fiocruz.br

Abstract. This paper presents an in-depth study on how a small group of deaf users reacted while learning abstract vocational concepts in the domain of librarianship, using mediated interaction supported by WNH, a Web Navigation Helper. WNH's purpose is to allow *helpers* to create mediation dialogs to enable or facilitate *helpees'* online interaction with Web pages. In our study, deaf employees at a Brazilian library were taught a lesson especially designed for WNH by a deaf librarian who is fluent in Brazilian Sign Language (LIBRAS) and Portuguese. Among the results we were able to see the huge gaps between what a library is for our deaf participants and what it is for non-deaf library professionals and customers. We could also appreciate the role of technologies like WNH in preparing deaf users to interact with Web systems in professional settings.

Keywords: Mediated communication, deaf learners, vocational education.

1 Introduction

Sign language is the first (native) language of most deaf people. Brazilian legislation recognizes LIBRAS as the official sign language in this country [1] and says that all deaf citizens must have access to full-length education in LIBRAS. Therefore there is a recommendation that teachers and other education professionals become proficient in LIBRAS [2]. This language, however, does not have a corresponding writing system. As a consequence, deaf Brazilian citizens must use Portuguese when they need to read or write, and Portuguese is a second language [3] for this population.

As is the case with any first language, LIBRAS shapes its speakers' cognition [4]. Thus communication in general and learning in particular are easier when deaf individuals can use sign language. Nevertheless, knowing no other language than LIBRAS can be severely restricting. Work places where deaf individuals must interact with non-deaf, for example, can be extremely difficult if not impossible to access. Vocational training must therefore develop a deaf learner's ability to communicate in a conventional natural language (through lip reading, writing, or other form). Only by being reasonably skilled in communicating with non-deaf customers, for instance, can deaf employees be successful as sales persons, service supervisors or managers.

C. Stephanidis and M. Antona (Eds.): UAHCI/HCII 2013, Part III, LNCS 8011, pp. 213–222, 2013.

This paper presents an in-depth study with a group of deaf participants taking a lesson to learn abstract domain-related concepts as part of a vocational librarianship training activity. The lesson was delivered with the aid of a special technology, namely the Web Navigation Helper (WNH) [5]. WNH is a script-based user agent implemented as an extension of Firefox. With it, Web users who are challenged by interaction patterns used in some application that they need to use can step through *rephrased* scripted interaction especially designed to remove challenges. This is possible because WNH allows *helpers* (*i. e.* savvier users with no difficulty to interact with the application at hand) to create mediation dialogs that enable or facilitate online interaction between challenged users (the *helpees*) and the application. As most content in the Web is delivered in written language, mediation dialogs in WNH tend to follow the pattern and use essentially textual material, too. However, as is also the case in the Web, videos and images can be part of mediation dialogs.

In a previous study [6] with WNH, the author showed that dialogs created by a LIBRAS interpreter could effectively help deaf users overcome certain accessibility barriers and interact with an organizational system designed for non-deaf users. The interpreter used direct instructions in simplified Portuguese and helped deaf users fill out long forms required by an administrative process in their organization. They were able to understand what they had to do with the system and to provide the required information by themselves. Our study makes one step forward and investigates whether WNH can successfully mediate communication about *conceptual tasks*, rather than *operational tasks*. To this end, we studied a group of deaf employees at a Brazilian public research institution's library. The goal of the activity proposed to them was to search a library's online catalog. To be successful, they would have to understand and be able to answer questions about basic librarianship concepts required for the task. Participants carried out this learning activity supported by WNH. The mediation dialogs for the study were created by a deaf librarian who was fluent in LIBRAS and Portuguese.

Our study confirmed that LIBRAS is a fundamental requirement in teaching this sort of content to deaf users. The main findings go thus a few steps beyond this. We found clear instances of huge gaps between how deaf participants conceive of library objects and processes compared to the typical conceptualizations made by librarians and library customers. Additionally, we found that WNH is a promising technology for this kind of vocational training. Not only can it be skillfully used to elicit learning requirements for vocational training targeted at this specific population, but it can also be subsequently used to support vocational training practices.

In the next section we present the methodology and procedures of our study. Next, we discuss the main results. In our concluding remarks we point at interesting research topics that can be explored along this path.

2   Methodology, Participants and Procedures

We used qualitative methodology given the exploratory nature of our study. Participants worked at well-known public health research institution with branches in various Brazilian states. It has a permanent social project aiming the inclusion of deaf people in the labor market, which is carried out with outsourcing services. At the time of our study, there were 168 deaf workers in their branches.

We followed four major steps of investigation. First, we interviewed the coordinator of the institutional library network to learn about the context and activities carried out by deaf employees. Second, we asked a deaf librarian to elaborate a mini course on library basic concepts needed to use their online catalog. He should use WNH to compose and deliver his mini course. Third we asked three deaf employees to take the lesson using WNH, to do an exercise based on its content and finally to answer a small quiz. Last, we made a semi-structured post-activity interview with participants.

The library network coordinator (henceforth *P-I*, for interviewee), was an experienced librarian, having worked in the institution for many years. She was thoroughly familiar with the challenges faced by deaf employees at the institution's library. The deaf librarian (henceforth *P-C*, for Creator) is deaf since the age of twelve, when he had already learned how to speak, read and write in Portuguese. He can do lip reading and speaks relatively well. P-C learned LIBRAS late, when he joined the institution, because there were many other deaf employees there. P-C holds a degree in librarianship and works in one of the institution's most important libraries.

The remaining participants (henceforth $P\text{-}S_n$, for Student$_n$) were three deaf employees who volunteered to take P-C's mini course. We recruited volunteers with the following characteristics: 1) profound levels of deafness, from birth or early age; 2) advanced knowledge of LIBRAS and reasonable knowledge of Portuguese; 3) basic computer literacy; 4) working at one of the institution's libraries. These participants' profiles are detailed in Table 1.

Table 1. Deaf participants profile

	Gender	Age	Schooling	Time working at library	Mastery of Portuguese
P-S1	Male	40 years old	High-school	14 years	Low
P-S2	Female	27 years old	High-school	6 months	Moderate
P-S3	Male	40 years old	Incomplete high-school	6 years	High

Mediation dialogs for P-C's mini course were created in two separate 90-minute sessions. Contents and vocational training needs emerged from the interview with P-I. Fig. 1 presents three snippets from the website in reference for the mini course (the library's online catalog). Following conventions in this domain, users type terms search (left side snippet) and results are subsequently shown and browsed at will (center and right snippets). The numbers in Fig. 1 index some of the concepts that were explored in the WNH-supported lesson, indicating the dialog where each was used (see Table 2 for illustrations).

$P\text{-}S_{1\text{-}3}$ took the lesson separately, by running WNH mediation dialogs previously created by P-C. Each dialog talked about some specific library concept that was used on the corresponding page of the online catalog system. The student should carefully read the dialog and click on "Continuar" (continue) to move on to the next dialog. Fig. 2 shows the dialog that explains the localization code used to identify books on library shelves (see left side bar). Notice that, thanks to scripted navigation, the word "Localização" (localization) is automatically highlighted in the webpage, pointing out the exact element that the dialog refers to. In addition to the text used in dialogs, WNH supported additional explanatory and illustrative resources. In Fig. 3 we show an extra dialog accessed through the "Ver exemplo aqui" (See example here) link in the main dialog (Fig. 2). In Fig. 4 we show the screen shown when the "Dúvidas" (doubts) button is pressed. The screen includes short videos with the LIBRAS translation of words appearing in mediation dialogs. P-C conceived of his dialogs in LIBRAS (the first language of his *helpees*) and then he phrased them in simplified Portuguese. In some cases, P-C found it very challenging to express meanings in Portuguese. He then asked to use images and word translations into LIBRAS[1].

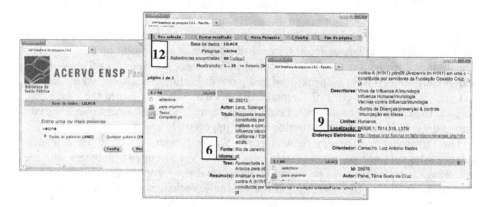

Fig. 1. Search website results page

Fig. 2. Localization mediation dialog   **Fig. 3.** Extra dialog   **Fig. 4.** LIBRAS

The whole lesson was communicated in 13 mediation dialogs. P-C's mini course had two goals: to teach basic library concepts (author, title, abstract, language, descriptors, localization code and link to download); and to teach how to make a basic search in the online catalog system (search terms, search activation, number of returned results and printing of selected results). In Table 2 we see some samples of

---

[1] All videos in LIBRAS embedded in WNH dialogs were obtained from an online LIBRAS dictionary (http://www.acessobrasil.org.br/libras/).

the final dialogs designed by P-C. They should by no means be taken as the actual corresponding text in English, written by or to deaf individuals. Samples are plainly evocative. We followed certain syntactic patterns of simplification that were verified in Portuguese just to give the reader an idea of the differences in written communication. For information about the English grammar as used by deaf users see [7]. Dialog numbers point to the corresponding element on the system's page (Fig. 1).

Table 2. Samples of content of library lesson dialogs

Dialog 1 (Welcome dialog)
We here learn service library, look for books. Start how to look for books, first seek Library staff. Ask how find book. Tell book name or person name who write book. Library staff look for book in computer. Wait he find book. He pick up book. Find not, staff say not have book, Ok! / Look for book in computer, yourself. Ask staff not need. / Open internet page and put [url] / In lesson I explain how to look for book or journal yourself. Ask help library staff not need. / Have doubt and not know meaning word, press doubt button. Words appear in Libras, video explain what word mean. When no doubts button, no word in Libras ok?

Dialog 6 ("Idioma" – language)
Language, you speak. Portuguese or English or Spanish. See pt (Portuguese) or en (English) or es (Spanish). Book or journal write Portuguese, English or Spanish.

Dialog 9 ("Localização" – localization)
Where you search book or journal library. See number and search. Example: 362.10972 (main book number), M542m (author letter and number, person write book) / See example here

Dialog 12 ("Sua seleção"– your selection)
Your selection/ When search book or journal many things appear. Select what good to see after see everything. Many book or journal appear? You lose important journal or book. When finish select, press selection. What you select before appear.

3   Reception of Lesson with Conceptual Notions in Librarianship

We made close observation of how P-S$_{1-3}$ took their lessons individually, interacting with WNH. The duration of the activity was approximately 50 minutes. A LIBRAS interpreter, also a permanent employee at the institution, who knew all participants, helped us to communicate with P-S$_1$ and P-S$_2$. P-S$_3$ could read lips and speak understandably, so we did not need the presence of an interpreter. Also, one of us is a co-worker of P-S$_3$'s, and thus we could communicate satisfactorily with this participant.

The dynamics of the activity was as follows. Before starting the lesson, the interpreter explained the activity to the participant. Then the participant interacted with WNH. At the end of the lesson, the participant was asked to take a quick test, where we could see how much was learned. The test included a few questions and a short task that participants should perform. The interpreter orally translated the content of test questions into LIBRAS.

An observation of how participants read the WNH-supported lesson in simplified Portuguese gave us valuable insights. P-S1 was the fastest reader (approx. 8 minutes to cover the whole material). He moved quickly from one dialog to the next. Only when he was reading the dialog explaining the "electronic address" field (with a link to download journal article), he seemed to closely follow guidelines presented in the dialog (like "you press blue color computer"). He clicked on the link, downloaded the file, opened it and browsed its pages. Our own reading of P-C's intent in such cases was that he just intended to tell the student about what he *might do* when he saw the link (not that he actually *did it*). Accessing the link was not a point in lesson. This observation, should be further investigated in view of the use of verbal modality in the simplified Portuguese displayed in P-C's dialogs (for example, we should investigate the differences in communication of what you *must* do and what you *might* do).

P-S$_2$ took about 15 minutes to complete the entire lesson. Various aspects of her interaction with WNH caught our attention. To begin with, she gesticulated spontaneously as she read the lesson. In the interpreter's word: "She translated what she was reading into LIBRAS." This is powerful evidence of the cognitive burdens of having to handle communication in a *second language* (compared to her more *native* LIBRAS). On some occasions, P-S$_2$ had doubts about the text produced by P-C. For example, at some point she asked the interpreter if she was supposed to click on a link (which we could take again as a question related to the use of modal verbs in P-C's simplified Portuguese).

In the document language dialog (6 in Table 2), she confirmed the meaning of the words "English" and "Portuguese" with the interpreter. She intriguingly interpreted the word "Spanish" as meaning "United States". The interpreter corrected the misunderstanding by translating "Spanish" into LIBRAS. Possibly the confusion sprang from both words starting with the same letters in Portuguese ("ESpanhol" and "EStados Unidos"). To us, this is a pointer to an interesting research question, related to the *iconic* reading of written words, so to speak. Similarity of form (starting with the same letters) might prevail over semantic relatedness (being a spoken language).

P-S$_2$ struggled to understand the dialogs explaining how to print selected books (12 in Table 2 is part of those). She apparently missed a script step in between subsequent dialogs, which caused the web page to change content. She did not realize that the page content had changed from one step to the other. This is an important finding to fine-tuning WNH for this context of use.

P-S$_3$ needed 11 minutes to finish the lesson. In the dialog about searching, he typed the word "disease" directly on the system's page textbox. This was literally the instruction written in the dialog ("You put name search want. Example: you write disease and press search button"), but the WNH script would have done it automatically for him. P-S$_3$ moved quickly through the remaining dialogs, apparently not reading the content in them. This comfortable situation changed when he reached the dialog about selecting of books. Even if he clearly noticed referred elements being automatically highlighted in the web page, he read and reread the text, very carefully. He also accessed the doubts area. At the end of the second dialog about this topic (12 in Table 2), he explicitly said that he did not understand what was being said. The interpreter gave him additional explanation and P-S$_3$ seemed to understand. In the last dialog of the lesson, P-S$_3$ did the same as P-S$_2$, he read the text and instantly translated it into LIBRAS.

Once the lesson was finished we proposed an exercise to participants. They should search for the word "vaccine", analyze results and then answer 6 questions (Table 3).

Table 3. Questions about activity

1	How many books or journals about "vaccine" were found?
2	Who wrote the first returned item? Say complete name in the right order (first, second and last name)
3	Find the numbers and letters you need to localize the first returned item on the library's shelves.
4	Can the first book be accessed in the internet? How do you know it?
5	Find a book or journal that was written in English. How did you figure that out?
6	Select two books or journals that were written by more than one author and prepare them for printing.

The general performance of participants is summarized in Table 4. Column 1 indicates the result of the first attempt of answer (Success/Failure). Column 2 corresponds to the result after the interpreter rephrased the question or the participant reread the corresponding dialog. In order to have a coherent interpretation about this table, it is useful to know what concepts the participants already knew before they took the lesson. They are summarized in Table 5.

Table 4. Participants performance in activity

	Questions	P-S1		P-S2		P-S3	
		1	2	1	2	1	2
1	Find References	F	F	S		S/F	S
2	Author (find name)	F	S	S		S	
2	Author (order name)	F	F	F	F	S	
3	Localization	F	F	F	S	S	
4	Electronic address	S		S		S	
5	Language	F	F	F	S	S	
6	Selection (find authors)	F	F	F	F	S	
6	Selection (prepare print)	F	F	F	F	S/F	S

Table 5. Previous known words

		P-S1	PS-2	PS-3
1	Reference	Yes	No	Yes
2	Author	Yes	No	Yes
3	Localization	Yes	No	Yes
4	Electronic address	No	No	Yes
5	Language	Yes	No	Yes
6	Title	No	Yes	Yes
7	Abstract	No	No	Yes
8	Descriptors	No	No	No

Table 4 shows that participants' performance differed significantly, which is good for an exploratory study designed to probe the depth of an unknown situation. Although P-S$_1$ read the lesson more quickly than others, the only question that he could answer correctly in his first attempt was about "electronic address". Suggestively, this concept was explored in the dialog where he spent most time exploring links, etc. As shown in Table 5, P-S$_1$ did not know what "electronic address" was before he took the lesson, from which we conclude that he learned this during the activity. However, even after rereading the corresponding dialogs, he failed answer most of the other questions correctly. At a second attempt, he managed to tell the name of the author of the first returned item (Table 4). P-S$_2$ gave three correct answers at her first attempt (Table 4), all of them involved unknown concepts (Table 5). With further help, she could correctly answer two more questions. Not surprisingly, P-S$_3$ did very well. "S/F" in Table 4 indicates that P-S$_3$ answered the question correctly but did not strictly follow what was taught in lesson. As a courtesy, in cases of repeated failure, the interpreter explained the answer in LIBRAS to the participant.

It took all participants some time to give a correct answer. They either looked for a clue in the webpage or engaged in "trial and error" mode. For example, to answer the question 1 (Table 3) P-S$_1$ spent considerable time scrolling the webpage up and down. Eventually, the interpreter offered some help, saying that the dialog explained how he could find the number of items returned by the search. We asked P-S$_1$ if the text was difficult and he said that it was complicated. In the dialog explaining localization on shelves, the interpreter told us, on the side: "This should be easy for him. It's his job:

to look for books on the library's shelves". Nevertheless, P-S$_1$ failed. After a number of unsuccessful turns, the interpreter directly asked: "What do you need to know in order to find a book on the shelf?" She then translated his answer to us: "He said he needs the title, the page number... He did not understand [the concept]." When the interpreter eventually explained the right answer to him, P-S$_1$ said the numbers and letters were very small, hard to see, and he was used to doing something different.

In the dialog about the document's language, after the first failure, the interpreter asked if one of the books was written in Portuguese or in English. P-S$_1$ correctly said that it was Portuguese. When asked how he knew it, he pointed to the English version of the book's title and said: "Only this in English". As most information in the item's entry was written in Portuguese, he concluded that the item's language must be Portuguese. At one point, he said another document was written in Spanish because he saw to the word "México" in one of the entry's fields. This kind of *metonymic* reasoning, taking the country of publication or the language of information in entry fields for the language of the document is an interesting cognitive strategy to be further explored in research. Its significance for vocational training is clear. Along these lines, P-S$_1$'s reasoning to answer question 6 (Table 3) was also revealing. At first, he looked through the webpage, searching for some clue to find an item with more than one author. His first attempt was to point at the content of the "Descriptors" field. The second was to point at content of the "Author's keywords" field. The latter was probably due to the presence of the word "author" in that field. But the former was only elucidated during the interview. When we asked if he knew the word "descriptors" before he took the lesson, he answered: "person wrote book". It then became clear that he was confused with the similarity between two words in Portuguese: "descritor" (descriptor) and "escritor" (writer). The cognitive gaps in this case were considerable, since the content of the "Descriptors" field were apparently taken as valid author names.

P-S$_2$ also gave us evidence of interpretive issues. In the dialog about localization, P-S$_2$ focused in fields whose content had sequences of numbers and letters. She used the sign "tag" to ask the interpreter if she was supposed to search for the localization code shown on books *tags*, but even then she failed to find the answer. After rereading the dialog, she finally understood that she should be looking for the "Localization" *field* and gave the right answer. The dialog on language (6, in Table 2) was again a source of insights. P-S$_2$ tried to guess the language by looking at words in field contents, but not reading what the "Language" field said. After a while the interpreter pointed to "pt" and asked her what it meant. She answered she did not know this word (she missed or forgot the content of the lesson). In the question about co-authored items, she tried to answer by counting the words in a single author's name, instead of counting how many authors were listed in the field.

P-S$_3$ gave us unexpected but correct answers for two questions. In question 1, he told the correct number of results, but he inferred this from the repetition of the number "60" in each of the listed items: "1/60", "2/60", "3/60", etc. He did not look for the value of "Referências encontradas" (found references) field, which was what the lesson said should be done in this case. Likewise, he selected books and journals as a side effect of clicking on individual print buttons, rather than selecting them in the way the lesson indicated.

The post-test interviews finally gave us important evidence of challenges faced by participants. For example, although P-S$_1$ started saying that the lesson was easy and that he had no problems, when asked about the content of textual explanations he said that he understood "more or less, a little bit". He also told us that he could learn the words "language" and "localization", which he did not know before.

P-S$_2$ confirmed during her interview one of the points raised by the library's coordinator (P-I), that alphabetical and numerical ordering is a recurring problem faced by deaf workers in the institution libraries. In the interview, P-S$_2$ said that the single activity she considered difficult in her job was dealing with localization codes. She said: "A, B, C, D, sometimes I read wrong and there are the numbers..." Her opinion about the textual material in the lesson, in general, was quite positive. She considered the text easy and understandable. The Portuguese was simple and she appreciated the correspondence between the dialog content and what happened on the system's webpage.

P-S$_3$'s opinions were expressed even before the interview started. While he was still running the lesson he said that after careful reading he could finally understand but that the activity was difficult at first time one use it, it is difficulty. He thought some practice was needed to really be able to learn. When asked if he thought other deaf students would understand explanations presented in the lesson, he said that if there was someone to show how it worked, it would be easier, because, in general, deaf people have problems to read and understand sentences. However, he said that he liked the text and the explanations that he learned some words (like "select" and "descriptors"). He also learned how to print more than one book. The problem with the lesson's format, in his opinion, was that: "one reads the first time, one learns content, but after some time, one forgets". This is a clear recommendation for lessons with more fixation tasks.

4   Concluding Remarks

Hearing impairment can be more critical than others mainly because it affects one of our most important abilities – communication. According to the world report on disability [8] "individuals with communication difficulties, such as hearing impairment or speech impairment, are at a significant social disadvantage, in both developing and developed countries." (p.172)

Our study confirmed what we already know, that is, that sign language is the main form of communication for deaf users, and that it must be used in vocational training. However, our perspective on vocational training was to investigate the potential of WNH as a means to leverage the linguistic skills of deaf individuals whose job requires that they interact with hearing people who do not know LIBRAS. Moreover, professional progress in their case requires that they learn to use computer technology (online catalogs, for example) that is designed to attend the needs of the majority of the library's customers. Even if there were optimal accessibility tools in place to allow deaf employees to understand and use this technology effectively, part of their job would be to help non-deaf customers use the system and/or to communicate with the through the system. In short, if vocational training must enable professional growth and progress in the context of our study, then it should prepare deaf learners to communicate more effectively with non-deaf co-workers and customers.

Our reported findings show the magnitude of cognitive gaps persisting over considerable periods of time (see "Time working at library" in Table 1) in our participants' conceptualization of the work place around them. It also shows the amount of effort that deaf individuals may be willing to make when trying to learn something. It is noteworthy that none of our participants said they simply did not know the answer to a question and gave up looking for an answer. Quite contrarily, they tried again and again until they succeed by themselves or we explained to them how to find the correct answer. Our in-depth observation shows that the teaching and learning of abstract concepts with the aid of computer technology was much harder than teaching and learning operational procedures, which has been done in a previous study [6].

Nevertheless, WNH proved to be a very promising tool for vocational teachers engaged with deaf learners. At first it can be used to *probe* the needs of learners in terms of communicative skills, domain content and learning strategies. Afterwards, it can be used to *support and effect* the teaching-learning process with considerable advantages. For instance, as a Web-based tool, WNH can easily integrate multiple modalities of communication like text, images and video. It can also let the learners pace their learning as it best fits them, on an individual basis. Finally, the Web infrastructure can be used to introduce deaf learners smoothly into the communicative realm of non-deaf Web users. In the context of our study, for example, advanced vocational training might teach deaf library workers how to carry out simple asynchronous computer-mediated communication protocols with library clients. The social benefits of a successful initiative along these lines would be invaluable.

Acknowledgement. Authors thank FAPERJ, CNPq and IBM Research for supporting this research.

References

1. Brasil. Lei n. 10.436, de 24 de abr. de 2002. Dispõe sobre a Língua Brasileira de Sinais – Libras e dá outras providências (2002)
2. Brasil. Decreto N° 5.626 de 22 de Dezembro de 2005. Regulamenta a Lei no 10.436, de 24 de abril de 2002 (2005)
3. Kozlowski, L.: O modelo educacional Bilíngue no INES; Anais do VI Seminário Nacional do INES - Surdez e diversidade social: 2001; VI Seminário Nacional do INES, Rio de Janeiro (2001)
4. Silva, V.: Educação profissional para surdos: uma vivência político-pedagógica no Centro Federal de Educação Tecnológica de Santa Catarina. Ponto de vista: Revista de Educação e Processos Inclusivos 5, 151–178 (2003)
5. Monteiro, I.T.: Acessibilidade por diálogos de mediação: Desenvolvimento e avaliação de um assistente de navegação para a Web, MSc Dissertation, p. 198. Pontifícia Universidade Católica do Rio de Janeiro, Rio de Janeiro (2011)
6. Alves, A.S.: Estudo do uso de diálogos de mediação para melhorar a interação de surdos bilíngues na Web, MSc Dissertation, p. 156. Universidade Federal do Estado do Rio de Janeiro, Rio de Janeiro (2012)
7. Berent, G.P.: The acquisition of English syntax by deaf learners. In: Handbook of Second Language Acquisition, pp. 469–506 (1996)
8. World Health Organization (WHO). The world report on disability. World Health Organization (2011), http://www.ncbi.nlm.nih.gov/pubmed/22726850

The Effects of Projector Arrangement
on Children Physical Activity

Loan Ngo and Fong-Gong Wu

Department of Industrial Design, National Cheng Kung University, Tainan, Taiwan (R.O.C.)
paid13@yahoo.com

Abstract. In kindergarten education, effective teaching is defined to be successful when children are learning while playing. As a combination of indoor and
outdoor activities, the purpose of kindergarten education is to develop children
physically, psychologically and socially. However, there are always some limitations from the surrounding environment that prevent kindergarten education
from achieving its purposes. This study considers the effect of changing infrastructure inside the classroom on children's learning through physical activities,
in particular, the effect of projector arrangement inside classrooms on kindergarten children's physical activities. This study is conducted in three different
environments: "outdoor environment," "one-projector environment," and "two-
projector environment" with the aim to learn about the effect of each environment on children's learning process through physical activities. The results
point to a confident relationship between children's physical development and
in class physical activities through interacting with projector images.

Keywords: Accessibility of Smart Environments, physical activities, children,
projector.

1 Introduction

Kindergarten is the foundation for a child's life where he has most of his early childhood experiences. Therefore, kindergarten environment must be a safe place where
children are protected from potential danger and are easily supervised. It is where the
important physical activities of the day take place such as playing, eating, and sleep-
ing. Beyond the basics, kindergarten is also important to help implementing and supporting the education program's philosophy and curriculum.

According to the World Health Organization (WHO), childhood obesity is one of
the most serious public health challenges of the 21st century. Globally, in 2010, the
number of overweight children under the age of five is estimated to be over 42 million. Close to 35 million of these are living in developing countries [1]. For children,
a major contributing issue to obesity is that they are leading more sedentary lifestyles
[2]. The rise in obesity has been attributed to sedentary behaviors, decreased in daily
physical activities, and in daily physical education classes. Researchers have investigated the levels of physical activity, the amount of physical education and the level of
fitness in relation to obesity. It is important to increase physical activities which also

C. Stephanidis and M. Antona (Eds.): UAHCI/HCII 2013, Part III, LNCS 8011, pp. 223–230, 2013.

at the same time reducing sedentary activities like watching television, playing video games or playing toys. However, for kindergarten, outdoor activities are not possible to conduct during gloomy weather, especially as mentioned, Southeast Asia region has extended rain seasons for almost half a year. During that period, teaching curriculum for kindergarten to have enough physical activities is even harder. In-class activities require more insight to organize because indoor environment is very limited.

2   Benefit of Physical Activity for Children

Kindergarten teaching focuses on helping children establish social relationships with each other through playing and doing group activities. Because the nature of learning at this age is through interacting with visual objects, the process of learning must be a combination of physical development and social relationship development. Scientific studies have demonstrated that physical activities improve on brain functions at every age level. It is also emphasized that physical activities enable the cells in the brain to be optimal, which maintain and improve brain functioning, and therefore give us the ability to learn and focus [3].

Developing control of muscles and movement is important for the infant's and child's ability to interact with her environment. Movement contributes to the organization of neural circuits that develop through the process of synaptogenesis, which permits children to learn to develop control over their sensory abilities and motor functions. Cognitive functioning is also facilitated by the process of myelination stimulated by movement. In addition, the cerebellum is affected by children's movement especially in the first few years of life as cells are forming functional circuits in the cerebellum which in turn affect spatial perception, memory, selective attention, language, handling of information, and decision making [4].

These findings are the positive effects of the structure and function of brains to improved memory and physical developments during time children learn and play with physical activities.

3   Physical and Mental Development during Early Childhood

3.1   Study Objective

"Early childhood" is generally defined in the developmental psychology as children age between two and six, namely, the sum of toddling children and preschool children. Children at this stage have been obviously changing in body and receiving great promotions in motor skills and cognitive abilities [5]. Meanwhile, those changes are closely related to biological factors as well as environmental factors which have some important impacts such as furniture, board and educational tools. That is the reason why we should choose the right education tools to combine with environment for kindergarten classrooms. The environment we choose will have decisive impacts on the way children feel about their studies. That will help organize the activities in classrooms and give children a clear idea of where they need to be at specific times during the day.

In reality, most classrooms in kindergarten are not multi-functional, convenient or have enough space to help children completely develop. So how can we help children get more energy with physical activities during their times in class? In which way could existing persuasive principles in combination with context-aware systems be applied to motivate children to do exercise?

3.2   Element Necessary for Children Development in Kindergarten Classroom

Children's learning is an active process. To accommodate this active learning process, figure 1 shows the elements necessary for classroom to help children develop. This conceptual model could be applied to understand the influences upon physical activities in children's learning behavior.

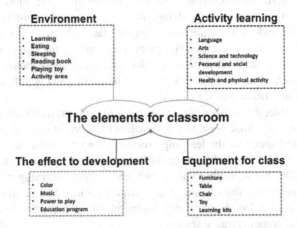

Fig. 1. The element necessary for children development in kindergarten classroom

4   Diagnosis of Children's Behavior in Kindergarten Classroom through Observation and Interview

First kindergarten classroom, which had 3 to 4 year-old children and their teachers, were selected from the Red School House in Singapore to participate in the study. I chose this classroom for the study because the population of Singapore is really high comparing to the country area. There isn't enough room for children to do activities. This kindergarten classroom was selected for the observation and interview.

The second kindergarten classroom, which had 5 to 6-year old children and their teachers, were selected from the Flower kindergarten in Vietnam. This classroom was chosen for the study because the weather in Vietnam only has two reasons – the rainy season and the dry season. There was limitation to organize children to do physical activities outdoors during rainy season. This kindergarten classroom was selected for the observation, interview and the experiment on physical activities and projector arrangements.

There are no significant differences in the environment of kindergarten classrooms when I did the observation and interview. The data was achieved through the use of questionnaire for teachers and children's activity log in kindergarten.

The space and environment in classroom are the most important factors to help teachers organize activities. Some kind of physical activity and entertainment are organized outdoor such as exercise, sport, science and natural studying. Children like to play outdoors where they can have more activities, but it is hard for teachers to control all of them outdoors. When the class has outdoor activities, teachers need more help to control her children.

During extended rain and cold weather when outdoor activities are not possible, physical activity indoors should be increased by reducing sedentary time. Normally in this time, teachers want to organize physical activities that produce overall physical, psychological and social benefits for children. For example, 15 minutes of physical education outdoors is replaced by doing on-site exercises or on-site step dancing. During the on-site indoor activities, according to data measured, the average energy burned is 40% less than the average energy burned while doing outdoor physical education. Teachers also said that it was best for children's development during spring when the weather was not rainy and warm; children had good health, came to school more often without absent due to sickness.

During class time, it has been observed that children are really interested in computer related lessons. Those lessons are visualized and vivid enough to attract children's attention and speed up the learning process. Using projectors as teaching equipment has been adopted in kindergartens in Singapore and Vietnam. However, applying the relationship between physical activity and children learning process into kindergarten teaching curriculum is still a new concept. Only 15 minutes of exercise is not enough for a complete physical development, not to mention the environmental limitation when it comes to rainy seasons.

5   Experiment on the Relationship between Projector Arrangement and Children Physical Activity

5.1   Participants

Twelve children 3 to 6 year-olds (7 boys and 5 girls) (n=12) and their teachers were selected from the kindergarten classroom in Vietnam to participate in the experiment. They attended kindergarten at a child development center at Dalat City. This kindergarten is chosen for the study because the weather of Dalat city and the size of the classroom met the criteria described earlier in this paper. Among these children, two of them are 3 year olds and ten others are 5 to 6 year-olds (5 boys and 5 girls). They are in the same class and at the beginning of their experiences with the projector classroom.

All but one child's family indicated that they had computers at home; however, in most cases, parents reported to know just a little about software that helps develop physical activities for their kids. Parents also mentioned that no more than 30 minutes of computer access a day for their kids, and the main purpose of the home computer was mainly for adult use. So children don't really have physical activities or exercises at home.

5.2 Experiment Environments

In order to increase the level of physical activities for children, I did an experiment in the school environments on physical activities in kindergarten classrooms with three environments in a lesson on exercising. Twelve children (n=12, 7 boys, 5 girls) attended in three different environments: outdoor, indoor with 1 projector and indoor with 2 projectors.

Outdoor environment: children do exercise outdoors. It is 15 minutes morning physical education (PE) exercises with music. Under the instruction of teachers, children run around in circles and do traditional kindergarten exercises.

Fig. 2. Illustration of outdoor environment

One projector classroom: Children do on-site PE exercises in class following the images of projector on the classroom wall. The projector projects an animated video clip that has the instructions for PE exercises by cute characters with audio music. Also, there are markers on the classroom floor to help children recognize where to put their feet according to movements require long distance and large steps.

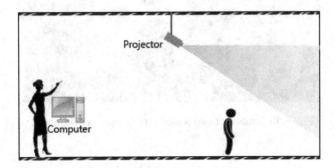

Fig. 3. Projector arrangement for one projector classroom

Fig. 4. Illustration of one projector classroom environment

Two-projector classroom: Children do on-site PE exercise in class with the support of two projectors. One projects on the classroom wall an animated video clip that has the instructions for PE exercises by cute characters with audio music. Another projector projects on the floor blinking steps that children need to follow along with the PE exercises.

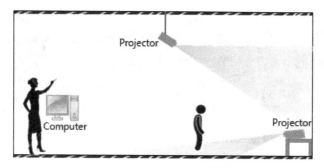

Fig. 5. Projectors arrangement for two projectors classroom

Fig. 6. Illustration of two projectors classroom environment

6   Result and Discussion

In this study, we focused on a novel kindergarten classroom-based environmental approach to the activity in children. We first compared physical activity levels, measured (using validated technology using Calorie Scanner Omron on children) energy dissipation, amount of fat burn and the movement steps during the PE exercises in the three experiment environments.

The dependent variable was the Calorie of energy dissipation (Kcal) between three environments. In the three environments (refer to table 1), outdoors showed the largest consumption of calories and under the one projector condition, children took the lowest consumption of calories.

Table 1. Dependent variable between environments

Independent Variables	Conditions	Calorie (Kcal)
Environments	Outdoor	19.50
	One projector	14.25
	Two projectors	19.25

Through repeated measures ANOVA, it was discovered that different environments had significant difference ($F_{2, 22}= 54.91$, $p< 0.001$). With least significance difference (LSD) applied to make a comparison, and there were two significant differences. It was revealed that the one-projector condition used up less calories than outdoors ($p= 0.000< 0.001$) and the two-projector ($p= 0.000< 0.001$) conditions.

According to my observation, in the first environment (outdoor), children do more physical activities than the second environment (one-projector classroom) because they have a bigger area to move, jump and run around. In the third environment (two-projector), children even have more physical activities than the second one. The second and third environments are both indoors, same classroom and same PE exercises. The only difference is the marker on the floor. In the second environment, there are simple and fixed markers while the markers in the third environment are dynamic and blinking. Children are more enjoyable in the third environment with two projectors than the second one. With the help of projector's image on the floors, children move faster and still can follow the rhythm of the exercise without looking at the one on the wall when they can't focus on both projector images at the same time.

According to the data collected, the calories of energy dissipation in the outdoors and the 2-projector environment are the same. The 1-projector environment dissipates less energy than the other two. Although the energy dissipation for the outdoors and the 2-projector environment is the same, the amount of fat burnt in the 2-projector environment is higher than the outdoor environment. This result is because during the PE periods, although the movement steps are less than in the outdoor environment due to limitation of available room to move, children move and jump with more intense movements and there are more forces acting on their bodies due to those intense movements. To recap, the two-projector environment has higher energy dissipation and higher amount of fat burnt although it has less movement steps due to space available for indoor PE.

The advantage of outdoor PE is that the environment supports the best physical development for children. Indoor PE with two projectors has limitation on the available space but we can accommodate this. Although the two-projector environment is not the best, it's still good for physical development. It also supports children learning process because while watching instruction video, they can recognize simple alphabets or numbers showing in the video. Additionally, children can also develop their perceptions on the relation between audio instructions and visual images. This two-projector environment can be used to promote more physical activities combining with regular lessons. Doing that will decrease the probability for children to get sick when having outdoor activities during cold and rainy seasons, saving a lot of teacher's effort on monitoring children outdoors. This environment also promotes children's interest in learning with vivid and playful video and images.

7   Conclusion

Physical activity is not only needed for children's physical development but also help speed up the brain activity during the learning process. With the limitation of outdoor activities due to cold and rainy weather, physical education for kindergarten children should be conducted inside classrooms with the support of computerized equipment. Since kindergartens are already equipped with projectors as a tool of teaching, taking advantage of the use of projectors to promote physical activities indoor should be considered in the kindergarten teaching program. The purpose of this study is transforming physical activities into applications for indoor classrooms. In the future, this new teaching environment will help teachers in encouraging children to do more physical activities. Projectors will be used to change the classroom environment as a tool for teaching and also support physical activities. It is also an economic way to save on cost for actual tools for indoor physical activities.

References

1. Childhood Overweight and Obesity. WHO. N.p., n.d. Web (December 26, 2012),
   http://www.who.int/dietphysicalactivity/childhood/en/
2. Sibley, B.A., Etnier, J.L.: The relationship between physical activity and cognition in Children: A meta-analysis. Pediatric Exercise Science 15, 243–245 (2003)
3. Ratey, J.J.: SPARK: The Revolutionary New Science of Exercise And The Brain. Little, Brown and Company, New York (2008)
4. Sibley, B.A., Etnier, J.L.: The relationship between physical activity and cognition in Children: A meta-analysis. Pediatric Exercise Science 15, 254–256 (2003)
5. Early Childhood. UNICEF. N.p., n.d. Web (December 26, 2012),
   http://www.unicef.org/earlychildhood/index_3870.html

Addressing Learning Disabilities
in Ambient Intelligence Educational Environments

Stavroula Ntoa[1], Margherita Antona[1], George Margetis[1],
and Constantine Stephanidis[1,2]

[1] Foundation for Research and Technology – Hellas (FORTH) - Institute of Computer Science
N. Plastira 100, Vassilika Vouton, 700 13 Heraklion, Crete, Greece
[2] University of Crete, Department of Computer Science
{stant,antona,gmarget,cs}@ics.forth.gr

Abstract. Learning disabilities (LD) affect not only an individual's academic skills, but also many aspects of life for a large population percentage. As a result, understanding individuals with learning disabilities and addressing their needs is an active topic of research, although it has been studied for several years. On the other hand, Ambient Intelligence (AmI) is an emerging field of research. AmI environments are claimed to be among other things sensitive, caring and adaptive to their inhabitants. In the context of education, AmI can adopt a student-centric approach and support the education activities that are taking place adapting to the individual learner's needs. This paper proposes an approach for AmI educational environments to assist in identifying, monitoring, and providing adapted instruction to students with LDs.

Keywords: learning disabilities, ambient intelligence, smart classroom.

1 Introduction

Learning disabilities (LDs) are gaining increased interest during the last decades, as they affect a large population percentage. According to the U.S Department of Health and Human Services [1], in 2010 almost 5 million children aged 3-17 had a learning disability (8%). Furthermore, learning disabilities constitute the most common disability among 3- to 21-year-olds served under the Individuals with Disabilities Education Act (IDEA) [2].

LD is a lifelong disorder that affects individual's academic skills and can impede learning to read, write, or compute. As a result, LD affects many parts of a person's life, such as school or work, daily routines, family life, and social contexts. For instance, according to a study carried out by the U.S. National Center for Learning Disabilities [3], students with LD go on to postsecondary education at a much lower rate than their nondisabled peers, and of those who do, few seek support in college and few earn undergraduate or advanced degrees. According to the same study, while more than two-thirds (69%) of students with LD had a transition goal of obtaining competitive employment after high school, only 46% had regular paid employment when surveyed within two years of leaving school. However, with appropriate support

C. Stephanidis and M. Antona (Eds.): UAHCI/HCII 2013, Part III, LNCS 8011, pp. 231–240, 2013.

and intervention, individuals with LDs can overcome barriers through alternative ways of learning, accommodations, and modifications.

Ambient Intelligence is an emerging field of research and development that is rapidly gaining wide attention by an increasing number of researchers and practitioners worldwide, and in Europe in particular [4]. According to Aarts and Wichert [5], Ambient Intelligence (AmI) is about sensitive, adaptive electronic environments that respond to the actions of persons and objects and cater for their needs, while the option of extended and more intuitive interaction is expected to result in enhanced efficiency, increased creativity and greater personal well-being.

In the domain of education, AmI is often claimed to bring a significant potential [6]. More specifically, the Smart Classroom has been defined [7] as a responsive intelligent environment that enhances collaborative learning by introducing the concept of situation awareness, where a number of attributes are monitored (i.e., PDAs' locations, levels of noise and luminance, etc.) to determine system response. However, a smart classroom, besides supporting a variety of technologies, should adopt a student-centric approach [8] and support educational activities through taking advantage of the advanced monitoring mechanisms, technology pervasiveness and the available knowledge and reasoning facilities, and adapting to each individual learner's needs. The system proposed in the context of this work aims to address the needs of students with learning disabilities in AmI educational environments by: (i) identifying students with potential LDs (ii) monitoring LD students' progress (iii) ensuring that appropriately adapted instruction is provided for each individual student and (iv) providing compensating and remediating technological assistance in students' daily classroom activities.

The remainder of this paper is organized as follows. Section 2 discusses issues related to learning disabilities, namely the definition of the term, classification models and assessment strategies. The currently available assistive technologies for supporting the needs of persons with LDs are introduced in Section 3. Section 4 introduces a systematic approach for addressing the requirements of students with LDs in the context of smart educational environments. Finally, Section 5 concludes this work and provides directions for future research.

2   Learning Disabilities

Learning Disabilities is not a simple concept to define. The first definition was provided in 1962 [9], and until recently different definitions or amendments to existing definitions have continued to arise. A recent definition was provided by the Individuals with Disabilities Education Act (IDEA) in 2004 [10], according to which the term 'specific learning disability' (a) means a disorder in one or more of the basic psychological processes involved in understanding or in using language, spoken or written, which disorder may manifest itself in the imperfect ability to listen, think, speak, read, write, spell, or do mathematical calculations, (b) including such conditions as perceptual disabilities, brain injury, minimal brain dysfunction, dyslexia, and developmental aphasia, (c) not including a learning problem that is primarily the result of visual, hearing, or motor disabilities, of mental retardation, of emotional disturbance, or of environmental, cultural, or economic disadvantage. In summary, the definitions that have been provided for learning disabilities aimed to (i) on the one hand identify the academic skill deficits exhibited by children with LDs, either by means of inclusion (what LD is) or by means of exclusion (what LD is not) and (ii) on the other hand to outline a model for identifying LDs.

More specifically, in the area of LD, classification occurs at multiple levels: in identifying children as LD or typically achieving; as LD versus cognitively disabled; and within LD, as reading versus math impaired [11]. The most distinguished classification models are aptitude-achievement discrepancy, low achievement, intra-individual differences and Response to Instruction (RTI).

According to the aptitude-achievement discrepancy model, learning disabilities can be identified by detecting a discrepancy between the achievements and the intellectual abilities of a person, with the IQ-achievement discrepancy criterion being the most controversial and best-studied approach [11]. Discrepancy-based approaches have received a lot of criticism (e.g. [12]), mainly since discrepancy has become the primary criterion in the LD identification process, and not because it does constitute an important concept related to LD [13].

Another model proposed as an alternative to aptitude-achievement discrepancies refers to identifying individuals as learning disabled based on absolute low achievement [14]. Despite evidence for their validity, definitions of LD based solely on low achievement models remain controversial, mainly due to the fact that because the purpose of the LD construct is to identify a unique group of low achievers whose underachievement is unexpected, it is questionable as to whether such an approach could ever identify individuals with LDs without additional criteria [15].

The intraindividual differences model proposes using intraindividual differences as a marker for "unexpected underachievement" and presumably the absence of variability (a flat profile) as a marker of "expected underachievement" [15], differentiating thus students with learning disabilities from students with low achievement. Several studies have been devoted to discussing the validity of this model, as summarized in [15]. A major concern according to the aforementioned study is that the model is based on the assumption that identification based on performance profiles will lead to enhanced treatment of individuals with LD. However, there is little evidence that instruction addressing strengths and weaknesses in cognitive skills is related to intervention outcomes, and as a result this assumption is unsupported.

An alternative approach is that of Response to Intervention (RTI), which involves the following phases [16]: (i) a classwide assessment to determine whether the overall rate of responsiveness for the class indicates that the instructional environment is sufficiently nurturing to expect student progress (ii) identification of students whose level of performance and rate of improvement are dramatically below those of classroom peers (iii) for the children identified at risk, classroom adaptations are designed and tested to enhance individual responsiveness in the general education setting. Students who cannot benefit from the instruction adaptations can be identified as having an intrinsic deficit (i.e., disability) and require special education. The RTI model constitutes an important landmark in the process of defining and modeling LDs, and as a result several studies have been devoted to discussing its results as applied during the educational process, as well as its validity. For instance, Kavale [17] identifies several criteria that are needed for a model to be deemed valid, which the RTI model fails to address. Namely, according to Kavale, the RTI model, among other issues, mostly focuses on phonological processing neglecting other LD-related academic deficits, emphasizes on early identification and not a cross-age spectrum, and may lead to overidentification, since the initial pool of students represents the lowest 25% in reading achievement in a kindergarten or first-grade population.

Henceforth, some new models have been proposed aiming to take advantage of the potential of the RTI model and to address the disadvantages that have been identified. Fletcher [18] recommended a model that is based essentially on a hybrid involving RTI, intraindividual differences in the achievement domains from both a low achievement and intraindividual perspective, and consideration of exclusionary factors. Kavale and Forness [19] proposed a five-level model, according to which the presence or absence of underachievement is documented in the first level, the second through fourth levels unravel the complex and multivariate nature of LD, while the final level establishes LD as a discrete and independent condition. Based on the previous model, Flanagan et al. [20] proposed an improved version, incorporating modern intelligence theory for theoretical and empirically supported grounding of LD and embedding the RTI model as well.

An important characteristic of LDs, which affects both their assessment and the provided intervention, is their heterogeneity. As a result, LDs may affect different domains of achievement, such as reading, math and written expression. In particular, five domains of academic deficiencies have been consistently identified in research and are assessed in existing assessment tests [18], namely word recognition, reading fluency, reading comprehension, math computations and problem solving, and written expression. Fig. 1 presents these academic domains, as well as the specific academic skills that are usually tested in order to identify a deficit in a specific domain.

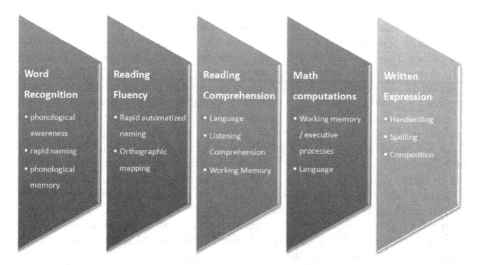

Fig. 1. Achievement domains that can be used as LD indicators and specific progress monitoring metrics

The approach proposed in this paper conforms to the RTI model and the methodology proposed in [18] and partly addresses the requirements of the model proposed in [19]. Furthermore, it supports all of the aforementioned tests in the five academic domains. Its advantage is that repetitive tests are easy to be carried out, that students' progress can be constantly monitored and the actions that are planned can be adapted as required in order to optimally address the needs of students. Finally, an important asset of the proposed system is its extendibility, making it possible to incorporate additional models in the future and to provide statistics regarding their validity and efficiency.

3   Assistive Technologies

Assistive Technology can offer powerful tools to students with learning disabilities by providing remedial or compensatory support in the classroom and for independent learning. A compensatory approach might be when a student listens to a taped version of the book for the English class to answer questions about it, with the goal of bypassing a reading problem, not learning to read. If the student listens to the tape of the book or has a computer reading a scanned version of the book while following along with the text and trying to learn unfamiliar words, this would be a remedial approach, designed to improve areas of deficiency.

For each individual, a different combination of assistive technologies might be the most suitable for facilitating learning according to his/her characteristics. An example illustrating the characteristics of an individual with reading learning disabilities and the support that can be provided by assistive technology is provided in Fig. 2.

Besides the type of learning disability that it compensates for, assistive technologies for LDs can be classified as low tech (e.g. pencil grips, graph paper, highlighting pens) and high tech (e.g. screen readers, spell checkers etc.). In summary, the

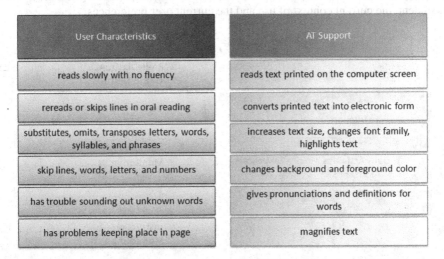

Fig. 2. Characteristics of a user with reading learning disabilities and related assistive technology solutions

categories of high-tech AT that can be used to address the needs of students with LDs include: alternative keyboards, portable word processing devices, tape recorders, reading pens, word processors, outlining programs, spell checkers, proofreading programs, abbreviation expanders, word prediction, screen readers, speech recognition software, concept mapping software, multimedia presentations and authoring software, talking calculators or electronic math worksheets.

4   Addressing the Needs of Students with Learning Disabilities in Ambient Intelligence Educational Environments

This paper proposes the design and implementation of a system aiming to address the needs of students with Learning Disabilities in Ambient intelligence educational environments, and in particular identify them as potentially LD, monitor their progress over time, as well as provide appropriate and personalized instruction and assistance in daily classroom activities (see Fig. 3).

In more details, students with potential LDs may be identified through an initial screening process. The screening tests can be carried out as part of regular exercises, transparently to the student, while the system will guide the student through the test, will monitor the student's answers, will calculate the score and will finally produce detailed reports with the results in order to inform the teacher. During the tests, multimodal interaction will be available, which may differ from one test to another. If necessary, the tests can be repeated over time periods without any burden for the classroom and the individual students.

Students identified as potentially LD should receive appropriate treatment, in terms of the educational process as well as in terms of assistance from the environment in their daily activities. The technology support will be adapted according to the individual student, the current context of use and the current user preferences.

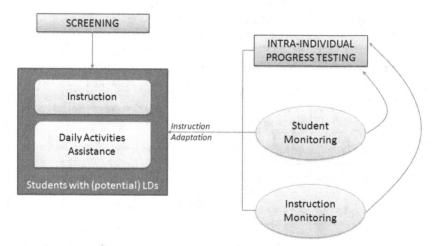

Fig. 3. Smart Classroom activities for effective identification, instruction and monitoring of students with LDs

The educational intervention adaptation will be suggested by the system individually for each student, according to their learning profile, the problems that have been identified and the interventions that have been applied so far. An appropriate reasoning mechanism will be used for this purpose, taking into account the individual student profiles and progress assessments, as well as the available instruction models. The teacher will have the possibility to accept, reject or modify accordingly the proposed adaptations. Besides the instruction adaptation guide, teachers will be supported through a suite of tools, including tools for designing and recording tests, as well as for monitoring students' performance.

Moreover, instruction activities as well as the students' progress and behavior in the smart classroom will be monitored by the AmI environment. As a result, the AmI environment will guide educators to adapt instruction activities as required, will carry out appropriate tests to assess the student's academic skills progress, also providing feedback on the effectiveness of the performed adaptations, and will provide assistance to student's daily activities as needed. An overview of the proposed system is presented in Fig. 4.

The target users, i.e., students and teachers, will be able to interact with the system through various devices, such as smartphones, laptops, tablets, etc. Furthermore, interaction with the system will be supported via any AmI artifacts, such as for example a smart desk, a smart board, an interactive display etc. Interaction will also be supported via physical objects, such as paper and pencil.

Users will be able to interact with a suite of applications. In summary, students will use screening and progress assessment applications, as well as assistive applications aiming to compensate or remedy their identified deficiencies. Both progress

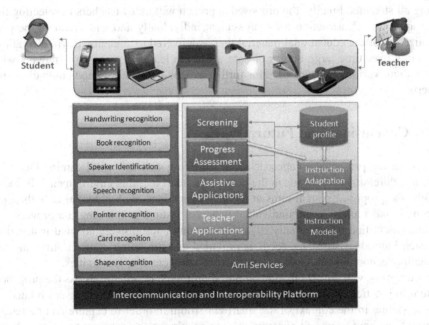

Fig. 4. Proposed system overview

assessment and assistive applications will be personalized for each student individually according to their profile. Teachers will be interacting with screening, progress assessment applications as well as specialized applications aiming to inform them of their students' progress and to allow them to plan the instruction adaptations when necessary. Finally, instruction adaptation will occur based on the progress assessment results, the individual student profile, as well as the teacher's input when necessary.

The applications' suite will use several services, implementing fundamental functionality using data from cameras and sensors. Such indicative services that will be used include book and pointer recognition [21], card recognition [22], and handwriting recognition services [23]. Finally, intercommunication needs between sensors / actuators and primary services will be addressed by a generic services interoperability platform [24], providing the necessary functionality for the intercommunication and interoperability of the heterogeneous services hosted in an AmI classroom environment.

The benefit of the suggested approach is that it ensures greater validity and reliability than other traditional LD identification approaches, since students can be identified as potentially Learning Disabled quite early and they can be seamlessly tested repeatedly if necessary. Additionally, they will be able to receive appropriate instruction, and their academic skills progress will be monitored constantly in order to correctly classify them as LD and further identify the exact educational activities in which they need support. Furthermore, the process is transparent to the student, who will not be psychologically affected by formal screening and LD-diagnosis tests, since these will be undertaken in the context of daily class activities and not as formal LD diagnosis tests. Furthermore, the approach is applied at a classroom level, thus benefitting all students. Finally, the proposed approach will assist teachers in selecting the most appropriate instruction for each student individually and will facilitate the personalization of the educational material that is delivered to students. It will also allow collecting over time large bodies of data about the learning process of students with and without various types of LDs for further processing, analysis and comparison by experts.

5   Conclusions and Future Work

This paper has presented an approach for identifying students with Learning Disabilities and addressing their needs in the context of smart learning environments. In more details, the proposed system aims at identifying students with potential LDs through screening and repetitive intraindividual progress testing, monitoring the progress of students identified as potentially LD, ensuring that appropriately adapted instruction for each individual student's needs is provided and providing compensating and re-mediating technological assistance in students' daily classroom activities.

Future work will aim at creating an initial prototype in order to assess the proposed system in practice. More specifically, forthcoming efforts will study issues related to user modeling in the context of the smart classroom in order to capture and represent information about users and contexts so as to enable the environment to adapt to both.

Furthermore, a detailed study of LD screening and progress monitoring tests and a selection of an indicative set of tests that will be embedded in the system will follow, as well as modeling of instruction approaches in order to address the changing needs of an LD learner. Based on the above, a working prototype of the system will be created and tested with experts and representative users.

References

1. Bloom, B., Cohen, R.A., Freeman, G.: Summary health statistics for US children: National Health Interview Survey, 2010. Vital and health statistics. Series 10, Data from the National Health Survey 250, 1 (2011)
2. Aud, S., Hussar, W., Kena, G., Bianco, K., Frohlich, L., Kemp, J., Tahan, K.: The Condition of Education 2011. NCES 2011-033. National Center for Education Statistics (2011)
3. Cortiella, C.: The state of learning disabilities. National Center for Learning Disabilities, New York (2009)
4. Ducatel, K., Bogdanowicz, M., Scapolo, F., Leijten, J., Burgelman, J.C.: Ambient intelligence: From vision to reality. IST Advisory Group Draft Rep., Eur. Comm (2003)
5. Aarts, E., Wichert, R.: Ambient intelligence. Technology Guide, pp. 244–249 (2009)
6. Abrami, P.C., Bernard, R.M., Wade, C.A., Schmid, R.F., Borokhovski, E., Tamim, R., Surkes, M., Lowerison, G., Zhang, D., Nicolaidou, I., Newman, S., Wozney, L., P.: A review of e-learning in Canada: A rough sketch of the evidence, gaps and promising directions. Canadian Journal of Learning and Technology/La Revue Canadienne de L'apprentissage et de la Technologie 32(3) (2008)
7. Yau, S.S., Gupta, S.K.Z., Karim, F., Ahamed, S.I., Wang, Y., Wang, B.: Smart classroom: Enhancing collaborative learning using pervasive computing technology. II American Society of Engineering Education (ASEE) (2003)
8. Antona, M., Leonidis, A., Margetis, G., Korozi, M., Ntoa, S., Stephanidis, C.: A student-centric intelligent classroom. In: Keyson, D.V., Maher, M.L., Streitz, N., Cheok, A., Augusto, J.C., Wichert, R., Englebienne, G., Aghajan, H., Kröse, B.J.A. (eds.) AmI 2011. LNCS, vol. 7040, pp. 248–252. Springer, Heidelberg (2011)
9. Kirk, S.A.: Educating exceptional children. Houghton Mifflin, Boston (1962)
10. Public Law No. 108-446, 118 Stat. 2647 "The Individuals with Disabilities Education Improvement Act of 2004"
11. Fletcher, J.M., Lyonm, G.R., Barnes, M., Stuebing, K.K., Francis, D.J., Olson, R.K., Shaywitz, S.E., Shaywitz, B.A.: Classification of learning disabilities: An evidence-based evaluation. Lawrence Erlbaum Associates Publishers (2002)
12. Stanovich, K.E.: The future of a mistake: Will discrepancy measurement continue to make the learning disabilities field a pseudoscience? Learning Disability Quarterly, 103–106 (2005)
13. Kavale, K.A.: Discrepancy models in the identification of learning disability. Identification of Learning Disabilities: Research to Practice, 369–426 (2002)
14. Siegel, L.S.: An evaluation of the discrepancy definition of dyslexia. Journal of Learning Disabilities 25, 618–629 (1992)
15. Fletcher, J.M., Denton, C., Francis, D.J.: Validity of Alternative Approaches for the Identification of Learning Disabilities Operationalizing Unexpected Underachievement. Journal of Learning Disabilities 38(6), 545–552 (2005)

16. Vaughn, S., Fuchs, L.S.: Redefining learning disabilities as inadequate response to instruction: The promise and potential problems. Learning Disabilities Research & Practice 18(3), 137–146 (2003)
17. Kavale, K.A.: Identifying Specific Learning Disability Is Responsiveness to Intervention the Answer? Journal of Learning Disabilities 38(6), 553–562 (2005)
18. Fletcher, J.M., Lyon, G.R., Fuchs, L.S., Barnes, M.A.: Learning Disabilities: from identification to intervention. The Guilford Press, New York (2007)
19. Kavale, K.A., Forness, S.R.: What Definitions of Learning Disability Say and Don't Say A Critical Analysis. Journal of Learning Disabilities 33(3), 239–256 (2000)
20. Flanagan, D.P., Ortiz, S.O., Alfonso, V.C., Dynda, A.M.: Integration of response to intervention and norm - referenced tests in learning disability identification: Learning from the Tower of Babel. Psychology in the Schools 43(7), 807–825 (2006)
21. Margetis, M., Ntelidakis, A., Zabulis, X., Ntoa, S., Koutlemanis, P., Stephanidis, C.: Augmenting physical books towards education enhancement. In: The Proceedings of the 1st IEEE Workshop on User-Centred Computer Vision (UCCV 2013), Tampa, FL, USA, January 16-18 (2013)
22. Korozi, M., Leonidis, A., Margetis, G., Koutlemanis, G., Zabulis, X., Antona, M., Stephanidis, C.: Ambient educational mini-games. In: Proceedings of the International Working Conference on Advanced Visual Interfaces, pp. 802–803. ACM (2012)
23. Margetis, G., Zabulis, X., Koutlemanis, P., Antona, M., Stephanidis, C.: Augmented interaction with physical books in an Ambient Intelligence learning environment. Multimedia Tools and Applications, 1–23 (2012)
24. Georgalis, Y., Grammenos, D., Stephanidis, C.: Middleware for ambient intelligence environments: Reviewing requirements and communication technologies. Universal Access in Human-Computer Interaction. Intelligent and Ubiquitous Interaction Environments, 168–177 (2009)

Ludic Engagement Designs: Creating Spaces for Playful Learning

Eva Petersson Brooks

Centre for Design, Learning and Innovation, Department for Architecture and
Media Technology, Aalborg University Esbjerg, Niels Bohrs Vej 8,
6700 Esbjerg, Denmark
ep@create.aau.dk

Abstract. The learning within and the design of a learning (or therapeutic) situation constitutes a situated activity with inherent actions and interventions. The participant profile influences the facilitator's decisions on how to set up the attributes of the environment relative to the desired learning process and the expected outcome of that process. This paper presents a model which was developed relative to the development, use and evaluation of interactive spaces for playful learning. However, the model has a more generic value as it has been used in learning situations where other forms of resources and/or methods have been used. Thus, the general results upon which the present model is created, indicate that a playful learning tool may be construed by an open-ended design, in the sense that its (im)material affordances should in a flexible way support inclusion of different forms of emergent interaction and forms of play.

Keywords: playful learning, design, semiotic interplay, facilitation.

1   Introduction

This contribution introduces the concept of 'Ludic Engagement Designs' [1, 2]. The body of work includes an emerged model for design and intervention that transcend and cross-inform in learning and rehabilitation situations. The term 'Ludic' relates to the designed for fun/playful participant-experience for both participant (learner) and facilitator (teacher/healthcare professional). 'Engagement' refers to the targeted immersion of the participant that is achieved through the adaptation of the available environment design features so that personalisation is optimised and, thereby, creating attention and consistency through agency and by means of navigation; a semiotic interplay. In other words, ludic engagement designs include the creation of spaces for playful learning.

The paper discusses affordances of interactive environments targeting learning and rehabilitation situations as well as the participants' playful engagements and inherent semiotic interplay. In doing so, the author will use examples from a wide range of empirical material (observations, video recordings, interviews) where interactive environments have been used for learning and training in the contexts of schools, museums and rehabilitation. The participants are children and young people; typically

C. Stephanidis and M. Antona (Eds.): UAHCI/HCII 2013, Part III, LNCS 8011, pp. 241–249, 2013.

developed and with special needs. The methods used were based on a participatory design approach.

2   Ludic Engagment Designs

It has been shown in previous research that explorations are involved in the mastery of tools and in the growth of competence [3, 4, 5, 6]. In the study presented in [6], the children (with severe special needs) were dynamically exploring what was occurring as a result of their empowered control. Their discovery of the interactive space involved range, speed, and directional variation of their gestures. Children especially indicated an early awareness, observed as improved concentration, which was a result of the direct correspondence and control to the physical movement of the robotic head and the subsequent movement of the light. Such self-achievement is a rare commodity for these children. This is relative to [3] where the absence of negative consequences encouraged the participants' exploration, which resulted in development of unemployed skills. This can also be applied to the parallel findings in [5] where the children with social and behavioral disabilities felt so safe and relaxed so that, for example, they closed their eyes in front of everybody when they were asked to do so, without any questioning or unwillingness. They were engaged in the interactive situation without expectations or rules, which resulted in creative achievements through exploration and expression. Through exploring the interactive environment the participant could acquire new abilities, interactions, expressions and emotions, enabling a mastering of tasks and practicing of skills. As such, explorative actions in the interactive environment created action cycles that had the potential to evoke the child's interest in practicing otherwise limited skills, which is vital in facilitation of achieving an optimal experience. Thus, I would like to suggest, that through practicing of skills the participant experienced a sense of control and, thereby, mastery and consciousness of the therapy situation and beyond.

2.1   Transformation of Actions

As described in [4] the initial patterns of actions became the constituents for new patterns of action through exercise. [7] extends this theory by emphasizing that the introduction of mediating tools created an imbalance in the systemic organization of the actions, which enhanced changed action patterns. Similarly, findings from the studies presented in [5, 6, 8, 9] demonstrated individual variation in action cycles. For example, one of the participant in [5] showed through his facial expressions that he went through different phases of interaction where intense concentration was balanced by relaxation, yet all aspects of the physical movements were intentional within his limits. The early sessions with a participant in [8] had instances of significance where his actions signaled his desire to participate more fully with increasingly extended instances of hand gestures. The participants involved in the study presented in [6] varied the range, the speed, and the direction of their gestures. The spatial movements by the participants in the study presented in [9] demonstrated variations in actions through range, intentionality, and shift of gestures. the support from the system encouraged the participants to reach beyond their limits; thus, achieving an extenuation of the participant's potentials. Thereby, I suggest that the transformation became apparent through the form of creative actions. I see a differentiation between creative and routine actions, where the creative actions are connected to the possible and the routine actions are connected to the existing. The functions of creative actions are the generation and creation of something new. Creative actions are not only characterized by motives, goals, and operations, but also by acts that generate new motives, goals, or operations [10]. By facilitating a safe environment creative actions are enhanced within the interactive space as an important prerequisite for playful learning processes. By this, I see action cycles as precondition for playful engagement.

2.2   Traits of Playful Learning

In his writings [11] has pointed to play as a source of the child's development through the Zone of Proximal Development (ZPD) which is defined by the distance between the child's actual level of development and the potential level of development. [12] characterizes play as a precondition to flow, which means an integration of physical, emotional, and mental functions. This was supported by the play activities as described in [5, 6]. As emphasized by [13] exploration goes hand in hand with play, but is not the same as play, rather explorations serve as a precondition to play. This is exemplified by the findings presented in [5] where the system offered exploratory and expressive elements, which was defined as an activity in which the participants were engaged in for fun and for their own sake; just like play situations – without expectations or rules. [14] underlines that interest has a motivating character that channels the child's choices involved in `doings`. By this, the interest had an immediate character, which placed the participant in the midst of the play experience; that is to say that the participants became absorbed by the `here and now`, as in a flow state. As pointed to in [5] the findings demonstrated play in the form of creative achievements originating from explorations and expressive elements that motivated the sense of flow. As such the interactive play situations indicated an enhancement of the quality of play and learning, which, in turn, facilitated engaging explorations that were utilized in the therapy. This is to say that play had a motivational potential achieved from the interactive environment, which was apparent through the participant's concentration when interacting within the environment.

Findings from the participants' exploration and play within the interactive environment pointed towards awareness and enjoyment as the interaction empowered them to manipulate the technical device. The physical relationship of synchronized participant movement within the interactive space reinforced the participants' actions. This finding was supported by the studies presented in [8, 9]. I argue that this reinforcement of actions is directed by the participant or by the facilitator's concern with overcoming of restrictions and with the development of new and improved actions. In the study presented in [9] findings showed that the participants' use of the body when navigating within the computer game environment as well as the immediate feedback in the form of game content had the potential to reduce the physical load in the daily physical rehabilitation. Findings reported in [6] emphasize the immediate feedback that supported the participant to incrementally push their movement limits. All in all, these results point to playful learning potentials from actions and interactions within interactive environments. I consider play as a crucial foundation for playful learning and it was evident in the findings that the interactive play was closely connected to learning aspects exemplified mainly through the effects of the participant's feed-forward (movements) resulting in self achievement, which is commonly rare for individuals with severe disabilities. The findings pointed to the components of (i) the merging of action and awareness, (ii) concentration, and (iii) the melting together of actions and consciousness. The fourth component of flow, according to [12], concerning the transformation of time was indicated by the facilitators in the form that the participants tended to continue to interact until they were more or less exhausted even after the end of the session.

My conclusion from this is that the use of the body in the interaction was motivating and created curiosity among the participants so as to continue their play and to practice their otherwise limited skills. This extends the concept of autotelic activity to also embrace the concept of aesthetic resonance. [15] refers to interactions such as reported in this paper as instrumental exploration, motivated and learned by the cause and effect and surprise exploration awaked by pure and simple novelty. This is to say that the instrumental and the surprise exploration achieved from the interactive environment are relational as forms of motivation due to the novelty [15].

3   Spaces for Playful Learning

This section discusses design features that influence learning in interactive environments by emphasizing open-ended interfaces and adaptation of the system through facilitator intervention. Previous research has defined the quality of intuitiveness as a crucial usability factor so as to be easy to learn and use [16]. This finding is supported by the studies presented in [5, 6, 8], where the participants put fewer loads on cognitive processing through the immediate and aesthetically adapted feedback from the system used in the studies.

Findings presented in [17] showed that tactile, visual, and audio feedback encouraged exploration and gestures, which was identified as open-ended features of design through the alterative opportunities in the interaction that was offered through these different modalities. Affordances in the form of shapes and surfaces offered information and creative values for the interaction. The findings presented in the previous paragraph (relative to findings from [5, 6, 8]) add to the fact that the situation within the kinesphere [18] – augmented as a volumetric information space where the participants' gestures were mapped, translated by the interface as control data to respond with selectable multimedia content manipulation in an immediate manner – clearly offered invisible affordances for the participant to act upon. This fact was enhanced by the non-intrusive interface, which, according to [19], offers the qualities of transparency and reflectivity through the mirroring of the participant's complexity of needs and desires. Thus, I conclude that the invisible affordances of the interface exhibit a tactile character through the manipulation, both direct and immediate, encouraged the participant's actions within the space. This extends the definition of an open-ended interface to also embrace the invisible gestural modality of the system. These findings are relative to the findings presented in [5, 6, 8] where the participants experienced safety and control when they interacted within the responsive environment, which empowered them to make own choices. The connection between these studies is supported by [20] `actant´ theory, where he emphasizes that other people as well as objects are equivalent as actants from the individual's perspective. The main point is that these aspects of intervention, including (i) adaptation of the system, (ii) creation of user profile, (iii) and intersubjectivity, represent different levels of practice and realization. Each of them contributes to the quality assurances based on the facilitator's judgements in and on action [21].

4   Composition of Playful Learning and Design

Previously in this paper it has been argued that the interactive environments used in the studies included in the paper, can be seen as a specific accessible technology allowing movement empowered by non-invasive technology. In this section an encapsulation of learning and design features within an interactive environment is presented through a model which, on the basis of the findings presented in the previous sections, describes the state and space of optimized motivation. The model which is proposed describes playful learning in interactive environments based on [12] theory on flow, Leont'ev's three level model of activity [23], and [22] theory on the Zone of Proximal Development (ZPD) in learning situations, and modified in order to better describe the processes that are dealt with here. The model was applied to better understand the findings from the individual empirical studies, but also to be able to take these findings a step further and develop a more comprehensive understanding of ludic engagement designs.

The model (fig. 1) is based on a boundary of the zone of optimization, which contains the on-going action cycles between the subject and the system as well as the continuous interventions from the outside agent to the system. These interventions can cause an ambiguity in the situation due to the fact that the goal of the action is equilibrium for a moment. The outside agent makes on-going judgements in and on the situation, i.e. when to intervene and how to adjust the multimedia feedback to fit the subject's wishes, desires, and level of competence. In this way the challenge with inherent surprises for the subject becomes optimal. The ambiguity in the situation is in the creation of an intersubjective activity , which is based on asymmetry rather than symmetric functioning. Bakhtin [25] dialogic concept of polyphony is representational of what is being approached in this situation. In other words, through the intervention more than one voice in the communication is active, the outside agent's through the intervention, the subject through the feedforward, and the system, which represents a distinct voice through the feedback. This can be thought of as a jointly created dialogue. When an increased level of shared situation takes place [26] a transfer of responsibility of the task is accomplished; i.e. the intra-subjective process. The

ZPD is defined as the distance between the actual level of development, - which is determined through the child's own way of solving problems - and the potential level of development, - which is defined through guidance of the adult [22]. Outside the borderline is a zone representing the aesthetic resonance grow zone and the edge zone, which is relative to the ZPD [22] in that the support from the outside agent and the system as mediating tools in order for the subject to reach beyond his or her limits is emphasized; aesthetic resonance.

In this way, the state of aesthetic resonance constitutes a bridge between inter and intra-subjective processes. This also includes an intra-subjective process according to the outside agent. The outside agent is involved in multifaceted judgements and re-sponsibilities. He or she is not only focused on achieving a specific activity, but also on the minimally required intervention (adaptation of system and/or guidance – phys-ical or verbally) so as to best maintain the subject's interest and engagement in the situation. An understanding relative to the importance of interest, curiosity, and en-joyment are inherent as resources for learning. According to [10] the model is repre-sentational of creative processes rather than as a sequential routine as the participant within the activity situation is involved in exploring and extending their skills, inten-tions and ideas. Thus, my preference is to create the conditions and design the activi-ties that most likely will lead to the desired learning I have in mind. In terms of [27] this should be focused upon the qualities as integral to the experience that leads to learning. To do this, activities that encourage actions and interaction are designed. This complexity is illustrated in Fig. 1 below.

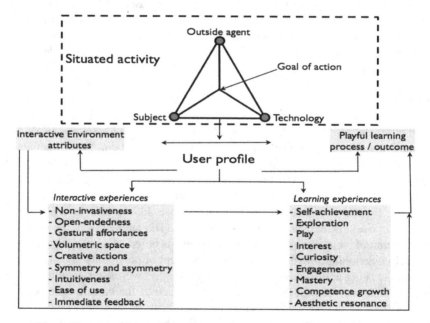

Fig. 1. The composition of learning and design in interactive environments

The learning within and the ludic engagement design constitutes a situated activity, with inherent actions and interventions. The goal of action is established according to the user by the facilitator determining a user's initial profile, which is incrementally refined as a result of session analysis. The profile influences the facilitator's decisions on how to set up the attributes of the virtual environment relative to the desired learning process and the expected outcome of that process. These decisions influence the learning process and the outcome of that process. All in all, this is an iterative process, which supports a holistic view on the design of interactive environments towards learning.

5   Conclusions

The goal of this paper was to offer an approach to and definition of the concept of 'Ludic Engagement Designs'. By scrutinising affordances of interactive environments targeting learning and rehabilitation and participants' playful engagements through actions, a model was proposed describing ludic engagement designs as an approach to create spaces for playful learning. The model constitutes a foundation for the contemplation of design issues that have emerged as having a generic outcome that offers opportunities and potential for other interactive environments that have been designed as remedial play environments for children.

Multimedia feedback was synchronously manipulated from sourced data movement information from each participant. The data was sourced through invisible volumetric non-invasive sensor technology [30]. The results highlighted positive effects of the interaction within the responsive environment by those with severe disabilities as well as typically developed participants, and conclude at the potential of the concept as a supplement to traditional learning and therapy techniques. Furthermore, the results highlighted the intervention strategy with the facilitator as a key person and having a prerequisite for targeting the participant's motivated engagement and ludic experiences. The attributes of the technology and of the interactive environments supported playful learning and I reflect on the central principle of learning without expectations or rules: creating spaces that build upon and is influenced by the participant's interest. Interventions create opportunities for the facilitator to learn from his or her own involvement as they support and encourage the participants to learn.

This creation of this paper has been an act of iterative reflection and analysis. Using this approach, interpretations and understandings can be made and differences in impact of using different feedback to the user can be examined. Thus, in closing, I state that it is not possible to capture or describe other peoples' experiences, nor is it possible to understand the world exactly like it is for others. However, it is possible to strive from the perspectives of our own lives to understand how the other person experiences something and then to compare it with situations we are aware of from our own experiences.

References

1. Petersson, E.: Editorial: Ludic Engagement Designs for All. In: Digital Creativity, vol. 19(3), pp. 141–144. Routledge, London (2008)
2. Beach, F.A.: Comparison of Copulatory Behaviour of Male Rats Raised in Isolation, Cobahitation, and Segregation. Journal of Genetic Changing World 60, 121–136 (1942)
3. Bruner, J.S.: Organization of Early Skilled Action. Child Development 44(1), 1–11 (1973)
4. Brooks, A., Petersson, E.: Recursive Reflection and Learning in Raw Data Video Analysis of Interactive 'Play' Environments for Special Needs Health Care. In: Proceedings of Healthcom 2005. 7th International Workshop on Enterprise Networking and Computing in Healthcare Industry, Busan, Korea, pp. 83–87 (2005)
5. Brooks, A., Petersson, E.: Humanics 2: Human Computer Interaction in Acquired Brain Injury Rehabilitation. In: Proceedings of HCI International 2005. Lawrence and Erlbaum Associates, Las Vegas (2005)
6. Petersson, E., Brooks, A.: Non-formal Therapy and Learning Potentials through Human Gesture Synchronized to Robotic Gesture [HRI] within a Virtual Environment [VE]. Universal Access in the Information Society 6, 166–177 (2007)
7. Wertsch, J.V.: Mind as Action. Oxford University Press, New York (1998)
8. Brooks, A., Petersson, E.: Raw emotional signalling, via expressive behaviour. In: Proceedings of the 15th International Conference on Artificial Reality and Telexistence, Christchurch, New Zealand, pp. 133–141 (2005)
9. Brooks, A., Petersson, E.: Play Therapy Utilizing the Sony EyeToy®. In: The Proceedings of Presence 2005, London, UK, pp. 303–314 (2005)
10. Tikhomirov, O.K.: The Theory of Activity Changed by Information Technology. In: Engeström, Y., Miettinen, R., Punamäki, R.-L. (eds.) Perspectives on Activity Theory. Cambridge University Press, Cambridge (1999)
11. Vygotsky, L.S.: The Genesis of Higher Mental Functions. In: Wertsch, J.V. (ed.) The Concept of Activity in Soviet Psychology. Sharpe, New York (1981)
12. Csikszentmihalyi, M.: Flow: The Psychology of Optimal Experience. Harper Perennial, New York (1991)
13. Bruner, J.S.: Nature and Uses of Immaturity. In: Bruner, J.S., Jolly, A., Sylva, K. (eds.) Play - Its Role in Development and Evolution. Basic Books, United States (1976)
14. Rogoff, B.: Apprenticeship in Thinking. Cognitive Development in Social Context. Oxford University Press, New York (1990)
15. Berlyne, D.E.: Novelty and Curiosity as Determinants of Exploratory Behaviour. Brittish Journal of Psychology 41, 61–80 (1950)
16. Bærentsen, S.: Intuitive User Interfaces. Scandinavian Journal of Information Systems 12, 29–59 (2000)
17. Petersson, E., Brooks, A.: Virtual and Physical Toys – Open-ended Features towards Non-formal Learning. Cyber Psychology and Behavior 9(2), 196–199 (2006)
18. Laban, R.: Modern Educational Dance. MacDonald and Evans, Bungay (1963)
19. Bolter, J.D., Gromala, D.: Windows and Mirrors. Interactive Design, Digital Art, and the Myth of Transparency. The MIT Press, Cambridge (2003)
20. Latour, B.: Technology is Society Made Durable. In: Law, J. (ed.) A Sociology of Monsters. Essays on Power, Technology and Domination, Routledge, New York (1991)
21. Löwgren, J., Stolterman, E.: Thoughtful Interaction Design. A Design Perspective on Information Technology. The MIT Press, Cambridge (2004)
22. Vygotsky, L.S.: Mind in Society. The Development of Higher Psychological Processes. Harvard University Press, Cambridge (1978)

23. Leontév, A.N.: Activity, Consciousness and Personality. Prentice-Hall, Englewood Cliffs (1981)
24. Lave, J., Wenger, E.: Situated Learning. Legitimate Peripheral Participation. Cambridge University, NY (1991)
25. Bakhtin, M.M.: The Dialogical Imagination: Four Essays. In: Holquist, M. (ed.) (1994)
26. Wertsch, J.V.: Vygotsky and the Social Formation of Mind. Harvard University Press, Cambridge (1985)
27. Rogoff, B.: Becoming a Cooperative Parent in a Parent Cooperative. In: Rogoff, B., Goodman Turkanis, C., Bartlett, L. (eds.) Learning Together. Oxford University Press, New York (2001)
28. Brooks, T., Camurri, A., Canagarahah, N., Hasselblad, S.: Interaction with Shapes and Sounds as a Therapy for Special Needs and Rehabilitation. In: Proceedings of the 4th International Conference on Disability, Virtual Reality & Associated Technologies, pp. 205–212 (2002)
29. Brooks, A., Hasselblad, S.: CAREHERE - Creating Aestetically Resonant Environments for the Handicapped, Elderly and Rehabilitation: Sweden. In: Sharkey, P., McCrindle, R., Brown, D. (eds.) 5th International Conference on Disability, Virtual Reality & Associated Technologies, pp. 191–198 (2004)
30. Brooks, A.L.: Virtual Interactive Space (V.I.S.) as a Movement Capture Interface Tool Giving Multimedia Feedback for Treatment and Analysis. In: The International Symposium for Integrative Medicine & Expressive Therapies, pp. 3–22 (1999)

Supporting Accessibility in Higher Education Information Systems

Arsénio Reis[1], João Barroso[2], and Ramiro Gonçalves[2]

[1] University of Trás-os-Montes e Alto Douro, Vila Real, Portugal
ars@utad.pt
[2] INESC TEC (formerly INESC Porto) and University of Trás-os-Montes e
Alto Douro, Vila Real, Portugal
{jbarroso,ramiro}@utad.pt

Abstract. Higher education institutions (HEI) and students are highly dependent of information systems, implemented as web applications. Students must be able to access this applications, thought accessible web interfaces, in order to perform their academic activities. This paper presents an overview of a typical set of web applications used by students and the main concerns regarding accessibility compliance. The analysis was conducted using the systems at the University of Trás-os-Montes e Alto Douro.

Keywords: Higher education institutions, Accessibility, W3C, Moodle, DSpace.

1 Introduction

Higher Education is a complex business, highly supported by Information Technology and Information Systems. Some of these information systems have web interfaces that enable students to access faculty services that, in some cases, were previously available as human interactions. The electronic interface, mainly the web, is now the default interface for accessing faculty services and, in some cases, the human infra-structure was restructured and is non-existent, leaving the electronic interface as the only interface. In this scenario, the electronic interface must be accessible by all students with no exception [1].

Higher education students are a special set of the population in terms of age and intellectual capability. Most information systems and software packages used in HEI are well typified in terms of business model and software implementation, so in addition to applying the common standards for accessibility, it´s interesting to analyze this population and the information systems used at the university in greater detail. Another interesting particularity of HEI is the fact that teachers are content creators and sometimes class designers with different perceptions of the concept of accessibility and the role they play on assuring that same accessibility.

C. Stephanidis and M. Antona (Eds.): UAHCI/HCII 2013, Part III, LNCS 8011, pp. 250–255, 2013.
© Springer-Verlag Berlin Heidelberg 2013

In this paper we follow a simple three steps method:

1. Characterize a typical set of information systems used in higher education institutions, of which the University of Trás-os-Montes e Alto Douro (UTAD) is well representative, as well as a user population, in regard to special accessibilities needs. In this case, the UTAD students.
2. Analyze the information systems [2], [3], regarding their compliance to W3C standards.
3. Conclude on the degree of accessibility provided by the university electronic services available to students and on some recommendations on how to effectively act to ensure accessibility.

1.1   Web Accessibility

Web accessibility can be defined as a practice of design, develop and edit web sites usable by all people without regard for their level of ability or disability, thus, granting equal access to information and functionality has normal people would have [4]. According to Jim Thatcher and Shaw Henry, web accessibility goal is to provide people with disability, the ability to perceive, understand, navigate and interact with the Web, including visual, hearing, physical, cognitive, speech or neurological impairments [5], [6].

1.2   Student Population

The Portuguese National Institute of Statistics (INE) developed a demographic study, in 2002, about the Portuguese population, regarding disabilities. According to this study, there were 634.000 Portuguese citizens with some kind of disability. This number accounts for about 6% of the country population, of about 10 million people [7].

The student's population of UTAD consists of about 7.000 students. According to the national percentage of citizen with disability, of 6%, there should be about 420 students with some kind of special access need.

At registration, each student is asked to voluntarily declare any disabilities. The sole purpose of this declaration is to provide proper access and support for a normal student's life on campus. Unfortunately a large number of students with light disabilities chooses not to declare them.

1.3   Information Systems in Higher Education Institutions

In Higher Education Institutions (HEI) there is a set of information systems, used by students that are implemented by distinct software systems. These systems are characterized by their purpose and sometimes by their proprietary within the institutional organics.

A well representative set can be found at the University of Trás-os-Montes e Alto Douro (UTAD) as described in the following topics.

Scientific Repository. The scientific repository purpose is to archive the documents related to research activities of the institution, including, articles, book chapter, thesis, etc. This system is a key element of the open access movement and institutional policies.

At UTAD the software package used is DSPACE [8], one of the most popular software packages built for this specific purpose.

Elearning. The elearning component purpose is to provide support for the teaching and learning activities. Teachers and students can manage content, activities and administrative tasks on this platforms. Although designated as "elearning", most times it is used for general pedagogical class management, also including b-leaning and traditional learning. At UTAD the software package used is Moodle [9].

Library. The library component purpose is to provide management support for the HEI library. It is used by the library staff for their management activities and it is used by students when interacting with the library services, such as, book requesting, catalog search, etc.

UTAD uses the Porbase software package [10], develop and distributed by the Portuguese National Library and widely used in Portuguese libraries. The student interaction with this component is fairly low and it's mostly used by library staff.

Student Portal. The student portal component is a web portal dedicated to provide information and services, related to the students' academic life, such as: course registration; fees payment; class scheduling; student grades, etc. It is used by all students and professors, on a daily basis and is one the most important components for the faculty regular activities. It is also used by some non-teaching staff. In some institutions, this component is integrated with the eleaning component.

At UTAD this portal is an in-house development project, named SIDE, using LAMP (Linux, Apache, Mysql and PHP), that implements the business model processes related to students, teachers, learning, teaching and administration. The SIDE Portal has a broad spectrum of usage and is tailored to meet the students and teachers information needs. Accessibility is a most important issue in this portal, as any student failing to access SIDE's information will not be able to execute his daily activities.

Institutional Portal. This component is the HEI web portal and its main purpose is to act has a communication channel from the HEI to the general public. Some parts of this portal are focused on the HEI business interests, such as, attracting students, publicizing research achievements, etc.

At UTAD the portal is implemented using the Microsoft sharepoint 2010 platform as a web site content manager.

Table 1. Systems used by students and their purposes

Purpose	System
Scientific repository	DSpace
E-learning	Moodle
Learning and student management	SIDE
Library	Porbase
General information	Website

2   Accessibility Concerns

For this analysis, the systems, previously described, were grouped in two. The first include Moodle and DSpace; the second includes the in-house developed web portals.

2.1   Moodle and DSpace

The tests performed with Total Validator [11] were somehow ambiguous, as it is difficult to separate the pure software platform from the usage practice made by administrators, content creators and external web developers. In a strict sense, we didn't found a single point of total inaccessibility in this platforms, although some had to be tackled by the user.

As an example, in moodle, if the user uses a screen-reader, it will have to turn off the HTML editor on the user profile. As a software platform, moodle has a configuration option for the administrator and the user to choose an external editor. So although there is a latent accessibility problem the software has the necessary configuration options to overcome the problem. In this scenario, it is the administrator practice that dictates the accessibility.

In another example, the teacher role, as a content creator, is determinant on accessibility: if the teacher decides for a poor choice of colors, such as, pale green text over a yellow background; not to write proper alt-text for images; upload video and audio without proper transcript; etc. On this example, the content will not be accessible at all and accessibility will not be platform dependent.

2.2   Student Portal and Institutional Portal

These portals were developed in-house. The student portal is based on a LAMP infrastructure and the institutional portal is based on a sharepoint platform. On the student portal it is the developers responsibly to ensure and enforce accessibility. The design does not allow for administrator or user configuration, capable of changing accessibility. As previously stated, this portal is an in-house project and it is of most importance for the university daily life. The user interface is very simple in order to ensure user access and compatibility across browser and hardware platforms. UTAD is the only Portuguese university with a graduation on Accessibility, so the university most important web application is always under scrutiny regarding its accessibility compliance and usability [12].

On the institutional portal, the sharepoint 2010 platform is well documented as a platform for achieving accessibility [13], and it the template designer and developer responsibility to ensure an accessible interface.

3   Conclusion

The analysis has shown that the three platforms in use (moodle, dspace and share-point) didn't presented intrinsic accessibilities issues. The platforms are generic and flexible enough and it is up to the developers and administrators to ensure proper development and configuration practices. In the moodle case, it also the teacher role that must follow good accessibility practices. Teachers and administrators are a large group of people and a strategy should be designed to ensure the desire accessibility compliance. In such a large group, the correct practice should evolve to a cultural sustainable practice.

In the web portals group it was shown that the accessibly compliance depends solely on the designers and developers practice. Thus it can be predetermined has a design and implementation requirement, which can also be tested prior to the system acceptance and deployment. In the SIDE portal, beside accessibility, usability is also an issue and the design options were taken to accommodate both concepts together [14] [15].

References

1. Accessibility vs. Usability vs. W3C Web "Standards", Accessibility and Usability at Pen State, http://accessibility.psu.edu/usability (accessed on February 2013)
2. Freire, A.P., Fortes, R.P.M., Turine, M.A.S., Paiva, D.M.B.: An Evaluation of Web Accessibility Metrics based on their Attributes. In: SIGDOC 2008. Proceedings of the 26th ACM International Conference on Design of Communication, Lisboa, Portugal, vol. 1, pp. 73–80. ACM Press, New York (2008)
3. Evaluating Accessibility, W3C Web Accessibility initiative, http://www.w3.org/WAI/eval/Overview.html
4. Yonaitis, R.: Understanding Accessibility: A Guide to Achieving Compliance on Web Sites and Intranets. HiSoftware, New Hampshire (2002)
5. Thatcher, et al: Constructing accessible web sites, http://tocs.ulb.tu-darmstadt.de/202240762.pdf

6. Gonçalves, R., Martins, J., Pereira, J., Mamede, H.: Portuguese Web Accessibility in Electronic Public Procurement Platforms. In: 2010 5th Iberian Conference on Information Systems and Technologies (CISTI), June 16-19 (2010)
7. INE, Censos 2001 – População residente com deficiência Segundo o grau de incapacidade e sexo (2002)
8. DSpace project, http://www.dspace.org
9. Moodle project, http://www.moodle.org
10. Porbase project, http://porbase5.mind.pt
11. Total Validator (2012), http://www.totalvalidator.com/ (accessed on December 2012)
12. Guide for developing usable web sites, http://www.usability.gov/ (accessed December 2012)
13. Fleming, R.: Achieving Accessibility in SharePoint 2010 (2012),
http://blogs.msdn.com/b/education/archive/2012/02/28/
achieving-accessibility-in-sharepoint-2010.aspx (accessed February 2013)
14. Web Accessibility and Usability Working Together,
http://www.w3.org/WAI/intro/usable (accessed on February 2013)
15. Roe, P.: Bridging the Gap. Access to telecommunications for all people. Comissão Europeia, Suíça (2001)

Social Media as Online Mentoring Tools
for STEM Students With and Without Disabilities

Robert L. Todd

Georgia Institute of Technology
CATEA
490 10th Street
Atlanta, GA 30318
USA
robert.todd@coa.gatech.edu

Abstract. Considerable attention has been given to the need for educating a diverse workforce in science, technology, engineering, and mathematics (STEM). Public and regulatory institutions have stressed the importance of efforts to recruit and retain students chronically underrepresented in STEM fields. Individuals with disabilities are among the most marginalized of these groups and face significant barriers to accessing higher education STEM programs. This paper will discuss affordances for e-mentoring of students in STEM education, with a focus on universal design for online learning and inclusion of all students, especially those with functional limitations due to disability. Preliminary data from ongoing research will be reviewed and discussed.

Keywords: e-mentoring, STEM, disability, social media, virtual worlds.

1   Introduction

Considerable attention has been given to the need for educating a diverse workforce in science, technology, engineering, and mathematics (STEM). United States National Science Foundation reports (NSF 1996, 2000, 2004) stress the importance of efforts to recruit and retain students chronically underrepresented in STEM fields. Individuals with disabilities are among the most marginalized of these groups (Wolanin & Steele, 2004) and face significant barriers to accessing higher education STEM programs (Burgstahler, 1994; NSF, 2000). This paper will discuss affordances for e-mentoring of students with disabilities (SwD) in STEM education as an important component in the solution to this lack of representation.

Students with disabilities and their teachers use a variety of social media and computer-mediated communication (CMC) tools in mentoring relationships through electronic mentoring (e-mentoring) (Todd, 2012). As e-mentoring can occur asynchronously, it has benefits not found with face-to-face (FtF) programs. While traditional FtF mentoring is often conceived as a dyadic relationship in which a senior, experienced individual provides support and guidance for a less-experienced one (Gay, 1994), e-mentoring has contributed to an expansion of this concept to include

C. Stephanidis and M. Antona (Eds.): UAHCI/HCII 2013, Part III, LNCS 8011, pp. 256–265, 2013.

lateral, hierarchical, group and asynchronous versus synchronous mentoring and to applications in expanded contexts (Ensher, Heun & Blanchard, 2003).

A growing literature base describes e-mentoring programs and their usefulness in educational, business, human resources, and social environments (Gregg, Chang, & Todd, 2012; O'Neill & Harris, 2004; Single & Single, 2005) and e-mentoring has demonstrated positive impacts on at-risk students' educational and personal goals (iMentor project, MentorNet 2012, Todd, 2012). Furthermore, e-mentoring has shown benefits through removal of geographic boundaries, including international collaborations, and positive effects through multiple cohorts of students of different educational levels and inclusion of professionals (McCarthy, 2012). E-mentoring also has demonstrated advantages for numerically small, isolated members of underrepresented groups in specific STEM fields, empowering communication, support, information exchange and other mentoring activities where otherwise impossible (Jefferson, Hannula, Campbell, et al., 2010).

2   Computer-Based Social Media Mentoring

Potentially, any form of computer-mediated communication, from relatively early formats such as listservs and email to the latest applications can provide means for e-mentoring. But as social media platforms and tools (as typified by user-generated content (Agichtein, et al., 2008)) become more powerful and ubiquitous, options for e-mentoring continue to expand. McCarthy (2012) reports on the successful use of Facebook as an e-mentoring tool among students and professionals, across international boundaries and among multivariate cohorts. Jefferson, Hannula, Campbell, et al., (2010) discuss the affordances of online blogging tools as a means of mentoring among diverse and underrepresented geoscientists. Voice over IP (VoIP) tools like Skype have seen growing use as e-mentoring tools, both in one-on-one and group mentoring situations, and with disability-related support such as mentoring of special education teachers (Smith & Israel, 2010). In addition, dedicated mentoring platforms, both software and browser-based, have grown in number and breadth of application, such as SocialLearn, as reported by Liu, Macintyre & Ferguson (2012). In many e-mentoring programs, combinations of tools, processes and applications are employed to provide custom e-mentoring experiences, and researchers provide students with disability-specific solutions to accessibility challenges (Todd, 2012).

3   Virtual Worlds

Among the newer CMC technologies, virtual worlds, or simulated 2-D and 3-D online environments (e.g. Second Life), have become an increasingly common software platform for education and training applications during the last decade (cf. Chou & Hart, 2012; Cremorne, 2009; deNoyelles & Kyeong-Ju Seo, 2012; Kingston, 2011; Taylor, 2002; Jones, 2007; Brown & Bell, 2004; Gerald & Antonacci, 2009) including e-mentoring (Todd, 2012; de Freitas, 2008). Virtual platforms can present their own challenges to full accessibility, but proper design and use of assistive technologies can make them usable and effective for SwDs (Todd, Baker & Pater, 2012; Folmer, Yuan, Carr & Sapre, 2009; Forman, Baker, Pater & Smith, 2012; Mancuso, Chlup, & McWhorter, 2010; Stendal, Molka-Danielsen, Munkvold & Balandin, 2011).

One common finding about the educational uses of virtual worlds is that immersion, or "the subjective impression that one is participating in a comprehensive, realistic experience" (Dede, 2009) can enhance the learning experience. Researchers have also observed that virtual worlds offer possibilities for experiential learning through specific mentoring activities; an approach that encourages students to engage in problem solving activities within a flexible environment that facilitates collaborative and constructivist learning (Cremorne, 2009). Educators have also been drawn to the potential that virtual worlds offer for distance mentoring through social interaction and learner engagement (Chou & Hart, 2012). In these applications, the presence of avatars can enhance "engagement and learning beyond computer-mediated communication without such agents" (Jarmon, 2008). Researchers have also noted the capacity of virtual worlds to facilitate experiential learning (Jarmon, Traphagan, Mayrath & Trivedi, 2009) via simulations, role-playing, and group work that can be used within mentoring activities (Duncan, Miller & Jiang, 2012; Inman et al., 2010).

4   Mobile Devices

Like many CMC solutions, virtual worlds are still most easily accessed from traditional personal computers (PCs), but there are opportunities to supplement PC based e-mentoring with mobile devices. Within the CMC rubric, modern students are increasingly turning to mobile computing platforms to stay connected when away from a PC, and the most commonly used devices are smartphones (Herrington, 2009). As a CMC platform, the smartphone is rapidly maturing. According to a yearly survey of college students, 99% own a cell phone, 69% of which are smartphones (Hanley, 2012). Hanley also reports that 99% of students use short messaging service (SMS), also known as "texting," many of whom text even while in class. Research suggests that SMS classroom communication can be educationally effective when properly implemented (Markett, Sanchez, Weber, Tangney, 2008), and instructors are taking advantage of texting to implement anonymous response systems, polling, and just-in-time communication techniques that have been used in mentoring (McClean, Hagan, & Morgan, 2010). While smartphone accessibility is far from perfect, studies indicate a growing trend for accessible input and output in these devices, increasing their use by SwDs (Lippincott, Morris & Mueller, 2011).

Smartphones also enable students to stay connected to social media on the go, including aforementioned tools such as Facebook. Patten, Sanchez and Tangney (2006) have identified several other common uses of smartphones by students, including video chatting and Tweeting. Research indicates that a majority of students use their smartphones for social stimulation, to remain continually available, to leave memos and reminders, and for time-keeping (Tindell & Bohlander (2012). These tools all have potential benefits for mentoring (Todd, 2012; Khalil, 2008).

5   Preliminary Results from BreakThru Research

Funded by the National Science Foundation Research in Disability Education division (award # 1027655), the Georgia STEM Accessibility Alliance provides online mentoring to secondary and post-secondary students with disabilities in STEM education through its BreakThru project. BreakThru studies the use and effectiveness of online mentoring in high schools, two-year college and university settings and on students with a wide range of disabilities, including learning, mobility, dexterity, health, sensory and cognitive concerns. Students are paired with mentors who are STEM instructors, graduate students, or professionals employed in the STEM workforce. Mentors provide guidance, support, information and networking assistance to enrolled students, with all contact effected through social media methods, including a 3-D virtual world island, e-mail, Skype (audio-only and video with audio), SMS (texting via smartphone), and telephone voice communication. BreakThru has created virtual world islands through the medium of Second Life, providing accessibility modifications and features to include all participants. Students and mentors in the program are allowed to freely choose their preferred methods of communication from the aforementioned tools. In addition, some student/mentor pairs include limited face-to-face contact, where appropriate.

The following project data is formative and preliminary, excerpted from Fall 2012 BreakThru results, but may help to shed light on the ways in which students, teachers and professionals can incorporate social and online media into mentoring activities. More complete interpretive and summative data from BreakThru will be published in future.

Thirty mentees completed a survey in Fall 2012 that was designed to gauge their satisfaction with mentoring. The following constructs were assessed on the mentee survey:

1. **Personal Responsibility:** degree to which mentor enhances interpersonal development among mentees
2. **Satisfaction:** sense of fulfillment in the mentoring relationship
3. **Communication-quantity:** satisfaction with frequency and duration of communication (extent)
4. **Communication-quality:** satisfaction with the quality of communication
5. **Support Seeking:** degree of support provided (academic and personal)

Additionally, the mentee survey explores the types of communication mediums being utilized and the level of satisfaction with each medium.

5.1   Results and Discussion

Table 1 summarizes mentees' average responses to the constructs listed above. It is evident that all constructs were rated above the optimal average of 4 on a 5-point likert scale where 1 signifies strongly disagree and 5 signifies strongly agree. The results show that participants enjoyed and saw the benefits of the mentor/mentee program, especially in the communication realm. For example, all 30 of the mentees indicated that they always felt respected and supported during sessions with their mentors.

Table 1.

Constructs	Mean	Strongly Disagree (1)	Disagree (2)	Neither (3)	Agree (4)	Strongly Agree (5)
Personal Responsibility	4.34	0%	1%	10%	44%	46%
Satisfaction	4.53	0%	0%	7%	33%	60%
Communication-*quantity*	4.40	0%	0%	12%	36%	52%
Communication-*quality*	4.68	0%	0%	3%	25%	71%
Support Seeking	4.41	0%	0%	9%	42%	49%

The same students responded to measures of engagement in the mentoring process via Second Life and other BreakThru social networking tools, such as Facebook, Twitter, email and Skype). Results indicated generally positive engagement, but suggested that Second Life may require further training or experience to be used most effectively. Students were, in general, less experienced and confident in use of the virtual world platform as opposed to more familiar affordances, and expressed some difficulties with technical issues, such as audio input and output in Second Life.

Table 2.

Engagement	n	Mean	Strongly Disagree (1)	Disagree (2)	Neither/ Neutral (3)	Agree (4)	Strongly Agree (5)
a. Using Second Life for mentoring was a positive experience for me.	30	3.37	10%	10%	33%	27%	20%
b. I feel comfortable using Second Life for my mentoring.	29	3.31	10%	10%	31%	34%	14%
c. Using social networks (such as Facebook, Twitter, email, Skype) helped me build a relationship with my mentee.	30	4.27	7%	0%	10%	27%	57%

Table 2. (*continued*)

d. My background/ experiences allow me to relate to my mentee.	29	4.31	3%	0%	0%	55%	41%

Frequency of use of communication media and student self-report indicate that they tended to use the tools most familiar to them and most readily "at-hand," including tools available through portable mobile devices such as smartphones.

Table 3.

Check all the ways you communicate with your mentor (Please check all that apply.)	n	%	Rank
Second Life	14	47%	4
Email	29	97%	1 (highest)
Facebook	10	33%	5
Twitter	0	0%	8(lowest)
Skype	9	30%	6
Texting	18	60%	3
Telephone	23	77%	2
In person	7	23%	7
Other	0	0%	8 (lowest)

Results with students and mentors indicated a need for training on multiple levels, but especially in the use of the virtual world platform of Second Life, largely unfamiliar to all respondents. A 1.5 hour virtual training session was conducted with project participants in Fall 2012, and results from one cadre of 21 students and 12 mentor trainees are summarized below. Trainees were instructed in basic movement of avatars, communicating with others, and advanced features, such as accessing web media through Second Life, group communications, manipulating in-world objects and travelling to alternate destinations.

On average, participants rated all of the agenda items above the critical limit of 3.5 or higher. Overall, the participants rated the agenda topics as a 3.75 for informative, a 3.85 for useful, and a 3.74 for engaging on a 4-point likert scale where 1 signifies "not at all" and 4 signifies "very much." Given that the primary goal of Second Life is to interact and learn with other participants, reinforcing the importance of communicating with other avatars may warrant further training.

Table 4.

	Mean[1]	Rank
Basic Movement (forward, backwards, turning, jumping)	3.91	1 (*highest*)
Communicating with other users	3.68	3 (*lowest*)
Advanced features	3.70	2
Overall average	**3.76**	

In responses to the open-ended questions, participants indicated that they need additional technical assistance in creating and navigating their avatars, and in reconciling audio problems encountered during the training session(s).

Table 5.

Modules		N	Mean	1 (not at all)	2	3	4 (to a great extent)
Basic Movement (forward, backwards, turning, jumping)	Informative	20	3.95	0%	0%	5%	95%
	Useful	19	3.89	0%	0%	11%	89%
	Engaging	18	3.89	0%	0%	11%	89%
Communicating with other users	Informative	19	3.74	0%	5%	16%	79%
	Useful	19	3.74	0%	5%	16%	79%
	Engaging	19	3.58	0%	11%	21%	68%
Advanced features	Informative	20	3.55	5%	5%	20%	70%
	Useful	18	3.78	0%	0%	22%	78%
	Engaging	17	3.76	0%	6%	12%	82%

In terms of comfort using the Second Life platform for e-mentoring, the training indicates that both students and mentors can quickly achieve a reasonable level of satisfaction, but further training and experience may be necessary to achieve a target mean of 3.5 or higher, which would indicate "great extant" of comfort.

Table 6.

Based on today's training, I...	n	Mean	1 (not at all)	2	3	4 (to a great extent)
Am more comfortable using Second Life	21	3.48	0%	10%	33%	57%
Am better able to use Second Life to support students.[1]	12	3.50	0%	8%	33%	58%
Am comfortable with the amount of support the trainers provided.	21	3.62	0%	5%	29%	67%

6   Conclusion

CMC solutions, including virtual worlds and smartphone technologies, open new possibilities for e-mentoring SwDs. Virtual worlds include technology, accessibility and learning challenges for many students, but can provide a rich mentoring experience with increased sense of immersion, with proper training. Mobile computing platforms such as smartphones can supplement more traditional PC-based e-mentoring, and in some cases can provide equivalent affordances to typical CMCs, such as e-mail, Skype, Facebook, browser-based applications, and other social media tools. They also have the advantage of convenience and nearly ubiquitous access for many students.

Overall, the preliminary BreakThru results suggest that mentoring activities gravitate to media that are familiar and comfortable to participants. The top 3 media for communicating with mentors were: Email, Telephone, and Texting. It is also possible that because of technical complications (i.e. audio problems), mentors and mentees have made less use of the virtual world option than may otherwise have been the case.

References

1. Agichtein, E., Castillo, C., Donato, D., Gionis, A., Mishne, G.: Finding High Quality Content in Social Media, with an Application to Community-Based Question Answering. In: Proc. ACM Web Search and Data Mining (WSDM), Stanford, CA, USA (2008)
2. Brown, B., Bell, M.: CSCW at play: 'There' as a collaborative virtual environment. In: Proceedings of the 2004 ACM Conference on Computer Supported Cooperative Work, CSCW 2004, pp. 350–359. Association for Computing Machinery, New York (2004)
3. Burgstahler, S.: Increasing the representation of people with disabilities in science, engineering and mathematics. Journal of Information Technology for Development 4(9), 1–8 (1994)
4. Chou, C.C., Hart, R.K.: The Pedagogical Considerations in the Design of Virtual Worlds for Organization Learning. In: Yang, H., Yuen, S. (eds.) Handbook of Research on Practices and Outcomes in Virtual Worlds and Environments, pp. 551–569 (2012)
5. Cremorne, L.: Interview—Denise Wood, University of South Australia. Metaverse Journal—Virtual World News (November 2, 2009)
6. Dede, C.: Immersive Interfaces for Engagement and Learning. Science 323(5910), 66–69 (2009)
7. de Freitas, S.: Serious virtual worlds: a scoping study. JISC, Bristol (2008), http://www.jisc.ac.uk/media/documents/publications/seriousvirtualworldsv1.pdf (retrieved February 4, 2009)
8. de Noyelles, A., Kyeong-Ju Seo, K.: Inspiring equal contribution and opportunity in a 3D multi-user virtual environment: Bringing together men gamers and women non-gamers in Second Life. Computers & Education 58(1), 21–29 (2012)
9. Duncan, I., Miller, A., Jiang, S.: A taxonomy of virtual worlds usage in education. British Journal of Education Technology (2012)

10. Folmer, E., Yuan, B., Carr, D., Sapre, M.: TextSL: a command-based virtual world interface for the visually impaired. In: Proceedings of the 11th International ACM SIGACCESS Conference on Computers and Accessibility, Assets 2009, pp. 59–66. Association for Computing Machinery, New York (2009)
11. Forman, A.E., Baker, P.M.A., Pater, J., Smith, K.: The Not So Level Playing Field: Disability Identity and Gender Representation in Second Life. In: Livermore, C. (ed.) Gender and Social Computing: Interactions, Differences, and Relationships. IGI Global, Hershey (2012)
12. Gerald, S., Antonacci, D.M.: Virtual World Learning Spaces: Developing a Second Life Operating Room Simulation. Educause Quarterly 32(1) (2009),
    http://www.educause.edu/EDUCAUSE+Quarterly/EDUCAUSEQuarterly
    MagazineVolum/VirtualWorldLearningSpacesDeve/163851
    (retrieved June 21, 2011)
13. Gregg, N., Chang, Y., Todd, R.: Social Media, Avatars, and Virtual Worlds: Re-Imagine an Inclusive Learning Environment for Adolescents and Adults with Literacy Barriers. Procedia Computer Science Journal 10 (2012) (in press)
14. Hanley, M.: Ball State University Student Cell Phone Usage February 2009 - February 2012. International Journal of Mobile Marketing (2012) (in press)
15. Herrington, A.: Using a smartphone to create digital teaching episodes as resources in adult education. In: Herrington, J., Herrington, A., Mantei, J., Onley, I., Ferry, B. (eds.) New Technologies, New Pedagogies: Mobile Learning in Higher Education, pp. 28–35. University of Wollongong, Wollongong (2009), http://ro.uow.edu.au/
16. iMentor project: iMentor Program Impact (2009),
    http://www.imentor.org/what/impact.php#eval_out (accessed September 2012)
17. Inman, C., et al.: Use of Second Life in K-12 and Higher Education: A Review of Research. Journal of Interactive Online Learning 9(1) (2010)
18. Jarmon, L.: Pedagogy and Learning in the Virtual World of Second Life. In: Rogers, P., Berg, G., Boettcher, J., Howard, C., Justice, L. (eds.) Encyclopedia of Distance and Online Learning (2008)
19. Jarmon, L., Traphagan, T., Mayrath, M., Trivedi, A.: Virtual world teaching, experiential learning, and assessment: An interdisciplinary communication course in Second Life. Computers & Education 53(1), 169–182 (2009)
20. Jefferson, A.J., Hannula, K.A., Campbell, P.B., et al.: The internet as a resource and support network for diverse geoscientists. GSA Today 20(9), 59–61 (2010)
21. Jones, D.E.: I, Avatar: Constructions of Self and Place in Second Life and the Technological Imagination. Gnovis, the Peer-Reviewed Journal of Communication, Culture and Technology 6 (2007)
22. Kingston, L.: Virtual world, real education: A descriptive study of instructional design in Second Life. Capella University (2011)
23. Lippincott, B., Morris, J., Mueller, J.: Keeping in Touch: Smartphone Touchscreens and Customers with Disabilities. Rehabilitation Engineering Research Center for Wireless Technologies (Wireless RERC), Atlanta, Georgia (2011)
24. Liu, H., Macintyre, R., Ferguson, R.: Exploring qualitative analytics for e-mentoring relationships building in an online social learning environment, Vancouver, Canada. Paper Presented at LAK12: 2nd International Conference on Learning Analytics and Knowledge (April 2012), http://oro.open.ac.uk/33632 (retrieved June 12, 2012)
25. Mancuso, D.S., Chlup, D.T., McWhorter, R.R.: A study of adult learning in a virtual environment. Advances in Developing Human Resources 12(6), 681–699 (2010)

26. Markett, C., Sanchez, I., Weber, S., Tangney, B.: Using short message service to encourage interactivity in the classroom. Computers & Education 46(3), 280–293 (2006)
27. McCarthy, J.: International design collaboration and mentoring for tertiary students through Facebook. Australasian Journal of Educational Technology 28(5), 755–775 (2012)
28. McClean, S., Hagan, P., Morgan, J.: Text Messaging for Student Communication and Voting. Bioscience Education (2010),
   `http://www.bioscience.heacademy.ac.uk/journal/vol16/`
   `beej-16-4.aspx` (accessed May 2012)
29. Khalil, M.A.: Promoting Success: Mentoring Students with Disabilities Using New Technologies in Higher Education. Library Hi Tech News 25(1), 8–12 (2008)
30. National Science Foundation (NSF): Shaping the future: New expectations for undergraduate education in science, mathematics, engineering, and technology (NSF 96-139) (1996)
31. National Science Foundation (NSF): Land of plenty: Diversity as America's competitive edge in science, engineering and technology. Author., Arlington (2000)
32. National Science Foundation.: Women, minorities, and persons with disabilities in science and engineering (NSF 04-317) (2004)
33. O'Neill, D.K., Harris, J.B.: Bridging the perspectives and developmental needs of all participants in curriculum-based telementoring programs. Journal of Research on Technology in Education 37(2), 111–128 (2004)
34. Patten, B., Sanchez, I.A., Tangney, B.: Designing collaborative, constructionist and contextual applications for handheld devices. Computers & Education 46(3), 294–308 (2006)
35. Single, P.B., Single, R.: E-mentoring for social equity: Review of research to inform program development. Mentoring and Tutoring 13, 301–320 (2005)
36. Smith, S.J., Israel, M.: E-mentoring: Enhancing special education teacher induction. Journal of Special Education Leadership 23(1), 30–40 (2010)
37. Stendal, K., Molka-Danielsen, J., Munkvold, B.E., Balandin, S.: Initial Experience with Virtual Worlds for People with Lifelong Disability: Preliminary Findings. Nokobit, pp. 105–118. The University of Nordland (2011)
38. Taylor, T.L.: Living Digitally: Embodiment in Virtual Worlds. In: Schroeder, R. (ed.) The Social Life of Avatars: Presence and Interaction in Shared Virtual Environments. Springer, London (2002)
39. Tindell, D., Bohlander, R.: The use and abuse of cell phones and text messaging in the classroom: a survey of college students. College Teaching 60(1), 1–9 (2012)
40. Todd, R.: BreakThru Research Data Autumn 2012. Georgia Institute of Technology, Center for Assistive Technology & Environmental Access (2012),
   `http://www.georgiabreakthru.org` (accessed December 2012)
41. Todd, R., Baker, P., Pater, J.: (In)Accessible Learning in Virtual Worlds. Virtual Worlds in Online and Distance Education. Athabasca University Press, Edmonton (2012)
42. Wolanin, T.R., Steele, P.E.: Higher education opportunities for students with disabilities. The Institute for Higher Education Policy, Washington, DC (2004)

Pupils' Satisfaction in Using Netbook

Fong-Gong Wu[1], Chii-Zen Yu[1,2], and Chiu-Min Yen[3]

[1] Department of Industrial Design, National Cheng Kung University, Tainan, Taiwan
[2] Department of Animation and Game Design, Toko University, Chiayi, Taiwan
[3] Department of Network System, Toko University, Chiayi, Taiwan
ycz@mail.toko.edu.tw

Abstract. E-learning is promoted in elementary school, and netbook is one of the equipment in e-learning. This study adopted questionnaire survey to discuss the pupils' satisfaction towards the usage of netbook. The data were analyzed by SPSS for descriptive statistics, independent sample t-test, and one-way ANOVA. The results are as follows: The order of the satisfaction degree of the pupils toward netbooks is portability, design, applications, e-learning, online search, keyboard, and screen. Except for screen, all other aspects are satisfactory. Regarding the influence of learning background and user experience on satisfaction, the degree of satisfaction of students who started to use computers early is lower, and that of students who had more experiences in using computers is also lower. The order of the influence degree of variate is gender, computer learning background, and computer using experience.

Keywords: Netbook, Satisfaction, Learning background, User experience.

1   Introduction

E-learning includes many kinds of electronically supported learning. It is promoted in elementary school, and netbook is one of the equipment in e-learning. This study adopted questionnaire survey to discuss pupils' satisfaction in using netbook. The data were analyzed by SPSS for descriptive statistics, independent sample t-test, and one-way ANOVA.

Customer satisfaction is generally defined as an evaluative response to the perceived outcome of a particular consumption experience [7, 10]. Anderson investigate the nature and strength of the link that between customer satisfaction and economic returns [9]. Churchill proposed an investigation into the determinants of customer satisfaction. The results suggest the effects are different for nondurable product and durable product [8]. There are several approaches for customer satisfaction in using netbook or notebook. Wu presents that brand image, service quality, product quality, price will have forward influence to customer degree of satisfaction [3]. Yushin presents that university Students would put more emphasis on quality, price, weight of the product, electricity-saving device, duration of battery, and the feel of using the input device in Tokyo [4]. Tseng wonder that what those consumers would consider base on purchasing behavior. When most consumers buy netbook, consider the

C. Stephanidis and M. Antona (Eds.): UAHCI/HCII 2013, Part III, LNCS 8011, pp. 266–271, 2013.

electricity, convenient, the brand, screen size and price [5]. The study results conclude that product design, product quality, and marketing methods are three major dimensions of the hierarchical framework for the KSF of netbook [6]. Wu presents four female consumer types through the process of segmentation. And there exists significant difference between market segmentation [1]. Pan presents that consumer prefer convenient and price of the netbook [2].

2   Method

This research aims to investigate the satisfaction degree of the use of netbooks by three-grade elementary school students. According to portability, design, applications, e-learning, online search, keyboard, and screen are the seven main aspects influencing the satisfaction degree of using netbooks. The students were divided into several groups according to gender, computer learning background and computer using experiences. The data were analyzed by SPSS for descriptive statistics, independent sample t-test, and one-way ANOVA. The students' satisfaction degree of the above seven aspects were surveyed. The Likert five-point scale was adopted to calculate the points.

The procedure of the research survey is as follows:

a. Pre-test: Using Cronbach α coefficient to examine internal consistency of the questionnaire.
b. Analyzing the result of pre-test: After retrieving the questionnaire, we conduct reliability analysis and consult professionals' advice to revise the questionnaire. The ultimate questionnaire is formed.
c. Formal test: Proceed with the survey of the 180 questionnaire.
d. Analyzing the result: Proceed with statistical analysis.

3   Result

After retrieving the questionnaire, we go on to data analysis and presenting statistical data. The participants are 98 boys and 82 girls. In the item of computer learning background, 91 students have learned computer in kindergarten, and 89 haven't. In the item of computer using experiences, 123 students have using experiences of netbooks or notebooks, and 57 students have none of them.

Divided by gender, the average of boys toward satisfaction degree of netbooks are higher than that of girls, as shown by Table 1. Students with different gender have same identity order with the aspects. It is shown in Table 2 that there are significant difference in gender in the aspects of online search and screen by variant analysis of independent sample t-test.

Divided by computer learning background, except for the aspect of "screen", the average of elementary school students who have learned computer in kindergarten toward satisfaction degree of netbooks are lower than that of the students who haven't learned computer in kindergarten, as shown by Table 3. Students who contacted computer in earlier ages have lower satisfaction degree toward netbooks. Students with different computer learning background have same identity order with the aspects. It is shown in Table 4 that there is significant difference in computer learning background in the aspect of portability by variant analysis of independent sample t-test. Students who haven't learned computer in kindergarten have much higher satisfaction degree in the "portability" aspect than those who have learned computer in kindergarten.

Divided by computer using experiences, students who have experiences of netbooks or notebooks have lower satisfaction degree toward netbooks, as shown by Table 5. In most aspects, students who have using experiences of neither netbooks nor notebooks have higher satisfaction degree toward netbooks. It is shown in Table 6 that experiences of using netbooks and notebooks make significant difference in factors of design, online search, and applications by variant analysis of one way ANOVA.

Table 1. The influence of students' gender on the satisfaction degree of netbooks

Aspects	Boy		Girl	
	Mean	SD	Mean	SD
Portability	4.59	0.30	4.54	0.29
Design	4.45	0.45	4.41	0.47
Applications	4.44	0.37	4.34	0.54
E-learning	4.33	0.42	4.26	0.45
Online Search	4.25	0.47	4.06	0.54
Keyboard	4.10	0.61	3.90	0.74
Screen	3.09	0.82	2.56	0.54
Total	29.25	3.44	28.07	3.57

Table 2. T-test of the difference of students' gender

Aspects	Gender（N）	SEM	T-test	P
Online Search	Boy（98）	.415	5.074	.000**
	Girl（82）	.296		
Screen	Boy（98）	.191	2.539	.012*
	Girl（82）	.239		

*P <0.05   ** P <0.01.

Table 3. The influence of students' computer learning background on the satisfaction degree of netbooks

Aspects	The students who have learned computer in kindergarten		The students who haven't learned computer in kindergarten	
	Mean	SD	Mean	SD
Portability	4.52	0.31	4.61	0.27
Design	4.42	0.47	4.44	0.45
Applications	4.35	0.47	4.44	0.44
E-learning	4.24	0.47	4.36	0.39
Online Search	4.14	0.56	4.19	0.46
Keyboard	3.91	0.69	4.11	0.65
Screen	2.87	0.88	2.83	0.61
Total	28.45	3.85	28.98	3.27

Table 4. T-test of the difference of students' computer learning background

Aspects	Have learned computer in kindergarten（N）	SEM	T-test	P
Portability	Yes（91）	.130	-2.15	.033*
	No（89）	.114		

*P <0.05.

Table 5. The influence of students' computer using experiences on the satisfaction degree of netbooks

Aspects	Students have using experiences of netbooks or notebooks		Students have none of netbooks and notebooks	
	Mean	SD	Mean	SD
Portability	4.57	0.31	4.56	0.27
Design	4.49	0.41	4.30	0.53
Applications	4.35	0.45	4.49	0.46
E-learning	4.26	0.45	4.38	0.40
Online Search	4.12	0.51	4.29	0.47
Keyboard	4.00	0.68	4.03	0.68
Screen	2.89	0.79	2.76	0.68
Total	28.68	3.60	28.81	3.49

Table 6. Variant analysis of one way ANOVA of computer using experiences

Aspects		SS	df	MS	F-test	P
Design	between groups	24.475	2	12.237	3.721	.026*
	within groups	582.075	177	3.289		
	total	606.550	179			
Applications	between groups	13.376	2	6.688	3.643	.028*
	within groups	324.935	177	1.836		
	total	338.311	179			
Online Search	between groups	51.956	2	25.978	6.584	.002**
	within groups	698.372	177	3.946		
	total	750.328	179			

*P <0.05   ** P <0.01.

4   Conclusions

The results of the research are as follows:

1. The order of the satisfaction degree of the three-grade students toward netbooks is portability, design, applications, e-learning, online search, keyboards, and screens. Except for screens, all other aspects are satisfactory.
2. The influence of students' computer learning background on the satisfaction degree of netbooks and notebooks is as below. Students' who have learned computer earlier have lower satisfaction degree toward netbooks, and so are those who have more computer using experiences. It's possible that students who have learned computer earlier and have more computer using experiences are more familiar with computer, which make them more aware of functional limitations of netbooks.
3. Students who have learned computer in kindergarten have lower satisfaction degree toward the screen of netbook than those who haven't. It's possible that students who have learned computer earlier have better adaptation to smaller screens.
4. The order of the influence degree of variate is gender, computer learning background, and computer using experience.

References

1. Wu, S.: A Study on Purchasing Patterns of Female Consumers and Marketing Strategy — Notebook Computer as an Example, Master's thesis, Department of Business Administration, National Taipei University, Taiwan (2004) (in Chinese)

2. Pan, Y.T.: Applying consumption value theory to analysis consumer behavior of the netbook, Master's thesis, Department of Business Administration, National Chengchi University, Taiwan (2009) (in Chinese)
3. Wu, Y.N.: A Study of the Brand Image, Service Quality, Product Quality, Price on the Customer Satisfaction and Loyalty of the Notebook PC, Master's thesis, Department of Logistics and Technology Management, Leader University, Taiwan (2007) (in Chinese)
4. Yushin, T.: Consumer Behavior to Notebook Computer Illustration with the University Students' Purchasing of Notebook Computer in Twenty-three areas in Tokyo, Master's thesis, Department of Business Administration, National Chung Hsing University, Taiwan (1998) (in Chinese)
5. Tseng, A.: The Influence of Green Product Design on Customer Purchasing Behavior of Netbook, Master's thesis, Department of Industrial Engineering and Enterprise, Huafan University, Taiwan (2010) (in Chinese)
6. Yen, P.S.: A Study of the Key Success Factors for the Netbook PC – The Cases of Asus, Acer and MSI, Master's thesis, Department of Business Administration, Kun Shan University, Taiwan (2010)
7. Westbrook, R.A., Oliver, R.L.: The dimensionality of consumption emotion patterns and consumer satisfaction. Journal of Consumer Research 24, 84–91 (1991) (in Chinese)
8. Churchill, R.A., Surprenant, C.: An Investigation into the Determinants of Customer Satisfaction. Journal of Marketing Research, 491–504 (1982)
9. Anderson, E.W., Fornell, C., Lehmann, D.R.: Customer Satisfaction, Market Share and Profitability: Findings from Sweden. Journal of Marketing 58, 53–66 (1994)
10. Cadotte, E.R., Woodruff, R.B., Jenkins, R.L.: Expectations and norms in models of consumer satisfaction. Journal of Marketing Research 24, 305–314 (1987)

Effectiveness of Learning Chinese Character Using Tablet Technology

Chao-Yang Yang, Ting-Yi Chiu-Huang, and Yu-Ting Wu

Chang Gung University, Department of Industrial Design, 259 Wen-Hwa 1st Road,
Kwei-Shan Tao-Yuan, Taiwan, 333, R.O.C.
Team0213@hotmail.com

Abstract. Bad handwriting often results in bad academic performance and discourages students from learning. Tablet technology has given character learning a new form such as writing by fingertip and various selection of background color. Without holding a pen, it is less stress and more intuitive for character-learning children. With certain background color, child seems pay more attention on writing. In this research, we piloted an evaluation to which we investigated whether learning by the tablet features is better than traditional paper-and-pencil learning. A third-year elementary student who is in the age of first learning Chinese characters was employed to this study. Different background color, stroke thickness and writing methods were tested. The results show that no significance between but aesthetics. There are steady stroke, slanted character, ratio and distance. And these aesthetics appear in specific colors strokes and background, thick and thin strokes or by finger and stylus writing.

Keywords: handwriting, tablet, color, stroke, background.

1 Introduction

In Taiwan, Chinese character writing is one of the many major aspects of an elementary school student's school life. Outside of Chinese class, Chinese writing is also a tool intensively used for learning in other classes, such as taking lecture notes and exams. Each elementary school student does a tremendous amount of writing every day.

Although writing itself is the means, not the objective, (Hallahan, Kauffman, & Lloyd, 1996), low effectiveness of handwriting results in poor academic performance and weak learning confidence (Mather & Roberts, 1997). Young students often struggle to pay attention in class, and the lack of focus contributes to their inefficiency in writing activities. To increase students' learning effectiveness, multimedia technologies have been integrated into lectures, taking the dullness out of classrooms. For example, competitive games motivate students to learn spontaneously; tablet PCs have become popular and have replaced traditional PCs' unintuitive input using the mouse and keyboard (Donker & Reitsma, 2007).

C. Stephanidis and M. Antona (Eds.): UAHCI/HCII 2013, Part III, LNCS 8011, pp. 272–280, 2013.
© Springer-Verlag Berlin Heidelberg 2013

Technologies have been gradually applied to teaching and learning as assistive tools over the years. Tablet PCs are the most preferred as they are light-weighed, generate immediate feedback, and provide intuitive handwriting functions, allowing students to practice and learn on one electronic gadget. Roslyn High School in New York, United States purchased US$750 iPads for their two experimental classes, and hopes to eventually provide iPads to all 1,100 of its students. A school in Virginia, United States uses iPads to improve interdisciplinary learning (Allen, 2011), and even their kindergarten students have started to use them for educational games. The Taiwan Ministry of Education will enhance teachers' integration of information technology into teaching as a policy of the year (Ministry of Education, 2011). And Taiwan's National Science Council and the Ministry of Education have launched experimental programs to promote the use of e-books, and the implementation outcome will be evaluated in elementary schools. For example, the electronic experimental class at Cambridge Primary School in Taipei County chooses iPads as its electronic teaching tools because of the long-lasting power and rich functionalities. Because of the popularity, light weight, the handwriting-featured touch screen and the well-developed assistive writing software that overcomes traditional teaching's limitations (Hulls, 2005; Yu, Zhang, Xue, & Zhu, 2010), we select tablet PCs as our main tool for studying students' handwriting characteristics.

2   Literature

Characters serve as the medium of communication in written Chinese. The ability to write reflects children's academic achievement at school (Morris, 1982). Chinese characters are complicated and do not necessarily represent pronunciation. Traditionally, learning Chinese characters requires a lot of imitation and practice using pen and paper. As technology advances, "finger writing" has replaced the traditional method of learning characters; however, little research has explored the efficiency of learning characters using finger writing. This is a pilot research aiming to investigate whether using different writing tools (finger and pen) will affect a student's writing performance.

2.1   Writing Skills in Children

Language is a critical medium for teachers to convey knowledge and to build students' understanding. Language skills include listening, speaking, reading, and writing, and writing ability is built on the other three abilities. Writing is usually used to show students' learning outcomes (e.g. answering questions in a test) (Morris, 1982; Smith, 1991) and to remember information. Although handwriting has been mostly replaced by typing, it is still the most intuitive, convenient and essential tool in everyday life.

Johnson and Myklebust (1967) addressed four fundamental abilities acquired before one can write effectively:

- Hearing: auditory memory, phonetic ability, auditory discrimination, the ability of following instructions, and the ability of processing sensory information.
- Vision: visual orientation, scanning skills, visual perception, visual memory and imagery.
- Movement: gross and meticulous motor coordination.
- Language acquisition: semantic network and linguistic experience.
- According to Taiwanese special education scholar Lin (2001), there are three major issues in children's Chinese character writing as they develop:
- Writing errors.
- Writing behaviors: the difficulty to focus, slowness, and carelessness.
- Writing gestures: awkward pen grips, excessive strength, and poor postures (Lin, 2001).

2.2   Using Tablet PCs for Learning

Tablet PC is a new multimedia tool. It can be used not only as an e-book reader, a gaming device, and an Internet browser, but also as an instructional tool in multiple forms. For example, reading stories to kindergarten children using sound effects and animation on a tablet PC enables them to actually experience story plots.

Hulls (2005) indicates that young students are more able to focus in class when they write on tablet PCs using strokes of different colors. Consequently, students receive better grades in class. He compares the advantages and disadvantages between using traditional teaching equipment and tablet PCs (Hulls, 2005).

Chalks and Blackboard

- Advantages: It is easier for instructors to draw students' attention to a specific spot. Instructors can also maintain direct interactions with students in the classroom.
- Disadvantages: There is a difficulty inherent in presenting complexity. Pictures and schematics are sometimes too complicated to be drawn on the board (Felder & Brent, 2005; Hulls, 2005). It can possibly yield errors in students, since they have limited time understanding the material during class and may not see the importance of subtle details. It is unlikely for students to retain what is exactly presented on the board for future reviews (for the purposes of doing assignments and preparing for exams); it is also impossible for instructors to record the lectures for future updates or revisions.

PowerPoint Presentation

- Advantages: They are attractive and in a clear format. Students can access to class materials both digitally and physically.
- Disadvantages: Being able to obtain lecture notes beforehand can reduce students' motivation to learn in class, and the multimedia features may also distract students.

Electronic Projection

- Advantage: It is convenient to show supplementary materials (e.g. animation, videos).
- Disadvantages: Its presentation is not as clear as that of a blackboard, and it decreases direct interaction between the instructor and students. It can be time-consuming.

Electronic Projection and Digital Ink

- Advantages: It can demonstrate lecture materials clearly as well as attract students' attention. It also generates feedback, motivates students, and increases in-class interaction. It supports the presentation of animation, videos, and visual effects. It is great for the retention of teaching materials, which can also be sent electronically to students.

Tablet PCs can also be used educationally as tools to improve reading ability.

McClanahan et al. (2012) studied a child with attention deficit hyperactivity disorder (ADHD); in their study, they helped him recognize compound words and comprehend reading. They downloaded applications on an iPad and used it as a teaching tool to help the ADHD child learn. The child was able to use applications to record himself reading and replay it. Those applications also helped him to identify the parts he read with his fingers. The researchers found that the ADHD child performed better in literacy and reading afterwards, and he learned to slow down his reading rate in order to correctly pronounce words and to understand main points. His learning attitude became more positive (McClanahan, Williams, Kennedy, & Tate, 2012).

2.3   Effect of Using Stimulus

Writing is a complex task (Amundson & Weil, 1996). Poor writing performance often leads to extended homework hours in children. Illegible handwriting can even affect interpersonal relationships when working in groups (Racine, Majnemer, Shevell, & Snider, 2008). Scholars have used stimuli in studies (e.g. colored screens and animation have positive effects on a ADHD patient's mathematics in-class learning (Lee & Zentall, 2002) and handwriting skills (Imhof, 2004)). Studies show that stimuli enhance the effectiveness of learning, especially in special education settings.

3   Method

To avoid unstable performance (Li, 2000), one male third grader, aged 9, from an elementary school in Taiwan was selected as the participant for this study. He had basic understanding of Chinese character structures, had already learned the characters used in this study, and had experience using an iPad.

3.1   Testing Environment

An Apple iPad was used as the writing platform and the participant's behavior was recorded on three cameras from different angles simultaneously (Figure 1). The participant was tested individually in a clean and quiet room to avoid distractions.

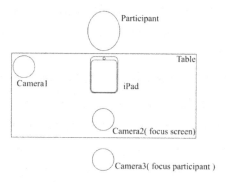

Fig. 1. Testing room arrangement

3.2   Tasks

The participant was asked to complete two tasks(Table 1) on Tablet PC screen by using finger and stylus (Table 2). In second task, the participant was asked to copy writing the given characters as proximal copying (Hallahan et al , 1996).

Table 1. Task description

First task	Second task
Drawing lines and geometric shapes. (triangle, quadrangle and circle)	Writing given Chinese characters.

Table 2. Tools

Two tools to write with:	
Writing on the iPad with a finger.	Writing on the iPad with a stylus.

Three characters (Table 3) for copying were selected from a list of commonly miswritten words (Yang, 2002) and printed in the 300-point BiauKai font on A4-sized papers (Li, 2000). We observed and recorded the participant's writing behaviors, test performance, correctness of the strokes, attention level, and performance rate. The child had already learned the selected characters in his first two years of school, therefore there was no learning effect involved. Additionally, we observed his attention focus by watching his head movements instead of using eye tracking equipment to lower children's psychological or physical stress.

Table 3. List of Chinese characters

Chinese Characters	Meaning in English
媽	Mother
姊	Sister
爸	Father

In the writing process of the Tablet PC, We will change in the different stimulant: color, stroke, writing way. And we divide strokes into two ways (thick strokes and thin strokes). The combination is as Table 4:

Table 4. Color options

Background color on the screen	Stroke color
White	Black
Red	Red
Blue	Blue

4   Results

Overall, the results show that there is no significantly different outcomes when using different stimuli combinations but it yielded aesthetic issues, such as steadiness, slant, proportion, and distance between strokes.

Lin (2001) addressed a few writing issues often found in school-aged children's writing: inaccurate distance between strokes and disproportion between parts. Imhof addressed a criterion used to determine ADHD children's writing performance: slant. Thus, we selected three criteria to evaluate the participant's handwriting performance. The quality of writing is relatively low and unstable when the participant wrote in thinner strokes, as shown in Figure 2.

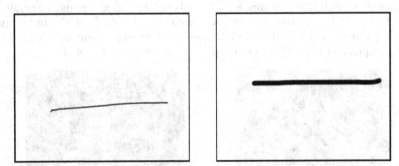

Fig. 2. Comparison of thick and thin horizontal strokes

The character appears to be more slanted when written with a finger than with a stylus (Figure 3).

Fig. 3. Left: written with a finger; Right: written with a stylus

As shown in Figure 4 (left), written in blue strokes on a red background, the upper half and lower half of the character are unbalanced in proportions. In Figure 4 (right), the distance between the left and right halves is too wide.

Fig. 4. Left: The upper half is too big; Right: the left half is too big and the distance between the two halves is too wide

When writing with black strokes on differently colored backgrounds, the results are similar (Figure 5).This results are consistent with that of Imhof's study. In his study, the control group (non-ADHD children) presented no significant difference either writing on a piece of white paper or on a piece of colored paper (Imhof, 2004).

Fig. 5. There is no significant difference between writings in black strokes with a stylus on a red and a blue background

5   Discussion and Conclusions

An interview with the participant showed that he preferred to write in blue strokes on a red background, but he did not perform differently using this combination nonetheless. His handwriting remained legible even though he changed stimuli repeatedly. Therefore, the stimuli did not affect writing results but maintained longer attention during learning. With multimedia technolgy, children can do work while having fun. We suggest that technology can compensate for the limitations of traditional learning methods and it contributes to higher learning efficiency.

In conclusion, from this study, we find that stimuli (background colors, stroke colors and types, and writing tools) do not significantly enhance a child's writing performance. We also suggest that a tablet PC is an appropriate technological device for learning Chinese character writing. Our future research topic of interest will be the study of learning distractions and the role of multimedia in stimulating students' motivation.

References

1. Allen, R.: Can mobile devices transform education. Education Update 53(2), 2 (2011)
2. Amundson, S.J., Weil, M.: Prewriting and handwriting skills. Occupational Therapy for Children 3, 524–541 (1996)
3. Bao-gui Lin, B.-X.C.: Elementary school of child writing language test preparation. Journal of Special Education and Rehabilitation (8), 53–74 (2000)
4. Donker, A., Reitsma, P.: Young children's ability to use a computer mouse. Computers & Education 48(4), 602–617 (2007)
5. Felder, R.M., Brent, R.: Random Thoughts: Death by Power Point. Chemical Engineering Education 39(1), 28–29 (2005)
6. Hallahan, D.P., Kauffman, J.M., Lloyd, J.: Introduction to learning disabilities. Allyn and Bacon, Boston (1996)
7. Hulls, C.C.W.: Using a Tablet PC for classroom instruction. Paper Presented at the Frontiers in Education, FIE 2005. Proceedings 35th Annual Conference (2005)
8. Imhof, M.: Effects of color stimulation on handwriting performance of children with ADHD without and with additional learning disabilities. European Child & Adolescent Psychiatry 13(3), 191–198 (2004)
9. Iovino, I., Fletcher, J.M., Breitmeyer, B.G., Foorman, B.R.: Colored overlays for visual perceptual deficits in children with reading disability and attention deficit/hyperactivity disorder: Are they differentially effective? Journal of Clinical and Experimental Neuropsychology 20(6), 791–806 (1998)
10. Johnson, D.J., Myklebust, H.R.: Learning Disabilities, Educational Principles and Practices (1967)
11. Lee, D.L., Zentall, S.S.: The Effects of Visual Stimulation on the Mathematics Performance of Children with Attention Deficit/Hyperactivity Disorder. Behavioral Disorders 27(3), 272–288 (2002)
12. Li, Y.-D.: The cognitive components relating to handwriting performance of students with and without Chinese handwriting difficulties. National Changhua University of Education (2000)

13. Lin, Q.-H.: Attention to the problem of elementary school children's writing. Elementary special education (2001)
14. Mather, N., Roberts, R.: Informal assessment and instruction in written language: A practitioner's guide for students with learning disabilities. J. Wiley (1997)
15. McClanahan, B., Williams, K., Kennedy, E., Tate, S.: A Breakthrough for Josh: How Use of an iPad Facilitated Reading Improvement. Tech.Trends 56(3), 20–28 (2012)
16. Ministry of Education, 100 annual policy objectives (2011),
    http://www.edu.tw/secretary/
    content.aspx?site_content_sn=23762
17. Morris, N.T., Crump, W.D.: Syntactic and vocabulary development in the written discourse of learning disabled and normal children and adolescent. Dissertation Abstracts International (SECA) 41(01), 140 (1982)
18. Racine, M.B., Majnemer, A., Shevell, M., Snider, L.: Handwriting performance in children with attention deficit hyperactivity disorder (ADHD). Journal of Child Neurology 23(4), 399–406 (2008)
19. Rubia, K., Noorloos, J., Smith, A., Gunning, B., Sergeant, J.: Motor timing deficits in community and clinical boys with hyperactive behavior: the effect of methylphenidate on motor timing. Journal of Abnormal Child Psychology 31(3), 301–313 (2003)
20. Smith, C.R.: Learning Disabilities: The Interaction of Learn, Tasks, and Setting. Allyn and Bacon, Boston (1991)
21. Yang, K.-T.: Learning disabilities, teaching materials. Wu Nan Psychological Publishing, Taipei (2002)

Part III

Universal Access to Text, Books, eBooks and Digital Libraries

AcceSciTech: A Global Approach to Make Scientific and Technical Literature Accessible

Alex Bernier[1] and Dominique Burger[2]

[1] Association BrailleNet
9, quai Saint-Bernard
75252 Paris Cedex 5, France
alex.bernier@upmc.fr

[2] INSERM UMRS_968, Université Pierre et Marie Curie
9, quai Saint-Bernard
75252 Paris Cedex 5, France
dominique.burger@upmc.fr

Abstract. In this paper, we introduce AcceSciTech, a research and development project which addresses the challenges faced in providing access to scientific and technical literature for the visually impaired and, more broadly, for those who are not able to read conventional print. Based on XML formats, this project aims to develop a coherent set of tools to produce, edit, deliver and to render complex documents accessible to impaired people.

Keywords: accessible publishing, Braille, DAISY, ebooks, EPUB, PEF, print-disabled persons, scientific documents, workflow, XML.

1 Introduction

In this paper, we introduce AcceSciTech and its first results, a three years research and development project funded by the French national research agency started in September 2012 involving three partners : Université Pierre et Marie Curie (Paris), BrailleNet and Eurobraille.

The AcceSciTech project addresses the challenges faced in providing access to scientific and technical literature for the visually impaired and, more broadly, for those who are not able to read conventional print. The project aims to develop coherent tools to create, edit, deliver, to render and to interact with complex documents. In this context, scientific and technical literature refers to all written text (articles, handouts, slides, books, etc.) that include complex elements such as mathematical formulae, graphs, charts, diagrams, notes, etc. These documents can cover both "exact sciences" and social sciences, and be of university level or aimed at the general public.

Visually impaired readers access text in a number of ways: by touch through the use of Braille (either as static text embossed on paper or dynamic text generated by a Braille display device); by listening to text read by a narrator or a speech synthesiser; or by sight through large print. These different means of

C. Stephanidis and M. Antona (Eds.): UAHCI/HCII 2013, Part III, LNCS 8011, pp. 283–290, 2013.
© Springer-Verlag Berlin Heidelberg 2013

accessing information are not exclusive: a student, for example, may find it useful to learn to read a sentence in Braille while listening to the same sentence. XML-based formats (mainly DAISY [1] and EPUB [2]) are used in this project because they allow to separate the content and the presentation of a document. Also these formats provide a general framework to render documents using various means (touch, listening or sight). EPUB and DAISY also provide mechanisms to enable, for example, the user to navigate from section to section or from chapter to chapter with ease, or to opt whether or not to read certain elements of a book such as footnotes or page numbers.

In order to introduce the problems associated with accessing scientific and technical literature, the following questions may be asked:

- How can one efficiently produce highly structured documents that originate from various sources (scans, PDF or LaTeX files provided by a publisher, etc.)?
- For documents containing many images, in which publishing environment should experts be invited to provide descriptions as and when the user needs them?
- How does one translate a mathematical formula into spoken words and/or Braille?
- How can a young visually impaired pupil with limited computer skills access a mathematics textbook with ease?
- How can one read and navigate with ease in a complex document using a Braille terminal or new touchscreen-based devices?

In many countries, the law grants approved organisations the right to ask publishers to provide source files used in the production of printed works subject to copyright, so that they may be adapted and distributed to people with disabilities. In order to take advantage of this favourable legal environment, an optimal technical environment that will facilitate and increase the production and distribution of accessible texts must be created. The AcceSciTech project proposes to do this, in the context of scientific and technical literature.

In the first sections sections, we will focus on production steps required to create accessible documents: after introducing the formats on which are operating the production chain in section 2, we will describe pre-processing steps required to detect and enhance the structure of a document in section 3, the various possibilities offered to edit accessible documents in section 4, and, in section 5, the softwares used to produce final documents, ready to be delivered to the end-user. In section 6, we will introduce the Helene platform, the core of an online library service for visually impaired people. Two new modules added to this platform will be described, allowing to dynamically generate and to distribute documents via Web services. Last, in section 7, we will highlight the features required in a rendering system based on touch to ease the reading of complex documents.

2   Formats

The first thing we did to find efficient solutions to answer the question "How can one efficiently produce highly structured documents that originate from various sources?" was to find common formats able to take the variety of representable documents into account. The different tools developed in the AcceSciTech project mainly rely on two formats: ZedAI for the production and EPUB 3 for the distribution. We extensively described these two formats and why they can be candidates to be part of high-quality document production chain in a previous paper ([3]). Let us introduce them briefly:

ZedAI (Z39.98 Authoring and Interchange [4]) is designed by the DAISY consortium to replace the XML DTBook format defined in the previous DAISY specifications (Z39.86-2005 [1]). On the DAISY consortium website, ZedAI is presented as "a specification that defines an XML-based framework with which content producers can represent various types of information in an extensible, standards-compliant way, suitable for the transformation into multiple output formats" [5]. The important point here is that ZedAI is not a format defined by a grammar like XML DTBook, but ZedAI is a framework to define grammars.

EPUB 3 is a standard distribution format (i.e. for the end-user of the content) for digital publications and documents. An EPUB 3 document is basically a single compressed file (the container) embedding HTML5 files, CSS, images, metadata and other resources. The accessibility related features (synchronisation mechanisms, skippable and escapable contents) available in DAISY 2005 have been fully integrated into this new version of the EPUB format.

Both ZedAI and EPUB 3 embed vocabulary association mechanisms based on RDF. This means that it is possible to transfer semantic inflections of elements from a ZedAI document into EPUB 3 using common concepts shared by ZedAI and EPUB 3 or linking ZedAI-specific vocabularies to the EPUB 3 document when concepts defined in these vocabularies are not already available in EPUB.

ZedAI and EPUB 3 are also good candidates to handle complex documents because their specifications allow to use MathML for representing formula and SVG for the graphical contents.

3   Pre-processing Steps

Because it is rich and extensible, we have selected ZedAI to be the core format of the production tool chain we design in the AcceSciTech project. The main requirement for this production chain is to be able to manage a wide range of source documents formats. The pre-processing steps are those done to convert a document provided at the input of the chain into a ZedAI file. They are as follow:

Document acquisition: the objective of this step is to obtain an electronic version of the document by digitising the printed version or by getting a source file from the publisher/author. If a source file is provided, it can be in a wide range of formats: LaTeX, PDF, Microsot Word, XML (using various DTD), etc. This step is implemented thanks to a high speed document scanner for book digitisation and using the PLATON platform provided by the French national library which allows accredited organisations to request source files corresponding to printed books. BrailleNet, as one of the accredited organisations, has noted two major difficulties using PLATON in a real production context: it hard to predict when the files will be uploaded by the publisher and once uploaded, in which format. Legally, publishers have to upload source files corresponding to a printed book no later than two months after the document has been requested. But in practice, some publishers do not respect the delay, and when they do, their responsiveness is quite variable. Regarding the formats, approximately 70% of the uploaded files are in PDF, 25% in XML, 4% in Microsoft Word an the last 1% in various other formats (LaTeX, InDesign, etc).

Conversion into readable format: if the document has been digitised or provided using an image-based format, it should be processed by an Optical Characters Recognition (OCR) software to be converted into readable text format. This step is implemented using the ABBYY FineReader SDK [7] for "simple" documents and the InftyReader [8] for documents with math.

Structure detection: to enable users to easily navigate inside a document, its structure should be known (chapter, section, footnotes, etc). Nowadays, some OCR tools (like FineReader) are able to detect some structural elements of documents like headings, footnotes, tables, etc. Unfortunately, this kind of detection is not efficient enough with complex layout or with complex document structure. So, an additional tool is currently being developed, to improve the results of structure detection. This tool is used the ALTO format as input and produce an annotated version as output, based on matching with document description models.

Conversion into ZedAI: finally, the resulting documents of previous processes should be converted into the core format. We are developing various converters to manage the input formats (annotated-ALTO, XML from publishers), integrated in one global tool. Some experimentation is also done to test existing converters from LaTeX: TRALICS [9] and TeX4ht [10].

4   Edition Tools

Because creating fully accessible documents will still require manual work (for example to describe images), AcceSciTech also addresses issues related to publishing, by providing various possibilities to edit document. We are working on three solutions:

A collaborative environment with an user interface dedicated to adapting books. This environment is based on a Wiki platform allowing users to work simultaneously on the same book divided into pages. The Wiki supports XML DTBook and ZedAI is added. Production management tools are also currently developed to improve the global efficiency of the platform, making possible to easily follow what kind of work has been done on a book (proofreading, structure improvement, image description, etc). Support for math formula is included using the TeX language. The Wiki is designed to adapt educational material which can be partially adapted by several teachers.

Oxygen with a ZedAI module: Oxygen [11] is an XML editor. Natively, it provides WYSIWYG features to edit DocBook, XHTML and TEI files. It can be extended to support new formats. For example, MathFlow is a plug-in which allows users to edit equations in the MathML format. As part of the AcceSciTech project, a module to handle ZedAI in Oxygen is under development. This solution is targeting users with some knowledge of XML and is well designed to be integrated in a production workflow, to adapt whole documents.

ODT2DAISY [12] is a plug-in for OpenOffice.org/LibreOffice.org to convert ODF-text files into DAISY. Currently, ODT2DAISY supports the XML DT-Book formats. We plan to modify it to handle natively the ZedAI format. Math equations can be created with an equation editor and are internally stored using the MathML format. This edition solution will be helpful for the users who are not familiar with XML and who would like to use a "standard" word-processor to create specific documents.

5   Production of Documents in Distribution Formats

The previous steps aimed to to create a structured and rich ZedAI document. Because ZedAI is an authoring format, such a document should be converted in a format more appropriate for distribution purposes like EPUB 3 or Portable Embossable Format (PEF) [20]. This task is done using the DAISY Pipeline [6] 2, an an "XML-centric open source cross-platform framework for the automated processing of various digital formats" [13] developed by the DAISY consortium. It uses XProc [14], an XML Pipeline language designed by W3C to create conversion workflows which can be based on the ZedAI format. Two working group have been set up: one dedicated to the production of Braille document and the other to the audio generated by Text-To-Speech (TTS) documents.

The AcceSciTech project will contribute to the developments of the DAISY Pipeline 2. Our efforts will focus on the two following aspects: production of complex Braille documents and efficient production using TTS.

Our main goal regarding the Braille production module is to support the French Braille code specification (both contracted and non-contracted codes) and to be able to produce Braille math from MathML equations. To include MathML support in the Braille module, three open-source softwares are evaluated: UMCL [15], LibLouis [16] + LibLouisXML [17] and NAT Braille [18]. Our evaluation covers efficiency (processing speed), input format and output code coverage. Depending of the results, one of these tools will be selected to be integrated into the DAISY Pipeline Braille module, or it will be decided to improve one of them or develop a new one.

The possibility to produce audio documents from XML DTBook using TTS is already provided by the Narrator module available in the first version of the DAISY Pipeline. We are participating in in the design of a new version of this module to be integrated in the DAISY Pipeline 2. Our main objectives are the following:

Providing support for the ZedAI Format
Optimising the production process to take advantage of multi-CPU computers
Handling math by contributing a library to convert MathML to SSML (a language designed to be processed by a TTS software [19])

6 Delivering Documents

After the adaptation and production processes, accessible documents are ready to be delivered to end-users. We use an online library (based on the Helene platform provided by BrailleNet), dedicated to visually impaired people.

The online library is based on Koha, an open-source library management system we have extended to support features required to manage digital documents [21]. More complex is the delivered document, more useful is it to for the end-user to be able to customise it corresponding to his/her specific needs. For example, it can be helpful to get a manual with the main text pronounced by a voice, footnotes by a different one, and math equations by a third. Th user should be able to select voices according his/her preferences.

It is already possible with the Helene platform to customise books on-demand, to deliver PDF version (for large-print), DAISY text-only and XHTML. Our objective is now to add this feature for audio books produced by TTS. The main issue here is to properly manage resources allowed to produce the requested books: scheduling, monitoring and caching mechanisms are implemented to make the system efficient and robust to deliver customised books to a large number of users.

Currently, the online library is accessible via Internet using a Web browser: the user search a book in the catalogue, download it and should copy it manually on its reading system. These operations require to be familiar with computers. It can be helpful, especially for young children, to make this process easier: this is the purpose of DAISY Online Delivery Protocol (DODP) [22] which is being implemented on the Helene platform. DODP specifies Web services to allow direct communication via Internet between a connected reading system and an online library management system. Two contents elections methods are proposed: "Out-of-band" and "Browse Content". The first is well-suited to deliver periodicals contents or books selected by a librarian: basically, the user has only to start hies/her reading system and the list of contents available will be presented automatically. The second method allow the user to search the catalogue (using the keypad of the reading system) and to browse it by categories thank to a dynamic menu mechanism.

7 Rendering Complex Documents and New Interactions Possibilities

Last, a multi-modal reading software is developed to render complex documents in Braille, audio and on a regular screen. It should have the following features:

Support DAISY (2.02 and 3.0) and EPUB 3 formats
Fine synchronisation of audio, Braille and visual outputs
MathML rendering
DAISY Online client

This software is designed to be multi-platform with constraints of embedded systems in mind: our objective is to integrate it in a portable Braille notebook (Esytime by Eurobraille) and into iOS and Android platforms with the goal to create new prospects for improving the reading efficiency of visually impaired users. Indeed, Esytime embeds a video-card to be plugged on a screen, a text-to-speech software and a new hardware mechanism able to detect fingers movement of the user on the Braille display thanks to optical sensors fixed on every Braille cell of the device. The sensors allow to recognise sequences of movement made by the user and to process these sequences to execute appropriate commands. Almost all the iOS and Android phones/tablets use touchscreen as the primary input device. To take advantage of these new possibilities, we are designing gesture libraries (in one and two dimensions) to experiment new interactions methods aiming to improve reading speed and to ease the navigation inside complex documents.

8   Conclusion

One of the main concerns of AcceSciTech is to reduce the gap between the number of accessible documents for print-disabled people and the number of documents available into the mainstream publishing market. This gap is significantly greater for scientific and technical literature because of the high costs involved to produce this kind of accessible material. Based on standard and extensible formats, AcceSciTech aims to create tools and to participate to the development of existing open-source projects, to contribute to the global effort required to make complex documents more accessible.

Acknowledgement. This work is supported by the Agence Nationale de la Recherche (AcceSciTech project: 2012 CORD 008 02). We are grateful to the Alcatel-Lucent company for their support and cooperation.

References

1. National Information Standards Organization (NISO). ANSI/NISO Z39.86-2005. Revision of ANSI/NISO Z39.86-2002. Specifications for the Digital Talking Book, http://www.daisy.org/z3986/2005/Z3986-2005.html
2. International Digital Publishing Forum. EPUB 3: http://idpf.org/epub/30
3. Bernier, A., Burger, D.: XML-Based Formats and Tools to Produce Braille Documents. In: Miesenberger, K., Karshmer, A., Penaz, P., Zagler, W. (eds.) ICCHP 2012, Part I. LNCS, vol. 7382, pp. 500–506. Springer, Heidelberg (2012)

4. National Information Standards Organization (NISO). ANSI/NISO Z39.98-2012. Authoring and Interchange Framework for Adaptive XML Publishing Specification, http://www.daisy.org/z3998/2012/z3998-2012.html
5. DAISY Consortium: ZedAI Introduction, http://www.daisy.org/zw/ZedAIIntroduction
6. DAISY Pipeline, A framework for document-related pipelined transformations, for the DAISY Consortium community: http://code.google.com/p/daisy-pipeline/
7. ABBYY FineReader SDK: http://www.abbyyeu.com/sdk/
8. Fukuda, R., Ohtake, N., et al.: Optical recognition and Braille transcription of mathematical documents. In: ICCHP, pp. 711–718 (2000)
9. TRALICS: a LaTeX to XML translator: http://www-sop.inria.fr/marelle/tralics/
10. TeX4ht, http://tug.org/tex4ht
11. Oxygen XML Editor, http://www.oxygenxml.com/
12. Strobbe, C., Engelen, J., Spiewak, V.: Generating DAISY Books from OpenOffice.org. In: Miesenberger, K., Klaus, J., Zagler, W., Karshmer, A. (eds.) ICCHP 2010, Part 1. LNCS, vol. 6179, pp. 5–11. Springer, Heidelberg (2010)
13. Deltour, R.: XProc at the heart of an ebook production framework. XLL Prague (2013)
14. XProc: An XML Pipeline Language, http://www.w3.org/TR/xproc/
15. Archambault, D., Fitzpatrick, D., Gupta, G., Karshmer, A.I., Miesenberger, K., Pontelli, E.: Towards a Universal Maths Conversion Library. In: Miesenberger, K., Klaus, J., Zagler, W.L., Burger, D. (eds.) ICCHP 2004. LNCS, vol. 3118, pp. 664–669. Springer, Heidelberg (2004)
16. Liblouis, A Braille translation and back-translation library: http://code.google.com/p/liblouis/
17. LiblouisXML - A Braille transcription software for XML documents: http://code.google.com/p/liblouisxml/
18. NAT Braille: A free universal Braille translator, http://natbraille.free.fr/
19. Speech Synthesis Markup Language (SSML) Version 1.0., http://www.w3.org/TR/speech-synthesis/
20. Håakansson, J.: PEF 1.0 - Portable Embosser Format Public draft, http://files.pef-format.org/specifications/pef-2008-1/pefspecification.html
21. Bernier, A., Burger, D.: Helene, an Open-Source and DAISY Compliant Digital Library Management System. In: CSUN Conference, March 14-19 (2011)
22. DAISY Online Delivery Protocol: http://www.daisy.org/projects/daisy-online-delivery/drafts/20100402/do-spec-20100402.html

Exploration of Picture E-Book Design for App Web

Cheih-Ying Chen[*] and Hung-Chieh Chang

Department of Cultural and Creative Industries, National Pingtung University of Education,
Pingtung City, Taiwan, R.O.C.
cychen@mail.npue.edu.tw

Abstract. The objective of this study is to investigate the interactive relationship between picture e-book design and children with the interface of APP web for mobile devices. In order to achieve the objective, the focus of this study is in applying APP technology to picture e-book. Also, APP web interfaces based on both smartphone and tablet via picture book are designed in the study. Furthermore, this study discusses children interface satisfaction in reading the e-book. It shows that both the interactive process and the result differ in smartphone and in tablet. It seems to be the best way for children to read the picture e-book if they can easily touch the buttons on the screen of a tablet.

Keywords: Picture e-book, APP web design, smartphone, tablet.

1   Introduction

With the development of information technology and the utilization of network, children play on the computers and digital devices increasingly in Taiwan. Children are growing up in an ever-changing electronic media environment. The multi-functional electronic media for children combines video and audio, and children can enjoy e-books, music, animations and films.

A picture book most often attracts young children. The images in picture books are illustrative with verbal narratives. With the digital media, a picture book can be designed with picture, language, audio and animation. There is a digital fever for books right now, and picture e-book is being developed rapidly in the web. There are many learning webs providing a lot of picture e-book for young children. Young children read picture e-book on personal computers and smart phones. It is difficult for children to surf the general web with smart phones having to zoom in and zoom out. Therefore, I am exploring the following topics: what is difference between the application of APP web and general web for picture e-book? How to take advantage of the existing picture e-book and incorporate into a smartphone device? How children can easily navigate and interact with smartphone and enjoy the information of audio and video in order to learn and play from the e-book web.

---

[*] Corresponding author.

C. Stephanidis and M. Antona (Eds.): UAHCI/HCII 2013, Part III, LNCS 8011, pp. 291–296, 2013.
© Springer-Verlag Berlin Heidelberg 2013

2   Picture E-Book Design

In 2007, Apple Inc. introduced the original iPhone, one of the first mobile phones to use a multi-touch interface. The iPhone was notable for its use of a touchscreen for direct finger input as its main method of interaction, instead of a stylus, keyboard, or keypad that were typical used with smartphones at the time. In July 2008, Apple introduced its second generation iPhone with a much lower listed price and 3G support. Simultaneously, the APP Store was introduced which allowed any iPhone to install applications (both free and paid) over a Wi-Fi or cellular network, without requiring a PC for installation; applications can be added, browsed through and downloaded directly. Featuring over 500 applications at launch [1], the APP Store was very popular, and achieved over one billion downloads in the first year[2]. Following the success of Apple's APP Store other smartphone manufacturers quickly launched application stores of their own. Google launched the Android Market in October 2008. For several years, the demand for smartphones has outpaced the rest of the mobile phone market [3]. According to a 2012 survey, around half of the U.S. mobile consumers own smartphones and could reach about 70% of all U.S. mobile devices by 2013 [4]. In profit sense, worldwide smartphones profitability far exceeds that of non-smartphones. As of December 2012, the worldwide smartphone market had Android as its top operating system, counting on 68.3% of market share, followed by iOS with 18.8% and Blackberry with 4.7% [5].

A tablet is a one-piece mobile computer, primarily operated by touchscreen; the user's finger acts like the mouse, and the cursor moves around screen as if a virtual keyboard and buttons are integrated into the display. The virtual integrated keyboard and functional buttons that can be hidden by a swivel joint or slide joint, jumps out only when the user commons the screen for touch virtual keyboard operation. In 2010, Apple Inc. released the iPad with iOS operating system which gained commercial success due to its extremely large fan base. Other manufacturers have produced tablets using a variety of operating systems such as, Android, Windows, and QNX, and most frequently use capacitive touch screens with multi-touch. The tablet focuses on media consumption together with internet, and provides a platform for audio-visual media, including electronic books, periodicals, films, music, computer games, and presentations [6]. The tablet has an optional e-books application, which displays books downloaded from the e-book store or internet. E-books are usually read on dedicated e-book readers, tablets and many smart phones using e-reader applications. Mobile availability of e-books may be provided for readers with a mobile data connection, so that these e-books need not be stored on the device. Additionally, e-books allow for readers to look up words or find more information about the topic immediately [7]. In Taiwan, a great share of picture e-books are available online for free, minus the minimal costs of the electronics required.

3   Methods

3.1   Interface Arrangement

In this research, we design the picture e-book for APP web, and test 30 children from 5-8 years old to compare two types with smartphone and tablet. Children use fingers to touch the screen, and read more information on the same APP webpage.

An idealized picture e-book design for APP web (Fig.1.) was divided into three sections: story text, game and author. In this study, one story was designed for the picture e-book to offer children reading.

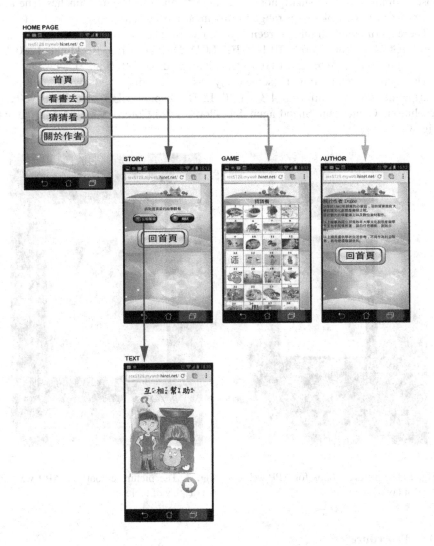

Fig. 1. The picture e-book design for APP web

3.2   Participants

The 30 children (5-8 years old) were experimented with smartphone or tablet. All children had color vision test and were found none to be color blind.

3.3   Apparatus

Screens on smartphones and tablet in both display size and display resolution. The most common screen of smartphone sizes range from 3 inches to 5.5inches. The most common screen of tablet sizes range from 7 inches to 12inches.

The experimental stimuli (screen layouts) were displayed by a multimedia tablet (Acer ICONIA Tab A500, 10.1" TFT LCD Display LED Backlight 1280x800 Resolution, Nvidia Tegra 250 1 GHz Dual Core, Android 3.0) (Fig. 2).

The experimental stimuli (screen layouts) were displayed by a multimedia smartphone (Asus Platform, 4.3" TFT LCD Display LED Backlight 960x540 Resolution, Qualcomm Snapdragon S4 8260A Dual-Core 1.5 GHz, Android 4.0) (Fig. 3).

Fig. 2. The picture e-book for APP web on the display of smartphone

Fig. 3. The picture e-book for APP web on the display of tablet

3.4   Procedure

Each subject played with each of the 2 interfaces for smartphone and tablet, and read the uniform picture e-book completely. To prevent bias, 15 subjects were tested with smartphone first, and the rest 15 subjects were tested with tablet first, both finish reading the story with both kind of mobile devices, each subject was asked 6 questions at the end:

1. Have you ever used a smartphone or tablet?
2. Which one do you think is more convenient to reading picture story? smartphone or tablet?
3. Which one has buttons that are easier to touch? Smartphone or tablet?
4. Which one can you read picture story more comfortably? Smartphone or tablet?
5. Which one can you read picture story more comfortably? Smartphone, tablet or book?
6. Which one attracts you to read picture story more? Smartphone, tablet or book?

4   Results and Discussion

The result for the interactive relationship between picture e-book design and children with the interface of APP web for mobile devices are given in Table 1.

Table 1. Overall user interface satisfaction of all participants

question	smartphone	tablet	book	Both (smartphone and tablet)
1. have ever used	20%	3%		77%
2. more conveniently	7%	93%		
3. touch the buttons easily	30%	70%		
4. more comfortably	20%	80%		
5. more comfortably	0%	67%	33%	
6. attract	3%	80%	17%	

All children have used smartphone or tablet; 97% of the children have used smartphone (20%+77%) and 80% children have used table; 93% of the children consider reading picture story more conveniently with tablet than smartphone, because the display of tablet is bigger than smartphone; 70% of the children consider sliding their fingers to touch the buttons is easier on that tablet than on smartphone, because the buttons on the display of a tablet is bigger than on a smartphone; 80% of the children consider reading picture story is more comfortable on a tablet than on smartphone, because the text and picture on the display of tablet is bigger than smartphone; 67% of the children consider reading picture story is more comfortable on a tablet than reading a book, and 80% of the children consider reading picture story is more attractive than reading picture story on tablet than on book and smartphone, because they like to play with the tablet.

5   Conclusion

In this experiment, we observe those children how they operate the mobile devices. Children slid their fingers on the screen to access the web on smart phone and tablet. They read simple and clear information on tablet but have difficulty reading it on smartphone. Because the screen of smartphone is too small, information is read with much smaller font and it is easy to touch the wrong button on the screen. To avoid touching the wrong button, APP web design must be simple and remove redundant information.

A good picture e-book design for children using APP web has three principles: 1. Easy to use 2.Simple target 3.Smooth Operation. The main purpose of picture e-book is how to guide children to read and make the device easy to use. It doesn't need much function and object for children. Children can understand and use the interface immediately, while they browse the good picture e-book design for APP web first time. Children like to use the tablet, because the display of tablet is bigger than smartphone. They feel that it is convenient and more comfortable to read the picture e-book on tablet, so the smartphone can't replace the tablet in picture e-book. Children also consider reading the picture book is more comfortable than reading the picture e-book with smartphone, and they really don't like to read the story with small fonts and tiny display on the smartphone.

References

1. Bowcock, J., Pope, S.: iPhone 3G on Sale Tomorrow. Press Release. APPle Inc. (2008), http://www.apple.com/pr/library/2008/07/ 10iPhone-3G-on-Sale-Tomorrow.html
2. Kerris, N., Bowcock, J.: APPle's APP Store Downloads Top 1.5 Billion in First Year. Press Release. APPle Inc. (2009), http://www.apple.com/pr/library/2009/07/14Apples-App-Store- Downloads-Top-1-5-Billion-in-First-Year.html
3. Smart phones: how to stay clever in downturn. Deloitte Telecommunications Predictions (2009), http://www.deloitte.com/assets/ Dcom-Montenegro/Local%20Assets/Documents/ me_Telecomunications_Predictions-2009.pdf
4. Smartphones Account for Half of all Mobile Phones, Dominate New Phone Purchases in the US, http://blog.nielsen.com/nielsenwire/online_mobile/ smartphones-account-for-half-of-all-mobile-phones-dominate- new-phone-purchases-in-the-us/
5. Graziano, D.: Android projected to own the smartphone market for the next four years (2012), http://bgr.com/2012/12/04/mobile-market-share-2012- android/
6. Eileen, G., Musto, R.G.: The Electronic Book. In: Suarez, M.F., Woudhuysen, H.R. (eds.) The Oxford Companion to the Book. Oxford University Press, Oxford (2010)
7. Saylor, M.: The Mobile Wave: How Mobile Intelligence Will Change Everything. Vanguard Press, New York (2012)

Read-Aid - An Assistive Reading Tool for Children with Dyslexia

Suvarna Rekha, Sai Gollapudi, Harini Sampath, and Bipin Indurkhya

International Institute of Information Technology,
Hyderabad, India
{suvarna.rekha,sai.gollapudi,harini}@research.iiit.ac.in,
bipin@iiit.ac.in

Abstract. We developed a software application, *Read-Aid* to help improve reading pattern in children with Dyslexia with visual processing problems. We hypothesized that after a dyslexic child's interaction with our application, there will be an improvement in their reading speed and comprehension. We compared our results with existing masked-reading intervention approach. A between-group study was conducted with 15 children. Results were significant ($p = 0.026$) suggesting that our Read-Aid tool has potential as an assistive technology application.

Keywords: Non-linear reading, Assistive technology, Learning disabilities.

1 Introduction

Developmental dyslexia is a specific and significant impairment in reading abilities of children and adults who otherwise possess adequate intelligence and motivation. The prevalence rate is estimated to be around 5% to 10% in school-age children. Dyslexia can be comorbid with language difficulties, writing and mathematics disorders.

There have been multiple theories [1, 2] attributing dyslexia to difficulties in visual perception, auditory perception and phonological processing. Many studies on visual processing in dyslexic readers [3–6] have established that the eye-movement pattern of dyslexic readers is different from that of typical readers. The general finding is that while the eye-movement pattern of typical readers follows a linear pattern, the pattern is arbitrary in case of dyslexic readers.

In particular, Geiger *et al.* [7] proposed that dyslexic readers tend to have a wider spatial attention. In their experiment that required dyslexic and typical readers to recognize centrally and peripherally presented stimuli, they found that dyslexics recognized letters visually farther in the periphery better than typical readers. They posit that this wider spatial attention results in difficulties in picking one word from others. For intervention, they used a specially designed mask to be laid on the text being read, and found that training with the mask improved reading performance.

C. Stephanidis and M. Antona (Eds.): UAHCI/HCII 2013, Part III, LNCS 8011, pp. 297–304, 2013.

2   Read-Aid Tool

Inspired by the masked-text technique, we developed the Read-Aid Tool, which was built with a QT GUI front-end and a C++ backend. The GUI consists of two simple tabs: A start tab for setting the view, and a read tab to read the target text. (Fig. 1) shows the start tab of the tool. The read tab shown in (Fig. 2) is essentially blank except for a centered word or two of the text. The number of words, their font style and size are all set in the start tab. Read-Aid Tool replicates the masked-text technique by having only one word in the center, and then gradually increasing it to have more than one word during the course of intervention.

The input file of the text to be displayed is entered in the file name widget of the start tab, which is also used to set non-default font settings, and non-default number of words to display. If the default settings are acceptable, then the user needs to just enter the input or the source file to be browsed. The interaction between the Read-Aid Tool and the user is thus simplified, and the focus is shifted from tool interaction to the target text comprehension.

The effectiveness of the masked-text technique stems from having only one word in the center, and then gradually increasing it to have more than one word, and the Read-Aid Tool replicates it in the digital form.

Fig. 1. Read Aid - Teacher Interface

To evaluate the effectiveness of the ReadAid Tool, three null-hypotheses were identified.

1. (H1) A manual masked-text intervention for dyslexics with reading difficulty does not improve their reading skills
2. (H2) A software implementation of a similar masked-text technique also does not provide an improvement for reading skills for dyslexics
3. (H3) The quantum of improvement in reading skill for software technique is worse than the manual approach

Fig. 2. Read Aid - Student Interface

3   Evaluation

To test the *Read-Aid* tool, a between-groups experiment was setup. The participants were divided into three groups as below:

– Group 1 - No intervention control group
– Group 2 - Manual masked-technique group and
– Group 3 - Read-Aid Tool group

We identified three parameters to operationally measure the reading skill as follows:

Reading Speed is measured as the number of error-free words divided by reading time, where error-free words are the number of read words minus errors made in reading them; reading duration is measured as overall time taken for reading, which is the time lapse between the first-word utterance attempt and the completion of the last-word utterance.

Reading Errors Number of erroneous word-utterances during reading (not mispronunciations but incorrect word choices)

Reading Comprehension aggregate score in word recollection and word remembrance tests.

Pre- and post-tests were conducted to capture the quantum of reading skill improvement (dependent variable) observed due to the type of intervention (independent variable) applied.

4   Participants

Fifteen children (eight boys and seven girls) participated in the experiment, with their ages ranging from 8.5 to 11.5 years. Twelve of these children were diagnosed to be dyslexics in prior testing by an expert using DTLD [8] and Schonnell spelling test [9] . Three children who were not Dyslexics were used for comparison and evaluation purpose. Their scores were not part of the result analysis, but instead used for guiding the design of the experiment. For the dyslexics, average chronological age was 9.67 years (var=0.76), average reading age was 7.1 years (var=1.3), and average spelling age was 6.8 years (var=1.2). All participants were secondary school students with an expected fourth-grade level fluency in English. There were three children in Group 1 (control with no intervention), three in Group 2 (manual intervention), and the remaining nine children were in Group 3 (software intervention).

Table 1. DTLD and Schonell Spelling Test Scores

Age(Mean)	Manualmasking	Read Aid
ChornonlogicalAge	9.44	10.6
Spelling Age	7	8
Reading Age	6	8

5   Stimuli

For measuring reading skills, a full page of text at the fourth-grade level was chosen. The text was reviewed and found appropriate by a fourth-grade teacher. Stimuli consisted of three stories [10]. The first story was used to conduct the pre-test. The second story was used for practice (in the manual intervention Group 2 and in software intervention Group 3). The control Group 1 received no intervention. The third story was used for the post-test.

6   Procedure

All three groups followed the same procedure. First, a reading task (the first story) was given, during which the student's voice was recorded on a Zoom H1 MP3 audio recording device for measuring the reading speed, reading errors and comprehension errors. Next, a test was given to evaluate the child's reading level. Then the children in each group were treated with their respective interventions. The intervention sessions lasted for three days with two hours a day. The second story was used for this. Finally, a reading task (the third story) was given, during which the student's voice was recorded for measuring the reading speed, reading error and reading comprehension.

The instructions for both pre- and post-tests were given to the participants verbally. Pre- and post-tests were similar, and they consisted of an equal number of recall retention questions based on the stimuli stories. The questions were presented in the multiple-choice format. Both questions and answers were read to the child, and the child's answers were recorded for subsequent analysis.

7 Retention and Recall Tests

For all three groups, there were only three interactions with the child. In the first interaction, the pre-test was conducted, in the second, the intervention treatment was conducted, and in the third, the post-test was conducted. Prior to doing the pre- and post-tests, a reading task was given by asking the child to read aloud a given piece of text. The audio of the read text was recorded for subsequent analysis. After the reading task, as part of the pre- or the post-test, the children were asked to answer a series of questions, which measured either the content recall or information retention. The recall and retention tests were verbally read to all the children after completion of their reading task. These two tests consisted of instructions, followed by multiple-choice questions. For the retention test, the instructions read to all the children were: *You will now hear four words. These words might be similar in sound, but only one was used in the paragraph that you have just read. Can you tell me which of these four words was read by you just now?*. After this instruction, the researcher starts with the first question, followed by the next question, and so on, until all the five questions are exhausted.

For the recall test, simple factual questions about the story were asked. The children were instructed as follows: Listen to the question carefully and identify the correct answer from a given set of four possible answers. Note that the answers might be similar but only one is correct. So pick what you believe to be the correct answer. Questions were phrased in the form of *Who entered Billy's room?* or *How did father feel when he saw the puppy*. Multiple-choice answers were given.

All the phrases and words were derived from the just-read text. The apropriateness of these tests was confirmed in two ways: First, a fourth-grade teacher was asked to review the tests and her suggestions were incorporated; and second, a non-dyslexic fourth-grade student was asked to take the test for comparison.

8 Results

Overall, eleven of the fifteen participants produced over 110 minutes of MP3 audio and 160 answers to the pre- and post-test questions. The MP3 audio was analyzed using BS.Player v2.62, and also with Audacity v2.02 equipped with a LAME MP3 encoder, to measure time, quantity of words read, and the errors made in reading. A judge (school teacher, who is not involved in the execution of the experiment) counted the words and errors in reading. Mispronounced words were not counted as errors. Only incorrect words and un-articulated words were counted as errors. In some cases because of the non-linearity in reading, the skipped words were harder to count.

Reading speed was calculated by extracting the number of words read, the number of errors made in reading them, and the time taken to read them. It was calculated as $ReadingSpeed = (wordsread - errorsmade)/time$ For this experiment, the reading speed for Groups 2 and 3, respectively, was 13.1% and

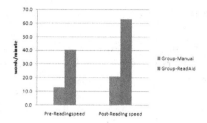

Fig. 3. Reading-Speed

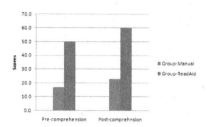

Fig. 4. Reading-Comprehension

40.3% in pre-tests, and 20.9% and 62.9% in post-tests (Fig. 3). It is important to mention that one set of dyslexics (Group 1) could not even read one word in the allocated five minutes. So, their speed was counted as 0 for our pre-test calculations. Reading errors were calculated by dividing the number of errors made by the overall number of words read. $ReadingError$ is represented in percentage. $ReadingError = (number - of - words - read - erroneously/all - words - read)$

The reading error for Groups 2 and 3, respectively, was 40% and 16% in pre-tests, and 36% and 7% in post-tests (Fig. 4). Because the children in Group 1 struggled to read, and could not even read a small portion in the allocated five minutes, so their error was set at 100 for the pre-test.

Improvement in the comprehension scores was calculated by summing up the correct answers given to the recall and retention questions posed in the pre- and post-tests.

$ComprehensionScores = (Recall + RetentionScores)$

The values of reading comprehension for Group 2 and 3, respectively, were 5.5 points and 4 points for pre-tests, and 7 and 4.4 points for post-tests (Figure 4). For Group 1 that struggled with the reading task itself, the recall and retention tests were overwhelming and unanswerable. Their scores were set to 0.

9   Discussion

Based on the results of the experiment, we found that with intervention there is a definite improvement in the reading speed, and reading comprehension scores, and the reading errors go down. With manual intervention the reading speed was observed to improve by approximately 41%. With Read-Aid Tool intervention, there is a further 3% increase. So, dyslexic children do benefit with either the manual masked-text approach, or with the ReadAid Tool approach. Amongst the two techniques, ReadAid is showing more improvement at 62.9%, a post-test value, which is a 44% improvement over the score of 40.3%. When it comes to reading errors, there is a 57% drop for the participants who used ReadAid Tool. That is, the Group 3 score dropped from a value of 16 to a new post-test value of 7. This is better than Group 2 (manual intervention) changes. For Group 2, the values also dropped, but not as much as the Group 3. Here the reduction for Group 2 was from 40% to 36%, which is a change of 9% Reading comprehension scores also showed a similar trend. The manual intervention and ReadAid Tool interventions showed a jump of 2.7 points and 2.2 points respectively. The Group 2 of 5.5 points improved to 7.7 points, and the Group 3 went from 4.0 points to 4.4 percent. However the overall result appears to be statistically significant ($F = (46.52, 37.17) = 5.632$ and $p = 0.026$).

10   Conclusion

Taking the overall pattern of measurements into consideration, we can clearly see that manual masked-text intervention yields an improvement over the control group (Table 1). Results also indicate that Read-Aid Tool intervention yields an improvement over the control group. With this we reject the null hypothesis H2, which states that a software implementation of a similar masked-text technique also does not provide an improvement for reading skills for Dyslexics. And finally, based on the collected data we see that Read-Aid Tool does show better results over the manual approach. With this we reject the final H3 hypothesis, which states that the quantum of improvement in reading skill for software technique is worse than the manual approach.

11   Future Work

This pilot study was designed primarily to explore the potential and promise of the Read-Aid Tool. As the results are promising, we feel that next steps would be to (1) repeat the experiment with more subjects, (2) do the treatment for a longer duration, and (3) do eye-tracker studies to establish the improvement in reading pattern. The current version of the tool is intended as a prototype. It can be further improved to contain more color control and text-to-speech features.

References

1. Ramus, F., Rosen, S., Dakin, S.C., Day, B.L., Castellote, J.M., White, S., Frith, U.: Theories of developmental dyslexia: insights from a multiple case study of dyslexic adults. Brain 126(4), 841–865 (2003)

2. Stein, J., Talcott, J., Walsh, V.: Controversy about the visual magnocellular deficit in developmental dyslexics. Trends in Cognitive Sciences 4(6), 209–210 (2000)

3. Eden, G., Stein, J., Wood, H., Wood, F.: Differences in eye movements and reading problems in dyslexic and normal children. Vision Research 34(10), 1345–1358 (1994)

4. Henderson, J.M., Ferreira, F.: Eye movement control during reading: Fixation measures reflect foveal but not parafoveal processing difficulty. Canadian Journal of Experimental Psychology 47(2), 201 (1993)

5. Pavlidis, G.T.: Eye movements in dyslexia their diagnostic significance. Journal of Learning Disabilities 18(1), 42–50 (1985)

6. Biscaldi, M., Gezeck, S., Stuhr, V.: Poor saccadic control correlates with dyslexia. Neuropsychologia 36(11), 1189–1202 (1998)

7. Geiger, G., Cattaneo, C., Galli, R., Pozzoli, U., Lorusso, M.L., Facoetti, A., Molteni, M.: Wide and diffuse perceptual modes characterize dyslexics in vision and audition. Perception 37(11), 1745 (2008)

8. Smriti, S., Mehta, D.: Behavioral Screening Device For Learning Disabilities. Department of Special Education, SNDT Women's University, Juhu Campus, Mumbai (1991)

9. Schonell, S.F.J., Wise, P.: Essentials in teaching and testing spelling. Macmillan, Basingstoke (1985)

10. Fourth grade reading comprehension, http://www.superteacherworksheets.com/, http://4th-comprehension.html (last accessed September 15, 2012)

Comparison of the Effectiveness of Different Accessibility Plugins Based on Important Accessibility Criteria

Alireza Darvishy and Hans-Peter Hutter

ZHAW Zurich University of Applied Sciences InIT Institute of Applied Information
Technology Winterthur, Switzerland
alireza.darvishy@zhaw.ch, hans-peter.hutter@zhaw.ch

Abstract. This paper compares two new freely available software plugins for MS PowerPoint and Word documents that we have developed at the ZHAW with similar tools with respect to important accessibility criteria. Our plugins [1, 2, 3] allow the analysis of accessibility issues and consequently the generation of fully accessible PDF documents. The document authors using these plugins require no specific accessibility knowledge. The plugins are based on a flexible software architecture concept [1] that allows the automatic generation of fully accessible PDF documents originating from various authoring tools, such as Adobe InDesign [5], Word or PowerPoint [6, 7]. Other available plugins, on the other hand, need accessibility knowledge in order to use them properly and effectively.

Keywords: Document accessibility, automatic generation of accessible PDF, screen reader, visual impairment, accessibility, tagged PDF, software architecture, PowerPoint and Word documents, PDF accessibility ISO standard.

1   Introduction

There are millions of PDF documents on the internet which are inaccessible to users with visual impairments using screen readers. In many cases, authors use authoring tools, such as Microsoft PowerPoint and Word [6, 7], to create these PDF documents. But all too often the resulting PDFs are not correctly tagged and therefore have to be manually post-processed in order to be turned into accessible PDFs. PDF tags provide a hidden structured textual representation of the PDF content that is interpreted by the screen readers. This meta-information has no effect on the visual presentation of the PDF file but is invaluable for screen readers. Manually post-processing incorrectly tagged PDFs is inefficient, very time consuming, and tedious. In addition, a separate solution is needed for each authoring tool because there is no single software solution that can be used with all the different authoring tools. A flexible software architecture was introduced in [4] to overcome these problems. The suggested architecture can be extended to include any authoring tool capable of creating PDF documents. For each authoring tool, a software accessibility plugin must be implemented that analyzes the logical structure of the document and creates an XML representation of it. This XML

C. Stephanidis and M. Antona (Eds.): UAHCI/HCII 2013, Part III, LNCS 8011, pp. 305–310, 2013.
© Springer-Verlag Berlin Heidelberg 2013

file is used in combination with an untagged non-accessible PDF to create an accessible PDF version of the document.

Recently, researchers at the ZHAW developed two software accessibility plugins for Microsoft Word and PowerPoint based on the suggested architecture. The typical accessibility issues that arise when creating a PDF document with an authoring tool such as Microsoft PowerPoint or Word are, for example, missing alternative text for images, missing table headers, heading structure and document language, or incorrect reading order. Although newer versions of Microsoft PowerPoint and Word provide facilities to overcome some of the above-mentioned issues, authors are still required to have specific accessibility and authoring tool knowledge in order to fix them. The newly developed plugins for PowerPoint and Word require no special knowledge either of accessibility issues or of fixing them.

There are also some other tools available for checking accessibility issues of Microsoft Word and PowerPoint documents, which are briefly described here.

— Accessibility Checker for MS Office: The Accessibility Checker functions like a spell checker, in that it highlights any accessibility issues that may be present in a document, including hyperlinks, document structure, font, and closed captioning on any inserted audio and visual [9].
— AccessODF: AccessODF is an extension for LibreOffice Writer which helps authors to evaluate and solve accessibility issues in OpenDocument texts, including color contrast, text alternatives for images and other objects, as well as the use of proper heading styles instead of big bold text to identify headings [10].

This part describes important criteria for comparing the effectiveness of currently known accessibility plugins for MS-Word and PowerPoint documents. These plugins allow authors using MS-Word and PowerPoint to check their documents in terms of accessibility issues, to facilitate correcting them, and finally to generate accessible PDF documents.

The suggested criteria are divided into two categories:

— General criteria,
— Technical criteria.

1.1   General Criteria

This category contains the following criteria:

— Transparency: This defines whether the accessibility software for MS-Word and PowerPoint is immediately visible to the user. The ZHAW accessibility plugin is visible in the usual MS-Office 2010 Ribbon-style. This is important for the user to be aware of the available functionality constantly while working with MS-Word and PowerPoint. For the MS-Office Accessibility Checker this is not the case: The user has to look and find out the location of the functionality.

— Accessibility Know-How: The ZHAW accessibility plugin requires no special know-how in terms of accessibility and knowledge to fix the accessibility issues shown in the plugin. With the MS-Office plugin the user only gets messages and descriptions about accessibility issues, however she or he must know how to fix the issues in MS-Word and PowerPoint themselves.
— Learning Curve: As the ZHAW accessibility plugins require no special accessibility knowledge, using them can be learned quickly.
— Accessibility Working Set: The ZHAW accessibility plugins provide an integrated set of tools to ensure accessibility: Checking accessibility issues, providing the user with accessibility conform styles, a facility to define accessibility conform MS-Word templates, and a shortcut for creating accessible PDF documents are all in one place.

1.2   Technical Criteria

All tools produce different message types in order to alert the document creator about errors, warnings or hints. The following tables illustrate these in comparison.

The first table compares accessibility plugins for MS-Word, the second one for MS-PowerPoint.

2   Comparison of Different Plugins Based on Important Accessibility Criteria

In Table 1 we present a comparison of three different accessibility checking plugins for Word documents. Table 2 presents the comparison of two different accessibility checking plugins for PDF documents.

3   Conclusion

This paper compared two newly implemented accessibility plugins for Microsoft Office 2010 with other similar tools. These plugins are freely available and help authors of MS-Word and PowerPoint 2010 documents to check their documents in terms of accessibility, fix them easily and finally create accessible PDF documents. Microsoft Accessibility checkers enable authors to check accessibility issues, however, authors must still know how to fix these issues. AccessODF has similar features to the ZHAW Word Accessibility plugin but it is only available for Open Office Writer documents. The ZHAW Accessibility plugins provides authors with an analysis tool as well as facilities to fix them and create accessible PDF documents in one place.

Table 1. Comparison of three different accessibility checking plugins for Word documents

Accessibility Test Item	ZHAW Word Accessibility Plugin	MS Accessibility Checker	AccessODF (OpenOffice.org Writer Plugin)
Check if document title exists	Checks if document title exists (Error).	-	Checks if document title exists (Warning).
Check if table header is specified	User should specify whether the first column or first row or both are table headings or whether the table is only for layout purposes. (Error/Warning).	No header row specified (Error). No alt text for a table (Error). Table rows or columns are blank (Warning).	Checks if table heading row(s) are present (Warning).
Check if alt text is set	No alternative text provided (Error). User can mark it as decorative or informative; if it is marked as informative then there should be also an alternative text.	No alternative text for picture or object (Error).	Image has no text alternative (Title and/or Description). (Error).
Check hyperlinks	No hyperlink Screen Tip is set (Warning). User can add "Screen Tip text" or mark it as "Screen Tip not required"	No hyperlink Screen Tip is set (Warning).	Language of a hyperlink set to „None" (Error).
Check heading hierarchy	Heading order is not correct (Error). User can set a heading to "style body", "text style", or "outline level".	Heading order is not correct (Hint).	Heading order is not correct (Error).
Check language settings	Language settings can be checked.	-	Checks for missing language identification for the document and for language changes inside it (Warnings).
Check Contrast	-	-	Checks for insufficient contrast between background and font color (Error).

Table 2. Comparison of two different accessibility checking plugins for PDF documents

Accessibility Test Item	PowerPoint Accessibility PlugIn	MS Accessibility Checker
Check if slide title exists	Checks if slide title exists (Error).	Checks if slide title exists (Error).
Check if alt text is set	No text provided (Error). User can mark it as decorative or informative; if it is marked as informative then there should be also an alternative text.	No alternative text is specified (Error).
Check if table header is specified	User should specify if first column or first row or both are table headings or the table is a layout table (Error/Warning).	No header row specified (Error). No alt text for a table (Error). Table rows or columns are blank (Warning).
Check language settings	Is language set correctly (Question). User can mark it as correct, as the exact language or as default language.	-
Check reading order	Is Reading order correct (Question)	Is reading order correct (Hint).
Check if hyperlink Screen Tip is set	No Screen Tip provided (Question). User can specify if "no Screen Tip is required" or "add a text".	Unclear Hyperlink text (Warning).
Check font size	Different font sizes (Warning). User can mark it as verified or change it.	-

References

1. Darvishy, A., Hutter, H.-P., Horvath, A., Dorigo, M.: A Flexible Software Architecture Concept for the Creation of Accessible PDF Documents. In: Miesenberger, K., Klaus, J., Zagler, W., Karshmer, A. (eds.) ICCHP 2010, Part 1. LNCS, vol. 6179, pp. 47–52. Springer, Heidelberg (2010)
2. Darvishy, A., Leemann, T., Hutter, H.-P.: Two software plugins for the creation of fully accessible PDF documents based on a flexible software architecture. In: Miesenberger, K., et al. (eds.) ICCHP 2012, Part I. LNCS, vol. 7382, pp. 621–624. Springer, Heidelberg (2012)
3. PowerPoint- and Word Accessibility Plugin Download,
   `http://www.zhaw.ch/fileadmin/user_upload/`
   `engineering/_Institute_und_Zentren/INIT/HII/Accessibility/`
   `AccessibilityAddins/MSOfficeAccessibilityAddInsSetup.zip`
4. Darvishy, A., Hutter, H.-P., Mannhart, O.: Web Application for Analysis, Manipulation and Generation of Accessible PDF Documents. In: Stephanidis, C. (ed.) Universal Access in HCI, Part IV, HCII 2011. LNCS, vol. 6768, pp. 121–128. Springer, Heidelberg (2011)
5. Adobe InDesign, `http://www.adobe.com/products/indesign/`
6. Microsoft Office Word, `http://office.microsoft.com/word/`
7. Microsoft Office PowerPoint, `http://office.microsoft.com/powerpoint/`
8. A New Standard for PDF Accessibility: PDF/UA,
   `http://blogs.adobe.com/accessibility/2012/08/pdf-ua.html`
9. Microsoft Accessibility Checker,
   `http://office.microsoft.com/en-us/word-help/`
   `check-for-accessibility-issues-HA010369192.aspx`
10. AccessODF, `http://sourceforge.net/p/accessodf/home/Home/`

Nonvisual Presentation and Navigation within the Structure of Digital Text-Documents on Mobile Devices

Martin Lukas Dorigo[1], Bettina Harriehausen-Mühlbauer[2], Ingo Stengel[1], and Paul S. Haskell-Dowland[1]

[1] Plymouth University, Plymouth, United Kingdom
[2] University of Applied Sciences Darmstadt, Darmstadt, Germany
martin.dorigo@plymouth.ac.uk

Abstract. This paper introduces a novel concept for an assistive technology in support of blind and visually impaired persons for nonvisual presentation and navigation within the structure of digital text-documents on mobile devices (smart phones, internet tablets, etc.) which enables them to get a fast overview over the structure of an entire document. The advantages compared to state of the art screen readers are that it enables them to identifying the type, position, length and context of each logical structure element, the current cursor position within the document as well as to accessing any structure element at any time in an arbitrary order. For the nonvisual presentation of the document structure elements auditory icons, tones and vibration feedback are used. Navigation and cursor routing is provided by performing gestures on the touch screen. There is no expensive special hardware required.

Keywords: Assistive technology, nonvisual, presentation, navigation, cursor routing, mobile devices, smart phone, internet tablet, auditory icon, tone, vibration feedback, touch screen, gestures, logical structure, overview, skimming and scanning, document accessibility, blind, visual impairment.

1 Introduction

There are thousands of digital text-documents such as websites or PDF files available on the Internet. Especially for large and highly structured documents like newspaper articles or scientific literature the structure is very important. If the reader has on overview over the structure of the entire document in mind, he is able to efficiently skimm and scann over the document and to quickly find relevant information within the document's content, he is searching for.

On visual media like screen or print, each logical structure element is physically presented by a specific visualisation, allowing sighted readers to recognise the structure at a glance. This structure can be quite complex. Therefore most user agents for the reading of digital text-documents provide a visual overview function, where the structure of the document is only (without the content) visually presented at a higher level of abstraction. The content (text and graphics) is substituted by place holders like dots, lines and thumbnails, indicating the length and size of it [Fig. 1].

C. Stephanidis and M. Antona (Eds.): UAHCI/HCII 2013, Part III, LNCS 8011, pp. 311–320, 2013.
© Springer-Verlag Berlin Heidelberg 2013

Blind and visually impaired persons on the other hand can not see this visual physical presentation of the logical document structure.

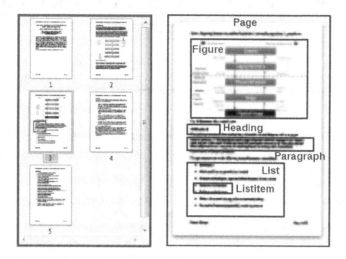

Fig. 1. Visual presentation and navigation over the structure of digital text-documents

2   State of the Art

Blind and visually impaired persons are using screen readers like Apple VoiceOver [1], Google TalkBack [2] or JAWS for Windows [3] for the nonvisual reading of digital text-documents [Fig. 2.].

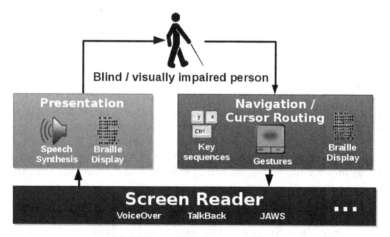

Fig. 2. State of the art screen reader

The screen reader uses speech synthesis or a braille display for presenting the text to the user. These output methods are mainly purposed for presenting text (document content) but not for the presentation of non-text data like the logical document structure.

Navigation and cursor routing commands are provided by performing key sequences on the keyboard, using the cursor routing keys of the braille display or by performing gestures on a multitouch pad or touchscreen. These commands enable the user to identify which element types and number of each type are contained within the document for e.g. by browsing the list of headings, list of graphics, list of hyperlinks, etc. But they do not provide any information about the position, length and context of a structure element and the current cursor position within the document. Furthermore it is not possible to access any structure element at any time in arbitrary order.

In addition to these commands, VoiceOver allows the user to explore which element of the currently visible portion of the document is visually physically rendered at which position on the screen by touching the touchpad or touchscreen at an arbitrary position and by sliding horizontally or vertically. But the knowledge of this physical structure does not necessary implicate the understanding of the logical structure behind it.

Several research projects aim to present various types of structured non-text data in a nonvisual way: Presenting HTML structure in audio [4], haptic cues to aid nonvisual structure recognition [5], nonvisual overviews of complex data sets [6], document structure presentation and navigation using a braille display [7], spatial exploration of web pages [8], intelligent non-visual navigation of complex HTML structures [9] and navigation of hierarchical structures [10].

But at the moment there is no solution for nonvisual presentation and navigation within the structure of digital text-documents on mobile devices.

3   Preliminary Results

My relevant survey [11] among 205 blind and visually impaired persons proved the need for a novel concept for nonvisual presentation and navigation within the structure of digital text-documents on mobile devices.

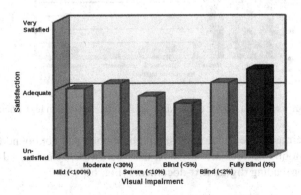

Fig. 3. Satisfaction with their current situation as to the reading of digital text-documents

At the moment all categories of blind and visually impaired persons are not very satisfied with their current situation as to the reading of digital text-documents [Fig. 3]. There is serious need for action required.

The logical document structure is very important for them as to the reading and navigation of a text-document [Fig. 4]. All of the participants would wish to have a better overview over the structure.

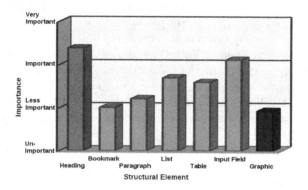

Fig. 4. Importance of logical structure elements for blind and visually impaired persons

Keyboard and mouse (for the categories who are not fully blind) are the most used input methods for the reading and navigation within digital text-documents [Fig. 5]. The participants would wish to have a more easy, intuitive and standardised method.

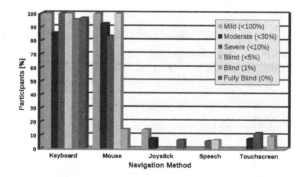

Fig. 5. Input methods used for the reading and navigation within text-documents

In addition their assistive technology should be mobile and not bound to a fixed location because mobile devices are the most used hardware by blind and visually impaired persons for reading digital text-documents [Fig. 6].

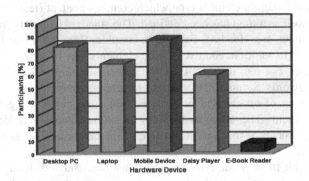

Fig. 6. Hardware devices used by blind and visually impaired for reading text-documents

4 Novel Concept

The following concept for nonvisual presentation and navigation within the structure of digital text-documents on mobile devices has been developed as a result of the state of the art and the initial survey [Fig. 7]:

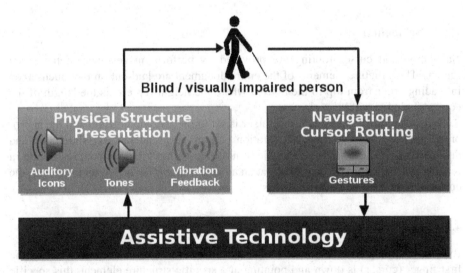

Fig. 7. Concept for nonvisual presentation and navigation within the structure of digital text-documents on mobile devices

4.1 Presentation

The logical document structure is physically presented in a nonvisual way serving the aural and the tactile human sense.

For each logical structure element type which contains content (text or graphic) an auditory icon as well as a tone has been defined. The standard elements, valid for any type of text-document, are: Heading, Paragraph, Graphic, Hyperlink, List-item, Table-row and Table-cell. In addition, context specific elements may be defined for specific types of documents. For e.g. in case of scientific literature these additional elements are: Abstract, Keywords, Summary, Conclusions, References, etc.

The auditory icon of an element is rendered when the cursor (finger) enters or passes by the element. The appropriate tones are simultaneously rendered for all nested structure elements at the current position of the cursor as long as the cursor is within an element.

The pitch at with these auditory icons and tones are rendered describes the hierarchy level of an element. Level 1 starts at musical note C4 (261.63 Hz). For each level, the pitch is increased by one note until B4. This allows the presentation of a maximum of 7 (resp. 12 if half tones are included) distinguishable hierarchy levels.

As with the aural medium, for each logical structure element containing content a vibration pattern has been defined. The appropriate vibration patterns are simultaneously rendered for all nested structure elements at the current position of the cursor as long as the cursor is within an element.

The speed at which the vibration pattern is rendered describes the hierarchy level of the element.

4.2   Navigation

Navigation and cursor routing are provided by performing gestures on the touch screen. The structure elements of the entire document are laid-out on the touchscreen in reading order from top to the bottom where the height represents the length of the content included within an element.

By putting down one finger, the cursor is set to the specific position and the appropriate auditory icons, tones and vibration patterns are rendered. By sliding up and down with one finger, the user is able to navigate within the document's structure in reading order forward and backward at an arbitrary speed. By lifting up the finger, the cursor is removed and rendering stops.

4.3   Cursor Routing

By single tapping with one additional finger anywhere on the touchscreen during the first finger (cursor) is down and pointing at a specific structure element, this specific element can be selected and the system cursor routed to it. This can be used for e.g. for reading the content contained in the selected element (text or textalternative for graphics) to the person using speech synthesis.

4.4   Advantages

The advantages of this proposed concept compared to state of the art screen readers are that it enables blind and visually impaired persons to:

1. Identify the **type** of each structure element and number of each type contained within the document
2. Identify the **position** of each structure element within the document
3. Identify the **length** of the content contained in each structure element
4. Identify the **context** of each structure element
5. Identify the current **cursor position** within the document
6. **Access** any structure element at any time in an arbitrary order

There is no expensive special hardware required. All features used are included in mobile devices out of the box. However the concept is not limited to mobile devices. It can also be used on a regular laptop or desktop PC by connecting a standard multi-touch pad and vibration feedback device to it.

In addition to blind and visually impaired the concept also benefits persons without disability in situations where the visual sense is in use by other activities and since the displays of mobile devices are much smaller than on regular laptop and desktop PCs.

Furthermore the concept is not limited to the context of text-documents. It can be used for nonvisual presentation and navigation within any hierarchical structure containing any kind of content (for e.g. program source code or file systems).

5   Evaluation Methodology

As proof of concept, a prototype App has been implemented for conducting a quantitative analysis. A pilot test with the implemented prototype is going on among blind and visually impaired participants online via Internet.

5.1   Research Questions

The hypotheses in [Chapter 4.4] lead to the following research questions. Does the proposed novel concept enable blind and visually impaired persons to:

1. Identify the type of each structure element and number of each type contained within the document ?
2. Identify the **position** of each structure element within the document ?
3. Identify the **length** of the content contained in each structure element ?
4. Identify the **context** of each structure element ?
5. Identify the current **cursor position** within the document ?
6. **Access** any structure element at any time in an arbitrary order ?
7. Receive **additional value** compared to using state of the art screen readers ?
8. Improve their **satisfaction** as to the reading of digital text-documents compared to the initial situation [Chapter 3] ?

5.2   Procedure

After the participants have downloaded, installed and started the prototype App on their own mobile device, the following procedure will be initiated [Fig. 8].

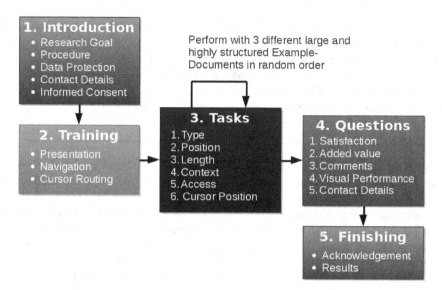

Fig. 8. Evaluation Methodology Procedure

At the beginning an introduction gives detailed description of the research containing all relevant information, a person requires to decide, if the person would like to participate within the pilot test or not. This includes: Research goal, procedure, data protection, contact details of the researcher as well as of the supervisory team and ethical approval. If the person decides to participate into the pilot test, he or she gives informed consent and confirming the minimal age 18 years.

The introduction is followed by a training of the novel auditory icons, tones and vibration pattern for the aural and tactile presentation of each structure element as well as the gestures for navigation and cursor routing.

After the training the participant is asked to perform the following tasks. This part will be repeated with 3 different large and highly structured example documents in random order. In addition, the time as well as finger movements performed are recorded.

1. Identifying which element **types** and number of each element type are contained within the document.
2. Routing the cursor to the **position** of a specific element within the document
3. Routing the cursor to the **longest** as well as to the **shortest** element
4. Finding the element within a specific **context**. For e.g. the graphic within a third subsection followed by a list
5. Locating the current **cursor position** within the document
6. **Accessing** different structure elements in an arbitrary order. For e.g. selecting an element in the middle, afterwards one at the end and finally one at the beginning of the document.

Subsequent to the tasks, the participants are asked to answer the following questions:

1. Does the proposed concept provide an **additional value** for them compared to using state of the art screen readers ?
2. How **satisfied** are the participants with their current situation as to the reading of digital text-documents using this novel concept ?
3. Additional **comments** like advantages, disadvantages and ideas for further improvement ?
4. Which **visual performance** do the participants have ?
5. Optionally **contact details** like e-mail, phone number or address. This is used for further questions and for sending the published results.

In the end, the participants are acknowledged for their participation in this pilot test and they are informed how they can obtain the published results. After that the App will be automatically terminated and the result will be sent back via Internet.

5.3   Prototype App

A prototype App, that implements the presented test procedure, has been developed. This App is freely available for anyone who is interested in testing this novel concept and in participating in this pilot test using their own mobile device. It can be downloaded from the Apple App Store on iTunes for iOS devices as well as from Google Play for users of the Android operating system.

5.4   Pilot Test

At the moment a pilot test is going on among 163 blind and visually impaired persons using the implemented prototype App online via Internet using their own mobile devices. First results successfully proved that the proposed concept provides a potential solution and may be a great contribution to the field of document accessibility. The results of this pilot test will be published in further publications.

6   Conclusions

The logical structure of large and highly structured text-documents is very important for the reader but blind and visually impaired persons can not see the visual physical structure presentation. At the moment, there is no solution for nonvisual presentation and navigation within the structure of digital text-documents on mobile devices. Therefore a novel concept has been developed using auditory icons, tones and vibration feedback for presentation and gestures on the touch screen for navigation and cursor routing. First results of an ongoing pilot test among blind and visually impaired participants using an implemented prototype App successfully proved that the proposed concept provides a potential solution and may be a great contribution to the field of document accessibility.

References

1. Apple, VoiceOver for iOS,
   http://www.apple.com/accessibility/voiceover (last accessed: January 28, 2013)
2. Google TalkBack: An Open Source Screenreader for Android,
   http://www.google.com/accessibility/products/ (last accessed: January 28, 2013)
3. Freedom Scientific, JAWS for Windows Screen Reading Software,
   http://www.freedomscientific.com/products/fs/
   jaws-product-page.asp (last accessed: January 28, 2013)
4. James, F.: Presenting HTML Structure in Audio: User Satisfaction with Audio Hypertext. In: Proceedings of the International Conference on Auditory Display, ICAD 1996, Palo Alto, CA, USA, November 4-6 (1996)
5. Jay, C., Stevens, R., Hubbold, R., Glencross, R.: Using haptic cues to aid nonvisual structure recognition. Journal ACM Transactions on Applied Perception (TAP) 5(2), Article No. 8 (2008)
6. Kildal, J., Brewster, S.A.: Non-visual overviews of complex data sets. In: Proceedings of the ACM SIGCHI Conference on Human Factors in Computing Systems, CHI 2006, Monréal, Québec, Canada, April 22-27 (2006)
7. Minatani, K.: Development of a DAISY Player That Utilizes a Braille Display for Document Structure Presentation and Navigation. In: Miesenberger, K., et al. (eds.) ICCHP 2012, Part I. LNCS, vol. 7382, pp. 515–522. Springer, Heidelberg (2012)
8. Petit, G., Dufresne, A., Robert, J.-M.: Introducing tactoWeb: A tool to spatially explore web pages for users with visual impairment. In: Stephanidis, C. (ed.) Universal Access in HCI, Part I, HCII 2011. LNCS, vol. 6765, pp. 276–284. Springer, Heidelberg (2011)
9. Pontelli, E., Gillan, D., Gupta, G., Karshmer, A., Saad, E., Xiong, W.: Intelligent nonvisual navigation of complex HTML structures. In: Universal Access in the Information Society, vol. 2(1), pp. 56–69 (2002)
10. Smith, A.C., Cook, J.S., Francioni, J.M., Hossain, A., Anwar, M., Fayezur Rahman, M.: Nonvisual tool for navigating hierarchical structures. In: Proceedings of the 6th International ACM SIGACCESS Conference on Computers and Accessibility, ASSETS 2004, New York, New York, USA, October 18-20 (2004)
11. Dorigo, M., Harriehausen-Mühlbauer, B., Stengel, I., Dowland, P.S.: Survey: Improving document accessibility from the blind and visually impaired user's point of view. In: Stephanidis, C. (ed.) Universal Access in HCI, Part IV, HCII 2011. LNCS, vol. 6768, pp. 129–135. Springer, Heidelberg (2011)

Usability of Web Search Interfaces for Blind Users – A Review of Digital Academic Library User Interfaces

Tapio Haanperä and Marko Nieminen

Aalto University School of Science, P.O. Box 15400, 00076 AALTO, Finland
{tapio.haanpera,marko.nieminen}@aalto.fi

Abstract. In this paper we report our findings on the usability of four digital academic library databases when used by blind individuals using a screen reader. Our interaction level analysis shows that despite improvements in accessibility guidelines and technologies web search interfaces still lack good usability for screen reader users. Accessibility issues appear to have been addressed from the angle of technical readability instead of usability or user experience. As a result of the analysis we present design suggestions for making a web search interface more usable for screen reader users: 1) Highlighting search results (e.g. using headings), 2) No unnecessary elements before search results, 3) Search edit field and button in the beginning, 4) Descriptive labeling of search elements, 5) Abstract right after the search result title.

Keywords: accessibility, usability, screen readers, web search, user interface.

1 Introduction

Digital academic library databases (DALD) are standard and everyday tools for researchers and students. Without these, efficient research work is not possible anymore. Therefore, many academic and research institutions have provided gateways and access to these databases as part of the modern offering of their library services. The access to these databases is, however, not straightforward and consistent between different database providers and publishers. The search interface is the key element in providing a smooth user experience for the users of the databases and services.

Modern search interfaces are widely considered easy-to-use. However, this is not the case with all users. Even though 92% of sighted users share this easy-to-use experience, only 7% of the non-sighted users agree with this (Buzzi et al. 2004). Therefore, in addition to the visual appearance of the search interface, the invisible screen-reader accessible structure is similarly important.

In this paper, we analyze the usability of search interfaces for non-sighted persons using a screen reader. We have analyzed the user interfaces of four popular DALDs emphasizing not just accessibility but also usability. At the end of the paper we outline suggestions for screen-reader-friendly search interfaces.

C. Stephanidis and M. Antona (Eds.): UAHCI/HCII 2013, Part III, LNCS 8011, pp. 321–330, 2013.
© Springer-Verlag Berlin Heidelberg 2013

2   Concepts and Related Research

2.1   Using Screen Readers

Screen readers are software tools that enable visually impaired and blind individuals to use a computer. A screen reader interprets the visual content on a display and describes this information to the user using synthesized speech. The content is read to the user in a serial manner so that a user only interacts with one element at a time.

A sighted user can scan the page quickly to get an overview of the page structure and find the relevant content quickly. However for a non-sighted user this is usually a major challenge and can be a time consuming and frustrating process. (e.g. Rakesh et al., 2009; Lazar et al., 2007; Di Blas et al., 2004)

A screen reader user uses the keyboard to interact. Screen readers have several different keyboard commands that enable more efficient manners of interaction. On a web page the screen reader starts to read the page from the beginning (i.e. from the top left corner of the display). This is not a very efficient way of reading considering the amount of irrelevant content a single page typically includes. However the user does not need to read every single element on a web page. Screen readers allow users to use keyboard commands to browse through and jump over different elements. A blind individual can, for example, go through all the links, headings, lists, tables, form fields, edit fields, and graphic elements of a web page. This makes browsing a web page and accessing relevant and interesting content more efficient.

WebAIM (2012) conducted a survey of 1782 screen reader users in 2012. The study showed how differently screen reader users browse the web stating that - "there is no typical screen reader user". This can be a major design challenge for web developers trying to make their sites not only accessible but more usable for screen reader users. In this paper we aim to bridge this gap through analyzing the use of search interfaces with screen readers from the usability viewpoint.

Screen reader users mentioned to try navigating through headings (60.8% of the respondents) first in order to find information (WebAIM (2012). Navigating through links was mentioned by 13.2% of the respondents. Landmarks were used by 2.3%.

2.2   Accessibility

Accessibility can be considered as "reachability". Accessibility enables the non-sighted users to access and use the website or service mainly from the technical viewpoint. Accessibility ensures the "technical readability" for the non-sighted users. However, this is not a sufficient level of operation for optimal efficiency. In a study by Christopher et al. (2012) only 50.4 % of all the problems that non-sighted users encountered were addressed by Success Criteria in the WCAG 2.0. In order to achieve the more advanced levels of usage, we need to address both usability and user experience of the service when used with a screen reader (e.g. Buzzi et al. 2004; Di Blas et al. 2004 & Byerley et al. 2005).

2.3   Usability

Usability has been defined in ISO 9241-11 standard (1998) as "the extent to which specified users can achieve specified results with specified effectiveness, efficiency, and satisfactions". In addition to this definition, some research-originated definitions of usability are widely used, namely the one published by Nielsen (1993). We use the following integrated metrics from both of these definitions while reviewing the four web search interfaces:

Effectiveness – Are the basic search tasks technically achievable using a screen reading software?

Learnability – How efficient is it for the user to perform basic tasks successfully at the first time?

Efficiency – How quickly can a user perform tasks after learning to use the search interface?

Memorability – How efficiently can a user use the search interface after not having used the service for a while?

Satisfaction – How pleasant is it to use the search interfaces?

2.4   Search Engine Interfaces Used with a Screen Reader

Research has been done on search engine interfaces and how they can be accessed using a screen reader (Buzzi et al. 2004, Leporini et al. 2004A, Leporini et al. 2004B Andronico et al. 2006 and Ivory et al. 2004). The challenges of these interfaces are very similar to those when browsing any other web page – i.e. navigating and finding relevant and interesting content on a web page efficiently. In a survey by WebAIM (2009) Google was the "favorite web site" among screen reader users. This was for all web sites and not just for search engines.

Most screen reader users do not believe that search engines are easy-to-use (Ivory et al. 2005). In a study by Buzzi et al. (2004) only 7% of non-sighted users felt that search engines are easy-to-use. In comparison 92% of sighted users considered the same search user interfaces easy-to-use. For non-sighted users it was harder to find the information they were looking for. Reading the additional information provided for each search result is also harder for non-sighted users (Ivory et al. 2005).

Leporini et al. (2004A) have set some instructions on how to design a more usable search engine interface for screen reader users. Below are listed the guidelines that are the most relevant regarding our review and the tasks we conducted on each DALD:

1. Search elements such as search fields and buttons should be labeled correctly and placed at the top of the page. This makes accessing them more rapid.
2. The result area should be highlighted using a heading before the results.
3. The search results should be placed in a numbered list so that each list item is a link to the result. Also a summary of the result should be placed here. The results list should be placed just after the result notification.

3   Our Study: Analysis of Four Search Interfaces

A search task was performed for four different DALDs: IEEE Xplore, ACM, Scopus and Google Scholar. The search term used was "user experience" in order to ensure a vast amount of search results. The aim of this was to find out how a non-sighted individual can find relevant and interesting information (e.g. research articles) from these databases. Table 1 presents the four tasks that were conducted on each of the four digital academic library database.

Table 1. Tasks performed for each DALD

Task #	Task description
1	Performing a simple search: This included finding the search elements (i.e. search edit field) from the site and performing a simple search. The search term used was "user experience".
2	Finding the title of the first search result: This task included finding the first search result from the results page.
3	Browsing the result titles one-by-one: This task included going through the titles of the search results one-by-one. This task was performed after the user had navigated to the title of the first search result.
4	Accessing and reading the additional information: This included accessing and reading additional information about a search result. This was done in the result page without having to leave the page. All sites provided at least the following information: authors, publisher, publication year and a short summary or the abstract of the search result. This information was displayed below the title.

The review was done by one non-sighted and skillful screen-reader user. The analysis includes a low-level description of the interaction a non-sighted individual is required to do in order to complete the four basic tasks. The screen reading software tells the number of headings and links of a web page automatically after a page is loaded. This information is presented in this paper as well.

We applied the most used methods of navigating a web page described in the WebAIM (2012) survey to the web search interfaces we reviewed. These methods were only used for browsing the search results (tasks 2 and 3). Task 4 was accomplished using the down arrow key and spacebar if links had to be opened in order to complete the task successfully.

The review was conducted using Microsoft Windows 7 operating system and Internet Explorer 9 web browser. The screen reading software used, was JAWS (version 13.0.1006) by Freedom Scientific. These were chosen since they are all the most popular among screen reader users (WebAIM, 2012). Other assistive technologies such as braille displays were not used in this study.

Leporini et al. (2004A) and Leporini et al. (2004B) suggested the use of list elements displaying the search results. For this reason we used lists as well when trying to navigate the web search interfaces. We also tried to find the most efficient way (i.e. least amount of keystrokes – inputs from the user) of doing the four tasks described. The number of keystrokes needed by a user was recorded for each method and search interface. We start from the assumption that the number of user inputs correlates straightly to learnability and efficiency. Subjective satisfaction is affected by these two (Lazar et al. 2007).

In our study, the DALDs were accessed through the gateway of the Aalto University library which provides a full-text access to all the analyzed databases. The search user interfaces may vary if accessed through other gateways and proxies.

3.1   ACM Digital Library

After loading ACM Digital Library (ACM) the screen reader informed that there are 48 links and no headings on the first page. On the first page there is only one edit field that did not have a label indicating that what it is used for. After the edit box there is a button that is labeled "Search" that made the purpose of the edit field more apparent. After this performing a search task was accomplished easily.

The first results page contained 171 links and no headings. The search results were not highlighted as headings or as a list. Therefore, at the first time it was only possible to find the first result by going through links). This required 43 keystrokes since the 43rd link on that page was the title of the first search result. Navigating to a next search result through links required at least 3 keystrokes depending of the additional information (e.g. number of authors) between two result titles.

After getting more familiar with the site structure it came apparent that the search results are actually presented inside a table. The search result titles and other additional information about the result were presented on the second column. After this it was possible to browse the search results in a more efficient manner - requiring total of 5 keystrokes accessing the first search result and 3 keystrokes navigating to the next search result. (Navigating inside a table between columns requires three keys to be pressed simultaneously on the keyboard.)

Accessing the short summary of a search result required 10 keystrokes.

3.2   Google Scholar

The search page of Google Scholar had 13 links and no headings. After loading the page, the screen reader activated the edit field (apparently the Search box) automatically. The edit field did not have a label. The next element after the edit field was a link to advanced search and the element after that was a search button.

After performing a simple search the search results page contained 10 headings and 108 links. Each search result was highlighted using heading tags. This made it possible to navigate to the first search result and browse the titles of the search results one-by-one using just the 'H' –key on the keyboard. By default 10 search results were displayed per search result page. In the results page there were 3 lists as well. These lists contained sorting and filtering elements for the search results.

After the result title, authors and publisher, a short description including samples of the article was presented. Accessing this information required 3 keystrokes.

3.3   Scopus

The first page of Scopus contained 50 links and one heading. The only edit field on that page was activated automatically by the screen reader. The edit field was labeled "Search term". The search button was the fourth element after the edit field.

The first search result page contained 269 links and 1 heading. The search results were not highlighted using headings or lists. For this reason the first result on that page was found by going through links. This required 43 keystrokes. Browsing through all of the links one-by-one it was possible to find the next results as well. This required 7 keystrokes.

We were able to find a more efficient way of finding the first search result by first navigating to the first combo box on that page (the 'X' –key), then navigating to the next check box (the 'C' –key) and then pressing the down arrow key twice. Navigating to a next search result could be done similarly without navigating to a combo box. This method reduced the number of keystrokes needed and made performing tasks 2 and 3 more efficient.

After each result title there was additional information regarding the result. It was possible to open the full abstract on the same page without having to leave the site. This required 16 keystrokes. There was also a link to show all the abstracts of each search result which revealed abstracts' of each search result displayed.

3.4   IEEE Xplore

The first page of IEEE Xplore contained 61 links and 7 headings. On this page there was only 1 edit field which was labeled "Search term". After the edit field was the search button.

On the first result page there was 326 links and 34 headings. Each search result was highlighted and tagged as headings. The first result was the fourth heading on that page. Finding the first search result in this site required 4 key strokes. Browsing to the next search result required 1 key stroke.

The full abstract of a search result could be opened in the results page. This required 22 keystrokes. This way the user did not have to leave the results page in order to read the abstract from another page.

4   Analysis

All of the web search interfaces reviewed performed very different from each other using a screen reader. All sites had their advantages and disadvantages. All of the databases reviewed were technically accessible – i.e. they all could be operated using a screen reader.

A challenge users of a screen reader typically face is finding the relevant and interesting content in a web page. Navigating to the first search result and browsing through the rest of the results showed some major differences between each site in terms of usability.

Google Scholar and IEEE Xplore highlighted each search result with a heading tag. This made finding the search results and browsing the result titles extremely efficient since the user can navigate to the next result by just pressing one key on the keyboard.

Accessing the short preview of a search result showed some differences in terms of efficiency and the method this was accessed. ACM and Google Scholar displayed a short preview of the abstract and article. Scopus and IEEE Xplore provided a link that revealed the whole abstract. The abstract on these both sites opened on the same page. This is not as efficient but the user accesses the whole abstract this way without having to leave the search result page. Accessing the full abstract from Google Scholar or ACM requires leaving the result page and finding the abstract from another page which can be a time consuming process. Scopus also provides the user a possibility to show the abstracts of all the results in the results page.

Table 2 presents the number of keystrokes a screen reader user is required to do in order to find the first title of the first search result from the results page. This was done from the top of the page. The methods used are presented in the first column. We tried navigating through headings, links, landmarks, and lists. None of the sites used landmarks to present the search results area. IEEE Xplore was the only page that could have been operated using lists. However, the screen reader used read the list items in an almost non-understandable manner because the highlighting of the search term in each search result corrupted the fluent screen reading. Due to this, lists are excluded from this review.

Table 2. Number of keystrokes required for navigating to the title of the first search result

	ACM	Google Scholar	Scopus	IEEE XPlore
Headings	N/A	1	N/A	4
Links	43	21	43	43
Optimal	5 (second row and second column of the first table on the page)	1 (first heading on the page)	4 (first combo box, next check box and pressing the down arrow key twice)	4 (using headings)

We also tried to find the most optimal method of performing tasks 2 and 3. The optimal method in this review presents the most efficient way (i.e. least amount of keystrokes needed) of browsing through the search results. Finding the most efficient method took time and effort since the page's structure and its elements had to be studied first.

Table 3 presents the number of keystrokes a screen reader user has to do in order to get to the next search result from another search result. The methods used are presented in the first column.

Table 3. Number of keystrokes required when navigating search result titles one-by-one

	ACM	Google Scholar	Scopus	IEEE Xplore
Headings	N/A	1	N/A	1
Links	3	7	7	10
Optimal	3 (Ctrl + Alt + Down arrow key)	1 (headings)	3 (combo box -> 2 x down arrow key)	1 (headings)

Below are the results for the usability of each web search interface.

Effectiveness – For the four tasks presented in this paper we found that each web search interface was technically accessible for a blind user using a screen reader. In practice this means that all the tasks could be accomplished despite the time it took to learn and master the DALD search user interface.

Learnability – We consider learnability as the efficiency of interaction when using the DALD for the first time. Finding the first result on the result page and browsing through the results one-by-one showed some significant differences in terms of first-time use efficiency. Going through headings is by far the most used method to navigate a web page by screen reader users. Google Scholar and IEEE Xplore were the only search interfaces that used headings to highlight result titles. These search interfaces were the most efficient when using them for the first time considering that the user expects to find relevant information through headings in the web page. Another method some screen reader users use to navigate a web page is going through links one-by-one. Using this method Google Scholar was the most efficient one.

Efficiency – After having learned the structure of a DALD user interface, the most efficient services in tasks 2 and 3 were Google Scholar and IEEE Xplore. However, after using ACM and Scopus and investigating the structure of the result pages it was possible to find much more efficient workarounds to accomplish tasks 2 and 3.

Reading a short preview of the full text provided below the result title on the result page could be accomplished most efficiently with Google Scholar (3 keystrokes) and ACM (10 keystrokes). Scopus (16 keystrokes) and IEEE Xplore (22 keystrokes) provided the user an option to reveal the whole abstract on the results page which could not be accomplished as efficiently. However, using this method the user does not have to leave the search results page and navigate to the full abstract in another page. For accessing the full abstract Scopus and IEEE Xplore were the most efficient.

Memorability – Google and IEEE use headings for navigation. This supports good memorability. The workarounds that were found for Scopus can be forgotten easily. The most efficient method finding the first search result in Scopus required the user to navigate to the first combo box, then to the next check box and after this pressing the down arrow key twice. ACM uses a table for the search results. This requires the user to navigate to the first table and then to the second row and second column of that table. These methods of navigating a web page when trying to find interesting and relevant information are not used by screen reader users typically (WebAIM 2012).

Satisfaction – Lazar et al. (2007) found in their research that the time lost frustrates screen reader users when trying to accomplish a task. For tasks 2 and 3 Google Scholar and IEEE Xplore can be considered the most pleasant to use.

For accessing a short summary of a search result Google Scholar and ACM were the most pleasant to use (i.e. they were the most efficient). Even though IEEE Xplore and Scopus were not as efficient, they provided a possibility to read the full abstract without having to leave the page, For a user who wishes to read the full abstract and not just a short summary, IEEE xplore and Scopus are the most efficient and therefore the most pleasant to use for this.

5   Conclusions and Discussion

Based on the results of our review with the basic search tasks we present following suggestions on the design of usable screen-reader-accessible search interfaces:

1. Highlighting each search result – Finding and browsing through the search results can be a burdensome and time consuming task. We suggest that every search result would be highlighted as headings on the search results page. There should be none or only a few headings before the first search result.
2. Reducing the number of unnecessary elements before the search results - Many screen reader users browse through links or read through the whole web page in order to find interesting and relevant information and content. For this reason the number of links and other unnecessary elements before the first search result should be minimal so that the search results could be accessed more rapidly.
3. Search elements first - The search elements (i.e. search edit field and button) should be placed at the top of the page – preferably they should be the first elements on that page.
4. Descriptive labeling of search elements – All of the search elements (e.g. search fields and buttons) should have a label indicating for what the element is used for.
5. Abstract below the search result title – Each search interface we reviewed provided a short preview of the full text or the whole abstract. This information should be presented just after result title for a quicker access. Preferably the user should be able to access the full abstract on the results page. This eliminates the need of finding the abstract from another page and thus providing a more efficient method of finding interesting information for the user.

For designing usable search interfaces developers must understand how blind users navigate the web with screen readers. For sighted users, the visual appearance of different search pages may be identical even though the structure to produce the layout varies a lot – which is faced by the non-sighted users. These structural inconsistencies between the search interfaces create additional barriers that do not support learning across sites. Our results point out the need for structural consistencies between search user interfaces so that also screen readers interpret the sites similarly.

Despite many constraints, however, even larger amount of content in a search results page does not necessarily decrease the efficiency of the page if the page is structured correctly. For example displaying the full abstract for all the results in a page would not make the page less efficient to use for a screen reader user since the user does not have to interact with every single element on a web page.

Improving the search interface of the DALDs to better serve a non-visual user using a screen reader would not require major changes to the site structures and the visual appearance would not be affected greatly. We argue that these improvements would enhance the usability – and even the user experience – of these search interfaces for non-sighted individuals.

References

1. Andronico, P., Buzzi, M., Castillo, C., Leporini, B.: Improving search engine interfaces for blind users: A case study. In: Universal Access in the Information Society, vol. 5(1), pp. 23–40 (July 2006)
2. Babu, R., Singh, R.: Evaluation of Web accessibility and usability from blind user's perspective: The Context of Online Assessment. In: AMCIS 2009 Proceedings (2009)
3. Buzzi, M., Andronixo, P., Leporini, B.: Accessibility and usability of search engine interfaces: Preliminary testing. In: Proc. of 8th ERCIM UI4ALL Workshop (2004)
4. Byerley, S.L., Chambers, M.B.: Accessibility and usability of Web-based library databases for non-visual users, vol. 20(2). Library Hi Tech (2005) ISSN 0737-8831
5. Di Blas, N., Paolini, P., Speroni, M.: "Usable Accessibility" to the Web for blind users. In: Proceedings of 8th ERCIM Workshop: User Interfaces for All (2004)
6. ISO 9241-11; Ergonomic requirements for office work with visual display terminals (VDTs) Part 11: Guidance on Usability. ISO (1998)
7. Ivory, M.Y., Yu, S., Gronemyer, K.: Search result exploration: A preliminary study of blind and sighted users' decision making and performance. In: CHI EA 2004, Extended Abstract on Human and Computing Systems, pp. 1453–1456 (2004) ISBN 1-58113-703-6
8. Lazar, J., Allen, A., Kleinman, J., Malarkey, C.: What frustrates screen reader users on the Web: A study of 100 blind users. Proceedings of Int. J. Hum. Comput. Interaction 2007, 247–269 (2007)
9. Leporini, B., Andronico, P., Buzzi, M.: Designing search engine interfaces for the visually impaired. In: W4A 2004 Proceedings of the 2004 International Disciplinary Workshop on Web Accessibility (W4A), pp. 57–66 (2004A) ISBN 1-58113-903-9
10. Leporini, B., Paterno, F.: Increasing usability when interacting through screen readers. In: Universal Access in the Information Society, vol. 3(1), pp. 57–70 (March 2004B) ISSN 1615-5297
11. Nielsen, J.: Usability Engineering. Academic Press, Boston (1993) ISBN 0-12-518405-0
12. Power, C., Freire, A., Petrie, H., Swallow, D.: Guidelines are only half of the story: Accessibility problems encountered by blind users on the Web. In: CHI 2012, Proc. of the SIGCHI Conference on Human Factors in Computing Systems (2012) ISBN 978-1-4503-1015-4
13. WebAIM; Screen reader user survey, CPD – Center for Persons with Disabilities, Utah State University (2009),
    http://webaim.org/projects/screenreadersurvey/
14. WebAIM; Screen reader user survey #4. CPD – Center for Persons with Disabilities, Utah State University (2012),
    http://webaim.org/projects/screenreadersurvey4/

Design and Developing Methodology
for 8-dot Braille Code Systems

Hernisa Kacorri[1,2] and Georgios Kouroupetroglou[1]

[1] National and Kapodistrian University of Athens,
Department of Informatics and Telecommunications,
Panepistimiopolis, Ilisia, 15784 Athens, Greece
{c.katsori,koupe}@di.uoa.gr
[2] The City University of New York (CUNY),
Doctoral Program in Computer Science, The Graduate Center,
365 Fifth Ave, New York, NY 10016 USA
hkacorri@gc.cuny.edu

Abstract. Braille code, employing six embossed dots evenly arranged in rectangular letter spaces or cells, constitutes the dominant touch reading or typing system for the blind. Limited to 63 possible dot combinations per cell, there are a number of application examples, such as mathematics and sciences, and assistive technologies, such as braille displays, in which the 6-dot cell braille is extended to 8-dot. This work proposes a language-independent methodology for the systematic development of an 8-dot braille code. Moreover, a set of design principles is introduced that focuses on: achieving an abbreviated representation of the supported symbols, retaining connectivity with the 6-dot representation, preserving similarity on the transition rules applied in other languages, removing ambiguities, and considering future extensions. The proposed methodology was successfully applied in the development of an 8-dot literary Greek braille code that covers both the modern and the ancient Greek orthography, including diphthongs, digits, and punctuation marks.

Keywords: document accessibility, braille, 8-dot braille, assistive technologies.

1 Introduction

Braille code, employing six embossed dots evenly arranged in quadrangular letter spaces or cells [2], constitutes the main system of touch reading for the blind. Moreover, assistive technologies offer a number of devices with a braille keyboard. Limited to 63 possible dot combinations per cell, according to BANA's position "there are numerous examples, both historic and modern, in which the six dots of the traditional braille cell have proven inadequate for a particular task" [4]. Increasing the number of dots from six to eight has been proposed as an extension and a number of relative standards are progressing in this direction, as shown in the related work section. In fact, BANA recognizes that 8-dot braille systems have proven to be extremely useful, particularly in the STEM fields, i.e science, technology, engineering, and mathematics. Some believe that

C. Stephanidis and M. Antona (Eds.): UAHCI/HCII 2013, Part III, LNCS 8011, pp. 331–340, 2013.
© Springer-Verlag Berlin Heidelberg 2013

the ongoing progress in information technology will eliminate the need for embossers and braille displays that support 8-dot code. It is a fact that, although the majority of current embossers can be configured to produce 8-dot braille, the common practice is to print in 6-dot braille. Besides that, adopting an 8-dot braille code can lead to a number of challenges. However, additional advantages of rich screen displays have resulted in continuing the production of refreshable braille displays with 8-dot cells.

Despite the advancement in the domain of 8-dot braille codes for a number of languages, there is a lack of a systematic way to design these tactile systems. This work proposes a language-independent methodological approach, along with a set of principles, to assist in the development phases of new 8-dot braille codes. Furthermore, we present the results of the application of the proposed methodology for the design of an 8-dot literary Greek braille code, which covers both modern (monotonic) and ancient (polytonic) Greek writing systems, including letters, diphthongs, digits, diacritics, and punctuation marks.

2   Related Work

An 8-dot braille is only introduced as an extension to the 6-dot braille for specific tasks, where the 63 braille 6-dot cells (Fig. 1a) prove insufficient. The extended 8-dot braille character set, with 255 combinations, retains the structure of the 6-dot cell for the top 6 dots and adds dots 7 and 8, as shown in Fig. 1b. These characters are typically presented through a refreshable braille display, except for some historic examples (as described in [4]). An 8-dot braille code is not meant to substitute the 6-dot braille. This potentially raises some issues for braille readers, related particularly to the need of learning up to two codes, and switching between them. Some of these issues are: memory load, finger position adjustments, and reading style modification [17]. While the last two are related to the nature of the 8-dot braille itself, the memory load is partially dependent on the degree of similarity retained to the existing 6-dot code.

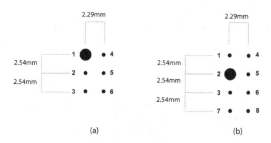

Fig. 1. Distances and labels of the dots in (a) a 6-dot braille, and (b) an 8-dot braille cell.

We can classify the existing 8-dot braille literature, as well as developed codes both for scientific and literary purposes, in two groups:

— The first group includes adopted standards related to 8-dot braille. Since September 1999, Version 3.0 of Unicode [19] has included the 256 combinations of an 8-dot braille cell (where the blank cell is counted too) with code points u+2800 to u+28ff. In addition, the encoding of 8-dot braille patterns was also supported by ISO/IEC 10646-1:2000 [8]. In 2001, ISO released ISO/TR 11548 [9-10] where it assigned semantics to the 8-dot braille patterns and produced a mapping for the Latin alphabet based character sets. In 2006, the Braille Authority of the United Kingdom added an 8-dot representation of Computer Braille in the already adopted 6-dot braille code [20].

— The second group involves other proposed 8-dot braille expansions. Some of these emphasizing on mathematical content, such as the Lambda Project [12-13], the DotPlus [18], and the GS8 [7] and others focusing on Computer Braille, e.g. [1] [3] [5] [6] [14].

3   Methodology

To successfully develop an 8-dot braille code, which could be adopted by 6-dot braille readers, we designed a methodology that results in a consistent, efficient, and unambiguous code. In this section, we define the required phases for developing the new code. In addition, we consider the design principles necessary for transitioning from a 6-dot braille code. In Section 4, we describe a successful application of our methodology to create a Greek 8-dot literary braille code.

3.1   Development Process Model

We group the development activities into three sequential phases, while incorporating feedback to resolve unexpected problems before proceeding to a subsequent phase.

First, the planning phase includes the following subtasks: (a) incorporating braille specialists and braille users of a specific language, along with its associated character set, at an early stage by recording their requirements and suggestions; (b) studying and comparing existing 8-dot braille codes with a focus on the adopted design principles and transition rules; and (c) defining the design principles for the extension of the existing 6-dot code (section 3.2).

Second, during the implementation phase, the results from the first phase are taken into account to specify the required transition rules from the 6-dot to the 8-dot braille system for the specific language. Then the following subtasks are considered necessary: (i) applying the transition rules to the existing 6-dot braille code; (ii) debugging each one rule e.g., eliminating any errors; (iii) checking for consistency between transition rules' results e.g., ensuring that application of two or more rules produces no conflicts; and (iv) providing a list of unbounded 8-dot characters available.

Finally, the evaluation phase focuses on: (1) checking the validity of the proposed code, (2) estimating its efficiency, and (3) examining its readability with users.

3.2   Design Principles

As in any system design, a crucial task in creating an 8-dot braille code for a specific language is extracting the user requirements. Braille users typically have an abstract idea of a desired result, but not how to get there. Considering users' needs, as well as other restrictions introduced by the nature of the 8-dot braille system, and the existence of a 6-dot braille code, we can recognize incomplete, ambiguous, or even contradictory requirements. We call these requirements design principles and, as mentioned in section 3.1, they have to be defined during the planning phase. Meeting these requirements is an essential milestone for the evaluation phase.

Development of the 8-dot braille code may be viewed as a problem constrained by design principles. Some principles may be contradictory, requiring a delicate balance during the specification and application of transition rules.

We propose the following design principles:

- **Compression:** map as many characters as possible to a single braille cell. Our aim is not only to save space but also to facilitate reading by avoiding the need to back-translate.
- **Intra-Similarity:** take into account the existence of a 6-dot code, which will likely coexist. It is essential that the logic behind the new code maintains ties with the 6-dot. Radical changes should only be made when unavoidable.
- **Inter-Similarity:** minimize the deviations between transition rules adopted by other (at least widespread) languages.
- **Unambiguity:** ensure that mapping of different characters to one representation only occurs when they have the same meaning or when the meaning is obvious from context. Ensure validity of the code when a combination of two or more 8-dot cells is assigned to a character.
- **Consistency:** apply the same transition rule(s) to characters of the same category e.g. capital letters. This way the mnemonic correlation between semantically related characters is taken into account.
- **Foresight:** consider possible expansions in other areas (e.g. scientific braille, computer braille) by providing unbounded cells or sharing characters.

4   Case Study – Greek 8-dot Braille Code

The National Association for the Blind in Greece estimates the number of visually impaired people in 2010 at 127.000, of which 27.000 are registered blind. A recent study [22] shows that 91,4% of the blind students in Greece use braille and 74,3% screen readers. The Literary braille code supports both the modern and ancient Greek orthography. Given the usage of diacritics, such as accents, breathings, subscripts, diaeresis, and their combinations, the majority of the symbols are mapped to two, three, or even four 6-dot braille characters. Therefore, an 8-dot extension would be beneficial for the braille display users. In this paper we propose a Greek literary 8-dot braille code following the methodology described in section 3 (see Table 1 for an overview). We arranged the presentation of the resulting code in four groups: (I) letters and diphthongs, (II) digits, (III) diacritics, and (IV) punctuation.

Table 1. Overview of the proposed Greek 8-dot braille code

Total number of characters supported	**528**
Number of characters that retained the 6-dot representation	127
Number of characters modified based on other transitions rules	387
Number of characters entirely modified	12
Number of 6-dot braille characters abolished	2
Reserved 8-dot braille characters	147

4.1   Phases of Development

We started the planning phase with a short questionnaire answered by 7 Greek professionals closely related to braille and assistive technologies for people with visual impairment. They were queried on: (i) the need for a Greek 8-dot braille code, (ii) the scope of this code, and (iii) suggestions and requirements for the design process. Valuable feedback included: minimizing the memory load on users, adopting other 8-dot braille codes supported by braille displays, and user testing before formalizing the code. We studied proposed extensions developed in other countries, discussed in the Related Work section, focusing on their common aspects such as the way they: compress capitalized letters and accents, represent digits and, map punctuation and other symbols such as the Euro symbol (€). Considering the existing 6-dot code and related 8-dot codes, we adopted the design principles proposed in Section 3.2 for the specification and application of the transition rules.

In the implementation phase, we defined five transition rules, described in section 4.2, and applied them to each of the subcategories inside the letters and diphthongs, digits, diacritics, and punctuations symbol groups. This can be seen as an iterative process: if a transition rule is applied to a subcategory, then all previously visited subcategories are checked to ensure they are conflict free. If a conflict arises then we decide which transition to preserve and modify the other subcategory accordingly. Debugging and checking for consistency were facilitated by maintaining an aggregate presentation of mapped symbols in two ways. At first, logically sorted symbols, by the subcategory and group they fit, were mapped to the 8-dot characters. Second, all the available 255 8-dot braille characters were mapped to the symbols that were represented. This last representation also allowed for easy identification of the unbounded 8-dot braille characters. The evaluation phase is an ongoing project; the results of this phase will be provided in future work.

4.2   Transition Rules

A transition rule is defined as the logic used for mapping one or more 8-dot braille characters to a symbol based on its 6-dot representation. We specified five distinct transition rules in the implementation phase. For each subcategory of symbols covered by the proposed code, one or more transition rules were applied consistently. The design principles met by each transition rule are covered below.

— **First Rule:** Retain the 6-dot representation. In this case, priority was given to the symbols mapped to one 6-dot cell. This rule was also applied in some exceptional cases where: even if a symbol was mapped to two or more 6-dot cells, the memory load of compressing it to fewer 8-dot cells would have been higher. For example, if a transition could not be applied to all symbols within a subcategory (contradicting *Consistency*). This rule focuses on maximizing the *Intra-Similarity*.

— **Second Rule:** Add dot 7 or dot 8 to the 6-dot representation. This has the effect of preserving the 6-dot representation while activating additional dots in the 8-dot cell. Restricted by the *Consistency* design principle, these rules are applied uniformly within a subcategory, e.g. capital letters. It aims to maximize *Compression*.

— **Third Rule:** Add dot 4 or dot 6 to the 6-dot representation. As in the previous rule, we preserve the 6-dot representation in the new code with the difference at the dot 4 or 6, which are activated. Similarly to the Second Rule, this satisfies the *Compression* design principle.

— **Fourth Rule:** Shift the 6-dot representation one row above or below. In this case, the 6-dot mapping is shifted vertically. This rule is required to resolve possible conflicts that arise after applying the preceding rules. Retaining a logical connection with the 6-dot representation, this supports *Intra-Similarity*.

— **Fifth Rule:** Entirely amend the 6-dot representation. Implementation of the last rule eliminates any logical connection with the 6-dot representation. It is usually required to achieve *Unambiguity* or to maximize *Inter-Similarity*.

4.3   Proposed Code

As mentioned in Section 3.2, some of the design principles contradict each other (e.g. intra-similarity and compression) and a delicate balance is required when applying the transition rules based on these principles. In this section we provide information on: (i) the symbol groups, (ii) the results after the applied transition rules, (iii) the relation to transitions adopted by other 8-dot codes, and (iv) a few examples for each of the symbol sub-categories.

Letters and Diphthongs: This group includes the small and capital letters, and the diphthongs that are common both in modern and ancient Greek. The small letters and diphthongs are the most commonly used characters and are mapped to a single 6-dot braille cell. Their 6-dot representation was retained (1st rule). The capital letters, and the diphthongs with a capitalized first letter, are mapped to two 6-dot braille cells; a capital indicator and the corresponding small letters. In this case the 2nd rule was applied: the indicator was removed, the 6-dot representation was copied to the 8-dot cells and, the dot 7 was raised, as shown in Fig. 2. A similar rule was applied in other proposed 8-dot extensions (e.g., [12]) and standards (e.g., [9-10]).

Symbol	6-dot	Braille 6-dots	8-dot	Braille 8-dots	Symbol	6-dot	Braille 6-dots	8-dot	Braille 8-dots
α	⠁	1	⠁	1	A	⠨⠁	46,1	⡁	17
β	⠃	12	⠃	12	B	⠨⠃	46,12	⡃	127

Fig. 2. Example of results of 1st rule for small (left) and 2nd rule for capital (right) letters

Digits: In the 6-dot representation of digits (0-9), a numeric indicator is used before each one of the digits. We investigated the proposed transitions in other extensions as shown in Fig. 3. However, given the restrictions of the existing Greek 6-dot braille code with previously reserved characters and the use of 8-dot for word stress, we were unable to follow any of these transitions exactly. Instead, we decided to combine part of their transition logic.

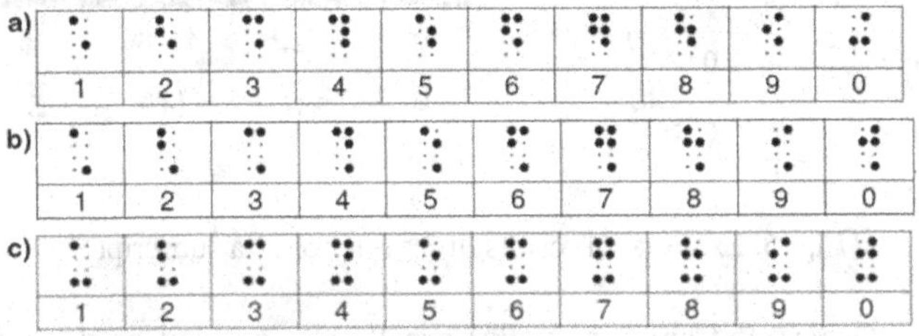

Fig. 3. Digits in 8-dot braille as adopted by: a) ISO [9-10] and most European Countries that participated in the Lambda project [12] b) Portugal [13] and c) GS braille [7].

For the 8-dot representation of digits, we first shifted their 6-dot representation one row below (4th rule) and then added dot 8 (2nd rule), as shown in Fig. 4. The result of this shifting corresponds to the digits in Nemeth braille code [15]. Given that Greece has officially adopted Nemeth for representing math [11], we minimized the memory load for braille readers by requiring them to remember only the raised dot 8.

Symbol	6-dot	Braille 6-dots	8-dot	Braille 8-dots
0	⠼⠒	3456,25	⢴	3568
1	⠼⠁	3456,1	⢂	28

Fig. 4. Example of results of 4th and 2nd rules for digits

Diacritics: This group includes accents, breathings, subscripts, and diaeresis, including small and capital letters, and diphthongs, on which these diacritics are applied. The most commonly used accent in both monotonic and polytonic Greek orthography is the acute accent, known also as tonos or okseia. Regardless of the difference on the Unicode mapping of tonos (U+0301) from okseia (U+1FFD), these two symbols are equivalent in the Greek language. In the proposed code, the acute accent is represented by the braille dot 8. The required indicator, used before the letter where the accent applies, is removed and the dot 8 is raised in the corresponding 8-dot representation (2nd rule), as shown in Fig. 5. As for the grave accent (vareia) and the circumflex (perispomeni), their 6-dot representations were maintained (1st rule).

Symbol	6-dot	Braille 6-dots	8-dot	Braille 8-dots
´		5		8
ά		5,1		18

Fig. 5. Example of results of 2nd rule for acute accent

The iota subscript (hypogegrammeni), applied solely to an alpha, eta, or omega, was represented in the 6-dot braille by an indicator immediately preceding the letter. We omitted the indicator and included the information in one braille cell, as shown in Fig. 6. For eta and omega, the dot 6 was added and for alpha, dot 4 was added (3rd rule).

ω ->   ῳ ->

η ->   ῃ ->

α ->   ᾳ ->

(a)

Symbol	6-dot	Braille 6-dots	8-dot	Braille 8-dots
ᾀ		4,1,35		4,14
ᾳ		1,35		14

(b)

Fig. 6. Example of results of 3rd rule for iota subscript

Both rough (daseia) and smooth (psile) breathings, as well as their combinations with other accents, maintained the 6-dot representation (1st rule). The only exception is the combination of psile with okseia, which is equivalent to okseia since psile can be inferred by the context. In this case, the letters to which this combination is applied follow the okseia transition rule.

The diaeresis, appears on the letters iota and upsilon indicating that a pair of vowel letters is pronounced separately, rather than as a diphthong. However, since a diphthong is given by one braille character and a pair of vowel letters by two braille characters with each corresponding to a letter, there is no need to represent diaeresis either in 6-dot braille or in 8-dot. The only exception occurs when it is not directly applied to a letter but combined with an accent, as shown in Fig. 7. In this sense, their 6-dot representation was maintained (1st rule).

Symbol	6-dot	Braille 6-dots	8-dot	Braille 8-dots
¨		5		8
ΐ		24		24
ΐ		5,24		248

Fig. 7. Example of representation of diaeresis when combined with okseia and vareia

Punctuation: Symbols in this group are punctuation marks and other symbols, such as the Euro sign (€). The 6-dot representation was maintained for most of the symbols represented by a single braille cell (1st rule). Exceptions made were a few symbols that either conflicted with the transitions results or required change to ensure unambiguity, e.g. to differentiate open with close parenthesis (in this case the 5th rule) were applied). As for symbols mapped to two or more 6-dot braille characters, most of them were reassigned to one 8-dot braille cell (5th rule). There were also a few cases where the 6-dot representation was intuitive (1st rule), e.g. ellipsis. In both cases, an attempt was made to follow similar representations with other codes when a change was required.

5   Discussion and Future Work

This paper has described a language-independent design methodology for the systematic development of an 8-dot braille code. Our methodology was successfully applied in the design of a Greek literary 8-dot braille code. We found that a set of design principles, such as compression of the braille representation, similarity with the 6-dot braille code and with 8-dot codes adopted in other countries, unambiguity, and consistency, is necessary to be defined and used in the development of the transition rules from the 6-dot to the 8-dot code.

We are currently working on the validity of the proposed code and estimating its efficiency by introducing a number of evaluation metrics that will allow us to quantify the level of conformance with the design principles, e.g. metrics based on Shanon theory [16]. In future work, we intend to conduct a user study to investigate the readability of the proposed code. Whereas many factors may contribute to readability [21], we plan to investigate how users would perform when reading 8-dot characters which: (i) retain the 6-dot mapping, (ii) result from other transition rules, and (iii) correspond to a new 8-dot mapping.

Acknowledgements. This research has been co-financed by the European Union (European Social Fund – ESF) and Greek national funds through the Operational Program "Education and Lifelong Learning" of the National Strategic Reference Framework (NSRF) under the Research Funding Project: "THALIS-University of Macedonia- KAIKOS: Audio and Tactile Access to Knowledge for Individuals with Visual Impairments", MIS 380442.

References

1. American Printing House for the Blind: 8-dot Computer Braille Table (2013), http://tech.aph.org
2. Braille Authority of North America (BANA): Definition of Braille. English Braille American Edition 1994 (2002) (Revised 2002)
3. Cranmer, T.V.: Code for Computer Braille Notation. In: Dixon's, J. (ed.) Braille into the Next Millennium. Library of Congress, Washington, D.C (2000)
4. Dixon, J.: Eight-dot Braille, A Position Statement of the Braille Authority of North America. BANA position (2007) (Adopted September 2007)
5. Durre, K.P., Tuttle, D.W., Durre, I.: A Universal Computer Braille Code For Literary And Scientific Texts. In: International Technology Conference (1991)
6. EuroBraille 8-dot Braille Table(s) for Refreshable Braille Displays (2013), http://www.eurobraille.com

7. Gardner, J., Salinas, N.: The Science Access Project. GS Braille (2013),
   http://dots.physics.orst.edu/gs.html
8. ISO/IEC 10646-1:2000. Information technology – Universal Multiple-Octet Coded Character Set (UCS) – Part 1: Architecture and Basic Multilingual Plane (2000)
9. ISO/TR 11548-1:2001, Ed. 1: Communication aids for blind persons–Identifiers, names and assignation to coded character sets for 8-dot Braille characters – Part 1: General guidelines for Braille identifiers and shift marks. International Standards Organization. Zurich, Switzerland (2001)
10. ISO/TR 11548-2:2001, Ed. 1: Communication aids for blind persons–Identifiers, names and assignation to coded character sets for 8-dot Braille characters – Part 2: Latin alphabet based character sets. International Standards Organization. Zurich, Switzerland (2001)
11. Kouroupetroglou, G., Florias, E.: Greek Braille Scientific Notation – Application in Information Systems for the Blind. Education and Rehabilitation Center for the Blind, Athens (2003) (in Greek) ISBN 960-87918-0-4
12. Edwards, A., McCarthey, H., Fogarolo, F.: Lambda: A multimodal approach to making mathematics accessible to blind students. In: Proc. of ASSETTS 2006, pp. 48–54 (2006)
13. Lambda Project. Linear Access to Mathematics for Braille. Device and Audio-synthesis. IST-2001-37139. Deliverable 3.7. 8-dot Maths code. Integration Table (2005)
14. Nair, N., Pitre, N., Doyon, S., Mielke, D.: Access to the Console Screen for Blind Persons using Refreshable Braille Displays. North American Braille Computer Code (NABCC) Table. BRLTTY Reference Manual (2012)
15. Nemeth, A.: The Nemeth Braille Code for Mathematics and Science Notation 1972 Revision. American Printing House for the Blind (1972)
16. Shannon, C.E.: A Mathematical Theory of Communication. The Bell System Technical Journal 27, 379–423 (1948)
17. The Science Access Project. GS Braille. Structure of Braille (2005),
    http://dots.physics.orst.edu/gs_braillestructure.html
18. The Science Access Project. DotsPlus Braille. Oregon State University (2005),
    http://dots.physics.orst.edu/dotsplus.html
19. The Unicode Standard 3.0. Braille Patterns, Range 2800-28FF (1999)
20. UK Association for Accessible Formats. Braille Computer Notation. Braille Authority of the United Kingdom 1996, Registered Charity No. 1001157, Printed by Royal National Institute for the Blind, Peterborough. Registered Charity No. 226227 (2006)
21. Wetzel, R., Amos, W.: Under the auspices of the Braille Authority of North America (BANA): Research on Readability of the Nemeth Uniform Braille System, NUBS (2009)
22. Papadopoulos, K., Koutsoklenis, A.: Reading Media Used by Higher-Education Students and Graduates with Visual Impairments in Greece. Journal of Visual Impairment & Blindness 103(11), 772–777 (2009)

Effects of Environmental Illuminance
on the Readability of E-Books

Tatsuya Koizuka[*], Takehito Kojima, Shunta Sano,
Nobuhiro Ishio, and Masaru Miyao

Nagoya University, Furo-cho, Chikusa-ku, Nagoya, Aichi, 468-8603, Japan
koizuka.tatsuya@g.mbox.nagoya-u.ac.jp

Abstract. We carried out experiments to evaluate the readability of e-books using different display systems. We used two types of e-paper (Amazon KindleDX and 300dpiEPD), one type of backlit LCD (new iPad), and ordinary paper text. In the experiments, we conducted subjective evaluations and measured viewing distance. This study found a dependency between readability and illuminance of each device.

Keywords: Evaluation of Accessibility, Usability, User Experience, E-books, E-paper, KindleDX, iPad, Readability, Illuminance.

1 Introduction

In recent years, e-books have spread to many countries. E-books are available for tablet PCs (e.g. Apple iPad [1]) and E-readers (e.g. Amazon Kindle DX [2]), and are used in various illuminance environments. However, the readability of e-books depends on several factors including the characteristics of the display and environmental illuminance.

In this study subjects evaluated the readability of highly backlit LCDs in low illuminance environments. However, as the illuminance increased so did the reflection of the background light making it more difficult for subjects to read the LCD. In contrast, subjects rated the readability of e-paper as difficult under low illuminance, but as the illuminance increased so did the positive evaluations of readability. Thus, the reading of the backlit LCDs are more difficult to read under high illuminance, while e-paper is easier to read under high illuminance. Because of the increasing popularity of e-paper usage, we were interested in understanding at what exact point of illuminance would be satisfactory for the readability with both forms of media. Our initial conjecture was that this point rests between 1,000 lx and 3,150 lx of illuminance.

2 Method

2.1 Subjects

The subjects for this study included 130 healthy males and females between the age of 17 and 85 years. Those who needed glasses or contact lenses were permitted to use

---

[*] Corresponding author.

C. Stephanidis and M. Antona (Eds.): UAHCI/HCII 2013, Part III, LNCS 8011, pp. 341–347, 2013.
© Springer-Verlag Berlin Heidelberg 2013

them in order to simulate their normal reading situation in normal fashion. We obtained informed consent from all subjects and approval for the study from Ethical Review Board in the Graduate School on Information Science at Nagoya University.

2.2   Experimental Design

We carried out the experiments in a darkened room. In order to adjust to constant illumination, we used fluorescent lights and LED lights for reading. We put the reading devices in small compartments on a desk. The subjects read them in comfortable reading posture. In the experiments, we used two types of e-paper (Amazon Kindle DX and 300 dpi EPD), one type of backlit LCD (new Apple iPad) and an ordinary paper text, under five illuminance conditions (500, 750, 1,000, 2,000, 5,000 lx).

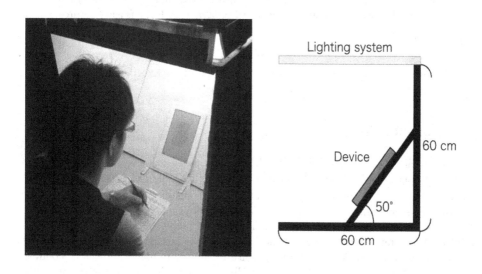

Fig. 1. The reading set up

The picture resolution was 150 dpi (monochrome, 16 gradation) with Kindle DX, 300 dpi (monochrome, 2 value) with the 300 dpi EPD, 264 dpi (color, 256 gradation) with the new iPad, and 1200 dpi (monochrome, 2 value) with the paper text. Each textual device was covered with white Kent paper in order to show only the display to the subjects, raised to the same height as the subject on a mounting board, and placed at a 50 degrees angle from the horizontal direction(Figure 1). Table 1 shows the measured illuminance values.

Table 1. Measured illuminance values (*lx*)

Illuminance	Measured value
500 *lx*	565
750 *lx*	803
1,000 *lx*	1,110
2,000 *lx*	2,080
5,000 *lx*	5,310

2.3   Task Design

The experimental task was to read aloud written text displayed on the devices (Figure 2).There were 34 characters in Japanese per line, and 13 lines in each text passage. The character font was 9-point Shuei-Mincho L. The text style was black/dark on a white/bright background color for screen polarity. The brightness level of the back-light of the LCD was set to the maximum. Table 2 shows the text contrast under the each condition of illuminance.

ジョバンニは何べんも眼を拭いながら活字をだんだんひろいました。六時がうってしばらくたったところ、ジョバンニは拾った活字をいっぱいに入れた平たい箱をもういちど手にもった紙きれと引き合せてから、さっきのテーブルの人へ持って来ました。その人は黙ってそれを受け取ってかすかにうなずきました。ジョバンニはおじぎをすると扉をあけてさっきの計算台のところに来ました。するとさっきの白服を着た人がやっぱりだまって小さな銀貨を一つジョバンニに渡しました。ジョバンニはにわかに顔いろがよくなって威勢いよくおじぎをすると台の下に置いたかばんをもっておもてへ飛びだしました。それから元気よく口笛を吹きながらパン屋へ寄ってパンの塊を一つと角砂糖を一袋買いますと一目散に走りだしました。ジョバンニが勢いよく帰って来たのは、ある裏町の小さな家でした。その三つならんだ入口の一番左側には空箱に紫いろのケールやアスパラガスが植えてあって小さな二つの窓には日覆いが下りたままになっていました。

Fig. 2. Example of text for reading task

In each of the five illuminances (500 – 5,000 lx), the participants read aloud a line of text, and we measured their viewing distance with a laser distance meter. After reading, the participants subjectively evaluated the readability of the text. The evaluations by the subjects fell into six groups (Table 3).

Table 2. The contrast ratio of each device for given illuminance

Illuminance	Kindle DX	300dpiEPD	new iPad	paper
500 lx	8.37	7.96	151	13.3
750 lx	8.46	7.95	126	13.2
1,000 lx	8.53	8.99	99.7	13.1
2,000 lx	8.67	7.92	53.0	13.7
5,000 lx	8.87	8.75	26.7	13.0

Table 3. Subjective evaluation of readability for tested texts

Level	Evaluation
0	Very hard to read
1	Hard
2	A little hard
3	A little easy
4	Easy
5	Very easy

3   Results

3.1   Subjective Evaluation

Figure 3 shows the comparison of subjective evaluation for each illuminance. Under 500 lx and 750 lx, significant differences were observed among e-paper, backlit LCD and paper text. The order from easiest to hardest to read was new iPad, paper text, Kindle DX, and the 300 dpi EPD. Under 1,000 lx, significant differences were observed among e-paper, backlit LCD and paper text. The order from easiest to hardest to read was paper text, new iPad, KindleDX, and the 300dpiEPD. Under 2,000 lx and 5,000 lx, the evaluation of the new iPad was significantly worse than the other devices. The order from easiest to hardest to read was paper text, Kindle DX, 300 dpi EPD, and the new iPad.

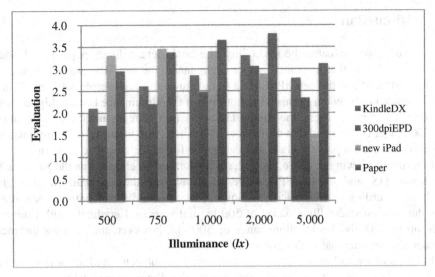

Fig. 3. Subjective evaluation for each illuminance

3.2   Viewing Distance

Figure 4 shows the comparison of viewing distance for each illuminace. No significant differences were observed in any conditions. Between 500 lx and 1,000 lx, the order from furthest to closest was the new iPad, paper text, Kindle DX and 300 dpi EPD. Under 2,000 lx, the order from furthest to closest was the paper text, new iPad, Kindle DX and 300 dpi EPD. Under 5,000 lx, the order from furthest to closest was the paper text, Kindle DX, new iPad, 300 dpi EPD.

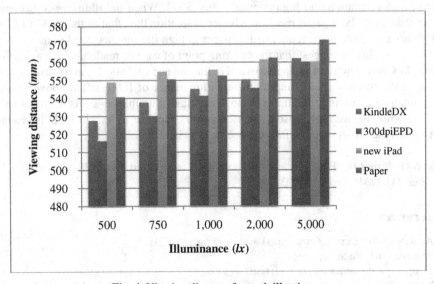

Fig. 4. Viewing distance for each illuminance

4   Discussion

In this study, we evaluated the readability of e-books and ordinary paper text. Under 500 lx and 750 lx, that is general indoor illuminance, the new iPad was evaluated to be the best. Because the new iPad has a light source and high resolution, readability was evaluated to be better in this condition. When the illuminance became higher than 2,000 lx, the subjects found the Kindle DX was easier to read, and the evaluation of the 300 dpi EPD exceeded that of the new iPad. Under conditions of high illuminance the new iPad cannot prevent glare, and the readability of the new iPad came down.

In terms of viewing distance, the order from furthest to closest was the paper text, the Kindle DX, and 300 dpi EPD, while the distance for the new iPad was found to fluctuate according to illuminace as follows. The viewing distance with the new iPad was the shortest under illuminance of 500 lx, and increased gradually with illuminance up to 2000 lx. Under illuminance of 5000 lx, however, the viewing distance became shorter than that in the case of 2000 lx.

In terms of overall ease of reading, a majority of subjects rated all devices to be easy to read (a little easy, easy, and very easy) under illuminance of 1000 lx and 2000 lx. Under illuminance of 2000 lx, the ease of reading evaluation of the Kindle DX and 300 dpi EPD exceeded that of the new iPad. Under illuminance of 5000 lx, the rating for ease of reading of the new iPad decreased significantly and the new iPad was more difficult to read than other displays and paper.

5   Conclusions

When the illuminance was lower than 1,000 lx, the backlit LCD received a better evaluation than that of e-paper. This is because the backlit LCD has its own light source, high resolution and high contrast ratio [3][4]. When the illuminance became higher than 2,000 lx, e-paper received a better evaluation than that of the backlit LCD. This is because glare is prevented with E-paper in high illuminance conditions.

The above results suggest that the crossing point of ease of readability between the Kindle DX and new iPad is approximately illuminance of 1600 lx, and between the 300 dpi EPD and new iPad is approximately illuminance of 1800 lx. The above values were obtained using interpolation without the actual illuminance levels of given values. Accordingly, we may presume that e-paper is superior to backlit LCD in readability when the environmental illuminance is 1800 lx or more.

Acknowledgments. This research was partially supported by JSPS Kakehnhi (B) Number 24300046 and 23300032.

References

1. Apple – iPad, http://www.apple.com/ipad/
2. Amazon – Kindle Store,
   http://www.amazon.com/kindle-store-ebooks-newspapers-
   blogs/b/ref=topnav_storetab_kstore?ie=UTF8&node=133141011

3. Kubota, S.: Lightness and contrast requirements for legibility of reflective liquid crystal displays. The Journal of the Institute of Television Engineers of Japan 50, 1091–1095 (1996)
4. Hasegawa, S., Fujikake, K., Omori, M., Matsunuma, S., Miyao, M.: Method to evaluate the legibility of characters on mobile phone LCDs and its application. In: Proceedings of Symposium on Mobile Interactions, pp. 59–64 (2007)

Verification of the Minimum Illuminance
for Comfortable Reading of an E-Paper

Takehito Kojima[1], Shunta Sano[1], Nobuhiro Ishio[2],
Tatsuya Koizuka[3], and Masaru Miyao[1]

[1] Graduate School of Information Science, Nagoya University,
Furo-cho, Chikusa-ku, Nagoya 464-8601, Japan
[2] Nagoya University Miyao Laboratory Collaborator, Japan
[3] School of Engineering, Nagoya University, Furo-cho, Chikusa-ku, Nagoya 464-8601, Japan
tkojima45@gmail.com, sano.shunta@c.mbox.nagoya-u.ac.jp,
miyao@nagoya-u.jp, chemist21@yahoo.co.jp,
tatsuya.koizuka@gmail.com

Abstract. Various e-paper devices also have been released (e.g. Amazon's Kindle DX^{TM}), and their features include paper-like display and low power consumption. In our previous studies, in high light conditions, readability of the backlight LCD dropped significantly, because of the glare of the surrounding background. On the other hand, the readability of the electronic paper is increased, it was easy to read than backlit LCD. The e-paper that have low contrast ratio, evaluation of readability was low. In low light, the evaluation of the readability of the backlit LCD was high. The aim of this experiment was to verify the minimum illumination for comfortable reading with e-paper in low illumination (300 or less lx).

Keywords: e-paper, backlight LCD, minimum illumination, readability evaluation.

1 Introduction

Recent advances in display technology have led to the introduction of a wide range of reading devices as alternatives to traditional paper made books. Various tablet devices with backlit LCDs have been released onto the market (e.g. iPad^{TM} [1]). These devices have many functions and can be used to read documents. Various e-paper devices also have been released (e.g. Amazon's Kindle^{TM} [2]), and their features include paper-like display and low power consumption. In 2012, new models equipped with an LED front light e-paper device and color e-paper were released. Thus, the choice of consumer e-book readers has further increased. One of the biggest differences between tablet devices and e-paper is the display system. Typical tablet devices, like the iPad, have mostly self-illuminating displays, while e-paper systems have reflective panels. However, the devices show different visibilities, partly affected by this difference in illumination. The general view is that under conditions of high illuminance,

C. Stephanidis and M. Antona (Eds.): UAHCI/HCII 2013, Part III, LNCS 8011, pp. 348–355, 2013.

the visibility of self-illuminating displays is poor. On the contrary, the visibility of reflective displays is as good as paper books under the same conditions. In this study, we carried out experiments with a reading test to evaluate the visibility of backlit LCDs and e-paper under various illuminance conditions. We used the Kindle DX and 300 dpi EPD (Electronic Paper Display) as e-paper devices and an iPad 2 as a backlit LCD device. For comparison, we also used conventional paper texts. In our previous study, self-luminous device under high illuminance, the readability is reduced by a significant reflection of the surrounding background. On the other hand, the evaluation of e-paper increased, it had become more than a backlight LCD. In low light, the readability assessment of self-luminous type LCD is high, however e-paper was lower rating. This is because the contrast ratio of the e-paper is low. Therefore, in this experiment we aimed to verify the practical allowable lower limit of environment illuminance for reading e-paper in low light (less than 300 lx).

2   Materials and Methods

For the experiment, we developed a presentation apparatus for use by the subjects in which the LED was the light source and illumination was increased in six steps (10, 20, 50, 100, 200, 300 lx). In addition, a diffusion board was installed under the light source to rectify the intensity luminous distribution. A board was set at an angle of 50 degrees inside the apparatus. The test media or test paper was mounted on the center of the board (Fig. 1, 2). The text displayed on each media was set at the same height. White Kent paper was affixed to the equipment and the object mounting board. Four types of media were used in the experiment: the e-paper devices were the Amazon Kindle DX and 300 dpi EPD; new iPad (back lit LCD); and a regular paper text as a control. The resolution of each medium was 150 dpi (monochrome 16 gradation) for the Kindle DX, 300 dpi (monochrome 2 value) for the 300 dpi EPD, 264 dpi (color, 256 gradation) for the new iPad, and 1,200 dpi (monochrome 2 value) for the paper text. In order to avoid any influence on the evaluation by the frame of each device, it was covered with white Kent paper and the subjects saw only the screen (Fig. 3).

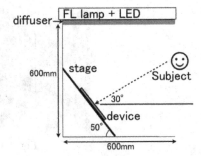

Fig. 1. Light source (left) D65 fluorescent lamp (right) FL lamp + LED

Fig. 2. Overview of the experiment

The experimental task was for the subject to read a text aloud as it was displayed on a device. There were 34 characters in Japanese per line and 13 lines in each text pas-sage. The font was 9-point Syuei Mincyo. The text color was black/dark and the background color was white/bright for screen polarity. The subjects were 130 people aged from 17 to 85 years old (average 46 years old). Subjects that needed glasses or contact lenses were allowed to use them in order to read as normal. The subjects were asked to read one line of text and the reading time and viewing distance between their eyes and the text was measured for the six illumination conditions of 10 to 300lx. After reading, the subjects subjectively evaluated the readability of the test device. The subjects rated readability as: (0): very hard (to read), (1): hard, (2): a little hard, (3): a little easy, (4): easy, and (5): very easy.

3   Results

3.1   Subjective Evaluations

Subjective evaluations in low light were higher in the order of the new iPad, paper, Kindle DX, and 300 dpi EPD. The 300 dpi EPD and Kindle DX were rated almost the same. The self-luminous new iPad had a nearly constant evaluation. On the other hand, the rating of e-paper and paper, which are reflection type media, dropped rapidly in light conditions less than 200 lx (Fig. 4).

3.2   Viewing Distance

The viewing distance with the iPad became longer as illumination decreased. On the other hand, the viewing distance with the three reflective type media decreased sharply with a low illuminance boundary of 50 lx. In addition, with illuminance between 10 lx and 50 lx the viewing distance with the paper was longer than with 300 dpi EPD, with illuminance between 50 lx and 100 lx the viewing distance was longer with 300 dpi EPD than with paper.

Fig. 3. bezel

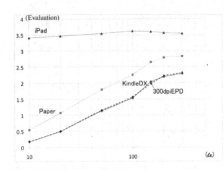
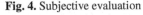

Fig. 4. Subjective evaluation

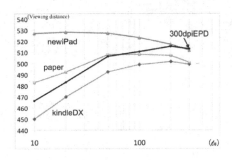

Fig. 5. Viewing distance

3.3   Contrast Ratio

With paper the contrast ratio decreases with low illuminance. Contrast ratio of KindleDX decreases with the decrease of illuminance. The case of 300dpiEPD, it rises with the decrease of illuminance. This is opposite to the paper. And, in most of illuminance, the contrast ratio is higher than KindleDX. The newiPad was set to maximize the brightness of the screen. Contrast ratio is very high compared to the other three models. Usually, the contrast ratio is reduced as environmental illuminance increases. Because with the increase of the light incident from outside, brightness of the black part also increases.

3.4   Subjective Evaluations by Age

Subjects were divided by age into a young group (up to age 43), middle-aged group (44-64 years), and advanced age group (65 years and older). Figures 6-8 shows the subjective evaluation by age. In all media, the highest Subjective evaluation of youth groups, and the second is middle-aged, advanced age was the lowest. From Figure 6-8, the results of the paper and the Kindle are very similar. However, the value of the evaluation of the paper is higher than KindleDX. Only the self-emitting iPad had nearly constant evaluations in all illuminance conditions.

3.5   Viewing Distance by Age

Figures 9-11 shows the viewing distance by age. In all media, the longest viewing distance is young groups, and the second is middle-aged, advanced age was the lowest. In addition, the viewing distance of advanced age was clearly shorter than the two other groups. The advanced age subjects wore glasses and so many subjects tended to have shorter viewing distances. The following is a reason for this. Lens accommodation power is weakened in the elderly due to the progression of presbyopia. In order to compensate for the lack of accommodative power due to the progression of presbyopia, the pupil is miosis Under high illuminance. As a result, the depth of field is deep. Thus, they can see the image without blur. However, under low illuminance conditions, miosis does not occur because the amount of light is insufficient with miosis of the pupil. So, viewing distance becomes short, because the subjects in order to close the face to the media in order to reliably read.

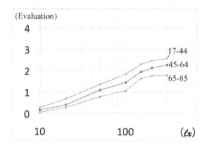

Fig. 6. Subjective evaluation (KindleDX)

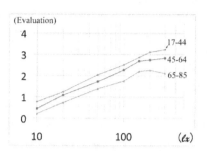

Fig. 7. Subjective evaluation (Paper)

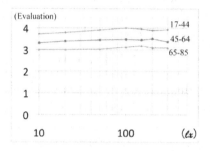

Fig. 8. Subjective evaluation (newiPad)

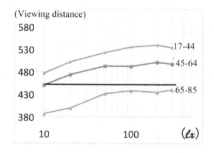

Fig. 9. Viewing distance (KindleDX)

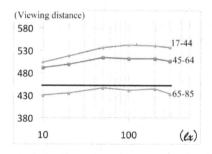

Fig. 10. Viewing distance (Paper)

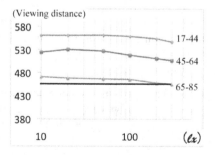

Fig. 11. Viewing distance (newiPad)

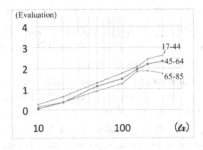

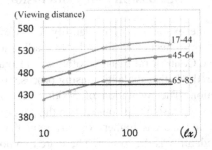

Fig. 12. Subjective evaluation (300dpiEPD)   **Fig. 13.** Viewing distance (300dpiEPD)

Table 1. Contrast ratio

(lx)	10	20	50	100	200	300
KindleDX	8.24	8.64	9.07	9.22	9.76	9.27
300dpiEPD	12.48	10.83	10.88	10.63	9.63	10.13
newiPad	695.2	657.7	602.9	603.3	543.1	492.7
Paper	9.73	8.51	6.53	11.08	12.45	11.88

3.6   The Results of Device 300dpiEPD Device

Because it was a device of the experimental stage, is shown in this section separately from the other three models are 300dpiEPD (Fig.12-13). Subjective evaluation of graph (Fig.12) is very similar to (Fig.7) the results of the paper. Graph (Fig.13) is very similar (Fig.10) the results of the paper the viewing distance. However, the number, which is a low value of about 0.5 to 1 than paper. Then, compare different device (Fig.4.5). Viewing distance of at least 100 lx is the longest in the reflective device. Viewing distance of 300 lx is longer than the iPad. However, Subjective evaluation was lowest in the most of illuminance.

Fig. 14. Enlarged image of the display surface, (left) KindleDX, 150dpi, black-and-white tone 16, (center) 300dpiEPD, 300dpi, black-and-white two-tone, (right) newiPad, 216dpi, 256 color gradation

4   Discussion and Conclusion

In the evaluation of readability, the viewing distance is also used as an indicator. When subjects feel difficulty in reading text, it is known that they move closer to the text. Contrast ratio and resolution is also a factor in readability. In addition, we considered whether the anti-aliasing process to the characters to affect the subjective evaluation. The resolution of 300dpiEPD, there are two times of KindleDX. Further, viewing distance is longer than the paper in the illuminance of 50 lx or more. Because this device has higher contrast ratio than paper. However, subjective evaluation of readability is the lowest. There are two possible reasons. First, screen display is black and white binary, and anti-aliasing has not been done in the font. Second, (see enlarged view of Fig. 14) during the display of the file that has been introduced from the outside, there is a possibility that the image is degraded (the middle of Fig. 14).

The viewing distance became a little shorter with the iPad as the illuminance level increased. On the other hand, paper and e-paper showed a tendency for the viewing distance to become longer with increasing illumination. It is suggested that paper and e-paper had an advantage in bright illuminance environments. In the present experiment, we used six different illuminations (10, 20, 50, 100, 200, 300 lx). In dark environments the iPad obtained good readability ratings, which decreased with increasing illuminance. Conversely, evaluation of e-paper and paper was poor in dark environments, and improved with higher illuminance. Ultimately, , the viewing distance was similar with all the media used in this experiment at illuminance of 200-300 lx. Considering the results of the present experiment, 200 lx might be a critical illuminance point where more than one third of subjects evaluated ease of reading at 3 or higher. Furthermore, in the 200 lx environment the viewing distance for the e-paper was similar to the backlit LCD and the regular paper text. Thus, we consider the 200 lx illuminance level to be the minimum optimum limit for comfortable reading of e-paper. E-book readers equipped with LED front light have begun to be released. These readers can compensate for the disadvantages of e-paper in low light. In the future, it will be necessary to evaluate those products and compare them with conventional products.

Acknowledgements. This research was partially supported by JSPS Kakenhi (B) Number 24300046 and 23300032.

References

1. Apple - iPad 2, http://www.apple.com/ipad/
2. Amazon's Original Wireless Reading Device (1st generation) Kindle Store, http://www.amazon.com/gp/product/B000FI73MA
3. Isono, H., Takahashi, S., Takiguchi, Y., Yamada, C.: Comparison of Visual Fatigue from Reading Between Electronic Paper and Conventional Paper, The Institute of Electronics, Information and Communication Engineers, Technical Report of IECE. EID, 104(666), pp.9–12 (2005)

4. Lee, D.S., Yeh, Y.Y.: Visual fatigue for using electronic paper displays. OIT Journal 27, 105–114 (2007)
5. Kang, Y.Y., Wang, M.J.J., Lin, R.: Usability Evaluation of E-books. Displays 30, 49–52 (2009)
6. Omodani, M.: Electronic Paper(<Special Section>Flat Panel Displays). The Institute of Electronics, Information and Communication Engineers 88(8), 659–665 (2005)
7. Shen, I.-H., et al.: Lighting, font style, and polarity on visual performance and visual fatigue with electronic paper displays. Displays 30, 53–58 (2009)
8. Isono, H., Takahashi, S., Takiguchi, Y., Yamada, C.: Measurement of visual fatigue from reading on electronic paper. In: IDW 2004, pp. 1647–1648 (2004)
9. Lee, D.-S., et al.: Effect of character size and lighting on legibility of electronic papers. Displays 29, 10–17 (2008)
10. Shieh, K.K., Lee, D.-S.: Preferred viewing distance and screen angle of electronic paper displays. Applied Ergonomics 38, 601–608 (2007)
11. Lee, D.-S.: Effect of light source, ambient illumination, character size and interline spacing on visual performance and visual fatigue with electronic paper displays. Displays 32, 1–7 (2011)
12. Siegenthaler, E.: Reading on LCD vs e-Ink displays: effects on fatigue and visual strain. Ophthalmic & Physiological Optics 32, 367–374 (2012)
13. Dillon, A.: Reading from paper versus screens: a critical review of the empirical literature. Ergonomics 35(10), 1297–1326 (1992)

Aging Effects on the Readability of Characters on E-Book Terminals

Ranson Paul Lege[1], Satoshi Hasegawa[2], Akira Hasegawa[3],
Takehito Kojima[4], and Masaru Miyao[4]

[1] Graduate School of Law, Nagoya University, Chikusa-ku Nagoya, Japan
[2] Faculty of Information and Media Studies, Nagoya Bunri University, Aichi, Japan
[3] Library Information Center, Nagoya Bunri University, Aichi, Japan
[4] Graduate School of Information Science, Nagoya University, Chikusa-ku Nagoya, Japan

Abstract. In recent years, e-book terminals are spreading rapidly. In the current aging society, there is an increasing need for elderly people to use information devices such as e-book. The readability of characters on e-book displays is important especially for elderly people. Few studies have measured subjectively the visibility of characters on e-book displays. In this study we examined the relationship between the readability of characters on e-book terminals compared with the characters printed on paper. The readability of characters on the displays of e-books deteriorates remarkably as the characters become smaller, especially when the user is an elderly person. Thus, makers of mobile text characters should consider aging so that e-book terminals are readable to all age groups.

Keywords: Readability, Visibility, iPad, Character, Aging Effects.

1 Introduction

E-book terminals are very popular in the world today. Tablet terminals with Liquid Cristal Displays (LCDs such as iPad: Apple Inc.) are also used as e-book reader as well as e-ink devices. Fairy tale picture books for children, digital textbooks for students, and general books for all age groups can be read on e-book terminals. E-book terminal are accessible to all ages. However, the readability of characters on such books is important for especially children whose visual functions are in the developmental stages and elderly with waning visual capabilities. While many studies standardized a recommended character size for personal computers as visual display terminal work criteria (VDT), few studies have focused on a subjective measure of the readability of characters on e-book displays. Thus, we researched the readability of characters on a car navigation display [1] and mobile phone display [2-6]. In this study we examined the aging effects [5] and the relationship between readability of characters on displays [7] of e-book terminals and compared this with the readability characters printed on paper.

C. Stephanidis and M. Antona (Eds.): UAHCI/HCII 2013, Part III, LNCS 8011, pp. 356–363, 2013.
© Springer-Verlag Berlin Heidelberg 2013

2   Method

2.1   Subjects and Measurement

The number of subjects was 112 (age: 17-89, average ±SD: 44.7±18.4) including 34 young individuals (17-29, 25.0±5.2), 50 adults in the middle age range (30-59, 47.3±4.2) and 28 seniors (60-89, 70.3±6.0). The subjects were all Japanese. All subjects read Japanese characters out loud from each terminal while sitting on a chair in a comfortable posture. The subjects held terminals or paper on a board with own hands (Fig. 1). The study included a measurement of the reading time (RT), viewing distance (VD) or the distance from eye to display. A Subjective evaluation (SE) was employed for each task of readability of the characters using a 7-point scale (3: very easy to read, -3: very difficult to read). Subjects who usually wore glasses for reading were allowed to use them for the experiment.

(a) Reading characters on iPad   (b) Measuring the viewing distance

(c) Reading characters on paper

Fig. 1. Reading experiment

2.2   Presented Characters and Display Devices

The Display devices used in this experiment were the third generation iPad (iPad3), iPad2 and paper. Three sizes of patterns (small, medium, and large) were displayed on iPad3 and paper. The iPad2 was used only for the medium size. Japanese characters (Fig.2) were used for the experiment in both an iPad (Fig. 1 a, b) and white paper (Fig. 1c).Various sentences were displayed with three different font sizes: small, 8 pt, (Fig. 2a); medium, 11.5 pt (Fig. 2b); and large, 18 pt (Fig. 2c). The Characters were laid out the same with 30 characters per line regardless of the size of the characters. A sufficient number of patterns with different contents were prepared as A-G (partly shown in Fig. 2). The patterns were displayed in random order so that no subject read the same content. The subjects read out loud three vertical lines from the right of each device: the iPad2 (only size M), iPad3 (S, M, L) and paper (S, M, L). The iPad2 has a 9.7 inch liquid crystal display (LCD) with a resolution of 1024 × 768 pixels (132dpi approximately). iPad3 LCD has a 9.7 inch display with 2048 × 1536 pixels (264dpi approximately). The environmental illuminance was 404.0±9.2 Lx (horizontal), 98.0±22.2 Lx (vertical) at the reading position.

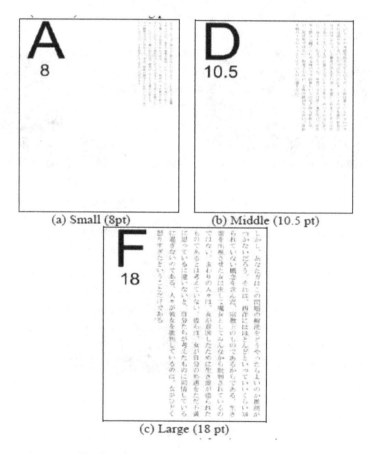

(a) Small (8pt)   (b) Middle (10.5 pt)

(c) Large (18 pt)

Fig. 2. Japanese text used for the experiment

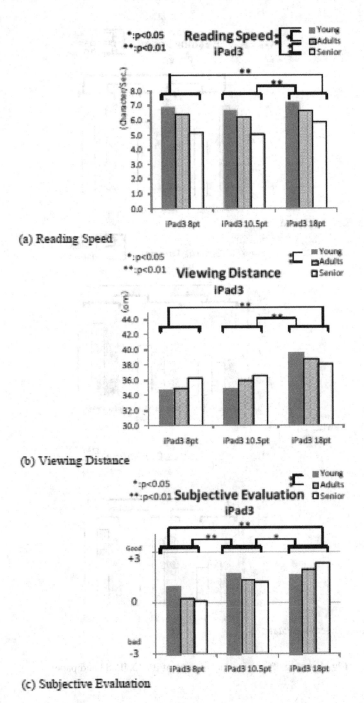

(a) Reading Speed

(b) Viewing Distance

(c) Subjective Evaluation

Fig. 3. Aging effects for each character size on iPad3

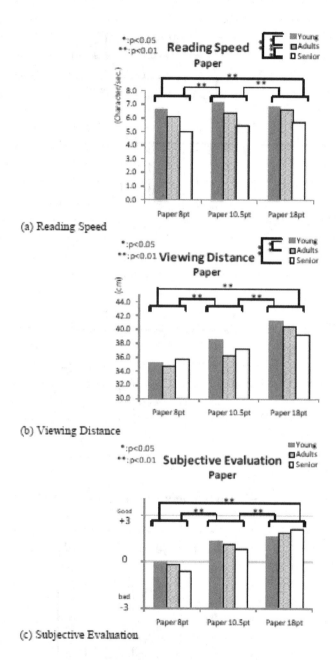

(a) Reading Speed

(b) Viewing Distance

(c) Subjective Evaluation

Fig. 4. Aging effects for each device of iPad2, iPad3 and paper

3   Results

The results of this study are shown in figures 3-5. The reading speed (RS) was calculated as 90 characters/RT. A significant difference in the average values is shown in these figures.

Figure 3 shows the results of the readability on the iPad3. The aging effects are shown significantly in the RS (Fig. 3a). The reading speed deteriorates for older subjects. Though larger characters helped slightly readability for the elderly, reading speed remained   slow even with 18pt characters (L). When the character size was small, the younger subjects shortened the viewing distance (VD) in order to maintain the viewing angle; however, the rate of shortening the VD was less in senior subjects (Fig. 3b). Presbyopia might have affected the elderly subjects. In the subjective evaluations (SE), the younger subjects rated the M size (10.5pt) most comfortable to read, while the middle aged adults stated the L size was easier (18pt) (Fig. 3c). As the character become larger, the ease of readability is stronger for the older subjects. Thus, larger size characters appear more suitable for senior individuals.

Figure 4 shows the results of the case of the reading on paper. The RS and VD show the significant effects on the reading by the aging (Fig. 4 a, b). The same tendency was seen in both the iPad3 (Fig.3) and paper (Fig.4), especially with the subjective evaluation (Fig 3c, 4c), although the iPad3 was slightly more readable than with paper.

A comparison of the iPad2, iPad3 and paper is shown in Figure 5. A medioum (M) character size was used in all devices. Significant effects of aging were seen in RS, VD and the SE. The VD was shortest with the iPad3 in younger subjects (Fig. 5b), while the elderly showed almost same values in the VD with all three reading devices. The SE of the younger subjects rated the iPad3 as highest (Fig. 5c). Though the elderly rated the iPad3 higher than reading from paper, the rating was not as high compared to younger subjects (Fig. 5c).

4   Discussion

For VDT work criteria [8], the International Organization of Standardization (ISO) [9] recommends that the minimum alphabetical or numerical character height should be 16 minutes of the arc, with preference for character heights of 20 to 22 minutes of the arc. In this study, this means the alphanumeric characters were approximately 3 mm height. Younger subjects in the experiment stated that the M font size of 10.5pt (3.7 mm) was more comfortable to read compared to the other sizes.

The larger sizes might suitable for seniors reading Japanese characters. The viewing distance increased with the age of the subjects due to the influence of presbyopia [2, 4, 10] so that larger character sizes was expected for the elderly persons. The aged may have difficulty in adjusting the viewing distance for reading to become optimal, at least in the adjustable range allowed by arm length (with a mobile terminal in hand).

The environmental illuminance was under 500 Lx in this experiment. In such a condition, an iPad is more readable than with paper or e-ink devices according to the recent research [11, 12]. The high resolution "Retina Display" (Apple Inc.) was superior for younger subjects to read the characters comfortably; however, the effect of the display resolution, or difference between the iPad3 and iPad2, was not as effective for the elderly. The character size displayed on the device might be more important for the elderly.

5   Conclusion

When characters are small, younger people ensure readability by shortening the viewing distance. However, elderly people find it far more difficult to see small characters. Small characters on an e-book might not be sufficiently legible for elderly even if there is a high resolution. The brightened LCD of an iPad is effective to help with the readability for the elderly in a relatively dark room.

In the current conditions of society, e-book terminals should be usable and harmless for people of all age groups with various visual abilities. A universal design that considers the visual abilities of older people is desirable.

References

1. Fujikake, K., Hasegawa, S., Omori, M., Takada, H., Miyao, M.: Readability of Char-acter Size for Car-Navigation Systems. Journal of mobile Interactions 1(1), 3–9 (2011)
2. Hasegawa, S., Miyao, M., Matsunuma, S., Fujikake, K., Omori, M.: Effects of Ag-ing and Display Contrast on the Legibility of Characters on Mobile Phone Screens. International Journal of Interactive Mobile Technologies (iJIM) 2(4), 7–12 (2008)
3. Hasegawa, S., Fujikake, K., Omori, M., Miyao, M.: Readability of characters on mobile phone liquid crystal displays. International Journal of Occupational Safety and Ergonomics (JOSE) 14(3) (2008)
4. Omori, M., Watanabe, T., Takai, J., Takada, H., Miyao, M.: Readability and characteristics of the mobile phones for elderly people. Behaviour & Information Technology 21, 313–316 (2002)
5. Hasegawa, S., Matsunuma, S., Omori, M., Miyao, M.: Aging effects on the readability of graphic text on mobile phones. Gerontechnology 4(4), 200–208 (2006)
6. Hasegawa, S., Sato, K., Matsunuma, S., Miyao, M., Okamoto, K.: Multilingual disaster information system: Information delivery using graphic text for mobile phones. AI & Society 19(3), 265–278 (2005)
7. Darroch, I., Goodman, J., Brewster, S., Gray, P.: The effect of age and font size on reading text on handheld computers. In: Costabile, M.F., Paternó, F. (eds.) INTERACT 2005. LNCS, vol. 3585, pp. 253–266. Springer, Heidelberg (2005)
8. ISO 9241-3. Amendment 1. International Organization for Standardization (2000)

9. ISO 9241-3. Ergonomic requirements for office work with visual display termi-nals (VDTs) Part 3: Visual display requirements. International Organization for Standardization (1992)
10. Miyao, M., Hacisalihzade, S.S., Allen, J.S., Stark, L.W.: Effect of VDT resolution on visual fatigue and readability: an eye movement approach. Ergonomics 32, 603–614 (1989)
11. Hasegawa, A., Miyao, M., et al.: Characteristics of Displays of e-Book Terminals on Text Readbility. In: IDW 2011, pp. 1131–1132 (2011)
12. Kanda, T., Miyao, M., et al.: Evaluation of e-paper Readability. In: IDW 2011, pp. 1135–1136 (2011)

Improving Communication of Visual Signals
by Text-to-Speech Software

Robert F. Lorch, Jr.[1] and Julie Lemarié[2]

[1] University of Kentucky
Lexington, Kentucky, USA
rlorch@email.uky.edu
[2] Université de Toulouse – Le Mirail, CLLE-CNRS
Toulouse, France
lemarie@univ-tlse2.fr

Abstract. Printed signals are well-documented aids to reading and memory for expository text. Despite their usefulness, many TTS applications fail to adequately communicate signaling. A theoretical framework called "SARA" provides an analysis of printed signals that identifies what specific information should be rendered in order to preserve the signaling function. Further, SARA identifies two important criteria – the availability criterion and the accessibility criterion – that should help guide the evaluation of alternative auditory renderings of signals.

1 Introduction

If a text consists of continuous prose (e.g., narrative), text-to-speech (TTS) software is very good at producing a clearly intelligible auditory rendering of the text [1-2]. However, much text contains non-sentential content: A set of instructions is likely to contain illustrations of the procedures to be carried out. A scientific article is likely to contain tables and graphs. Exposition of all types frequently contains various signaling devices (e.g., headings, typographical contrast) used by the author to emphasize specific content or to highlight aspects of the organization of a text. These non-prose sources of information in a text pose major challenges to attempts to render printed text in other modalities [1], [3-4]. It seems readily apparent that visual, analog nature of graphs presents obstacles to the goal of effectively communicating their content via a nonvisual representation. It may be less apparent that signaling devices such as headings and typographical contrast pose any problems for TTS, but they do [3], [5].

This article focuses on the question of how TTS applications might effectively communicate signaling devices in printed text. We organize our presentation as follows: First, we define signaling devices and briefly review the psychological literature documenting their influence on processing of expository text. Second, we describe our theoretical framework for analyzing signaling devices. We present our framework as an answer to the question of what information must TTS software communicate to effectively render a printed signaling device. Finally, we consider the other important question that must be answered if printed signals are to be effectively

C. Stephanidis and M. Antona (Eds.): UAHCI/HCII 2013, Part III, LNCS 8011, pp. 364–371, 2013.
© Springer-Verlag Berlin Heidelberg 2013

communicated by TTS software; namely, what forms of auditory representation might be used to effectively communicate visually signaled information?

2   Effects of Signals on Text-Processing

Understanding technical information or following the exposition of a complex argument are examples of common challenges faced by citizens in an educated society. Part of the challenge for a reader or listener is following the organization of an exposition, and part of the challenge is distinguishing more important from less important content. Authors often attempt to help their audiences by using signaling devices to highlight text organization and to emphasize important content [6]. In printed text, signals include writing devices such as: headings, outlines, topical overviews, typographical contrast, preview sentences, summaries and importance indicators.

There is an extensive literature in cognitive and educational psychology that documents a range of ways in which signaling devices support text-processing [7]. Signals that emphasize specific text content produce more attention and better memory for the signaled content. Specifically, the use of typographical contrast (e.g., boldface, italics, color) is effective at attracting attention to the signaled content [8] and improving memory for the content [8-10]. Similarly, the use of numbers to highlight a list results in more attention and better memory for the content [11].

Various signaling devices may be used singly or in combination to highlight text organization to the benefit of readers. Numbering a list of items produces better memory for the organization of the content [11].   Providing an overview of text topics speeds reading of sentences that introduce the topics later in the text [12-13] and improves recall of content [14] by aiding memory for the text topics [15-16]. Preview and review sentences that make connections between topics that are distant in the surface structure of a text result in greater attention to those connections and better memory for them after reading [17]. Headings, and headings in combination with topical overviews and summaries, have been repeatedly shown to support online processing and subsequent recall of text. The presence of headings in a text affects readers' calibrations of their progressive eye movements [18-19] and how they scan a text when searching it for the answers to questions [20]. Headings can facilitate the search for information in a text [21-22] and they serve as reference points for readers when they are reading to summarize a text [23-24]. In fact, the presence of organizational signals in a text can alter readers' text-processing strategies [25]. In the absence of signaling of text organization, even mature readers often construct a very linear representation of text structure that is minimally organized around the major text topics [16], [26-27]. When signaling devices emphasize text organization, readers construct a hierarchical representation of text structure that focuses on the major text topics [16], [26-27]. This change in text-processing strategy and the resulting effects on the nature of the text representation leads to better memory for the text topics and their organization and that, in turn, usually leads to better overall memory for text content [16], [26], [28].

Signaling devices are generally found to facilitate text processing but there is evidence that the extent of their benefits depend on both text and reader characteristics. Organizational signals are increasingly beneficial as text organization becomes more complex [28] or more difficult to perceive [15]. Readers who lack background knowledge relevant to understanding a text appear to depend more on signals to text organization [29] and content [30-31]. Finally, there is some evidence to suggest that poorer readers benefit more from the presence of signals than better readers [32].

To sum up, signaling devices are ubiquitous in expository texts. Authors use them to guide readers in their efforts to understand text organization and to sort important from less important content. The empirical literature demonstrates that signaling devices do, in fact, serve these purposes well. Given this state of affairs, it is desirable that printed signals be effectively communicated by TTS applications. To do this, two problems must be solved: (1) the information carried by printed signals must be identified and (2) effective means of auditorily communicating that information must be identified.

3   SARA: A Theoretical Framework for Analyzing Signaling Devices

The problem of identifying the information carried by printed signals is addressed by a theoretical framework we call "SARA", which stands for "signaling available, relevant, accessible" information [33]. The acronym stands for the three criteria that we hypothesize must be met in order for a signaling device to influence text processing: The signal must code information (i.e., make "available") in a way that is easy for the reader to use (i.e., "accessible") and the information must be pertinent (i.e., "relevant") to the reader's goals. The criterion of "availability" is our concern in the present context; that is, what distinct types of information does a given signal encode? We propose that 7 distinct types of information may be identified:

1. **Demarcation:** Some signaling devices indicate major boundaries in the structure of a text. This information is often communicated in a purely visual way (e.g., a line return).
2. **Emphasis:** Some signaling devices provide emphasis to text content, often by purely visual means (e.g., typographical contrast).
3. **Hierarchical Organization:** Outlines, topical overviews, systems of headings all typically carry information about the hierarchical organization of topics or themes within a text. This information can be coded verbally but it is also often communicated visually by variation in typography and spacing.
4. **Linear Organization:** Sequencing of related text sections is often signaled by numbering but it can also be communicated nonverbally (e.g., by bullets)
5. **Labeling**: Signals such as headings can be used to provide verbal labels for text sections. The labels facilitate reference to specific sections by the author or reader.
6. **Topic Identification:** Signals such as headings and preview sentences are often used to explicitly identify topics of a text section with verbal labels.
7. **Function Identification:** Headings, preview sentences and other devices can be used to explicitly identify the function of a text section (e.g., "introduction"). This also requires verbal coding.

To illustrate these "information functions" of signaling devices, imagine that the heading for the first section of this article had been:

I.   Introduction: Signaling Devices as a Challenge to TTS Software

This particular heading communicates all seven possible information functions. First, by the white space that precedes and follows it, the heading *demarcates* a boundary between distinct subsections of the text. Second, *emphasis* is applied to the heading in the form of boldface print. Third and fourth, information about both the *hierarchical* and *linear* position of the subsection is communicated by the Roman numeral "I." Fifth, the heading is a *label* for the subsection that may be used to refer uniquely to the subsection it heads. Sixth, the phrase "signaling devices as a challenge to TTS software" identifies the topic of the subsection. Finally, the label "introduction" establishes the function of the subsection. It is important to realize that not all headings serve all possible information functions. A heading usually serves only a subset of all possible functions. For example, the heading above might have been truncated to "Signaling devices as a challenge to TTS software" or simply "Introduction" or even more simply "I." All headings carry emphasis, and demarcate and label a subsection, but the other four information functions are optional where headings are concerned. Other signaling devices perform other combinations of information functions. For example: typographical contrast is often used solely to lend emphasis to specific content; preview sentences indicate a section boundary and identify a new topic; advance outlines identify topics and their hierarchical and linear organization. In short, an analysis of the information functions of various signaling devices is an important part of understanding the similarities and differences between distinguishable signaling devices.

Besides establishing the nature of similarities and differences among signaling devices, an analysis of the information functions of a given signaling device is a critical step in understanding how that signaling device might influence text-processing. The information functions of a signaling device mediate the effects of the device on text-processing. If a signal codes a particular type of information such that the information is readily accessible to cognitive processing, and if that information is relevant to the reader's goals, then that information function will influence text-processing. In a series of experiments, we have isolated each of the information functions under task conditions that make each highly relevant to task performance and shown that each information function has an influence on text processing [21, 22]. For example, if readers are asked to select sentences from a text to compose a summary, they are more likely to select a sentence from a paragraph if it is immediately preceded by a row of asterisks (i.e., demarcation) than if it is not; this is true even if the paragraph is not an appropriate source of summary information.

Of particular relevance in the present context is the observation that several information functions are often coded by purely visually means rather than verbally. It is in these cases that TTS applications often fail to render important information for the listener. Specifically, the information functions of emphasis, demarcation, hierarchical organization and linear organization are often (although not always) represented visually rather than verbally. In the heading example considered earlier, emphasis and demarcation information was coded by typographical contrast and spacing; hierarchical and linear organization was coded by a Roman numeral in that example but it is very common for the hierarchical organization of headings to be communicated solely by formatting conventions (i.e., spacing and typographical variation). To the extent that such information is useful to the listener in identifying important content and understanding the organization of the discourse, the loss of the information can be expected to disrupt text processing. In fact, we have found that if a TTS application fails to preserve emphasis, demarcating and hierarchical information for listeners, outlining performance is severely disrupted [5].

In sum, SARA provides a very useful analysis of the distinct types of information communicated by different signaling devices. Most importantly, SARA's identification of information functions is the appropriate level of analysis for understanding how signaling devices influence on text-processing. Thus, SARA provides an answer to the important question of: What information in signaling devices must be preserved when print is converted by a TTS application?

4   Implications for Auditory Rendering of Printed Headings

SARA does not address the question: How should visually communicated information functions be represented auditorially when a printed signal is converted by a TTS application? However, it does offer two criteria that are relevant to evaluating candidate solutions to this challenge. The first is simply that the auditory signal must preserve the information functions of the printed signal; we will refer to this as the "availability criterion." Second, it must do so in a way that allows efficient cognitive processing of the information functions; we will refer to this as the "accessibility criterion." Thus, given the choice of two alternative auditory codings of the same information functions, we would select the option that more effectively and efficiently communicates those functions to the listener.

Maurel and his colleagues [34-36] have elaborated a model, the Modèle d'Oralisation des Textes Écrits pour être Lus Silencieusement or "MOTELS", that describes four possible strategies to render text visual signals in the auditory modality. Their descriptive strategy simply describes the visual properties of the text content. For instance, the sentence: "TTS systems have now reached acceptable levels of **quality** and **naturalness**" could be transformed into: "TTS systems have now reached acceptable levels of quality and naturalness. The words quality and naturalness are in bold." We do not see this strategy as holding much promise because although it meets the first criterion of communicating the information function of emphasis, it does not meet the second criterion of communicating efficiently. We suspect that this strategy would be cognitively cumbersome. Further, the description of visual properties is not compatible with Design-for-All principles [37].

The second strategy in the MOTELS model is the discursive strategy. It is closely related to the descriptive strategy except that instead of describing the physical attributes of the text, the author's intentions in signaling are described. For the example above, the translation would be: "TTS systems have now reached acceptable levels of quality and naturalness. I emphasize quality and naturalness." This approach is compatible with Design-for-All principles. Although the current example would not appear to fare well when evaluated against the cognitive accessibility criterion, there may be instantiations of this general approach that would measure up well against both the availability and accessibility criterion. For example, preceding the verbalization of a heading with a simple verbal label such as "Level 1 heading" might be an effective and efficient way to communicate demarcation, function and hierarchical information.

The third, typo-phonic strategy represents the nonverbal properties of signals by tones or earcons. Going back to the preceding example, the words "quality" and "naturalness" could be preceded by a specific sound [38]. Alternatively, the fourth, prosodic strategy attempts to find or define a prosodic equivalent to the nonverbal information communicated by a visual signal. In our example, the boldfaced words "quality" and "naturalness" might be read more slowly, more loudly and/or at a different pitch than the rest of the sentence to contrast them with the rest of the text analogous to the way that typographical contrast is used in the printed text [39-40]. This approach has been used relatively effectively in communicating emphasis in TTS applications [3], [41]. The apparent advantage of both the typo-phonic and prosodic strategies is that both should allow efficient communication. The prosodic strategy is particularly attractive in this regard in that prosodic variation is integral to the speech signal rather than requiring the addition of other information (i.e., a tone or earcon or verbal label). The possible disadvantage of each strategy may derive from the implicit nature of both categories of devices. That is, there is no natural relationship between the hierarchical status of a heading in a text and either a set of tones or earcons or variation in prosody. Further, as the number of distinctions within a particular information function increases, implicit means of communicating the distinctions may become less effective. Again taking the hierarchical status of a heading as our example, it may be easy for a listener to understand variation in tones or earcons or prosody as signaling two different hierarchical levels; however, if there are four or five levels of headings in a text, the correspondence between the auditory cues and hierarchical level may be more difficult to learn and process.

5   Conclusion

Printed signals are well-documented aids to reading and memory for expository text. However, many TTS applications fail to adequately communicate signaling and the resulting loss of information can actually disrupt text processing. SARA's analysis of printed signals might be used to augment current TTS applications by identifying what specific information should be rendered in order to preserve the signaling function. SARA also identifies two important criteria that should help guide the evaluation of alternative auditory renderings of signals. However, much work needs to be done to identify effective and efficient ways to render printed signals in auditory form.

References

1. Fellbaum, K., Kouroupetroglou, G.: Principles of electronic speech processing with applications for people with disabilities. Technology and Disability 20, 55–85 (2008)
2. Schröder, M.: Expressive speech synthesis: Past, present and possible futures. In: Tao, J., Tan, T. (eds.) Affective Information Processing, pp. 111–126. Springer, London (2009)

3. Spiliotopoulos, D., Xydas, G., Kouroupetroglou, G., Argyropoulos, V.: Experimentation on spoken format of tables in auditory user interfaces. In: Proceedings of the 11th International Conference on Human-Computer Interaction (HCII 2005), pp. 361–370 (2005)

4. Spiliotopoulos, D., Xydas, G., Kouroupetroglou, G., Argyropoulos, V., Ikospentaki, K.: Auditory universal accessibility of data tables using naturally derived prosody specification. Universal Access in the Information Society 9, 169–183 (2010)

5. Lorch Jr., R.F., Chen, H.-T., Lemarié, J.: Communicating headings and preview sentences in text and speech. Journal of Experimental Psychology: Applied 18(3), 265–276 (2012)

6. Meyer, B.J.F.: The organization of prose and its effects on memory. North-Holland, Amsterdam (1975)

7. Lorch Jr., R.F.: Text signaling devices and their effects on reading and memory processes. Educational Psychology Review 1, 209–234 (1989)

8. Lorch Jr., R.F., Lorch, E.P., Klusewitz, M.A.: Effects of typographical cues on reading and recall of text. Contemporary Educational Psychology 20, 51–64 (1995)

9. Crouse, J.H., Idstein, P.: Effects of encoding cues on prose learning. Journal of Educational Psychology 63, 309–313 (1972)

10. Fowler, R., Barker, A.: Effectiveness of highlighting for retention of text material. Journal of Applied Psychology 59, 358–364 (1974)

11. Lorch Jr., R.F., Chen, A.H.: Effects of number signals on reading and recall. Journal of Educational Psychology 78, 263–270 (1986)

12. Lorch Jr., R.F., Lorch, E.P., Matthews, P.D.: On-line processing of the topic structure of a text. Journal of Memory and Language 24, 350–362 (1985)

13. Murray, J.D., McGlone, C.: Topic overviews and processing of topic structure. Journal of Educational Psychology 89, 251–261 (1997)

14. Glynn, S.M., DiVesta, F.J.: Outline and hierarchical organization for study and retrieval. Journal of Educational Psychology 69, 69–95 (1997)

15. Lorch Jr., R.F., Lorch, E.P.: Topic structure representation and text recall. Journal of Educational Psychology 77, 137–148 (1985)

16. Lorch Jr., R.F., Lorch, E.P.: Effects of organizational signals on text processing strategies. Journal of Educational Psychology 87, 537–544 (1995)

17. Glover, J.A., Dinnel, D.L., Halpain, D.R., McKee, T.K., Corkill, A.J., Wise, S.L.: The effects of across-chapter signals on recall of text. Journal of Educational Psychology 80, 3–15 (1988)

18. Cauchard, F., Eyrolle, H., Cellier, J.-M., Hyönä, J.: Vertical perceptual span and the processing of visual signals in reading. International Journal of Psychology 45, 40–47 (2010)

19. Cauchard, F., Eyrolle, H., Cellier, J.-M., Hyönä, J.: Visual signals vertically extend the perceptual span in searching a text: A gaze-contingent window study. Discourse Processes 47, 617–640 (2010)

20. Klusewitz, M.A., Lorch Jr., R.F.: Effects of headings and familiarity with a text on strategies for searching a text. Memory & Cognition 28, 667–676 (2000)

21. Lorch Jr., R.F., Lemarié, J., Grant, R.A.: Signaling hierarchical and sequential organization in expository text. Scientific Studies of Reading 15, 267–284 (2011)

22. Lorch Jr., R.F., Lemarié, J., Grant, R.A.: Three information functions of headings: A test of the SARA theory of signaling. Discourse Processes 48, 139–160 (2011)

23. Hyönä, J., Lorch Jr., R.F.: Effects of topic headings on text processing: Evidence from adult readers' eye fixation patterns. Learning and Instruction 14, 131–152 (2004)

24. Hyönä, J., Lorch Jr., R.F., Kaakinen, J.: Individual differences in reading to summarize expository text: Evidence from eye fixation patterns. Journal of Educational Psychology 94, 44–55 (2002)
25. Sanchez, R.P., Lorch, E.P., Lorch Jr., R.F.: Effects of headings on text processing strategies. Contemporary Educational Psychology 26, 418–428 (2001)
26. Lorch Jr., R.F., Lorch, E.P.: Effects of organizational signals on free recall of expository text. Journal of Educational Psychology 88, 38–48 (1996)
27. Mayer, R.E., Dyck, J.L., Cook, L.K.: Techniques that help readers build mental models from scientific text: Definitions pretraining and signaling. Journal of Educational Psychology 76, 1089–1105 (1984)
28. Lorch Jr., R.F., Lorch, E.P., Inman, W.E.: Effects of signaling topic structure on text recall. Journal of Educational Psychology 85, 281–290 (1993)
29. Surber, J.R., Schroeder, M.: Effect of prior domain knowledge and headings on processing of informative text. Contemporary Educational Psychology 32, 485–498 (2007)
30. Dee-Lucas, D., Larkin, J.H.: Novice strategies for processing scientific texts. Discourse Processes 9, 329–354 (1986)
31. Dee-Lucas, D., Larkin, J.H.: Novice rules for assessing importance in science texts. Journal of Memory and Language 27, 288–308 (1988)
32. Meyer, B.J.F., Brandt, D.M., Bluth, G.J.: Use of top-level structure in text: Key for reading comprehension of ninth grade students. Reading Research Quarterly 16, 72–103 (1980)
33. Lemarié, J., Lorch, R.F., Eyrolle, H., Virbel, J.: SARA: A Text-Based and Reader-Based Theory of Text Signaling. Educational Psychologist 43(1), 27–48 (2008)
34. Lemarié, J., Eyrolle, H., Cellier, J.-M.: Visual signals in text comprehension: How to restore them when oralizing a text via speech synthesis. Computers in Human Behavior 22, 1096–1115 (2006)
35. Maurel, F.: De l'écrit à l'oral: analyses et générations. In: Actes de la 11ème Conférence sur le Traitement Automatique des Langues Naturelles (TALN 2004), Fès, Maroc, pp. 289–298 (Avril 2004)
36. Maurel, F., Lemarié, J., Vigouroux, N.: Oralisation de structures visuelles: de la lexico-syntaxe à la prosodie. In: Actes du colloque national Interface Prosodique (IP 2003), Nantes, France, Mars 27-29, pp. 137–142 (2003)
37. Tsonos, D., Xydas, G., Kouroupetroglou, G.: Auditory accessibility of metadata in books: A design for all approach. In: Stephanidis, C. (ed.) HCI 2007. LNCS, vol. 4556, pp. 436–445. Springer, Heidelberg (2007)
38. McGookin, D.K., Brewster, S.A.: Understanding concurrent earcons: Applying auditory scene analysis principles to concurrent earcon recognition. ACM Transactions on Applied Perceptions 1, 130–155 (2004)
39. Giraud, S., Thérouanne, P.: Role of lexico-syntactic and prosodic cues in spoken comprehension of enumeration in sighted and blind adults. Presented at Multidisciplinary Approaches to Discourse, Moissac, France (2010)'
40. Giraud, S., Uzan, G., Thérouanne, P.: L'accessibilité des interfaces informatiques pour les déficients visuels. In: Dinet, J., Bastien, C. (eds.) L'ergonomie Des Objets et Environnements Physiques et Numériques, Hermes - Sciences Lavoisier, Paris (2011)
41. Argyropoulos, V.S., Sideridis, G.D., Kouroupetroglou, G., Xydas, G.: Auditory discriminations of typographic attributes of documents by students with blindness. British Journal of Visual Impairment 27, 183–203 (2009)

Online Digital Libraries at Universities:
An Inclusive Proposal

Amanda Meincke Melo and Joseane Giacomelli da Silva

Federal University of Pampa (UNIPAMPA), Alegrete – RS, Brazil
amanda.melo@unipampa.edu.br, jogiacomelli.cc@gmail.com

Abstract. Information accessibility at online digital libraries is an essential requirement so people can use them independently. These are very common systems at Universities for sharing academic knowledge and for supporting learning. However, information accessibility to people with disabilities is not properly taken into account when designing and maintaining end-user interfaces and content. This paper is part of a broader research that aims at contributing to the implementation of an accessible online digital library system at UNIPAMPA, Brazil, as well as at promoting the universal access on other on-line digital library systems. Based on the literature review and a case study in Human-Computer Interaction, this research proposes a set of accessibility guidelines to design and maintain online digital libraries. These guidelines should be part of inclusive educational settings.

Keywords: accessible online digital libraries, information accessibility, universal design, inclusive design, inclusive education, online learning, Brazil.

1 Introduction

Information and communication technologies (ICTs), including online digital libraries, extend the possibilities of information dissemination and access. Online digital libraries support publication and management of digital objects (e.g., technical reports, monographs, theses). At universities their content is made by different academic sectors and it is used for teaching, extension programs, research and management. University online digital library promotes the sharing of knowledge generated by the academia within it as well as with the outside community.

Online digital libraries should be designed with universal access in mind so each and every user could access them independently and on equal terms. However, it has not necessarily been true [7], [8], [12], [14]. Basic guidelines have been neglected, such as providing alternative texts to images or providing labels to forms [21]. Even though Universal Design [6][23] and Web Accessibility Guidelines [3], [24] are widely disseminated, it is still necessary:

To undertake or promote research and development of universally designed goods, services, equipment and facilities, as defined in article 2 of the present Convention, which should require the minimum possible adaptation and the least cost to meet the

C. Stephanidis and M. Antona (Eds.): UAHCI/HCII 2013, Part III, LNCS 8011, pp. 372–381, 2013.
© Springer-Verlag Berlin Heidelberg 2013

specific needs of a person with disabilities, to promote their availability and use, and to promote universal design in the development of standards and guidelines. [6]

This work aims at contributing to the implementation of an accessible online digital library system at UNIPAMPA, Brazil, and at promoting the universal access on other online digital library systems. Differently from other proposals [7], [12], [14], but deeply inspired by the universal design framework, this work deals with universal access of an online digital library from the very beginning of its development, starting with requirement elicitation, going through the assessment of candidate systems and a pilot prototyping of end-user interfaces. This paper also proposes a set of guidelines to support design and maintenance of accessible online digital libraries at Brazilian Universities.

2   Literature Review

An online digital library better suited to inclusive educational context shall allow every person – including users of assistive technologies – to browse its pages, to search within its content and to access and read publications in an equitable way. Academic managers should be able to maintain the system – according to each assigned role – with autonomy. From its conception to updating, Web Accessibility Guidelines should be followed, including the need for several types of end-users throughout the design process [13].

The Brazilian Decree 5.622/2005 states that eLearning courses should provide adequate libraries, with collections that comply with the student's needs [10]. According to the UN Convention on the Rights of Persons with Disabilities [6], information accessibility should be a basic requirement. However, it has not been fully achieved at online digital libraries of Brazilian Universities. Very often alternative texts to images or labels to forms are missing, what is a barrier to screen reader's users to perceive and to operate the user interface [21].

It is essential promoting universal access [2], [5] to make sure academic and external communities can broadly access and use digital objects available at online digital libraries. The concerns regarding the use of online digital libraries by people with disabilities put in evidence the importance of following accessibility standards in the development of accessible materials and the use of assistive technologies resources [8], [12]. However, in Brazil, these initiatives are still very limited to local collections access, to the retrofit of inaccessible systems or to specific groups of users with disabilities, such as blind and deaf people [7], [12], [14].

Moreira [14] presents an academic service to support information access to people who are blind or who have low vision, which offers specialized services, like coding texts to Braille and/or accessing assistive technologies. Although this service is a very important initiative, it isn't enough to provide online digital libraries access and use on equal basis.

Lira [12] reports on a project regarding physical and digital retrofit of Rio de Janeiro's National Library, suggesting that it could be a model to enhance information accessibility in libraries for people with disabilities and elders. The project also highlights the need to adapt the National Library's website to principles of accessibility as well as to carry out a process taking into account the content and the information accessibility, including alternative media to books.

Corradi and Vidotti [7] analyze accessibility resources available at online digital libraries, such as audio files for blind users and videos with sign language for deaf users. The authors argue that such resources could enhance information access and use to people with disabilities. However, the analyzed resources do not guarantee that each and every user could access the available information on equal basis, especially because among these resources one can find, for example, audio files without equivalent transcript, videos with no captions, and videos without audio to provide equivalent information for users who need them.

Digital Accessible Information System (DAISY) [9] has been recently adopted by the Brazilian Department of Education as a technical standard to deploy accessible books to blind students who are enrolled at public schools [19]. Although it is not mandatory standard in Brazil, digital talking books produced with this technical standard can provide synchronization of text, audio and images, thus providing information accessibility to people who are unable to read standard print [9]. On the other hand, the use of Printable Document Format (PDF) for publishing content at online digital libraries is very common [21]. Files published using this format should be edited providing accessibility at native document applications, such as Microsoft Word and LibreOffice Writer, before exporting to PDF format, which is just a destination file format [16], [20].

Although there are laws [6], [10] and widely known web standards [3], [24] to improve online access to people with disabilities, a great deal of contributions is still necessary to their effective practice. Universal access should be seriously considered in the design of online digital libraries to broad their access and use by people with disabilities on equal terms with any other people.

3   Method

A case study was carried out with a qualitative and exploratory approach at Federal University of Pampa (UNIPAMPA), Brazil. It was based on concepts and techniques from Software Engineering [22] (e.g., requirement elicitation, iterative development, brainstorming, questionnaire) and Human-Computer Interaction [1], [13], [16] (e.g. iterative design and assessment, end-user participation, prototyping, user interface accessibility assessment).

The case study started with a requirement elicitation regarding an online digital library. To do that, an online questionnaire was applied in ten University Campuses and a participatory meeting was realized to address different stakeholders (e.g., teachers, students, librarians, eLearning staff, and IT professionals). In this meeting, the brainstorming technique was used followed by requirements prioritization [21]. Table 1 summarizes the high-priorities user interface requirements to the online digital library.

Table 1. High-priority user interface requirements to an online digital library [20]

- Show user location on the website ("You are here:");
- Clear and simple options on Menus;
- Quick access to other portals (e.g., CAPES);
- High contrast options;
- Easy to use, with usability (observing usability heuristics);
- Accessibility (observing web accessibility recommendations, e.g., e-MAG):
  - o Address accessibility at website structure and content;
  - o Address accessibility at published files.
- Objectivity:
  - o Simple and objective pages.
- Navigability:
  - o *Layout* that helps guiding the user;
  - o Objective *links*;
  - o Uncomplicated operation.
- Colored and dynamic *layout*;
- Human responses.

The generated information in this former stage subsidized the definition of attributes to be observed in Free Software Systems available as infrastructure to online digital libraries development and maintenance (e.g., EPrints, DSpace, Fedora, TEDE, Greenstone). Some DSpace characteristics contributed to its choice among other systems [20]:

- possible interoperability with other digital libraries using OAI-PMH;
- recommendation by the Brazilian Institute of Information in Science and Technology (IBICT) for the deployment of institutional repositories at Brazilian Universities [11];
- successful cases of integration between Content Management Systems (CMS) and DSpace, e.g., Brasiliana USP [4];
- support material for its deployment and customization;
- case studies regarding integration of DSpace into eLearning plataforms, e.g., Moodle;
- qualified staff at University in the programming language used to develop it.

The low-fidelity prototyping, using the BrainDraw participatory technique [15], followed DSpace software choice. Finally, a high-fidelity prototype was designed, and a preliminary accessibility assessment was carried out on it. Prototyping and assessments are described hereafter.

3.1   Prototype Building and Assessment

A first prototyping was supported by BrainDraw participatory technique, which is a group elicitation method. This technique supports designers in prototyping so they can start from different perspectives instead of just theirs own. Usually its groups consist of 2 to 8 members [15].

Undergraduate students from Computer Science Course, who are also prospective users of online digital libraries and had been taking HCI classes, were invited to the initial prototyping. They were organized into three groups, each one with three or four members.

Before applying the BrainDraw technique, students received a short introduction of the research and the identified requirements. They also received some supporting materials: slides showing DSpace repositories so they could recognize some concepts like Communities and Collections; the high-priority requirements [20]; and Nielsen's ten usability heuristics [16].

The BrainDraw technique was started and each student drew an initial design. At the end of a minute, the participants handed her/his drawing to other student at her/his right side. After each paper had passed by each student twice, the drawings were analyzed within the groups and they supported a design proposal by the group. The three generated design proposals were analyzed to generate a low-fidelity prototype to the online digital library main page (Figure 1).

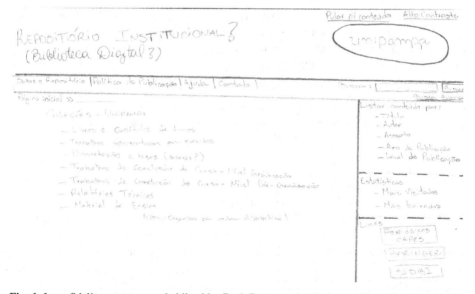

Fig. 1. Low-fidelity prototype subsidized by BrainDraw: main page structure and content to an online digital library [20]

Finally, a high-fidelity prototype (Figure 2) using DSpace software was produced to the online digital library taking into account the low-fidelity prototype, the infrastructure provided by DSpace system, and the identified requirements. The high-fidelity prototype is realistic enough to be assessed by experts and end-users, throughout different user interfaces techniques.

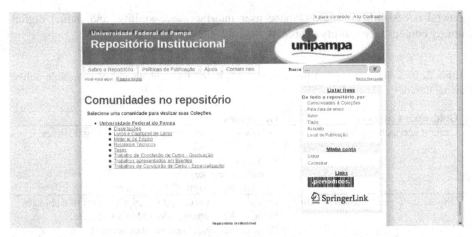

Fig. 2. High-fidelity prototype using DSpace system: main page structure and content proposal to UNIPAMPA online digital library [20]

During high-fidelity prototyping some accessibility problems – e.g., absence of header level 2 and the absence of the main language specification – were identified and solved. To conclude, a preliminary accessibility assessment was carried out by a junior HCI researcher supervised by an expert on web accessibility assessment. The assessment followed Web Accessibility Initiative (WAI) recommendations to preliminary review of web sites for accessibility [18].

A set of representative sampling of pages were selected, including main DSpace features, different layouts and functionalities (e.g., main page; search results; advanced search; navigation by author, title, subject, date and location; Community and Collections; a community page; a collection page; item visualization; and feedback form). Graphical and textual browsers (e.g., Firefox, Google Chrome, Opera, Lynx) as well as the NVDA screen reader supported the web content assessment – e.g., place of images, sequential equivalence. ASES semiautomatic tool helped to assess conformance level to e-government guidelines.

Although DSpace design follows web standards [20], the assessment pointed out the absence of labels to forms, the use of absolute font-size values instead of relative font-size values in CSS, and a poor use of the webpage title property. Such issues could compromise the use of online digital libraries by blind users and through small screen devices. Also, keyboard operation could be enhanced, providing skip links, direction links and access keys.

4   Results and Discussion

The literature review and the case study showed the necessity of proposing some guidelines to support the design and maintenance of accessible online digital libraries at Universities. These guidelines are organized in the following three categories:

general accessibility issues, DSpace user interface accessibility, and online digital library content accessibility (Table 2).

Table 2. Guidelines to support the implementation and the maintenance of accessible online digital libraries

Guidelines Category	Guidelines
General accessibility issues	Follow web accessibility standards and guidelines
	Provide skip links
	Provide direction links
	Provide access keys
	Validate the design with end-users
DSpace user interface accessibility	Provide informative and descriptive titles to webpages
	Identify the language adopted in a webpage
	Respect the logical sequence of headers
	Provide labels on forms
	Adopt relative values in CSS
Online digital library content accessibility	Post accessible videos
	Provide alternatives to audio
	Provide alternatives to images
	Publish accessible PDF files

Besides supporting the design and maintenance of online digital libraries, these guidelines aim at promoting DSpace system accessibility. It should be observed since the beginning of developing a new online digital library. It also should be taken into account when adding or updating content.

General guidelines can be applied to web based systems as well as to online digital libraries. These guidelines point out keyboard operation, web standards and accessibility guidelines, and the importance of assessment with users.

DSpace system is a reference to online digital libraries deployment at Brazilian Universities. In relation to guidelines to this system, changes should be made on it to avoid accessibility errors. These changes would allow some people with disabilities (e.g., users who are blind, users who have low vision, etc.), screen reader's users, and small screen users adopting online digital libraries built up DSpace system.

Content publication guidelines should be considered when producing and publishing the content, so it is flexible enough to different users. There are specific guidelines to produce accessible videos, audio, images and PDF files. Table 3 summarizes them.

These specific guidelines should be observed when producing content which is flexible enough to suit to different user needs on equal basis.

Table 3. Specific guidelines to promote online digital library content accessibility

Guideline	Description
Post accessible videos	Features that allow users to watch videos without sound or access to images and movements should be offered to make them widely accessible. E.g., captions are useful to users who are hard of hearing or who are in noisy environments; sign language window is useful for people who are deaf; audio description is useful for people who are blind, who have low vision or who have their vision busy with another activity. Local culture issues should also be taken into account when providing sign language window – e.g., Brazil has its own sign language that is known as LIBRAS.
Provide alternatives to audio	A text transcription to the audio should be provided so people who are deaf or hard of hearing could access its content. Whenever possible, sign language transcription should be provided to the audio material once many people who are deaf have a sign language as their first language.
Provide alternatives to images	Images inside a document should be properly described. Users who are blind and textual browser users could take benefit of this caution. W3C Accessibility Guidelines [24] and e-MAG [3] provide guidance on how to provide alternative texts to images. An alternative text should replace the meaning of an image in the context in which it is used.
Publish accessible PDF files	Documents – like technical reports, monographs, theses, etc. – should be properly structured within a text processor (e.g., Microsoft Word, LibreOffice Writer). This can be done applying styles to headings, lists, tables, etc. before converting them to PDF [16]. A tagged PDF improves accessibility to screen reader's users and to different screen sizes.

5   Conclusions

Online digital library systems are very common at Universities [8], [11], [20] to organize their publications and to support learning. On the other hand, universal access should be taken into account throughout their development so the needs of people with disabilities could be considered since the early beginning of requirement elicitation in an inclusive design approach, influencing design decisions.

W3C accessibility guidelines as well as end-user participation – e.g., students, teachers, University staff, and people outside University –, including people with disabilities, play an important role in the design of web systems for all. However, they have been neglected when building online digital libraries at Brazilian Universities. This paper presents some guidelines to address this problem.

The pilot prototype suggested in this research could support the further deployment of an online digital library at UNIPAMPA, Brazil. Its design considered contributions from end-users during requirement elicitation and Web Accessibility Guidelines [3], [4]. In the next steps, it should also be assessed by real users – including people with disabilities – as part of an iterative and inclusive design approach.

An important outcome of this case study is that eLearning staff is more aware about the necessity of information accessibility and it has influenced their practices.

Acknowledgements. Thanks to UNIPAMPA Academic Development Scholarship Program (PBDA). Special thanks to Rumenigue Hohemberger, Katia Vieira Morais and Susana Cristina dos Reis.

References

1. Bevan, N.: Quality in use for all. In: Stephanidis, C. (ed.) User Interfaces for all: concepts, methods, and tools, pp. 353–370. Lawrence Erlbaum, New Jersey (2001)
2. Bonacin, R., Melo, A.M., Simoni, C.A.C., Baranauskas, M.C.C.: Accessibility and interoperability in e-government systems: outlining an inclusive development process. Universal Access in the Information Society 9(1), 17–33 (2010)
3. Brasil. Ministério do Planejamento, Orçamento e Gestão. Secretaria de Logística e Tecnologia da Informação. e-MAG Modelo de Acessibilidade de Governo Eletrônico. V. 3.0. MP/SLTI, Brasília (2011)
4. Brasiliana USP, http://www.brasiliana.usp.br/
5. Colette, N., Abascal, J. (eds.): Inclusive Design Guidelines for HCI. CRC Press (2001)
6. United Nations. Convention on the Rights of Persons with Disabilities (2006), http://www.un.org/disabilities/convention/conventionfull.shtml
7. Corradi, J.A.M., Vidotti, S.A.B.G.: Elementos de Acessibilidade em Ambientes Informacionais Digitais: bibliotecas digitais e inclusão social. In: Seminário Internacional de Bibliotecas Digitais. USP, São Paulo (2007)
8. Cusin, C.A., Vidotti, S.A.B.G.: Acessibilidade Web em Bibliotecas Digitais Universitárias. In: Seminário Nacional em Bibliotecas Universitárias, São Paulo (2008)
9. DAISY Demystified, http://www.daisy.org/daisypedia/daisy-demystified
10. Decree 5.622/2005, http://www.planalto.gov.br/ccivil_03/_ato2004-2006/2004/decreto/d5296.htm
11. DSpace – Repositórios Digitais, http://dspace.ibict.br/
12. Lira, G.A.: Biblioteca Nacional: desenvolvimento do modelo brasileiro de biblioteca acessível para pessoas com deficiência e idosos. Inclusão Social, 2, 2 (abr./set), 10-13 (2007)
13. Melo, A.M., Baranauskas, M.C.C.: An Inclusive Approach to Cooperative Evaluation of Web User Interfaces. In: Eighth International Conference on Enterprise Information Systems. Paphos (2006)
14. Moreira, S.M.B.L.: Acessibilidade a informação aos deficientes visuais na Biblioteca Central Clodoaldo Beckmann da UFPA. In: Simpósio Nacional de Bibliotecas Universitárias, São Paulo (2008)
15. Muller, M.J., Haslwanter, J.H., Dayton, T.: Participatory Practices in the Sofware Lifecycle. In: Helaner, M.G., Landauer, T.K., Prabhu, P.V. (eds.) Handbook of Human-Computer Interaction, 2nd edn., pp. 255–297. Elsevier, Amsterdam (1997)
16. PDF Accessibility Overview, http://www.adobe.com/accessibility/products/acrobat/pdf/acrobat-xi-pdf-accessibility-overview.pdf

17. Preece, J., Rogers, Y., Sharp, H.: Interaction Design: beyond human-computer interaction. John Wiley & Sons (2002)
18. Preliminary Review of Web Sites for Accessibility, http://www.w3.org/WAI/eval/preliminary.html
19. Projeto MecDaisy, http://intervox.nce.ufrj.br/mecdaisy/
20. Reck, J.G.S.: Bibliotecas Digitais Acessíveis: promovendo o acesso à informação com recursos da informática. UNIPAMPA, Alegrete (2010)
21. Silva, J.G., Hohemberger, R., Melo, A.M.: Biblioteca Digital Inclusiva no Ensino Superior. In: Brazilian Symposium of Human Factors on Computer Systems, Belo Horizonte (2010)
22. Sommerville, I.: Software Engineering, 8th edn. Addison-Wesley (2006)
23. The Principles of Universal Design, http://www.ncsu.edu/project/design-projects/udi/center-for-universal-design/the-principles-of-universal-design/
24. Web Content Accessibility Guidelines (WCAG) 2.0, http://www.w3.org/TR/WCAG20/

Access to Books: Human Rights, Copyright and Accessibility

Abigail P. Rekas, Esq.[*]

Centre for Disability Law & Policy, National University of Ireland, Galway
abigail.rekas@nuigalway.ie

Abstract. This paper will explore the tension between the right to read (ensuring intellectual property does not create an unreasonable barrier to access) and the protection afforded to literary works by copyright, particularly how copyright policy can limit access to content. Using statutory analysis of international copyright law and human rights law, it will look at the way Human Rights treaties have addressed intellectual property in the past, and will compare them to the United Nations Convention on the Rights of Persons with Disabilities. This will be followed by a discussion the proposed World Intellectual Property Organization Treaty on Limitations and Exceptions for Visually Impaired Persons/Persons with Print Disabilities and how this proposed treaty will increase access to content for persons with disabilities. The conclusion of this analysis is that copyright policy must evolve in order to keep up with technology to enable equal access to content for persons with disabilities.

Keywords: WIPO, Accessibility, Copyright, Exceptions, Limitations, UNCRPD, Human Rights, Visually Impaired, Print Disabled, Disability, Dyslexic, Access to Knowledge, Access to Content.

1   Introduction

The right to read is fundamental. It is impossible to overstate the importance of literacy. Through the written word, past generations speak to the present, great ideas are expressed, language is learned, critical thought is developed, political movements rise and fall. Not only this, but reading provides pleasure and entertainment, and is valuable for this reason alone. It is nearly impossible to fully participate in cultural and community life without being able to access the written word.

There are many reasons why people are denied access to content, economic, social and educational opportunity to name a few. However, persons with print disabilities[1]

---

[*] Marie Curie Early Stage Research Fellow, Disability Rights Expanding Accessible Markets Project (http://www.nuigalway.ie/dream/), Ph.D. Candidate.

[1] For the purposes of this paper, the term Print Disability will encompass any disability that limits a person's ability to access standard text material. While there are many disabilities that affect a person's ability to read and understand print material, this paper is limited to those visual, perceptive and motor impairments that do not require substantive alteration to the content of a work to enable access.

C. Stephanidis and M. Antona (Eds.): UAHCI/HCII 2013, Part III, LNCS 8011, pp. 382–388, 2013.
© Springer-Verlag Berlin Heidelberg 2013

are faced with greater challenges. These challenges are not reflective of their impairment, but rather of policy. Persons with print disabilities are denied access to works protected by copyright. They are denied access even though there are technological tools to support universal access to content.

Historically, persons with print disabilities have been served by non-profit organizations working under exceptions and limitations to copyright to produce physically bulky accessible material using Braille, or accessible audio books in analog formats. The process to create these accessible format books was expensive in time and resources, and as a result, persons with print disabilities were extremely limited in what cultural materials they were able to access. The rise of digital technology has the potential to change all of this.

Digital technology allows the costs of creating accessible format material to drop significantly, and there has been some success in creating widely accepted standards for web accessibility, allowing for much greater access to cultural content that is available on the Internet. Engineers have created hardware and software that enables access for persons who had previously been unable, due to disability, to access much of this content. Refreshable braille readers and screen readers, as well as a multitude of cell phone apps and other developments have opened up a whole world of cultural content.

Unfortunately, international copyright law has not kept pace with these new technologies, and publishers have not embraced universal design in publishing. A great deal of content, particularly books, has been kept locked away through the territorial nature of copyright law and exceptions, through expansive protection for digital rights management protections/technical protection measures (DRM/TPM) and due to the publishers reluctance to engage in accessible publishing Without content, these enabling technologies are useless. There still exists, in this digital age, a book famine.

The term book famine refers to a World Blind Union (WBU) statistic that in the wealthiest nations only about 7% of all books published annually are converted into accessible formats (Braille, digital files with accessibility tools for DAISY readers and other devices, audio files, and other formats) for persons who are unable to access the written word (which encompasses digital format as well as hardcopy format material) in a standard format. In the developing world, this can be as low as 1%.

WBU estimates that there are 285 million blind and partially sighted persons living in the world. 90% of those people live in the developing world. This number grows every day as the global population ages and more people experience age-related disability.

2   Human Rights – The Right to Read

The ability to access the written word is essential to the realization of many human rights. It provides the foundation to the right to political involvement, freedom of expression, the right to education and the right to access culture and take advantage of scientific progress. These rights were articulated by the Universal Declaration of Human Rights (UDH), and reaffirmed through various treaties and conventions, most recently by the United Nations Convention on the Rights of Persons with Disabilities (UNCRPD).

The Universal Declaration of Human Rights initially had no legal force, and it required implementing treaties, the International Convent on Civil and Political Rights and the International Covenant on Economic, Social and Cultural Rights (ICESCR). The ICESCR Article 15 recognizes that access to culture is a fundamental human right, and that it is tied with the right to benefit from one's intellectual product. That relationship is extremely complicated. It implies that states must find a balance between those rights, but provides no guidance in how to do so.

The right to access culture until fairly recently has been largely ignored. Intellectual property and human rights are fields that have evolved separately and as each sphere has grown, they have begun to intersect more and more. This intersection has become increasingly important as the impact of extremely rigorous intellectual property protection on fundamental human rights has become more and more apparent.

3   The Balance

When most people think about this conflict, they generally think about access to medicine and food held in tension with patent protection. This is one of the most glaring intersections of IP and human rights and where there is highly publicized conflict. However, this is not the only area where intellectual property protection has the potential to effectively deny basic human rights to whole populations.

The intersection between access to content and copyright protection is another balancing act. While these issues may not seem to be as important as the right to adequate food and medical care, particularly in the developing world, it has been recognized that all human rights are reliant on other rights for their realization. The Vienna Declaration and Programme of Action, as adopted by the World Conference on Human Rights states: "All human rights are universal, indivisible and interdependent and interrelated. The international community must treat human rights globally in a fair and equal manner, on the same footing, and with the same emphasis." It is impossible to be effectively politically active if one has no food, it is difficult to have food if one has no education, and it is difficult to have education if one has no access to books.

Looking at the interaction between the right to access culture and education and the right of authors to benefit from the moral and material protection of their work becomes particularly challenging when one considers the above statement regarding the need to treat human rights in a fair and equal manner, on the same footing and with the same emphasis. It then becomes a balancing act between two fundamental human rights. The U.N. Sub-Commission on the Promotion and Protection of Human Rights recommends that governments recognize the "primacy of human rights obligations over economic policies and agreements." This guidance helps in some circumstances, particularly when dealing with large corporations, but that does not help when dealing with the rights of natural persons.

Why has this intersection between intellectual property and human rights become so important? It comes down to the purpose and mission of copyright protection.

Black's Law Dictionary defines copyright as follows: "The right to copy; specifically, a property right in an original work of authorship... fixed in any tangible medium of expression, giving the holder the exclusive right to reproduce, adapt, distribute, perform, and display the work..."

Copyright protects the rights of the author and copyright owner, but the purpose of copyright is to benefit the public. The US Constitution empowers Congress "To promote the Progress of Science and the useful Arts, by securing for limited Times to Authors and Inventers the exclusive Right to their respective Writings and Discoveries." This notion of using Intellectual Property to promote the public good hinges on the balance of protection, and access. If the balance swings too far one way, the protection hinders innovation and further creative activity. If it swings too far the other way, authors and innovators will not be able to support themselves doing their creative and innovative work.

This balance is extremely important, and it should be noted that no natural person is exclusively a creator or exclusively a consumer. Access and protection can both benefit a single person.

4   United Nations Convention on the Rights of Persons with Disabilities

The UNCRPD is the first treaty that explicitly requires states that have signed and ratified to examine the balance between the protections provided to rights holders and the right of the public to access content protected by intellectual property law. Article 30.3 requires that "States Parties shall take all appropriate steps, in accordance with international law, to ensure that laws protecting intellectual property rights do not constitute an unreasonable or discriminatory barrier to access by persons with disabilities to cultural materials." This reflects the tension between the rights guaranteed by the ICESCR Article 15 for the first time, and is a direct response to the book famine experienced by persons with disabilities.

All state parties who have signed and ratified the UNCRPD have an obligation to address the global book famine. Not only is it a moral imperative, it is also a legal one. Article 4(1) of the UNCRPD obligates the state parties to undertake "(a) to adopt all appropriate legislative, administrative and other measures for the implementation of the rights recognized in the present convention..."

Article 9 requires member states to "take appropriate measures to ensure to persons with disabilities access, on an equal basis with others (...) to information and communications..." Not only must member states legislate to make sure the printed work is accessible, they must also cooperate to promote the rights outlined in the UNCRPD.

Article 32(1) requires that "State parties recognize the importance of international cooperation and its promotion in support of national efforts for the realization of the purpose and objectives of the present Convention, and will undertake appropriate and effective measures in this regard, between and among states and, as appropriate, in partnership with relevant international and regional organizations and civil society, in particular organizations of persons with disabilities."

5   Copyright Protection Barriers to Access

Unfortunately, the digital revolution that has allowed for standard print materials to be made accessible is a double-edged sword. On one hand, accessible publishing and making available of works is simpler and cheaper than ever before. On the other hand, digital technology allows for content piracy. The publishing industry fears they will suffer the same fate as the record industry. This makes them extremely protective of proprietary content and resistant to harmonized exceptions and limitations internationally.

Added to this is the challenge of the territorial nature of copyright law. While some baseline protection standards have been set by international law through the various IP treaties (discussed below), copyright is a territorial right. The protection, and exceptions, is only valid within the physical territory of the protection nation.

The balance of interests in copyright law is, in part, maintained through a system of limitations and exceptions to the exclusive right of the owner of the copyright. Examples of exceptions are areas where copyright law does not apply in the same way, i.e. licensing fees could be limited or waived, authors may not have the right to prevent distribution in a certain format and so forth. Exceptions differ from country to country as the "nature and scope... has been largely left to national policy makers to determine within broad permissive areas" (WIPO Sullivan Study). Broadly speaking, they are created to allow for commentary or criticism, news reporting, academic research, teaching, archiving, and access for the print disabled community.

There has been very little international harmonization in national copyright laws, and by extension, exceptions to copyright law. Due to this lack of harmonization in exceptions, cross-border trade in digital accessible books created under these exceptions is a matter of uncertain legality. There has been some regional transfer of hard copy Braille format and analogue audio cassettes between nations, but that has been the extent of any sharing between nations, for instance, the National Council for the Blind in Ireland receives books from the Royal National Institute of Blind People in the United Kingdom and the Library of Congress in the United States. There is no clear law governing what types of distribution are within the scope of specific exceptions.

In addition "other aspects of the scope of the exceptions... such as who may act under the exception, how to determine whether or not the requirements about the end beneficiary of the exception are met, whether requirements that a work must have been published are met, whether or not only copies made under the exception may be distributed in the country and whether the same type of accessible copies in both importing and exporting countries are permitted" (WIPO Sullivan Study) complicates the issue even further.

Creators of accessible books do not wish to jeopardize themselves by making themselves liable for civil, and potentially criminal, penalties, by shipping books created under an exception into countries where they may be grey market goods. This has resulted in great redundancy in the world of accessible publishing. If the transfer of digital master files were clearly legal, the resources of organizations doing accessible publishing could be shared and more books could be unlocked for persons with disabilities, rather than multiple master files being created for each individual country. This means ONCE in Spain could share its more than 100,000 accessible titles with Spanish speaking countries in South America.

International copyright treaties establish baseline protections for the content industry that each member country must provide the intellectual property of citizens of other member states. The ones most frequently discussed in the intersection of copyright and human rights are the Berne Convention and the World Trade Organization TRIPS agreement.

6   "Draft Text of an International Instrument/Treaty on Limitations and Exceptions for Visually Impaired Persons/Persons with Print Disabilities"

None of these treaties listed above establish any mandatory exceptions or limitations to the rights of the content industry. As one WIPO study points out, "Much of the development of the international framework for copyright protection has, however, concentrated on defining rights needed to secure the aim of encouraging and rewarding creativity" (WIPO Sullivan Study). Until recently, the focus internationally has been stronger and stronger protection. Exceptions were acceptable as long as they complied with the three-step test established by the Berne Convention (and reiterated in the subsequent copyright treaties). "The three step test states that exceptions must only be in "certain special cases," it must not "conflict with the normal exploitation of a work," and must not "unreasonably prejudice the legitimate interests of the author" (Berne Convention, Art. 9(2)).

The World Intellectual Property Organization (WIPO) administers all copyright treaties except for TRIPS.[2] In December of 2012 in an extraordinary meeting, the General Assembly of WIPO made the groundbreaking decision to convene a diplomatic conference on a potential international instrument to increase access to copyright material for persons with print disabilities. This international instrument would be groundbreaking because it represents a significant shift in international intellectual property law policy. It is a response to the obligations placed on the UNCRPD member states, as recalled in the recitals, and to the book famine experienced by the millions of print disabled persons worldwide.

This treaty mandates exceptions to the baseline protections established by prior intellectual property treaties. It will harmonize exceptions in member states to remove legal uncertainty in the cross border exchange of books created under exceptions.

---

[2] WIPO is an agency of the United Nations, established in 1967. There are 184 member states, including China, the EU, the United States and the Russian Federation, and 250 accredited observers, including the World Blind Union and International Federation of Library Associations.

7   Conclusion

The book famine is a denial of fundamental human rights. Without legal access to content, all of the technology in the world will not allow enable people with disabilities to access content on an equal basis with others. Without that access, persons with disabilities are limited in their right to education, freedom of expression and speech, their right to political involvement, their right to work and the right to access culture.

The Draft International Instrument represents that the international community sees the denial of access to content to persons with disabilities, the so-called "book famine," is unacceptable. It is an example of human rights law working together with international intellectual property law to realize human rights objectives for persons with disabilities.

Accessible technology has created the possibility of an inclusive world where universal design allows everyone to experience content on an equal basis with others. Policy must evolve to keep pace. Universal access is possible, but only where copyright policy is flexible and responsive to emerging technologies.

Acknowledgments. The Author would like to acknowledge the support of the DREAM project, Marie Curie Actions, a Framework 7 research grant and the support of her colleagues at the CDLP. She also wishes to thank Mr. Gearóid O'Brien for his good sense.

References

1. UN Resources: Universal Declaration of Human Rights, art. 26, 27, 29 G.A. Res. 217 (III) A, U.N. Doc. A/RES/217(III). (December 10, 1948); Convention on the Rights of Persons with Disabilities, arts. 21, 24, 30, G.A. Res 61/106, U.N. Doc. A/RES/61/106. (January 24, 2007) [UNCRPD]; International Covenant on Economic, Social and Cultural Rights, (ICESCR) art. 15.1(c), Adopted December 16, 1966, 993 U.N.T.S. 3 (entered into force January 3, 1976); Vienna Declaration and Programme of Action, as adopted by the World Conference on Human Rights art. 5 (June 25, 1993); Intellectual Property Rights and Human Rights, Sub-Comm'n on Human Rights Res. 2000/7 par. 3, U.N. Doc. E/CN.4/Sub.2/RES/2000/7 (August 17, 2000) (Res. 2000/7)
2. U.S. Const. art. I, § 8
3. WIPO Resources: WIPO, SCCR, Study on Copyright Limitations and Exceptions for the Visually Impaired, 12, 15th Sess., SCCR/15/17 (September 11-13, 2006) [Sullivan Study]; The Berne Convention for the Protection of Literary and Artistic Works September 9, 1886, as last revised at Paris, July 24, 1971, 828 U.N.T.S. 221 (Berne Convention); WIPO, SCCR, Draft text of an international instrument/treaty on limitations and exceptions for visually impaired persons/persons with print disabilities, Special Session. SCCR/SS/GE/13/REF/SCCR/25/2 REV (February 22, 2013)
4. The Agreement on Trade-Related Aspects of Intellectual Property Rights, April 15, 1994, Marrakesh Agreement Establishing the World Trade Organization, Annex 1C, 1869 U.N.T.S. 299 (TRIPS)

Providing an Accessible Track Changes Feature for Persons Who Are Blind

John G. Schoeberlein and Yuanqiong Wang

Towson University, 7800 York Road
Towson, Maryland 21252-0001 USA
Jschoe4@students.towson.edu, ywangtu@gmail.com

Abstract. Collaborative writing applications are widely utilized in the work place to co-author documents and to exchange ideas. Unfortunately, persons who are blind have difficulty in identifying the changes and their related context, which prevents them from actively participating in collaborative writing. In order to expand on the knowledge gained from previous research, additional usability studies were carried out with participants who are blind utilizing Microsoft Word with the focus on track change and comment features. Based on results from all the previous usability studies, a Microsoft Word Add-In was proposed to solve the issues identified. This paper briefly presents the results of the usability studies, the prototype design of the Microsoft Word Add-In and a pilot review of the Microsoft Word Add-In for making the track change and comment features accessible and usable.

Keywords: Collaborative writing, accessibility, usability, blind.

1 Introduction

According to World Health Organization [13], about 285 million people are visually impaired worldwide, among them 39 million are blind. Collaborative writing in organizations has become essential for exchanging and sharing ideas. Unfortunately, persons who are blind have experienced accessibility and usability issues while interacting with popular collaborative writing applications, such as Microsoft Word and Google Docs [9].

As an early attempt on designing a more accessible collaborative writing application, several usability study sessions were conducted [9] to establish a baseline for the current collaborative writing features provided. However, most of the participants of these study sessions were experienced users of the collaborative writing tools.

In order to verify whether the baseline data collected from the previous usability study [9] is consistent with a more diverse user population and to identify the solution to the issues identified additional usability study sessions were conducted with persons who are blind with no residual vision to address the following questions.

C. Stephanidis and M. Antona (Eds.): UAHCI/HCII 2013, Part III, LNCS 8011, pp. 389–398, 2013.
© Springer-Verlag Berlin Heidelberg 2013

The following research questions were addressed:

- RQ1: What accessibility and usability issues do collaborative writing technologies, such as Microsoft Word, present for persons who are blind? And,
- RQ2: How should a collaborative writing interface be designed in order to be accessible and usable for persons who are blind?

This article builds upon the earlier work [9] and results from additional usability study sessions, exploring the design of a proposed Microsoft Word Add-in that can potentially solve the issues identified when answering the two research questions. After briefly presenting the usability studies that investigates the above research questions, this article presents the design of the proposed solution. The potential benefits of the proposed design, the pilot review of the Microsoft Word Add-In and the future research directions are discussed.

2   Related Work

Several usability studies were reported [9] which identified the issues that persons who are blind experience when using collaborative writing tools. Using Microsoft Word with the JAWS screen reader, participants from those studies were requested to complete a set of collaborative writing tasks including starting a collaborative writing session by opening a document and setting the "track change" feature, identifying the comments/changes in a given document, searching for a specific change/comment in the document, adding a change/comment to the document, accepting/rejecting a change in the document. All of the participants who are blind were expert users of both Microsoft Word and the JAWS screen reader. These studies showed that the majority of blind participants did not think Microsoft Word is flexible and understandable. They experienced problems when trying to identify specific changes/comments, and were not able to identify the context of the revisions and comments presented in the document. In addition, there was no direct access for blind users to operate on the existing changes in the document.

3   Additional Usability Study

Due to the lack of variance in the participants' previous experience levels in the prior usability studies, it is necessary to check whether the results can be applied to other users who have less experience with Microsoft Word and the JAWS Screen Reader. Therefore, additional usability study sessions were conducted to include participants with less experience using the same research instruments.

3.1   Participants

Participants were recruited from local universities and businesses, giving a total of eight participants for all usability studies. The genders of participants were evenly distributed, with four (50%) females and four (50%) males. The ages of the subjects were distributed from 19 to 59 years. The majority of the participants (62.5%) were between 19 and 39 years of age.

Half (50%) of the participants had twenty-one to thirty years of experience utilizing the computer and the JAWS Screen Reader. All of the participants utilized the computer daily (100%), and primarily used to computer at work (62.5%) or at school/college (37.5%). Half (50%) of the participants had eleven to twenty years of Microsoft Word experience.

3.2   Task Performance

All (100%) participants were able to successfully complete the tasks that requested them to open the document and start a "track change" session, add a change, delete and change text, and add a comment to the document. 37.5% of the participants did not complete the tasks related to searching for changes and accepting/rejecting changes.

The participants took the longest time when adding a change (252 seconds), adding a comment (202.5 seconds) and accepting/rejecting the remaining changes (249 seconds). There were big variations in terms of the time spent on completing the tasks. This was reflected in the big standard deviation observed. For example, the participants spent 155 seconds on average to search for changes, with a standard deviation of 67.82. Participants were able to finish the tasks in a shorter time when they deleted text (78.12), change text (70.62), accept a change (73) and reject a change (89).

Table 1 presents the categories identified based on the transcripts from the usability study audio/video recordings collected during the usability studies.

3.3   Results

Comparing to the original usability studies [9], the additional usability studies highlighted similar key areas where persons who are blind had difficulty in completing tasks related to searching for changes and accepting/rejecting changes.

The difficulty of searching the ribbon menu structure in order to search for changes was expressed as a reason for not being able to complete the searching changes and accepting/rejecting changes tasks. A participant commented that they are, *"Not familiar with the ribbon menus and finding the track changes menu items takes time, which can take some getting used to."*

In regard to the interactions with Microsoft Word's interface, 37.5% of the participants thought that the interactions with Microsoft Word's interface were not flexible, and 62.5% of the participants thought that Microsoft Word's interface was not clear and not easy to understand. The participants considered track changes difficult to distinguish and understand unless they accepted all of the changes before reviewing the document. The comments were also difficult to distinguish and understand because the contexts of the comments were not clearly presented.

37.5% of the participants who are blind thought that the tasks were not easy to complete, and they were dissatisfied with the time they took to complete the tasks.

50% of the participants who are blind disagreed that they were able to complete the tasks without any problems.

Based on all the usability studies conducted, the participants who are blind suggested the following improvements to make the application more accessible: (1) clearly differentiate the text from the comments; (2) provide the context of inserted/deleted changes and comments by providing paragraph content with the changes and comments; (3) notify the user when text is added/deleted or accepted/rejected; and (4) give the ability to review changes in their accepted form.

Table 1. Categories identified from audio/video recordings

Category	Annotated List Element
1. Searching techniques utilized	• Searching/reading word-by-word with the tab key • Scrolling up/down with the up/down-arrow keys • Tab key to parse menu items • Find / replace menu access key • JAWS hot keys (Insert/Shift/R) to search MS Word's Revisions' list
2. Selecting techniques utilized	• Selecting text with the alt-shift-right-arrow keys (word select) • Selecting letters with the shift-right-arrow keys • Selecting (tabbing) word-by-word
3. Editing techniques utilized	• Right-click (accept/reject list) • Copy (control-c)/Paste (control-v) keys • Typing text with a standard keyboard
4. Reading techniques utilized	• JAWS Screen reader to read text • Braille keyboard to read text (used in conjunction with standard keyboard)
5. Accessibility and usability issues	• Participants cannot determine the context of the comments • JAWS "Say All" feature doesn't always read the revisions/changes as revisions/changes (Cannot determine/identify the changes when read in the sentence) • Changes in the revisions list do not show context • Changes are entered in the incorrect position within the sentence/paragraph due to incorrect cursor position • Extra access time searching menus for features • Extra access time searching for text insertion point

4   Proposed Solution

Based on the data analysis from the usability studies, it is clear that providing the context for the revisions is the key for persons who are blind to successfully utilize track changes and comments features of Microsoft Word.

Since Microsoft Word is still one of the most frequently used editing tools in the work place, the solution needs to be able to work with Microsoft Word seamlessly. With Microsoft Word's Application Add-In [12], it is possible to provide context information more clearly. Therefore, we propose to develop a Microsoft Word Application Add-In [12].

4.1 Microsoft Word Application Add-In

A Microsoft Word Application Add-In is a tool or application that is developed to integrate with Microsoft Word in order to expand or enhance the features of Microsoft Word. In this case, A Microsoft Word Application Add-In will be designed to improve the access and use of track changes and comments features included with Microsoft Word. This Add-In would be set at the application level, allowing the developed features to be available for any Microsoft Word document. In order to access the revisions and comments, the Microsoft Word Paragraphs [4], Revisions [5] and Comments [6] Collections are accessed to present the revisions and comments within the context of their paragraphs.

4.2 Features Proposed

The proposed Microsoft Word add-in will be compatible with different versions of Microsoft Word and provides the following features:

1. Provide a comprehensive view of all revisions and comments.
2. Present the context (paragraph or sentence) of each comment and revision.
3. Identify each revision as an addition, a deletion, or a change.
4. Present each comment separately.
5. Select/highlight each revision/comment in series.
6. Providing direct access to the features of the Add-In through a Microsoft Word Command Bar.
7. Provide the "Final" view, as if the revisions are applied, for each paragraph or sentence.
8. Provide the "Revision" view, with the in-line revisions, for each paragraph or sentence.
9. Compatible with JAWS 13.
10. Provide optional audio feature as an alternative to JAWS.

The following sections discuss each feature in more detail.

Comprehensive View

To provide a comprehensive view of the revisions and comments, the Microsoft Word Add-In presents an overview of the total number of paragraphs or sentences, along with the total number of revisions and comments (Figure 1). This overview is necessary for any person to know immediately whether they have revisions or comments to review.

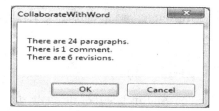

Fig. 1. Overview

Paragraph or Sentence Context

Based on the comments of the participants of the baseline usability study [9], it was determined that the context of a revision or comment was necessary to the understanding of the revision or comment being reviewed. However, Microsoft Word does not properly present the context of revisions or comments, making review difficult for persons who are blind [9]. In order to provide the proper context for revisions and comments, the paragraph (Figure 2) or the sentence containing the revision of comment is presented.

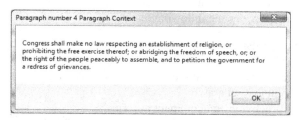

Fig. 2. Paragraph or Sentence Context

Revision Type

In addition to the context of a revision or comment, it is essential that the type of revision be identified. The developed Microsoft Word Add-In provides for addition, change and deletion revisions (Figures 3).

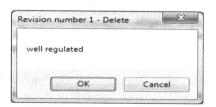

Fig. 3. Delete Revision

Present Each Comment

The comments in the document will be presented one by one when the user requests it.

Select Revision/Comment

In order to act upon any revision or comment, the revision or comment must be selected by the Microsoft Word Add-In (Figure 4). Once selected (highlight in blue), the revision can be accepted or rejected. The selected comment can be deleted.

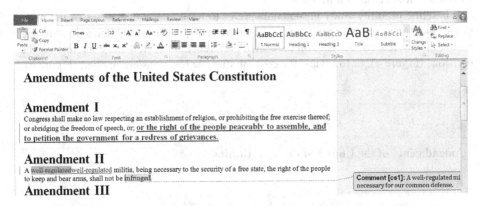

Fig. 4. Revision View with a selected revision (highlight in blue)

Provide Direct Access

Since accessing the Microsoft Word Ribbon Menu was a usability issue for the participants who are blind [9], and in order to provide seamless interface integration of the Microsoft Word Application Add-In [12] with Microsoft Word, the Microsoft Word Command Bar (Figure 5) [7] was utilized to add features necessary to provide improved access and use of the track changes and comments features of Microsoft Word.

Fig. 5. Microsoft Word Command Bar

The Microsoft Word Command Bar would allow the end-user the ability to avoid accessing the Microsoft Word Ribbon Menu by simply right-clicking anywhere on the document to access the Command Bar, to directly access the application's features.

Revision View versus Final View

The baseline usability study participants prefer to have alternative views of the paragraphs and sentences with revisions and comments [9]. Users should be able to toggle between two views depending on their own preference: to review the content with the revisions (Figure 4), or to review the content after the revisions are applied (Figure 6).

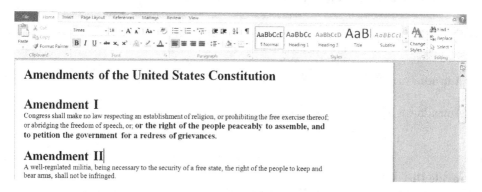

Fig. 6. Final View

JAWS and Built-In Audio

The JAWS Screen Reader [2] is the standard output device utilized by persons who are blind in order to interface with any computer application. Therefore, the developed Microsoft Word Add-In and Microsoft Word Command Bar have to be compatible with the JAWS Screen Reader. The Microsoft Word Add-In and the Microsoft Word Command Bar and the message boxes presented by the Add-In have been validated to work seamlessly with the JAWS Screen Reader.

Alternatively, a Microsoft Speech API was included in the development of the Microsoft Word Add-In, to provide audio output for persons who did not have access to the JAWS Screen Reader. No content is displayed on the interface, only the audio content representing the messages boxes that would otherwise display for the JAWS Screen Reader.

4.3   Microsoft Word Add-In Benefits

The proposed Microsoft Word Add-In provides many benefits to the users. Since the Add-In is a component of Microsoft Word, it will be seamlessly integrated into Microsoft Word. Users do not need any prior knowledge to utilize the Command Bar, since they can simply right-click anywhere on a document to have direct access to the commands. With this direct access feature, there is no need to memorize complex key stoke combinations when working on the document. Therefore, the cognitive load will be reduced to prevent overload. Since the Add-In will be applied at the application level, it will work with all Microsoft Word documents. It provides descriptive information regarding any comments/revisions including their sequence as well as type and content of the revisions. In addition, users will be presented with an overview of the document and context of the revision/comments so that users will be aware of the context of any action. The Add-In can be upgraded to different versions of Microsoft Word and is compatible with the JAWS screen reader. This eliminates the need for additional investment for the application to be accessible.

5   Pilot Usability Study

On January 17, 2013, a pilot usability study was conducted at the NFB with a participant who was blind with no residual vision, in order to examine and suggest improvements to the developed Microsoft Word Add-In. The participant had experience utilizing Microsoft Word (6 to 10 years) and the JAWS Screen Reader (11 to 20 years) on a daily basis. The participant's role at the organization was as a member of the public relations team which was responsible for correspondence with the public.

The participant "*agreed*" that the Microsoft Word Add-In interface was clear and understandable, and "*strongly agreed*" that the Microsoft Word Add-In interface was flexible and easy to use, improved performance, and enable tasks to be completed without any problems. Further, the participant "*strongly agreed*" that he was satisfied with the time he took to complete the study tasks, and that he would utilize the Microsoft Word Add-In interface in the future on a regular basis.

The participant reported that the Microsoft Word Add-In interface "*helps place the revision in context and identifies exactly what is being changed. It also provides easier access to the comments than just the screen reader.*"

The participant suggested "*some clarification of language on some menu options and message boxes*" as improvements to the Microsoft Word Add-In interface.

6   Conclusion

The prior usability studies [9] concluded that the participants who are blind were out-of-range when compared with the visually able participants in several collaborative writing tasks. Given the result from the prior usability studies, additional participants who are blind participated in usability studies to validate the baseline quantitative measures related to task completion times, the qualitative analysis on notes and audio recordings related to participants' preferences collected, and to expand on the experience and age demographics. What was discovered is that as the experience level drops, so does the ability to complete certain collaborative writing tasks related to revisions and comments. Based on these results, it was decided that an improvement to the Microsoft Word interface was necessary to improve access to revisions and comments and to provide the context of the revisions and comments.

The proposed solution, which includes a Microsoft Word Application Add-In [12], will enable all persons to review revisions and comments in any Microsoft Word document by directly accessing the Microsoft Word Command Bar [7]. Simply right-clicking anywhere on the document will prompt the Command Bar to be activated and direct access is available to the revisions, the comments, and the context of the revisions and comments. This direct access will promote ease of use and the ability of all persons to be able to complete all collaborative writing tasks.

The pilot usability study provided positive responses in regard to the access and use of the Microsoft Word Add-In interface, which now will undergo extensive review with additional participants. The Microsoft Word Add-In will be available at some future time for general distribution.

References

1. Cohen's Kappa (2010),
   http://www.experiment-resources.com/cohens-kappa.html
2. Freedom Scientific (JAWS),
   http://www.freedomscientific.com/products/fs/
   jaws-product-page.asp
3. Grounded Theory (2009),
   http://www.analytictech.com/mb870/introtoGT.htm
4. MSDN Paragraphs Collection, http://msdn.microsoft.com/en-us/library/
   office/aa679608v=office.10.aspx
5. MSDN Revisions Collection, http://msdn.microsoft.com/en-us/library/
   office/aa223078v=office.11.aspx
6. MSDN Comments Collection, http://msdn.microsoft.com/en-us/library/
   office/aa220940v=office.11.aspx
7. MSDN Microsoft Word Command Bar, http://msdn.microsoft.com/en-us/
   library/office/aa165324v=office.10.aspx
8. National Federation of the Blind. Assuring opportunities: A 21st century strategy to increase employment of blind Americans, http://www.icbv.net/National%
   20Issues/Opportunities.htm
9. Schoeberlein, J., Wang, J.: Accessible Collaborative Writing for Persons Who Are Blind: A Usability Study. In: Proceedings of ASSETS 2012, pp. 267–268. Boulder, Colorado (2012)
10. Schoeberlein, J.G., Wang, Y.: Examining the Current State of Group Support Accessibility: An Expanded Study. In: Stephanidis, C. (ed.) Posters, Part I, HCII 2011. CCIS, vol. 173, pp. 389–393. Springer, Heidelberg (2011)
11. Schoeberlein, J., Wang, Y.: Examining the Current State of Group Support Accessibility: A Focus Group Study. In: Stephanidis, C. (ed.) Universal Access in HCI, Part IV, HCII 2011. LNCS, vol. 6768, pp. 272–281. Springer, Heidelberg (2011)
12. Word Add-Ins,
    http://msdn.microsoft.com/
    en-us/library/office/aa189710v=office.10.aspx
13. World Health Organization,
    http://www.who.int/mediacentre/factsheets/fs282/en/

Improving the Accessibility of Digital Documents for Blind Users: Contributions of the Textual Architecture Model

Laurent Sorin[1], Mustapha Mojahid[1], Nathalie Aussenac-Gilles[1], and Julie Lemarié[2]

[1] Institut de Recherche en Informatique de Toulouse, Toulouse, France
{sorin,mojahid,aussenac}@irit.fr
[2] Laboratoire Cognition-Langues-Langage-Ergonomie, Toulouse, France
lemarie@univ-tlse2.fr

Abstract. This paper presents a framework which aims at describing text formatting, based on a model coming from the field of logic and linguistics, the Textual Architecture Model [23]. The goal is to improve documents accessibility for blind users. The project will later focus on evaluating the efficiency of different navigation and content presentation strategies, based on this framework.

Keywords: blind people, documents accessibility, visual signals, text structure.

1 Introduction

Accessibility of information contained in digital documents is a crucial challenge for visually impaired people, especially for blind users. Indeed, it is predicted that the number of blind people will drastically increase with the global ageing of world population. Besides, blind users should be in the center of design issues since Internet and new technologies are an unprecedented opportunity for them to perform tasks that they can hardly do without [8]. When figuring out how to give blind users access to information contained in digital documents, two general approaches may be considered.

The first approach is to change the environment; that is to say creating a new version of each document, media or web page that is entirely and specifically designed for blind users. This is what transcription companies do by offering for instance audio or Braille versions of books. However, this strategy is very rarely used because it is time-consuming and expensive; as far as digital documents are concerned, the always growing body of web pages and digital documents makes this approach impossible to generalize, and thus marginal.

The second possible solution is to include in the original document annotations and possibly additional information in order to make it accessible through assistive technologies. Instead of creating an alternate version of a document, the document designer will respect for instance the WAI accessibility guidelines for visually impaired

C. Stephanidis and M. Antona (Eds.): UAHCI/HCII 2013, Part III, LNCS 8011, pp. 399–407, 2013.
© Springer-Verlag Berlin Heidelberg 2013

people (e.g. to give each graphic presentation a textual counterpart), so that a blind user may easily access the information contained in the document.

Even though there has been much effort on designing assistive technologies and accessible information, the situation often remains frustrating for blind users (e.g. [10, 18]). According to [20], several reasons may explain why Internet is still not accessible to blind users. Among them, one should stress the fact that some types of contents are intrinsically visual and can hardly be represented using non-visual modalities. Another major reason is that Internet has a growing multi-task, multi-objects and multi-application logic which makes it particularly difficult for blind users to build a representation of the page layout.

Indeed, digital documents are primarily designed to be visually displayed, so that the expressive means offered by a spatial layout are often intensively used to create complex objects like tables, graphs, outlines, menus, etc. Consequently, it is very challenging to create adaptable contents, i.e. contents that can be presented in different ways without losing structural information and associated cognitive functions. Up to now, when a blind user accesses a document via an audio or a tactile device, he/she has very few clues about the original layout. For instance, Text-To-Speech software (TTS) tools are efficient to oralize a page of continuous text but still struggle with typical web pages [7] and text objects like headings [13].

Yet, many research works in educational and cognitive psychology have clearly shown the positive effects of text signaling devices revealing the text architecture (titles, headings, lists, overviews, etc.) on text processing (see [11] for a review). For instance, a recent study by [13] shows that it is possible to improve oralized texts comprehension by systematically rendering the information conveyed by text headings. In the first experiment, the effects of headings and preview sentences on outlining performances were compared to a control condition (no signal) for both a printed text version and an auditory TTS presentation. It was found that the task of reporting the text organizational structure (outlining task) is facilitated by preview sentences as compared to a no signals condition for both printed text and TTS audio rendering of the same text. Because of their entirely discursive nature, preview sentences are adaptable to audio presentation. In contrast, adding headings to the text was efficient for the printed text but poor for the audio presentation since speech synthesis can't communicate nonverbal information carried by headings in their visual form. In the second experiment, it was further investigated how headings could be rendered by TTS presentation using the analysis provided by [12] on the different information functions associated to headings. Prosodic cues like pauses and discursive indications were added to enrich the TTS presentation and mimic the printed text. The result was that outlining performance improved to levels similar to the visual headings condition of Experiment 1. This shows that giving access to information carried by visual signals in audio format can improve content comprehension.

In this context, the MathArchiTact project aims at allowing blind users to access a document's visual properties and logical structure and at designing new reading tools. We focus on mathematics text-books and try to improve their accessibility to blind high-school teenagers. The project is currently in its early stages.

2   Textual Architecture Model

2.1   Overview

To describe the visual properties of a document, we will use and enrich a model coming from the fields of logic and linguistics: the *Textual Architecture Model* (TAM) [16, 17, 22, 23]. TAM has been used in a computer science perspective for text-generation [14] and analysis [11, 21] and in a psycholinguistic perspective for modeling and predicting the effects of text signaling devices on cognitive processing [11]. Here, as a first step in the MathArchiTact project, we want to use this model to make text formatting available to blind people. Though the scope of this paper is to analyze the model contributions to our goal and examine how to implement it, the longer-term goal is to improve document navigation and content comprehension of documents described with TAM.

This model aims at providing a semantic analysis of text formatting properties that contribute to the "text architecture.

2.2   Key Concepts

According to TAM, a text is composed of (1) a **message** and (2) its specific **formatting**, those two components being separated in the model. A good analogy to understand is to compare it with the data/data-presentation separation, in computer science.

(1)The **message** is made up of the *content* the author intends to communicate to the reader (ideas and concepts), and their specific *linguistic expression* by the author's choice of wording, syntax, and so on, to convey the content. (2)The **text-formatting** properties refer to typography and disposition of the textual content. Those visually distinctive aspects of the text are called **textual objects**; in other words textual objects refer to text-formatting phenomena. For instance: headings, lists, paragraph structure, and any other visually identifiable entity in a text are textual objects.

Finally, the **text architecture** refers to the document textual objects and the relationships that exist between them. The underlying idea here is that text-formatting reflects the author's intention to organize and structure his message; this is why we speak of "architecture".

The text-formatting is represented in TAM as **metatext**, where the metatext is a coherent and cohesive set of metasentences with a specific grammar [17], each metasentence describing the intention that underlies the use of the corresponding text-formatting property. We use the term "**metasentence**", borrowed from Harris [9], to designate language used to describe language itself and its properties (here the text visual properties), as opposed to language referring to real world elements. For instance, "This article is divided into three parts" is a metasentence because it conveys information about the text rather than objects or events in the world.

Fig. 1 shows an example of how text-formatting can be described using metasentences with the TAM.

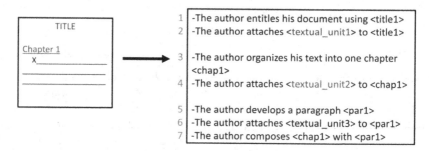

Fig. 1. Example of text-formatting representation using the TAM

As you can see, each textual object has a unique id in the metatext (title1, chap1, par1...). Metasentences 2, 4 and 5 shows how content is separated from textual objects, by attaching textual content (divided in textual units) to the corresponding textual objects. Notice that a textual-object may itself contain different textual objects; here the chapter contains a paragraph.

Concerning the relationships between textual objects, two categories appear. The first comprises all of the composition relationships which give the hierarchical structure of the text, as in the metasentence 3 in Fig. 1; they depict the text logical structure. The other category regroups all of the non linear relationships between objects, for instance a footnote annotating a paragraph.

Lastly, even though the previous example included only organizational textual objects for illustration purposes, the TAM allows describing very local formatting phenomena such as emphasizes.

2.3   Metasentences Properties

Metasentences are the key concept of the model and have several interesting properties that are worth being reported.

First, metasentences are generic: one metasentence can describe adequately one class of textual objects. For instance every possible "first level title" textual objects can be described with the same metasentence regardless of their visual form, considering a given content for this object.

Besides, a metasentence does not only describe one textual object, it constitutes its discursive form. In this way, a metasentence can be "reduced" to its visual form, the corresponding textual object. The concept of reducibility borrows from Harris's [9] proposal that metalanguage can be truncated from a complete sentence to a reduced sentence but that the reduction leaves traces in the utterance. Thus the property of reducibility is not specific to the realm of texts but is a general property of language. As a consequence, a metasentence may take various forms in the context of the TAM.

At one extreme, a metasentence may be left intact, appearing as a discursive statement in the text. At the other extreme, a metasentence may be reduced to the point where it is represented only by visual contrast in the text. The example below illustrates the concept of reducibility.

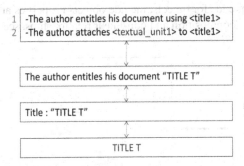

Fig. 2. Reduction / development of a set of metasentences

Fig. 2 shows how the original text at the bottom finds its discursive equivalent in the set of metasentences (in the first frame at the top). The traces left by the reduction process include syntactic transformations, lexical elements (e.g., the lexical content of a specific heading), typographical and spatial realization properties (e.g., italics, bold characters, indentation, blanks), and punctuation marks.

2.4   Technical Framework

After presenting the TAM, the next step in order to apply it to digital documents accessibility is to formally adapt this model, originally a linguistics model, to build a framework for accessing text-formatting semantics as described in the TAM.

Regardless of the original document format, segmentation of textual objects implies being able to annotate the content. Each textual object has its properties and potentially relationships with other objects. Those constraints make markup languages appropriate for implementing the TAM. This choice was also motivated by the wish to be compliant with the DAISY[1] standard which is widely use in digital libraries [6]. Most of DAISY audio-books are in HTML or XML format. The idea would be to keep their existing structure and annotate a duplicated file with the TAM, using the same html/xml ids, which could allow further navigation into textual objects.

For the moment, the annotation process is manual. Yet, depending on the original document format, semi-automatic methods could be proposed. For instance, in the case of web pages, we could use styles defined in CSS[2] to first segment textual objects. More generally, documents where formatting styles are well defined are easier to segment with the TAM. However, a reliable and fully automatic method to segment textual objects appears to be almost impossible since formatting isn't always consistent in one document. The most efficient approach would be to include TAM annotation in the documents production process.

The core of the TAM is the metasentences describing textual objects. Using XML or XHTML, the tags must keep the metasentences following properties: content/formatting

---

[1] International standard for audio books.
[2] Cascading Style Sheets: language used to describe the formatting of several markup languages.

separation, using unique ids for objects, include objects properties and describe relationships between objects (composition and non-linear relationships, see 2.2).

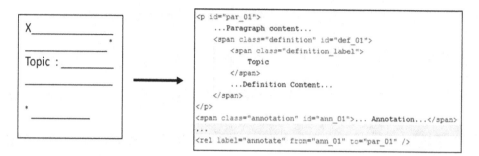

```
<p id="par_01">
    ...Paragraph content...
    <span class="definition" id="def_01">
        <span class="definition_label">
            Topic
        </span>
        ...Definition Content...
    </span>
</p>
<span class="annotation" id="ann_01">... Annotation...</span>
...
<rel label="annotate" from="ann_01" to="par_01" />
```

Fig. 3. TAM implementation in XML

Content/formatting separation is native with markup languages. Composition relationships emerge with the tags hierarchy and, for the headings, their order. Textual objects ids and properties are described with tags properties. Finally we use special tags and objects ids to note non-linear relationships as the annotation in the example above.

Currently, the DTD[3] is still under construction and should describe objects properties and relationships. For instance, in Fig. 3, the definition is tagged using the class property of the HTML tag "span", but could also be described using a new tag. A set of about twenty textual objects and relationships will be formalized; yet new textual objects can be encountered depending on the studied corpus. For instance with mathematics we can add theorems, lemma, demonstration, etc.

Concerning the reduction/development properties of metasentences (see 2.3), discursive equivalents are stored in a separate file for each textual object define, for later presentation purposes.

3   Contributions to Digital Documents Accessibility

This section presents how text formatting information made available with the TAM can contribute to accessibility of digital documents.

3.1   Accessing Content and Structure

As explained in 2.3, the TAM makes available discursive counterparts to text objects, ranging from fully discursive metasentences to more reduced forms. For each type of textual object of the model we store the different more or less discursive forms of the object in order to fit different presentation needs. For instance: "The definition of A is B" could also be presented with the sentence "A, B" (using prosodic cues). Those two

---

[3] Document Type Definition: tags definition, here for an XML file.

forms of the same object could each be useful depending on the user's task and the specific text object to render.

Currently, several approaches in document presentation for the blind try to give an overview of the content using keywords [1] or summaries [5]. This may be very useful for the user to build a first anchoring representation of the document content and structure, but accessing the visual structure of the document during reading is also crucial.

3.2   Document Navigation

DAISY readers allow basically two types of navigation: local and global navigation[4]. Local navigation refers to text reading control and includes actions such as jumping to the next paragraph or increasing the reading rate, whereas global navigation refers to navigation between text sections and headings. By segmenting documents with the TAM we could allow a new type of navigation through the textual objects relationships. Composition relationships would complete what DAISY call "global navigation" and non-linear relationship would give information about the text structure on a lower level.

Segmenting documents textual objects would also allow to reorganize the content regarding the relationships between objects. For instance, when reading a document, we could regroup textual objects according to their non-linear relationships to avoid cross references, e.g. a theorem with its demonstration and related annotations.

3.3   The case of Mathematics

In the context of the MathArchiTact project, we chose to work on a corpus of mathematics text-books to improve their accessibility for blind high-school teenagers. This choice was driven by the fact that mathematics courses have a very rich visual structure, richer than other courses. Besides, an extensive literature exist on complex mathematics objects access by blind people, mainly formulas [2, 3, 19], which could give us clues about content presentation and navigation.

4   Future Work and Perspectives

We proposed a framework for implementing the TAM in digital documents, in the perspective of their access by blind users.

The next step in the project will be to develop a reader with navigation and presentation techniques adapted to documents annotated with the TAM. Results obtained with this reader will be compared to existing software and methods. This reader will most likely include existing presentation conventions such as prosodic cues, earcons[5]

---

[4] See G. Kerscher: Theory behind the DTbook DTD,
   http://data.daisy.org/publications/docs

[5] Non-verbal sounds used to represent a specific event or convey other information.

and spearcons[6] which are often used in audio interfaces [4, 24]. It could also make use of a Braille output, depending on the user task and presented on textual objects.

Several ways could be explored in the later stages of the project: automatic segmentation of textual objects will be studied, as well as segmentation of the rhetorical structure of the text using the Rhetorical Structure Theory [15] combined with the TAM (merging the two models was already studied for text generation [14]). Thanks to the flexibility offered by markup languages, exporting metadata using web standards would be easy in the case of existing data model like "Learning object Metadata"[7], and constitute another interesting trail.

Finally, we should mention that the proposed framework could be used for other types of disabilities, such as cognitive impairments, or specific situations where the visual modality is not available (no screen, small screens, etc.) as it provides access to the logical structure of the content.

Acknowledgements. We would like to thank "l'Institut des Jeunes Aveugles de Toulouse" for their precious support in the MathArchiTact project. This work is funded by the "Region Midi-Pyrénées" and the "Pôle de Recherche et d'Enseignement Supérieur de Toulouse".

References

1. Ahmed, F., Borodin, Y., Puzis, Y., Ramakrishnan, I.: Why Read if You Can Skim: Towards Enabling Faster Screen Reading. In: Proceedings of the International Cross-Disciplinary Conference on Web Accessibility (W4A 2012), p. 39 (2012)
2. Alajarmeh, N.: Doing Math: Mathematics Accessibility Issues. In: Proceedings of the Interna-tional Cross-Disciplinary Conference on Web Accessibility (W4A 2012), p. 23. ACM (2012)
3. Awdé, A.: Techniques d'interaction multimodales pour l'accès aux mathématiques par des personnes non-voyantes. PhD Theses, University of Quebec (2009)
4. Bates, E., Fitzpatrick, D.: Spoken Mathematics Using Prosody, Earcons and Spearcons. In: Miesenberger, K., Klaus, J., Zagler, W., Karshmer, A. (eds.) ICCHP 2010, Part II. LNCS, vol. 6180, pp. 407–414. Springer, Heidelberg (2010)
5. Berger, A.L., Mittal, V.O.: OCELOT: a system for summarizing Web pages. In: Proceedings of the 23rd Annual International ACM SIGIR Conference on Research and Development in Information Retrieval, pp. 144–151. ACM, New York (2000)
6. Christensen, L.B., Stevns, T.: Biblus – A digital library to support integration of visually impaired in mainstream education. In: Miesenberger, K., Karshmer, A., Penaz, P., Zagler, W. (eds.) ICCHP 2012, Part I. LNCS, vol. 7382, pp. 36–42. Springer, Heidelberg (2012)
7. Fellbaum, K., Kouroupetroglou, G.: Principles of electronic speech processing with applications for people with disabilities. Technology and Disability 20(2), 55–85 (2008)
8. Giraud, S., et al.: L'accessibilité des interfaces informatiques pour les déficients visuels. In: Dinet, J., Bastien, C. (eds.) L'ergonomie des objets et environnements physiques et numériques, Hermes - Sciences Lavoisier, Paris (2011)

---

[6] Spoken audio samples speeded-up at very fast rates, which cannot be recognized as speech when listening.

[7] Data model used to describe a learning object.

9. Harris, Z.S.: Structures mathématiques du langage. Dunod (1968)
10. Lazar, J., Allen, A., Kleinman, J., Malarkey, C.: What Frustrates Screen Reader Users on the Web: A Study of 100 Blind Users. International Journal of Human-Computer Interaction 22(3), 247–269 (2007)
11. Lemarié, J., Lorch, R., Eyrolle, H., Virbel, J.: SARA: A Text-Based and Reader-Based Theory of Signaling. Educational Psychologist 43(1), 27–48 (2008)
12. Lemarié, J., Lorch, R., Pery-Woodley, M.-P.: Understanding How Headings Influence Text Processing. Discours 10 (2012), doi:10.4000/discours.8600
13. Lorch, R.F., Chen, H.-T., Lemarie, J.: Communicating headings and preview sentences in text and speech. Journal of Experimental Psychology: Applied 18(3), 265–276 (2012)
14. Luc, C.: Représentation et composition des structures visuelles et rhétoriques du texte. Approche pour la génération de textes formatés (2000)
15. Mann, W.C., Thompson, S.A.: Rhetorical Structure theory description and constructions of text structures. In: Kempen, G. (ed.) Natural Language Generation. NATO ASI Series, Series E: Applied Sciences, vol. 135, pp. 85–96. Martinus Nijhoff Publishers, Dordrecht (1987)
16. Pascual, E.: Integrating Text Formatting and Text Generation. Trends in Natural Language Generation: An Artificial Intelligence Perspective, pp. 205–221 (1996)
17. Pascual, E., Virbel, J.: Semantic and Layout Properties of Text Punctuation, 41–48 (1991)
18. Petit, G., Dufresne, A., Robert, J.-M.: Introducing TactoWeb: A Tool to Spatially Explore Web Pages for Users with Visual Impairment. In: Stephanidis, C. (ed.) Universal Access in HCI, Part I, HCII 2011. LNCS, vol. 6765, pp. 276–284. Springer, Heidelberg (2011)
19. Schweikhardt, W., Bernareggi, C., Jessel, N., Encelle, B., Gut, M.: LAMBDA: A European system to access mathematics with Braille and audio synthesis. In: Miesenberger, K., Klaus, J., Zagler, W.L., Karshmer, A.I. (eds.) ICCHP 2006. LNCS, vol. 4061, pp. 1223–1230. Springer, Heidelberg (2006)
20. Uzan, G., Wagtaf, P.: A Model and Methods to solve problems of Accessibility and Information for the Visually Impaired. In: Proceedings of the International Conference STHESCA, Krakow (2011)
21. Vigouroux, N., et al.: Problématique, enjeux et perspectives de la présentation orale de documents: une approche pluridisciplinaire. In: Inscription Spatiale du Langage structure et processus (ISLsp 2002), Toulouse, January 29-30, pp. 139–150. IRIT (2002)
22. Virbel, J.: Langage et métalangage dans le texte du point de vue de l'édition en informatique textuelle. Cahiers de grammaire. pp. 5–72 (1985)
23. Virbel, J.: Structured documents. In: André, J., et al. (eds.) Structured Documents, pp. 161–180. Cambridge University Press, NY (1989)
24. Walker, B.N., Nance, A., Lindsay, J.: SPEARCONS: Speech-based earcons improve navigation performance in auditory menus. In: Proceedings of the 12th International Conference on Auditory Display, pp. 63–68 (2006)

Adopting Open Protocols to Increase the Impact on Digital Repositories

Ligia Eliana Setenareski, Marcos Sfair Sunye, and Walter Shima

Universidade Federal do Paraná, Curitiba, Brazil
{ligia,sunye,shima}@ufpr.br

Abstract. Recently the discussion of technological standards became important due to the profusion of new technologies arising from the development of microelectronics, computing, telecommunications, etc. Sometimes, one standard can be adopted or not, depending on the way the competition unfolds. As it is well known, it is not necessarily the best standard which becomes dominant, neither are the consumers who choose it, but the standard from the firm that used the most efficient market strategies. Sometimes a standard takes a long time to become dominant or will not be established because the competition process forces the manufacturers to permanent innovation. Considering the development of digital libraries, the development of diffusion and preservation systems has followed another course, not based on competition, but through the exploration of the symbiosis between Free and Open Source Software (FOSS), Open Archiving Initiative (OAI), and following the Google dominance. From this initiative, the cost of interoperability among digital libraries has greatly diminished. The NSDL (National Science, Technology, Engineering, Mathematics and Education Digital Library) defines three levels of cooperation needed to achieve interoperability. The technical level is related to the capacity of each digital library for sharing their metadata and enabling a unified search. The level of correlated content allows distinct repositories to describe their contents uniformly. The organizational level allows the sharing of management and governance of the repositories. This case study describes the open protocols adopted by UFPR in the construction of its digital repository. The digital library's files on logs are used to analyse the increase in the accessibility and visibility of scientific production in this institution.

Keywords: Digital Library, Accessibility, First Mover, FOSS, Open Archiving, OAI-PMH, network externality, technological patterns, lock-in.

1 Introduction

The objective of this paper is to discuss the emergence and development of technological standards concerning digital repositories and their impact on the visibility and accessibility of scientific content. In addition, concepts such as Network externalities reached by technological standards and open source software used in digital repositories will be discussed as well.

C. Stephanidis and M. Antona (Eds.): UAHCI/HCII 2013, Part III, LNCS 8011, pp. 408–416, 2013.
© Springer-Verlag Berlin Heidelberg 2013

Recently the discussion of technological standards became important due to the profusion of new technologies arising from the development of microelectronics, computing, telecommunications, etc. Sometimes, one standard can be adopted or not, depending on the way the competition unfolds. In other words, the release of a new product by many manufacturers implies the commitment to the greatest number of suppliers and co-developers and a strategy to achieve the greatest numbers of consumers in order to create lock-in and path-dependence.

According to David [1], a path-dependent sequence of an economic change means that important though temporary and remote events may influence the final output. Such events may be defined by elements of luck instead of systematic forces, being full of uncertainty and immeasurability. Furthermore, historical accidents can not be ignored or isolated. In 1873, for example, the layout QWERTY was important for the sellers to impress the consumers when two words were typed fast: TYPE WRITE. It was also considered the best layout to avoid keys to be jammed - even not being so efficient as DVORAK or DHIATENSOR (David [1]). Those two accidental circumstances (not planned as a strategy to dominate a new industry) made the industry move forwards the adoption of QWERTY as universal. Simultaneously, typists were not trained to work on Dvorak because no employers used it..

The social benefit of switching standards may be greater than its social cost, but it is unattainable unless all users do it, It is too costly to coordinate all users' simultaneous switch. Thus, each random decision in favour of QWERTY would raise the probability that the next selector would favour QWERTY, which would result in decreasing costs of selection. Therefore, the type machine begun to belong to an interrelated complex system involving buyers, typists, training organizations for typists, manufacturers and suppliers of parts that used to grow spontaneously due to network externalities.

Network externalities are the benefit for the growing numbers of users who incorporate a technology that brings success to a network sponsoring firm. The users have a collective benefit from network because they exchange information and enjoy the future generation of improvements in such a technology. Other systems may be better, but they do not have the same diffusion and, consequently, do not have the same critical mass that enables incremental improvements to its development. In other words, newcomers do not have scale for development. The sponsoring firm's profits with growing number of buyers (users) increase and so does its network as long as its costs of development for improvements decrease. Specifically, in economic terms, the firm acquires economy of scale and its marginal cost tends to zero (Shapiro & Varian) [2].

Despite the historical circumstances that involved QWERTY standard, modern standards were established for new equipment and technologies due to efficient strategies of competition from a specific firm, which also depends on the users' technological expectations. The first movers have their own advantages, but the most important issue to consolidate the standard is the capability to find some element in or within the technology that persuades the market to presume that such a technology is going to be the standard. From that point on, a virtuous circle with an increasing support from the market begins. On the other hand, the opposite is also feasible, i.e. a vicious circle (Shapiro & Varian) [2].

Even with some key elements that determine the strategies, another important issue for the dominant standard firm is the architecture's opening or closing. At this stage, the important point is the technology valorisation and not the control per se, resulting in the increase in the number of users. This technology will probably be open when there is no capable firm to establish the standard and the complexity of the technology demands coordinated work between multiple developers and several new interfaces. At this moment, the earnings will be generated by network externalities, when more and more users and other developers connect to this open system and, consequently, create opportunities for more development with decreasing costs (Shapiro & Varian) [2]. The GSM open architecture for mobile communication became a dominant standard because more and more users and developers connected to it and the network value increased exactly because of the network externalities. Nowadays, the same situation happens to Android OS with disadvantages to proprietary systems as Symbian, RIM, Palm and also Apple. A proprietary technology in complex systems is very risky since the uncertainty does not encourage interface developers to work with specificity and restrictions.

The technologies for digital repositories did not arise from a private competition strategy, but from social movements by the academy against the enclosure of private editors of scientific journals. In 1991, Paul Ginsparg developed and implemented the arXiv [3] as a tool to enable the access to preprints[1] in physics. The objective was to facilitate and accelerate the access to high quality scientific content by the scientific community, who was also in charge of producing it. This initiative gave rise to a well known movement called Open Access whose main goal was to build open access networks for academic content, differently from the high cost of access to contents in private publishers' journals that tended more and more to cartelized behaviour. In 2001, this Movement established the OAI-PMH protocol (Open Archives Initiative – Protocol for metadata harvesting) [4] which created a low-barrier mechanism for repository interoperability, which rapidly enabled the adherence by the academy. In 2006, the main site OAI (OAIster) [5] had already more than 500 registered institutions that integrated its network. Nowadays, OAI-PMH and Dublin Core metadata are the main standard of the Open Access movement. Two other important initiatives that arose from the Open Access movement - the community FOSS (Free and Open Source Software) – were the software OAI-PMH protocol (Open Archives Initiative – Protocol for metadata harvesting) [4] which created a low-barrier mechanism for repository interoperability2 , which rapidly enabled the adherence by the academy. In 2006, the main site OAI (OAIster) [5] had already more than 500 registered institutions that integrated its network. Nowadays, OAI-PMH and Dublin Core metadata are the main standard of the Open Access movement. Two other important initiatives that arose from the Open Access movement - the community FOSS (Free and Open Source Software) – were the software Dspace [6] and the software OJS (Open Journal

---

[1] A scientific paper still to be published by a journal with peer review.
[2] Data Providers are repositories that expose structured metadata via OAI-PMH. Then Service Providers make OAI-PMH service requests to harvest that metadata. OAI-PMH is a set of six verbs or services that are invoked within HTTP (OAI-PMH) [4].

System) [7] that are currently the main systems for digital libraries and scientific journals' management respectively. They enable the sharing and management of scientific content and are responsible for the dissemination of open access digital repositories.

Therefore the scientific community, who developed interoperable standards, was never interested in competing with private editors or being a kind of potential entrant in order to expand its market share. Indeed, these standards worked as alternative solutions against the market monopolization by private editors. In other words, the editors' cartelized behaviour (supply) led the scientific community (demand) to create an alternative solution that was possible through the development of information and communication technologies. Such technologies caused the demand to adopt new behaviour against a restricted supply. The most important objective was not the establishment of path-dependence, positive network externalities, or a virtuous circle, but the possibility to divert from the restrictions imposed by private editors.

In 2004, an institutional digital repository was created at Universidade Federal do Paraná - UFPR. From that year on, the software Dspace has been used for theses, dissertations and videos, and the software OJS has been used for journals. UFPR was the first university in Brazil to deploy such software. This Chapter will show how the network externalities that came from the Open Access movement contributed towards the adoption of an Open Software by UFPR and how this choice was instrumental in increasing its visibility.

2   Open Protocols for the Digital Library Federation

The turn of the century saw the emergence of the organization of federations such as the Digital Library Federation that has worked with the standardization of metadata for digital libraries since 1996. This initiative was consolidated in 2001 with the emergence of the Open Archives Initiative (OAI) [4]. Two important standards were defined: the Dublin Core, which describes the minimum attributes that make up metadata in any digital library, and the PMH (Protocol for Metadata Harvesting) that standardizes the sharing of metadata.

The first goal of the standards promoted and developed by the Open Archives Initiative (OAI) was to provide accessibility to scholarship and scientific information produced by Academic Institutions. Therefore, this set of standards can be actually used by any institution that aims to manage its digital content. These standards are a formal foundation that allows the scientific community to build a network of digital libraries. An OAI-PMH federation is composed by two main agents: the Data Providers (DP) and the Service Providers (SP).

Data Providers are digital repositories that can be implemented by any system capable of inserting and recovering digital documents based on a single identifier. Besides, a Data Provider is expected to be capable of linking a document descriptor a.k.a. "metadata" with its correspondent document source. In the architecture of the OAI, the link between metadata and its original document is made by the insertion of a Permanent Uniform Resource Locator (PURL) in the metadata. This approach keeps the link between the original document (that is maintained in its original Digital Library) and the metadata, which can be distributed and copied by other systems.

Service Providers (SP) are systems that harvest metadata from Data Providers, grouping and indexing them in a database, which allows a unified search. The protocol PMH allows the communication between Service and Data Providers, as well as providing the synchronization between all Federations' metadata.

The OAI also proposes the standardization of the minimum description of attributes known as "Dublin Core" [9]. The Dublin Core standard has 32 attributes and Figure 1 shows their use at UFPR´s Digital Library.

As the only correspondence between metadata and its original document is given through a Permanent URL stored in the metadata, it is very common the adoption of a handle server. The function of a handle server is to translate dynamically the permanent address into its physical address. The Handle System [10] composes a major standard for Digital Object Identifier called DOI (www.doi.org) and it is used by the majority of Data Providers.

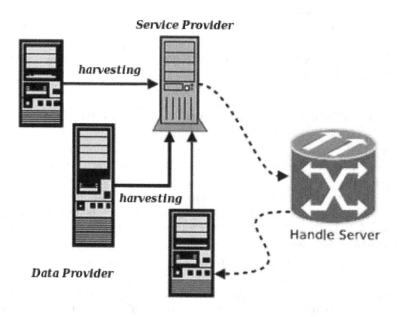

Fig. 1. OAI-PMH architecture and Handle System Server

2.1   Free Open Source Software (FOSS) for Digital Libraries

There is a great deal of Open Source Software that can perform the OAI protocols[8]: CDS-Invenio (Switzerland), DoKS (Belgium), DSpace (USA), EPrints (UK), FEDORA (USA), Greenstone (New Zealand), MyCoRe (Germany), OPUS (Germany), SciX (Slovenia). All of them use an Open Source Database Management System to store and search their metadata. The two most popular softwares for Digital

Libraries are Dspace that uses Postgresql and Eprints that uses MySql. The standard software for scientific journals is OJS (Open Journal System) that uses Postgresql.

As most Digital Libraries Systems run on Linux with an Apache server, the entire environment needed to maintain a Digital Library can be offered by the FOSS community.

3   The Adoption of Open Protocols by UFPR

The emergence of several open code systems for the management of digital libraries such as Dspace and Eprints as well as the implementation of these metadata searching systems (Google in 2008 started to index metadata through the standard OAI-PMH) have sustained the standard OAI-PMH, which has quickly become a reference. From this initiative, the cost of interoperability among digital libraries has greatly diminished. The NSDL (National Science, Technology, Engineering, Mathematics and Education Digital Library) defines three levels of cooperation needed to achieve interoperability. The technical level is related to the capacity of each digital library for sharing their metadata and enabling a unified search. The level of correlated content allows distinct repositories to describe their contents uniformly. The organizational level allows the sharing of management and governance of the repositories.

The Federal University of Paraná (UFPR) has adopted the standard OAI-PMH since 2004 when Dspace and OJS were implemented in its digital libraries, ensuring a technical interoperability of its digital collection. The insertion of a digital library for federations of theses and dissertations at UFPR, as it was the case of the server Oaister in 2005, has been ensuring the interoperability in sharing correlated content, allowing even the detection of duplicities of theses (when a researcher connected to the university defends his thesis in Europe and registers it in two collections). Finally, the construction of tools in order to integrate the physical and the Digital collection, started in 2008, has been allowing the backward scanning of works without increasing the cost of indexing at UFPR's digital library. .

The third level of interoperability, which includes the construction of agreements to enable the governance and the provision of coordinated services among various digital libraries, has been partially achieved by UFPR. Services such as the Handle System, which foresees a definitive and permanent identifier for each new digital object created, allows the repositories of UFPR to change its hardware and software without compromising any level of interoperability.

For instance, UFPR has changed its Library Management System (LMS) from Virtua [11] to Sophia [12] but the system remains interoperable with the Digital Library as the metadata of UFPR's Digital Library has been harvested from LMS through PMH.

3.1   UFPR's Choice of Open Protocols

The development of the digital library management software - from the symbiosis between the Open Access movement and the FOSS - rapidly expanded its positive network externalities with its dissemination in the academia, including university libraries. The university libraries, which are responsible for the preservation of printed scientific literature, were in search of suitable and affordable alternatives to store and manage content also in digital media. These positive network externalities were crucial for UFPR to build its digital repositories after analyzing available alternatives in the market. Thus, open and interoperable protocols started to be used to create a digital repository at UFPR taking the following aspects into account:

1. The increase in the visibility of scientific researches.
2. The publication of scientific production could be made by copyleft, with no costs of copyright.
3. The diffusion of knowledge produced at UFPR would be rapidly extended worldwide.
4. The absence or reduction of legal and institutional procedures in the adoption of open technologies in comparison to the vast number of procedures in the adoption of proprietary technologies.
5. A short estimated time to deployment.
6. A low estimated cost to deployment (whereas OJS and DSpace software are free and the only costs come from the hardware and the software customization).
7. The core competence inside the Department of Informatics at UFPR which was able to customize, deploy and train the first users of open technologies.

The purchase of the server, the software customization and the effective deployment of digital libraries for the first inclusion of digital objects took about a year to be finalized and cost approximately US $ 25,000.00. It is considered a short time and a relative low cost if compared to the time and cost of the computerization process of the UFPR´s library catalogs, which used proprietary software and took 7 years. This process demanded fundraising and specific bidding procedures - mandatory by the public sector in Brazil - for the acquisition of computer equipment and proprietary software, as well as for hiring the services of retrospective conversion of bibliographic records on paper (catalog cards) for the digital media. These steps along with the staff training had an approximate cost of US$ 750,000.00.

3.2   The UFPR's Digital Repository and Its Accessibility and Visibility

Due to the Open Access, the UFPR's digital repositories were accessed by more than 150 countries between March 2012 and February 2013 - detailed access logs are available at [13]. CHART 1 describes the number of files downloaded per country last year. Accesses within the Brazilian territory were excluded, as well as the hits from the U.S., because they could be confused by Google's Crawlers and, consequently would distort the number of hits to a higher level in these countries.

It is observed that the number of hits coming from Portuguese speaking countries is high. Besides being relatively high in numbers, hits from Portugal, Angola, Mozambique and Cape Verde have been continuous, revealing a constant habit of searching the UFPR's library by these countries. It is also important to point out that language is not a barrier to access the UFPR's digital repository. After Portugal,

Germany, China, France, Netherlands, Spain and Great Britain, in spite of not being a Portuguese speaking country, present the highest numbers of accessed files. The Portuguese speaking country that has the largest number of accessed files after Portugal is Mozambique, which has the 7th position after all the countries with other languages.

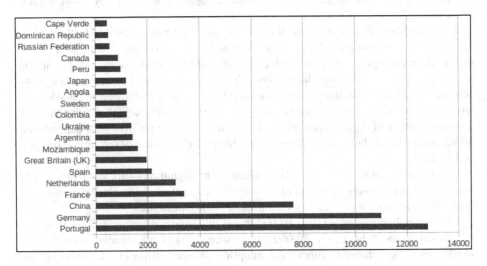

Chart 1. Number of accessed files per country, from March, 2012 to February, 2013

4   Conclusion

The main issue discussed in this paper is the level of accessibility to scientific content produced by the academia and not published by private editors, who more and more restrict the access by producers (researchers from universities who were expected to pay to publish their own papers) and to consumers (readers who were supposed to pay to access journals). Although OAI-PMH was a movement from the academia against the private editors' cartelized behaviour, it was not a strategy to establish a new technological standard as it can be seen in competitions when potential entrants establish new technological standards in emergent markets - for instance, the recent competition between Blu-ray DVD x HD-DVD). Therefore, the Open Access movement was not created in order to impose any kind of standard but it was a political and economic strategy that aimed a rapid diffusion of preprints and other scientific contents, which would never be accessed if they were in the hands of private editors. OAI-PMH rapidly expanded towards the universities, libraries and researchers and inevitably became one of the standard technologies for digital repositories. At the same time, FOSS also became an important interoperable standard in the Open Access movement.

The separation between digital documents and their metadata, as well as the free distribution of this metadata are the main features of the OAI-PMH approach. The simplicity of the protocol for metadata exchange quickly allowed large part of management software to implement digital libraries. Hence, most academic digital libraries became Data Providers, that is, an OAI federation.

Besides the free distribution of metadata that started with the separation of digital documents, the main feature of the OAI-PMH approach is the simplicity of the protocol for metadata exchange, which enabled a rapid deployment by most digital libraries.

Those technologies became the standard for digital repositories due to their open access and interoperability. They were marked by non-economic interests, and not meant to become proprietary technologies. Although the academic world had an interest in accessing and researching knowledge, it did not intend to appropriate technologies of diffusion as the private editors did. Thus, OAI-PMH became a standard with rapid positive network externalities as a virtuous circle, with an exponential growing number of digital repositories. This is the case of a positive path-dependence which brings about larger communities and high quality in the development of apps and solutions.

Due to the adoption of OAI-PMH standard in the digital repository at UFPR, there was a rapid and growing diffusion of its scientific content, not only among Portuguese speaking countries but also among countries of other languages.

UFPR has deployed more than 10,000 theses and dissertations as well as 38 scientific journals totalling nearly 20,000 titles since 2004. Undoubtedly, such figures would never be achieved without the adoption of open protocols, considering the characteristics, prices and enclosure from proprietary standards.

References

1. David, P.A.: Clio and The economics of Querty. American Economic Review 75, 332–337 (1985)
2. Shapiro, C., Varian, H.R.: A Economia da Informação: Como os Princípios Econômicos se Aplicam à Era da Internet. Elsevier, Rio de Janeiro (2003)
3. ArXiv, http://arxiv.org/
4. Open Archives Initiative Protocol for Metadata Harvesting, http://www.openarchives.org/pmh
5. The OAIster Database, http://www.oclc.org/oaister
6. Dspace, http://www.dspace.org/
7. Open Journal System, http://pkp.sfu.ca/?q=ojs
8. Madalli, D.P., Barve, S., Amin, S.: Digital Preservation in Open Source Digital Library Software. Journal of Academic Libraries 38, 161–164
9. Dublin Core Initiative, http://dublincore.org
10. Handles System Server, http://www.handle.net
11. Virtua VTLS, http://www.vtls.com
12. Sofia, Prima Informática, http://www.primasoft.com.br
13. Webalizer of UFPR digital library, http://calvados.c3sl.ufpr.br/webalizer

Part IV

Health, Well-being, Rehabilitation and Medical Applications

A Pilot Study: Integrating an Emergency Department with Indiana's Prescription Drug Monitoring Program

Hamed Abedtash[1] and John T. Finnell[1,2,3]

[1] School of Informatics and Computing, Indiana University, Indianapolis, IN 46202, USA
abedtash@iupui.edu
[2] School of Medicine, Indiana University, Indianapolis, IN 46202, USA
[3] Regenstrief Institute, Indianapolis, IN 46202, USA
jfinnell@regenstrief.org

Abstract. Rapid increase in abuse and overdose of controlled substances was the main driving force of implementing Prescription Drug Monitoring Programs (PDMP). We aimed to describe how the integrated Indiana's PDMP (INSPECT) data into an electronic health record (EHR) can improve clinical workflow within an emergency department (ED). After integration, upon patient arrival into the ED, a PDMP report containing history of dispensed schedule II-V medications is retrieved and stored in the patient's medical record. The evaluation of the new system among physicians showed high satisfaction of having access to the patients' medication history through the existing EHR. We show that the PDMP data was easily accessible and more informative in the new integrated system. The PDMP report alters the pattern of prescribing narcotic medications to patients. In conclusion, enhancing workflow through PDMP reports integration with the patients' EHR is valued by the clinicians and reduces the number of narcotic prescriptions.

Keywords: Opioid abuse, Prescription drug monitoring program, PDMP, Doctor shopping, EHR, Electronic health records, Effectiveness evaluation.

1 Introduction

Since early 1990s, prescribing opioids for chronic pain treatment has been widely accepted in the United States [1]. Endorsed by a report from Centers for Disease Control and Prevention [2], sales of opioid analgesics increased four times in the recent decade. Merely in 2010, 7.1 kg opioid analgesics per 10,000 people were sold in the United States equal to prescribe every adults in the United States with "5 mg of hydrocodone every four hours for one month" [2].

Along with the increase in the sale, the death from drug overdose has reached the epidemic level in the United States [3-5]. It has become the second principal cause of unintentional injury deaths after car accidents [2]. Opioid analgesics were responsible for more unintentional overdose deaths compared to the deaths from cocaine and heroin together. The severity of the situation in 20 states (e.g., Ohio) is such that the

C. Stephanidis and M. Antona (Eds.): UAHCI/HCII 2013, Part III, LNCS 8011, pp. 419–425, 2013.
© Springer-Verlag Berlin Heidelberg 2013

deaths from unintentional opioid overdose have exceeded deaths from motor vehicle accidents.

To respond to the epidemic situation of substances abuse, 44 states have established prescription drug monitoring programs (PDMPs) in recent years to collect and monitor prescribing, sale, and dispensing of controlled substances [6]. PDMPs have promoted patient care by reducing the supply of excess or misprescribed opioids leading to lower probability of abuse [7-9]. PDMP reports give physician a better image of patient's behavior of controlled substances use not only before starting chronic opioid therapy, but also during the treatment. Physicians recognize the patient is at risk of abuse based on the pattern of previous physicians and pharmacies visits, amount of prescribed controlled substances (opioids, sedatives, stimulants), and number of overlapped opioid prescriptions.

Indiana's PDMP, called INSPECT (INdiana Scheduled Prescription Electronic Collection & Tracking), is one of the first of its kind that tracks outpatient dispensed schedule II-V controlled substances statewide. INSPECT covers over 1,700 pharmacies across the state providing about 12 million medication records per year. Each pharmacy in Indiana State has to report dispensed prescribed controlled substances (schedule II-V) for Indiana residents to the INSPECT system within seven days [10].

Despite the usefulness of PDMPs, physicians are not interested in using the system [11]. PDMP data is accessible through a web portal that requires additional time to find an open workstation, recall credentials for system access, and having available patient demographic information to retrieve the report. To make PDMP data more accessible to the physicians, the Office of the National Coordinator for Health IT (ONC) has sponsored pilot programs to test the effects of expanding Indiana and Ohio states PDMP utilizing health information technology (HIT). In this paper, we describe integration of INSPECT with an emergency department's (ED) management system at Wishard Hospital in order to increase utilization of INSPECT reports. We also performed empirical research to evaluate effectiveness of the new integrated system.

2   Integration

Wishard Memorial Hospital, Indianapolis, Indiana is a Level 1 Trauma Center and tertiary referral center. There are over 108,000 emergency visits annually. Before implementing direct access to patients' history of prescribed controlled substances, physicians had to switch to Indiana's PDMP web portal, query patients' history, and prescribe narcotics based on the INSPECT data. However, since integration of INSPECT system into Indiana Network for Patient Care (INPC), the largest health information exchange in Indiana, the physicians have had real-time access to patients' INSPECT report through CareWeb, Wishard's ED electronic health record (EHR) system.

To perform the integration, the current connection between INSPECT and prescription monitoring program interconnect (PMPi) was used, through which INSPECT retrieves patients' data from other states.

Once a patient checks in ED, the registration application (McKesson) generates a Health Level 7 (HL7) ADT-A04 (patient registration) message. The INSPECT message processor module, which monitors ADT message, extracts the patient's name, birth date, sex, and medical record number from PID segment of the message. In the next step, Regenstrief Institute, the responsible entity for maintaining EHR system at Wishard Hospital, sends a request to PMPi using a HTTP POST operation. The query has two parts. One part is encrypted that identifies the patient. The other unencrypted part indicates which state is doing the query, which state is being queried, and who specific provider requested the medication history. In our case, it is not an individual provider, the hospital system acting as a provider. The message is in eXtensible Markup Language (XML) format in conformity with national PMIX (Prescription Monitoring Information eXchange) architecture. Once the PMPi interconnect hub validates that the particular requesting node is configured to make a request from INSPECT system, the Indiana's PDMP matches the supplied demographics against its known patients. If there is a match, the patient's history of prescribed controlled substances is returned in PMIX format to Regenstrief server. Then, it is sent to Wishard Hospital's repository to populate the clinical record via a simple HL7 message enclosed INSPECT report (Fig. 1 and Fig. 2).

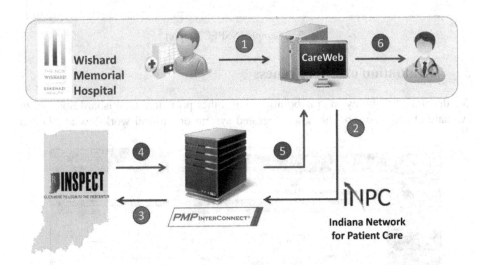

Fig. 1. Integrated workflow diagram. 1) Upon patient check-in, a request for patient's controlled substances history is sent to CareWeb. 2) CareWeb queries PDMP data from PMPi. 3) PMPi sends the request to INSPECT. 4) INSPECT responds with a PMDP report. 5) PMPi transfers the information to CareWeb. 6) CareWeb formats and stores PDMP report in EHR to be reviewed by physicians.

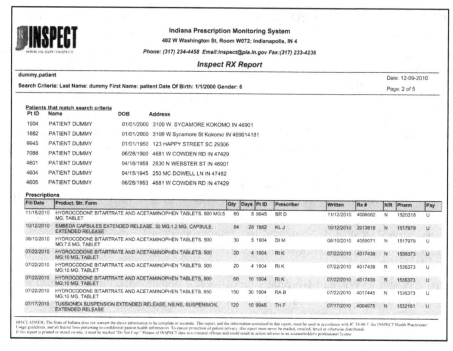

Fig. 2. A sample INSPECT report

3   Evaluation of Effectiveness

We developed a survey in collaboration with other providers at Wishard hospital to evaluate effectiveness of the new integrated system on clinical workflow at ED and

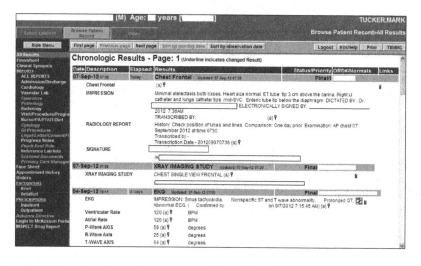

Fig. 3. A screenshot of CareWeb. "INSPECT Drug Report" link is accessible at the bottom left

physicians' behavior of prescribing opioids. The survey was designed to take less than one minute to fulfill. From July 9, 2012 to November 30, 2012, the physicians at Wishard Hospital's emergency department had access to the new INSPECT report delivered through the EHR interface (CareWeb) by clicking on a provided link only shown to physicians (Fig. 3). Providers were asked to answer to three optional questions after retrieving reports (Table 1).

Table 1. The survey to evaluate effectiveness of the new integrated system

Question	Possible answers
Was there information in the INSPECT report that you were not aware of? (Select one answer)	Yes Somewhat No
Will the INSPECT report modify your prescribing behavior? (Select one or more answers)	Yes, I will reduce the number of pills I prescribe. Yes, I will reduce the number of prescriptions I write. No, there will be no change in my prescribing behavior for this patient. Yes, I will increase the number of pills I prescribe. Yes, I will increase the number of prescriptions I write.
Did you find the INPSECT data easier to obtain through CareWeb? (Select one answer)	Yes Somewhat No

4   Results

Through the integrated system, CareWeb successfully accessed PMPi hub upon patient arrival at ED, retrieved INSPECT report, and stored a printable Portable Document Format (PDF) format of the report in EHR. Physicians could access patients' INSPECT report by selecting the provided link on patients' profile in CareWeb.

Over the five-month study, 488 providers accessed 3540 INSPECT reports through CareWeb that shows significant increase in number of providers contrary to previous nonintegrated system. Providers who retrieved the reports completed 866 surveys through the study. Ninety-eight percent (N=831) of the respondents indicated that having access to the PDMP data through the existing EHR was much easier to use. In addition, 85% (N=815) found information within the report that they were unaware of previously. In response to the question whether INSPECT report changed their narcotics prescribing pattern, 58% (N=455) of answers indicated reduction and 6% (N=50) specified increase in either number of prescriptions or number of narcotic pills prescribed, whereas 36% (N=280) of respondents stated that the PDMP data did affect their planned prescribing manner.

5   Discussion

Through this pilot study, we introduced an integrated EHR with PDMP administration system that successfully provided the physicians at Wishard Hospital's emergency department with immediate access to patients' history of controlled substances use. According to the providers, the integration could improve clinical workflow at emergency department and had effects on their planning for prescribing narcotics to patients.

The integration of EHR with PDMP not only brings convenience for the physicians, but also improves workflow. Centers for Disease Control and Prevention [12] reported that the demand for opioid analgesics at ED has increased severely in recent years. This increase in the requests amplifies the problem of identifying opioid abuser patients because checking patient's PDMP data is a time-consuming task causing suspension in clinical workflow. Most participant physicians (98%, N=831) found the new system easy to use and fit with clinical workflow at emergency department. The new integrated system facilitates providers' access to patients' history of controlled substances that help physicians rapidly and accurately identify abuser patients who visit emergency department requesting opioid analgesics.

In addition, the new formatted PDMP report led physicians to make a reasonable decision about prescribing opioid medications to patients. In more than half of cases (64%, N=505), physicians stated that accessing to the PDMP data changed their plans to prescribe narcotics for patients either increased or decreased prescriptions. On the contrary, physicians did not change their decision in 36% (N=280) of cases. This might be because the PDMP data endorsed physician's perception or could not provide enough evidence that the physician changes the prescription plan. Therefore, in accordance to other studies [13,14], PDMP reports alters medical practice by assisting providers to find doctor shopper patients to make the most appropriate decision regarding prescribing opioids.

6   Conclusion

Improving delivery of healthcare data within the existing workflow has tremendous payoffs. Integrating available EHR with PDMP data could ease of use, access to information that was previously unknown, with reduction in opioid prescribing. One of our physicians provided this comment: "I have to say that this is probably one of the more genius moves of the 21st century... having easy access to INSPECT without going to a totally different website and have it pop up instantly has taken a lot of time off of decision making for me."

The authors greatly acknowledge Mark Tucker for his contribution to this paper in particular describing the integrated system workflow.

References

1. Ballantyne, J.C.: Safe and effective when used as directed: the case of chronic use of opioid analgesics. Journal of Medical Toxicology 8, 417–423 (2012)

2. Centers for Disease Control and Prevention: Vital signs: Overdoses of prescription opioid pain relievers-United States, 1999-2008. Morbidity and Mortality Weekly Report 60, 1487–1492 (2011)
3. Paulozzi, L.J., Weisler, R.H., Patkar, A.A.: A national epidemic of unintentional prescription opioid overdose deaths: How physicians can help control it. Journal of Clinical Psychiatry 72, 589–592 (2011)
4. Robinson, R.C., Gatchel, R.J., Polatin, P., Deschner, M., Noe, C., Gajraj, N.: Screening for problematic prescription opioid use. Clinical Journal of Pain 17, 220–228 (2001)
5. Manchikanti, L., Helm, S., Fellows, B., Janata, J.W., Pampati, V., Grider, J.S., Boswell, M.V.: Opioid epidemic in the United States. Pain Physician 15, ES9–ES38 (2012)
6. Status of State Prescription Drug Monitoring Programs (PDMPs), http://www.namsdl.org/presdrug.htm
7. Baehren, D.F., Marco, C.A., Droz, D.E., Sinha, S., Callan, E.M., Akpunonu, P.: A Statewide Prescription Monitoring Program Affects Emergency Department Prescribing Behaviors. Annals of Emergency Medicine 56, 19–23 (2010)
8. Simeone, R., Holland, L.: An evaluation of prescription drug monitoring programs. National Criminal Justice Reference Service (NCJ217269), United States Department of Justice, Washington, DC (2006)
9. Simoni-Wastila, L., Qian, J.J.: Influence of prescription monitoring programs on analgesic utilization by an insured retiree population. Pharmacoepidemiology and Drug Safety 21, 1261–1268 (2012)
10. What is INSPECT?, http://www.in.gov/inspect
11. Feldman, L., Williams, K.S., Coates, J., Knox, M.: Awareness and utilization of a prescription monitoring program among physicians. Journal of Pain & Palliative Care Pharmacotherapy 25, 313–317 (2011)
12. Centers for Disease Control and Prevention: Emergency Department Visits Involving Nonmedical Use of Selected Prescription Drugs-United States, 2004-2008. Morbidity and Mortality Weekly Report 59, 705–709 (2010)
13. Green, T.C., Mann, M.R., Bowman, S.E., Zaller, N., Soto, X., Gadea, J., Cordy, C., Kelly, P., Friedmann, P.D.: How Does Use of a Prescription Monitoring Program Change Medical Practice? Pain Medicine 13, 1314–1323 (2012)
14. Sinha, S., Callan, E.M., Akpunonu, P., Baehren, D., Marco, C.: How Does Use of a Statewide Prescription Monitoring Program Affect Emergency Department Prescribing Behaviors? Annals of Emergency Medicine 54, S14-S15 (2009)

Can Ubiquitous Devices Utilising Reminiscence Therapy Be Used to Promote Well-Being in Dementia Patients? An Exploratory Study

Claire Ancient[1], Alice Good[1], Clare Wilson[2], and Tineke Fitch[1]

[1] University of Portsmouth, School of Computing, Portsmouth, United Kingdom
{claire.ancient,alice.good,tineke.fitch}@port.ac.uk
[2] University of Portsmouth, Department of Psychology, Portsmouth, United Kingdom
clare.wilson@port.ac.uk

Abstract. This exploratory study aimed to assess whether ubiquitous devices could be used to facilitate person-centred reminiscence therapy. In order to test this approach to delivering a reminiscence therapy intervention, a tablet application was designed (using participatory design) and tested by the carers of people with dementia. The study showed that there is the potential to utilise the recent advances in mobile technology to facilitate reminiscence therapy. However, it did not provide conclusive proof that the device would be effective in its delivery of reminiscence therapy, but further research will aim to explore this.

Keywords: Dementia, Reminiscence Therapy, Ubiquitous Devices.

1 Introduction

The aim of this study was to establish whether a mobile application could be used to facilitate personalised reminiscence therapy within the home environment by people with dementia and their carers.

Dementia is a devastating progressive disease. It is characterised by symptoms, including memory loss, mood changes and problems with reasoning and communication [1]. Current estimates suggest that over 800,000 people in the UK are living with dementia, with this figure set to exceed one million by 2021 [2].

With a rapidly increasing population of people with dementia and no cure on the horizon, steps need to be taken to try and manage the symptoms associated with the condition. Reminiscence therapy has the potential to do exactly that. By focusing on the early memories of an individual, it can help to create a sense of self, improve communication, improve one's mood and promote well-being [3].

1.1 Dementia

The main cause of dementia is damage to the brain, either due to certain diseases or a series of mini-strokes. There are four main types of dementia: Alzheimer's Disease, Vascular Dementia, Dementia with Lewy Bodies and Fronto-temporal Dementia.

C. Stephanidis and M. Antona (Eds.): UAHCI/HCII 2013, Part III, LNCS 8011, pp. 426–435, 2013.

Alzheimer's disease is the most common form of dementia, with 62% of people being diagnosed with this form [2].

Despite extensive research, there is currently no cure for dementia. Medications can be prescribed to people with Alzheimer's disease in order to slow the progression of the disease or temporarily alleviate the symptoms. However, these are only effective for a limited period of time (normally between six months and a year) [4].

It is estimated that between 80% and 90% of people with dementia present with neuropsychiatric symptoms, including depression, apathy and irritability [5]. Although medication can be used to mitigate these symptoms of dementia, they should only be used in extreme cases. The National Institute for Clinical Excellence (NICE) recommends investigating alternative interventions and using medication as a last resort [6].

Due to the growing number of people being diagnosed with dementia, the need to provide high quality person-centred mental health care aimed at mitigating some of the associated symptoms has become a critical issue.

1.2   Reminiscence Therapy

Reminiscence therapy is one type of intervention which is often used as a "simple non-drug treatment" in order to mitigate some of the neuropsychiatric symptoms associated with dementia [6].

Reminiscence therapy utilises tangible prompts as a way of promoting conversation about shared past experiences, activities and events [3]. These prompts can include photos, music, archive recordings, newspaper clippings and anything else which can be used to stimulate memories. It has been described as "one of the most popular psychosocial interventions in dementia care" which is "highly rated by staff and participants" [3] and research has suggested that it can have positive effects on the participants [3, 7-10]. However, these results are yet to be conclusively established, using robust and unbiased evaluation techniques. In addition to this, Cohen-Mansfield et-Al. [9], suggest that participants are more involved and engaged with reminiscence therapy when the subject matter is personalised to them.

Reminiscence can provide the person with dementia the opportunity to reconstruct memories gained throughout life and provide a stabilising function. It can also be used to help the primary care-giver remember the person as they used to be before the dementia took hold. It can extend the carer's knowledge of the background, achievements and personality of the person they are caring for, which could eventually result in an improved person-centred care plan.

The diagnosis of dementia often causes the person to look at their failings. By focusing on the early memories, which remain intact for longer, reminiscence therapy is able to focus on the person's strengths. It reduces the likelihood of failing to remember and thus can provide reassurance in light of decreasing capacity to retain recent memories. In addition to the positive (and in some cases pleasurable) emotions felt, the person with dementia also experiences improved communication skills and can confidently discuss their earlier memories [7].

Reminiscence therapy also has the potential to help people with "other mental health conditions where depression and general low mood are common" [11]. With waiting lists of up to two years for some talking therapies [12], ubiquitous devices implementing reminiscence therapy could provide an important self-soothing function for people with mental health problems.

1.3   The Use of Ubiquitous Devices

With their increased capacity and improved portability, ubiquitous devices have the potential to facilitate personalised reminiscence therapy.

Currently, reminiscence therapy is performed as a group activity using generic memory prompts. Preparation is a time-consuming process as facilitators must generate a theme for the week and gather relevant materials [13]. Reminiscence is rarely carried out as a one-to-one activity using personal memorabilia. In utilising the power of ubiquitous devices, reminiscence therapy could become person-centred through the use of the individual's own photos, thus enhancing the participant's interaction.

Research by Alm et al. [14], has shown that people with dementia are able to adapt to and interact with touch screen environments. With this in mind, a tablet PC could be used to provide mobility to the users, enabling reminiscence therapy to become an activity which can occur whenever and wherever it is appropriate and convenient.

2   Method

This study was approached from a user-centred perspective, with the carers of people with dementia included at all stages of the design process. It was split into four phases: an initial study, application design, a prototyping session and finally user testing.

2.1   Initial Study

The initial study aimed to assess the perceived nature of reminiscence therapy, identify the types of prompt which evoke memories for both the person with dementia and their carer and also identify usability issues experienced whilst using a computer or touch screen device.

Originally, the initial study was designed to be a focus group involving six carers over the age of 65, who were approached a week before the intervention. However, one participant was due to be away on the planned date for the focus group, but was keen to take part. This led to five participants taking part in the focus group and one interview.

Both the focus group and the interview were semi-structured, with a standard list of questions, enabling the possibility of modification to questions or to include supplementary enquiries for clarification. It also meant that should the participants feel that they were unable to answer some of the questions; these could either be missed out or rephrased.

2.2   Application Design

The application was designed based on the findings of a literature review together with additional information gained as part of the initial study. These designs were then evaluated by carers of people with dementia as part of the prototyping session.

2.3   Prototyping

Initially, two prototyping sessions were planned: a low-fidelity prototype session using paper-based designs and a high-fidelity session which employed the ubiquitous device. However, during the initial focus group, it came across that the carers of people with dementia were struggling to envisage the application. For this reason, it was decided that only high-fidelity prototyping should be carried out. This would allow the potential users to assess the actual usability of the application.

Five potential users were given a set of tasks to carry out as part of the prototyping session. These activities were designed to test all the possible ways the user could interact with the system. The users were observed as they completed the tasks, with any problems encountered recorded. On completion of the activities, the carers were encouraged to discuss their opinions of the system, together with any changes they felt would be beneficial.

2.4   User Testing

This phase of the study was designed to evaluate the perceived effectiveness of the application. Two potential system users, who both have extensive experience of caring for a person with dementia, were used to assess the system.

Similarly to the prototype testing, the user testing involved the completion of several tasks aimed at testing the basic functionality. They were also designed to ensure that the users had interacted with the system sufficiently to form an opinion on the feasibility of utilising the application to facilitate reminiscence therapy. During the testing session, the users were observed to determine whether there were any problems with interaction. Subsequent to the testing session, the carers were interviewed to allow them to discuss their thoughts of the system.

3   Results

3.1   Initial Study

Whilst the participants of the focus group felt that reminiscence therapy would have no effect on their partners at the current point in time, they did believe that it would have been beneficial at an earlier stage of the illness. By contrast, the interviewee considered reminiscence therapy to be useful at the point of execution, but felt it had no lasting effect on her partner.

During the focus group it became apparent that the carers had the perception that reminiscence therapy can only be done as part of a group session, for a specific amount of time. Although reminiscence therapy is often carried out as part of a group following a set 'prescription', it can be just two people remembering their past together at home. It follows that for the application to be useful the carer's preconceptions of reminiscence therapy need to be challenged and changed.

One couple had participated in a 12-week programme of group reminiscence therapy several years ago. The carer felt that her husband did enjoy the group and "came to life" during the sessions. She also commented that despite his worsening condition, music still provokes memories, with him often able to remember the words to songs from an earlier age.

It was generally agreed by the focus group that music effectively evoked memories for both the carer and the person with dementia. One carer stated that she has CDs containing old music which reminds them of when they first met and revives memories for her husband. The group did agree that photos do stir up memories; however, they were often inaccurate, for example, a person mistaking his grandchildren for his children. This caused the carers frustration, especially when their partners seem able to remember incorrect memories over actual recollections. In addition to this, the participants expressed that taking part in discussions prompted further memories, much like a spider-web fanning out. One participant found that her husband could clearly remember poems from when he was younger. Finally, they felt that there were times when a word would stimulate memories, the example given being "mardy" which reminded the participant of her northern upbringing.

Of the six participants only one person had previously used a tablet PC. He found that his wife became visibly distressed when he used a laptop computer. However, she appears to be unaffected by him using a tablet PC. An observation of the interviewee whilst using the tablet PC showed that she had considerable trouble when using the "pinch-zoom" functionality. This will need to be considered during the design process.

3.2   Application Design

Designing an application for use by people with dementia needs to consider not only the effects of the condition, but also the changes which naturally occur as a person ages. In addition to this, as a group of people ages, their individual needs become increasingly diverse [15].

Due to the declining short term memory of people with dementia, the application has been designed to reduce the volume of information which needs to be remembered. For example, if the user wants to change an item or remove it completely they are able to do this directly from the reminiscence screen. This eliminates the need to remember which item they intended to alter whilst changing their location in the application.

Often, mobile devices will have too much functionality [16]. This leads to increased cognitive load due to the complexity, however when it comes to older users, it is desirable to reduce the amount of effort placed on the brain, as this capacity is in decline. This is even more important for people with dementia whose cognitive skills will be dramatically reduced when compared to someone who does not suffer from the condition. By simplifying the functionality on each screen and increasing the size of elements, the cognitive load is reduced and the users will not be overwhelmed by the number of possible operations available to them [17]. It is however, important to remember not to simplify the navigation too much. By cutting the number of menu items shown on a screen to just one item, more harm may be done than good. It will stop the users from seeing the alternatives and will also hide the navigation structure from them [16].

In addition to this, as a person grows older there is a natural decline in their ability to extract relevant information in a field of distractors [18]. This is particularly important when trying to facilitate reminiscence therapy, as the focus should be on the memory prompt rather than the interface. Therefore, to avoid distractions, the interface has been designed to be as simple as possible, bearing in mind the dangers of over-simplification mentioned above. This ensures that the person with dementia focuses on the reminiscence item rather than the interface, promoting enhanced interaction with the process.

In order to maximise the readability of the interface, designers need to consider the colour of the background in relation to the foreground text. Research suggests that there should be a high contrast between background and foreground colours [19]. It is suggested that the best colours to use are black text on a white background [18]. However, Lorenz & Oppermann [20] agree that whilst the readability is best with the black text, white background combination, their users commented that the white background was too bright and made them uncomfortable. This led them to propose a grey or orange background with black, white or turquoise fonts. In this application, a white background has been chosen to maximise readability. However, to combat the discomfort caused by the harsh background, the interface components will be made as large as possible, without compromising the flow of the interface. This will allow the text size to be made as large as possible, which agrees with the suggestions made by Dickinson et al. [19].

The application allowed the users to link music and images together, in order to provide the potential for dual stimulation of memories. In addition to this, the users were able to name their memories and provide extra notes to act as supplementary memory prompts.

Figure 1 shows the interface for the main reminiscence screen. It provides all the functionality required to facilitate reminiscence therapy. In order to maintain the consistency of the layout when there is no music assigned to an item, the play, pause and restart buttons will be hidden allowing for no change in the positioning of the subsequent buttons. This will remove any frustration felt from buttons which appear to have no functionality, without requiring the users to search for buttons that are in different positions.

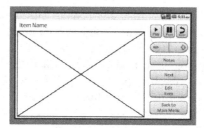

Fig. 1. Reminiscence screen

3.3   Prototyping

In general, the users felt that the system was easy to use. The prototyping session provided an insight into the problems which could be encountered by the users allowing adjustments to be made to the system in order to eliminate these issues.

The main issue identified by all the participants in the prototyping session was the colour scheme. Contrary to the findings of the literature review, they did not have a problem with the brightness of the white background; instead they felt that it was a "boring" colour scheme. The carers were encouraged to suggest the colours they would particularly like to see in the interface. The majority stated that calming pastel colours (such as light yellow or purple) would be the ideal option, as they would make the interface appear "cheerful".

The users struggled to identify the zoom buttons in the interface. Therefore by adding a label to the zoom buttons, this would allow the users to quickly identify their use. They did, however, like the ability to zoom into images as it enabled them to see additional detail which had been overlooked. This feature allowed the carer to emphasis parts of a photo to the person with dementia, such as the face of a loved one. The main reminiscence screen was adapted to take this suggestion into account, see figure 2.

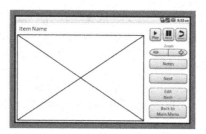

Fig. 2. Updated Reminiscence screen to reflect the labelled zoom button

All the participants had problems reading the notes before they disappeared from view. They quickly realised that if they kept pressing the notes button, the pop-up remained visible for longer. This is not an ideal solution; therefore, in the final system the length of time the pop-up remained on the screen needed to be increased.

When adding and changing items, the users struggled to decide which button related to each section of the interface. For example, the participants couldn't decide which button added an image. It was suggested that this problem would be eliminated by switching the position of the button with the text field (in the case of the music) and the image preview (for the photo). This made the associations clearer to the user.

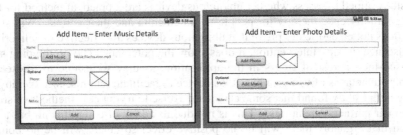

Fig. 3. Updated Add Music and Add Photo screens

3.4   User Testing

Both testers felt that the application would be beneficial to them for facilitating reminiscence therapy with their respective relatives. They commented that a large number of their photographs are already saved on their personal computer, and as such would be easy to transfer.

One tester commented that the initial input of personal memories would be extremely time consuming and quite difficult using the Android keyboard. However, after the first series of memories had been entered, it would simply be a case of maintaining the database and adding extra memories when necessary. Conversely, the other tester felt that the input process would provide an additional opportunity to reminisce, allowing input from the person with dementia, which could result in a more comprehensive set of memory prompts.

When asked to zoom in on an image, both users approached the task differently. One tester decided to use the buttons included on the interface, whereas the other user automatically exploited the pinch-zoom functionality. This justified the inclusion of both methods of enlarging the picture in order to reduce unassisted recall.

One user found it frustrating that having pressed the next button the ability to return to the previous image was absent. This was perpetuated by the buttons being situated in close proximity, as the user found it easy to accidentally press the adjacent button when intending to display the photo notes.

The testers felt the background colour scheme used had an overall calming effect. The testers commented that the background colour did not detract from the purpose of the screen, ensuring that the focus was maintained on the reminiscence item rather than the surroundings. Despite this, care needs to be exercised when concluding that the colours are appropriate, due to the variety of the potential users' visual needs.

Despite increasing the amount of time available for the notes to be displayed on the screen, both users still found difficulty in reading the entire contents of the pop-up before it disappeared. This suggests that either there needs to be an improved method of displaying the notes on the screen or the length of time that the pop-up is displayed should be increased further. The latter is possible; however, there is the risk that there will always be someone who reads the pop-up slower than others.

4   Conclusion

This study aimed to assess whether ubiquitous devices are a practical method for facilitating reminiscence therapy for people with dementia and their carers. Whilst this study does not categorically prove that ubiquitous devices are effective in delivering a reminiscence therapy intervention, it does show the potential. The prototyping stage increased the interest of carers in the application, as they were able to foresee the possible advantages of using a ubiquitous device to facilitate reminiscence therapy.

The initial study found that some carers are averse to trying new methods of stimulating their partners' memories. This is not due to a lack of commitment, but to the opinion that arguably there will be no positive effect so "there will be no point in trying". There also appears to be a belief that reminiscence therapy can only take place in a group, for a set period of time. This assumption needs to be challenged, as reminiscence can occur at any time.

Should reminiscence therapy be adopted during the earlier stages of dementia, a routine may be instilled which enables both the person with dementia and the carer to benefit from the recollection of shared memories. By developing the catalogue together, whilst their treasured memories remain intact, allows for increased participation. The burden of creating and maintaining the flow of conversation during reminiscence on the carer will be reduced [13].

Future research will investigate whether the application is designed sufficiently to be used by people with dementia. Once this has been established, the application will be tested to investigate whether it has a measurable effect on the well-being of people with dementia and their carers. In addition to establishing the use of ubiquitous devices to facilitate reminiscence therapy for people with dementia and their carers, further research will be completed to investigate use with other user groups (such as people with depression, borderline personality disorders and other mental health problems).

References

1. What is Dementia?,
   http://www.alzheimers.org.uk/site/scripts/
   documents_info.php?documentID=106
2. Demography,
   http://www.alzheimers.org.uk/site/scripts/
   documents_info.php?documentID=412
3. Woods, B., Spector, A.E., Jones, C.A., Orrell, M., Davies, S.P.: Reminiscence Therapy for Dementia. Cochrane Database of Systematic Reviews (2009)
4. Drug treatments for Alzheimer's disease,
   http://www.alzheimers.org.uk/site/scripts/
   documents_info.php?documentID=147

5. Steinberg, M., Tschanz, J., Corcoran, C., Steffens, D., Norton, M., Lyketsos, B.J.: The Persistance of Neuropsychiatric Symptoms in Dementia: The Cache County Study. International Journal of Geriatric Psychiatry 19, 19–26 (2004)
6. Drugs used to relieve behavioural and psychological symptoms in dementia, http://www.alzheimers.org.uk/site/scripts/documents_info.php?documentID=110
7. Thorgrimsen, L., Schweitzer, P., Orrell, M.: Evaluating Reminiscence for People with Dementia: a Pilot Study. The Arts in Psychotherapy 29, 93–97 (2002)
8. Hsieh, C., Chang, C., Su, S., Hsiao, Y., Shih, Y., Han, W., Lin, C.: Reminiscence Group Therapy on Depression and Apathy in Nursing Home Residents with Mild-to-Moderate Dementia. Journal of Experimental and Clinical Medicine 2, 72–78 (2010)
9. Cohen-Mansfield, J., Thein, K., Dakheel-Ali, M., Marx, M.S.: The Underlying Meaning of Stimuli: Impact on Engagement of Persons with Dementia. Psychiatry Research 177, 216–222 (2010)
10. Westerhof, G.J., Bohlmeijer, E., Webster, J.D.: Reminiscence and mental health: a review of recent progress in theory, research and interventions. Aging & Society 30, 697–721 (2010)
11. Good, A., Wilson, C., Ancient, C., Sambhanthan, A.: A Proposal to Support Wellbeing in People With Borderline Personality Disorder: Applying Reminiscent Theory in a Mobile App. In: The ACM Conference on Designing Interactive Systems. ACM Press, New York (2012)
12. The Fundamental Facts: The latest facts and figures on mental health, http://www.mentalhealth.org.uk/content/assets/PDF/publications/fundamental_facts_2007.pdf?view=Standard
13. Astell, A., Ellis, M.P., Bernardi, L., Alm, N., Dye, R., Gowans, G., Campbell, J.: Using a Touch Screen Computer to Support Relationships between People with Dementia and Caregivers. Interacting with Computers 22, 267–275 (2010)
14. Alm, N., Dye, R., Gowans, G., Campbell, J., Astell, A., Ellis, M.: Designing an Interface Usable by People with Dementia. In: Proceedings of the 2003 Conference on Universal Usability, pp. 156–157. ACM Press, New York (2003)
15. Gregor, P., Newell, A.F., Zajicek, M.: Designing for Dynamic Diversity - Interfaces for Older People/. In: Proceedings of the Fifth International ACM Conference on Assistive Technologies, pp. 151–156. ACM Press, New York (2002)
16. Ziefle, M.: Information Presentation in Small Screen Devices: The Trade-Off between Visual Density and Menu Foresight. Applied Ergonomics 41, 719–730 (2010)
17. Sayago, S., Blat, J.: Telling the Story of Older People E-mailing: An Ethnographic Study. International Journal of Human-Computer Studies 68, 105–120 (2010)
18. Hawthorn, D.: Possible Implications of Aging for Interface Designers. Interacting with Computers 12, 507–528 (2000)
19. Dickinson, A., Newell, A.F., Smith, M.J., Hill, R.L.: Introducing to the over-60s: Developing an Email System for Older Novice Computer Users. Interacting with Computers 17, 621–642 (2005)
20. Lorenz, A., Oppermann, R.: Mobile Health Monitoring for the Elderly: Designing for Diversity. Pervasive and Mobile Computing 5, 478–495 (2009)

Human Computer Confluence in Rehabilitation: Digital Media Plasticity and Human Performance Plasticity

Anthony Lewis Brooks

Aalborg University Esbjerg, Niels Bohrs vej 8, Esbjerg, Denmark
tb@create.aau.dk

Abstract. Digital media plasticity evocative to embodied interaction is presented as a utilitarian tool when mixed and matched to target human performance potentials specific to nuance of development for those with impairment. A distinct intervention strategy trains via alternative channeling of external stimuli that bypasses desensitized/dysfunctional sensory pathways to close the afferent/efferent loop. Designing method and apparatus to optimize participant motivation is core of the emergent model. Accessible play, fun, and creativity are central as user experiences, rather than traditional therapeutic approaches promoting mindsets and activities commonly considered enduring, mundane and boring. The concept focuses on sensor-based interfaces mapped to control tailored-content that acts as direct and immediate feedbacks mirroring input. These flexible, adaptive, and 'plastic' options offer facilitators new tool-kits for individualized interventions to supplement traditional approaches and strategies. Conclusions point to how required informal/non-formal training of such plastic approaches requires formal accreditation to realize potentials and adoptions.

Keywords: Digital Media & Human Performance Plasticity; Alternative channeling; HCI; Games; Creativity; Brain Plasticity; Afferent-efferent Neural Loop Closure.

1 Introduction

This paper presents a mature body of research exploring *digital media plasticity* mixed and matched to a participant's needs to question alternative channeling of stimuli to affect plasticity of the brain and consequentially plasticity of human performance. This is via achieving closure of the human afferent-efferent neural loop [1, 2, 3]. A supplement to traditional therapeutic/rehabilitation intervention has emerged. Following the introduction of the concept, method and apparatus, a discussion presents the argument of plasticity potentials and how ICT applied within intervention using games and creativity requires advanced training, learning and hands-on experiences. A critical reflection closes the paper stating the challenges of the informal/non-formal approach suggesting possible derailment through lack of authorized formal accreditation being in place to offer would be life-long learners new opportunities.

C. Stephanidis and M. Antona (Eds.): UAHCI/HCII 2013, Part III, LNCS 8011, pp. 436–445, 2013.
© Springer-Verlag Berlin Heidelberg 2013

2   SoundScapes Concept

Following prototype creation and many years of solo (author) fieldwork, a family of patents resulted on method and apparatus (5/5/2000: US 09/565,924[1]) – see [4]. The research was responsible for national (Denmark) and international projects that subsequently realized a product, commercial company, and dedicated research facility.

2.1   Background

The concept (now a registered company in Denmark) evolved from the author's artist/musician profile having an engineering education and a domestic history, and thus, intimate experiences of family members with profound impairment. The insights to individual traits, needs, desires and preferences led to exploration of digital media's plasticity enquiring adaptability, interconnect-ability, and tailor-ability applied across performance art (stage and installation) and rehabilitation (PMLD). Preliminary research on technological solutions for biofeedback (with a focus on direct cause and effect) led to various prototypes being created and tested in exploratory fieldwork. The devices were basic apparatus that used the MIDI (Musical Instrument Digital Interface) communication protocol that had recently been standardized (1983). Various test instruments were made – predominant was a touch-sensitive MIDI-Bass that could give digital and analogue mixed stimuli feedback (low-frequency audio, image etc.)

Research included inspirational tours, residencies and guest visits at Stanford University Music department; the Mechanical Engineering Department Design Group; the Palo Alto VA Health Care System, Rehabilitation Research and Development Center, California, USA; IRCAM, Paris, France; DIEM, Aarhus, Denmark; Steim, Amsterdam … as well as a number of commercial companies including Biomuse (Biocontrol Systems, Neuro Interactive Technology) [5], and Waverider[2] (MindPeak). These early biocontrol systems were based on electronic signals measured from electrodes precisely positioned on the surface of the skin then mapped to control a computer. Instrumentation amplifier circuits (IA) are used to measure the bioelectric signals from the electrodes that are then sent to a programmable gain amplifier (PGA). The signal is then sampled and processed by a specialized digital signal processing microprocessor in order to filter the signals and then perform specific pattern recognition operations. This processed signal is then sent to the computer using an optically isolated serial channel, which importantly protects the user from voltage spikes coming from the computer. Electronic information was thus sourced from the heart (ECG), brain activity (EEG), sweat (Electrodermal/GSR). More direct and immediately controllable signals, i.e. eye blinks/motion (EOG), muscle tensioning (EMG), were also sourced, reducing lag, optimising desired direct and immediate causality. An issue was that worn 'wet' on-body biocontrol sensors (at that time) required conducting gel

---

[1] United States Department of Commerce: United States Patent & Trademark Office document.
[2] http://www.mindpeak.com/WaveRider-Pro.aspx as performed by author at The EuropeanNetwork for Intelligent Information Interfaces, i3 gala dinner, Basel, 2001.

preparation of the participant that was enduring, uncomfortable, and requiring post-session cleaning. Alongside this was the problematic preciseness of positioning of the sensors for optimal Signal-to-Noise ratio (often abbreviated SNR or S/N), which equates to signal strength. These systems were evaluated as imposing a mindset of 'wired for therapy' and problematic due to need for specific training of possibly technophobic staff where specific knowledge of MIDI (or other) protocol was needed. Thus, a more user-friendly solution was sought.

It was found that if residual movement exists then an increased opportunity is offered to *directly and immediately control* data dynamically via non-worn sensors. A reduced lag factor was evident using off-body infrared sensors compared to worn sensors that source data from inner body signals (e.g. brain, heart, GSR) where 'control' is questionable. Thus, motion of an impaired individual has been the focus of data acquisition in this work to optimize the experience of control for the end-user.

Movement as unencumbered biocontrol. Awareness of one's body differs according to each person, and especially in the case of impairment, condition and situation. In line with this, research presented how the US Federal government acknowledged how pleasure derived from movement, alongside the empirically supported premise that the body, mind and spirit are interconnected has resulted in associations for dance and movement therapy where psychotherapeutic use of movement benefits the emotional, cognitive, physical and social integration of individuals[3]. The link between motion-pleasure to human performance was furthered via a U.S. National Science Foundation report from 2002, titled *Converging Technologies for Improving Human Performance* [6] where disability and healthcare issues are in focus. The plasticity of digital media is suggested in this report. It is this form of 'convergence of technologies' thinking, wherein innate flexible potentials to mix'n'match in order to address individual needs of impairment, that are in focus herein and in the author's earlier publications [e.g. 1, 2, 3, 4, 7, 8, 9, 15]. The SoundScapes research (including *ArtAbilitation, GameAbilitation, Ludic Engagement Designs for All [LEDA]*) therefore evolved to create devices and systems for investigation of non-worn sensors, in other words where unencumbered free gesture (nothing held, or attached) in an invisible sensing space - referred to as "Virtual Interactive Space" (VIS) [1] – generated control data. The focus on systems that required no participant preparation, discomfort, or post-session cleaning meant that participants could enter the session room and immediately begin before getting tired or distracted. The developed prototypes also required no strength or dexterity to operate as mapping software enabled scaling and other decisions related to multimedia content so that tailored solutions were apparent. A situation thus evolved where it was no longer questioned *what one could do with these systems* but rather design decisions had to be made as to *what not to do*. The decisions were determined on the participant/patient profile, therapist/doctor goal from sessions, and the available system components available e.g. interfaces, mapping software, multimedia content, and presentation equipment. The early interface sensors and system developments are outlined in the next section.

---

[3] http://www.adta.org/About_DMT

2.2   SoundScapes - Non-worn Biocontrol Sensor Systems

The development of the SoundScapes non-worn sensor-based interfaces focused on infrared technology with multiple sensor arrays (figure 1). Ultrasound, camera (figure 2), and later, laser technologies were integrated so that increased mixing and matching options were available to session designers and intervention facilitators.

Fig. 1. Infrared prototypes with 3 heads for RGB filter control of image; manipulation of three MIDI instruments; or three properties of robotic device or game control via gesture alone

Development was aligned with multimedia growth and advancements in sensor technologies, computer hardware and software. Alongside was increased ICT pervasiveness in society. The use of multiple interface technologies having differing sensing profiles (where the invisible space can be volumetric/3D, linear, or planar according to technology used - figure 2) preceded contemporary mixed-sensing inventions such as the Nintendo Wii and Microsoft Kinect (see later references in following sections).

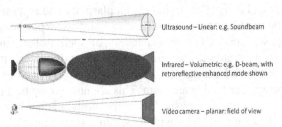

Ultrasound – Linear: e.g. Soundbeam

Infrared – Volumetric: e.g. D-beam, with retroreflective enhanced mode shown

Video camera – planar: field of view

Fig. 2. Non-invasive sensing profiles

2.3   Acceptance by Institutes

Following preliminary research that resulted in prototype creation, the early proof-of-concept was an enduring challenge to gain acceptance of the SoundScapes' sensor-based interfaces and gesture-control of games and art/creative play within rehabilitation and healthcare. However, demonstrations and subsequent residencies illustrated to healthcare professionals and families the end-user positive responses to the untraditional intervention with fun and creative activities. Following rigorous testing, assessments, and evaluations by various experts, SoundScapes was adopted into a select number of institutes in Denmark in the mid nineteen nineties. A product prototype was realized as a multi-institute commission in 1998/9 whereby intervention training and evaluation supported the author's apparatus and method concept. Adoption followed leading to product and company creation. The addressing of future society demographics through ICT was especially in focus, especially the predicted increased aged and impaired communities alongside associated service care industries. Unemployment is a related issue, which is detailed elsewhere in the author's publications. Models have thus emerged from SoundScapes that are offered for peer augmentation to improve on the method, apparatus and testing [7].

2.4   **Moving beyond Own-created Apparatus**

Following the early years of developing devices, it became clear that commercial equipment offered more affordable solutions providing that the mapping software could be programmed to control selectable open content to be adapted to an individual. Explorations of game peripherals included the Sony EyeToy [8] and Nintendo Wii [9]. However, both companies responded negatively to approaches to open the game content. More recently, 3rd party software[4] enables open environments for content creation and sensor data mapping. Even basic microprocessors (e.g. MakeyMakey/Arduino) can be mapped to easily constructed video games. The potentials of open-source peripherals has been made apparent by the Microsoft Kinect (and other available time-of-flight cameras and related devices), as evidenced by the huge community of developers creating an array of potential tools available for use in this field considering different needs of 'players'.

2.5   **Facilitator Competences and Need for Specific Training Programs**

With such progress and activity in digital media plasticity and its potentials in human performance plasticity, the question must be asked of the competences of those facilitating the training sessions. Their understanding of such systems and the required change to intervention strategies that are required to optimize use to maximize patient/participant benefit and progress of development clearly need to be in line with the goals of the therapist or healthcare team. This alignment may be a problem.

From experiences to date, it is posited that this question is not being asked enough as facilitators are utilizing such tools without specific schooling, extra curricula training or even thought (a tendency is to just include a game as an add-on). SoundScapes has thus invested in developing an accessible training/spa/learning-lab complex with accommodation in Denmark in line with life-long learning, games4health, and welfare society (which Denmark is renown for). This is set up as a travel-for-health retreat to train trainers (national/international) via programs on how ICT can be used in healthcare, intervention and learning. The next section overviews aspects of plasticity relating to the SoundScapes' philosophy on facilitator training needs.

---

[4] e.g. Osculator http://www.osculator.net -- Max/MSP/Jitter
  http://cycling74.com -- Eyesweb
   http://www.infomus.org/eyesweb_ita.php -- Isadora
   http://troikatronix.com, and others...

3   Plasticity

3.1   Digital Media Plasticity

The malleable aspect of digital media, in this work, is tied closely to variance in brain plasticity and of effect on human performance (next section). This research, through a history exploring the plasticity of digital media, creates adaptive situated experiences to stimulate meaningful causal interactions to supplement traditional intervention. It is posited from this research that the brain can be affected by designing specific interactions with stimuli to promote a nuance of participant microdevelopment [10]. An example of this is a case study questioning how the balance sense attribute of a patient with acquired brain injury was lost and then trained via sound that gave feedback according to the body position in space – thus training proprioception/balance [11]. Thus, the activity – be it gaming, creating (art-based), or other control - is optimal if it allows access to parameters for on-the-fly changes according to a participant needs profile, preferences, and progress. In this way it is imperative that a facilitator understands the system to match to the individual and to tailor/fine-tune to the session goal.

3.2   Brain- and Human Performance Plasticity

When one refers to brain plasticity (also commonly called neuroplasticity) it is the neuronal circuits, synapse activities, and malleable qualities of change and subsequent affect on the body's nervous system that are being discussed. These elements change throughout life [12]. When a person is subject to physical injury or impairment these elements and the sensitizing associated to the brain can become damaged [13] leading to disability and need for rehabilitation and therapeutic intervention that involves training and (re)learning. The involved cortical remapping is available into adulthood [14], which presents opportunities for promoting change via alternative channeling of stimuli. It is this alternative non-formal approach that is the core in SoundScapes. Whist fun and enjoyment are seen as the designed-for experience, behind is a profile-dependent purpose targeting nuance of development progress through focused intervention by SoundScapes' trained facilitators. Thus, SoundScapes has evolved from an original invent with a goal of adaptive apparatus and method (as per the published patent) to help as an assistive technology and technique to redirect foci to investigate relations between people and systems wherefrom models emerged both for specific intervention and holistic evaluations: People = Patients/Participants + Facilitators.

4   Discussions

Over the lifetime of this research, the increased plasticity of digital media - i.e. the abundance of opportunities for creation and application - has evolved to effect this work such that it became clear that one no longer questioned what one could do with these systems but rather design decisions had to be made as to what not to do. The redundancy decisions are determined on the participant/patient profile, therapist/doctor goal from sessions, and the available system components available e.g. interfaces, mapping software, multimedia content, and presentation equipment. An even greater factor is suggested as being who the facilitator is and their competence in applying ICT in this form within this context.

Analogizing - A musician has to pick from the available multitude of notes on his/her instrument and then perform with selected available nuances according to interpretation. A painter has to choose colors- raw, mixed and blended- from his/her palette and then apply to a canvas according to an envisioned result. Both are aware of how silence, space, and no color are crucial. These analogies relate to how the SoundScapes designer researches, consults, then selects, mixes, blends, matches and presents the tailored palette of components as an instrument or toolkit for the facilitator to use and improvise intervention in sessions. The delimited choices are created as presets to enable swift parameter change (sensitizing of feed-forward input, mapping, and content) to maintain maximum contact between the facilitator and the patient/participant. Improvised facilitator intervention is based upon the ZOOM (Zone of Optimized Motivation) model of in-action assessment of capacity and increment of challenge [7]. The system designer thus passes over what has been created by him/her for the facilitator to evoke an aesthetic response by mediating the patient/participant's ludic and creative engagement with the system, thus to achieve a representation of the targeted neuroaesthetic resonance [15].

Linking external aesthetic stimuli to affect on the brain and the inner resonance of the patient/participant and subsequent actions [7], a clear causal afferent-efferent neural loop closure is available for closure via the intervention. In line with this is how discussions with neurologists have influenced the author's understanding and direction in creating and evolving SoundScapes. Influence from this work is evident in projects involving neurologists, neuropsychologists, psychologists, physio/occupation therapists, etc. [7, 11] Similarly; other luminaries state the link between the neural and the artist wherefrom an improved understanding of the nature of man is posited, e.g.

> *... neuroscientists would do well to exploit what artists, who have explored the potentials and capacities of the visual brain with their own methods, have to tell us in their works. Because all art obeys the laws of the visual brain, it is not uncommon for art to reveal these laws to us, often surprising us with the visually unexpected. Paul Klee was right when he said, "Art does not represent the visual world, it makes things visible." // It is only by understanding the neural laws that dictate human activity in all spheres - in law, morality, religion and even economics and politics, no less than in art - that we can ever hope to achieve a more proper understanding of the nature of man [5]*

Relating the presented issues of plasticity and how technology offers opportunities to support and complement traditional strategies links directly to designing for specific interactions by people with different needs. Such embodied design of interaction is in line with Dourish [16] who states how "Embodied interaction is not a technology or a

---

[5] www.neuroesthetics.org/statement-on-neuroesthetics.php

set of rules it is a perspective on the relationship between people and systems. The question of how it should be developed, explored, and instantiated remain open research questions." (p. 192). Accordingly, and as stated earlier, the creation and evolution of the SoundScapes system apparatus and method [4] has at the core held focus on the relationship between people and systems; with the human at the center.

5   Conclusions

This contribution presents a mature body of research exploring digital media plasticity mixed and matched to the needs of a participant. The concept behind questioning and realizing alternative channeling of stimuli to affect the plasticity of the brain and simultaneously the plasticity of human performance is discussed.

Related outcomes involving closure of the human afferent-efferent neural loop is argued in line with the applied use of creativity, play and learning via video games and art as content/experience. Models are introduced, linked and proposed for peer elaboration and improvements. The impact in the field, including product, researches, company spinout, patent, and research laboratory achievements are shared. An ICT supplement to traditional therapeutic/rehabilitation intervention has resulted.

Digital media is discreet in form yet analogous to human use. The improvisation required by the facilitator with the given ICT tools involves a need for training where intimate acquaintance is involved. Innate to this claim are contemporary strategies involving role-play where the facilitator becomes the participant. A facilitator understanding of how inter-subjectivity works and the system linkage is not enough: A requirement for success is where intra-subjective affects are achieved from the inter-subjective – thus, establishing embodied interactions via alternative channeling of stimuli to promote stimulation of brain plasticity and neural re-mappings toward improvements and nuance of development.

The attitude is that the system designer should be creating a piece of art each time s(he) hands over the apparatus to the facilitator. The facilitator implements the apparatus under a method open for creativity and expression where a shared experience with the participant evolves. The participant's experience of ludic creativity and self-expression develops from embodied interactions with the apparatus. Thus, the method as detailed in the patent [4] has evolved to not solely rely on interface apparatus but to be able to adapt and mix'n'match such a design 'toolkit' via mapping software and creative vision of end result potentials. In this way the method, stated in the patent, has evolved to supersede the apparatus as prime invent for this unique communication form to assist in rehabilitation, therapy, and even life quality aspects of society.

To close a reflection is made on how this work has evolved from preliminary research on biofeedback involving the positioning of sensors on the body and head to generate data mapped to manipulate audiovisual representations. The research then created and investigated primarily with non-worn sensor systems to stimulate human affect and this is in line with how luminaries in human research report how media affects the brain [e.g. 17, 18, 19, 20]. Others inform of how perception and cognition are inherently predictive, functioning to allow anticipate consequences of current and/or potential actions [21]. Links to sensation and perception are clear [22], as are the connections between gesture-based communication and human-computer interactions [23]. Mirroring, as afforded by plastic digital media, offers customized means to perceive the self, which can lead to learning awareness, and subsequent training of e.g. psychological phenomena such as proprioception and kinesthesis to assist maintaining balance, coordinate actions, and basic perceptual and memory processes involved in navigation. Such digital mirroring is core to SoundScapes, and in line with [24, 25].

From the applied research to date it is evident that the alternative channeling approach of adapting media plasticity to human plasticity offers opportunities for training that engages participants at a different level than traditional methods. It is therefore concluded that a concentrated effort is needed in research to fully understand potentials. Alongside this is the author's committed investment to contribute by establishing a training facility for professionals and families to school their utilizing of ICT in healthcare, rehabilitation and therapy. A challenge in this is that such informal/non-formal schooling is not accredited so that funding maybe restricted to further or fully realize the potentials such an initiative would offer.

References

1. Brooks, A.L.: Virtual interactive space (V.I.S.) as a movement capture interface tool giving multimedia feedback for treatment and analysis. In: International Congress of The World Confederation for Physical Therapy (WCPT), Yokohama, Japan, May 23-28, WCPT/Science Links Japan (1999), http://sciencelinks.jp/j-east/article/200110/000020011001A0418015.php
2. Brooks, A.L., Camurri, A., Canagarajah, N., Hasselblad, S.: Interaction with shapes and sounds as a therapy for special needs and rehabilitation. In: Proc. International Conference on Disability, Virtual Reality and Associated Technologies, Veszprém, Hungary, September 18-20, pp. 205–212. Reading University Press, Reading (2002), http://www.icdvrat.rdg.ac.uk/2002/papers/2002_27.pdf
3. Brooks, A.L.: Robotic synchronized to human gesture as a virtual coach in (re)habilitation therapy. In: Proc. International Workshop for Virtual Rehabilitation, École Polytechnique Fédérale de Lausann, Lausanne, Switzerland, September 16-17, pp. 17–26. École Polytechnique Fédérale de Lausann, Lausanne (2004)
4. Brooks, A.L., Sorensen, C.: Communication Method and Apparatus. US patent US6893407 (2000/2005)
5. Knapp, R.B., Lusted, H.S.: A Bioelectric Controller for Computer Music Applications. Computer Music Journal 14(1), 42–47 (1990)
6. Roco, M.C., Bainbridge, W.S. (eds.): Converging technologies for improving human performance: nanotechnology, biotechnology, information technology and cognitive science. U.S. National Science Foundation (2002), http://www.wtec.org/ConvergingTechnologies/Report/NBIC_report.pdf
7. Brooks, A.L.: SOUNDSCAPES: The Evolution of a Concept, Apparatus and Method where Ludic Engagement in Virtual Interactive Space is a supplemental Tool for Therapeutic Motivation. PhD dissertation. University of Sunderland, UK (2006/2011)

8. Brooks, A.L., Petersson, E.: Play Therapy Utilizing the Sony EyeToy®. In: Proc. International Workshop on Presence, University College London (UCL), London, UK, September 21-23, pp. 303–314. The International Society for Presence Research (ISPR), Dept of Computer Science, UCL, London (2005)

9. Brooks, A.L., Petersson, E.: Perceptual Game Controllers and Fibromyalgia studies. In: Proc. Conf. Disability, Virtual Reality & Associated Technologies (ICDVRAT), pp. 439–441. University of Reading, Reading (2012)

10. Granott, N., Parziale, J. (eds.): Microdevelopment: Transition Processes in Development and Learning (Cambridge Studies in Cognitive and Perceptual Development). Cambridge University Press, Cambridge (2002)

11. Brooksm, A.L.: HUMANICS 1 – a feasibility study to create a home internet based telehealth product to supplement acquired brain injury therapy. In: Proc. International Conference on Disability, Virtual Reality and Associated Technologies, Oxford University, England, September 20-22, pp. 43–50. Reading University Press, Reading (2004)

12. Pascual-Leone, A., Amedi, A., Fregni, F., Merabet, L.B.: The plastic human brain cortex. Annual Review of Neuroscience 28, 377–401 (2005)

13. Pascual-Leone, A., Freitas, C., Oberman, L., Horvath, J.C., Halko, M., Eldaief, M., et al.: Characterizing brain cortical plasticity and network dynamics across the age-span in health and disease with TMS-EEG and TMS-fMRI. Brain Topography 24, 302–315 (2011)

14. Rakic, P.: Neurogenesis in adult primate neocortex: an evaluation of the evidence. Nature Reviews Neuroscience 3(1), 65–71 (2002)

15. Brooks, A.: Neuroaesthetic Resonance. In: De Michelis, G., Tisato, F., Bene, A., Bernini, D., et al. (eds.) ArtsIT 2013. LNICST, vol. 116, pp. 57–64. Springer, Heidelberg (2013)

16. Dourish, P.: Where the Action Is: The Foundations of Embodied Interaction. MIT Press, Cambridge (2001)

17. Trehub, S.E.: The developmental origins of musicality. Nat. Neurosci. 6, 669–673 (2003)

18. Trevarthen, C.: Musicality and the intrinsic motive pulse: evidence from human psychobiology and infant communication. Rhythms, Musical Narrative, and the Origins of Human Communication. Musicae Scientiae Special Issue 1999–2000, 157–213 (1999)

19. Peretz, I., Zatorre, R.J.: Brain organization for music processing. Annu. Rev. Psychol. 56, 89–114 (2005)

20. Schlaug, G.: The brain of musicians. A model for functional and structural adaptation. Ann. NY Acad. Sci. 930, 281–299 (2001)

21. Berthoz, A.: The Brain's Sense of Movement (trans. G. Weiss). Harvard Press (1997/2002)

22. Matlin, M.W., Foley, H.J.: Sensation and Perception, 4th edn. Needham Heights. Allyn and Bacon, Mass. (1997)

23. Camurri, A., Volpe, G. (eds.): GW 2003. LNCS (LNAI), vol. 2915. Springer, Heidelberg (2004)

24. Loveland, K.A.: Autism, affordances, and the self. In: Neisser, U. (ed.) The Perceived Self, pp. 237–253. Cambridge University Press, Cambridge (1993/2006)

25. Lewis, M., Brooks-Gunn, J.: Social cognition and the acquisition of self. Plenum, New York (1979)

Universal Conceptual Design Solution
for Built-in Orthopaedic Rocker-Bar Device

Robert C.C. Chen

School of Design, Faculty of Art Design and Humanities, De Montfort University, UK
RChen1@dmu.ac.uk

Abstract. Gout is an acute inflammatory joint disorder (Arthritis) caused by deposition of monosodium urate monohydrate crystals around joints, tendons, and other tissues. According to data from the Survey [1] of Taiwanese Epidemiology in 1999, residents have a 0.4% chance of developing gout disease with a rise of about 7.5% every year in Taiwan. In the UK, Gout affects about 1 in 200 adults. Men are more commonly affected than women and first attack of gout typically develops in middle age and there is a family history of gout in about 1 in 5 cases. In spite of being unacceptable in style, rocker-bar is always an effective treatment, this research is, therefore, focused on a universal design concept and fitting assessment in relation to the design of orthopaedic rocker-bar with new universal hidden built-in construction, which provides the best way to improve the appearance, comfort and strength, it is suitable not only for gout disorders, but also for those patients with standing, walking or shoe-fitting corrective requirements.

Keywords: Universal concept, Orthopaedics, Rocker-bar.

1   Introduction

Gout disorder has been discovered for a long time, but nowadays, it still exists too many known factors in its full field of symptom [2]. Gout is a heterogeneous collection of genetic and acquired diseases characterized by elevated levels of uric acid in the blood (hyper-uricemia) and recurrent arthritic attacks. These arthritic attacks result from the deposition of uric acid crystals in connective tissue and joints. Systemic manifestations consist of recurrent arthritic attacks, chronic tophaceous arthritis, tophi in soft tissue, and gouty nephropathy.

Based on recent Taiwanese medical statistical data, it shows that almost 99% of gout patients are male. It also presents that nearly 73% of these serious gout patients is at their ages between 41 and 60 in the rate of gender. This serious problem of gout disorder needs to be solved immediately.

This research focuses on the design and development of orthopaedic rocker-bar. Rocker-bar is a medical device, which is also an out-sole mechanical construction with a firm supportive sole, always used in the treatment of various foot conditions such as arthritis or inflammation of the foot bones and its associated joints, ligaments, muscles and tendons. In spite of being unacceptable in appearance and style, the

C. Stephanidis and M. Antona (Eds.): UAHCI/HCII 2013, Part III, LNCS 8011, pp. 446–452, 2013.

rocker-bar shoe is always an effective treatment used in various foot problems at bones and joints.

As we can imagine, the appearance of fashion shoe style is the first consideration when buying or wearing shoes. Without any alternative, most of the patients with foot disorders have to wear their shoes with orthopaedic assistive devices to prevent themselves from foot pains and post-injury.

In the case of the patient with gout foot disorder, it is obviously that the main purpose of a orthopaedic rocker-bar is to give a shoe-sole its rigid and fixed surface, and also provide a fitted toe-spring to perform the foot of its expected gait. However, it is impossible for the rocker-bar to have an exquisite shape as normal high street shoe does. This research is, therefore, aimed at concepts both in universal design and fitting assessment in relation to the design and development of orthopaedic rocker-bar construction and its footwear.

2   Related Work

SATRA Footwear Technology Centre has been doing research in shoe, last and foot assessment for several years. A number of experiments and reports have been published recently. However, under the conditions of their conservative and confidential principles, it is quite difficult to get the information, which is related to research work in this field.

Many groups have worked on the surface shaping of orthopaedic foot and last (Tuckman et al, 1992) [3]. Lord and Foulston (1991) reported and concentrated on the technical evaluation of a commercial shoe CAD system, which is already widely used in the volume shoe trade, to access its ability for orthopaedic shoe upper design. It is the first time that the commercial CAD is encouraging for its potential use with orthopaedic shoes and lasts successfully [4]. Also an interactive computer graphics system for the design of molded and orthopaedic shoe lasts was introduced by McAllister et al in 1991 [5]. Other commercial developments are noted but no publications reported.

An international research project "SELECT (EUREKA, EU-661)", in the Department of Medical Engineering and Physics, King's College London, which is purposed into feasibility and definition of integrated measurement, data-bases and computer-aided design for orthopaedic footwear. Although that is the first time that brings together medical researchers, specialists and orthopaedic footwear companies between the United Kingdom and the Netherlands [6], it was still focused on the shoe-uppers and last shapes. From the point of view of shoe-sole technology, there is no information enough, which is related to research work in this field too.

3   Aims and Objectives

The aim of this study is to develop a universal orthopaedic rocker-bar device, which is used for making special orthopaedic footwear for fitting the foot of gout patients. This research will provide a special built-in construction with well-fixed rocker-bar factors, which are toe-spring angle and heel-strike cut.

The specific objectives of this trial are:

1) to develop, design and make a series of trial shoes/sandals with different angles of toe-spring and adjustable heel-strike bars;
2) to measure the length of the foot at the weight-on position, i.e. standing position;
3) to assess fit from different graded toe-spring and heel-strike;
4) to identify tolerable allowance at forepart and back-part of the foot during gait assessment;
5) to provide recommendations for acceptable ranges of the toe-spring angle and heel-strike cut for new built-in orthopaedic rocker-bar design and manufacturing.

4   Trial Protocol

In this experiment, a number of techniques are required i.e. foot measurement, fit assessment skills and special trial shoes/sandals making with different ranged construction at their forepart and back-part of the bottom region. Seven different RBAs with their toe-springs ranged from 5mm to 35mm (within 5mm intervals) of the same men's notional size of 8G and five different HSCs ranged from 0mm to 20mm (within 5mm intervals) of heel-strike cut were developed according to British Standard Institution (BS-5943, 1980) [7]. Then these were trialed on a number of normal subjects of this notional shoe size. During experiment, the biomechanical studies, including fitting assessment, plantar pressure measurement and gait analysis, are also performed.

The stages in this trial can be identified as:

1) Orthopaedic rocker-bar trial shoes/sandals making (see figure 1).
   a. Different ranged RBA (rocker-bar angle also called toe-spring angle) making, modification and checking.
   b. Different ranged HSC (heel-strike cut) making, modification and checking.
2) Subjects selection and foot measurement.
3) Fitting trial (see figure 2)

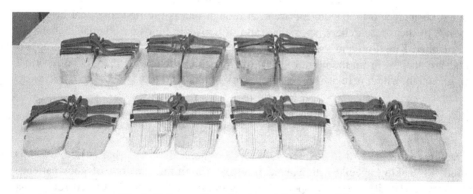

Fig. 1. Orthopaedic rocker-bar trial shoes/sandals

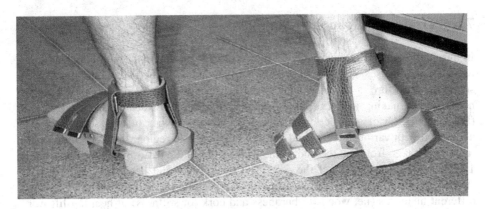

Fig. 2. Fitting trial shoes/sandals

5   Foot Measurement System and Observer Tests

A foot measurement system was adopted based on the orthopaedic standard BS-5943 and Clarks (C&J Clarks International Ltd.) system commonly used in fitting trials. In order to assess operator consistency, a trial was conducted involving the experienced author and his assistant who would subsequently take the measures and has received formal training offered to those staff from Taiwan Footwear Research Institute, an international research centre of footwear technology in Taiwan. Intra-observer tests were conducted by the assistant, who took measurements on a single subject three times over the course of a day. Inter-observer tests were done by both the author and the assistant, who took measurements on the same subject without reference to each other and then compared the results.

Before the trial was assessed, the reference points of foot ball joint (i.e. the 1st and the 5th Metatarsal-head), instep joint (i.e. dorsal medial cuneiform-head), short heel (i.e. talo-navicular) joint and back-heel height (i.e. back-top of calcaneum bone) were all determined and marked on those subjects' feet in order to ensure the same location for the measurements.

6   Subjects Selection

Based on recent Taiwanese medical statistical data, it shows that almost 99% of gout patients are male. National Yunlin University of Science and Technology, Graduate School of Design provided 20 usual fitting trial volunteers subjects. Their feet were measured by methods similar to those used in the volume shoe manufacture and orthopaedic trade including length, girth (width), and height measurements of the feet. The volunteers are all known to represent a good average of a given size, in this case of size 8G.

7   Trial Shoes (sandals) Making

In this study, due to the gout patient's foot is always rigidus in the foot bone and joint regions and it causes seriously hurt while moving and walking even at the position of standing. Therefore, a hard mechanical construction to support its out-sole firmly is necessary in making this trial shoes/sandals. In order to evaluate the shoed factors (RBA and HSC) of satisfaction, all the designed prototypes of trial shoes are well assembled with various heights and angles at the out-sole region. In figure 3, the RBA factor was taken from the toe-end of the trial sandal to the tread-line (at the bottom of 1st metatarsal-head point) of the sole. The toe-springs and heel strike cuts of trial shoes both were measured upright from the floor surface with 5mm increments. Two different materials (i.e. wood for hardness and cork for softness) of heel top-lift were used at the back-part of those trial sandals for getting better understanding.

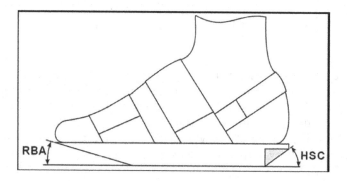

Fig. 3. Orthopaedic rocker-bar trial shoes/sandals making

8   Results and Discussions

The figure 4, 5 and 6 presented the detailed results of the suitability of fitting assessment on rocker-bar toe-spring (RBA) and heel-strike cut (HSC) factors. Figure 4 explains the relationship between the fitting assessments. It also indicates that the well-fit (acceptable) zone was found between 20mm and 30mm RBA (with the best-fit on 25mm RBA). Based on the best-fit of 25mm RBA, the HSC factor was assessed in both rigid (wood) and soft (cork) materials. The heel regions of those trial sandals were also designed to be replaceable (adjustable).

The figure 5 shows the suitability of HSC fitting assessment by using cork heel-lift; it indicates that the well-fit (acceptable) zone was found between 0mm and 15mm HSC with the best-fit on 5mm HSC. Figure 6 shows the suitability of HSC fitting assessment by using wooden heel-lift; it also indicates that the well-fit (acceptable) zone was found between 0mm and 15mm HSC with the best-fit on 5mm HSC. Although its well-fit (acceptable) zone is not so smooth as that in figure 5, the best-fit of 5mm HSC can be pointed out very clearly.

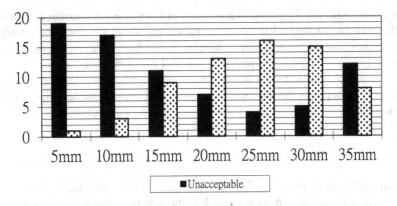

Fig. 4. The suitability of RBA fitting assessment

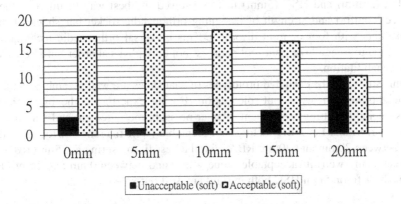

Fig. 5. The suitability of HSC fitting assessment by using cork heel-lift. (Based on the best-fit of 25mm RBA).

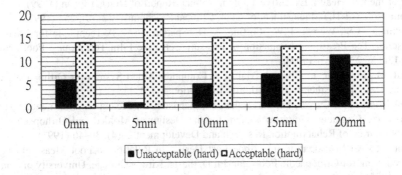

Fig. 6. The suitability of HSC fitting assessment by using wooden heel-lift. (Based on the best-fit of 25mm RBA).

Comparing with the 8mm of normal shoes in high street, to design and development the built-in constructed orthopaedic rocker-bar shoes for gout, the appropriate RBA is 25mm (ranged from 20mm to 30mm). It offers suitable toe-spring at forepart of shoe and makes the patient's problem foot feel comfort during walking, standing. This new built-in constructed rocker-bar with suitable RBA and HSC factors showed the best way to improve the appearance, comfort and strength of designing orthopaedic rocker-bar shoes for those gout patients with foot or joint disorders.

9 Conclusions

A special built-in orthopaedic rocker-bar construction was successfully developed for taking place of the old styled rocker-bar. It is the first time that the hidden rocker-bar construction has been developed. This new built-in constructed rocker-bar with suitable RBA (25mm) and HSC (5mm) factors showed the best way to improve the appearance, comfort and strength of designing orthopaedic rocker-bar shoes for those gout patients with foot or joint disorders. This universal orthopaedic technique can also be used to treat all the gout foot patients' not only physical order but also psychological rehabilitation.

In this study, all the designed prototypes of trial shoes are well assembled with various heights and angles at out-sole region. During experiment, the biomechanical studies, including fitting assessment, plantar pressure measurement and gait analysis, are also performed. For RBA factor, the acceptable (well-fit) range of toe-spring was found between 20mm and 30mm RBA with the best-fit toe-spring at 25mm RBA. For HSC factor, the well-fit (acceptable) zone was found between 0mm and 15mm HSC with the best-fit on 5mm HSC both in rigid and soft out-sole materials

References

1. Department of Health, Executive Yuan: in Annual Report of DOH, Taiwan (1999)
2. Emmerson, B.: The Management of Gout. Clinical Biochemistry 3(30), 253 (1997)
3. Tuckman, A.S., Werner, F.W., Fortino, M.D., Spadaro, J.A.: A Technique for Measuring Absolute Toe Pressures: Evaluation of Pressure-Sensitive Film Techniques. Foot and Ankle 13(14), 220–223 (1992)
4. Lord, M., Foulston, J.: Clinical Trial of A Computer Aided System for Orthopaedic Shoe Upper Design. Prosthetics and Orthotics International (15), 11–17 (1991)
5. McAllister, D.F., Carver, D., Devarajan, R., Harrison, L., Pietenpol, J.L., Yang, S.H.: An Interactive Computer Graphics System for the Design of Molded and Orthopaedic Shoe Lasts. Journal of Rehabilitation Research and Development 28(4), 39–46 (1991)
6. Chen, R.: An Investigation into Shoe Last Design in Relation to Foot Measurement and Shoe Fitting for Orthopaedic Footwear. Ph.D. thesis, King's College, University of London, UK (1993)
7. British Standard Institution: Methods for Measurement and Recording for Orthopaedic Footwear. BS-5943 (1980)

User Acceptance of a Community-Based Healthcare Information System Preserving User Privacy

Chien-Lung Hsu[1] and Ming-Ren Lee[2]

[1] Department of Information Management, Chang Gung University, Taiwan, R.O.C.
clhsu@mail.cgu.edu.tw
[2] Department of Information Management,
Taoyuan Innovation Institute of Technology, Taiwan, R.O.C.
D9009207@mail.ntust.edu.tw

Abstract. Community-based healthcare information systems (HIS) are developed to cope with the demand for home healthcare. However, the issue of privacy protection in HIS adoption has not been given sufficient attention. This study is to propose a privacy-enhanced framework and to investigate the role of privacy protection in HIS adoption. Our research model extends the unified theory of acceptance and use of technology by considering perceived security and information security literacy. Our experimental HIS is implemented according to our proposed privacy-enhanced framework which integrates healthcare applications and privacy protection mechanisms. The former includes health management, physiological monitoring, healthcare education, and healthcare consulting modules. The latter contains secure transmission, privacy protection and access control modules. Analyses indicate that user adoption of HIS is directly affected by social influence, performance expectancy, facilitating conditions, and perceived security. Perceived security has a mediating effect between information security literacy and user adoption.

Keywords: privacy protection, healthcare information system, UTAUT, perceived security, information security literacy.

1 Introduction

Population ageing has become a global trend because of rising life expectancy and declining birth rates. An American study in 2009[1] indicated that people older than 65 years old represent 12.9 percent of the U.S. population. In parts of Asia, elder persons accounted for 10.74 percent in Taiwan in 2010[2]. Japan, one of the most rapidly ageing countries, had the 20.8 percent of elderly population in 2006, and it will increase to 40 percent by 2050[3]. As predicted by the United Nations, the proportion of elders in the

---

Data source:
[1] Administration on Aging, U.S.A.
(http://www.aoa.gov/aoaroot/aging_statistics/index.aspx)
[2] Department of Statistics, Ministry of the Interior, Taiwan.
(http://www.moi.gov.tw/stat/)
[3] National Institute of Population and Social Security Research, Japan
(http://www.ipss.go.jp)

C. Stephanidis and M. Antona (Eds.): UAHCI/HCII 2013, Part III, LNCS 8011, pp. 453–462, 2013.
© Springer-Verlag Berlin Heidelberg 2013

world will reach 21 percent in 2050. The ageing phenomenon has caused rapid increase of the demand for health promotion and related services. In a report by the American Association of Retired Persons (AARP), approximately 85 percent of older people prefer to stay in their home when needing medical care [1]. This leads to a growing interest in using information systems to facilitate in-home healthcare and health management.

Research about healthcare information systems (HISs) usually addresses on the outcomes and benefit, but little attention has been given to privacy protection. For instant, several studies aimed to examine the impacts [2], time efficiency [3], benefit and contributions [4] of electronic health records (EHRs) on HISs. Vishwanath, Singh [5] also investigate whether EHRs could improve outpatient workflows. However, unlike other information systems, a HIS accesses a lot of sensitive data such as personal information, physiological parameters and health records. The end-users of a HIS nowadays have been extended from physicians in hospitals to patients (or their family) in home. Thus, challenge in a HIS is the transition from the stand-alone systems to the networked ones [6], but the issue of privacy protection has not been given the attention it needs.

This essay has two purposes. Firstly, for the networked HISs, the mechanisms of privacy protection are not in widespread implementation. One of our purposes is to propose a privacy enhanced framework for networked HIS. Secondly, whether a system is secure or not is related to human psychological cognition. A well-implemented IT system is not the guarantee of keeping a sense of safety because users' feeling of security does not completely reflect the technical security level [7]. Providers will work in vain if users are not aware of the precautions for their privacy. The second purpose is to investigate how users' psychological perception of privacy protection affects their adoption of HISs. To complete these purposes, we firstly design and develop a privacy-enhanced HIS as experimental platform to investigate user behavior. The essay would conclude with implications for research and practice. The proposed framework of experimental platform could provide insides for practitioners interested in HIS development; and the results of empirical survey would provide understanding of privacy protection in HISs adoption.

2   Theory and Hypotheses

To investigate user behavior toward health-related systems, we quoted the unified theory of acceptance and use of technology (UTAUT) [8] in support of our research model. UTAUT is one of the most influential models that have been used to evaluate the acceptance of a new technology. This theory posits that four major variables namely performance expectancy, effort expectancy, social influence, and facilitating conditions are of primary relevance in explaining the user intention to adopt an emerging innovation. Particularly, this study puts attentions on the users' psychological perception of privacy protection. Thus, we proposed perceived security and information security literacy as key indicators of using healthcare system. Figure 1 presents the model and its constructs.

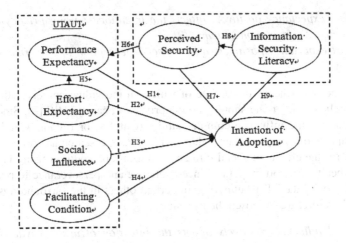

Fig. 1. Research model

2.1   Hypotheses on UTAUT

Modifying the definition given by Venkatesh, Morris [8], we defines performance expectancy (PE) as the degree of which an individual believes that using the privacy-enhanced HIS will help him or her to improves the performance of health management. When coming up with a technology innovation, one of the major concerns for individuals is whether they can benefit by using it. In prior research, PE was shown to possess strong influences on behavioral intention of adopting a new IT [9-11]. Healthcare information systems would advantage users to control over the determinants of their health and thereby improve their health. Especially for patients with chronic disease, the system let users be aware of physiological symptoms such as heartbeats, blood sugar, blood pressure, blood oxygen, and body temperature. Patients can perform regular examinations of self-health management at home or community center instead of going to a clinic. Besides, the health tracking functionality gives assistance to the control of health risk factors. Therefore, we proposed the hypothesis:

H1: Performance expectancy positively affects the intention of using privacy-enhanced healthcare information system.

Effort expectancy (EE) refers to the degree of an individual believes that using the privacy-enhanced HIS is free of effort [8]. Ease-to-use is considered as the essential element during the first time usage [10]. The less effort is required, the more willing users are to adopt a new IT. For example, Zhou and Lu [9] found that users will have more intention to adopt mobile banking system if its interface is easy to learn. Similarly, it takes time and efforts for a newbie to understand how to process healthcare related systems and to get familiar with them. In addition, the amount of effort needed will affect users' evaluation of whether a new IT can improve their job performances [12]. Therefore, we proposed the hypotheses:

H2: *Effort expectancy positively affects the intention of using privacy-enhanced healthcare information system.*

H5: *Effort expectancy positively affects users' perception of performance expectancy.*

Social influence (SI) means the degree of which an individual perceives that important others believes he or she should use the privacy-enhanced HIS [8]. Since human cannot live alone, the influence coming family, relatives, or friends would generate powerful impacts on changing their behavior [13]. Prior research has provided empirical support for the effects of social influence on user's behavior of using IT [14, 15]. In terms of health promotion, patients need patience and perseverance to perform the examinations every day. The support of important others in the surroundings is indispensable. Therefore, we proposed the hypothesis:

H3: *Social influence positively affects the intention of using privacy-enhanced healthcare information system.*

Facilitating condition (FC) is defined to the degree of which an individual believes that resources or knowledge exists to support use of the privacy-enhanced HIS [8]. The conduction of a new IT usually tends to run into many bottlenecks; it needs technological or organizational supports that help to remove barriers to use. Besides, the domain knowledge and skills are necessary for the operation of new IT. For a health-related system, basic healthy knowledge and skills will be required, such as the operation of a sphygmomanometer and the meaning of measured value. The amount of resources one has is considered as a key determinant of IT adoption [9, 16].

H4: *Facilitating condition positively affects the intention of using privacy-enhanced healthcare information system.*

2.2   Perceived Security and Information Security Literacy

Perceived security (PSY) refers to the degree of which an individual believes that using the privacy-enhanced HIS will be secure [7]. Rather than traditional systems, healthcare information systems cope with private and sensitive data which are directly related to identifiable persons [6]. A general situation is that people would refuse to give authorization of the electronic health records (EHRs) because of privacy concerns [17]. Hence, from the legal perspective, the Health Insurance Portability and Accountability Act of 1996 (HIPAA) emphasizes the necessity to establish the standards for use of electronic data interchange and confidentiality of health-related data.

However, Shin [7] noted that users' feeling of security does not completely reflect the technical security measures. A system with well secure protection will make a futile effort if users do not perceive the sense of precautions. Thus, previous research has indicated that security in cyberspace is subjectively related to human perception such as the image of risk affinity [18]. In e-commerce context, PSY has been considered as the key antecedence of shopping behavior [19]. In addition, PSY will prevent users from using an IT that copes with sensitive transaction such as a mobile wallet system [20]. Since a healthcare information system would conduct the transaction of EHRs, it is importance to investigate the role of PSY in health context. The proposed hypotheses aim to determine how PSY affects the intention to use HISs, directly or indirectly through performance expectancy.

> *H6*: *Perceived security positively affects users' perception of performance expectancy.*
>
> *H7*: *Perceived security positively affects the intention of using privacy-enhanced healthcare information system.*

The other privacy-related factor discussed is Information security literacy (ISL), which refers the ability and knowledge an individual possesses enabling him or her to protect information and systems [21]. Of the same physical security levels, the users' perceptions of security would be different because of their security literacy. Although a secure IT has given users the indication of precautions, individuals with higher ISL, rather than lower ISL, tends to be aware of the security awareness [21]. In addition, the degree of ISL is related to users' behavior of using the secure application [22]. As such, we thus propose relation between ISL, PSY, and the intention of using privacy-enhanced healthcare system.

> *H8*: *Information security literacy positively affects perceived security.*
>
> *H9*: *Information security literacy positively affects the intention of using privacy-enhanced health promotion system.*

3 The Development of Proposed Privacy-Enhanced HIS

The proposed framework has four logical phases: EHRs phase, privacy protection phase, healthcare application phase and multi-roles phase. Firstly, EHRs phase consists of databases storing sensitive information. Secondly, privacy protection phase contains three main modules, namely secure transmission module, privacy protection module and access control module. Thirdly, healthcare application phase includes individual health management module, physiological monitoring module, healthcare education module, and healthcare consulting module. Lastly, multi-roles phase means the users and devices. As shown in Figure 2, when a user performs the healthcare applications by using a PC or physiological testing equipment, all data access should be done through the privacy protection modules.

In healthcare application phase, the individual health management module enables users to manage personal long-term health record in a graphical layout. The physiological monitoring module provides immediate warning of users' physiological data if it does not meet the reasonable ranges. The healthcare education module recommends appropriate health education information to users. The healthcare consulting module enables users to leave an asynchronous message or consult a doctor via video phone synchronously.

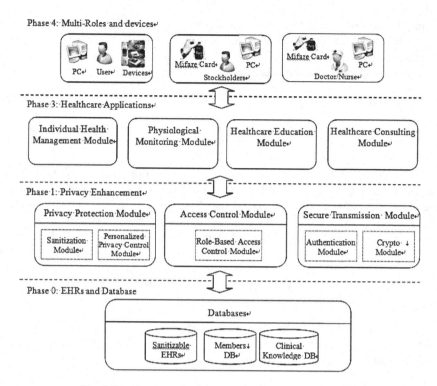

Fig. 2. The framework of proposed privacy-enhanced HIS

This study pays attention on privacy-enhanced functionality. Firstly, the secure transmission module prevents physiological information from being eavesdropped by malicious persons. Secondly, the privacy protection module protects user privacy by applying a sanitizable signature scheme. Lastly, the access control module ensures that only authorized users can access system resources, including community information, personal health records and knowledge bases. Secure transmission module is designed to provide a secure wireless transmission between server and physiological monitoring equipment such as body weight machine, blood pressure meter, blood glucose meter, and blood oxygen meter. As EHRs contain sensitive patient information, this study builds a crypto module and applies the Authentication Protocol in ISO standard [23] to identify the legitimacy of these devices as well as user identity. Besides, we encrypt users' physiological data by Advanced Encryption Standard (AES) algorithm to ensure the safety. Privacy protection module is to preserve the confidentiality, integrity, and availability. EHRs, which are mostly private records of patients, should not be leaked out to any third party unless the patients personally agreed to disclose the medical records. This module quotes the conception of sanitizable scheme [24] to shade private information before EHRs is shared within authorized users and in the meantime original digital certificate remains valid. Access control module assures system resources such as EHRs and knowledge bases are only accessed by authorized users. There are multi-roles in HIS system and each role has his own specific security permission. This module applies the Role-Based Access Control mechanism [25] that access permissions are determined by the level of user identity and access control policy.

4   Results and Discussions

The proposed privacy-enhanced HIS and devices were set up in the experimental classroom and totally 315 undergraduates were invited to participate in the experiment. Of the 315 participants, after removing incomplete or invalid questionnaires, we receive 280 usable samples and response rate is 88.9 percent. The participants' ages range from 18 to 29. In terms of gender, 62.9 percent are male and 37.1 percent are female. As for the frequency of going to a clinic for medical treatment, 18.9 percent of participants say they do so about once a week; 18.2 percent go once a month; 33.9 percent are about once a quarter; 17.5 percent only go once annually; 11.4 percent are less than once a year.

The examinations of constructs reliability and validity include factor loading, composite reliability, convergent validity, and discriminant validity. The results are shown in Table 1. Factor loadings, ranging from 0.71 to 0.95, were greater than the threshold value of 0.5. The minimum standard of composite reliability (CR) is 0.7 [26], and our values are between 0.88 and 0.96. The values of average variance extracted from each construct (AVE) were greater than the lowest bound of 0.5 [27]. These results imply that our constructs exhibited acceptable convergent validity. The square root of AVE is greater than any correlation among the constructs, implying that our constructs had acceptable discriminant validity.

The analysis of hypothesis test could give an understanding of what drives users to adopt a privacy-enhanced HIS like ours. Figure 3 presents the results of model testing. In short, all of our hypotheses are statistically supported except H2 (β = -0.02, $p >$ 0.01) and H9 (β = 0.10, $p >$ 0.01). This shows that there exists no direct effect of effort expectancy and information security literacy on the intention of adopting. However, the indirect effect analysis estimated by LISREL discovers interesting findings (see Table 3). First, the effort expectancy has indirect effect on behavioral intention (β = 0.15, $p <$ 0.001). Second, the indirect influence of information security literacy on adoption is also significant (β = 0.09, $p <$ 0.001). Our proposed model explains 65 percent of observed variance in the adoption of the privacy-enhanced HIS.

The study seeks to explore the role of privacy concerns on user willingness to use a healthcare information system. To achieve this purpose, we integrate several secure schemes and implement a privacy-enhanced HIS as our experimental platform. After the experiment about a week we receive 315 usable responses. The analysis results exhibits several findings. First of all, user intention toward using a privacy-enhanced HIS is directly driven by, in order of importance, social influence, perceived expectancy, facilitating conditions, and perceived security. This indicates that users attach great importance to others' suggestions while making a decision on HIS adoption. Thus, the strategy of word-of-mouth marketing would be effective for promotion. For example, providers should pay close attention to what is being said about their HISs in a social network service (SNSs) like Facebook and Twitter, especially negative comments. Meanwhile, they should consider facilitating conditions such as whether there exist sufficient resources supporting their HISs. In other words, the systems should be compatible with existing devices and follow existing international standard like Health Level Seven (HL7). Secondly, the impact of cost-effect on the privacy-enhanced HIS is different from traditional systems; ease of use has no directly impacts on user intention, but affects it indirectly by increasing perceived usefulness. The means performance expectancy might be the mediator variable between effort expectancy and user adoption; the user-friendly interface is not the guarantee of user adoption unless this HIS can improve their healthcare efficiency.

This study addresses on users' information security literacy (ISL) and users' perception of system security (PSY). The mean value of PSY is about 4.23, showing that our experimental HIS receives positive belief of security protection. Our system structure modules could give practitioners insides for developing similar privacy-enhanced HISs. The path analyses show that the increase of PSY could directly enhance intention of HIS adoption; ISL has no direct effects on adoption, but affects it indirectly through PSY, showing that PSY builds the relation between ISL and adoption. That means people with higher ISL would not generate more intention toward adopting HISs unless they are aware of well security protection. Besides, PSY also facilitates the belief of performance expectancy, which is one of the key factors for HIS adoption. In short, providers should endeavor to increase PSY and then make significant enhancement of performance expectancy and user adoption.

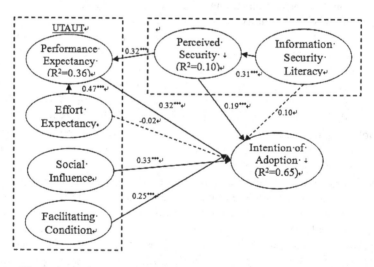

Fig. 3. Analysis results (Note: *:p<0.05; **:p<0.01; ***:p<0.001)

5   Conclusions

This study proposes several implications for research and practice. For academic researchers, this article extends UTAUT to user adoption of privacy-enhanced HISs by integrating the perspectives of perceived security and information security literacy, and the proposed model explains 65 percent of observed variance. Secondly, we find performance expectancy is a key moderator between effort expectancy and user adoption of privacy-enhanced HISs. Besides, perceived security plays an important role that could encourage user adoption as well as increase performance expectancy; security literacy affects user adoption indirectly by increasing the awareness of perceived security. For service providers, this article proposes a framework for a privacy-enhanced HIS and receives positive reactions in the experiment. The functionality of privacy protection, i.e. secure transmission module, privacy protection module, and access control module could give a reference for practitioners to design privacy-enhanced health systems. In practice, practitioners should take account of word-of-mouth effects and whether their systems are compatible with mostly medical testing equipment. There still exists a few limitations should be noted. The implications are suggested on the basis of an experimental study, so caution must be taken while generalizing to other types of systems. The suggestion is based on the 315 participants in the experiment, who are youths with well computer-skill and health-related knowledge; it needs further research if the decision maker of IT in a family is not a young man. Lastly, we take a short-term experiment for convenient and long-term observation can be reserved for further study.

References

1. McKelvey, V.: Spending More on In-Home Care (2010),
   http://www.aarp.org/relationships/caregiving/
   info-01-2010/spending-more-on-in-home-care.html
2. Häyrinen, K., Saranto, K., Nykänen, P.: Definition, structure, content, use and impacts of electronic health records: A review of the research literature. International Journal of Medical Informatics 77(5), 291–304 (2008)
3. Poissant, L., et al.: The Impact of Electronic Health Records on Time Efficiency of Physicians and Nurses: A Systematic Review. Journal of the American Medical Informatics Association 12(5), 505–516 (2005)
4. Williams, F., Boren, S.A.: The role of electronic medical record in care delivery in developing countries. International Journal of Information Management 28(6), 503–507 (2008)
5. Vishwanath, A., Singh, S.R., Winkelstein, P.: The impact of electronic medical record systems on outpatient workflows: A longitudinal evaluation of its workflow effects. International Journal of Medical Informatics 79(11), 778–791 (2010)
6. Sokratis, K.: Health care management and information systems security: awareness, training or education. International Journal of Medical Informatics 60(2), 129–135 (2000)
7. Shin, D.: Understanding purchasing behaviors in virtual economy: Consumer behavior of virtual currency in Web2.0 communities. Interacting with Computers 20(4), 433–446 (2008)
8. Venkatesh, V., et al.: User acceptance of information technology: Toward a unified view. MIS Quarterly 27(3), 425–478 (2003)
9. Zhou, T., Lu, Y., Wang, B.: Integrating TTF and UTAUT to explain mobile banking user adoption. Computers in Human Behavior 26(4), 760–767 (2010)

10. Davis, F.D.: Perceived usefulness, perceived ease of use, and user acceptance of information technology. MIS Quarterly 13(3), 319–339 (1989)
11. Pai, J.C., Tu, F.M.: The acceptance and use of customer relationship management (CRM) systems: An empirical study of distribution service industry in Taiwan. Expert Systems with Applications 38(1), 579–584 (2011)
12. Premkumar, G., Bhattacherjee, A.: Explaining information technology usage: a test of competing models. Omega: International Journal of Management Science 36, 64–75 (2008)
13. Park, C.W., Lessing, V.P.: Students and housewives: differences in susceptibility to reference group influence. Journal of Consumer Research 4(2), 102–110 (1977)
14. Karahanna, E., Straub, D.W., Chervany, N.L.: Information technology adoption across time: across-sectional comparison of pre-adoption and post-adoption beliefs. MIS Quarterly 23(2), 183–213 (1999)
15. Lewis, W., Agarwal, R., Sambamurthy, V.: Sources of influence on beliefs about information technology use: An empirical study of knowledge workers. MIS Quarterly 27(4), 657–678 (2003)
16. Taylor, S., Todd, P.A.: Understanding information technology usage: A test of competing models. Information Systems Research 6(2), 144–176 (1995)
17. Corey, M.A., Agarwal, R.: Adoption of Electronic Health Records in the Presence of Privacy Concerns: The Elaboration Likelihood Model and Individual Persuasion. MIS Quarterly 33(2), 339–370 (2009)
18. Dewan, S., Chen, L.: Mobile payment adoption in the US: A cross-industry cross-platform solution. Journal of Information Privacy and Security 1(2), 4–28 (2005)
19. Lwin, M., Wirtz, J., Williams, J.D.: Consumer online privacy concerns and responses: a power-responsibility equilibrium perspective. Journal of the Academy of Marketing Science 35(4), 572–585 (2007)
20. Shin, D.: Towards an understanding of the consumer acceptance of mobile wallet. Computers in Human Behavior 25(6), 1343–1354 (2009)
21. Wilson, M., Stine, K., Bowen, P.: National Institute of Standards and Technology (NIST) Special Publication 800-16: "Information Technology Security Training Requirements: A Role- and Performance-Based Model (Draft)" (2009),
   http://csrc.nist.gov/publications/drafts/800-16-rev1/Draft-SP800-16-Rev1.pdf
22. Lin, I.L., Liu, M.D.: An Investigation of High School Teachers' Cyber Security Literacy in Taiwan. In: Taiwan Academic Network Conference (TANET 2007) (2007)
23. ISO/IEC-9798-3, Information technology—Security techniques—Entity authentication mechanisms; Part 3; Entity authentication using a public key algorithm in International Organization for Standardization (1993)
24. Ming, Y., Shen, X., Peng, Y.: Identity-Based Sanitizable Signature Scheme in the Standard Model. Communications in Computer and Information Science 105, 9–16 (2010)
25. Ferraiolo, D.F., Kuhn, D.R.: Role Based Access Control. In: 15th National Computer Security Conference, pp. 554–563 (1992)
26. Nunnally, J.C.: Psychometric Theory, 2nd edn. McGrawHill, New York (1978)
27. Fornell, C., Larcker, D.F.: Evaluating structural equation models with unobservable variables and measurement error. Journal of Marketing Research 18(1), 39–50 (1981)

Application of Human Error Identification (HEI) Techniques to Cognitive Rehabilitation in Stroke Patients with Limb Apraxia

Charmayne M.L. Hughes[1], Chris Baber[2], Marta Bienkiewicz[1], and Joachim Hermsdörfer[1]

[1] Institute of Movement Science, Department of Sport and Health Science, Technical University of Munich, 80992 Munich, Germany
{charmayne.hughes,marta.bienkiewicz,joachim.hermsdoerfer}@tum.de
[2] Electrical, Electronic and Computing Engineering, The University of Birmingham, Birmingham, B15 2TT, U.K.
C.BABER@bham.ac.uk

Abstract. The aim of this study was to consider the potential uses of human error identification (HEI) techniques in the development of a Personal Healthcare System (PHS) capable of delivering cognitive rehabilitation of activities of daily living (ADL) for stroke patients with limb apraxia (i.e., CogWatch). HEI techniques were able to predict a number of apraxic errors, as well as the associated consequences. The results of the present study indicate that HEI analysis is a useful tool in the design of cognitive systems that seek to reduce or eliminate errors in apraxic populations. The results will be implemented in the Cog-Watch system and will be used to develop error reduction strategies that prevent errors from occurring, and to provide post-error feedback to help the user correct their actions.

Keywords: Human error identification, apraxia, activities of daily living.

1 Introduction

After a stroke incident as many as 24% of patients suffer from persistent impairments of limb apraxia [1], a cognitive-motor deficit characterized by impairment in the performance of skilled movement, which is operationally defined as a neurological disorder of learned purposive movement skill that is not explained by deficits of elementary motor or sensory systems [2]. Apraxia is frequently caused by relatively large lesions in the territory of the left middle cerebral artery (MCA), resulting in plegia of the contralateral right hand. In the case of right hand plegia, the patient has the use of only the ipsilateral left hand. Further, apraxia does not only affect the side of the body opposite to the cerebral lesion (contralateral limb), but also the ipsilateral side.

In general, research has demonstrated that patients with apraxia have difficulty performing many activities of daily living, often committing errors during action

C. Stephanidis and M. Antona (Eds.): UAHCI/HCII 2013, Part III, LNCS 8011, pp. 463–471, 2013.
© Springer-Verlag Berlin Heidelberg 2013

planning and execution [3-5]. For example, patients will often omit an action (e.g., turn on the coffee maker without having inserted water) or use an inappropriate object (using a knife to stir the tea) during the performance of ADL [6-7]. Several case studies have shown that some error types are more frequent than others [8-12]. For example, patients with left [6] and right hemisphere stroke [11] generally omit more steps and make more sequence errors during ADL performance. By comparison, addition errors, perseveration errors, quality or spatial errors, and semantic errors are less frequently observed than the more prominent errors.

1.1   Applying Human Error Identification (HEI) to Cognitive Rehabilitation Systems

Approaches to Human Error Identification (HEI) range from the generic taxonomies to task-specific failure mode approaches to probabilistic/fault-tree approaches. In Human Factors, perhaps the best known generic taxonomy is Reason's [13] Generic Error Modeling System (GEMS) which considers human error in terms of varieties of slips, lapses and mistakes. GEMS is based on a combination of diary study and accident review and provides a convenient means of classifying error at a high level. A potential problem with applying high-level descriptors of error is that this does not readily lend itself to the design of specific tasks or products; working at a generic level means that one is often left with guidance which is generic and not specific to the design under consideration. Consequently, task-based approaches consider the manner in which specific tasks could 'fail'. In his review of Human Error Identification techniques, Kirwan [14] identified two approaches which follow the broad approach of Failure Mode analysis, i.e., identify the ways in which a given product (or task) is likely to fail, which satisfy the criteria he laid out for a good HEI technique. These approaches were SHERPA (Systematic Human Error Reduction and Prediction Approach) [15], and PHECA (Predictive Human Error Cause Analysis) [16]. Finally, probabilistic approaches, such as HEART [17] seek to define the likelihood of an error occurring given combinations of Performance Shaping Factors.

The purpose of the present study was to ascertain the potential uses of human error identification (HEI) techniques in the development of a Personal Healthcare System (PHS) capable of delivering personalized cognitive rehabilitation of ADL for stroke patients (i.e., CogWatch). For the purposes of this paper, we apply a form of SHERPA to the tasks derived from a Hierarchical Task Analysis. The assumption behind SHERPA (and related forms of failure mode analysis of human error) is that each task a person performs can either result in the desired outcome or can fail in some categorizable manner. Thus, for example, if the goal is to 'pick up a cup' then SHERPA codes the potential failure modes in terms of actions which could be performed on the wrong object (so the person picks up a different object) or wrong actions on the right object (so the person performs another action with the cup, such as push it over) or the actions are not completed (so the person grasps the cup but does not lift it). It is important to note that SHERPA's categorization is agnostic as to the causes of these failures; it is only concerned with categorizing likely ways in which a particular goal is not achieved. In terms of reliability and sensitivity of techniques like SHERPA, Baber and Stanton [18] found an inter-rater reliability of 90%, a validity of 0.8 (with the observation that failure mode approaches tend to have a high 'false alarm' rate, i.e., to over-predict errors which might not be observed).

2   Procedure

2.1   Participants

Sixteen patients with limb apraxia resulting from lesions following a single cerebro-vascular accident (CVA) who also showed clear signs of apraxia in clinical tests (mean age = 55.13 y, SD = 12.65, 3 left-handed, 13 right-handed, 8 men, 8 women) were examined. Seven patients suffered a right hemisphere lesion which resulted in right hand hemiparesis and were able to perform the task with only the left hand. The remaining nine patients were able to use both hands to perform the task. Sixteen neurologically healthy individuals (mean age = 46.13 y, SD = 14.34, 3 left-handed, 13 right-handed, 8 men, 8 women) served as control participants.

2.2   Apparatus and Procedure

Participants sat at a table with a dimension of 100 cm x 60 cm. There were a total of 14 objects located on the work surface. Each participant was asked to perform a 2 cup tea-making task, in which one cup of tea required milk and two sweetener tablets, and the other cup of tea required a slice of lemon and one sugar cube. Subjects were informed that all the things required to make the tea are on the table, and that they were to inform the experimenter if they required help stabilizing an object. Two trials were performed. Actions were recorded by a video camera (Panasonic HDC-SD909) located 45° to the right side of the table.

2.3   Hierarchical Task Analysis

The first step in a HEI analysis is to obtain an appropriate HTA for the task. The HTA was drawn up by the lead author, and reviewed by the second author as well as two researchers from the Technical University of Munich. The root of the tree is referred to as the task end-goal. In this study the task end-goal was to make two cups of tea (cup1 required milk and 2 sweetener tablets, cup2 required a slice of lemon and 1 sugar cube). The actions required to complete this task (i.e., sub-goals) are shown in the second level of the hierarchy.

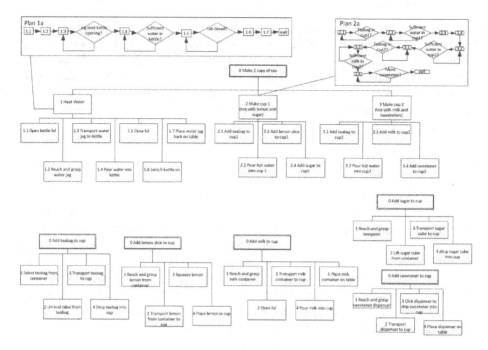

Fig. 1. Hierarchical task analysis (HTA) for the 2 cup tea-making task

2.4   Human Error Analysis

In order to conduct the error analysis it was necessary to develop an error production table for the two tea-making task. The table contained information regarding the sub-goal in which the error was made. The error analysis was not influenced by task inter-leaving, thus the HTA described in the previous section could be divided into three sub- goal levels (heat water, make cup1, make cup 2). We also classified errors based on severity. Level 1 refers to errors that are recoverable, such as not pouring enough hot water into cup1. Level 2 refers to errors that prevent the participant from success-fully completing the task (e.g., adding coffee to cup1). Level 3 refers to recoverable errors that result in potential harm to the participant (e.g., switching the kettle on be-fore pouring water into the kettle). Lastly, Level 4 errors are those that prevent the participant from successfully completing the task and also result in potential harm to the participant (e.g., dropping the kettle when moving it to position over cup1).

The error analysis prediction table (Table 1) was designed by the lead author, and reviewed by another researcher with apraxia error experience. Inter-rater reliability was calculated separately for potential errors, error severity, and sub-goal. The mean percent agreement was 93% (range 90-97%).

There were a total of 54 identified possible errors that could be executed. Potential errors were categorized based on sub-goal and severity (Figure 2A and 2B, black bars). It was predicted that 24% of errors would occur in the heat water sub-task, 38% in the make cup1 sub-task, and 44% in the make cup2 sub-task. When errors were categorized by error severity, it was predicted that 16% would be level 1 errors, 68% would be level 2 errors, 10% would be level 3 errors, and 14% would be level 4 errors. The table also contained a description of each error and error classification. Because it was not feasible to use standard HEI error classification systems to classify errors in the tea making task, errors of action were classified in 12 categories based on previous apraxia literature [7].

Table 1. Summary of action errors typically committed by apraxia patients, and the predicted and observed errors

Error Type	Definitions	Example
Sequence addition	Adding an extra component action that is not required in the action sequence	Adding instant coffee to cup2
Sequence anticipation	Performing a subtask earlier than usual	Turning the kettle on before pouring water into the kettle
Sequence omission	An action sequence in which one subtask is not performed	Turning on the kettle on without having inserted water
Sequence	Performing a subtask much later than usual	Switch kettle on after preparing both cups of tea
Ingredient omission	Failing to add an ingredient required to complete the task goal	Failing to put sugar into cup1
Ingredient substitution	An intended action carried out with an unintended ingredient	Pouring coffee grounds instead of sugar into cup2
Object substitution	An intended action carried out with an unintended object	Pour heated water into non-cup object
Execution	An error in the execution of the task	Dropping a cup onto the table
Misestimation	Using grossly too much or too little of some substance	Pouring half of the milk jug contents into cup2
Mislocation	An action that is appropriate to the object, but is performed in the wrong place	Pouring some liquid from the bottle onto the table rather than into the glass
Quality	The action was carried out, but in an inappropriate way	Putting the tea bag and the paper label into a cup
Perseveration	The unintentional repetition of a step or subtask	Adding more than one sugar cup to cup2

2.5   Consequence Analysis

Based on the possible errors developed in the previous section, it was possible to predict the consequences for each of the identified errors. For example, if the participant switched the kettle on without adding water (error) this would burn out the element in the kettle (consequence). The list of potential consequences was developed by the first author, and reviewed by a trained assistant. The level of rater agreement was 97%.

3   Results

3.1   Activity Sampling

To ascertain how apraxic patients and healthy controls perform the 2 cup tea-making task two individuals (lead author and a trained assistant) scored the recorded videos separately with respect to the sub-goals in Figure 1. Inter-rater agreement was 95.4%. Activity sampling provides an opportunity to describe alternative ways in which sub-goals can be sequenced. For ease of reading, specific information regarding plans have been omitted from the HTA diagram. That said, in general it was observed that control participants performed the sub-goal "heat water" using varying plans, whereas the apraxia patients always used the same plan. For the sub-goal "make tea" there was no clear preference for an action sequence plan for either control participants and for apraxia patients. Furthermore, there was a distinct difference in "make tea" plans between the groups, such that control participants preferred one set of action plans, whereas the apraxia patients preferred another set. Lastly, and perhaps most interestingly, both control and apraxic individuals used a different action plan for the first and second trial for the sub-goal "make tea."

3.2   Human Error Analysis

Analysis indicated that control participants successfully completed the task in 88% of trials. There were four errors committed, which was comprised of two ingredient substitution (adding sugar cubes instead of sweetener to cup2), and two ingredient omission errors (failing to add milk to cup2). In contrast, apraxia patients committed errors in 57.1% of trials, with a total of 50 errors recorded. The number of errors per trials ranged from 0 - 7 (mean = 2.84, SD = 2.0). Table 2 presents a summary of the HEI error analysis, restricted to errors which were observed on more than two occasions (due to the large number of possible errors that were committed).

The most frequently occurring error was that of ingredient omission (30% of errors), with patients typically failing to put tea bags into one or both cups, or adding one or both sweetener tablets to cup2. There were also a number of trials in which apraxia patients placed too much of too little of an ingredient into either cup (misestimation = 20%), omitted a step in the action sequence (sequence omission = 16%), or substituted an unnecessary ingredient for a necessary one (ingredient substitution = 16%). There was a small number for sequence addition (6%), quality (4%), execution (4%), sequence anticipation (2%) and sequence (2%) errors. Lastly, we did not observe any mislocation or perseveration errors.

Errors were also categorized based on sub-goal and severity. Analysis indicated that the number of errors produced by apraxia patients was higher for the "make cup2" (42%) and the "make cup1" (34%) sub-tasks, compared to the "heat water" sub-task (24%). When errors were classified by error severity, it was evident that the vast majority of errors (82%) resulted in a fatal error that prevented the successful completion of the task (level 2). There were also a small number of trials involving level 1 (recoverable error: 10%) and level 4 (fatal error that also resulted in potential harm to the user: 8%). There were no recoverable errors that resulted in potential harm to the participant (level 3).

Table 2. Outcome of human error analysis

Task Step	Error Category	Description	Consequence	Error Severity	# trials
1	SO	Fail to put water into kettle	Unable to heat water	4	3
	Q	Not waiting for water to boil	Water will not be hot enough to infuse tea ingredients	2	2
1.4	ME	Not pouring enough water into kettle	Unable to make 2 full cups of tea	1	3
2.1	IO	Fail to add teabag into cup1	Required ingredient not added	2	3
	IS	Add coffee instead of tea bag into cup1	Required ingredient not added, Incorrect ingredient added, tea will have incorrect taste	2	4
2.2	SO	Did not pour water into cup1	Incorrect ingredient added, unable to make a cup of tea	2	2
2.3	ME	Add more than one sugar cube	Incorrect ingredient added, tea will have incorrect taste	2	2
2.4	IO	Fail to add lemon to cup1	Required ingredient not added	2	4
3.1	IO	Fail to add teabag into cup2	Required ingredient not added	2	3
	IS	Add coffee instead of tea bag	Required ingredient not added, Incorrect ingredient added, tea will have incorrect taste	2	2
3.2	ME	Not pouring enough water into cup2	A full cup of tea will not be made	2	2
3.3	IO	Fail to add milk to cup2	Required ingredient not added	2	2
3.4	IO	Fail to add sweetener to cup2	Required ingredient not added	2	3
	IS	Add sugar instead of sweetener	Incorrect ingredient added, Required ingredient not added,	2	2
	EX	Drop sweetener tablet outside of cup2	Required ingredient not added, possible ingredient contamination	1	2

The observed errors were then compared to those predicted. That analysis revealed that HEI analysis successfully predicted 24 of the 26 observed errors. In our predictions we classified the act of adding coffee into cup1 or cup2 as an addition error (i.e., adding coffee *and* a tea bag), but did not consider the possibility that an individual would add coffee *instead* of a tea bag (ingredient substitution error). We also failed to include the "not waiting for the water to boil before pouring water" error (quality error). However, as is often the case in HEI, there were a number of predicted errors that were not observed (44%) in these trials. In contrast to our expectations, apraxic patients did not commit mislocation (e.g., pouring milk into water jug instead of cup1) or perseveration errors (repeatedly performing the pour water into the kettle sub-task).

3.3   Consequence Analysis

The HEI technique was particularly useful when the predicted consequences were compared with what was actually observed. With the exception of one error and its associated consequence (switch kettle on an incorrect time which leads to the burn out of the element), all consequences were observed after their respective error occurred (96.1% successful prediction).

3.4   Error Reduction Strategies

Based on the obtained results it was possible to generate a list of possible error reduction strategies that could implemented in a cognitive rehabilitation system in order to reduce or prevent errors in apraxic populations. These strategies were divided into *prospective* and *feedback*. Prospective strategies include verbal and visual spatio-temporal cues (via simulated avatars) that indicate the next most probable action sequence of the task. Feedback strategies include auditory messages generated by the CogWatch virtual task execution (VTE) module, and vibration signals (constant and pulsed) delivered through the CogWatch wrist device. The strength and the content of the feedback warning signal will depend on the error severity of the error committed.

4   Conclusions

In summary, the results of the present study indicate that HEI analysis is a useful tool in the design of cognitive systems that seek to reduce or eliminate errors in apraxic populations. HEI techniques were able to predict a number of apraxic errors, as well as the associated consequences. The apraxia results are to be implemented in the CogWatch system and will be used to develop error reduction strategies that prevent errors from occurring, and to provide post-error feedback to help the user correct their actions. The observed probabilities associated with action sequencing and error analysis will be integrated into the CogWatch action recognition task models.

Acknowledgments. The authors wish to thank Georg Goldenberg for access to patients, Saskia Steinl and Rhoia Neidenbach for help with data collection, Alexander Matschl for data analysis, and CogWatch cooperation partners for their insightful comments. This study was supported by a grant from the European Commission (FP7-ICT-2011-288912).

References

1. Bickerton, W., Riddoch, M.J., Samson, D., Balani, A., Mistry, B., Humphreys, G.W.: Systematic assessment of apraxia and functional predictions from the Birmingham Cognitive Screen. Journal of Neurology, Neurosurgery, and Psychiatry 83, 513–521 (2012)
2. Rothi, L.J.G., Heilman, K.M.: Apraxia: The Neuropsychology of Action. Psychology Press, East Sussex (1997)
3. Buxbaum, L.J., Schwartz, M.F., Montgomery, M.W.: Ideational apraxia and naturalistic action. Cognitive Neuropsychology 15, 617–643 (1998)
4. De Renzi, E.: Apraxia. In: Boller, F., Grafman, J. (eds.) Handbook of Neuropsychology, Amsterdam, pp. 245–263. Elsevier, New York (1989)
5. Buxbaum, L.J., Schwartz, M.F., Montgomery, M.W.: Ideational apraxia and naturalistic action. Cognitive Neuropsychology 15, 617–643 (1998)
6. Schwartz, M.F., Montgomery, M.W., Buxbaum, L.J., Lee, S.S., Carew, T.G., Coslett, H.B., Ferraro, M., Fitzpatrick-DeSalme, E., Hart, T., Mayer, N.: Naturalistic action impairment in closed head injury. Neuropsychology 12, 13–28 (1998)
7. Schwartz, M.F., Reed, E.S., Montgomery, M., Palmer, C., Mayer, N.H.: The Quantitative Description of Action Disorganization After Brain-Damage - A Case-Study. Cognitive Neuropsychology 8, 381–414 (1991)
8. Humphreys, G.W., Forde, E.M.E.: Disordered action schema and action disorganisation syndrome. Cognitive Neuropsychology 15, 771–811 (1998)
9. Morady, K., Humphreys, G.: Multiple task demands in action disorganization syndrome. Neurocase 17, 461–472 (2011)
10. Schwartz, M.F.: Re-examining the role of executive functions in routine action production. Structure and Functions of the Human Prefrontal Cortex 769, 321–335 (1995)
11. Schwartz, M.F., Buxbaum, L.J., Montgomery, M.W., Fitzpatrick-DeSalme, E., Hart, T., Ferraro, M., Lee, S.S., Coslett, H.B.: Naturalistic action production following right hemisphere stroke. Neuropsychologia 37, 51–66 (1999)
12. Schwartz, M.F., Montgomery, M.W., Fitzpatrick-desalme, E.J., Ochipa, C., Coslett, H.B., Mayer, N.H.: Analysis of a disorder of everyday action. Cognitive Neuropsychology 12, 863–892 (1995)
13. Reason, J.T.: Human Error. Cambridge University Press, New York (1990)
14. Kirwan, B.: Human error identification in human reliability assessment. Part 1: overview of approaches. Applied Ergonomics 23, 299–318 (1992)
15. Embrey, D.: SHERPA: a systematic human error reduction and prediction approach. In: Proceedings of the International Topical Meeting on Advances in Human Factors in Nuclear Power Systems, Knoxville, Tennessee (1986)
16. Whalley, S.P.: Minimising the cause of human error. In: Proceedings of the 10th Advances in Reliability Symposium. Elsevier, Amsterdam (1988)
17. Williams, J.C.: HEART: a proposed method for assessing and reducing human error, Birmingham. Presented at 9th Advances in Reliability Technology Symposium, Birmingham (1986)
18. Baber, C., Stanton, N.A.: Human error identification techniques applied to public technology: predictions compared with observed use. Applied Ergonomics 27, 119–131 (1996)

Facilitators and Barriers to Patients' Engagements with Personal Health Records: Systematic Review

Abdulrahman Jabour and Josette F. Jones

Health Informatics Department, Indiana University-Purdue University Indianapolis, USA
ajabour@imail.iu.edu, jofjones@iupui.edu

Abstract. The purpose of this paper is to identify the facilitators and barriers to patents' engagement with Personal Health Records (PHR). We performed systematic review searching Pub Med, IEEE, and Google Scholar for studies published between January, 2001 to September, 2012. Among the 508 articles identified, 14 articles included in the result. We extracted the key study characteristics and categorized facilitators and barriers using the Technology Acceptance Model (TAM). In total, there were 10 barriers, and 6 facilitators identified. The 6 facilitators were related to both perceived usefulness and ease of use, where the barriers were mostly related to ease of use. Recruited participants were mostly older patients with chronic diseases. The result of this review indicates that patients in general recognize the value of PHR but they appear to have technical difficulties.

Keywords: Systematic review, Personal Health Records PHR, Patients' engagement, Facilitators and Barriers, PHR Design.

1 Introduction

Personal Health Records (PHR) have the potential to contribute to solving many common problems in the American health care system such as cost, fragmentation, safety, medical errors, and inequality [2],[3]. The communication capabilities that PHR provide can keep both patients and providers on track with the recommended health plan. It was identified as "the missing link needed to bridge the patient-provider health information gap"[4].

With PHR, patients will have the tools to be involved in their healthcare and be more responsible and conscious about their health condition [1]. They will have the freedom to seek or choose between health providers. They will also be able to continually monitor their health condition more closely as well as understand their medical history, current situation, and progress. PHR can assist in creating a more complete and balanced view of patient's status by giving patients the opportunity to enter or edit information like demographic data, medical history and other health data.

1.1 Users Engagement

Patient engagement is more than simply using a system. It is a process of active participation where users invest time and attention. Successful engagement strategy

C. Stephanidis and M. Antona (Eds.): UAHCI/HCII 2013, Part III, LNCS 8011, pp. 472–481, 2013.

needs to consider people, process and technology [5]. Aligning technology and process with users' preference and need will increase the chance of users' engagement [5]. The National e-Health Collaborative created a framework for patients' engagement. The framework consists of five major stages that can be used as a roadmap to assist healthcare organizations in their patient engagement process [23].

The framework specified the technology and process needed to inform and engage patients. But it is the developers' job to translate the framework into design. The designer's understanding of users' psychology and the interpretation of this understanding into the system development will determine the acceptance of the system.

1.2   Users' Centered Design

Many PHR models have been released and tested, but very few achieved the desired outcome. In many cases the technology of these systems is advanced and the required functionalities are available. However, the adoption rate is still below the expectation. User centered design is frequently discussed in healthcare information systems but rarely applied when it comes to patients [6]. Many PHR studies evaluated the system by incorporating designers', physicians' and health professionals' feedback where in many cases patient perspectives were neglected or underestimated [6]. Understanding the end users is a critical part for a system's usability where every patient's need should be addressed.

Where many of the previous studies discussed the barriers to PHR adoption, very few studies have evaluated the situation by incorporating both positive and negative factors [7]. Investigating both positive and negative factors will help us generate a more holistic view and understanding of the underlying causes. In this paper we will conduct a systematic literature review to identify the factors associated with PHR adoption. We will focus on how PHR is perceived by patients, and we will summarize and draw an overall view of the facilitators and barriers to PHR adoption in the previous studies.

2   Method

The searched databases utilized in this study were IEEE, PubMed, and Google Scholar. The search was conducted using combinations of "PHR" and "Perception" synonyms (Table 1). The search was limited to English language articles published from January, 2001 to December, 2012. Initially, the number of articles generated was 150, 262, and 150 from Google Scholar, Pubmed, and IEEE respectively. The total number of results retrieved by our keyword combination from PubMed was included in our primary result. Both Google Scholar and IEEE started to show irrelevant results by the 90s and 80s, and we included the first 150 to increase the sensitivity of our result. Then all the results were imported into an Excel spreadsheet and filtered to remove duplicated articles.

Table 1. Search keywords

Personal health record PHR synonyms	Attitude synonyms
Patient health records PHR	Behavior
Electronic patient record EPR	Acceptance
Personal Health Information Management System	Perceptions
Web-based patient-centered personal health record	Satisfaction
Computer-based Patient Record	

Two reviewers reviewed the title and abstract of the remaining 508 articles independently. In this step the inclusion/exclusion criteria applied were as follows:

- The included article has to be an original study, not a review.
- The included study has to use PHR as defined by Healthcare Information and Management Systems Society (HIMSS). HIMSS defined PHR as "a universally accessible, layperson comprehensible, lifelong tool for managing relevant health information, promoting health maintenance and assisting with chronic disease management via an interactive, common data set of electronic health information and ehealth tools. The ePHR is owned, managed, and shared by the individual or his or her legal proxy(s) and must be secure to protect the privacy and confidentiality of the health information it contains. It is not a legal record unless so defined and is subject to various legal limitations" [8].
- Studies have to discuss users' attitudes, behaviors, acceptance or satisfaction. Studies that focus on PHR design, technology or functionalities were excluded.
- Users have to be patients. Studies that recruited physicians, designers, or medical students as primary sources of data were excluded. The recruited patients also have to be system users. Prospective users or readiness assessment studies were excluded.
- Studies have to include quantitative data.

After merging the results from each reviewer, 40 articles remained. The full texts of the remaining articles were reviewed comprehensively During the review, 17 of the 40 articles were excluded due to one of the following reasons: full text was not in English, the study did not require participants to use the system, the study was system design focused, or the study focused on physicians and nurses.

For the remaining 23 articles, we applied 14 questions we developed for quality ranking. The list included questions about recruited participants, the system applied, and study design. The questions were yes or no questions where every question answered yes was weighted as one point. Then we set a cutoff point with 10 of 14 for quality ranking. Articles with10 points or below were excluded from the study for not meeting the quality requirements. At this step, 9 articles were excluded and 14 articles remained.

The remaining 14 articles were summarized and key information extracted (Table 2). We also extracted the facilitators and barriers used in these studies and grouped them into similar categories (Table 3).

Facilitators and barriers were categorized using the Technology Acceptance Model (TAM). This model was used to analyze users' attitudes toward information systems for the purpose of predicting their use. In this model, the influencing factors are grouped into two main categories, "perceived ease of use" and "perceived usefulness"(Figure 1).

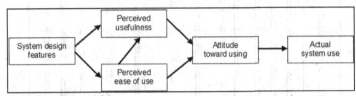

Source: Davis, et, al, (1989).

Fig. 1. Technology Acceptance Model (TAM)

3   Results and Discussion

The identified study characteristic of the 14 articles was participant related information (age, socioeconomic status, level of computer literacy, health condition), study related information (study design, system description, tethered capability), facilitators, barriers and outcome (Table 2).

One of the most relevant characteristics was the chronological condition of the diseases that participants had. Seven studies reported the condition as chronic, with two specified as diabetes and two cardiovascular diseases [9], [10], [15], [18]. Another frequent disease was HIV, with frequency of two [21], [22]. The majority of the recruited participants in most of the 14 studies included were elderly. As most participants were patients with chronic diseases, one explanation might be the association between chronic diseases and age. This could also be attributed to the clinical significance of PHR in managing chronic diseases that proportionally increase with age.

Other important characteristics were socioeconomic status and the level of computer literacy, which seem correlated. The level of computer literacy was reported in 9 of the 11 studies. The participants' socioeconomic status was reported in 10 of the 14 studies, 5 of which reported this level as low [9], [11], [12], [14], [22]. All 5 studies that reported low socioeconomic status also reported a low level of computer literacy [9], [11], [12], [14], [22]. Only 5 of the PHR systems used in the 14 studies were tethered [13], [15], [17], [20], [21]. In general, the systems supported most of the basic PHR functions such as entering, viewing, managing, and tracking health related information.

Table 2. Study Summary

Reference	Title	Participants age	Computer literacy	Socio-economic status
Kim 2010 [9]	Digital Divide: Use of Electronic Personal Health Record by Different Population Groups	site 1: mean of 63; site 2: mean of 47; site 3.	low in old patients at site 1 and 2 and higher in site 3.	(site 1) low income, (site 2) no data, (site 3) college students
De Clercq 2003 [10]	A consumer health record for supporting the patient-centered management of chronic diseases.	N/A	daily PC users. More computer literate than average	N/A
Lober 2006 [11]	Barriers to the use of a personal health record by an elderly population.	49 to 92 mean 69	low	low-income
Kim 2009 [12]	Challenges to using an electronic personal health record by a low-income elderly population.	mean 63	low	low-income
Nazi 2010 [13]	Veterans' voices: use of the American Customer Satisfaction Index (ACSI) Survey to identify My HealtheVet personal health record users' characteristics, needs, and preferences	>31	medium to high	N/A
Kim 2005 [14]	Evaluation of Patient Centered Electronic Health Record to Overcome Digital Divide	mean 65	low	low-income
Hess 2007 [15]	Exploring Challenges and Potentials of Personal Health Records in Diabetes Self-Management: Implementation and Initial Assessment	mean 55	N/A	majority have at least some college
Weitzman 2010 [16]	Sharing Medical Data For Health Research: The Early Personal Health Record Experience	groups mean 45 & 71.	N/A	high levels of education and moderately high levels of income
Yamin 2011 [17]	The Digital Divide in Adoption and Use of a Personal Health Record	>18	N/A	varied widely
Karsh 2011 [18]	Factors affecting home care patients' acceptance of a web-based interactive self-management technology	mean 62	varied	varied widely
Denton 2001 [19]	Will Patients Use Electronic Personal Health Records? Responses from a Real-Life Experience	35 to 85	N/A	N/A
Tom 2012 [20]	Integrated Personal Health Record Use: Association With Parent-Reported Care Experiences	mean 36	N/A	at least college degree
Hilton 2012 [21]	A Cross-Sectional Study of Barriers to Personal Health Record Use among Patients Attending a Safety-Net Clinic	mean 46	Medium 29%; high 51%	N/A
Luque 2012 [22]	Bridging the Digital Divide in HIV Care: A Pilot Study of an iPod Personal Health Record	mean 48	low	mostly low educational level, and low income

Table 2. (*continued*)

Health condition/disease	Study Design	PHR description	Tethcard	Barriers
Site 1 mostly chronic; Site 2 Cardiovascular; Site 3 mostly Diabetes	survey and usage activities	collect, and manage health information as well as enhancing communication	No	1- low computer literacy)
Diabetes	survey and usage activities	web-based system to enter, view and edit the information.	No	1-patients didn't fill some of the information where they didn't see the advantage of doing so.
Chronic diseases	patients observation and monitoring usage activities	organize self-reported patient histories, and facilitate referral management.	No	1-Computer literacy, 2- computer anxiety, 3- cognitive barriers that limited their ability to use the computer,4- difficulty in memorizing password, user name or the PHIMS URL, 5-Health literacy (i.e. diseases and conditions, medications, terminology), 6- physical limitations of the upper extremities and; 7- other conditions like hearing and vision impairments.
Chronic diseases	survey and usage activities	enter and manage health information	No	1- digital divide includes a technical divide based on the availability of ICT infrastructure, hardware and software, 2- social divide resulting from the skills required to manipulate and utilize technical resources , 3- fear over computers and the Internet 4- health information understanding related barriers. 4- limited physical/cognitive abilities.
N/A	survey	complete traditional services and improve managed care	Yes	1- One time in Person Authentication (IPA) at local VA facility required to access all features. 2- Many users not familiar with authentication process. 3- Must have internet access. 4- Computer literacy a problem. 5- Secure messaging only available for a limited number of participants (not everyone who has taken the time to complete the IPA has access to everything) 6- Not everyone who used the system was invited to participate in feedback 7- Navigation was difficult. 8- Medication information not available to users
N/A	survey and monitored activities	store and retrive demographic and clinical data	No	1- Residents need access to Internet to use Personal Health Information Management System (PHIMS)
Diabetes	focus groups and mentoring communication activities	centralized information about diabetes management, report BS readings, appointment reminders	Yes	1- Lost or unknown user names and passwords. 2- Patients unaware of the features of UPMC Health Track such as glucose tracking. 3- Conclusion noted that "Simply placing resources within an environment is inadequate to stimulate patient use"
N/A	exit surveys; structured protocol from PCHR usability testers; focus groups monitored usage	login view their information	No	1- only contains views of a regionally sampled, nonrepresentative set of subjects and a specific form of health record
Disease varies	survey, phone interviews	access medications lists, lab results, appointment information and communicate with providers	Yes	1- Racial/minority patients adopted a PHR less frequently than whites 2- "Living with a chronic disease is associated with decreases in Internet access rate by 50%" 3- Patients had to register for PHR on website and activate their account online
Cardiovascular disease	survey, phone interviews		No	N/A
Spine disorders	survey		No	N/A
Chronic diseases	survey	record viewing, secure messages, medication management, and appointment management	yes	1- no time, 2- forgot login password, 3- access, 4- did not knew about it, 5- did not have computer device, 6- difficult to use.
HIV	survey	populate selected data from EMR	yes	N/A
HIV	self-rated questionnaire	IPod device with PHR application allow store, and retrieve, medical information and allow reminders for appointments and medication.	no	not specified

Table 2. (*continued*)

Facilitators	Outcome
1- assistance were available	The study find that younger individuals used the PHR system without any difficulty compare to elderly participants.
1- system was updated with layout that could differentiate between fields or parts that required by patients or physicians (as users requested). 2- The screens were designed on the basis of existing forms that were regularly discussed with the patients.	The development of such patient-centered health records is crucial for improving the patient's self-awareness regarding managing chronic diseases.
1- PowerPoint slides to explain the system. 2- Displaying posters and flyers to promote participation. 3- Assistance made available.	Elderly and disabled residents of the EHA were able to create and maintain a PHR when assistance were available.
1- Informational sessions to explain what the PHIMS was and to demonstrate how to use it.	The majority of the low-income elderly would not be in a position to benefit from PHR.
1- The ability to delegate access to all or selected parts of the PHR. 2- New features are released often 3- Secure messaging available for some users. 4- Site redesign was planned for 2009 to make navigation easier 5- Program will continue to focus on meeting the needs of all users by ensuring compatibility with dial-up access 6- Ability to view and/or manage appointments was added. 7- Local education and training initiatives have been deployed at many VA facilities to address the need for computer literacy.	identified priority areas for improvement and provides important information about users' characteristics, preferences, and needs
1- Public computers 2- Internet access. 3- Graduate Nursing students available to assist participant. 3- support printing and saving on CD, USB drive 4- system response timings were modified.	the system positively influenced their ability to manage health records and created more awareness about their health
1- Links to information about diabetes. 2- Communication with office practice.	PHR has potential to improve chronic disease management and to link pt to physician office
1- health demonstration	clear advantages to exploring use of PCHRs as a vehicle for collecting health information germane to public health research
N/A	patients with chronic diseases were 25% more likely to adopt PHR than those without. Racial digital divide exists
1- free computers; 2- training from visiting nurses.	Perceived usefulness, perceived ease of use; subjective norms and, healthcare knowledge predict most of the variance in patients' acceptance and use of the system
1- Made free and available to all patients in practice.	30% of patients with spinal conditions will express interest in obtaining EPHRs
N/A	Parents were willing to use PHR for their children.
1- training	Mental health condition and substance abuse were not barriers to patients use of PHR.
1- Participants provided with IPod devices, 2- two PHR apps were piloted to chose the easiest one, 3- one to one training sessions, 4- disease management classes.	PHR was generally accepted by users.

3.1   Facilitators and Barriers

The main purpose of this review is to better understand patients' attitudes toward PHR as well as investigating the facilitators and barriers applied in previous studies. This review did not directly include PHR design studies, but it includes deeper understanding of user characteristics and preferences. Users' understanding is the first step for designing a user centered system. Studies indicated that most of the available PHR did not incorporate users' perspectives [6]. Vendors', physicians', and designers' input is definitely important, but they have different levels of computer skills and health understanding than patients [6].

In this study, we identified the variables that may influence patients' acceptance of PHR. The identified barriers and facilitators along with the frequency of each were presented in Table 3. The conceptual framework TAM was used to synthesize the facilitators' and barriers' findings. This model infers that user acceptance of technology can be predicted by the perceived usefulness and ease of use. In total there were 10 barriers and 6 facilitators identified. By categorizing the facilitators and barriers into perceived usefulness and ease of use, we found that 10 barriers and 4 facilitators were related to ease of use, and 1 barrier and 4 facilitators were related to the perceived usefulness (Table 3).

Table 3. Barriers and facilitators categories

Barriers	Frequency	Perceived usefulness	Perceived ease of use
Physical limitation (like upper extremities impairment)	2		x
Health Condition (vision, hearing,)	2		x
Not Knowing about the system or some of the system features	5	x	x
Access (username, password, URL, account registration, and activation)	5		x
Computer literacy	4		x
Social Divide	2		x
Digital divide	4		x
Computer anxiety	2		x
Cognitive barriers	1		x
Health literacy	2		x
Facilitators	**Frequency**	**Perceived usefulness**	**Perceived ease of use**
Promotional adds	2	x	
System modification to user preference	3	x	x
Training and education	6	x	x
Staff assistance	4		x
Communication features	2	x	
Providing free devices	1		x

The most frequent barriers were; not knowing about the system (5) and access related barriers (5). Not knowing about the system included issues such as participants' unawareness of some of the available system functions or the inability to utilize them. Other frequent barriers were digital divide and computer literacy (4). Conversely, the most frequent facilitators were training sessions (6), staff assistance availability (4), and modifying system to user preference/need (3).

In our finding, only 4 of the 14 studies included system modification or selection to user preference. Three of them were modifying the system and adding features based on patient input, and one piloted two applications for patients to choose from. The first three studies were mainly concerned with providing patients with the features and functionalities they need whereas the last one was to find the easiest interface [10], [13], [14], [22].

As shown in Table 3, all barriers (except system feature awareness) were related to the perceived ease of use. Most of the barriers found were technical factors, such as difficulties in using the computer, certain applications, or Internet and unfamiliarity with computers or the technology in general. Generally, computer skill-related factors seem to be more common with elderly users. Younger or more educated groups tend to be more computer savvy than older or less educated users. Since the PHR use is mostly recommended for chronic disease management, those user groups are more likely to be older.

4   Conclusion

The purpose of this review was to better understand facilitators and barriers to PHR adoption. The result showed that patients in most studies are experiencing technical difficulties with PHR. However, no significant barriers were identified in their level of awareness of the system value and importance. They appear to be willing to accept and use PHR when they can.

References

1. Ball, M.J., Smith, N.C., Bakalar, R.S.: Personal Health Records: Empowering Consumers. Journal of Healthcare Information Management 21(1), 77 (2007) (print)
2. Hess, R., et al.: Exploring Challenges and Potentials of Personal Health Records in Diabetes Self-Management: Implementation and Initial Assessment. Telemedicine and e-Health 13(5), 509–518 (2007) (print)
3. Kim, E.H., et al.: Challenges to Using an Electronic Personal Health Record by a Low-Income Elderly Population. Journal of Medical Internet Research 11(4) (2009) (print)
4. Noblin, A.M., Wan, T.T., Fottler, M.: The Impact of Health Literacy on a Patient's Decision to Adopt a Personal Health Record. Perspectives in Health Information Management/AHIMA, American Health Information Management Association (Fall 9, 2012) (print)
5. Selig, G.J.: Implementing IT governance: a practical guide to global best practices in IT management. Van Haren Pub. (2008)
6. Rodriguez, M.M., Casper, G., Brennan, P.F.: Patient-Centered Design: The Potential of User-Centered Design in Personal Health Records. Journal-Ahima 78(4), 44 (2007) (print)

7. Tang, P.C., et al.: Personal Health Records: Definitions, Benefits, and Strategies for Overcoming Barriers to Adoption. Journal of the American Medical Informatics Association 13(2), 121–126 (2006) (print)
8. Healthcare Information and Management Systems Society. HIMSS' PHR, ePHR definition (June 25, 2009), at
   http://www.himss.org/ASP/topics_FocusDynamic.asp?faid=228
9. Digital Divide: Use of Electronic Personal Health Record by Different Population Groups. In: 2010 Annual International Conference of the IEEE Engineering in Medicine and Biology Society (EMBC). IEEE (2010) (print)
10. De Clercq, P., Hasman, A., Wolffenbuttel, B.: A Consumer Health Record for Supporting the Patient-Centered Management of Chronic Diseases. Informatics for Health and Social Care 28(2), 117–127 (2003) (print)
11. Lober, W.B., et al.: Barriers to the Use of a Personal Health Record by an Elderly Population. In: AMIA Annual Symposium Proceedings 2006, p. 514 (2006) (print)
12. Kim, E.H., et al.: Challenges to Using an Electronic Personal Health Record by a Low-Income Elderly Population. Journal of Medical Internet Research 11(4) (2009) (print)
13. Nazi, K.M.: Veterans ' Voices: Use of the American Customer Satisfaction Index (Acsi) Survey to Identify My Healthevet Personal Health Record Users' Characteristics, Needs, and Preferences. Journal of the American Medical Informatics Association 17(2), 203–211 (2010) (print)
14. Kim, E., et al.: Evaluation of Patient-Centered Electronic Health Record to Overcome Digital Divide. IEEE, 593–596 (2005) (print)
15. Hess, R., et al.: Exploring Challenges and Potentials of Personal Health Records in Diabetes Self-Management: Implementation and Initial Assessment. Telemedicine and e-Health 13(5), 509–518 (2007) (Print)
16. Weitzman, E.R., Kaci, L., Mandl, K.D.: Sharing Medical Data for Health Research: The Early Personal Health Record Experience. Journal of Medical Internet Research 12(2) (2010) (print)
17. Yamin, C.K., et al.: The Digital Divide in Adoption and Use of a Personal Health Record. Archives of Internal Medicine 171(6), 568 (2011) (print)
18. Calvin, O., et al.: Factors Affecting Home Care Patients' Acceptance of a Web-Based Interactive Self-Management Technology. Journal of the American Medical Informatics Association 18(1), 51–59 (2011) (print)
19. Denton, I.C.: Will Patients Use Electronic Personal Health Records? Responses from a Real-Life Experience. Journal of Healthcare Information Management 15(3), 251–260 (2001) (print)
20. Tom, J.O., et al.: Integrated Personal Health Record Use: Association with Parent-Reported Care Experiences. Pediatrics 130(1), 183–190 (2012) (print)
21. Hilton, J.F., et al.: A Cross-Sectional Study of Barriers to Personal Health Record Use among Patients Attending a Safety-Net Clinic. PloS One 7(2), e31888 (2012) (print)
22. Luque, A.E., et al.: Bridging the Digital Divide in Hiv Care: A Pilot Study of an Ipod Personal Health Record. Journal of the International Association of Physicians in AIDS Care, JIAPAC (2012) (print)
23. National eHealth Collaborative. Patient Engagement Framework (2012),
   http://www.nationalehealth.org/patient-engagement-framework

Complexity Analysis of a Transfer Center

Josette F. Jones[1], Michelle Lenox[1], Tami Raute[2], Shelly Maersch[2],
Cortney Gundlach[2], and Mark Pfaff[1]

[1] Indiana University School of Informatics and Computing, Indianapolis
{jofjones,mlenox,mpfaff}@iupui.edu
[2] Indiana University Health, Indianapolis
{traute,smaerch,cgundlac}@iuhealth.org

Abstract. Patient throughput and the reduction of wait times for care are critical to improve patient outcomes in life-threatening emergencies. The concept of patient throughput underpins many wait time improvement techniques currently being implemented by healthcare providers across the industry as well as at Indiana University (IU) Health. Without the ability to implement effective patient throughput process improvement solutions, healthcare providers will struggle to reduce wait times and meet strategic goals of improved patient outcomes.

IU Health launched its first patient transfer program between intensive care units. A level 1 vascular emergency program in August 2009; the initiative was soon complemented by other patients transfer programs. The success of the program showed a significant drop in median emergency department-to-operating room time, reductions in time spent at referring hospitals and in transit. Despite the successes, the program is left with increasing demand (volume & acuity) and a need for interactive care pathway or delivery of care solutions to streamline the patient throughput and to adequately measure impacts on patient outcomes and capacity management.

The paper will present a preliminary analysis of (1) observations of current workflows and their complexity, and (2) based on the observations suggest patient throughput simulation in order to identify bottlenecks and test potential solutions and protocols before actually implementing them in practice.

1   Introduction

Interfacility and intrafacility transfers can be immensely challenging, time-consuming, and detrimental to patient safety if not managed properly. According to Strickler et al. (2003), transfers can be a key piece of the overall hospital business process, employee and patient satisfaction, yet it is mostly an invisible aspect of hospital work. Traditionally, transfers were made on the basis of bed availability, not on service or patient acuity [1]. The arrival times were predominantly unknown and the patients' needs were assessed upon arrival at the receiving hospital [2, 3]. This problematic and delayed process clearly endangers the welfare and outcomes of patients especially those with life-threatening emergencies.

C. Stephanidis and M. Antona (Eds.): UAHCI/HCII 2013, Part III, LNCS 8011, pp. 482–489, 2013.

Patient Transfer Centers were established in recent years due to the growing need to streamline inter-facility transfers. One such center was instituted by Indiana University (IU) Health (then Clarian) in August of 2009 with its level 1 vascular emergency program. "The foundation of the transfer program is the one-call streamlined process for patient throughput "where upon an outside emergency department (ED) physician's diagnoses of an emergency, the following factors are facilitated: transportation for the patient either by air or ground, activation of appropriate surgeon(s) and treatment team including the operating room (OR) charge nurse and accepting surgeon, physician-to-physician communication and nursing report, and a guaranteed bed placement for the patient. According to a report by the Society for Vascular Surgery [4], IU Health's program dramatically decreased the overall door-to-treatment time from 183.5 minutes to 157 minutes, emergency department-to-operating room time from 35 minutes to 23 minutes, non-significant reductions in time spent at the referring hospital from 150.5 to 110 minutes and in transit times from 52 to 35 minutes.

The IU Health transfer center's success also brings with it many challenges. Since this service in healthcare is fairly new, there are a negligent amount of studies in published literature that researchers as well as health professionals can derive from as basis. Questions as "What type of staff, how many per call, staffing ratios at different times …" remain unanswered. Then there is the issue of cost such as determining full-time employees (FTE) needed and cost allocation. Other areas include bed management, transportation, education requirements, and quality assurance. How does an organization determine their activity and how many transfers do they facilitate a month/ week/day/year? How can you track for acuity or service line?

Data and meaningful trends for such systems are prominently sparse. Calls were made to various transfer centers across the nation and found that benchmarks and standards do not exist. Some facilities have registered nurses who are ICU and ED experienced and certified while others have non-clinical staff; transfer protocols are a concatenation of existing "provider preferences" to non-existing. There are no standards or metrics for effective patient throughput so most of the facilities are hoping they are maintaining quality without even knowing the benchmarks for effectiveness and efficiency of the practices.

The proposed study is collaboratively conducted by nurses in the 24/7 Patient Transfer Center and a research team of the School of Informatics. The aims of this exploratory study presented are:

- To describe observations and contextual inquiry into the current information and workflow in a large 24/7 transfer center
- To identify current challenges in the workflow and information sharing between settings
- To model the workflow and information of the transfer center's activities using open source simulation software [5, 6].

2   Research Design

2.1   Methods

The research design is a mixed-methods study using qualitative and quantitative approaches to develop and evaluate care coordination between care settings using principles of sociotechnical design [7-9] and distributed cognition [10, 11].

These principles include:

1. focusing on the users and tasks in context
2. measuring care coordination and throughput empirically
3. visualizing all processes, current and proposed.

This approach brings attention to the end users, physical and cognitive resources, organizational policies, and institutional rules embed and surrounding the information system, as well as how these various elements interact and interface with one another. Our analysis will also involve evaluating the care coordination processes and identifying areas for improvements in efficiency and effectiveness. Figure 1 illustrates the analysis framework we will use, one that will place the user interaction within the complex, diverse health information systems.

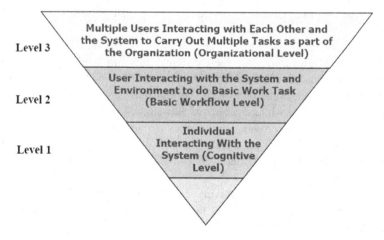

Fig. 1. Framework for conducting cognitive-socio-technical analysis at three levels of a system (adopted from E.H. Borycki et al 2010)

2.2   Setting

The setting for this pilot study is the 24/7 Patient Transfer Center at a Midwest teaching hospital system. The transfer center originally is established in 2009 as part of a protocol for Level 1 vascular emergencies requiring transport (LifeLine) services. It is currently evolving to manage all inter- and intrafacility transfers within its six core hospitals and ambulatory services.

The transfer center is staffed with nurses with extensive critical care experience providing the following functionality for patient flow:

- • Providing interfacility transfers **among** its healthcare system, from any location
- • Providing intrafacility transfers **within** its healthcare system
- • Additional services include transport (air and ground)

2.3   Preliminary Findings

Observations and a Contextual Inquiry into the Current Information and Workflow

In healthcare organizations, many complex, non-trivial processes and workflows, of various duration and objectives, are performed to help achieve the goal of providing quality care to patients. Over a period of five months our team visited the center five times for a total of 14 hours. The observed workflows are dissimilar, flexible and often involve several medical and non-medical departments such as bed-management as well as clinical and non-clinical staff. The workflows observed consist of a range of tasks using specific resources (e.g., Cerner EHR, Teletracking XT, IM, AmCom paging,..) , technology (2 displays, notebook, phone,..) and tools ("flow" flip book, phone book, transfer worksheet), within a physical environment (part of room)   and within organizational conditions and goals of optimal care coordination.

The transfer process and its supporting tasks are fragmented, composed of separate but inter-twined cycles running at different speeds and as thus prone to several worka-rounds such as the phone "chain problem" or bypassing electronic bed requests.

Adding to the complexity of this activity is that much of the transfer processes are tacit; the individual mind is the locus of knowledge, problem solving, and information processing ultimately responsible for (intelligent) actions. So understanding the workflow means identifying, ordering and prioritizing the different tasks involved in the transfer process, as well as defining the information and communication patterns needed by transfer center nurses in achieving their care coordination goals through repeated observations and think-aloud using the naturalistic inquiry approach.

Feasibility of Unobtrusive Technology Integration into the Workflow

As part of our initial study our team investigated the use of technology with minimal or no impact on the workflow. Our team evaluated the smart pen technology for its (1) efficiency and accuracy in capturing written text and (2) its fit into the workflow of transfer center. The smart pen is a paper-based mobile computing solution that bridges the gap between paper and digital note taking. The smart-pen can automatically capture entries on the paper transfer worksheets used by Transfer Call Nurses. Real time electronic capture will benefit the transfer center tasks by (1) decreasing the workload as the need to transcribe data by hand into the systems is removed through the auto-population of the captured electronic data (2) increasing the currency and availability of clinical data captured in clinical information systems, and (3) allow for the development of HIT solutions tied to real-time transfer data.

The preliminary findings on the smart pen are promising:

- Use of the pen is intuitive and needs minimal or no training
- Dot paper expensive but can be easily reproduced with 600dpi printer
- Apps needed to convert the written text to Word, Excel, etc .are inexpensive desktop applications and
  - Creation of tables are easy yet each record need separate paper
  - Conversion written text to electronic documents is straight forward.

The accuracy of capturing of numeric characters ranges from .49 to .98; for alpha numeric characters the range is from .80 to .87. Yet for special characters the accuracy only reaches .50 (table 1)

Table 1. Accuracy of Conversion

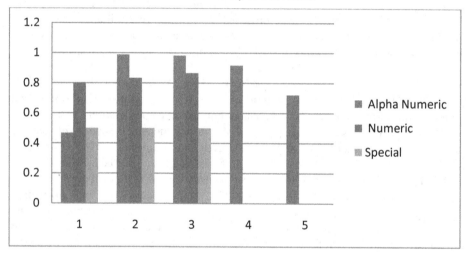

In addition to the smart pen, the research team also evaluated how to better utilize existing technologies (functionality within their current EHR) or adopt innovative mobile applications (Diagnotes™) supporting the coordination of care across settings. Diagnotes™ (http://www.diagnotes.net/) facilitates communication among providers via secure text messaging and supports immediate encounter documentation and provider follow-up actions decreasing the transcription task but more importantly making the documents available real time.

Implement through Simulations, Solutions to the Challenges Identified, and Information and Workflow Modeling

After investigating several open source models for workflow simulation and re-engineering, we propose to model the processes using Petri-Nets (with additional rules) that model patient throughput and flow process behavior [12], While these process-nets (PNs) may be syntactically correct, PNs have shown not always to provide meaningful models of how organizations (i.e., 24/7 Transfer Center) conduct their processes [13]. Moreover, the processes represented by these nets may not be feasible to execute or reach the transfer centers goals when executed. Therefore we propose to use the approach by Soffer et al. (2010) for mapping the "understanding of patient throughputs and flows" derived by attaching ontological semantics to the process-net models (figure 2). These rules guide the construction of process-nets, which are meaningful in that their nodes and transitions are directly related to the modeled patient throughputs. Furthermore, the proposed semantics imposed on the process models constraints that guide the development of valid process models, name-ly, models that assure that the process can accomplish its goal when executed [13].

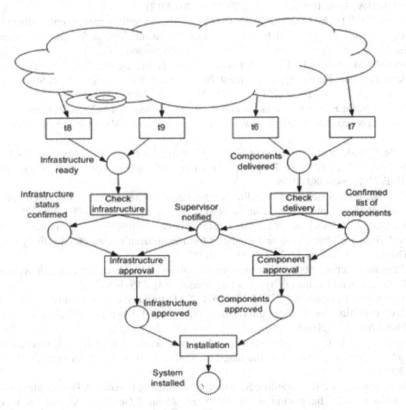

Fig. 2. Framework for Assigning Ontological Semantics to Process Net (Soffer et al. ,2010)

3   Discussion

This study presented provided an understanding of how patient throughput and flow is a key piece of the overall hospital business process, clinician satisfaction [14], and patient satisfaction, yet it is mostly an invisible aspect of hospital work. The aim of our study was an understanding of the complexity of the workflow, improving processes and predicting potential bottlenecks in transfer processes by creating actionable models of transfer center activities. Findings regarding technologies and processes to best coordinate patient flow among and within health care systems can be modeled and tested prior to implementation. Additionally the simulations suggest standards and metrics for care coordination in terms of patient outcomes and capacity management compliant with Meaningful Use quality objectives.

References

1. Barnett, M.L., Song, Z., Landon, B.E.: Trends in Physician Referrals in the United States, 1999-2009. Arch. Intern. Med. 172(2), 163–170 (2012)
2. Tortorella, F.R., et al.: Developing a transfer center in a tertiary cancer center: streamlining access and communication to accommodate increasing demand for service. Journal of Healthcare Management 56(3), 199–210 (2011); discussion 210-1
3. Hatfield, M., et al.: 131: Use of A Transfer Center To Manage the Transfer of Pediatric Patients From the Emergency Department To the Intensive Care Unit: A Pilot Study. Critical Care Medicine 39(12), 27 (2011), 10.1097/01.ccm.0000408627.24229.88
4. Wendling, P.: Protocol shrinks Ruptured AAA Treatment Times,Transfer from ED to OR time improved. The Official Newpaper of the Society for Vascular Surgery (September 2011)
5. Leite, C.R.M., et al.: Modeling of Medical Care with Stochastic Petri Nets, pp. 1–4 (2010)
6. Murata, T.: Petri nets: Properties, analysis and applications. Proceedings of the IEEE 77(4), 541–580 (1989)
7. Hasvold, P.E., Scholl, J.: Flexibility in interaction: Sociotechnical design of an operating room scheduler. International Journal of Medical Informatics 80(9), 631–645 (2011)
8. Yanchar, S.C.: Using numerical data in explicitly interpretive, contextual inquiry: A "practical discourse" framework and examples from Engestrom's research on activity systems. Theory & Psychology 21(2), 179–199 (2011)
9. Carayon, P., et al.: Sociotechnical systems analysis in health care: a research agenda. IIE Transactions on Healthcare Systems Engineering 1(3), 145–160 (2011)
10. Hazlehurst, B., Gorman, P.N., McMullen, C.K.: Distributed cognition: an alternative model of cognition for medical informatics. International Journal of Medical Informatics, 2008 77(4), 226 (2008)
11. Xio, Y.: Artifacts and collaborative work in healthcare: methodological, theoretical and technological implications of the tangible. Journal of Biomedical Informatics 38, 26–33 (2005)
12. Terenziani, P.: In: Rinderle-Ma, S., Sadiq, S., Leymann, F. (eds.) A Hybrid Multi-layered Approach to the Integration of Workflow and Clinical Guideline Approaches Business Process Management Workshops, pp. 539–544. Springer, Heidelberg (2010)
13. Soffer, P., Kaner, M., Wand, Y.: Assigning Ontological Meaning to Workflow Nets. Journal of Database Management 21(i3), 35 (2010)
14. Amedee, R., Maronge, G., Pinsky, W.: Improving the Transition of Care in Patients Transferred Through the Ochsner Medical Center Transfer Center. The Ochsner Journal (2012)
15. Barnett, M.L., Song, Z., Landon, B.E.: Trends in physician referrals in the United States, 1999-2009. Arch. Intern. Med. 172(2), 163 (2012)

16. Hatfield, M., et al.: 134: Impact of A Transfer Center to Manage Transfer of Pediatric Patients From the Emergency Department to the Intensive Care Unit in An Academic-Based Setting .... Critical Care ...(2012)
17. Hatfield, M., et al.: 131: Use of A Transfer Center To Manage the Transfer of Pediatric Patients From the Emergency Department To the Intensive Care Unit: A Pilot Study. Critical Care ...(2011)
18. Tortorella, F., et al.: Developing a transfer center in a tertiary cancer center: streamlining access and communication to accommodate increasing demand for service. Journal of Healthcare Management/American College of Healthcare Executives 56(3), 199 (2011)

Analysis of User-Generated Multimedia Data on Medication Management and Consumption Behavior Using Data Mining Techniques

Chaiwoo Lee, Lisa A. D'Ambrosio, Richard Myrick, Joseph F. Coughlin, and Olivier L. de Weck

AgeLab, Engineering Systems Division, Massachusetts Institute of Technology, Cambridge, MA 02139, United States
{chaiwoo,dambrosi,dmyrick,coughlin,deweck}@mit.edu

Abstract. Technology-enabled tools have been suggested as a solution to assist older adults in the management and consumption of medications. However, existing systems and studies are often limited by incomplete understanding of the potential users' behaviors. This study uses a web-based survey and photo submission system to collect and analyze user profiles and behavioral characteristics. Various data mining techniques, including association rules, clustering and classification, are used on quantified data to find important behavioral patterns, group users with similar characteristics, and discern factors related to risky medication management behaviors. This paper presents the process and results of analysis, including a detailed description of coding scheme and model development. Practical and methodological implications are also discussed.

Keywords: Medication compliance, assistive technology, user observation, survey research, design for aging population.

1 Introduction

An average older American takes 3 to 5 medications [1-2]. Of all older adults seeing a physician, 61% are prescribed at least one medication [3]. However, older adults often experience limitations in terms of physical and cognitive capabilities, making it challenging for them to manage and consume their medications as directed. As a result, noncompliance, which can cause serious problems in terms of health outcomes and healthcare costs, is reported to be prevalent in up to 59% of older adults [4].

As a solution, technology-enabled tools for medication management and their potential benefits have been discussed and explored in various academic disciplines. For example, studies in artificial intelligence mainly looked at sensor technologies and algorithms to track information related to medication management and consumption [5]. In engineering design, the configuration of system architecture and the design of devices and interfaces have been the major topics [6]. In addition, relevant research from human factors perspectives has focused on the interactions between users and the tools [7].

C. Stephanidis and M. Antona (Eds.): UAHCI/HCII 2013, Part III, LNCS 8011, pp. 490–499, 2013.

While current products and systems are developed to aid older adults' management and consumption of medication, many are based on insufficient understanding of user behaviors and use cases. For example, systems were often developed with a focus on performance and reliability, while the match among the interface design, information flow, and actual user behaviors has not yet been fully discussed [8].

Although medication compliance is an important topic and a complex concept, there exists little information on the ways that people, especially older adults, manage their medications. This study aims to observe and analyze older adults' behaviors in storing, managing and consuming their medications. A novel web-based photo collection survey was conducted for a remote yet detailed observation of medication management and user characteristics. A data mining approach was used to discern behavioral characteristics and patterns from the survey data and photo submissions. To find behavioral patterns, describe characteristics related to risky behaviors, and build taxonomy of users, various data mining techniques were used.

This paper describes the process of data collection, the characteristics of data and its variables, and the methods used for data mining analysis. The results and their implications are also presented. With the comprehensive investigation of user characteristics and behavior in managing medications, this study is expected to contribute by providing implications to the design of medication management systems as well as suggesting an effective method of participatory user study.

2   Data Collection

The purpose of this study is to find important characteristics and patterns that can inform the design and delivery of medication management systems. For the study, a survey method was used to ask people about their medication management behaviors and characteristics. Also, for a remote observation, a photo submissions system was added to the survey. The collected data were tabulated and coded for quantitative analysis. This section describes how the data were collected and processed, as well as what fields and values the dataset included.

2.1   User Survey and Photo Collection

A web-based user survey was conducted for collection of data. Individuals in the MIT AgeLab participant database, who have agreed to be contacted with studies they may be eligible to participate in, were emailed with information about the survey. The email included a link to the survey web page that included the instructions, the survey, and the photo uploading tool. Figure 1 shows a portion of the survey web page.

The survey included a brief questionnaire about the participants, including demographics and living situation. They were asked to answer questions on their consumption and management of medications, including the types of medications that they take, the amount of time they spend on managing and taking medications, and their perceived difficulty of managing.

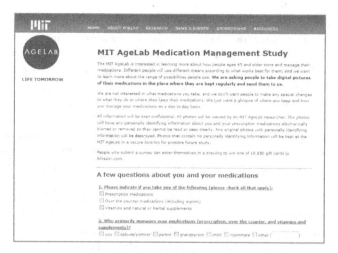

Fig. 1. Survey web page

In order for the survey to be submitted, participants were required to upload at least one photo that describes where and how they store their medications. They were asked to take one or more photos that show the medications and their surroundings including the room and the containers. Figure 2 shows a sample of collected photos.

Fig. 2. Photo collection sample

The survey was distributed only to people who are 45 or older to focus the interest of the study on the older adult population. As they are a significant population of users who consume various types of medications, they, and their caregivers, face a complex task of managing multiple medications. Thus, the topic of medication management applies more importantly to this population.

2.2   Coding and Pre-processing

Data were first pre-processed to remove any personal identifying information such as names and addresses in the collected photos. Any irrelevant data, such as photos without any medication information in them, were removed prior to analysis.

The information in the collected photos was coded quantitatively according to a comprehensive set of descriptor variables, including the room that medications are stored in, whether or not they are in an enclosed space, characteristics of packaging, display of risky storage behaviors, and more. The complete set of variables for meta-data coding is summarized in Table 1.

Table 1. Coding scheme for photo information quantification

Category	Description	Binary (yes or no) variables
Location	The type of the room where medications are being stored as shown in the photo	— Kitchen — Bathroom — Bedroom
Enclosure	The type of space or container where medications are stored or enclosed as shown in the photo	— Enclosed cabinet, drawer or box — Open container or shelf — Tabletop — Bags or purses
Combination	The method of which medications are kept individually or mixed with other drugs as shown in the photo	— Individually kept — Mixed in bulk — Mixed by dose
Packaging	The method of which medications are kept in their original packaging or repackaged by the user as shown in the photo	— Kept in original packaging — Kept in a pill minder — Kept in some other bottle or box
Space sharing	Items or products that are kept in the same space as the medications as shown in the photo	— Medications alone — Kept with food — Kept with bath/ beauty products — Kept with healthcare products — Kept with office supplies — Kept with flatware and/or utensil
Risky behaviors	Whether or not any behaviors undesirable for appropriate management of medications are shown in the photo	— Medications kept near heat — Medications kept near water — Medications kept with the lid open

2.3   The Dataset

The data includes 112 observations, or responses from 112 individuals. As some people submitted more than one photo, the total number of photos collected was 213. For those who submitted multiple photos, the information from the photos were collectively merged into one row. For example, if a person submitted a photo showing medications in a bathroom and another photo showing medications in a kitchen, the row corresponding to the individual was marked with the value 1 under both variables of *Kitchen* and *Bathroom*.

A total of 36 variables, including participant ID and basic demographics, are included in the data. Out of the 36, 21 binary variables, as described in Table 1, are used for quantitative description of photos collected. More binary variables were also used for describing if the respondents take prescription medications, over-the-counter medications and/or supplements. Categorical variables were used for marital status, living situation, and other people that a person manages medications for. Ordered categorical variables were used for age, time spent managing medications and perceived difficulty. A ratio scale was used for describing the number of people in household.

3   Analysis and Results

A number of different data mining techniques were used to investigate find behavioral patterns, group users, and to describe predictors of risky behavior. XLMiner, a data mining program operated on Microsoft Excel, was used for applying the techniques. This section describes the specific goals, methods and results of the analysis.

3.1   Medication Management Behavior Patterns

For the objective of finding important and common behavioral patterns in management and consumption of medications, the associations between variables were investigated. Association rules analysis was used on the binary variables to see if some behavioral and user characteristics are associated with others.

Variables with binary values were used for the association rules analysis. Some relevant categorical and continuous variables were transformed into binary format. For example, the variable *Number of People Living With* was transformed into *Live with Others*, with value 0 for living alone and 1 for living with someone. Also, one observation that had missing values was removed prior to analysis.

Using XLMiner, association rules with the minimum support of 20 and minimum confidence of 80% were generated. The initial result generated many rules were redundant and didn't contain meaningful information. For example, one rule stated that "90.91% of females who keeps prescription medications individually and mixed by dose also consume supplements and use both the original packaging and pill minders." This rule is meaningful in illustrating that in some cases people employ multiple methods and use multiple containers to manage their medications. However, the specific causal order may not have a significant meaning, especially since the related variables were found in different orders in other rule statements. Due to the limitations of directly interpreting the raw results, this part of the study focused more on identifying and examining the co-occurring relationships that were common in many rules. A subset of the result is summarized in Table 2.

Table 2 lists several rules that were found by examining the common co-occurring associations. The first rule suggests that when prescription medications are organized by dose, pill minders are used 97% of the time. However, only 75% people who use pill minders organized their prescription medications by dose. This rule indicates that while pill minders are the primary strategy in organizing medications to keep the regimen, they are not always correctly used. The second rule states that 71% of the time when pill minders are used, they are kept in an enclosed space. Since pill minders are intended to be used as an accessible, simple and often portable means for complying with medication regimen, one can expect to see pill minders in a more open space, such as tabletops, or near a purse. However, pill minders were very often kept deep inside big boxes and cabinets, which, along with the first rule, suggests that people who have pill minders may not be using them as intended. The third rule states that 66% of people who use pill minders and keep their medications mixed by dose are females, which is higher than the overall proportion of females in the sample. This indicates that people who employ more strategized and planned method of organizing medications are largely females. The fourth rule states that 80% people who manage medications for other people in the household are females living with others. Although it was not statistically tested, rules 3 and 4 may be related in how females are often faced with more complex tasks and may seek ways for easier management. The fifth rule states that 69% of people who live with others and take both prescriptions and supplements keep their medications in individual, original packaging in enclosed spaces. No gender association is stated in this rule, but it may have implications similar to rule 4 in that it suggests the relationships between complexity of task and simplicity of management methods.

Table 2. Association rules (a subset of secondary analysis results)

A	B	Confidence[1] A→B	Confidence[1] B→A	Lift ratio[2]
Dose-mixed, Prescription	Pill minder	97%	75%	2.25
Pill minder	Enclosed	71%	50%	1.16
Female	Pill minder, Dose-mixed	44%	66%	1.18
Female, live with others	Manage for others	28%	80%	2.07
Live with others, Prescription, Supplement	Enclosed, Individual, Original packaging	69%	44%	1.16

3.2   User Groups

The second part of the data mining analysis concerns the variety in user characteristics and types of user behaviors related to medication management. This aims to categorize and group users to build a taxonomy of users according to their behavioral characteristics. For this part of the study, clustering analysis was used.

Prior to the analysis, variables that were thought not to contribute directly to medication management behavior were excluded. These include *ID*, *Marital Status*, *Pets*, *State* and *Race*. Hierarchical clustering was first applied to see the overall structure in which the observations can be clustered or set apart. Based on the hierarchical clustering result, it was determined that five distinct clusters can be formed with the data.

---

[1] The confidence of rule A→B shows the proportion of events A that also meet consequent B.
[2] The lift shows the performance of a rule compared to random, independent occurrences. A lift higher than 1 indicates positive dependence between events.

Accordingly, a k-means clustering with k=5 was conducted. The result from the k-means clustering analysis is summarized in Table 3.

From the k-means clustering results, with k=5, it can be seen that respondents can be grouped based mainly on the types of medications, their age, the number of people in household, whether or not they manage medications for someone in the household, the primary storage location, their use of pill minders and reorganization of medications, and the things that they store their medications with.

Table 3. K-means clustering result (K=5)

Cluster no.	No. of observations	Distinguishing characteristics based on cluster centers
1	4	— Spend the most time managing medications — Live alone and among the oldest of the sample — Store medications in kitchen — Mixes by dose and don't keep original packaging
2	51	— Don't reorganize medications in any way — Manage only for self
3	24	— Take both prescriptions and supplements — Mostly female — Store medications in kitchen and bathroom — Manage for others in household
4	15	— Take over-the-counter medications — Keep original packaging
5	17	— Take both prescriptions and supplements — Use pill minders to organize medications

3.3   Behavior Classification

Another objective of this study is to identify and describe characteristics related to undesirable, or risky, behaviors such as storing medications near heat, near water, or with the lids open, as exemplified in Figure 3. With the identification of common characteristics, safety measures and tools can be targeted to help people with the identified characteristics. For this part of the study, classification methods were used to develop models that classify risky and non-risky users based on the data.

The response variable was newly defined to integrate the variables describing risky behaviors - *Near Heat*, *Near Water*, and *Container Open*. If a person had 1 under one or more of the three variables, the person was marked with a 1 under the new variable *Risky Behavior*. That is, the new variable *Risky Behavior* had two values - 0 for no sign of risky behavior and 1 for display of some risky behavior. Variables that were hypothesized to be irrelevant, or found to have little variance in its values were excluded from the analysis. For example, only 4 observations had value 0 for the variable *Original Packaging*, and the difference in the value of this variable was found not to be associated with risky behaviors. Thus the variable *Original Packaging* was removed before classification. In the same manner, variables *Individual, Bags* and *Bulk-mixed* were excluded from classification analysis.

Fig. 3. Examples of risky medication management behaviors

For this supervised approach, the data was partitioned into a training set and a validation set. Prior to the classification analysis, 60% of observations were randomly labeled as training data, and the other 40% were grouped into the validation set. The training set was used for developing classification models, and the trained model was applied to the validation data for evaluation.

A total of five different methods - naïve Bayes, k-nearest neighbors, logistic regression, discriminant analysis and neural networks - were used to develop classification models. For the k-nearest neighbors model, k=3 was used for analysis as it was found to be the best k with the lowest validation error. For logistic regression, a best subset selection was done using an exhaustive search, and a model with 11 predictor variables was selected. During the neural networks analysis, 100 networks were first generated and a simple model with the lowest error was selected. Classification tree method was also used, but was not included in the final comparison as it generated a model where all observations were predicted to belong to the majority and didn't base the decision on any of the behavior variables. The error results from the five classification models are summarized in Table 4. In Table 4, class 1 error refers to the probability of incorrectly classifying risky individuals in the validation set as non-risky.

Table 4. Classification model comparison

Classification model	Training error	Validation error	Class 1 error
Naïve Bayes	8.96%	22.73%	100.00%
k-nearest neighbors	14.93%	18.18%	100.00%
Logistic regression	10.45%	22.73%	62.50%
Discriminant analysis	11.94%	20.45%	75.00%
Neural network	4.48%	20.45%	87.50%

While the k-nearest neighbors model showed the lowest overall validation error, it classified all risky individuals in the validation set as non-risky. If higher costs are associated with the class 1 error, this result can be very costly. On the other hand, the logistic regression model showed the best performance in correctly identifying individuals with risky behavior, although it showed a somewhat higher overall validation error. If one was to develop a product or service targeted at individuals who are more likely to show risky behavior, the logistic regression model may be chosen to best inform related design decisions. The logit model below, as developed from with the logistic regression analysis, shows that individuals who consume supplements, store medications in bathroom or open tabletops with various other products, have a pill minder, and live with other people are more likely to show risky behaviors. On the other hand, it shows that people who keep medications in enclosed spaces are less likely to show risky behaviors.

$$\text{Logit} = -4.23 + 1.80 \times Supplements + 0.87 \times No.\ of\ people\ living\ with + 1.81 \times Bathroom$$
$$- 4.68 \times Enclosed - 1.79 \times Open\ box + 1.99 \times Tabletop + 2.07 \times Pill\ minder +$$
$$2.25 \times With\ food + 2.77 \times With\ bath\ or\ beauty + 2.82 \times Flatware\ utensil$$

4   Discussion and Conclusion

In this study, user-generated data were analyzed using various data mining techniques to find results that can inform the design of medication management systems. The goal of this study was to find important behavioral characteristics and patterns that people, especially older adults, show as they manage and consume medications. Along with the survey data, information coded from a collection of photos was used for a comprehensive analysis. To find patterns, investigate user characteristics, and determine what leads to risky behaviors, association rules analysis, clustering analysis, and various methods of classification, respectively, were applied.

Through association rules analysis, this study found co-occurring associations among variables. The results can be expected to inform designers as they analyze use cases, investigate possible errors, and set specific development goals. For example, medication management tools that can be used by a whole family can be targeted a female adult user, since they are more likely to be actually in charge of managing medications. This study then took a step in building a taxonomy of users and their behavioral characteristics using hierarchical and k-means clustering. The result of clustering can be useful as designers write scenarios and detailed use cases around system interactions and interfaces. The clusters can inform practitioners if they need to target certain behaviors or specific groups of people. The third part of the study concerned classifying users into risky and non-risky groups based on their behavioral characteristics. Five different methods were used to find classification models, which were analyzed comparatively based on their performance. In order to make medication support tools more beneficial and effective, targeting the behavioral characteristics associated with risky behaviors can be helpful. For example, systems can be designed with an enclosed storage space without requiring users to organize medications into pill minders to lower the likelihood of showing risky behaviors.

This study has implications not only for developers and designers of medication management tools, but also for practitioners in other fields. For example, pharmaceutical companies can use the result of clustering analysis for targeting their products at a more specific segment of customers. Healthcare professionals such as physicians and nurses can better advise their patients to store and manage their prescription medications in a less risky manner. Also, home care personnel can be informed to assist their customers and patients in managing their medications in a safer way.

A novel web-based research approach was used for data collection. Previous studies aimed at studying medication consumption behaviors were based on home visits and direct observations [8-9]. While such methods allow a close analysis, they may not be ideal for studying the heterogeneity and variance of behavioral characteristics, and can be costly for studying a larger sample. As the use of information and communications technology become prevalent among older adults, the user-driven remote observation method can be effectively and efficiently utilized. Also, the process of metadata coding can inform development of algorithms for analyzing graphic media. The definition of variables and attributes, as well as the process of quantification, can inform ways in which features are extracted and analyzed in multimedia data mining.

In short, this study extends the current understanding of potential users of medication management systems, especially older adults, by investigating the variance and patterns in their behavioral characteristics. The use of a new user-driven approach, application of quantitative data mining techniques, and the findings from the study can be expected to inform system designers, healthcare providers and caregivers, as well as researchers and scholars in the disciplines of user studies and data mining.

References

1. Giron, M.S.T., Wang, H.X., Bernsten, C., Thorslund, M., Winblad, B., Fastbom, J.: The Appropriateness of Drug Use in an Older Nondemented and Demented Population. J. Am. Geriatr. Soc. 49(3), 277–283 (2003)
2. American Society of Health-System Pharmacists (ASHP): Snapshot of Medication Use in the U.S., ASHP Research Report (2000),
   http://www.ashp.org/s_ashp/docs/files/PR_snapshot.pdf
3. Rathore, S.S., Mehta, S.S., Boyko, W.L., Schulman, K.A.: Prescription Medication Use in Older Americans: A National Report Card on Prescribing. Fam. Med. J. 30(10), 733–739 (1998)
4. Malhotra, S., Karan, R.S., Pandhi, P., Jain, S.: Drug Related Medical Emergencies in the Elderly: Role of Adverse Drug Reactions and Non-Compliance. Postgrad. Med. J. 77(913), 703–707 (2001)
5. Sadri, F.: Multi - Agent Ambient Intelligence for Elderly Care and Assistance. In: Proc. Internat. Electron. Conf. Comput. Sci., pp. 117–120 (2007)
6. Silva, J.M., Mouttham, A., El Saddik, A.: UbiMeds: A Mobile Application to Improve Accessibility and Support Medication Adherence. In: Proc. ACM SIGMM Internat. Workshop Media Stud. Implement. Help Improv. Access Disabl. Users, pp. 71–78 (2009)
7. McGee-Lennon, M.R., Wolters, M.K., Brewster, S.: User-Centred Multimodal Reminders for Assistive Living. In: Proc. ACM SIGCHI Conf. Hum. Factors Comput. Syst., pp. 2105–2114 (2011)
8. Geetanjali, N.: Prospective Randomized Survey Study on Assessment and Education of Home Medicine Cabinet among General Population of Community, Doctoral Thesis. Rajiv Gandhi University of Health Sciences, Bangalore, India (2010)
9. Palen, L., Aaløkke, S.: Of Pill Boxes and Piano Benches: "Home-Made" Methods for Managing Medication. In: Proc. ACM SIGCHI Conf. Comput. Support. Coop. Work, pp. 79–88 (2006)

Motion Sensing Technology on Rehabilitation for Children with Physical Disabilities

Chien-Yu Lin[1,*], Ming-Chi Lin[2], and Shu-Hua Chen[3]

[1] Department of Special Education, National University of Tainan, Tainan, Taiwan
[2] National Tainan Special School, Tainan, Taiwan
[3] Guei-Nan Elementary School, Tainan, Taiwan
linchienyu@mail.nutn.edu.tw

Abstract. This research is focus on application of hand-eye coordination of motion sensing for children with developmental disabilities. Based on the base technology of interactive technology, thereby bringing the children the experience of the interactive technology application. There are 2 demonstrations on this research. The equipments are actually applied on children with developmental disabilities, the research focus on using low-cost equipment, then the relative activities will be easy follow for children. In this research, the devices relied upon user-friendly design, reducing the working load. The projector will be presented other children to participate and share interactive content, extended deep Tablet PC application. The aim of this study was to evaluate whether training via interactive effect enhances the motivation of CP children. These findings suggest that training of sense of hand-eye coordination could help to increase the motivation of training for children with different needs.

Keywords: intuition, hand-eye coordination, high tension, resource class, children, disabilities, cerebral palsy.

1 Introduction

Cerebral palsy is a very common congenital or acquired disorder that causes coordination problems. It is important for medical professionals and patients to understand the different types in order to create the best symptom management and physical rehabilitation plans. The most common form of the disorder, comprising about 75 percent of all diagnosed cases. The defining characteristic of spastic cerebral palsy is unusually high tension in muscles, which makes it difficult or impossible to bend, relax, and control muscles. Children with cerebral palsy (CP) show alteration of perceptual and cognitive abilities in addition to motor and sensory deficits [1].The main purpose of the study is to develop new tools according to children with developmental disabilities requirements special for children with CP. This study focus on using interactive activities as a assistive process in their rehabilitation treatment.

---

* Corresponding author.

C. Stephanidis and M. Antona (Eds.): UAHCI/HCII 2013, Part III, LNCS 8011, pp. 500–507, 2013.
© Springer-Verlag Berlin Heidelberg 2013

Assistive technology is an interactive visual and auditory material which is basically intended to improve hand-eye coordination, increase attention duration, and decrease reaction time. Coordinated movements represent a distinct category of instrumental movements, which give to the subject the possibility to economize effort, motor action, in predictable situations (stereotypical)[2],hand-eye coordination is very important for children in cognition and action coordination. Interactive technology is a new interface on rehabilitation, for teaching purposes with a number of software features, offer children a wealth of information and promote the teaching of students in the classroom attention, abstract understanding of memory after school[3]. Computer games developed to improve hand-eye coordination require ability to use mouse or keyboard, and therefore are usually unsuitable for special education because many of disabled individuals lack the capacity to use these kinds of computer peripherals[4]. Integration of visual and auditory feedback that get the more positive thinking about their motivation. Interactive whiteboard to promote the ability of understanding in the teaching materials, links the experience of learning styles[5].Disable children which prevent them from using base computer control devices, but custom made alternative devices always more expensive[6], one kind of solution is to explore the application of devices used in contemporary gaming technology[7], there are many studies about using wii remote in hand as a model is promising for integration into clinical and home-based rehabilitation exercise therapy systems[8],but the weight of the wii remote maybe too heavy to control for children with high tension in muscle. Infrared camera is generally used in tracking systems and this leads to costs often not affordable, particular, wii remote used as infrared cameras[9].Some research combined remote and infrared emitter to create low-cost interactive whiteboard[10], so that teachers enable to design teaching materials enhance the motivation of rehabilitation for children with developmental disabilities. The interactive technology focus on decrease the device weight and slow-speed interactive effect. Combined low-cost gear to create a cheaper device, the laptop could be controlled by the infrared emitter that functions much like click the left button of a mouse, The Nintendo wii remote is a compact, readily accessible position, orientation, and motion sensing technology with blue tooth wireless communication[11]. the application of a virtual interface and infrared light emitter is similar like make a mouse in the participant's hand but enhance the application field[12]. In addition, children with developmental disabilities special CP with high tension in muscle always didn't have the ability to control the correct not only could taste new teaching method but also are impressed by them. Virtual interface design has an advantage in that the application is able to not only game but also on rehabilitation treatment. However, through the virtual interface and infrared emitter, the process becomes uncomplicated for the children; only operate the tool using the sense of tuition.

2   Method

In the past experiments indicated the children with developmental delay took the infrared emitter near the projective wall, they always face to the screen, the path from wii remote and infrared emitter could be interfere by their body, it is not a good operate method for children with learning delay, specially most of children with CP could not stand by the wall, they always stand via upright stander or positioning chairs. This study want to used an intuition method, that the children face the screen and operate the interactive model by their body. Therefore, the first part of this study was improved for the devices, the subjects do not have to come to the wall is projected to operate the IR pen, but rather, against the participation of children in the wii remote, at the time during calibrated moment, the research consider the scope of the children's body could stretch as the operation of the virtual range. In this way, the projected image still on the walls, but the subjects can seat in a chair, holding a infrared emitter pen as a pc mouse in the learning process, just as Fig. 1. The purpose of this research is to help children with developmental disabilities have some opportunities enjoy happiness on their learning process. Assistive technology is a helpful method for learning, which has prominent influences on helping teachers explain difficult concepts, giving access to a huge range of examples and resources, and inducing pupils to engage in learning easily. This research showed appreciation with many experts who devote their technology about interactive whiteboards using the remote. Wii remote is a handheld device just like a television remote, a high-resolution high speed IR camera and wireless Bluetooth connectivity, the camera is sensitive only to bright sources of infrared light emitter; tracked objects must emit a significant amount of near infrared light to be detected [13]. With infrared emitter and wii remote could be create an effect just like pc mouse, it's a low-cost and custom-made tool[14]. Therefore, the study is able to integrate the feedback of flash software and power point and to develop teaching materials for children with developmental disabilities.

2.1   Hardware Set-Up(Virtual Space)

Infrared emitter could be design to different tools for different needs, this study applied the modified tools to be body training tools for children with disabilities. Consider to make an intuitive operation that the participant could stand in front of the screen, the calibration method could be modify, this study set the remote toward the operator, the operator first create a virtual concept plane positioning operation in this area, the screen interactive effect. In this research, the virtual interface displays the function of infrared receiver. It is a simple tool for children to control the micro switch, and the teaching material could be modified for other courses. When the research set up the device in the classroom, the children with developmental disabilities only take an infrared pen behind the virtual interface could use the interactive effect. Participants could operate the system in an intuition method, and then the study could set infrared emitter in different tools from different teaching materials. Based on the requirement for children, the weight of the device that children hold is only a simple pen with micro switch. The display mode of this method is an intuitive learning tool.

Fig. 1. Hardware setup-virtual space

2.2   Hardware Set-Up(Table Space)

It's difficult to ask for children with cerebral to hold on a tool to train the muscular endurance, set remote on the top area of the operator's hand that could be put on the table , so that the sensing area in the user's hand can be touched, since the remote can track sources of infrared light emitter, so the research make a virtual interface, there is a virtual operate range, when the children press the micro switch in this area, the infrared emitter just like a mouse to control to system. Through infrared emitter, re mote could track the location of infrared emitter, so, the function of the infrared pen just like a pc mouse, the children with developmental disabilities could touch the board instead of a mouse as a controller, just as Fig. 2.

Fig. 2. Hardware setup- table space

2.3   Infrared Tool

The devices included infrared emitter and a wii remote, the principle of infrared emitter en focus on 4 micro switches at 4 corners. when the child with cerebral palsy press the board, the board will emit infrared light, the remote will detect the signal. This kind of tools that design for those who could not control their body, there are 4 micro-switches could control the infrared emitter, it was special designed for high tension in muscle problem, just as Fig3.

Fig. 3. 4 micro-switches infrared tool

3   Case Study

This 2 cases are custom made for children with cerebral palsy so as to increase their intention on rehabilitation treatment. Using virtual interface, infrared light emitter could make a simple interactive interface design, which is able to increase the applicative field on rehabilitation process. there are 2 cases demonstrate on this study. The research performed how to use the assistive tool, the child used intuition operate process. Case 1. The participant of case 1 is a boy. He is 13 years who's obstacle category belongs to moderate mental retardation, the tool is homemade infrared transmitter samurai sword. the power of his wrist is weaker than normal children, and his palm parts is always in involuntary tremor. Hand movements need a longer operating time, poor performance in finer finger movements. Assessed by occupational therapists in schools, it is recommended to strengthen the training of the students of the upper arm, and the arm strength, and force the proficiency to reduce barriers on hand tremor, this study provided an interactive game and test the operational flexibility of the student in the use of the sword-type infrared emitter; Observed from the test, he was the positive response of the tool, the intention and effect of hand-eye coordination, and control the use of appliances are also good, but there are some goal need enhance that is control of the direction and control and wrist forces. At the first step, this study use normal game, although this study setup the first level ,but it is also difficult for children because their high tension in muscle, so we redesign the program, the content is using the participant's pictures as the material to design an interactive effect, at the beginning ,there are no figure show on the screen, this study put on an infrared emitter on his hand, ask for the participant try his best to move his hand, when he do that, we can see that he scratch part of the picture because he move his hand. Another participant is a girl who is 13 years ,Category obstacle for the multiple severe barriers (cerebral palsy),her limb belongs to involuntary high tension, the parts of neck, back and waist belongs to the low-tension. Therefore, the student use positioning wheelchair in the classroom class, she only can wave her left hand, her left palm also belongs to high tension, she only control herself better part is the index finger. There was a special table boarding the classroom, she could only operate a small range that almost $20 * 20 \text{ cm}^2$,it's difficult for her to control herself to touch the 4 corner of the table. In this event, we used the upright stander to help the student could stand in an fix area, the self-made infrared emitter sword maybe suit obstacle category belongs to moderate mental retardation but it's too heavy to student with cerebral palsy, we also observe that the speed of the game content is too fast to control for participant 2.

Fig. 4. CP child tried interactive rehabilitation via upright stander

Using virtual interface on the ground and table and infrared light emitter like a board could make a simple interactive design, which is able to increase the applicative field. there are 2 cases demonstrate on this study. The research performed how to use the assistive tool, the child was asked for to push the board by their hand or foot. When she press the micro switch on the board of the infrared pen, the user could heard the reflections that the picture show. The research performed how to use the assistive tool, the child was asked for to push the board by their hand or foot. When she press the micro switch on the board of the infrared pen, the user could heard the reflections that the picture show. In this case, she sat on a wheelchair, and assist with a positioning cushions provide the better seating solution whether the need is for upper body support, lower body support, this positioning options are available which extend usefulness to almost any situation. This positioning chairs encourage sitting skills while the child is participating in other activities. Proper seating allows children to participate with peers at eye level but not allow her to operate the normal whiteboard or interactive white board. the relative infrared tools on the table, so the participant easy to push them, set the infrared emitter on the virtual interface range, when the girl push the board with micro switch of the infrared emitter, just like she operate the left button of a mouse. Case 2 is one kind of teaching materials for child with cerebral palsy, the research put on 4 interactive tools before the participant could touch them, and set up the relative sound as feedback. we want to enhance the stretch ability of the hand, so we arrange the 4 boards on a large range, when the girl push the board, she could hear the relative sound, and she know she could control the situation by herself, in this Fig. 5, the study remove 2 interactive board and set 2 interactive boards at the far position to train her hand strength. The case is not only a custom-made teaching materials design but also a real-time feedback. Fig. 2. shows the pictures in the experimental process. This case focuses on using low-cost assistive technology could make interactive effect, child with cerebral palsy could do the rehabilitation by a interesting method. By this way, children to train their body active ability by virtual interface design with interaction.

Fig. 5. CP child tried interactive rehabilitation via virtual table

4   Conclusion

Just as the application of low cost and custom-made interactive technology, the emphasis is focus on the application of rehabilitation, it's the sensor from the infrared emitter could transmit the signals to the wii remote then at the same time connect to the computer. Because resource class don't have enough resource, and the children need different help, so this study combine some tools to make it. The main purpose is to instruct children in the application of physical activities. There will be more application on the field of interface, because the interface design focus on easy operate and easy use, moreover ,the interface design provide not only real-time feedbacks but also lower price could overcome the high tension in muscle. It is real and quite assistance to design interactive teaching materials for parents, resource teacher and physical therapist. Based on the fundamentals of making the operating interface simpler and burden-free. Some games are very interesting but the original design for normal person, so they t consider how difficult of the game and always design different level for users, sometime we can use the basic level for children with CP, but we also consider the high tension of muscle, if the children with high tension in muscle, the designer could redesign the content to fit the children. There are many interactive games just Fruit Ninja game could be redesign for children with physical disabilities, and consider the equipment on hand to redesign a system for children with physical disabilities just as the high tension in muscle. In terms of the hardware, the infrared emitter is modified to different type that children could be have high interested to be used, so that the projected images are interactive in real-time. Furthermore, the introduction of interactive, assistive technology also facilitates the children's rehabilitation. When help children with physical disabilities to do the regular rehabilitation, the interactive material is modified according to their needs. The development of the study may cater to more children with diverse needs;. The development of digitization possesses high potential; as far as children are concerned, not only is the application of digital content refreshing, since the rehabilitation materials emphasize methods such as interaction and coordination, children will become more interested while training their body coordination, which in turn generates a sense of accomplishment. Therefore, the development of interactive interface to assist the children's rehabilitation is a direction of thinking and execution. This study let the content present on the wall or floor via wii remote, so that the operator does not have to focus on the screen but in a more intuitive way to let the limb movement. To create activation of the teaching content , and by the process of the game into the technology of interactive technology. Therefore, throughout the process, children with high tension also could participant some kind of interactive effect, not only on the rehabilitation process but also could enhance their self confidence.

Acknowledgement. This work was supported by the National Science Council, Taiwan , under the Grant NSC 100-2410-H-024-028-MY2.

References

1. Ritterband-Rosenbaum, A., Christensen, M.S., Nielsen, J.B.: Twenty weeks of computer training improves sense of agency in children with spastic cerebral palsy. Research in Developmental Disabilities 33, 1227–1234 (2012)

2. Grigore, V., Mitrache, G., Predoiu, R., Roşca, R.: Characteristic of instrumental movements – eye hand coordination in sports. Procedia - Social and Behavioral Sciences 33, 193–197 (2012)
3. Coyle, Y., Yanéz, L., Verdú, M., Verdú, M.: The impact of the interactive whiteboard on the teacher and children's language use in an ESL immersion classroom. System 38, 614–625 (2010)
4. Sahin, Y.G., Cimen, F.M.: An interactive attention board: improving the attention of
5. Individuals with autism and mental retardation. The Turkish Online Journal of Educational Technology 10, 24–35 (2011)
6. López, O.S.: The digital learning classroom: improving English language learners' academic success in mathematics and reading using interactive whiteboard technology. Computers & Education 54, 901–915 (2010)
7. Vidal, J.C., Mucientes, M., Bugarn, A., Lama, M.: Machine scheduling in custom furniture industry through neuro-evolutionary hybridization. Applied Soft Computing 11, 1600–1613 (2011)
8. Wuang, Y.P., Chiang, C.S., Su, C.Y., Wang, C.C.: Effectiveness of virtual reality using Wii gaming technology in children with down syndrome. Research in Developmental Disabilities 32, 312–321 (2011)
9. Taylor, M.J.D., McCormick, D., Impson, R., Shawis, T., Griffin, M.: Activity promoting gaming systems in exercise and rehabilitation. Journal of Rehabilitation Research and Development 48, 1171–1186 (2011)
10. Amici, S., De, S.A., Lamberti, F., Pralio, B.: A Wii remote-based infrared-optical tracking system. Entertainment Computing 1, 119–124 (2010)
11. Lee, J.C.: Hacking the Nintendo Wii Remote. Pervasive Computing, 39–45 (2008)
12. Azcarate, G., Savage, R., Savage, S., Sucar, L.E., Reinkensmeyer, D., Toxtli, C., Roth, E., Molina, A.: Nintendo wii remote for computer simulated arm and wrist therapy in stroke survivors with upper extremity hemipariesis. Virtual Rehabilitation, 74–74 (2008)
13. Lin, C.Y., Jen, Y.H., Wang, L.C., Lin, H.H., Chang, L.W.: Assessment of the application of Wii remote for the design of interactive teaching materials. Communications in Computer and Information Science 235, 483–490 (2011)
14. Standen, P.J., Camm, C., Battersby, S., Brown, D.J., Harrison, M.: An evaluation of the Wii Nunchuk as an alternative assistive device for people with intellectual and physical disabilities using switch controlled software. Computers & Education 56, 2–10 (2011)
15. Lin, C.-Y., Wu, F.-G., Chen, T.-H., Wu, Y.-J., Huang, K., Liu, C.-P., Chou, S.-Y.: Using interface design with low-cost interactive whiteboard technology to enhance learning for children. In: Stephanidis, C. (ed.) Universal Access in HCI, Part IV, HCII 2011. LNCS, vol. 6768, pp. 558–566. Springer, Heidelberg (2011)

A Surgery Planning System by Visualizing 3D Profile of the Knee during Motion for Anterior Cruciate Ligament Reconstruction

Kouki Nagamune[1,2], Yuichiro Nishizawa[2], Daisuke Araki[2], Koji Nishimoto[2], Yuichi Hoshino[2], Ryosuke Kuroda[2], and Masahiro Kurosaka[2]

[1] University of Fukui, Fukui 910-0017, Japan
[2] University of Kobe, Kobe, Hyogo, 650-0017, Japan

Abstract. Anterior cruciate ligament (ACL) reconstruction is one of the surgeries to recover the knee function. The ACL reconstruction attach the grafts which is harvested from other parts to the femur and tibia. The grafts connects the femur and tibia by passing through the bone tunnels. One of the techniques makes the bone tunnel of the femur and tibia in one line at a proper knee flexion angle. If the angle is improper, the bone tunnel is made at high risk of infection. So, it is important to visualize the virtual bone tunnels at various knee angle as a planning system. This paper proposes a new method to visualize 3D profile of the knee and the virtual bone tunnels during motion with 3D scanner and 3D electromagnetic sensors.

Keywords: surgery planning system, visualization, orthopaedics.

1   Introduction

In the medical fields, dynamic motion of the profile of the bone is required for diagnosis. In case of failure of the anterior cruciate ligament (ACL), the motion of the knee is deferent from the normal knee. An expert doctor can clinically diagnose the difference by manual. However, the evaluation is subjectively and ambiguous information. Therefore, some systems have been developed for providing quantitative information. KT-1000 can mechanically measure an anterior position of the tibia relative to the femur [1]. Rolimeter (OS Inc., Hayward CA, USA) can measure a similar information with an electrogoniometer [2]. We also have developed a system can measure six degree of freedom of the knee motion with electromagnetic sensors [3]. However, these system cannot obtain information derived from surface of the bone (e.g., gap of the bones, motion of the ligament) which is one of the important criterion for diagnose. On the other hand, MRI and 3DCT can acquire profile information of the objects (e.g., bone, muscles, ligaments, fat tissue). A study [4] have reported bone relationship measured at each position. Naturally, the result of this method is different from the real dynamic. A study have reported that the bone relative information can be analyzed with fluoroscopy and 3DCT [5]. This method could accurately produce

C. Stephanidis and M. Antona (Eds.): UAHCI/HCII 2013, Part III, LNCS 8011, pp. 508–515, 2013.
© Springer-Verlag Berlin Heidelberg 2013

the contact point of the femur to the tibia. However, a kind of this method requires much time to registration due to image matching. This paper proposes a new method to analyze a relative motion of the bones and to visualize the virtual bone tunnels with 3D scanner and 3D electromagnetic sensors. The detail of the method is represented as follows.

2   Preliminaries

2.1   3D Scanner

The 3D laser scanner (FastSCAN Cobra, Polhemus) was employed to obtain 3D profile of the knee [6], [7]. This device consists of a receiver with laser scanner, a transmitter and signal processing unit (Fig. 1). The laser scanner has laser indicator and camera. The laser indicator radiates a broad-ranging beam to a target object. The beam is distorted by the target object, and captured by the camera. Then, the transmitter transmits a magnetic wave so that the receiver could calculate the position and pose of a space. The laser scanner obtained 3D profile of the target by manual moving the receiver.

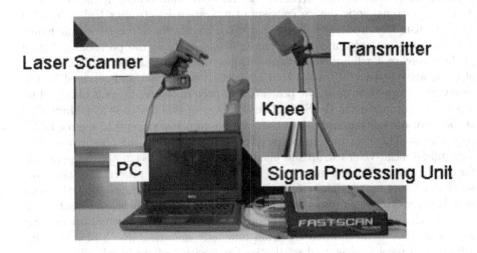

Fig. 1. 3D laser scanner

Measurement data is 3D numerical data that represents mesh structure of the target profile. A primitive mesh shape is triangle. The proposed method is applied for this obtained mesh data. An example of a measurement data of the knee is shown in Fig. 2. In the transmitter was placed near a cadaveric knee by using a tripod (Fig. 1). The effective area of the transmitter is 1000 mm.

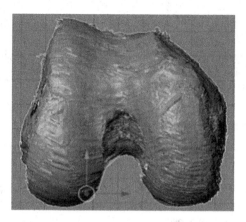

Fig. 2. An example of measurement data

2.2   3D Magnetic Sensor

A 3D magnetic sensors system consists of a personal computer, an electromagnetic device (Polhmus Inc., LIBERTY), and stylus and braces as shown in Fig. 3. The electromagnetic device consists of a System Electronics Unit (SEU), a single transmitter, and one to four receivers. The relationship between the femur and the tibia are calculated using the information from the position and pose of the receivers. Each analyzed value was provided and recorded at 240 Hz. The electromagnetic wave is transmitted from the transmitter, and received by the receivers. Information from the position and pose of the receivers is obtained by a personal computer via the SEU. The accuracy of this device is as follows. The static error of position and orientation are 0.8 mm RMS and 0.15 degree RMS, respectively. The electromagnetic receivers are attached to the plastic braces by a circumferential Velcro strap and placed approximately 13 cm above the patella for the femur and approximately 10 cm below the tibial tubercle for the tibia so as not to interfere with examination maneuvers. The braces allow the non-invasive measurement of knee kinematics. The operating theater was set up so that the electromagnetic devices are positioned within the optimal operational zone and there is no interference from magnetic materials [8]. A plastic stylus affixed by a receiver was used to digitize the position of landmarks.

3   Methods

Firstly, 6 DOF (degrees of freedom) of the knee motion should be analyzed from 3D magnetic sensors. The 6 DOF is important information for knowing relative motion between the femur and tibia. Finally, the anatomical landmark which is obtained from the femur and tibia, is used for registration of motion and profile data. Each detail is explained at following sections.

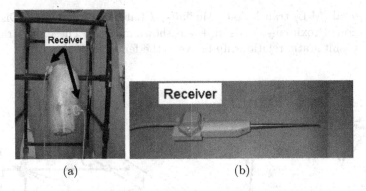

(a)   (b)

Fig. 3. 3D magnetic sensors

3.1   Calculation of 6 DOF

The anatomical reference points were digitized by pointing a probe equipped with an additional receiver before 6 DOF kinematics measurement. All reference points were indicated at 90 degree of knee flexion using the stylus affixed by the receiver, because at 90 degree the distance between the transmitter and receivers is within optimal range and anatomical reference points are most distinguishable. The reference points were (P1) the greater trochanter of the femur, (P2, P3) the medial and lateral epicondyles, (P4) intersection between the knee joint line and the medial collateral ligament, (P5) the proximal edge of the fibula, (P6, P7) the distal edges of the medial and lateral malleoli of the ankle as shown in Fig. 4 (a). In acquiring the kinematics data, the reference points were calculated from position and pose information of the receivers.

The coordinate systems on the femur and tibia are defined as follows (Fig. 5). The center of P2 and P3 is used as the origin of the femoral coordinate system. The bone axis of the femur (Z) is the line between P1 and the origin of the femur. The medial and lateral (M-L) axis of the femur (X) is the projected line of the line connecting P2 and P3 on the perpendicular plane to the bone axis. The anterior and posterior (A-P) axis of the femur (Y) is the line, which is the cross product of the bone and M-L axes. The center of P4 and P5 is used as the origin of the tibial coordinate system. The bone axis of the tibia (z) is the line connecting the center of P4 and P5 with the center of P6 and P7. The M-L axis of the tibia (x) is the projected line of the line connecting P4 and P5 on the perpendicular plane to the bone axis. The A-P axis of the tibia (y) is the line, which is the cross product of the bone and ML axes.

The 6 DOF in knee kinematics were calculated by modifying the principle of the joint coordinate system proposed by Grood and Suntay [[9]] using the bone axis of the femur instead of the mechanical axis as shown in Fig. 4. The 6 DOF consists of three rotations (Flexion-Extension (F-E) rotation: Flexion(+) / Extension(-), Valgus-Varus (V-V) rotation : Valgus(+) / Varus(-), External-Internal (E-I) rotation : External(+) / Internal(-)), and three translations (Anterior-Posterior (A-P) translation : Anterior(+) / Posterior(-),

Medial-Lateral (M-L) translation : Medial(-) / Lateral(+), Proximal-Distal (P-D) translation : Proximal(-) / Distal(+)) as shown in Fig. 6. These six parameters represent a joint static relationship between the femur and tibia.

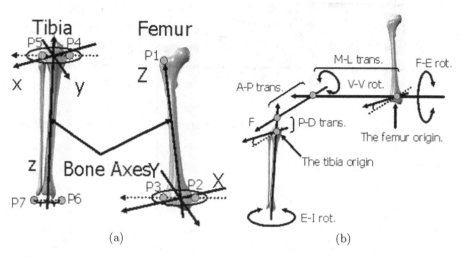

(a)   (b)

Fig. 4. Coordinate systems

3.2   Registration of Motion and Profile Data

Registration of motion and profile data is performed with three reference points for each bone. The three reference points makes a triangle. The profile data is transformed so that the triangle of the profile is corresponding to the triangle of the motion. In this study, we employ medial and lateral epicondyles, and posterior surface of middle of the femur for the femur, and posterior edge of medial and lateral condyle, and anterior surface of middle of the tibia for the tibia. We consider three points matrix A of the profile data, and B of the motion data, and transformation matrix M. Each matrix is expressed as the following equations.

$$A = \begin{bmatrix} x_{a1} & x_{a2} & x_{a3} \\ y_{a1} & y_{a2} & y_{a3} \\ z_{a1} & z_{a2} & z_{a3} \end{bmatrix} \tag{1}$$

$$B = \begin{bmatrix} x_{b1} & x_{b2} & x_{b3} \\ y_{b1} & y_{b2} & y_{b3} \\ z_{b1} & z_{b2} & z_{b3} \end{bmatrix} \tag{2}$$

$$M = \begin{bmatrix} x_{11} & x_{12} & x_{13} \\ y_{21} & y_{22} & y_{23} \\ z_{31} & z_{32} & z_{33} \end{bmatrix} \tag{3}$$

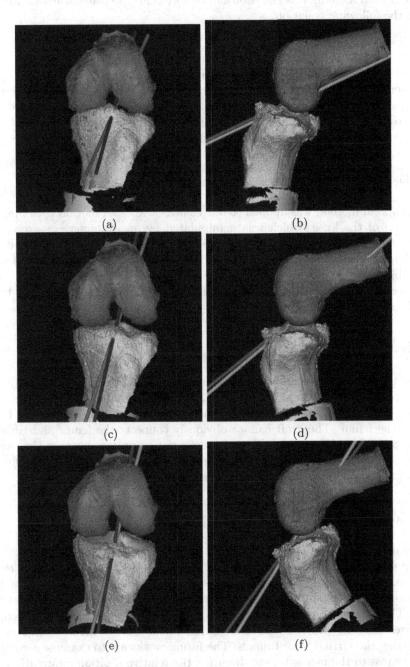

(a)

(b)

(c)

(d)

(e)

(f)

Fig. 5. Virtual bone tunnels

where $B = MA$. Here, this equation can be solved for the transformation matrix M as the following equation.

$$M = BA^{-1} \tag{4}$$

Then, each mesh of the profile can be translated to the position of the 3D magnetic sensor by using the transformation matrix M. Then, the translated profiles of the femur and tibia, and each anatomical reference points are calculated. Finally, the virtual bone tunnels are visualized by connecting anteromedial (AM) and posterolateral (PL) attachments of the each bones.

4   Experiments

The proposal method was applied to one cadaveric knee. A motion with flexion-extension of the knee, which was manipulated by an examiner, was recorded by 3D magnetic sensor. The reference points of registration and AM and PL attachments were also recorded. Then, the soft-tissue surrounding the femur and tibia was completely removed. The profiles of the femur and tibia were acquired by 3D scanner. In this experiment, the virtual bone tunnels and bone relationships were visualized.

5   Results

The virtual bone tunnles and bone relationships were shown in Fig. 5. The figures are corronal and sagittal at 70, 90, and 110 knee flexion angle, respectively. In case of 70 degree, the virtual bone tunnel runs obviously parallel to the bone axis of the femur. The graft cannot obviously connects the femur and tibia in this relationship. Also in case of 90 degree is not so proper, because the extra-articular point of the virtual bone tunnel has a risk for infection. The case of 110 degree is the most safety in comparing with other angles.

6   Conclusion

This study was to propose a registration method of 3D profile and motion data and to visualize the virtual bone tunnels obtained by 3D scanner and 3D magnetic sensors. Especially, a solving method about a transformation equation was presented. In the experiment, the proposal method was applied to one cadaveric knee. The virtual bone tunnel and bone relationships was visualized. Then, it indicates that the proposed method could show a risk for medical doctors by visualizing the virtual bone tunnels. The future works are to examine a contact point, stress to the meniscus, etc. by using the relative position information.

References

1. Fox, J.M., Sherman, O.H., Markolf, K.: Arthroscopic anterior cruciate ligament repair: preliminary results and instrumented testing for anterior stability. Arthroscopy 1(3), 175–181 (1985)
2. Vergis, A., Gillquist, J.: Sagittal plane translation of the knee during stair walking in healthy volunteers measured by an electrogoniometer chain. J. Scand. J. Med. Sci. Sports 5(6), 353–357 (1995)
3. Kuroda, R., Hoshino, Y., Nagamune, K., Kubo, S., Nishimoto, K., Araki, D., Yamaguchi, M., Yoshiya, M.S., Kurosaka, M.: Intraoperative Measurement of Pivot Shift by Electromagnetic Sensors. Operative Techniques in Orthopaedics 18(3), 190–195 (2008)
4. Arno, S., Chaudhary, M., Walker, P.S., Forman, R., Glassner, P., Regatte, R., Oh, C.: Anterior-posterior stability of the knee by an MR image subtraction method. Knee 19(4), 445–449 (2012)
5. Lu, T.-W., Tsai, T.-Y., Kuo, M.-Y., Hsu, H.-C., Chen, H.-L.: In vivo three-dimensional kinematics of the normal knee during active extension under unloaded and loaded conditions using single-plane fluoroscopy. Medical Engineering and Physics 30(8), 1004–1012 (2008)
6. Edgar, D., Day, R., Briffa, N.K., Cole, J., Wood, F.: Volume measurement using the Polhemus FastSCAN 3D laser scanning: a novel application for burns clinical research. J. Burn. Care. Res. 29(6), 994–1000 (2008)
7. McKernan, B., Bydder, S.A., Deans, T., Nixon, M.A., Joseph, D.J.: Surface laser scanning to routinely produce casts for patient immobilization during radiotherapy. Australas Radiol. 51(2), 150–153 (2007)
8. Milne, A.D., Chess, D.G., Johnson, J.A., King, G.J.: Accuracy of an electromagnetic tracking device: a study of the optimal range and metal interference. J. Biomech. 29(6), 791–793 (1996)
9. Grood, E.S., Suntay, W.J.: A joint coordinate system for the clinical description of three-dimensional motions: application to the knee. J. Biomech. Eng. 105(2), 136–144 (1983)

Data Reduction for Continuum of Care: An Exploratory Study Using the Predicate-Argument Structure to Pre-process Radiology Sentences for Measurement of Semantic Similarity

Eric Newsom[1] and Josette F. Jones[2]

[1] Indiana University Health, Indianapolis, IN, USA
enewsom@iuhealth.org
[2] Indiana University-Purdue University Indianapolis, Indianapolis, IN, USA
jofjones@iupui.edu

Abstract. In the clinical setting, continuum of care depends on integrated information services to assure a smooth progression for patient centered care, and these integrated information services must understand past events and personal circumstances to make care relevant. Clinicians face a problem that the amount of information produced in disparate electronic clinical notes is increasing to levels incapable of being processed by humans. Clinicians need a function in information services that can reduce the free text data to a message useful at time of care. Information extraction (IE) is a sub-field of natural language processing with the goal of data reduction of unstructured free text. Pertinent to IE is an annotated corpus that frames how IE methods should create a logical expression necessary for processing meaning of text. This study explores and reports on the requirements to using the predicate-argument statement (PAS) as the framework. A convenient sample from a prior study with ten synsets of 100 unique sentences from radiology reports deemed by domain experts to mean the same thing will be the text from which PAS structures are formed. Through content analysis of pattern recognition, findings show PAS is a feasible framework to structure sentences for semantic similarity measurement.

Keywords: Information Extraction, Predicate-Argument Structure, Semantic Similarity.

1   Introduction

Today's knowledge worker has far too much published information to review for conducting his/her professional practice [1]. In healthcare, the majority of knowledge is in the form of free text such as professional journals and patient clinical notes [2]. These forms of free text have been linked to profits [3] and are central to a health system reliant on an integration of services to deliver patient centered care over a continuum [3,4]. Informational continuity forms from past events and personal circumstances [6] allowing for the clinician to establish a personal relationship and

C. Stephanidis and M. Antona (Eds.): UAHCI/HCII 2013, Part III, LNCS 8011, pp. 516–525, 2013.
© Springer-Verlag Berlin Heidelberg 2013

cooperation [7]. These clinical notes, therefore, provide the patient specific data necessary for continuum of care. The continuum of care can be greatly enhanced if means exist to synthesize from disparate clinical notes a meaningful message at the point in time for delivery of care. Analyzing these unique forms of knowledge by a machine-driven mechanism in order to decrease the knowledge worker's burden of reading is a goal of natural language processing (NLP). For data reduction to occur as a normal function in continuity of care, NLP methods use information extraction (IE) methods [2], which depend on an annotated corpus [1] to model structuring of unstructured text as a pre-process before semantic comparisons. To accomplish this, an annotation method has to be used that can retain the semantics of the entire sentence. One method uses a form of semantic role labeling (SRL) called predicate-argument structures (PAS) for IE of free text and appears to be the most commonly researched and used method for analysis of entire sentence structures [1,8-18].

For this study, PAS will serve as the annotation framework, but the measurement that will be used to determine the semantic equivalence for data reduction between two PAS elements will be semantic similarity. Semantic similarity is degree of closeness between two different texts and attempts to replicate how humans represent relationships within these varying vocabulary expressions to formulate meaning of experiences [19]. This study will evaluate the feasibility to use PAS as a pre-processing step for comparing semantic similarity of sentences.

1.1   Problem Statement

To test semantic similarity, concepts need to be represented at the atomic level in order to understand how broad or narrow one text element is to another [20]. Successful studies that have tested for semantic similarity have focused on terms or lexical elements [21-24]. These studies attest to the idea that less complexity of an expressed thought the easier it is to measure semantic similarity. In another study that comes closest to evaluating sentential semantic similarity through a method called Named Entity Recognition (NER), the method in [25] fails with issues of complex synonymy, overlapping text span, and structured interpretations. [25] attempts to look at the whole meaning of a sentence, but the study underlines the difficulty of comparing the equivalency between two sentences when dissected and chunked into smaller parts. In a PAS annotation study that closely resembles this one, annotation of semantics is not evaluated for semantic similarity [26]. It remains to be evaluated if PAS frames can rise to a level of complexity to analyze sentential semantic similarity.

2   Review of Literature

The contribution of PAS to IE is its ability to retain structure of sentences [11], contribute to inductive learning [16], and facilitate mapping of arguments to ontological references [15]. These are three components essential for successful NLP [3]. Typically, PAS development is guided by guidelines introduced through the Propbank project [18,26] whereby a usage of a predicate's sense is referenced by a RolesetID frame (see.01, be.02) in its knowledgebase. The RolesetID frame provides argument definitions to mark textual boundaries in sentence annotation.

While guidelines instruct a process of annotation of PAS, literature suggests the annotation process incorporate certain considerations. [15,16] contend that modification of a PAS frame is encouraged to correctly identify observations of a domain's structure necessary for semantic translation. For a corpus of radiology reports, a study by [27] frequently encountered missing predicates and implied concepts. These findings concerning a radiological corpus could mean that annotation will identify arguments and predicates not anchored in text. However, if domain experts make this kind of inference then the purpose of annotation serves to mimic the process of human judgment. For sentences lacking a predicate, this study will have to determine a method in the annotation process for measuring successfulness of constructing complete sentences from incomplete sentences and inferring implied/incomplete text.

If method of annotation is PAS, then focus is on the predicate, and to assure that predicates function to guide argument development, [12] argue that verbs should be classified based on syntactical structures present in corpus. For example, does the predicate accept a direct object or does it not. Such syntactical analysis of how a sentence is structured around specific verbs could help understand the arguments. Another issue that has to be addressed before annotating PAS frames is to understand how the corpus handles nominalization of verbs [13]. Nominalized verbs take different forms, such as gerunds, and these forms may have arguments despite not being the predicate of the sentence. This study will have to make a conclusion if the Propbank annotation guidelines and knowledge base can serve as the formal schema to build a PAS frame from a corpus that has unique usages of verbs and how those usages have to be annotated. The complexity of using PAS as a formal schema to measure sentential semantic similarity lies not in forming syntactical phrases but in examining similarity of text phrases of one sentence to text phrases of another. This kind of measurement goes beyond the discreteness of word to word comparison and requires a representational scheme to assist with matching which phrase of one sentence should be compared to a phrase of another sentence. To adhere to principles of semantic similarity, this representational scheme not only has to address syntax and conceptual needs in a sentence, but it has to provide a foundation to capture the accumulative sense formed by concepts in the sentence [15]. The goal, then, is to have a representational scheme whereby the output of syntactical phrases formed from one sentence are appropriately matched and compared to those of another sentence, and this representational scheme will serve as the basis for pattern discovery of synonymy [28].

Creating this scheme could pose the biggest obstacle to using the PAS. [27] state PAS cannot scale; however, it is not known if this statement is true or not. The problem of scalability of PAS is presented when two semantically equivalent sentences have two different predicates. In such cases, it is possible that content of the arguments and modifiers of one sentence may not match to the other predicate's corresponding arguments and modifiers. In some cases, there may be no text to compare. Table 1 shows how three semantically equivalent sentences present the problem of scalability with three difference predicate senses.

Table 1. --Scalability Problem of PAS

Sentence 1	The lungs demonstrate left basilar atelectasis or infiltrate.		
Sentence 2	There is interval clearing of the left lower lobe infiltrate.		
Sentence 3	The left lower lobe infiltrate is identified.		
	Sentence 1	Sentence 2	Sentence 3
RolesetID	demonstrate.01	be.02	identify.01
Predicate Use	*'show off'*	*'existential'*	*'label, call'*
Arg0	The lungs		
Arg1	**atelectasis or infiltrate**	interval clearing	**infiltrate**
Arg2			
ArgM-Locative	left basilar	of the left lower lobe	The left lower lobe
ArgM-Cause		**infiltrate**	

In each sentence, PAS annotates the complete syntactical structure of the sentence; therefore, the complete sense of each sentence is maintained. But when the goal is to compare the semantics across each role, problems arise from the fact that each predicate assumes a different structure for role assignments. It is evident that when trying to measure semantic similarity of varying predicates, not every role will contain like content. Arg1 of sentence 1 & 3 have semantic similarity but Arg1 of sentence 2 is not semanticly similar despite the fact that the defined roles of the verb places the actual content that could be compared in the modifier 'cause'. The question then is how is it possible to 'cross' compare arguments for a synset comprised of various predicates? Is it possible to compare differing semantic roles? This study will investigate patterns among synsets with varying predicates for feasibility of an algorithm allowing cross comparing of semantic roles.

3 Methods, Design, and Sampling

This study used a traditional annotation schema for clinical corpus [29]. Guidelines for the schema were adopted from the Propbank annotation [30] and used the Unified Verb Index [31]to facilitate construction of PAS frames. The reader is directed to [30] for further understanding of PAS. While the study is primarily an exploratory, non-experimental, methodological study, it will use a content analysis process for pattern recognition of meaning in text developed for NLP [32].

A convenience sample from a prior study [27] is used as the data set. The data set represents ten synsets. Each synset has 100 randomly selected sentences (n=1000) from original synsets containing more than 1,000 sentences of an ongoing annotation project. A propositional sentence serves as the representing sentence for the synset (see Table 2).

Table 2. --Proposition Sentences of Synsets

Synset	Propositional Sentence of Synset
1.	The endotracheal tube is above the carina.
2.	There is no pneumothorax.
3.	There is a left lower lobe pulmonary infiltrate(s).
4.	The pulmonary vessels are prominent.
5.	A posterior anterior (PA) chest x-ray was performed.
6.	The gray white matter differentiation of the brain is normal.
7.	The intervertebral disc heights are normal.
8.	There are pelvic phlebolith(s).
9.	There is small vessel ischemic disease of the brain.
10.	The lungs are diffusely hazy bilaterally.

3.1   Data Analysis/Content Analysis

One researcher validated and analyzed the data but used alternative means reported in [33] to address validity. The content analysis method was adapted from [15] to address the dominant problem of scalability. In that study, development of PAS begins by identifying the NP and VP. In this study, the NP and VP was annotated (see Figure 1) for each of the proposition sentences of the 10 synsets and extended to annotate respective modifiers.

Synset Proposition: The endotracheal tube is above the carina.
                NP   VP

Fig. 1. Synset 1 in Table 2

The intent is to establish a baseline for possible pattern recognition of semantically equivalent phrases not annotated to identical arguments in PAS frames due to varying uses of predicates.

4   Findings

For sentences with missing predicates, a process was applied whereby the annotator transformed the incomplete sentence to a complete, firstly, with the predicate RolesetID 'be.02' ('there are'/'there is'<NP>). If the sentence did not make sense with 'be.02' usage, 'be.01' RolesetID was applied (<NP> 'is'/'are'<VP>). If that transformed structure did not make sense, the annotator used any predicate that made the sentence understandable. 260 sentences were missing a predicate and the results are reported in Figure 2. The summary indicates that a radiology sentence missing a predicate can more than likely be completed with 'be.02'.

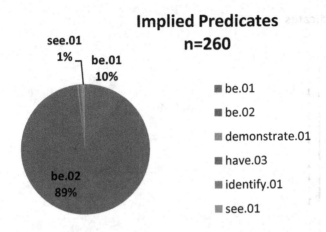

Fig. 2. Summary of All Synsets for Sentences Missing A Predicate

Figure 3 shows a frequency summary of predicate usage across sysnsets that clearly shows the dominate usage of the predicates 'to be', be.01 and be.02. With over 2/3 of the predicates expressed in the dataset using an existential form of 'to be', it is evident that Arg0 is absent. In fact, with non-'to be' predicates, less than 1% annotated text to Arg0. Arg0 represents the role of an agent or someone doing the action. In contrast, all sentences annotated with Arg1 (entity that receives action). According to [30], this indicates that predicates in this dataset are 'externally caused'. With externally caused predicates, the explanation for the motive or stimulate in the sentence is implied. The implication that predicates in a corpus are externally-caused vs. internally-caused suggests that the writer has a great deal of leniency to express a thought. There is an element that use of language in such a corpus is generalizable. A radiology report merely has to present observations and interpretation of those observations. It does not have to explain the actions of the disease process requiring use of internally-cause predicates. Because of the generalizability of text annotated to an argument for externally-caused predicates, it is possible to compare the content of an argument with a 'defined' semantic role label to content of an argument of a differently 'defined' semantic role label.

If comparison of differing semantic role labels is feasible in a radiology corpus, then a predictable pattern is necessary to establish an algorithm for IE processing. For each of the sysnets, a flowchart was developed to indicate based on the RolesetID, where the content of NP, VP, and modifiers of proposition sentence is annotated in candidate sentences. An example of the flow chart is Figure 4. Across all synsets, it is estimated that the uncovered pattern will be an algorithm with a content coverage of no less than 96%. Based on a predicate's usage (RolesetID), the necessary content of

**Unique Predicates
n=33**

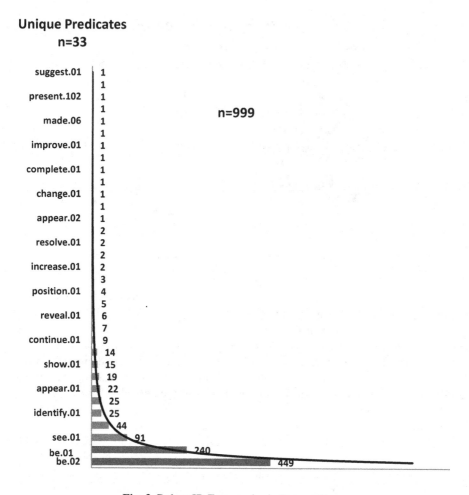

Fig. 3. RolesetID Frequencies in Dataset Corpus

arguments/modifiers of the candidate sentence needed to compare to those of the proposition sentence can be predicted. For RolesetIDs 'be.01' and 'be.02', conflicting patterns were often found; however, in all cases, patterns of usage determine what circumstances apply to one usage sense vs. another. In Figure 4, the VP concept of proposition sentence is found in Arg2 as long as Arg2 does not have the terms 'place', 'position', and 'present'. Otherwise, for RolesetIDs 'be.01' and 'be.02', the VP concept is found in the PAS modifier 'Locative' of the candidate sentence.

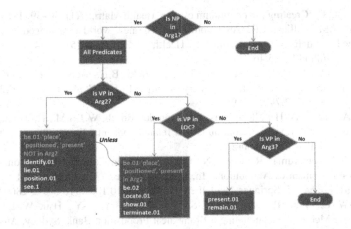

Fig. 4. --Algorithm Predicting Location of Equivelent Content of Proposition NP/VP for Synset 1 (See Figure 1) Based on RolesetID

5   Conclusions/Future Directions

This study looked at using the PAS as a pre-processing function to structure unstructured text for evaluation of semantic similarity of two unique sentences. Findings from content analysis showed a way to manage incomplete sentences, justify comparison of differing arguments, and predict pattern for mapping appropriate differing arguments. What remains to be tested is if the methods discovered in this study are repeatable with equivalent synsets from another radiology corpus. It is hypothesized, however, that new predicates would not drastically change the prediction patterns as the distribution or curve (See Figure 3) of predicates is not expected to vary. While a radiology corpus is not entirely representative of the content clinicians will have to review to assure continuum of care, a radiology corpus does provide a good context for NLP experimentation because of its content predictability. Future experiments will have to broaden the clinical corpus content, and those findings based on annotation methods in this study may have different results [26]. Future experiments with this dataset will have to take the annotated PAS corpus and conduct experiments of semantic similarity to determine if the logical representation of the proposition sentence is truly semantically representative of sysnet to accomplish data reduction.

References

1. Zweigenbaum, P., Demner-Fushman, D.: Advanced literature-mining tools. In: Edwards, D., Stajich, J., Hansen, D. (eds.) Bioinformatics, pp. 347–380. Springer, New York (2009)
2. Demner-Fushman, D., Chapman, W.W., McDonald, C.J.: What can natural language processing do for clinical decision support? Journal of Biomedical Informatics 42, 760–772 (2009)
3. Friedman, C., Hripcsak, G.: Natural language processing and its future in medicine. Academic Medicine 74(8), 890–895 (1999)

4. Evashwick, C.: Creating the continuum of care. Health Matrix 7(1), 30–39 (1989)
5. Shortell, S.M., Gillies, R.R., Anderson, D.A.: The new world of managed care: Creating organized delivery systems. Health Affairs 13(5), 46–64 (1994), doi:10.1377/hlthaff.13.5.46
6. Haggerty, J.L., Reid, R.J., Freeman, G.K., Starfield, B.H., Adair, C.E., McKendry, R.: Continuity of care: a multidisciplinary review. BMJ 327(7425), 1219–1221 (2003), doi:10.1136/bmj.327.7425.1219
7. Uijen, A.A., Schers, H.J., Schellevis, F.G., van den Bosch, W.J.H.M.: How unique is continuity of care? A review of continuity and related concepts. Family Practice 29(3), 264–271 (2012), doi:10.1093/fampra
8. Tan, H., Kaliyaperumal, R., Benis, N.: Ontology-Driven Construction of Domain Corpus with Frame Semantics Annotations. In: Gelbukh, A. (ed.) CICLing 2012, Part I. LNCS, vol. 7181, pp. 54–65. Springer, Heidelberg (2012), doi:10.1007/978-3-642-28604-9_5
9. Chou, W.-C., Tsai, R.T.-H., Su, Y.-S., Ku, W., Sung, T.-Y., Hsu, W.-L.: A Semi-Automatic Method for Annotating a Biomedical Proposition Bank, Sydney, Australia. Paper Presented at the Proceedings of the Workshop on Frontiers in Linguistically Annotated Corpora (2006)
10. Tsai, R., Chou, W.-C., Su, Y.-S., Lin, Y.-C., Sung, C.-L., Dai, H.-J., et al.: BIOSMILE: A semantic role labeling system for biomedical verbs using a maximum-entropy model with automatically generated template features. BMC Bioinformatics 8(1), 325 (2007)
11. Cohen, K.B., Hunter, L.: A critical review of PASBio's argument structures for biomedical verbs. BMC Bioinformatics, 7(suppl. 3), S5 (2006)
12. Godbert, E., Royaute, J.: PredXtract, A Generic Platform to Extract in Texts Predicate Argument Structures (PAS), Valleta, Malta. Paper Presented at the LREC 2010 Proceedings (2010)
13. Kilicoglu, H., Fiszman, M., Rosemblat, G., Marimpieti, S., Rindflesch, T.: Arguments of Nominals in Semantic Intepretation of Biomedical Text, Uppsala, Sweden. Paper Presented at the BioNLP 2010 (2010)
14. Kogan, Y., Collier, N., Pakhomov, S., Krauthammer, M.: Towards Semantic Role Labeling & IE in the Medical Literature. Paper Presented at the Annual AMIA Symposium (2005)
15. Miyao, Y., Ohta, T., Masuda, K., Tsuruoka, Y., Yoshida, K., Ninomiya, T., Tsujii, J.I.: Semantic Retrieval for the Accurate Identification of Relational Concepts in Massive Textbases. Paper Presented at the Proceedings of the 21st International Conference on Computational Linguistics and the 44th Annual Meeting of the Association for Computational Linguistics, Sydney, Australia (2006)
16. Surdeanu, M., Harabagiu, S., Williams, J., Aarseth, P.: Using Predicate-Argument Structures for Information Extraction. Paper Presented at the Proceedings of the 41st Annual Meeting of the Association for Computational Linguistics, Sapporo, Japan (July 2003)
17. Tsai, R., Chou, W.-C., Su, Y.-S., Lin, Y.-C., Sung, C.-L., Dai, H.-J., Hsu, W.-L.: BIOSMILE: A semantic role labeling system for biomedical verbs using a maximum-entropy model with automatically generated template features. BMC Bioinformatics 8(1), 325 (2007)
18. Wattarujeekrit, T., Shah, P., Collier, N.: PASBio: Predicate-argument structures for event extraction in molecular biology. BMC Bioinformatics 5(1), 155 (2004)
19. Samsonovic, A.V., Ascoli, G.A.: Principal semantic components of language and the measurement of meaning. PLoS ONE 5(6), e10921 (2010)
20. Caviedes, J.E., Cimino, J.J.: Towards the development of a conceptual distance metric for the UMLS. Journal of Biomedical Informatics 37(2), 77–85 (2004)

21. Chaves-González, J.M., Martínez-Gil, J.: Evolutionary algorithm based on different semantic similarity functions for synonym recognition in the biomedical domain. Knowledge-Based Systems 37, 62–69 (2013), doi:
    http://dx.doi.org/10.1016/j.knosys.2012.07.005
22. Builtelaar, P., Sacaleanu, B.: Ranking and Selecting Synsets by Domain Relevance. Paper Presented at the Proceedings of WordNet and Other Lexical Resources (2001)
23. Elhadad, N., Sutaria, K.: Mining a Lexicon of Technical Terms and Lay Equivalents. Paper presented at the Proceedings of the Workshop on BioNLP 2007: Biological, Translational, and Clinical Language Processing, Prague, Czech Republic (2007)
24. Mihalcea, R., Corley, C., Strapparava, C.: Corpus-Based and Knowledge-Based Measures of Text Semantic Similarity. Paper Presented at the Proceedings of the 21st National Conference on Artificial intelligence, Boston, Massachusetts (2006)
25. Savova, G.K., Masanz, J.J., Ogren, P.V., Zheng, J., Sohn, S., Kipper-Schuler, K.C., Chute, C.G.: Mayo clinical Text Analysis and Knowledge Extraction System (cTAKES): Architecture, component evaluation and applications. Journal of the American Medical Informatics Association 17(5), 507–513 (2010), doi:10.1136/jamia.2009.001560
26. Albright, D., Lanfranchi, A., Fredriksen, A., Styler, W.F., Warner, C., Hwang, J.D., Savova, G.K.: Towards comprehensive syntactic and semantic annotations of the clinical narrative. Journal of the American Medical Informatics Association (2013), doi:10.1136/amiajnl-2012-001317
27. Friedlin, J., Mahoui, M., Jones, J., Jamieson, P.: Knowledge Discovery and Data Mining of Free Text Radiology Reports. In: 2011 First IEEE International Conference on Paper Presented at the Healthcare Informatics, Imaging and Systems Biology, HISB, July 26-29 (2011)
28. McCrae, J., Collier, N.: Synonym set extraction from the biomedical literature by lexical pattern discovery. BMC Bioinformatics 9(159) (2008)
29. Xia, F., Yetisgen-Yildiz, M.: Clinical Corpus Annotation: Challenges and Strategies, Istanbul, Turkey. Paper Presented at the Third Workshop on Building and Evaluating Resources for Biomedical Text Mining Workshop Programme (2012)
30. Babko-Malaya, O.: Propbank Annotation Guidelines (2005),
    http://verbs.colorado.edu/~mpalmer/projects/ace/
    PBguidelines.pdf (retrieved November 7, 2010)
31. Unified Verb Index (2012),
    http://verbs.colorado.edu/verb-index/index.php (retrieved December 12, 2012)
32. Yu, C.H., Jannasch-Pennell, A., DiGangi, S.: Compatibility between text mining and qualitative research in the perspectives of grounded theory, content analysis, and reliability. The Qualitative Report 16(3), 730–744 (2011)
33. Holden, R.J.: Physicians' beliefs about using EMR and CPOE: In pursuit of a contextualized understanding of health IT use behavior. International Journal of Medical Informatics 79(2), 71–80 (2010)

Ontological Model for CDSS in Knee Injury Management

Kanitha Phalakornkule, Josette F. Jones, and John T. Finnell

School of Informatics and Computing Indiana University- Indianapolis, USA
{kpa,jofjones,jfinnell}@iupui.edu

Abstract. Due to the increased adoption of Electronic Health Records (EHR) and its integrated clinical decision support (CDS) tools, health information technology (HIT) is a key influence in Medicine. The main challenges in healthcare are to integrate the information across care units and to increase the quality of continuity of patient care. There are three types of knowledge sources in medicine: (1) Evidence Based Practice (EBP), (2) Practice Based Evidence, and (3) Medical Textbooks. Information in these sources is presented and organized in different formats. Ontology may allow us to integrate knowledge discovered from two separate data sources without platform restrictions. The knowledge can be reusable and sharable without the need of technology. Further, this paper also combines the strengths from both EBP and PBE on knee treatment. The hybrid knowledge model will derived from real practices while integrating existing external knowledge discovered and reported in published literatures.

1   Introduction

Since the early 1990s, health information technology (HIT) has played an important role in the improving and continuity of health care delivery globally. One of the main influences comes through the introduction of Electronic Health Record Systems (EHRs) facilitating continuity of care throughout patient's lifespan, and across regional, national, and global healthcare systems. Clinical Decision Support (CDS) Systems play an important key in EHRs by computing and analyzing stored EHR data. CDS systems (CDSS) facilitate decision making at the point of care by advising or alerting clinicians with analyzed information that is in its knowledge model. Based on its knowledge model, CDSS can influence how a clinician makes their decision at at the point of care. Moreover, CDSS can assist clinicians in advising the best evidence or warning of potential risks which the clinicians have not encountered before. Therefore, the knowledge model in the CDSS is a critical key to its performance. The efficiency and accuracy of the knowledge model remain to be fully understood, which prevents CDS in EHR to be fully realized.

There are two types of dynamic knowledge sources for CDSS: (1) Evidence Based Practice (EBP) and (2) Practice Based Evidence. Knowledge from the Evidence Based Practice or EBP collects and utilizes the best available academic research evidences as data, while Practice-Base knowledge is derived from the learning through clinicians' own experiences in the day-to-day profession (Barkman and Mellor-Clark

C. Stephanidis and M. Antona (Eds.): UAHCI/HCII 2013, Part III, LNCS 8011, pp. 526–535, 2013.
© Springer-Verlag Berlin Heidelberg 2013

2003). EBP has been in Medicine for decades and is more commonly used in CDSS so it tends to bring many promises. However, EBP should not be used by itself without requiring additional new information about each different patient, each singular clinician and hence each dissimilar practice, since its knowledge is based on aggregated data from a specific group of population of specific interest in a controlled environment which does not likely exist in a real practice. Additionally, many of compound variables in research studies are not published in articles; therefore, the influences of these variables are unknown and are not taken into account when the CDSS's knowledge model based on EBP is applied in the real practice. This is why the efficiency of EBP has been questionable.(Green 2006 & 2008)

On the other end, Practice-Base Evidence (PBE) only utilizes clinical expertise and gathers data from the evidence during practices. PBE mainly collects evidence from routine practices with similar, if not the same, aims and outcomes in uncontrolled environment. Outcomes resulted from a practice-based study have higher external validity because they are based on routine practice. With a PBE approach, the experiences gained in individual practices will be reviewed and learned at the point-of-care. PBE is a more patient-specific approach than EBP because the compound factors in its knowledge model are the same as in the practice. Nevertheless, while PBE approach seems to be a great model to follow, PBE implementation requires large amount of data in order to build a knowledge model. It needs to be able to share its finding and integrate new knowledge to its knowledge base across multiple practices.

Opportunistically, with current EHRs and other technologies, the development of a knowledge network is possible and can be deployed and dispersed rapidly within healthcare organizations. Even though knowledge representation is independent from platform and database systems, the structure of knowledge representation could be based on individual practice's workflow and organization structure in order to be more meaningful and suitable for individual practice (Dang, Hedayati et al. 2008). Ontological concepts and a knowledge editor such as Protégé by Stanford University are well-known tools used in semantic network representing and integrating knowledge models. Using an ontologic approach will allow us to integrate and re-use knowledge discovered from multiple separate data sources without platform restrictions. The hybrid knowledge model will be derived from a real practice setting while integrating existing external knowledge discovered and reported in published literature. This will enhance the performance of the CDS to be patient-specific while being aware of any unknown knowledge and adaptive with high external validation. The innovative focus of this study is to bring both EBP and PBE approaches, along with an ontological knowledge model to CDS's functionality. As of now, there have been no studies published explaining the extraction and value of both EBP and PBE from existing clinical practice data using in CDS, while many studies have demonstrated how to build evidence-based practice (EBP) and its value to clinical practice.

2   Background

In information science, an ontology knowledge framework is known for representing a hierarchical-structure knowledge model that consists of classes, properties or slots, relationships between classes and individuals (or instances) (Gruber 2009) due to its ability to cluster many transaction-level concepts into a domain level (T. Mabotuwana 2009). It's structure is in hierarchical or in topology format similar to a human making a decision (Milgrom 2010). Many studies in medicine implemented an ontologic approach in order to measure qualitative outcomes. Another main benefit of the ontologic framework is that it allows the domain knowledge to be independent from technology. In other words, it can be run on multiple platforms with different capabilities (Farion, Michalowski et al. 2009). An ontology knowledge model allows a separation between logic knowledge and software design. It represents a set of concepts and the relationships among them in a hierarchical format. This format can be referenced in the reasoning rules in machine learning. Therefore, when the knowledge is changed, only the reasoning is changed without any changes to the software system. Because of these characteristics, an ontologic approach is beneficial for data sharing in EHRs. It isolates medical knowledge from technology. It allows patient's information to be exchanged across health institutions regardless of the EHRs' technology or operation.

One of the well-known uses of ontology in healthcare is terminology server such as UMLS (Unified Medical Language System), SNOMED and LOINC. These servers are well-structured systems in order to offer standardized communication, documentation and classification of health/medical vocabularies (Cole 2004). However, even these terminology systems are all based on a standard structured framework; there are still inconsistencies and incompatibilities among their concepts (B. Bolbel 2006). The terminology structure in UMLS was used as a starting ground for the medical ontology construction. In order to connect the ontologic concepts with the UMLS terms, a special class of UMLS synonyms was built inside the ontology that is linked to the original guideline term through a "UMLS synonym" property. This ontology was used to build structure for automated systems to provide classification within clinical notes. Using this ontology, existing terminology domains can be shared and integrated into existing definitions and terminologies across healthcare level (D. Pappa 2006). It is a key prerequisite for sematic interoperability, especially in the context of knowledge representative and terminologies. (Blobal 2006 & 2007).

An important distinction: medical ontologies differ from terminology ontology frameworks. (Peleg 2008) While the ontology for terminology servers are based on static structures used for knowledge reference and its databases are categorized based on its linguistic concepts, the medical ontology combines all of the relevant concepts. These concepts are related to the diagnostics, treatment, clinical procedures, patient data and outcome prediction (Jovic, Prcela et al. 2007). The ontology in medicine/patient-care environment has to consider changes and temporal factors, especially when it is applied to EHRs. This is because EHRs are patient-center, longitudinal, comprehensive and prospective (S Garde 2007). The existing ontology models also have to be reusable and adaptable to new changes easily. Moreover, there are several stakeholders in medicine. In the same domain, the ontology can be organized in different ways based upon its purpose of design. Consequently, the ontology in medicine can be more complex to design and to share. In some other papers, ontology could be used as a new implementation for a knowledge framework for connecting systems together. Since medicine is a complex system, all studies have to focus on a niche knowledge domain. In order to link or apply these knowledge frameworks to a larger framework, an ontology has to be designed to connect their common interests.

The further use of ontology in EHRs is a framework for clinical decision support functions (CDS). (Sim 2001) The additional requirement for CDS requires statistical methodologies to run reasoning rule-base utilities (Montani, Bellazzi et al.). However, there have not been many studies on the application of CDS in EHR based on individual practices. Nevertheless, the content of patient-centric CDSS implementation can be applicable. This is an important requirement for CDS in EHRs due to the Meaningful Use (http://himssclinicaldecisionsupportwiki.pbworks.com).

In summary, the modern EHRs require a framework to support their enhanced functionalities (S. Mersmann 2004). When the demand of using EHRs expands from local to multiple institutions, a standard framework is in need. Ontology can bring many benefits in the knowledge sharing and can make its knowledge assumptions explicated and independent from operational systems. Ontology can increase EHR's functionalities in standardizing medical terms, knowledge sharing, and support for automatic reasoning using in decision support systems(3). Equally the Era of Patient Safety Implications for Nursing Informatics Curricula paper (J. Effken 2002) concluded that Ontology plays a main role in CDSS, integration and standard for patient safety in clinical environment.

3   Methodology

The implementation of this study consists of two main steps: (1) Developing Ontological Knowledge Framework based on Practice-Based Evidence, and (2) Integrating Evidence-Based Information to the Knowledge Model

1. Developing Ontological Knowledge Framework based on Practice-Based Evidence

The first stage of the study is to capture existing knowledge, then transform it to an Ontological knowledge framework. In this study, our current knowledge is derived from experts and patient-record in a EHR system. The data in EHR systems is recorded in a relational database (RD) formats. RD is mainly utilized for storing and querying high volumes of data, but cannot represent the knowledge behind its database structure. On the other hand, an ontology presents the structure of knowledge in a specific domain, but lack of ability to store and query data. The ontology portion has the universal flexibility to be shared and reused regardless of database systems.

1a) Represent Knowledge with Predicate.
In this paper, the knowledge was not imported directly from EHR system, but it was abstracted through human interpretation and a guideline from domain experts. Based on the study by Jones (2011), the knowledge structural model for patient care is initiated by a high level abstraction of a "healthcare event". The concepts of healthcare events are structured in triplets of subject -> predicate -> object and based on the following description logic premise as shown in Figure (1).

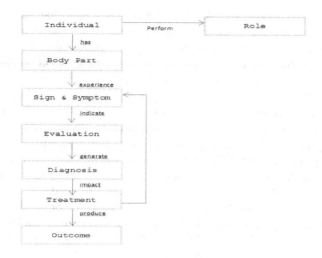

Fig. 1. Health Event Diagram

In this paper, the healthcare events are structured as:

> An entity -> has role as -> a patient
> The patient -> experiences-> Knee injury
> Knee injury -> is evaluated by -> Knee exam
> Knee exam-> generates result -> ACL tear
> ACL tear -> requires -> ACL reconstruction surgery
> ACL reconstruction surgery -> needs -> post-op rehab
> Post-op physical rehab -> has an impact on-> Range of Motion
> Range of Motion -> effects -> Return to Activity

Now, the main concepts of the domain are captured. These will be used to represent main classes in the ontologic model. The sub concepts will represent choices of their parent concepts. For example, the body part composes of left knee and right knee, while the class "ACL reconstruction surgery" has subclasses based on location of graft (Ipsilateral VS Contralateral).

1b). Implement Ontological Framework in Protégé

Protégé 4.1 (OWL) by Stanford University is used as an ontological editor in this study. There are 9 main classes derived from practiced based evidences as mentioned above.

Class1: Entity

Since this study will merge knowledge from both real practices and publications, the entity class will have two main sub classes: Article and Human.

Class2: Role

There are three categories of the Role class: Patient, Clinician and Study. In the future, the set of roles should be expanded to cover more relationship with patients such as family.

Class3: Body Part

The study treats left knee and right knee as individual class instead of two subclasses of knee class. The knee class is designed as knee anatomy of bone, ligament and soft tissue as shown in Figure 2.

Class4: History

The history class represents history and chief of complaint in EHR. This information is based on patient's own knowledge and history (Figure 3)

Class5: Sign and Symptoms

The sign and symptom class represents physical observation at the current time by clinical staff (Figure 4).

Class5: Evaluation

The Evaluation class includes results from any lab tests, subjective and objective scores (Figure 5).

Class6: Diagnosis

The Diagnosis class represents the summary of patient's information binding to clinician's knowledge. Then the clinician will make a conclusion what disease or health issue the patient is facing (Figure 6).

Class8: Treatment

The treatment class shows the treatment that the patient is received based on the diagnosis. Here, two main subclasses of the treatment plans are surgical and non-surgical treatment (Figure 7).

Class9: Outcome

The concept of Outcome class is to find a set of variables validating if the patient has a good or bad outcome from the treatment.

In addition to the 'heath-event' classes, two new classes are added on the knowledge model: Categories and Sports. The categories class is used to binding information from EBP to PBE. It is not uncommon to find a result reported in articles as qualitative outcomes rather than quantitative outcomes.

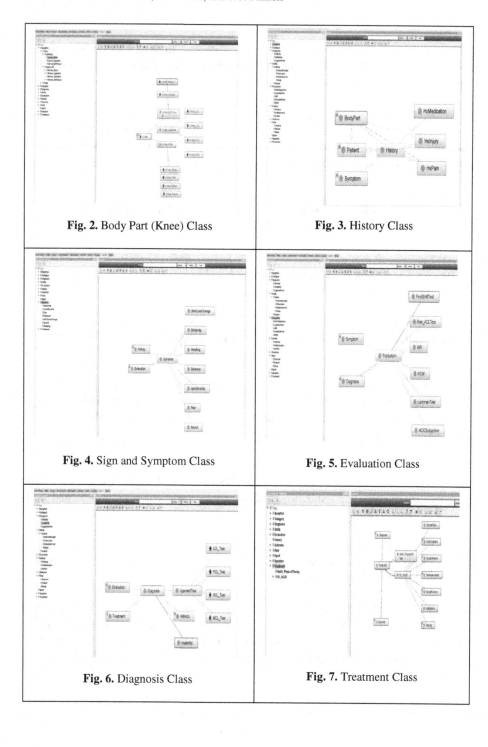

Fig. 2. Body Part (Knee) Class

Fig. 3. History Class

Fig. 4. Sign and Symptom Class

Fig. 5. Evaluation Class

Fig. 6. Diagnosis Class

Fig. 7. Treatment Class

4   Integrating Evidence-Based Information to the Knowledge Model

4.1   Measuring Quality of Publications

The challenge in using data from publications are (1) Validating the reported outcomes (2) Merging contradicted outcomes. These two issues could be deflated by comparing the quality of publications. The quality of studies will be evaluated for strength of evidence, validity and reliability. The strength of evidence well be graded 10 levels as listed (Cercone 2011).

- 1A Systematic Review of Randomized Controlled Trials
- 1B RCTs with Narrow Confidence Interval
- 1C All or None Case Series
- 2A Systematic Review Cohort Studies
- 2B Cohort Study/Low Quality Studies
- 2C Outcomes Research
- 3ASystematic Review of Case-Controlled Studies
- 3B Case-Controlled Study
- 4 Case Series, Poor Cohort Case Controlled Studies
- 5 Expert Opinion

The studies will be evaluated for validity and reliability through a Cumulating Evidence Score weighted by the quality of the study (Miller 2009). As a result, the stronger methodological quality and better design research will have higher scores than weaker ones. A database will then be designed in order to record the researches along with its rank into machine-interpretable formats suitable of CDS.

4.2   Developing a Formula for Weighting Publication's Outcomes

The detail in this step is omitted from this paper. The aim is to develop a methodology using Bayesian Network (BN) to calculate the most suitable publications for each individual patient. BN is an appropriate tool for Ontology due to its probabilistic ability and directed acyclic graph (DAG). (Bucci 2011) Then, BN's probabilistic model will be used as a rule in Protégé.

4.3   Implement Rules Representing Knowledge from Evidence-Based

In this step, Rules will be added to the knowledge model. Specific knowledge can be imbedded in the model through rules. This approach will allow the model to be flexible and modify existing knowledge without changing the knowledge structure. For example, one of the rules in this study represented as (Figure 9)

Symptome(?s), signJoinGiveout(?s, "positive") -> RecommendedTest(?s, "LachmanTest")

This is interpreted as

"Any patient having a symptom of join give out, the Lachman test will be recommended for diaganosis".

In the future, if the practice decides to add more tests for the patient, a new rule will be added without changing the knowledge structure.

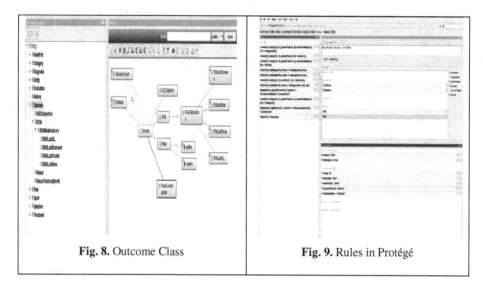

Fig. 8. Outcome Class   **Fig. 9.** Rules in Protégé

5   Conclusion

The paper illustrates how we can capture and synthesize different types of knowledge resources that complement each other. The key tasks for the study presented are (1) design the knowledge model and (2) defy a formula for merging information in publications. Designing a knowledge model is intricate because we have future use and reuse more than just to represent current knowledge. There are many ways to model knowledge, but there are only few that can be applied for a specific use. Binding PBE and EBP knowledge together offers more accurate and patient-focus support in clinical decision system. This will allow us to enhance the benefit from EHR systems and improve care.

References

1. Blobal, B.: Educational Challenge of Health Information Systems's Interoperability. Methods Inf. Med. 46, 52–56 (2007)
2. Bucci, G., Sandrucci, V., Vicario, E.: Ontologies and Bayesian Networks in Medical Diagnosis. In: HICSS 2011, Proceedings of the 2011 44th Hawaii International Conference on System Sciences, pp. 1–8 (2011), doi:10.1109/HICSS.2011.333
3. Cole, C.: Using a Terminology Server and Consumer Search Phrases to Help Patients Find Physicians with Particular Expertis. MedInfo (2004)

4. Dang, J., Hedayati, A., Hampel, K., Toklu, C.: An ontological knowledge framework for adaptive medical workflow. Journal of Biomedical Informatics 41(5), 829–836 (2008), doi:10.1016/j.jbi.2008.05.012
5. Green, L.: Public Health Asks Of Systems Science: To Advance Our Evidence-Based Practice, Can You Help Us Get More Practice-Based Evidence? American Journal of Public Health 96(3), 406–413 (2006)
6. Green, L.: Making Research Relevant: if it is an evidence-based practice, where's the practice-based evidence? Practice Advance Access (25), 20–24 (2008)
7. Jones, J., Phalakornkule, K., Fitzpatrick, T., Iyer, S., Ombac, C.Z.: Developing Protégé to Structure Medical Report. In: Stephanidis, C. (ed.) Universal Access in HCI, Part IV, HCII 2011. LNCS, vol. 6768, pp. 356–365. Springer, Heidelberg (2011)
8. Effken, J., Carty, B.: The Era of Patient Safety: Implications for Nursing Informatics Curricula. J. Am. Med. Inform. Assoc. (2002)
9. Milgrom, L.: Toward a Topological Description of the Therapeutic Process. The Journal of Alternative and Complementary Medicine 16(12), 1329–1341 (2010)
10. Montani, S., Bellazzi, R., Riva, A., Larizza, C., Portinale, L., Stefanclli, M.: Artificial Intelligence Techniques for Diabetes Managements: the T-IDDM Project
11. Peleg, M., Denekamp, K.S.,, Y.: Mapping computerized clinical guidelines to electronic medical records: knowledge-data ontological mapper (KDOM). J. Biomed. Inform. 41(1), 180–201 (2008)
12. Sim, I., Gorman, P., Greenes, R., Haynes, B., Kaplan, B., Lehman, H., Tang, P.: Clinical Decision Support Systems for the Practice of Evidence-based Medicine. Journal of the American Medical Informatics Association 8(6), 527–534 (2001)

Content Analysis of Specialist Interviews in the Development of the Music Therapy Activity System

Kevin C. Tseng[*] and Chieh-Yun Liu

Product Design and Development Laboratory, Department of Industrial Design,
College of Management, Chang Gung University, Taiwan (R.O.C)
ktseng@pddlab.org

Abstract. The study aims to define the needs and specification of a music therapy system based on music therapy programs designed for elderly dementia patients. The mobile music therapy system proposed from this study will allow music therapy to no longer be restricted by location, time, and instrument needs, while at the same time preserving the emphasis of music therapy on personalization, wide choice, and options of both active and passive activities. In order to evaluate whether the designed activities meet the needs of dementia patient and their caregivers, the present study utilized a semi-structured interview format to collect perspectives from three different music therapists on the system; the vocabulary content of the responses were then subjected to linguistic analysis to determine the suitability of the system structure for user needs. The results demonstrated that music therapists approved of the system functions and confirmed its suitability for its target populations.

Keywords: content analysis, dementia, elderly, music therapy, system.

1 Introduction

Dementia is a common condition among the elderly and includes symptoms of memory loss and mood instability, among others. In addition to medical therapy for symptomatic control, music therapy is a common alternative mode of treatment. It has the benefit of significantly improving the memory loss and mood problems that dementia patients suffer from. However implementations of music therapy are too often restricted by time, space, instrument supply, and human resources. Due to these limitations, music therapy has yet to become broadly integrated into the lives of dementia patients. While music therapy can effectively halt the memory loss process and improve mood in dementia patients, it is limited by the fact that it requires an experienced therapist and multimedia tools, and as such cannot be implemented widely amongst dementia patients. Therefore, the current research combined current music therapy practices and modern technologies in the hopes of integrating and producing a novel system to facilitate the implementation of musical therapy.

The goal of music therapy is to improve an individual's symptoms through the involvement of music. The emphasis is not on advancing specialist, music-theoretical

---

[*] Corresponding author.

C. Stephanidis and M. Antona (Eds.): UAHCI/HCII 2013, Part III, LNCS 8011, pp. 536–543, 2013.
© Springer-Verlag Berlin Heidelberg 2013

knowledge, but rather on the reactions elicited in patients and whether clinical symptoms improve as a result. At present, music therapy is commonly delivered either individually or in a group setting. Group therapy has the benefit of increasing social interactions amongst dementia patients, while individual therapy can be tailored to each patient's special needs. In dementia patients, the typical responses observed are smiling and singing along to songs from earlier in their lives [1]. Even with memory loss, it appears that memories of music persist [2], highlighting the relative importance of the demand for individualized therapy sessions.

Music therapy has been shown to effectively improve memory [3], mood stability [4], and family interactions amongst dementia patients. But considering music therapy's emphasis on individualization, it must provide multiple options to patients and allow a combination of active and passive modes of delivery. Also relevant are the need for flexibility in activity content and the complex planning bridging content design and therapy delivery. At present, there are many obstacles in expanding implementations of music therapy from the settings of nursing homes and hospitals to those with families and at other locations, which can maximize the opportunities for interaction between patients and their family members and friends.

The present study aims to define the needs and specification of a music therapy system based on music therapy programs designed for elderly dementia patients. It utilizes current music therapy practices as its structure, and consolidates complex procedures and multimedia tools into a music therapy system. In order to evaluate whether the designed activities meet the needs of dementia patient and their caregivers, a semi-structured interview format to collect perspectives from three different music therapists on the system was conducted; the vocabulary content of the responses were then subjected to linguistic analysis to determine the suitability of the system structure for user needs. This paper is organized as follows: section II describes the music therapy activities system; section III elaborates on the content analysis of specialist interviews; and finally, sections IV and V introduce discussion and conclusions.

2   Music Therapy Activities System (MTAS) Description

We confirmed the goals of our system design through literature review, and demonstrate commonly used music therapy practices for dementia patients in the flow diagram below. The yellow parts indicate the scope of MTAS as designed in the present study, while the other areas represent individual evaluations carried out by music therapists (Figure 1).

The system design is based on commonly used music therapy activities targeting dementia patients, including activity items, song lists, and instruments. Activity design accommodates both active and passive forms of delivery: active forms include playing an instrument and singing along to a song, while passive forms include music appreciation, with the option of a guessing a song's name at its conclusion. Each activity has a role in alleviating clinical symptoms. For example, music appreciation can utilize songs from the patient's youth or tailored to their interests and mood. Instrument playing can be divided into polyphonic, monophonic, and percussion instruments, chosen based on user interests.

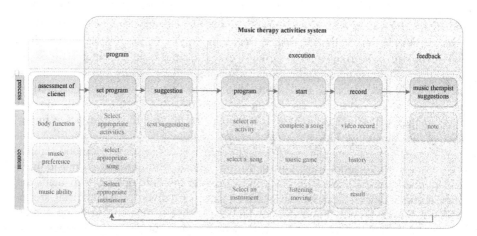

Fig. 1. Current Music Therapy Practices Flow Diagram

3   Content Analysis

In order to evaluate whether the designed activities meet the needs of dementia patient and their caregivers, semi-structured interviews were conducted with three music therapists and the results subjected to linguistic analysis.

3.1   Specialist Interviews

Answers to pre-set questions were collected from three therapists who had particular experience in employing music therapy with elderly dementia patients in a semi-structured interview. Researchers recorded the conversations in their entirety and later transcribed it for analysis.

(1) Interview Subjects
Three music therapists with clinical experience in the treatment of dementia patients were selected (see Table 1).

Table 1. Specialist Interview Summary

Music therapist	Specialty	Experience
Zhao-Wen Yang	music therapist for dementia elders	Chang Gung medical foundation
Siang-Ling You	music therapist for dementia elders	Cedar Falls Lutheran Home
Pei-Qi Wang	music therapist for dementia elders and children	Chang Gung medical foundation

(2) Interview Tool
The study utilized a semi-structured interview format for information collection. The questions referenced and inquired about aspects that the therapists considered important when evaluating a music therapy treatment style, and also about their

thoughts on directions and developments in technology-assisted music therapy. After obtaining consent from the interviewees, the conversations were recorded and later transcribed.

(3) Information Processing and Analysis

Utilizing vocabulary analysis[5] as part of content analysis, the conversation recordings were first transcribed. Referencing Chinese vocabulary ranges used in information processing previously published in *Academia Sinica*, the interviews were subjected to manual vocabulary truncation and the words categorized according to a Supplementary Resource from the Taiwan Department of Education: Chinese Language Commonly Used Vocabulary (Edition 3). For example, the phrase "can be considered for use in children" would be categorized as "can" (verb), "consider" (verb), "use" (verb), "for" (preposition), "children" (noun). However, as the conversation was colloquial, some vocabulary words unable to be categorized (e.g., English vocabulary, or phrases unable to be simplified) were processed according to the meanings of the constituent nouns, verbs, and adjectives. Those that appeared greater than five times throughout the interview were subjected to manual filtering by subject and highly relevant phrases in order to identify the keywords for subsequent categorization.

3.2   Interview Analysis and Outcome

The results of vocabulary analysis show a vocabulary density of 0.63, and the categorization of vocabulary from the three interviews are documented below as percentages according to the aforementioned Taiwan Department of Education Supplementary Resource (Table 2).

Table 2. Vocabulary Categorization Summary

	Grammar	N	%
Content word	nouns	311	18.7
	adjectives	93	5.6
	verbs	426	25.6
	adverb	82	4.9
	pronouns	92	5.5
	quantifier	27	1.6
Function word	preposition	203	12.2
	conjunction	174	10.5
	particle	7	0.4
	interjection	7	0.4
Punctuation	，	150	9.0
	、	19	1.1
	。	39	2.3
	；	2	0.1
Mathematical symbols	%	3	0.2
Number	number	12	0.7
Others	spoken language	14	0.8

There were 311 nouns, 93 adjectives, and 150 verbs. After manual filtering and confirmation of original meanings, 364 phrases with high relevance to the current research topic were sorted and categorized into 30 key phrases; the results are shown in Figure 2.

The words "elderly" (x32), "children" (x2), "family" (x10), "person" (x5), and "therapist" (x9) comprised 21.7% of the total words; they are categorized as system target user- and time frame-related vocabulary system target user-related vocabulary.

"Multimodality (x5), "different" (x8), "increase" (x5), "self-operate" (x13), and "guidance" (x6) comprised 12.91% of the total words; they are categorized as system multi-modality-related vocabulary.

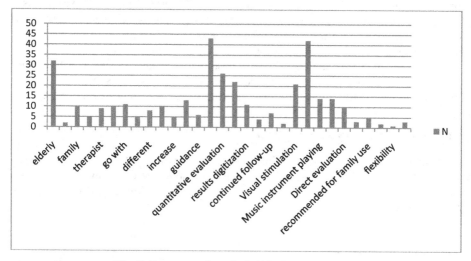

Fig. 2. Summary of vocabulary frequency analysis

"Visual stimulation" (x21), "auditory stimulation" (x42), and "tactile stimulation" (x1) comprised 17.58% of the total words; they are categorized as sensory stimulation-related vocabulary.

"Music instrument playing" (x14), "music tempo" (x14), "tone" (x4), and "understanding" (x3) comprised 9.62% of the total words; they are categorized as system activity suggestion-related vocabulary.

"Results evaluation" (x43), "quantitative evaluation" (x26), "qualitative evaluation" (x22), "results digitization" (x11), "results display" (x4), "continued follow-up" (x7), and "therapist-collected results" (x2) comprised 31.59% of the total words; they are categorized as system evaluation recommendation-related vocabulary.

"Direct evaluation" (x10), "easy to operate" (x3), "recommended for family use" (x5), "interesting" (x2), "flexibility" (x1), and "convenient" (x3) comprised 6.59% of the total words; they are categorized as system feedback-related vocabulary.

System evaluation recommendation-related vocabulary (31.59%) was the most frequently mentioned by therapists evaluating the program, followed by system target user and implementation (21.7%), sensory stimulation-related (17.58%), system multi-modality-related (12.91%) , system activity suggestion-related (9.62%), and system feedback-related vocabularies (6.59%).

4   Discussion

Through vocabulary analysis, the content of the specialist interviews were collected into six categories for discussion: 1) System target user and implementation, 2) system multi-modality, 3) sensory stimulation, 4) system activity suggestions, 5) system evaluation recommendations, and 6) system feedback.

System target user and implementation: The research goal of the present study is clearly apparent here. "Therapists" design and recommend activity content for the "elderly" patients and their "family", who then jointly carry out the activities and thus increase interpersonal "interactions". The therapists recommended the present system be used "in conjunction" with existing music therapy activities, and not replace them. Consistent with our research goal, while carrying out music therapy activities, it is important to bear in mind that the interaction is not between the individual and a touch screen, but rather between individuals: in this way, we will not lose sight of the original purpose of music therapy.

System multi-modality: All therapists agreed that the system provides a novel activity medium for elderly dementia patients in the realm of music therapy. The software provides much in the way of song content, instrument types, and activity types, allowing users to freely choose their desired activities and increase their confidence in the process.

Sensory stimulation: The MTAS program increases visual and auditory stimulation for elderly dementia patients, and these stimulations allow for continued neural stimulation and association between the visual and auditory organs. For example, listening to a particular song can lead to visual imagery in the mind of the listener. However, the tablet format is unable to provide tactile stimulation, and therefore therapists suggested that the program be used in conjunction with original formats of music therapy to increase multi-modal sensory stimulation for elderly dementia patients.

System activity suggestions: The therapists suggested that the music tempo employed by MTAS may have been too fast, as dementia patients' hand-eye coordination is slower than that of the average population. Moreover, the therapists suggested deficiencies in the areas of "tone" and "music theory". For example, the elderly may sing along to a song, but the range of the default scale (C major) may extent too high for users to sing along with, and so should consider lowering the default key to G major. Second, often when users without prior understanding of keyboard instruments see a music note appear on top of a key, they tend to immediately press it without regard for the correct tempo, and thus produce music out of sync. Future design alterations may consider adding a guiding note that informs users to wait with respect to the correct tempo before hitting a key.

System evaluation recommendations: therapists gave positive feedback regarding the digitized results display, which permitted the rapid communication of music therapy progress to both users and family, and also has the added benefits of tracking progress and monitoring long-term outcomes. However, the quantitative values provide only improvement trends or regressions; qualitative evaluations would still require further analysis and explanation from a therapist. Only when evaluations take into consideration both quantitative and qualitative assessments can a holistic picture of user progress through music therapy be generated.

System feedback: overall therapists gave positive feedback, indicating the system to be user-friendly and a convenient tool. Therapists stated they would recommend the software for use amongst elderly patients, and also suggested the tool as appropriate for children because of their high interest in new technology. Future development of MTAS might consider a music therapy system tailored to children.

While the present system used digitization to provide numerous benefits to the users, there remain areas that require further modification. For instance, the results evaluations require therapist input in addition to quantitative values if a meaningful overview is to be obtained. Main activities may need to adjust the default music tempo and scale in order to better meet the needs of elderly users. All these adjustments require music therapist input, and therefore the system should be viewed as a complementary tool to current music therapy practices, since it is somewhat lacking as an independent tool.

5   Conclusion and Recommendations for Future Study

In summary, the present study conducted a semi-structured interview with music therapy specialists and subjected the interview contents to vocabulary analysis. The results suggest that the novel MTAS system serves the functions envisioned in its initial research goals and is generally approved of by specialists. The program emphasized addressing the need for a multitude of choices in its design, which allowed for a greater degree of sensory stimulation via engaging and interesting activities. In addition, its quantitative results display permits easy visual comprehension of progress and long-term follow-up outcomes. Future music therapy systems will be tested by dementia patients and their families in order to further assess whether they meet the needs of real-world users.

Acknowledgement. This research work was supported in part by the research grants of the National Science Council of Taiwan, Republic of China under grant numbers NSC100-2410-H-182-023-MY2 and NSC101-2218-E-182-002. The funders had no role in study design, data collection and analysis, decision to publish, or preparation of the manuscript.

References

1. Sung, H.C., Chang, A.M., Lee, W.L.: A preferred music listening intervention to reduce anxiety in older adults with dementia in nursing homes. Journal of Clinical Nursing 19, 1056–1064 (2010)

2. Cuddy, L.L., Duffin, J.: Music, memory, and Alzheimer's disease: is music recognition spared in dementia, and how can it be assessed? Medical Hypotheses 64, 229–235 (2005)
3. Bruer, R.A., Spitznagel, E., Cloninger, C.R.: The temporal limits of cognitive change from music therapy in elderly persons with dementia or dementia-like cognitive impairment: a randomized controlled trial. Journal of Music Therapy 44, 308–308 (2007)
4. Witzke, J., Rhone, R.A., Backhaus, D., Shaver, N.A.: How sweet the sound: research evidence for the use of music in Alzheimer's dementia. Journal of Gerontological Nursing 34, 45–52 (2008)
5. Patton, M.: Qualitative evaluation methods. Sage Publications, Beverly Hills (1980)

Supporting the Continuum of Care for Combat Wounded Patients: Adaptive Interfaces for Personal Health Records

Harry D. Tunnell IV and Aeshvarya Verma

Grappa Lab, Indiana University School of Informatics (Indianapolis)
hadtunne@iupui.edu

Abstract. In this paper, we describe a concept for an adaptive interface for a military Personal Health Record (PHR). PHRs are electronic records used by people to manage their personal healthcare information. In the Military Healthcare System, combat wounded patients encounter a range of challenges due to the unique nature of the military environment and the severity of their wartime injuries. These factors affect how people interact with a computer interface. In many instances, combat wounded patients eventually have assistance from family members, professional caregivers, and others. This forms a disparate end-user population. Because the pool of potential users includes people with a wide range of cognitive and physical capabilities, an adaptive interface that considers attributes of health can improve user experiences.

Keywords: Adaptive interfaces, ability-based design, Personal Health Record (PHR), combat wounded, military informatics.

1 Introduction

In order to meet the needs of disparate users within the Military Healthcare System, the concept to provide multiple unique interface options to access one person's Personal Health Record (PHR) is relevant. Devising PHRs to support different types of user has been identified as an important and critical challenge of system design [1]. To overcome the challenge of accessibility to a PHR, we propose that a single record have multiple interfaces based upon user cognitive and physical ability. The users envisioned for this PHR are people who support the continuum of care for wounded in action (WIA) military personnel such as patients, family members, and professional caregivers.

Traditional human-computer interaction (HCI) approaches include examining individual differences, but not in the context of single patient multi-user systems with multiple interfaces. Understanding individual differences is important for HCI models to improve a single interface and experiences for multiple users, design adaptive interfaces that change based upon the interaction of a single user, or to recognize patterns of search interaction to improve web search [2, 3]. Our proposed approach is different because it suggests multiple interfaces for a single system based upon

C. Stephanidis and M. Antona (Eds.): UAHCI/HCII 2013, Part III, LNCS 8011, pp. 544–552, 2013.
© Springer-Verlag Berlin Heidelberg 2013

individual differences. The objective is to deliver the right interface to users based upon the specific end-user's ability to interact with the system. For example, patients may use an interface based upon ability-based designs while family members and caregivers rely on more typical user-centered designs. Here we outline the role of PHRs in this context, highlight the military informatics environment that defines usability requirements, and describe a concept for a PHR adaptive interface.

2   Personal Health Records to Support Combat Wounded

2.1   The Role of Personal Health Records

There are various types of electronic records within the healthcare domain. PHRs and Electronic Health Records (EHRs) are among the most common. Each is used to manage patient information, but they have different roles and audiences. The PHR is typically designed for one person who can grant access to others. PHRs are web-based applications that people use to manage and share their health data or access the records of others (as long as they have the proper credentials) [4, 5]. PHRs are commercial (e.g., Medefile, Microsoft HealthVault) or institutional (e.g., MyHealtheVet) products. The EHR, on the other hand, is a repository of computer processable information that can be securely transmitted and that multiple users can use to access information about a single patient [6]. An EHR is used by medical professionals and is accessed using an institutional system (hospital, medical practice, clinic, etc.) [4].

2.2   The Military Informatics Environment

There have been nearly 50,000 combat wounded service members since September 11, 2001 [7]. Military professionals realized that traditional information systems to track patients were inadequate due to the pace of combat operations, casualty acuity, and casualty load in a complex healthcare environment [8]. Military informatics is the design of information systems (IS) for a military audience to accomplish military-related goals. A military informatics based PHR, incorporating interfaces that change based upon end-user cognitive and/or physical capability, can help people navigate the complex Military Healthcare System.

Wounded personnel within the Department of Defense (DOD) receive treatment at the point of injury and are evacuated to an acute care facility in the combat theater [8, 9]. The next evacuation center is often a non-theater hospital such as Landsthul, Germany [8-10]. Patients are then evacuated to medical facilities in the U.S. or returned to their military unit. Patients are transferred to a different medical system such as the Veteran's Administration (VA) upon discharge or medical retirement [10]. Solutions such as the Joint Patient Tracking Application, which tracks real-time patient status, have been implemented as a result of the volume of wounded patients and complexity of the military healthcare environment [8].

The military; however, has yet to implement a comprehensive patient-facing IS, preferring to incorporate PHR-like features into existing systems. For example, the U.S. Army includes deployment health information in its Army Knowledge Online

(AKO) application, but soldiers also use the system for e-mail, training and clothing records, and other aspects of military information management. AKO is a document based system that requires users to have domain knowledge about U.S. Army organization and culture which makes navigation and searches difficult for newcomers and outsiders [11]. Relying on AKO in lieu of a PHR fails to recognize that AKO is not intuitive and requires patients to recall complicated domain specific information during periods of cognitive impairment due to injury or medication. Family members and caregivers likely do not have the requisite domain knowledge to find patient health information within AKO. A PHR with an adaptive interface can provide important tools to support the continuum of care for combat wounded patients.

Combat wounds often result from an adversary's employment of advanced weapons and munitions typically not available to civilians (e.g., an Explosively Formed Penetrator, which is commonly known as an EFP). Despite technical advances in weaponry, American military personnel are less likely to be killed in action today than earlier wars due to improved protective equipment, early damage-control surgery, and rapid evacuation out of the combat theater [9]. There has been a reduction in patient mortality from 22.8% during WWII to 8.8% today [8]. Even formerly catastrophic injuries are survivable; four military patients endure as quadruple amputees [12]. The fact that people live with increased cognitive and physical impairment means they may rely upon a network of family and professional caregivers for help. This is complicated by the international and cross-healthcare system nature of military health information management. The need for a military informatics derived multi-user PHR within the defense medical ecosystem is essential.

2.3   Information Sharing and Accessibility

Even though PHRs are designed primarily for a patient to manage their own data, many have features that allow healthcare providers to add data to the record. Furthermore, some commercial PHRs have built-in functions that allow a person to share their PHR outside of the medical community [13]. Usability testing consistently shows people want the ability to share PHR information with medical providers and others outside of the healthcare profession [1, 5, 14]. This also supports the concept of a PHR for one patient that can be shared among several people.

About 70 million people in the U.S. use some form of PHR [4]. Despite the popularity of PHRs, testing indicates that significant usability problems remain [1]. Recent innovations regarding PHRs tend to focus on security, end-user privacy, and content. Fortunately, the scope of PHR innovation is expanding to include aspects such as intelligence. The goal of an intelligent PHR is to automatically provide users with personalized healthcare information [15]. Additionally, research by Liu, Shih [1] indicates that PHRs should consider accessibility designs so that end-users with disabilities can customize the system to suit their specific needs. In the next section, we examine customization as a means to support combat wounded patient PHR needs.

3   Discussion

3.1   End-User Types

One of the challenges of design is having the right information about users [16]. Demographic information for combat wounded personnel such as age, race, gender, and injury is highly documented and simplifies data collection because there is precision in the knowledge about the wounded population [17]. For example, there were 1,286 amputations during the period 2001-2009 [17]. An amputee registry has been created to track and manage military patient care and needs, which tend to be different from the needs of elderly patients who lose a limb due to vascular disease [10]. Traumatic Brain Injury (TBI) has a greater rate of injury than amputation with 43,779 personnel diagnosed between 2003 and 2007 [17]. Unfortunately, research to support designs for cognitively dysfunctional users is inadequate [16]. Yet the rate of TBI compared to other wounds highlights an immediate need to support cognitively impaired users. In addition to the wounded population of end-users, family members and caregivers who are not disabled are potential users. Traditional HCI methods of interface design are acceptable for this population.

3.2   Interface Customization

Interface customization has become a normal part of the user experience. It is common in both client-side and server-side applications. Marathe and Sundar [18] define interface customization as an activity that a user performs to change the presentation and functionality of an interface to increase its personal relevance. Customization is increasingly popular because it is tied to the user's sense of identity and sense of control—as many as 92% of research participants customize an application in some manner [18, 19]. Even though there is high acceptance of customization, user choices are typically limited because customization is a difficult programming task and requires significant extra work for developers [19]. There are generally two options for customization: functional and cosmetic. Marathe [20] notes that functional customization pertains to work practices and cosmetic customization pertains to embellishments surrounding the work practices. Customization can improve user experiences for family members and caregivers. Unfortunately, customization does not support the wide disparity in cognitive and physical ability common among the combat wounded population. Fortunately, adaptive interface capabilities can go beyond customization.

3.3   Adaptive Interfaces

Adaptive user interfaces present a number of solutions that can be matched to the changeability of users and the environment [21]. This is significantly different from an interface that presents a single solution for multiple users. For example, a Microsoft Windows interface that emphasizes WIMP-style (windows, icons, menu, and pointer) interaction through a graphical user interface (GUI) and allows users to modify the color, size, and position of backgrounds and icons is customizable but not adaptive. The Microsoft Windows 8 GUI, on the other hand, lets users transition between WIMP and tile touch screen—this an example of an interface that has characteristics of being customizable and adaptive.

Even though interfaces that employ WIMP, touch screen, speech, gesture, and other forms of interaction are not new, they are increasingly available to the public on commercial personal use systems. However, the end-user must manually select the style of interaction. Montague [22] proposed a framework that provides a user with the most suitable interaction experience based upon their needs at the time they operate the interface. In the framework, web services update the client model without requiring calibration exercises or manual configuration of the interface [22]. This approach could have utility for PHR adaptive interfaces.

The typical approach to adaptive interfaces and users with disabilities has been to focus almost exclusively on accessibility concerns or interfaces that run on different devices (e.g., mobile or desktop) [23]. Regarding specific disability, Newell [16] states that blindness is the priority in accessibility research and this has resulted in a lack of support for the large population of people with other disabilities. The approach proposed herein is a multimodal presentation of interfaces based upon users that may or may not have a disability. This allows a user to employ an interaction option based upon their physical condition, mental state, or level of medication for instance. Additionally, an adaptive interface that incorporates intelligence can recommend modifications to the patient based upon the healthcare data managed within the PHR. For example, once data about a change in medication is entered into the PHR, the intelligence feature presents the patient with interface options based upon how the medication affects cognition (e.g., changing from Percocet to Ibuprofen).

Ability-based design is a new concept that offers opportunities to improve the user experience for wounded personnel. Rather than focus on user disability (the dominant approach), ability-based designs emphasize what a person can do and the system is designed around their capability to interact with an IS rather than an inability to use hardware and software [24]. Multimodal interfaces that consider end-user ability rather than disability allow a user to select, or have presented to them, the interaction style they prefer to use for their tasks [25]. A library of adaptive interfaces can include designs by modality for a specific disability. The library provides an integrated yet changeable solution for a single IS with multiple users based upon cognitive and physical ability rather than aesthetic preferences or workflow.

An interface library is important because the patient's capability may change as they undergo treatment and rehabilitation. For example, a person who survives an EFP attack may suffer multiple injuries resulting in amputation and a diagnosis of TBI. Their cognition might be affected initially by the explosion and/or powerful pain medications. Speech recognition technology is relevant in this case because speech interaction is important for people with cognitive disabilities who have difficulty remembering the mapping of menu items [25]. As the patient's medication and capability changes based upon cognitive improvement, lack of chronic pain, use of prosthesis, or successful limb transplantation surgery, they may wish to modify their interaction style. Customization does not support dramatic fluctuations in patient ability but a library of interfaces based upon impairment type, matched with interaction style, may improve the user experience. Furthermore, an ability-based methodology promotes long-term adaptive approaches (e.g., when a patient transitions from treatment to rehabilitation the interface is modified to reflect enhanced ability).

Yahoo!, an early leader in interface personalization, developed a massive User Database (USB) to support scalability and improve the speed and efficiency of personalization [26]. Designers of a PHR for combat wounded, on the other hand, potentially have access to details about the complete wounded population and thus have an opportunity to design interfaces accordingly. Once interfaces are implemented using a server-side distributed system, a dialogue record that contributes to the interaction knowledge base can be maintained for each user interaction [21]. In a manner reminiscent of the UDB, as the interaction knowledge base grows, changes are made to the library [21]. In this way, designers learn from actual user interaction with the system.

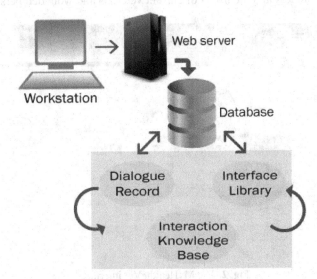

Fig. 1. A PHR adaptive interface architecture example

3.4   Implications for Design

Accessibility for web based technologies is considered an important part of the design process by HCI professionals [27]. Unfortunately, the actual implementation of accessibility features is limited, and visual impairment is the most common disability considered in accessibility designs [16, 27]. The lack of implementation and the focus on visual impairment does not meet the needs of the population of young combat wounded patents who will require extensive long-term care.

In addition to advances in technology and better knowledge about the military disabled population, it is important for designers to have better access to military patients during development. A major problem of interface design for assistive technologies is that it is difficult to recruit disabled people to test a new design [28]. The nature of military service allows commanders to make some decisions about testing. This means that leaders within DOD may be able to authorize and direct usability testing.

4   Limitations and Future Work

Despite the fact that there is a significant number of healthcare IS within DOD that store and retrieve documentation about casualties, there is not a comprehensive and coherent single user interface available to access the multitude of legacy systems, so there are limitations to the quality of casualty information [9]. Fortunately, the VA has been a leader in PHR development and MyHealtheVet (the VA's web-based PHR) has undergone usability testing with older veterans [5]. This provides a frame of reference to understand the needs of current veterans and wounded personnel.

Fig. 2. The MyHealtheVet interface

5   Conclusion

Disabled users are often overlooked during design and testing [25]. A PHR for a military audience needs to include the combat wounded population early. A framework that incorporates military informatics and HCI can lead to adaptive designs that provide satisfactory user experiences for combat wounded personnel as they progress through the continuum of care.

It is only recently that non-cost prohibitive technology that is reliable, easy to use, and includes multimodal input devices on a single system has become widely available to the public. This offers new possibilities to design for a better user experience. Adaptive interfaces improve accessible technology by identifying user needs and providing a dynamically personalized user interface [23]. These ideas extend to the civilian community because people often have multiple disabilities—UK government research indicates that 80% of people with a sensory disability (e.g., visual) also have another disability (e.g., motor) [29].

Acknowledgements. The authors thank Jason Saleem for providing feedback on the initial concept and Mark Pfaff and Michael Lewis for commenting on drafts of the paper.

References

1. Liu, L.S., Shih, P.C., Hayes, G.R.: Barriers to the adoption and use of personal health record systems. In: Proceedings of the 2011 iConference, pp. 363–370. ACM, Seattle (2011)
2. Benyon, D.: Accommodating individual differences through an adaptive user interface, Computing Department. Open University, Milton
3. Buscher, G., et al.: Large-scale analysis of individual and task differences in search result page examination strategies. In: Proceedings of the Fifth ACM International Conference on Web Search and Data Mining, pp. 373–382. ACM, Seattle (2012)
4. Señor, I.C., Alemán, J.L.F., Toval, A.: Personal Health Records: New means to safely handle health data? Computer 45(11), 27–33 (2012)
5. Haggstrom, D.A., et al.: Lessons learned from usability testing of the VA's personal health record. Journal of the American Medical Informatics Association 18(suppl. 1), i13–i17 (2011)
6. Sachdeva, S., Bhalla, S.: Semantic interoperability in standardized electronic health record databases. Journal Data and Information Quality 3(1), 1–37 (2012)
7. Department of Defense, U.S. Casualty Stats. US Government, Washington, DC (2012)
8. Eastridge, B.J., et al.: Trauma system development in a theater of war: Experiences from Operation Iraqi Freedom and Operation Enduring Freedom. The Journal of TRAUMA Injury, Infection, and Critical Care 61(6), 1366–1373 (2006)
9. Gerhardt, R.T., et al.: Out-of-hospital combat casualty care in the current war in Iraq. Annals of Emergency Medicine 53(2), 169–174 (2009)
10. Peake, J.B.: Beyond the Purple Heart - Continuity of care for the wounded in Iraq. The New England Journal of Medicine 352(3), 219–222 (2005)
11. Douglas, L.: An object and performance framework for implementation of web-based knowledge sharing technology. Journal of Theoretical and Applied Electronic Commerce Research 4, 57–71 (2009)
12. Ruane, M.E.: Johns Hopkins Hospital performs double arm transplant on Army soldier. The Washington Post (2013)
13. Martino, L., Ahuja, S.: Privacy policies of personal health records: An evaluation of their effectiveness in protecting patient information. In: Proceedings of the 1st ACM International Health Informatics Symposium, pp. 191–200. ACM, Arlington (2010)
14. Baird, A., North, F., Raghu, T.S.: Personal Health Records (PHR) and the future of the physician-patient relationship. In: Proceedings of the 2011 iConference, pp. 281–288. ACM, Seattle (2011)
15. Luo, G., Tang, C., Thomas, S.B.: Intelligent personal health record: Experience and open issues. In: Proceedings of the 1st ACM International Health Informatics Symposium, pp. 326–335. ACM, Arlington (2011)

16. Newell, A.F.: Accessible computing – past trends and future suggestions: Commentary on Computers and People with Disabilities. ACM Transaction in Accessible Computing 1(2), 1–7 (2008)
17. Fischer, H.: United States military casualty statistics: Operation Iraqi Freedom and Operation Enduring Freedom, C.R. Service, Editor, US Government: Washington, DC (2009)
18. Marathe, S., Sundar, S.S.: What drives customization?: Control or identity? In: Proceedings of the SIGCHI Conference on Human Factors in Computing Systems, pp. 781–790. ACM, Vancouver (2011)
19. Lee, L.-C., Lutteroth, C., Weber, G.: Improving end-user GUI customization with transclusion. In: Proceedings of the Thirty-Third Australasian Conference on Computer Science, vol. 102, pp. 163–172. Australian Computer Society, Inc., Brisbane (2010)
20. Marathe, S.S.: Investigating the psychology of task-based and presentation-based UI customization. In: Extended Abstracts on Human Factors in Computing Systems, CHI 2009, pp. 3129–3132. ACM, Boston (2009)
21. Benyon, D.: Adaptive systems: A solution to usability problems, Computing Department. Open University, Milton
22. Montague, K.: Interactions speak louder than words: Shared user models and adaptive interfaces. In: Adjunct Proceedings of the 25th Annual ACM Symposium on User Interface Software and Technology, pp. 39–42. ACM, Cambridge (2012)
23. Peissner, M., et al.: MyUI: Generating accessible user interfaces from multimodal design patterns. In: Proceedings of the 4th ACM SIGCHI Symposium on Engineering Interactive Computing Systems, pp. 81–90. ACM, Copenhagen (2012)
24. Wobbrock, J.O., et al.: Ability-Based Design: Concept, Principles and Examples. ACM Transactions on Accessible Computing 3(3), 9:1–9:27 (2011)
25. Kortum, P. (ed.): HCI beyond the GUI: Design for haptic, speech, olfactory, and other nontraditional interfaces. Morgan Kaufmann Publishers, Boston (2008)
26. Manber, U., Patel, A., Robison, J.: Experience with personalization of Yahoo! Communications of the ACM 43(8), 35–39 (2000)
27. Putnam, C., et al.: How do professionals who create computing technologies consider accessibility? In: Proceedings of the 14th International ACM SIGACCESS Conference on Computers and Accessibility, pp. 87–94. ACM, Boulder (2012)
28. Mankoff, J., Hayes, G.R., Kasnitz, D.: Disability studies as a source of critical inquiry for the field of assistive technology. In: Proceedings of the 12th International ACM SIGACCESS Conference on Computers and Accessibility, pp. 3–10. ACM, Orlando (2010)
29. Kienle, H., et al.: Ten years of access for all from WSE 2001 to WSE 2011. In: 13th IEEE International Symposium on Web Systems Evolution (2011)

Design Guidelines for an Integrated PHR System: An Approach for UI Designers to Break Down Individual-Level Barriers to PHR Adoption

Shu-Wen Tzeng and Yuan Zhou

Department of Industrial and Graphic Design, Auburn University, Alabama, USA
szt0004@auburn.edu, yzz0007@tigermail.auburn.edu

Abstract. The significance of the quality of healthcare information has been recognized in the health care field. How will health information reach people, including patients, health care providers, employers, and etc.? How can information flow seamlessly among systems in a secure environment? In the case of individuals, how can one access, manage and share his/her health information with authorized health providers? To answer those questions, PHR (Personal Health records) plays a crucial role here. User interface design is essential for improving the usability of interactive systems like PHRs. In this study, two PHR applications are examined; rules will be applied to a PHR system design prototype to demonstrate how constructing and integrating of intuitive graphic design is carried out, and how to make PHRs more user-friendly by incorporating users' daily activities into personal health decision making and medical care.

Keywords: Integrated PHR System, User Interface, Design Guidelines.

1 Introduction

"The Obama administration has set a goal of computerizing all of America's medical records within five years (2011) as a means of improving efficiency, quality, and safety and ultimately money saving. The economic recovery package recently signed into law by President Obama will provide bonus payments of $44,000 to $64,000 to physicians who adopt and effectively use Electronic Health Record (EHR) systems from 2011 through 2015, and it is likely that penalties will then be introduced for physicians who do not adopt the technology.

The significance of the quality of healthcare information has been recognized in the health care field. How will health information reach people, including patients, health care providers, employers, and etc? How can information flow seamlessly among systems in a secure environment? In the case of individuals, how can one access, manage and share his/her health information with authorized health providers? To answer those questions, PHR (Personal Health Record) plays a crucial role here. Since user interface design is essential for improving the usability of interactive systems like PHRs, creating design guidelines and principles for PHR systems is an

C. Stephanidis and M. Antona (Eds.): UAHCI/HCII 2013, Part III, LNCS 8011, pp. 553–562, 2013.
© Springer-Verlag Berlin Heidelberg 2013

emerging need for the UI designers. To help UI designers recognize the UI responsi-bilities in the process of PHR system design, this study examined two highly recom-mended PHR applications, identified the rules that will break down individual-level barriers to PHR adoption, and eventually created the design guidelines for making an integrated and more efficient healthcare system in the United States.

2   The Definition and Benefits of Integrated PHR

The so-called PHR (Personal Health Record) is a system that patients, doctors, and other health care providers could securely access through the Internet no matter where a patient is seeking medical care [1]. In most scholarly articles, PHRs are described as ''an electronic application through which individuals can access, manage and share their health information, and that of others for whom they are authorized, in a private, secure, and confidential environment [2].'' In today's parlance, a PHR typically refers to a computer-based record – either a free-standing/ independent/stand-alone product that are accessible on the Internet or on a USB drive, or one that is integrated with the provider's Electronic Health Record (EHR) system. While the uptake of free-standing/ independent/ stand-alone PHRs has been slow, a growing number of patients actively use integrated PHRs [3].

KEY POTENTIAL BENEFITS OF INTEGRATED PHR SYSTEMS	
ROLES	**BENEFITS**
Consumers, Patients and their Caregivers	❑ Support wellness activities ❑ Improve understanding of health issues ❑ Increase sense of control over health ❑ Increase control over access to personal health information ❑ Support timely, appropriate preventive services ❑ Support healthcare decisions and responsibility for care ❑ Strengthen communication with providers ❑ Verify accuracy of information in provider records ❑ Support home monitoring for chronic diseases ❑ Support understanding and appropriate use of medications ❑ Support continuity of care across time and providers ❑ Manage insurance benefits and claims ❑ Avoid duplicate tests ❑ Reduce adverse drug interactions and allergic reactions ❑ Reduce hassle through online appointment scheduling and prescription refills ❑ Increase access to providers via e-visits
Healthcare Providers	❑ Improve access to data from other providers and the patients themselves ❑ Increase knowledge of potential drug interactions and allergies ❑ Avoid duplicate tests ❑ Improve medication compliance ❑ Provide information to patients for both healthcare and patient services purposes ❑ Provide patients with convenient access to specific information or services (e.g., lab results, Rx refills, e-visits) ❑ Improve documentation of communication with patients
Payers	❑ Improve customer service (transactions and information) ❑ Promote portability of patient information across plan ❑ Support wellness and preventive care ❑ Provide information and education to beneficiaries
Employers	❑ Support wellness and preventive care ❑ Provide convenient service ❑ Improve workforce productivity ❑ Promote empowered healthcare consumers ❑ Use aggregate data to manage employee health
Societal/Population Health Benefits	❑ Strengthen health promotion and disease prevention ❑ Improve the health of populations ❑ Expand health education opportunities

Fig. 1. Key Potential Benefits of PHRs and PHR Systems (Source: HHS, 2006)

Integrated PHRs are essentially portals into the EHRs of patients' health care pro-viders. They are populated with patient information from a variety of sources, includ-ing EHRs, insurance claims, pharmacy data, and home diagnostics and can provide consumers as well as providers with a more complete view of relevant health information. In 2006, the US Department of Health & Human Services [4] released a report on the key potential benefits of integrated PHR Systems, which are summarized in Figure 1. This report reveals the potential benefits brought from integrated PHR systems to the patients, healthcare providers, health insurance companies, employers, and the related societies. Many experts believe that integrated PHR systems are more than just static repositories for patient data; they combine data, knowledge, and software tools, which help patients to become active participants in their own care [5].

3   Barriers to PHR Adoption

It is quite obvious that integrated PHRs are beneficial for both consumers and clinicians. However, there are a number of obstacles to overcome for wide-scaled PHR adoption, including technical issues, environmental barriers, legal concerns, and individual-level barriers. First, technical issues include difficulties with data exchange, authentication of information, and summarization tools. The second barrier, environmental, results from the fact that currently health information on each patient resides in multiple locations. Thus, integrated PHRs must reach across organizational boundaries to interface with multiple EHR systems. A related and equally problematic barrier is that EHRs must not only exist in individual offices and hospitals, but must also be able to communicate with various PHRs. Economic and market forces are obstacles to PHR (and EHR) adoption. Another sensitive issue is that of legal concerns. While consumers appropriately desire protection of their private health information, aggressive protection measures might hamper PHR access by patients and clinicians and impede optimal care. Finally, individual-level barriers impede adoption of PHRs.

At the level of the individual, healthcare consumers must understand and accept their roles and responsibilities related to their own healthcare. However, consumer-related interfaces, technology, and access issues specific to PHRs are not yet well understood. Also, the workflow models for both providers and patients are poorly understood. An understanding is necessary of how the PHR can fit into the existing flow of day-to-day activities for both providers and patients. Part of this process includes providers and patients developing different mindsets and levels of trust of each other. In the case of PHR adoption, change management issues involve providers, consumers, and regulators. In each case, there must first be a motivation to change.

4   Understanding and Breaking Down the Barriers to PHR Adoption

The two main mechanisms for breaking down the barriers to PHR adoption are education and research. Behavioral research can identify optimal educational strategies. Provider sites that currently offer integrated PHRs offer a good starting point to determine which individuals tend to use the PHR, how frequently, and for what purposes, as well as impacts on healthcare and workflows. Therefore, two user behavioral researches were conducted by surveying 1849 adult representatives on consumers and health information technology adoption and by observing users' interaction with two different types of PHR tools that were chosen from the results of national survey.

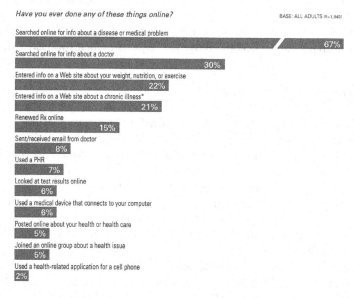

Fig. 2. The tendency of PHR adoption among 1849 adult users

The national survey results reveal the tendency of PHR adoption among 1849 adult users (Fig. 2) and their expectations of the functions in an integrated PHR system (Fig. 3). The survey summary is listed as follows:

- About 7% of those surveyed say they have used a PHR — more than twice the proportion identified two years earlier in separate research.
- Users are most likely to have a PHR supplied by their health insurer, followed by their doctor/ health care provider.
- Half or more of users indicate that the ability to look at test results, renew their prescriptions online, or email their providers is somewhat or very useful. Making sure their information is correct ranks highest in terms of usefulness.
- Although higher-income individuals are the most likely to have used a PHR, lower-income adults, those with chronic conditions, and those without a college degree are more likely to experience positive effects of having their information accessible online.
- Two-thirds of the public remain concerned about the privacy and security of their health information, but the majority of those who are using a PHR are not very worried about the privacy of the information contained in their PHR.
- Most PHR users and non-users say privacy concerns should not stop learning how health IT can improve health care.

- More than half of adults are interested in using online applications to track health-related factors, and almost half are interested in medical devices that can be connected to the Internet. Of those who do not have a PHR, 40% express interest in using one.
- Having trust in the organization that provides the PHR is a top factor in signing up for one. More than half of non-users say they would or might sign up if their doctor expressed confidence in the safety of information in a PHR.

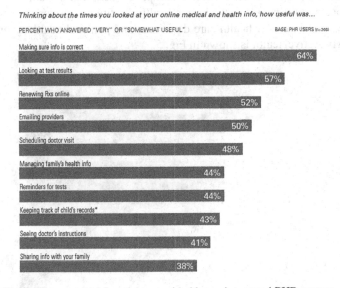

Thinking about the times you looked at your online medical and health info, how useful was...

PERCENT WHO ANSWERED "VERY" OR "SOMEWHAT USEFUL"   BASE: PHR USERS (n=268)

Making sure info is correct — 64%
Looking at test results — 57%
Renewing Rxs online — 52%
Emailing providers — 50%
Scheduling doctor visit — 48%
Managing family's health info — 44%
Reminders for tests — 44%
Keeping track of child's records* — 43%
Seeing doctor's instructions — 41%
Sharing info with your family — 38%

Fig. 3. The expected functions provided by an integrated PHR system

From studying the reviews and feedback from actual users, we were expecting to learn how both mobile users and web users interact with personal health management applications on different platforms. Based on popularity and availability, two products representing two types of PHRs were Nike+GPS and My ActiveHealth.

Fig. 4. The UI design of Nike + GPS- a mobile phone based PHR tool

Nike+ GPS maps user's runs, tracks the progress and Provides the motivation user needs to go even further. It plays mid-run cheers every time a user's friends like or comment on the run status or outruns them in a game of Nike+ Tag. With this app in hand, a user can track every indoor and outdoor workout easily, without a sensor. A user can also record the pace, distance and run route using the iPhone's GPS and accelerometer technology to see the progress over time and push him or herself to go even further. The UI design of Nike+ GPS is shown in Fig. 4.

My ActiveHealth manages to offer a complete integrated system of services that includes coaching for people with chronic health conditions, services that help doctors and patients make smarter health care decisions, and personal health records. The UI design of My ActiveHealth is shown in Fig. 5.

Fig. 5. The UI design of My ActiveHealth- a Website based PHR tool

After observing users' interaction with these two PHR systems respectively and conducting in-depth studies on the UI design on both PHR systems, the users' needs and frustrations with these tools were identified and analyzed by different themes. The theme analysis revealed the following facts:

- Users' privacy is the biggest concern in the adoption of PHR systems.
- There is a lack of motivation to the use of PHR.
- Excessive information is always hard to manage.
- Information transition between personal devices and medical care providers is hard to manage.
- The efficiency and usability of PHR systems decide the level of user satisfactions.

5   The Design Guidelines for an Integrated PHR System

As discussed in the previous section, three key issues inhibit the use of PHRs: privacy concerns, lack of motivation, and operational difficulty. However, in addition to the individuals, provider group and health plan organizations emphasizing PHR adoption highlight the value of using the PHR focusing on consumer-to-PHR and PHR-to-consumer interactions as levers to improve health and reduce costs [6]. Before discussing any design guidelines, the following common types of PHR interactions should be considered as each of them will affect the choices of adoption of PHRs. The first, consumer-to-PHRs connections, enable users to update their record with new information from connections such as a home monitoring device. The second, PHRs-to-consumer interactions, should include ways of sending automated notices for upcoming events from the system to the users. The third type of connections, consumer-to-consumer, promote online social networks such as emails and health forums. Finally, PHR-to-PHR connections allow transfer of information between PHRs, promoting usability by gathering and grouping user activities and experiences. These four types of PHR interactions are illustrated in Fig. 6.

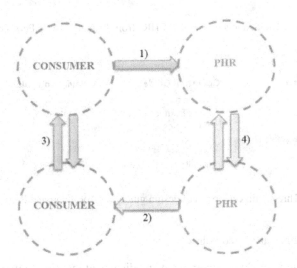

Fig. 6. Four types of PHR interactions

After considering the types of connections, the sequence of use for primary users should be planned. Based on previous research, the ideal sequence is as follows (Fig. 7):

After understanding the problems inhibiting users from the adoption of PHR systems, the different types of PHR interactions and the sequence of use in PHRs, some design guidelines can be generated and suggested to the UI designers for creating an integrated PHR system. To make these guidelines more systematic and easy to understand, they are developed accordingly in regard to a PHR's visual purpose, operational purpose and navigational purpose as shown in Fig. 8.

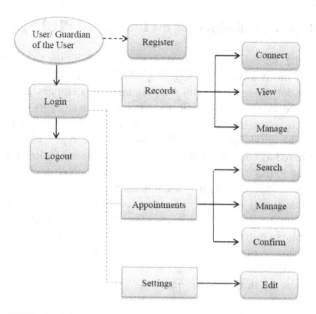

Fig. 7. The Sequence of Use in PHRs from Primary User's Perspective

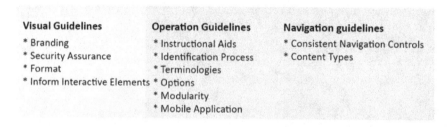

Fig. 8. Three main categories of design guidelines for integrated PHR systems

These guidelines are listed below:

- All information should be generalized and displayed in a simple manner.
- The use of navigation should remain consistent throughout the site unless there are areas requiring custom control unique to a specific function.
- The PHR site and application should include instructional aids such as text, illustrations or videos, to define the services provided and explain the process if applicable.
- An integrated PHR system should assure users of the privacy and security of the system by providing educational description and illustrations regarding how users' identity and information will be used and protected.

- An integrated PHR system should process identification information in a secure and timely manner.
- The PHR system should speak the users' language, with words, phrases and concepts familiar to the user, rather than official medical terms.
- User information received from medical care providers must be organized and displayed in a format that is easy to view and assistive to decision making for users.
- The PHR site or application should distinguish content types from general content to current page content by text, colors, contrast, or graphic cues.
- When there are interactive elements, there should be changes in colors or size to highlight or indicate the interaction.
- Multiple options should be provided to users in order to achieve the maximum of functionality and flexibility.
- Users should have the ability to adjust their privacy preferences.
- An integrated PHR system should be modular so as to add more components to accommodate customers with specific needs.
- Because mobile devices may serve as an entry point for customers to access their PHRs, studying the characteristics of mobile platforms accordingly before designing a mobile application is a must.

6   Suggestions for Guidelines Application

This set of design guidelines were geared towards designing a user-centric and integrated PHR system. They can always support guiding designers along the design process. In addition, they could be used in designing other user-centric or personal information management systems.

With the fast developing pace of mobile industry, the relationship between a PHR site and a PHR mobile application may change. Policies for health information may be improved to facilitate a better environment for the adoption of PHR systems. These guidelines can always be modified when necessary and used for provide direction for design, in both general and concrete terms.

References

1. Health Information Privacy. HHS. Gov. Press (2005)
2. Tang, P.C., Lee, T.H.: Your doctor's office or the internet? Two Paths to Personal Health Record. 2009 Massachusetts Medical Society. New England Journal of Medicine 360(13), 1276–1278 (2009)
3. Detmer, D., Bloomrosen, M., Raymond, B., Tang, P.: Integrated Personal Health records: Transformative Tools for Consumer-Centric Care. BMC Medical Informatics and Decision Making 8, 45 (2008)

4. HHS. National Cancer Institute. National Institutes of Health. National Center for Health Statistics. Centers for Disease Control and Prevention. Personal Health Records and Personal Health Record Systems - A Report and Recommendations from the National Committee on Vital and Health Statistics, Washington, D.C. (2006)

5. Tang, P.C., Ash, J.S., Bates, D.W., Overhage, J.M., Sands, D.Z.: Personal Health Records: Definitions, Benefits, and Strategies for Overcoming Barriers to Adoption. Journal of the American Medical Informatics Association 13(2), 121–126 (2006)

6. Kahn, J.S., Aulakh, V., Bosworth, A.: What It Takes: Characteristics of The Ideal Personal Health Record: Wider adoption of PHRs will require greater computer competency, Internet access, and health literacy. Health Affairs 28(2), 369–376 (2009)

Evaluation of User Interface of Computer Application Developed for Screening Pediatric Asthma

Maryam Zolnoori[1], Josette F. Jones[1], Mostafa Moin[2], Hassan Heidarnejad,
Mohammad Reza Fazlollahi[2,3], and Masoud Hosseini[1]

[1] School of Informatics, IUPU University, Indianapolis, Indiana, USA
[2] Immunology, Asthma, and Allergy Research Institute,
Tehran University of Medical Science, Tehran, Iran
[3] Masih Daneshvari Hospital, Shahid Beheshti University of Medical Science, Tehran, Iran
{mzolnoor,jofjones,hosseini}@iupui.edu,
{MMoin,fazlollahi}@sina.tums.ac.ir,
Heidarnazhad@ams.ac.ir

Abstract. Asthma is a chronic disease which has a negative effect on the quality of life of (1.4% to 27.4%) people around the world. Unfortunately in many countries, because of limited access to pulmonary physicians, and laboratory tests, asthma is usually under diagnosed especially at the first stages of this disease. The purpose of this study is to report a patient –centered computer application for diagnosing pediatric asthma. Techniques of semantic networks, production rules, fuzzy logic, and decision trees have been applied for representing evidence-based research knowledge. User-Interface of this system is evaluated by nurse practitioners. Result of this evaluation reinforces that this system meets requirements of user interaction satisfaction.

Keywords: Asthma, diagnosis, decision tree, semantic network, fuzzy logic, user interface evaluation.

1 Introduction

In 1984, asthma was defined as a chronic disease that remains under-diagnosed and undertreated [1]. Despite improvement in pathological and clinical knowledge for diagnosing asthma, in 2012, asthma is defined as a global health problem that economically and socially has a huge negative effect on families and societies[2]. Asthma under-diagnosing [3, 4] especially in children is accompanied by low quality of life. Sleep disturbance, activity limitation, and missing school days, and eventually emergency department visits, which may result in hospitalization[5].

However, evidence-based medicine proposes a systematic solution for diagnosing and treatment of disease [6, 7], and evidence-based guidelines developed for diagnosing diseases relevant to respiratory symptoms are heavily dependent on laboratory tests [8] which are not widely accessible to many primary care settings or physicians 'office. Patient-centered tools such as questionnaires which are provided to diagnose symptom-related asthma do not collect sufficient information about the patient's

C. Stephanidis and M. Antona (Eds.): UAHCI/HCII 2013, Part III, LNCS 8011, pp. 563–570, 2013.
© Springer-Verlag Berlin Heidelberg 2013

respiratory symptoms [9, 10]. These questionnaires usually are applied in population-based studies to estimate the prevalence of asthma [11, 12].

Medical informatics is the intersection of medical practice, computer and cognitive science[13] providing solutions to deal with inconsistencies, insufficiencies, and uncertainties in medicine. Cognitive science [14] involves an in-depth analysis of a problem and its diagnostic in terms of identifying algorithm of decision making and principles of system usability.

As solution of this problem, we combined techniques of knowledge representation (computer science), process of medical judgment (cognitive science), and the patient's view to model empirical knowledge obtained from asthma evidence-based research (medical science). This model serves as patient-centered decision support system for diagnosing childhood asthma.

This paper is phase 2 of the project of developing decision support system for diagnosing (screening) pediatric asthma. In this paper, we present the results of evaluation of a user interface of this system. The rest of this paper is as follows: developing conceptual model (section 2), knowledge representation (section 3), system testing (section 4), user interface evaluation (section 5), and conclusion (section 6).

2   Developing Conceptual Model of the System

The conceptual model of this application is developed based on a framework of problem solving at different level of medical care [15]. This framework consists of four stages as follows:

1. Observation: observation is considered as variables that disturb daily activities of patients. Patients can recognize the variables and usually search for solutions to eliminate them.
2. Findings: Findings are a set of variables that patients have confirmed as having been observed. Findings have potential clinical significance.
3. Facet: Facet is a cluster of medical findings in every module to indicate underlying medical problem that can serve as part of the knowledge needed for decision making. Facets are used to divide information obtained from users into sets of manageable sub-problems.
4. Diagnosis: Diagnosis is the aggregation of obtained results in every module.

Epidemiological and pathological knowledge of asthma disease is represented based on this conceptual model.

3   Knowledge Representation

Techniques of knowledge representation used for modeling knowledge of asthma disease include semantic network, decision tree, and fuzzy logic.

3.1   Knowledge Representation Using Semantic Network

The epidemiological and pathological knowledge of asthma can be constructed as a casual relationship using semantic network serving to classify knowledge into manageable clusters of information. Knowledge collected from evidence-based research is reformed based upon the patient's view. Patient observations and findings are limited to symptoms and history. Therefore, for developing the semantic network based on the patient's view, we eliminate all variables that patients do not have access to (including laboratory and atopy tests). In this model, genetic factors, medical factors, environmental factors, associated disease, symptoms appearance and symptoms hyper-responsiveness are considered as main nodes representing cause and effect variables.   This semantic network is depicted in figure 1.

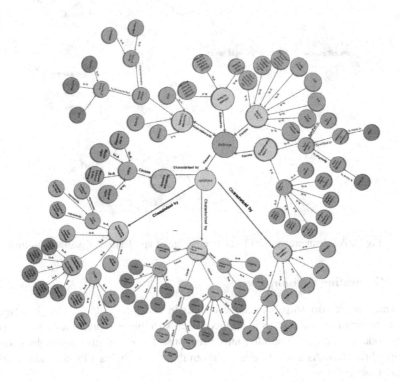

Fig. 1. semantic network based on patient view

Every main node in this module summarizes findings of patients for a class of variables such as medical history or associated diseases.

3.2   Developing Algorithm of Decision Making

Stages 3 and 4 of the conceptual model serve as a guiding framework for developing the algorithm for decision making. Every main node in semantic network consists of a facet of knowledge for diagnosing asthma. The possibility of asthma would be calculated from the aggregated results obtained from each module. Figure 2 depicts algorithm of decision making serves as inference engine of diagnosing asthma.

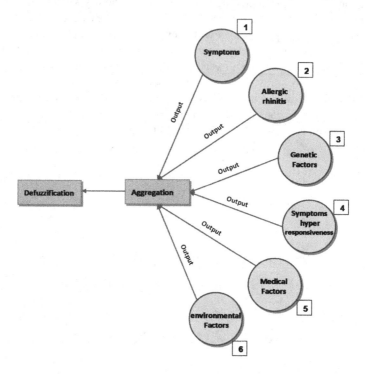

Fig. 2. A schematic view of Inference engine of application of pediatric asthma

3.3 Generating Decision Trees

To model the relationship between variables in every module (depicted in figure 2), the technique of decision trees is applied. Each variable is represented as a question in every node of the tree. The alternative response for every question split nodes into multiple branches. As a result, every path in the tree includes a facet of knowledge for decision making.

Rules which are used for developing decision trees of this application are as follows:

- Heuristic Meta rules: Heuristic Meta rules are used to determine the initial nodes in trees, and manage constraint on module and sub-module. For Example, in module of respiratory symptoms, seven decision trees are used to represent relationship between variables.
- Directive Meta Rules: Directive Meta rules determine the sequence of the variables in the branches of tree. For example, if someone has wheeze - then ask for seasonal variation of symptom.

- Statistical rules: Specificity and sensitivity of variables calculated in epidemiological research are used to estimate possibility of asthma for a set of medical finding in every path of trees. End nodes in each branch include possibility of asthma which is represented in linguistic statements in a continuum from very low to very high.
- Fuzzy logic: Fuzzy logic is used to represent the uncertainty of linguistic statements in a continuum (0-10).

4   Evaluation of System Result

This system has been tested on 139 asthmatic patients and 139 non-asthmatic patients who had respiratory symptoms and were referred to the immunology, Asthma, Allergy Research Institute of Iran. The specificity and sensitivity of this system, with a cut of value of 0.7 are 100% and 88% respectively.

5   Designing User Interface

One of the fundamental challenges with health information systems is to consider the human computer interaction [16, 17]. In fact, effectiveness of a piece of a software developed in medicine is not an internal attribute of the software, but is determined by the user's interpretation, and it depends on the user's specific context [18] . In medicine, user specific context can be considered in two ways: patient-centered view or health care providers' view. To design decision support for childhood asthma, interaction between this system and users is considered from the point of view of the parents who have direct relationship with the children having problematic respiratory symptoms.

The underlying premises which are considered for designing this interaction are: 1) People who are going to use this software have a little technical knowledge of computer systems, 2) they have minimal knowledge of medicine (They can recognize symptoms, and their pattern, and have a history of child).

To improve user-friendliness and intuitive data point of this system, we considered the following features in developing user interface:

1. To create the first interaction between the system and user, we give general information about the system and the type of questions that the user will be required to answer in the login page.
2. Modular base structure of this system helps user to concentrate on the specific type of questions
3. To start interaction with every module, a brief introduction of the module is provided before presenting questions in the screen.
4. To give users some information about the questions they are supposed to answer, semantic network and decision tree of every module is presented in the page of every module.

5. To prevent the system from appearing awkward or cumbersome, we used some co-lorful objects in every page related to the type of questions in every module.
6. To minimize the process of learning needed for working with this system, a part of every page is setup to guide users.

These features help users to feel confident (by getting probably sufficient information about this system) and keep him/her motivated to go through all the modules, answer questions, and finally see the possibility of asthma for a patients with respiratory symptoms.

To facilitate the process of data entry, multiple choice questions are considered. Users can read the questions and choose one of the options that highly match with the patients' background or current situation. However, this type of questions may limit interactions between the system and users, but will improve accuracy of entered data. Figure 3 presents some snapshots of user interface of this application.

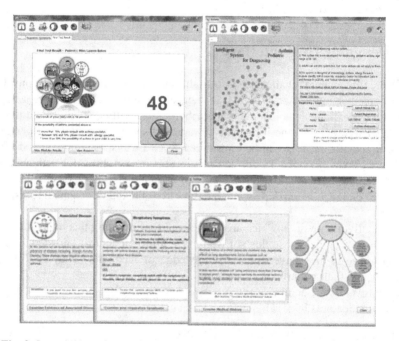

Fig. 3. Screen shots of user interface of application for diagnosing pediatric asthma

5.1   Evaluation of User –Interface

After obtaining IRB approval (#1302010660) five nurse practitioners who have had direct communication with asthmatic patients participated in this project.

Instrument. A modified version of QUIS (Questionnaire for User Interaction Satis-faction) [19] was used to evaluate user interface of this software. This questionnaire consists of five parts. Part 1 concerns general experience of working with this application. Part 2 concerns the windows layout of the system, Part 3 the terminology used, Part 4 the learnability of the interface (how easy it is to learn), and Part 5 system capabilities. Each part is evaluated by some relevant criteria. A 9-point Likert Scale (0-9) is applied to assess each criterion.

Result of the Evaluation. Five nurses were asked to run this application, register a patient and go through all the modules and answer questions appeared on the user interface. Then they filled in QUIS questionnaire regarding to their evaluation.

To analyze the results of the evaluation for each part, an average of marks given to each criterion by the nurses was calculated. This result for each part is as follows:

Part 1 (general experience): 7, part 2 (windows layout): 7, part 3 (terminology): 8, part 4 (learnability): 7, and   part 5 (system capabilities): 7.

These values show that user interface of this application meet the requirement for user-interaction satisfaction.

6   Conclusion

In this paper, we evaluated user interaction satisfaction of an application developed for diagnosing pediatric asthma. Five nurse practitioners participated in this project. The overall results of this evaluation indicates that the system meets the requirement of user satisfaction, the criterion of "designed for all level of users" in the part of system capabilities received an average score of only 4. Feedback from the nurses indicates that patients need more medical information to answer the questions. Thus, this application should be upgraded to provide more medical knowledge related to the questions asked.

Acknowledgement. I would like to gratefully acknowledge Professor Linda Gilman who provided me with the opportunity to evaluate user interface of this application. I thank Sophia Kusch for reviewing this paper.

References

1. Rees, J.: ABC of asthma. Definition and diagnosis. British Medical Journal (Clinical research ed.) 288(6427), 1370 (1984)
2. Wahn, U., Matricardi, P.M.: Toward a definition of asthma phenotypes in childhood: Making a long way shorter? Journal of Allergy and Clinical Immunology 130(1), 111–112 (2012)
3. Annesi-Maesano, I., et al.: Factors related to under-diagnosis and under-treatment of childhood asthma in metropolitan France. Multidisciplinary Respiratory Medicine 7(1), 24 (2012)
4. Yeatts, K., et al.: Who gets diagnosed with asthma? Frequent wheeze among adolescents with and without a diagnosis of asthma. Pediatrics 111(5), 1046–1054 (2003)
5. Yeatts, K., et al.: Health consequences for children with undiagnosed asthma-like symptoms. Archives of Pediatrics & Adolescent Medicine 157(6), 540 (2003)

6. Sackett, D.L., et al.: Evidence based medicine: what it is and what it isn't. BMJ 312(7023), 71–72 (1996)
7. Satterfield, J.M., et al.: Toward a Transdisciplinary Model of Evidence-Based Practice. Milbank Quarterly 87(2), 368–390 (2009)
8. Dicpinigaitis, P.V.: Chronic cough due to asthma ACCP evidence-based clinical practice guidelines. CHEST Journal 129(suppl. 1), 75S-79S (2006)
9. Weiland, S., et al.: Phase II of the International Study of Asthma and Allergies in Childhood (ISAAC II): rationale and methods. European Respiratory Journal, 2004 24(3), 406–412 (2004)
10. Shin, B., et al.: A new symptom-based questionnaire for predicting the presence of asthma. J. Investig. Allergol. Clin. Immunol., 2010 20(1), 27–34 (2010)
11. Yang, C.L., et al.: Verifying a questionnaire diagnosis of asthma in children using health claims data. BMC Pulmonary Medicine 11(1), 52 (2011)
12. Hong, S.-J., et al.: The validity of the ISAAC written questionnaire and the ISAAC video questionnaire (AVQ 3.0) for predicting asthma associated with bronchial hyperreactivity in a group of 13-14 year old Korean schoolchildren. Journal of Korean Medical Science 18(1), 48–52 (2003)
13. Patel, V.L., Arocha, J.F., Kaufman, D.R.: A primer on aspects of cognition for medical informatics. Journal of the American Medical Informatics Association 8(4), 324–343 (2001)
14. Kaufman, D.R., et al.: Conceptual knowledge and decision strategies in relation to hypercholesterolemia and coronary heart disease. International Journal of Medical Informatics 55(3), 159–177 (1999)
15. Evans, D.A., Gadd, C.S.: Managing coherence and context in medical problem-solving discourse. In: Evans, D.A., Patel, V.L. (eds.) Cognitive Science in Medicine: Biomedical Modeling, pp. 211–255. MIT Press, Cambridge (1989)
16. Kuhn, K., Giuse, D.: From hospital information systems to health information systems. Methods of Information in Medicine 40(4), 275–287 (2001)
17. Coiera, E.: Interaction design theory. International Journal of Medical Informatics 69(2), 205–222 (2003)
18. Fieschi, M., et al.: Medical decision support systems: old dilemmas and new paradigms. Methods Inf. Med. 42(3), 190–198 (2003)
19. Chin, J.P., Diehl, V.A., Norman, K.L.: Development of an instrument measuring user satisfaction of the human-computer interface. In: Proceedings of the SIGCHI Conference on Human Factors in Computing Systems. ACM (1988)

Part V
Access to Mobile Interaction

Engaging Students with Intellectual Disabilities through Games Based Learning and Related Technologies

David Brown[1], Penny Standen[2], Maria Saridaki[3], Nick Shopland[1], Elina Roinioti[4], Lindsay Evett[1], Simon Grantham[1], and Pauline Smith[1]

[1] Interactive Systems Research Group, School of Science & Technology,
Nottingham Trent University
{david.brown,nicholas.shopland,lindsay.evett,
simon.grantham,pauline.smith}@ntu.ac.uk
[2] University of Nottingham, Division of Rehabilitation and Ageing,
B Floor Medical School, QMC, Nottingham NG7 2UH p.
standen@nottingham.ac.uk
[3] Technologies Laboratory in Communication, Education and the Mass Media (UoA NTLab),
National and Kapodistrian University of Athens
msaridaki@gmail.com
[4] Panteion University of Social and Political Sciences,
Dept of Communication, Media and Culture
helen_roi@yahoo.com

Abstract. Studies within our research group have shown that Digital Games Based Learning (DGBL) can have a positive effect on some of the core development needs of people with intellectual disabilities and associated sensory impairments. Of current interest is the expansion of DGBL activities on mobile platforms. The RECALL Project describes the development and evaluation of a novel route learning system for people with disabilities using location based services (on the Android OS). Research has shown that route guidance systems suppress cognitive map development, and for a target audience described as having 'poor spatial skills', systems that develop route learning rather than guidance are required. Two studies are reported here. The first demonstrates that there were less navigational errors made, and less help required, in the more independent usage of the system, than in the earlier training stages. The second focusses on more qualitative evaluation of soft skills and personal development via the use of the system, and of the gamified version of the software. It looks specifically at how a playful approach can aid the understanding of map based representations.

Keywords: route learning, mobile, digital games based learning, disability.

1 Game Based Learning: Effectiveness and Motivation

It is agreed that learning is both an emotional and cognitive process (Piaget, 1951), and when players are engaged in activities that are intrinsically motivating, they are

C. Stephanidis and M. Antona (Eds.): UAHCI/HCII 2013, Part III, LNCS 8011, pp. 573–582, 2013.
© Springer-Verlag Berlin Heidelberg 2013

more prone to demonstrate deep learning (Habgood et al., 2005). Digital games have been reported to stimulate the students' interest, while motivating them to deploy control, curiosity and imagination (Malone, 1981; Staalduinen, 2011). One of the most important qualities of games is their ability to adapt to user's abilities and time-frames, thus avoiding feelings of anxiety, inadequacy, boredom and stress (Malone, 1980; Sedighian, 1997; Baker et al., 2010; Toprac, 2011). Research has also shown that video games are particularly effective in engaging students with low self efficacy and low motivation (Amon &Campbell, 2008; Brown et al, 2007; Carr & Blanchfield, 2009; Saridaki & Mourlas 2011). Research has also shown that DGBL can have a positive effect on some of the core development needs of people with Intellectual Disabilities and associated sensory impairments. These include improved measures of choice reaction time (Standen et al 2009), decision making (Standen et al, 2009), memory (Brown et al, 2008), and functional skills (Brown et al, 2011a). However until recently, digital games have been predominantly used in the classroom for users with cognitive impairments as a reward and as a tool for external motivation (Fitros, 2005, Saridaki et al 2011).

The aim of the current study was to investigate the potential of using location based services to teach route learning to students with disabilities, and to combine this with a 'playful' approach, to investigate whether this approach is effective in route learning, and in the developing of the underlying key skills required by people with disabilities for their inclusion in society (and especially towards employability).

When developing navigational skills in people with disabilities there are several key issues that should be considered. First, route guidance systems suppress cognitive map development (Oliver and Burnett, 2008). For a group of people who are de-scribed as having 'poor spatial skills' route learning should be adopted so as not to further suppress the development of these key navigational skills (Brown et al, 2011b). Second, the importance of developing a full spatial representation cannot be over stated. External frames of reference and map-based strategies allow more effi-cient representation which enables flexibility, so that alternative routes can be taken, shortcuts can be made and destinations changed, because they encompass a more complete representation of the environment (Golledge et al, 1996; Evett et al, 2009). Third, learning should be combined with fun and use approaches that are motivating to enhance effectiveness (Habgood et al., 2005). Cartwright (2006, p. 33) also states that "We have a need to produce artifacts that provide the stimulus for humans to create a mental map or a synthetic world." Today's mobile devices, like smartphones and PDAs, are often used as gaming instruments. There has been a recent explosion in the number of creative new games that are facilitated by mobile devices in such a way that the game activity evolves according to players' location. Mobile location-based games, are described as compelling for young players as well as adults with or with-out disabilities (Quinn, & Cartwright, 2011).

Admiraal et al (2009) reported that "mobile games are excellent ways to combine situated, active and constructive learning with fun" (p 302). The mobile games be-come learning experiences when embedded in places of information such as museums or street settings, since they create an augmented reality setting which helps people to better experience the environment. According to Hinske et al, (2007)) the four main characteristics that contribute both to the mobile game's appeal and to the emotional attachment that players feel are the physical experience, mental challenge, social experience, and immersion. Finally, the feeling of immersion in the game setting provides the main entertainment factor (Ardito et al, 2010).

2   Recall Project and Route Mate Application: A Playful Approach

The RECALL Project describes the development and evaluation of a novel route learning system for people with disabilities using location based services (on the Android OS) and is the output of a major EU award (504970-LLP-1-2009-1-UK-KA3-KA3MP). Route Mate (the major route learning app of the project) is an accessible location based application developed to help people with Intellectual Disabilities and other sensory and physical disabilities to learn simple routes (Brown et al, 2011b). It provides the user with the option to create a new route through their mobile device or through a desktop console, as well as load and modify an existing route with the help of a parent, caretaker or trainer. There are three modes of RECALL: Plan, Use and Challenge. Plan and Use allow the development of a new route and its practice. This system doesn't guide the user; rather it scaffolds their journey should they make navigational errors (time or geographical divergence) by comparing current progress with their first (ideal) use of a newly planned route. The Challenge Mode provides a range of playful activities to help people with disabilities understand the connection between map-based representations and their corresponding real world locations. The Plan and Challenge Setting mode are available via the 'Console'.

The playful narrative approach takes the form of digital scavenger hunts, by extending the landmark style and interactions in different ways, and using them to scaffold different phases of use of the application. This approach seeks to teach and reinforce the concept of maps and route learning, as well as promoting the connection between the map representation and its real world counterpart.

During the Plan mode and by using different icons that promote narrative, playful storytelling and safety, the facilitator can easily design playful games using many different narratives. For example: Pirates – associated with route planning and creation activities while locating treasure and possible enemies in an urban setting; and Ninjas – a "scavenger hunt" to find as many treasure items as possible, associated with being road cautious and aware of ourselves, of other pedestrians and staying safe and on route while using Route Mate.

3   Evaluating Effectiveness and the Playful Approach

3.1   Effectiveness

In an earlier version of the Route Mate App, the Use Mode was separated into two Modes – Practice (for early stage heavily scaffolded use), and Use (more independent use). It was predicted that the number of error and help events produced by each individual would be lower in the Use Mode than the Practice Mode. If this hypothesis is accepted, it would support the view that with practice participants can use Route Mate to develop increasingly more effective navigational skills and do so more independently.

3.1.1 Methodology

Within subjects mixed methods. Quantitative data was captured using a repeated measures assessment of error and help events. Qualitative data took the form of notes based upon the quantitative measure and other events (Grantham, 2010).

Participants: Eight participants with Intellectual Disabilities (see table 1 - abilities based on 'P' levels 1-8 scales are sub-national curriculum, levels 1c-2a go onto National Curriculum levels) were accompanied by an assistant who gave help or explanation when necessary. Testing only took place on days with fine weather conditions as rain could have a detrimental on the device and participant ability. Prior to the creation of the experimental design several preliminary sessions took place so outcomes could be factored into the experimental design and data capture methodology used (Nemeth, 2002). Each participant was given an initial training session.

Task: Each participant was given the task of navigating between the same two start and end points. A number of points called "Road Sign" were created and placed at positions where road name signs were obviously visible. Each user navigated through the route twice, first in the Practice Mode and secondly in the Use Mode. Repeated measures for Error and Help events were recorded on the Data Capture sheet. Qualitative observational notes recorded any utterances, input from the assistant and other miscellaneous observations. As the Practice Mode began the user was pointed in the correct direction, when they reached the first of the Decision Points they were prompted to look at the map (on device) and to make a decision about the direction they should head in. If an incorrect directional decision was made they were asked to re-think their decision and this was classed as one occurrence of requiring 'Help'. At each Decision Point explanation of navigation decision, more complicated explanations, and failure to properly communicate decisions were recorded

Table 1. Participant's abilities based on P-Levels

ID	English				Maths		
	Read	**Write**	**Speaking**	**Listening**	**Number**	**U + A**	**SS +M**
1	2B	2C	2A	2A	1C	1	2A
2	1C	1C	P7	P7	2B	1	2C
3	1C	2C	2A	2A	2A	2A	2A
4	1C	P8	1C	1C	P8	1	1C
5	P8	1B	1A	1A	P8	1	P8
6	2A	2C	2B	2B	2C	2	2C
7	1B	1B	1C	1C	1C	P8	2B
8	P6	P7	P8	P8	P6	P8	P7

Once completed in the Practice mode the route was re-run using the Use mode. Observations and any Error or Help occurrences were recorded. As in the Practice phase the participants were left to make their own independent navigation decisions. If the user made an incorrect navigational decision they were asked to reconsider and provide a justification. If they still wanted to make the same navigational decision they were corrected.

Error and Help Events: A frequency count was used to record the number of instances of help and error events. A help event is where the user asked for help or where it was judged that help was required (e.g., when a user loses their position on the map or is reminded of how to move the map). An error event would be where the participant incorrectly uses Route Mate or the device (e.g., presses the wrong button on the device). An error event may also trigger a help event to occur, for example, if the participant incorrectly used the device or the application and subsequently required help to correct the situation this would be recorded as an error event for the original incorrect use and as a help event for the assistance required in correcting the error. Notes were also recorded on the nature of each help and error event. Spontaneous feedback from the participant and their replies to directed questioning were also recorded (also from assistants).

3.1.2   Results
Quantitative Measures: Table 2 shows the number of help and error events for both the Practice and Use tests. There was a reduction in the mean number of help events from the Practice (mean = 4.5, SD = 2.8) to the Use phase (mean = 3.4, SD = 3.2) but a paired t-test indicated that this did not reach significance. Similarly for errors there was a reduction in the median number of errors from the Practice phase (3.0, range 0 – 5) to the Use phase (median = 1, range = 1 – 8) and a Wilcoxon test (errors non-normally distributed) indicated this reduction did not reach significance either.

Table 2. Number of help and error events for both the Practice and Use tests

ID	Practice		Use	
	Help	Errors	Help	Errors
1	6	3	2	1
2	9	5	11	8
3	3	2	1	1
4	7	4	4	3
5	5	3	2	0
6	3	1	3	1
7	3	0	3	1
8	0	3	1	0

3.2   Playful Approach

3.2.1   Methodology

A Case Study Methodology was adopted via a mixed qualitative and quantitative analysis for a period over two months.

Participants: 43 end users in four different countries, by five different research partners (UK, Greece, Romania and Bulgaria). Participants worked together with their caretakers and parents together with one or two researchers. Gender balance: 55.8% male, 44.2% female. Ages ranged from 8 to 68 years. Ethnicity: 15 were British, 1 Pakistani British, 9 Bulgarian, 7 Romanian and 8 Greek. 45.2% were beginners (referring to technical knowledge), 45.2% were average users and 9.5% (4 out of 43) were described as experienced users. 34.9% experienced learning disabilities, 14% with autism and 4.7% communication problems. Cognitive, physical disabilities and sensory impairment were recorded in almost equal rates ranging from 25.6% to 27.9%.

Evaluation Tools: At this later stage of evaluation (in comparison with 3.1) three phases of evaluation were conducted. First, a Soft Outcome Star measurement tool was used (MacKeith, 2011) to gather and systemize qualitative observations focusing on eight basic areas (Confidence, Engagement, Self-esteem, Concentration, Attendance, Participation and Timekeeping), applied before and after user trials to establish a baseline and to measure the application's impact. The second stage took place in real settings using qualitative methods of analysis. Routes were created with Route Mate in Caretaker or teachers/end user dyads. An observation checklist for six areas of interest (Satisfaction with usability/accessibility features, General attitude towards RouteMate, Verbal and non-Verbal expressions, Caretaker/teacher and end-user interaction and communication, User's progress, Impact/change after use), was used to order to organize the field notes. In depth analysis of selected cases was also included. The third stage used a Likert-scale questionnaire to measure the carers' evaluation of Route Mate, comprising 19 items in three sub-scales. Two supplementary methods took place that are worth mentioning. "Recreating the Route" was a way to test the construction of cognitive maps through the use of mobile assistive technologies. After the end of a journey each group gathered around and with the guidance of the researchers and the help of the caretakers, recreated the trip using markers and a printed Google map copy of the general area. The aim was to recall the entire journey, stop-by-stop and draw them on the map. In this way the researchers could test whether or not the end-users could create a cognitive line of their trip and if Route Mate helped them to do so. The "Where-to-go-next" screen in Route Mate and the playful concept of choosing photos was also evaluated.

The "Ninja Game Route" was an example of a gamified user experience research method. The basic concept was to implement a game narrative structure in the session and create goal-orientated actions. The narrative here was a Ninja scavenger hunt game where participants had to "unlock" and thus collect hidden diamonds. The diamonds were "unlocked" each time a predefined stop was reached and were given to the participant who could recall that stop at the end of the session. All diamonds were placed upon a wooden sword. Incorporating game-like elements, such as this, made the journey not only more fun but also helped the users to concentrate and be more cautious while walking, and could also contribute to spatial map formation.

3.2.2   Results

The data analysis showed a possible link between the level of satisfaction while using Route Mate and previous technological knowledge, while the reliability of the application - defined both as the actual problems that may occur during a test trial and as the negative expectation based on personal experience - seemed to play an important role. Stress levels correlated with user's confidence and in turn became an encouraging/discouraging motivational factor for using Route Mate. During the piloting sessions, as the technical problems started to be resolved, stress levels decreased whilst participants' confidence increased and their intrinsic motivation to use Route Mate motivated them to learn new routes (see Figure 1). The stress levels of the more experienced users are significantly lower. An interesting aspect was that in some cases getting to know and use the technology triggered the desire for self-improvement and learning other skills (independence, learning to read, finding similar programs and information about assistive technologies).

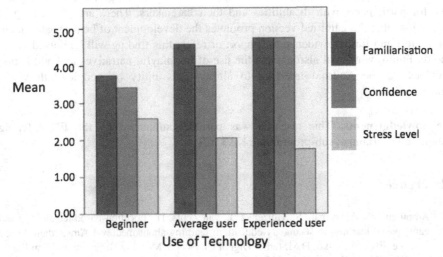

Fig. 1. General means for Outcome Star Scores for participants with varying levels technology experience

The role of Route Mate as an educational tool was evaluated by caretakers and in some cases parents. 83,7% of the responders agreed that Route Mate is a useful tool for training disabled people, while the 79,1% answered that mobile assistive technologies can be a potential educational method. Finally, responses from users with Intellectual Disabilities show no qualitative differences in contrast with individuals with no Intellectual Disabilities (but with other kinds of impairments/disabilities) regarding usability/accessibility, impact and change after use and attitudes to use, providing an important indication that Route Mate can be an equally useful as a learning and assistive tool for both categories. Interestingly, preliminary qualitative results and focus groups at the end of each playful session concluded that users retained information much better when using Route Mate as a scaffolding game than when using it as an assistive route learning application. More research data is required in order to determine that the playful use of Route Mate improved the understanding of map based representations. An increase in self-determination, motivation and memory was also recorded in participants at the gamified piloting sites.

4   Conclusions

The RECALL project has led to the development of a Console – a web based route planning device that can push routes to the Route Mate App. The App itself can be used to plan and practice routes. A series of playful narratives have been created to engage users in independent travel training. In evaluating the route learning modes of App participants require less help and make fewer errors in later stages of route learning than in earlier stages, showing that it is an effective semi-independent route learning system. A qualitative evaluation showed that use of the system can increase measures of self-determination, motivation and memory with high motivational qualities for participants with disabilities and their caretakers. There are also emergent indications that the gamified version promotes the development of better spatial mental models and further evidence to support or refute this finding will be pursed in the future. Future work will also expand the use of the playful narratives and add haptic feedback to the Android interface to allow accessibility by people with visual impairments.

Acknowledgements. This research was partially supported by the EU Lifelong Learning Programme: sub-programme KA3 ICT.

References

1. Admiraal, W., Akkerman, S., Huizenga, J., van Zeijts, H.: Location-based technology and game-based learning in secondary education: learning about medieval Amsterdam. In: de Souza e Silva, A., Utko, D.M. (eds.) Digital Cityscape: Merging Digital and Urban Playspaces, pp. 302–320. Peter Lang, New York (2009)
2. Amon, K., Campbell, A.: Biofeedback video games to teach ADHD children relaxation skills to help manage symptoms. Patoss Bulletin (2008)
3. Ardito, C., Sintoris, C., Raptis, D., Yiannoutsou, N., Avouris, N., Costabile, M.F.: Design Guidelines for Location-based Mobile Games for Learning. In: Proc. Int. Conf. on Social Applications for Lifelong Learning, Patras, Greece (2010)
4. Baker, R., D'Mello, S., Rodrigo, M., Graesser, A.: Better to be frustrated than bored: The incidence and persistence of affect during interactions with three different computer-based learning environments. International Journal of Human-Computer Studies 68(4), 223–241 (2010)
5. Brown, D.J., Shopland, N., Battersby, S.J., Lewis, J., Evett, L.: Can Serious Games Engage the Disengaged? In: European Conference on Games-Based Learning, University of Paisley, Scotland, pp. 35–46 (2007)
6. Brown, D.J., McIver, E., Standen, P.J., Dixon, P.: Can Serious Games Improve Memory Skills in People with ID? Journal of Intellectual Disability Research 52(8-9), 678 (2008)

7. Brown, D.J., Shopland, N., Battersby, S., Tully, A., Richardson, S.: Game On: Accessible Serious Games for Offenders and those at Risk of Offending. Journal of Assistive Technology 3(2), 13–25 (2009)

8. Brown, D.J., Ley, J., Evett, L., Standen, P.J.: Can participating in games based learning improve mathematic skills in students with intellectual disabilities? In: IEEE 1st International Conference on Serious Games and Applications for Health (seGAH), pp. 1–9 (2011a)

9. Brown, D.J., McHugh, D., Standen, P., Evett, L., Shopland, N., Battersby, S.: Designing Location based Learning Experiences for People with Intellectual Disabilities and Additional Sensory Impairments. Computers and Education 6(1), 11–20 (2011b)

10. Carr, J., Blanchfield, P.: A game to aid behavioral education. In: European Conference on Game-Based Learning, Graz (2009)

11. Cartwright, W.E.: Exploring games and gameplay as a means of accessing and using geographical information. Human IT 8(3), 28–67 (2006)

12. Csikszentmihalyi, M.: Flow: the psychology of optimal experience. Harper and Row, New York (1990)

13. Evett, L., Battersby, S., Ridley, A., Brown, D.J.: An interface to virtual environments for people who are blind using Wii technology - mental models and navigation. Journal of Assistive Technologies 3(2), 30–39 (2009)

14. Fitros, K.: IT in special education. In: 2nd National Conference of Educational Technologies, Siros, Greece (2005)

15. Golledge, R.G., Klatzky, R.L., Loomis, J.M.: Cognitive mapping and wayfinding by adults without vision. In: Portugali, J. (ed.) The Construction of Cognitive Maps. Kluwer Academic Publishers, Netherlands (1996)

16. Grantham, S.: Usability Analysis of the Route Mate Software. Undergraduate Thesis, NTU (2010)

17. Habgood, M.P.J., Ainsworth, S.E., Benford, S.: Endogenous fantasy and learning in digital games. Simulation & Gaming 36(4), 483–498 (2005)

18. Hinske, S., Lampe, M., Magerkurth, C., Röcker, C.: Classifying pervasive games: on pervasive computing and mixed reality. In: Concepts and Technologies for Pervasive Games - A Reader for Pervasive Gaming Research, vol. 1, pp. 11–38. Shaker Verlag, Aachen (2007)

19. Klawe, M., Philips, E.: A classroom Study: Electronic Games Engage Children as Researchers. In: Proc. of CSCL 1995 Conf., Bloomington, Indiana, pp. 209–213 (1995)

20. MacKeith, J.: The Development of the Outcomes Star: A Participatory Approach to Assessment and Outcome Measurement. Housing Care and Support: A Journal on Policy, Research and Practice 14(3) (2011)

21. Malone, T.W.: Toward a theory of intrinsically motivating instruction. Cognitive Science 5(4), 333–369 (1981)

22. Nemeth, C.P.: Human Factors for Design - Making Systems Human-Centered. Taylor & Francis, London (2002)

23. Oliver, K.J., Burnett, G.E.: Learning-oriented vehicle navigation systems: a preliminary investigation in a driving simulator. In: Proc. of the 10th Int. Conf. on Human–Computer Interaction with Mobile Devices and Services, pp. 119–126 (2008)

24. Piaget, J.: Psychology of Intelligence. Routledge and Kegan Paul. Provenzo, London (1951)

25. Pivec, M.: Play and learn: potentials of game-based learning. British Journal of Educational Technology 38(3), 387–393 (2007)

26. Quinn, B., Cartwright, W.E.: Location based mobile games for learning and decision making. In: 24th International Cartographic Conference, p. 8. International Cartographic Association, Springer, Paris, Heidelberg (2011)
27. Saridaki, M., Gouscos, D., Meimaris, M.: Digital Games-Based Learning for Students with Intellectual Disability. In: Stansfield, M., Boyle, L., Connolly, T. (eds.) Game-Based Learning Advancements for Multi-Sensory Human Computer Interfaces: Techniques and Effective Practices. Information Science Reference Publications (2009)
28. Saridaki, M., Mourlas, C.: Motivating the demotivated classroom: gaming as a motivational medium for students with intellectual disability and their educators. In: Felicia, P. (ed.) Handbook of Research on Improving Learning and Motivation Through Educational Games: Multidisciplinary Approaches. IGI Global, Hershey (2011)
29. Staalduinen, J.: A First Step Towards Integrating Educational Theory And Game Design. In: Felicia, P. (ed.) Handbook of Research on Improving Learning and Motivation Through Educational Games: Multidisciplinary Approaches. IGI Global, Hershey (2011)
30. Sedighian, K.: Challenge-driven learning: A model for children's multimedia mathematics learning environments. In: ED-MEDIA 1997: World Conference on Educational Multimedia and Hypermedia, Calgary, Canada (1997)
31. Staalduinen, J.: A First Step Towards Integrating Educational Theory And Game Design. In: Felicia, P. (ed.) Handbook of Research on Improving Learning and Motivation Through Educational Games: Multidisciplinary Approaches. IGI Global, Hershey (2011)
32. Standen, P.J., Brown, D.J., Anderton, N., Battersby, S.: A systematic evaluation of current control devices used by people with intellectual disabilities in non-immersive virtual environments. Cyberpsychology and Behavior 9(5), 608–613 (2006)
33. Standen, P.J., Karsandas, R.B., Anderton, N., Battersby, S., Brown, D.J.: An evaluation of the use of a computer game in improving the choice reaction time of adults with intellectual disabilities. Journal of Assistive Technologies 3(4), 4–11 (2009)
34. Standen, P.J., Rees, F., Brown, D.J.: Effect of playing computer games on decision making in people with intellectual disabilities. Journal of Assistive Technologies 3(2), 4–12 (2009)
35. Toprac, P.: Motivating by design: an interesting digital-game based learning environment. In: Felicia, P. (ed.) Improving Learning and Motivation Through Educational Games: Multidisciplinary Approaches. Idea Group Reference, Hershey (2011)
36. Williams, C., Wright, B., Callaghan, G., Couglan, B.: Do Children with Autism Learn to Read more Readily by Computer Assisted Instruction or Traditional Book Methods? Autism (6), 71–91 (2002)

Multimedia Information Delivery
on Mobile Cultural Applications

Heloisa Candello

University of Brighton, Watts Building, Lewes road, Brighton, BN24GJ, United Kingdom
Universidade Anhembi Morumbi, Roque Petroni Jr., 630, São Paulo – Brazil
heloisacsp@gmail.com

Abstract. In this paper we describe a user evaluation that aims to understand the use of multimodal features in mobile cultural guides. The object of the study was a mobile guide prototype that delivers cultural heritage information about sculptures in the city of Brighton – UK. The study was taken in situ with 32 participants from diverse nationalities. Participants followed a short sculpture tour using a touch-screen mobile phone to access the application. The data was analyzed using descriptive statistical methods and qualitative methods. Relevant findings were identified, such as: the presence of the volume controls on the screen, multitask functions and visibility of hyperlinks. The length and quantity of information accessed by users was proportional to their familiarity with the content, language skills and time available. Pictures assisted in learning about subject history and way finding. Additionally, audio served the purpose when participants want to see the details of the sculpture or light conditions were not proper to visualize the screen. Video was suitable for before or after the tour. Those results served the base to formulated design recommendations for developing audiovisual cultural heritage guides.

Keywords: user interface design, mobile HCI, mobile cultural guides.

1 Introduction

This work is part of a PhD research situated in the field of Mobile HCI and interaction design applications for cultural heritage visitors in outdoor settings. The scope of this research is restricted to the activity of using a touch screen mobile phone to access multimedia content at real points of interest and provide design recommendations to develop such systems. In this paper, we focus on the mobile phone potential to deliver multimedia content and users' expectations of using it in outdoor settings. A prototype mobile guide was developed in order to study the role of multimedia features (text, pictures, video and audio) play when accessed by visitors. This system was based on a previous study [2], [3], [5]. On the basis of this material, a low-tech prototype was developed, followed by a high-tech prototype for evaluation with experts [4], and users in outdoor settings. This paper concentrates on the user evaluation. The objective of user evaluation was to examine the usability of the prototype and identify users' preferences with regard to multimedia information delivery on mobile

C. Stephanidis and M. Antona (Eds.): UAHCI/HCII 2013, Part III, LNCS 8011, pp. 583–592, 2013.

applications in outdoor contexts. The city of Brighton & Hove, on the South Coast of England, was chosen to be the setting of the study. Brighton, the larger part of Brighton & Hove, is a lively city and welcomes a diverse visitor population throughout the year.

2   Background

Much recent research on mobile city guides has been focused on the kind of technology applied to supply historical and cultural information. Location-based technologies help visitors and also residents to localize themselves and receive historical, cultural and entertainment information at a particular point of interest [6] and [16]. Location-based games are another means of presenting the history of a city in an entertaining way [14]. Cell ID and Wi-Fi help to identify user location and enable context-sensitive information access [1]. Sensors are employed to enhance the use of maps and the interaction of visitors with systems input [13], [12], [15], [17]. Moreover, the use of augmented reality in the cultural heritage field allows users to find out what certain locations and monuments were like in the past [9], [8]. Overall, the application of technologies has to make sense and involve visitors culturally and historically. In this way, visitors and residents alike might have new experiences, be entertained and learn more about historical cultural sites. Not only must appropriate technology be chosen for handheld mobile cultural guides, but also interfaces need to be well designed to provide information to visitors. Additionally, the research in mobile multimodal interfaces in cultural heritage settings is still weak in understanding how people perceive, handle and interact with mobile systems in outdoor location-based contexts. Research in this area is particularly needed at this point as the number of mobile applications is increasing substantially. In three years (from 2007 to 2010) over 300,000 mobile apps have been developed. In 2010 these applications were downloaded 10.9 billion times [10]. On the other hand, one in four mobile application downloaded is never used again [18]. It may be that users abandon an app because of usability problems, because it did not meet their expectation or because it lacked engaging content and interactivity. Travel services were identified as being among the top ten mobile consumer services in 2010 [7] and kept their place on the prediction list for 2012 [11]. Location-based services and mobile search are also on the list. More apps available in the market increase competition and boost development of better mobile interfaces designed with focus on user experience. Design recommendations for developing mobile cultural multimedia apps are scarce. Therefore, this work may give some insights of how to use some multimedia functions such as: audio, text, video and pictures to transmit cultural heritage content.

3   Mobile Cultural Guide Prototype

The prototype was developed for the HTC Hero phone, using the Android platform. In order to test users' preferences in content presentation, two versions of the content were part of the high-tech prototype (Figure 1). One version had a more complete set of multimedia features (Queen Victoria content) and another had fewer multimedia features (George IV content). The first content had text with hyperlinks, informal audio with two speakers discussing about the monument, pictures of the monuments with extra information and a shorter video length. The second content had a long text without hyperlinks, formal speaker in the audio file, pictures of the subject, and a video of George IV's life. This offered room for researching overall user preferences with regard to multimedia presentation of content.

Fig. 1. Two versions of text display in the app

4   Method

Participants followed a short sculpture tour using a touch-screen mobile phone to access the application. The application was available on the mobile phone via mobile broadband in the Internet browser. It was launched in full screen format and ready for the users to access at the beginning of the study. The application had a map with points of interest[1] and two versions of content. The researcher asked participants to go to one of the monuments from their current position. Eighteen participants started the tour seeing "Queen Victoria statue" and the remainder "George IV statue" to counterbalance any effect of content access order. In the first part of the tour, participants were free to access any content that sparked their interest. In the second part of the tour, the researcher motivated them, if necessary, to look at any information that they hadn't accessed before. The researcher marked down the sequence of multimedia content accessed during the tour on a form. The researcher accompanied the participants and asked them to use the think aloud technique. Questionnaires were filled in before and after the tour. Before the tour, demographic information and consent for the study were requested. After the tour, participants answered questions related to prototype interface design and their preferences for media. Observational data was also gathered during the tours. Participants wore a video head camera, which recorded their interaction with the prototype and any sound occurring on the tours. The observation data was analysed supported by the notes the researcher took during the tours.

4.1   Participants

Overall thirty-two participants did the user tests in June and July 2010. The age range of the participants was between 18 to 71 years old. However, most of the participants were between 23 and 29 years old. This meant that the majority of participants either had touch-screen mobile phones or had used them before. According to the data, 50% of the participants used touch-screen mobile phones every day, 37.5%

---

[1] http://www.cmis.brighton.ac.uk/users/hcdspc10/mo.html

not frequently and 12.5% had never tried this kind of mobile phone before. The data was diversified when looking at nationality. Participants were from three main continents: Europe (56%), South America (25%) and Asia (19%).

4.2   Data Analysis

Descriptive statistical analysis was carried out to analyse the data from the questionnaires - demographic data, semantic scales and design preferences. Tables and cross tabulation were applied to compare the results among participants and the use of the system. The transcriptions of the video observations, important notes taken during the fieldwork and suggestions given by participants while they were answering the questionnaires were considered. Research questions were established to guide the analysis, such as:

- What are the preferences for media usage and why?
- How much will users access text, audio, video and hyperlinks in front of the monuments?
- Is there any difference in interaction or preferences among diverse users profile?

These questions were kept in mind while the data was classified and codified. The main independent variables were: age, residence, level of English, familiarity with touch screen mobile devices, previous experience with mobile tour guides, time availability and environmental factors. Independent variables were used to investigate differences in participants' interaction with the application. Dependent variables, the issues we aimed to measure, were primarily the use of multimedia features on the mobile phones in outdoor settings. While carrying out the video observation, a table wasused to identify which features participants accessed during the tour and in which order functions were accessed. Only the first stage of the experiment was examined at this level, i.e. in other words, the stage participants were able to choose functions they wanted.

4.3   Findings

The findings are described here according to the use of multimedia features. Overall, participants accessed about four features (4.5 median) to gather information in the first part of the tour. They prioritized: text (56%), audio (28%), picture gallery (13%) and looked at the pictures in full screen mode (9%).

Text. Half of the participants started the tour by reading the text of the monuments. Others scanned the text and accessed other features. They also used their fingers to follow the text and found the typeface of George IV text was quite small to read. It was an interesting issue since the typeface was the same as Queen Victoria text. Users who identified this as a problem were over 47 years old and did not use touch-screen phones frequently. In spite of this, the evaluation of the type size for the whole system was satisfactory. The text of George IV was also difficult to follow, according to users. The main reasons were the use of arrows to scroll the text and the uneven transition of the text. Touch screen device users expected to scroll the text when tapping on it, zoom in with double tap or press and drag to scroll the test. Novice users of this technology were lost in the text and mentioned that they needed to memorise the last word read before scrolling the text. When asked for choose the presentation of the text, ten participants (31 %) preferred to scroll the text instead of having hyperlinks.

Hyperlinks. Twenty-two participants (69%) reported they prefer to have hyperlinks on the text than scroll it. They mentioned they did not want to read long texts in front of the monuments, so that, with hyperlinks they can choose what they want to know more. In spite of this, eleven participants did not try the hyperlinks in the first stage of the experiment. Besides, external hyperlinks and links to the system were rarely selected. Participants from South America and Asia accessed links much later in the tours or did not access this function at all (90%). They were in majority visitors and spent a day in Brighton. United Kingdom participants read the hyperlinks more often (80%). They were residents of Brighton and were particularly familiar with the subjects. Visitors did the tour after a day of sightseeing or between touristic activities. They looked for basic information and wanted to move on. On the other hand, residents, who had some familiarity with subject, searched for additional information in the hyperlinks. The scarce access of this function in the first part of the tour might be related to unintuitive presentation of hyperlinks. Participants commented that most of the time they saw the highlighted words but did not realised that there was a hyperlink in the first place. In their understanding, the colours were used to emphasise the words. Their suggestions were to use standards from the early stages of the WWW, i.e. underline words and make them blue. Additionally, twelve people did not access the external hyperlink in orange. The ones who accessed mentioned it the colours were very flashy and that is why they clicked on the words. Some of them mentioned that they did not realise it was an external link despite the word "website". Suggestions were given to make this function more transparent, such as add an icon - ↗ beside the word highlighted.

Pictures. Accessing the picture gallery during the tour was considered a secondary activity. When visiting the first sculpture, 18 participants (56%) did not interact with the picture gallery. Otherwise, it is evident they saw the first picture on the way to the sculpture or in front of the monument. Some of the participants used the pictures of the statue to localise themselves. When asked their preference for having pictures of the subject or the sculpture on the app, 14 participants (41%) would like to have both kinds of pictures for every sculpture. They justified their choice affirming that one picture of the statue was enough to recognise it, and more pictures of the subject were necessary to give context and make the history alive. Besides, participants suggested having ancient pictures of the sculpture, when it was unveiled or pictures that showed the surroundings in the past. The rest were divided in their choices. Eleven participants (34%) opted for the subject picture and 8 participants (25%) opted for the sculpture picture. The ones who preferred the subject mentioned they were able to see the real sculpture on the spot; consequently they do not need illustration. However, in the observation studies it became clear that even those participants also used the pictures to identify the statue. Seeing pictures in full screen mode, according to the questionnaire results, is an extremely important function. (Table 1).

Table 1. Important functions for users

	I didn't try	Not essential	Neutral	Essential
Pictures in full screen mode	___	1	3	28
Audio	___	2	4	26
Subtitles	8	3	2	19
Video	2	9	5	16

It is worth mentioning that even though they rated this function as very relevant in the questionnaire, they did not access full screen pictures very often. In the first part of the tour, just eleven participants tapped to see the pictures in full screen. This may be because certain participants did not identify the possibility of seeing full screen pictures, despite the message: "Tap to see full screen". This message was present in the first thumbnail picture. Sometimes, participants tapped on the arrows to change the pictures, and did not always notice the message or were confused about it.

Audio. In the prototype, two audio files were available. The first was the Queen Victoria audio that was recorded by two British speakers having a conversation about the sculpture. The second was delivered by one speaker with an American, international accent telling the history of George IV. George IV audio was an overview about the figure of George IV and history. In the Queen Victoria audio the speakers had an informal conversation about the sculpture. It was clear the audio was an option expected on mobile cultural guides. Audio was the second most important feature chosen by users as a feature to have on mobile guides. Having eyes free was the main justification for this must-have feature. Eighty percent of the participants tried the audio files in the first part of the tour. The twenty percent who did not try the audio files were also not familiar with touch screen mobile phones; however, most of them had used audio guides in museums and galleries. The tour was very short: as a consequence, novice users might find it difficult to overcome the technology barrier. In this case, a help function or information on how to use the app would benefit these users. In general, participants listened to the audio files until the end. Each audio was approximately two minutes and twenty seconds. While listening to the audio, they explored other sessions on the app or followed the instructions written down on the audio screen to appreciate the monument. In the first case, the audio file did not stop when they accessed other parts of the system. This was an error: nevertheless they appreciated the possibility to have multi task functions on the app – listening to the audio while accessing other functions. The only problem was when they wanted to stop the sound and needed to return to the audio page to select this function. Ten participants who were not familiar with the device did not know how to increase the volume of the audio. The volume controls were essential as the playback buttons and fundamental on the mobile phone screen. In addition, some participants listened to the audio and explored the system on their way to the monuments. The researcher had to attract their attention several times while crossing the streets or merely walking in crowded places. Problems with traffic and crowded environments also appeared in the previous study with a mobile device [5]. To motivate users to look at the monuments, we added a suggestion in the audio screen: "While you listen to the audio move closer to appreciate the monument". Twenty-one participants (67%) followed the suggestion. A few touched the monuments as well. It was pertinent to notice that the George IV statue was very high, so participants followed the instructions to get closer, but after a few seconds some distanced themselves to see the overall statue. Instructions clearly need to be given in a tailored way depending on the type of the monument. Perhaps audio or text suggestions should be given to lead visitors to stand in the best spot to appreciate the monument.

Video. The use of video in outdoor settings is a cumbersome activity. These include long latency while transmitting multimedia data over networks, mobile device decoding power, media formats and memory capacity. Some of these factors were also identified in the evaluation of the prototype. The videos in the application were streamed over mobile network and occasionally participants had to wait for watching it. Users familiar with the technology tried to forward the video, but were not successful. Likewise in the audio session, participants who were not familiar with the device had difficulties finding the volume controls that were not on the screen. Participants also had problems in understanding how the playback controls appeared by tapping on the screen. This action was learned by trial and error. For participants video was the least important feature to have in mobile guides. Additionally, not all the participants watched the video until the end. According to the sample studied, twenty-seven participants (85%) had never watched videos on mobile phones. Similarities of choices were found among eight participants who also did not mark video as an essential feature to have on mobile guides.

5   Discussion

Interesting facts are not only the ones that had high scores in the prototype evaluation. The qualitative analysis of videos and questionnaires highlighted issues present in designing multimedia mobile guides for use in outdoor settings. To summarise the findings, first the higher score of strengths of evidence will be discussed followed by the low scores highlighted in the evaluation. Few high score issues were related to technology and problems not possible to solve in the prototype development. Problems with Internet connection such as loading audio and video files, coming back from external links and the location tracker functions were primary in this category. Following these, it was the impossibility of scrolling the map, switching it according to the route taken and zooming in/out the map. These were features users expected to have in the guide based on their background using desktop applications and mobile applications.

Other higher score issues were more relevant to multimedia mobile interface and content design. For instance, the lack of volume controls on the screen, visibility of hyperlinks and instructions of how to go back from full screen pictures. In the first case, participants who were familiar with the type of the device did not mention this issue. Secondly, more evidence in the hyperlinks presentation was requested based on the user's technology background. Although the hyperlinks were in different colours, as in certain Webpages, participants needed more evidence of it on mobile devices. Thirdly, coherence of controls was expected in all the pages of the app. In this case, the majority were not frequent users of touch screens. They often relied on the back button of the phone when they did not know how to proceed. Returning to the previous state of the system offered them confidence. However, they had difficulties to get back from full screen, by trial and error they learnt how to do this action. Certain actions appeared to be instinctive and intrinsic to the context. It was also true when participants by instinct turned the screen to landscape to see a video. Multitasking was also a trend observed in this study. Participants appreciated being able to listen to the audio and at the same time interact with other functions on the system. The text was recognised as the feature that requested more users' attention. Occasionally users had to restart reading the text in order to focus. They also identified the importance of messages to lead participants to see other parts of the system or observe carefully points of interest. Although international and visiting participants were sometimes overwhelmed with content and diverse ways of presenting it, it was found relevant to have diversity of choices. Availability of multimedia choices is not only related to a participant's profile but also with environmental context. Environmental issues were observed with participants in the field but were not possible to duplicate in the lab tests. Text was preferred when there was noise in the surroundings. Audio was supported by the use of subtitles in the same conditions. Additionally, audio was more strongly indicated when participants wanted to explore the environment with visually, observing the details of the sculpture or when light conditions were not proper to visualise the screen. Video was suitable for before or after the tour, in their words, to be accessed in a comfortable place. Overall, participants watched the video not more than two minutes. The length of the tours and the quantity of sections visited was proportional to the familiarity with the content, language skills and time availability. Locals and UK residents spent more time in the tour and accessed more functions than Internationals and/or visitors. Participants who did not easily identify how certain functions worked requested the presence of a help system. In their opinion this should include information on: how to backtrack from full screen pictures, explaining the colour words were hyperlinks, how to close the application and interact by tapping instead of pressing on the screen. The presence of hyperlinks was positively identified as a factor to improve their experience. Text with hyperlinks was considered more organised and easier to understand than the other option. For the most part, the users' evaluation gave references on how to use multimedia features on mobile devices in outdoor settings. The presence of diverse ways to deliver information was essential to cater for the public of touristic and historical places. Tourists, locals and residents do not always have the same language, background and time available to visit the places. The use of tailored systems would facilitate and customise those applications. However, it is not straightforward to develop applications for a very mixed public. In the second part of the study international visitors were requested to interact more with the system. In real situations, they would not access those functions, as was attested in the first part of the tour. Moreover, it was valuable for residents and locals to have more options to explore the system. Likewise, subtitles were relevant for those without advanced English. Native and advanced speakers were not uncomfortable with the presence of this feature. Ideally, a system that has equilibrium of essential functions, for the clusters identified in this study, is the best option.

6   Conclusion

This paper described the user evaluation studies of the mobile guide prototype. Throughout, it was clear to see the variety of users' characteristics present in this study. A balance of essential issues for this diverse public should be utilised for developing mobile applications for outdoor settings. The environmental context played an important role in user experience. It affected the use of multimedia in outdoor settings in conjunction with user characteristics, such as residence, language skills and familiarity with technology. These issues would not have been possible to identify in lab tests. Moreover, it is relevant to mention that this research focused on user's characteristics and those tailored the application was tested. For instance, the use of subtitles/ transcriptions with audio and video files assisted international users to better understand the content in noisy environments. Requirements were confirmed during this last research stage and turn out to be some recommendations to develop future mobile guide apps.   More requirements might emerge if this research methodology were applied in a different setting with other user's characteristics. In diverse outdoor settings, such as Zoos or public parks, might appear, for example, requirements about how children or elderly people interact with mobile devices to consult information. Therefore, this research has the potential to be extended in the future, in other cultural and tourist settings.

This study served the base to build a framework of elements identified that influenced the user experience when visiting historical places in outdoor settings and a toolkit with a list of recommendations to help designers developing multimedia outdoor mobile guides. As this work described, the full list of recommendations is part of a PhD research named as Design for Outdoor Mobile Multimedia: representation, content and interactivity for mobile tourist guides, approved in March 2012.

Acknowledgements. This work would not be possible to complete without the funding provided by the Programme AlBan, the European Union Programme of High Level Scholarships for Latin America, scholarship no (E07D401646BR); and the support of the University of Brighton and incentive of my supervisors Lyn Pemberton and Richard Griffiths.

References

1. Arts, M., Schoonhoven, S.: Culture Around The Corner And Its Location-Based Application. Museums and the Web. Archives & Museum Informatics, Vancouver (2005)
2. Candello, H., Pemberton, L.: Gathering Requirements to Develop Outdoor Mobile Cultural Guides inthe Field. In: WCCA 2011 - World Congress on Communication and Arts, São Paulo (2011)
3. Candello, H., Pemberton, L.: Modelling Behaviour in Guided Tours to Support the Design of Digital Mobile City Guides. In: MLearn 2008. University of Wolverhampton, Ironbridge Gorge (2008)

4. Candello, H.: Métodospara a avaliação de guiasculturaismóveispara o usoemespaçosaber-tos. In: CIDI‖ 5° CongressoInternacional de Design da Informação, 2011, Florianópolis. Anais do 5° CongressoInternacional de Design da Informação, vol. 5 (2011)
5. Candello, H., Pemberton, L.: Analysing the experience of being guided by a mobile guide app. Revista GEMInIS 2, 21–52 (2011)
6. Cheverst, K., Mitchell, K., Davies, N.: The role of adaptive hypermedia in a context-aware tourist GUIDE. Communications of the ACM 45, 47–51 (2002)
7. Comscoremobilens, Inaugural report the 2010 Mobile Year in review, comScoreMobiLens (2011),
   http://www.comscore.com/Press_Events/Press_Releases/2011/2/comScore_Releases_Inaugural_Report_The_2010_Mobile_   (accessed May 12, 2011)
8. Dahane, P., Karigiannis, J.N.: Archeoguide: System Architecture of a Mobile Outdoor Augmented Reality System. In: Proceedings of the 1st International Symposium on Mixed and Augmented Reality. IEEE Computer Society (2002)
9. Demiris, A.M., Vlahakis, V., Ioannidis, N.: System and infrastructure considerations for the successful introduction of augmented reality guides in cultural heritage sites. In: Proceedings of the ACM Symposium on Virtual Reality Software and Technology, Limassol, Cyprus. ACM (2006)
10. Ellison, S.: IDC Forecasts Worldwide Mobile Applications Revenues to Experience More Than 60% Compound Annual Growth Through 2014, IDC,
    http://www.idc.com/about/viewpressrelease.jsp?containerId=prUS22617910&sectionId=null&elementId=null&pageType=SYNOPSIS (accessed May 2011)
11. Gartner. Gartner Identifies the Top 10 Consumer Mobile Applications for 2012 (2009),
    http://www.gartner.com/it/page.jsp?id=1230413 (accessed May 12, 2011)
12. Hardy, R., Rukzio, E.: Touch & Interact: touch-based interaction with a tourist application. In: Proceedings of the 10th International Conference on Human Computer Interaction with Mobile Devices and Services. ACM, Amsterdam (2008)
13. Hull, R., Melamed, T.: Report on the Beyond GPS Workshop at mscapeFest 2007 (2007)
14. Kim, H., Schliesser, J.: Adaptation of Storytelling to Mobile Entertainment Service for Site-Specific Cultural and Historical Tour Book Information and Communication Technologies in Tourism 2007. Springer, Vienna (2007)
15. Kriiger, A., Jiang, X.: Improving Human Computer Interaction through Embedded Vision Technology. In: IEEE Int. Conference on Multimedia and Expo. IEEE, Beijing (2007)
16. Krosche, J., Baldzer, J., Boll, S.: MobiDENK-Mobile Multimedia in Monument Conservation, vol. 11, pp. 72–77. IEEE MultiMedia (2004)
17. Linge, N., Parsons, D., Booth, K., Bates, D., Heatley, L., Holgate, R., Webb, P., Spicer, S.: mi-Guide @school - A Mobile Learning Application in a Museum Context. In: MLearn 2008, Ironbridge Gorge, Shropshire, UK, University of Wolverhampton (2008)
18. Localytics. First impressions matter 26 percent of apps downloaded and used just once,
    http://www.localytics.com/blog/2011/first-impressions-matter-26-percent-of-apps-downloaded-used-just-once/ (accessed May 12, 2011)

Creativity, Mobile Multimedia Systems, Human and Social Factors in Software: Communicability Excellence for All

Francisco V. Cipolla Ficarra[1,2], Alejandra Quiroga[3], and Valeria M. Ficarra[2]

HCI Lab. – F&F Multimedia Communic@tions Corp
[1] ALAIPO: Asociación Latina de Interacción Persona-Ordenador
[2] AINCI: Asociación Internacional de la Comunicación Interactiva
Via Tabajani, 1 – S. 15 (7), 24121 Bergamo, Italy
ficarra@alaipo.com, info@ainci.com
[3] Universidad Nacional de La Pampa
c/ Angel Baixeras, 5 – AP 1638, 08080 Barcelona, Spain
ficarra@alaipo.com, alejandra.quiroga.unlp@gmail.com

Abstract. We present a first set of results and trends in the formal and factual sciences aimed at reaching excellence of communicability for all in the second decade of the new millennium. Through a set of heuristic evaluation techniques and strategies for the analysis of communicability we present the first causes facing the presence and absence of creativity in the south of Europe, with regard to the contents for the mobile multimedia systems such as the PC tablets and the multimedia phones. Finally, a special case of human and social factors related to the web attacks is presented to foster local and international business in the multimedia publishing sector.

Keywords: Creativity, Communicability, Multimedia, Education, Human Factors, Evaluation.

1   Introduction

The current mobile multimedia systems are playing the same role as the multimedia videogames of the 90s, especially if the economic data in the European multimedia industry are considered. That is to say, they make up the vanguard of the R&D in the European ITC sector, especially in the north of the continent. Now the intersections in the multimedia context refer to the quality of the software, whereas the union on media refers to the hardware. A quality of the software that is presented to the users through audiovisual interfaces, since audiovisual communication still prevails among human beings and the new technologies of the new millennium. That is, in the second decade of the new millennium, the audiovisual and touch prevail above other means of interaction such as the vocal or the visual (movement of the components of the human eye). Although currently there are plenty of studies aimed at the cognitive models and the search of the interaction of interactive systems straight from the brain,

C. Stephanidis and M. Antona (Eds.): UAHCI/HCII 2013, Part III, LNCS 8011, pp. 593–602, 2013.
© Springer-Verlag Berlin Heidelberg 2013

the digital divide among the users makes that in the immediate future [1–5] and for cost reasons they will still use keyboards, mouse, joysticks, microphones, etc. as main means of input of the data that the CPU (Central Processing Unit) must process. In principle the creativity of the computer environment focuses on the interactive design, ergonomics, the potential of the operating system, the variety of applications (commercial or not), the compatibility of the different files that make up the data bases, telecommunications, etc. [7]. Some of these components are visible to most of the users of those devices, for instance, the icons of an interface. However, the time used to locate a street on an automotive navigation system (satellite navigation system) makes the different types of users agree, when the issue of the quality of the interactive system arises. The quality of the system is inversely proportional to the time used to find the digital information that one is trying to find. Another element linked to quality is the originality of the interactive system starting by the design categories. Currently we are working with the following design categories: presentation or layout, structure, navigation, parochialism, connection and content. The interested reader may delve into their main characteristics in the following bibliography. Now the latter of them, the content, is where one of the sources of conflicts is located when we speak of human factors in the era of the expansion of communicability, such as the lack of excellence in the contents of the online and/or offline interactive systems. The excellence of those contents stems not only from the multimedia industrial sector, but also from the university educational context. That is, those university studies akin to communicability, usability, interactive design, software, hardware, telecommunications, etc. which should train the future professionals of the sector, with wide cardinal or essential tools of knowledge not only in the present or the past, but also in the immediate or short term future, show that there is clearer hierarchy in the multimedia information architecture. That width of knowledge must be vertical and horizontal. Vertical when there is a specialization of the new technologies (videogames programming, multimedia engineering, interactive systems design, among other examples) without forgetting horizontality or transversality of knowledge and/or experiences to reach a 360 degrees vision of the main formal and factual sciences of those degrees.

2   Creativity and Heuristic Evaluation

From the point of view of the "genius conception" of creativity creative [7] thinking is regarded as an extraordinary occurrence which demands explanation. The reason for such statement is a consequence of the notion that creative thinking requires an explanation because it is taken for granted that humans do not have the need to think creatively in the course of the daily events, such as the research centers, university education, technology transfer, industrial design, etc. in many places of Southern Europe [8]. Not for nothing the hardware industry in multimedia mobile phones of the last generation is located in the Scandinavian peninsula, for instance. That is, that in the working life of those places everything is a trivial series of common events, which are familiar and which can be dealt with without resorting to creative thinking.

Theoretically, only in extraordinary circumstances, such as the global financial crisis, it is necessary to resort to creative thinking. These are the circumstances that make the best of human thinking emerge and it is this superior way of thinking which currently demands a greater attention, from the point of view of the analysis of the social sciences, including the economic aspect. An analysis of the social sciences which reveals how in that geographic environment positive creativity is not applied towards the ICT (Information and Communications Technology), but rather to the destructive human and social factors. Our work has been based on the techniques and methods of the social sciences, software engineering, specially software quality, descriptive survey and the adaptation of works by Nielsen, J. [9] [10], Mehlenbacher, B. [11], Wiklund, M. [12] They make the following classification of methods and techniques which complement the notions stemming from the social sciences, for instance: heuristic evelation, pluralistic walkthroughs, the Wizard of Oz technique, and direct observation [9].

The set of techniques and methods has been applied to the universe of study of online information, such as university websites and digital newspapers of Southern Europe and Latin America. The period of analysis starts in 1990 down to our current days. The analyzed university websites in Southern Europe have been randomly chosen, through a draw, in regard to a quality attribute turned into metrics at the end of the first decade of the current century, such as credibility, transparency and accessibility of the information in the university portals (figure 1) [13]. Reviewing again the portals that showed a low quality and bearing in mind the design breakthroughs stemming from the Web 2.0 it has been seen that the quality still remains low in 85% of the analyzed cases in the 2007–2008 period. These universities have again been the object of study from the point of view of creativity, for instance. The universe of study has been widened to other universities in the American continent. Consequently, our universe of study in the current work is made up by the universities in figure 6.

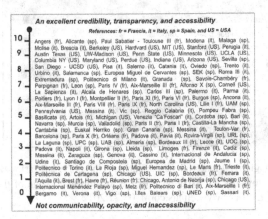

Fig. 1. The value scale goes from 10 to 0 (10 being the highest mark and 0 lowest score) for example: opaqueness of the portals information universities in the last lines

3   Multimedia Educational Mercantilism versus Excellence

The multimedia educational mercantilism in public, private, mixed or hybrid universities (the latter widely described in [14]) fosters and spreads the linguistic formula "educational excellence", not only in the local environment, but also globally with the virtual campus, e-learning, etc. Now this linguistic formula lacks veracity when in the local context we have realities such as one of the highest unemployment rates in a continent (figure 2), the plagiarism in the tools aimed at education (figure 3) or the obtainment of university diplomas such as a master or a PhD degree (figures 4 and 5).

Fig. 2. Spain's unemployment crisis ranges (almost six million out of work). The Spanish educational model is very negative. Digital newspaper –El Pais (www.elpais.com), 01.24.2013.

Fig. 3. The use of plagiarized material for education (University of Carlos III, Spain) shows the total lack of interest towards the excellence of the institutional image of the university centre. Digital newspaper – El País (www.elpais.com), 03.22.2012.

Fig. 4. This example shows the total lack of controls in the issuing of titles at the highest academic level in the German university system (PhD). Digital newspaper –El País (www.elpais.com), 02.09.2013.

Fig. 5. A candidate to prime minister who withdraws from the Italian elections (2013) because he inserts in his curriculum online a master he never got in the U.S.A. or two B.A. in Italy. Digital newspaper –Il Fatto Quotidiano (www.ilfattoquotidiano.it), 02.20.2013.

4 Syllogisms and the Union of Negative Human Factors

One of the disadvantages of the main Latin languages is the wealth of vocabulary when it comes to plagiarize contents without counting the different regional dialects or languages that there are for instance in the south of Europe. The linguistic factor fosters what Saussure called the belfry spirit which is opposed to the strength of the interchange or interrelations [15]. That is, that two sets of forces of a contrary effect operate over any language at the same time. The belfry spirit is strongly traditionalist, redolent of localism and locked, and it prompts the resistance by the speakers to any use that is alien to their own tradition. While the strength of interchange spreads the linguistic changes from the moment in which they take place to avoid that a communication blockage occurs, that is, something that would be unavoidable if every subgroup of speakers limited themselves to their own habits or transformations, as it happens in the first set. According to Saussure [15], these two opposite forces make a language keep its balance and stability over time. Traditionalism as well as the ability to accept novelties are necessary for any language to play its role in human societies. Now from the 90s onwards the mercantilism in the multimedia sector in the Southern Mediterranean linked to the belfry spirit generated parochialism in the context of the new technologies. All those professionals who did not develop their activities in the context of the training and/or experiences such as the graduates in mathematics, fine arts, physics, industrial engineers, etc. with the momentum of the offline multimedia first and then online automatically styled themselves as "experts" in e-learning, scientists in computer graphics, masters in interactive design, specialists in auditing of multimedia contents, and a myriad syllogisms stemming from the wealth of words in the lexicon of the Latin languages. In the first decade of the new millennium they were already self-styled "professionals" in usability engineering and design creativity. Currently all of them have become "innovators". Obviously, if all these self-denominations were true only in 1% of cases, the unemployment in figure 2 and the total lack of controls in universities (figures 3, 4, and 5) those societies would be one of the highest in the developed world. These figures indicate the presence of educational antimodels in university sector [8]. Therefore, creativity and innovation do not exist in those communities with the data and the statistic figures shown in figure 2, for instance.

In others words, from a sociological perspective related to software engineering and the new technologies, some of the human factors are interrelated with the working place conditions, such as the stability of the academic and non-academic staff, whether they are local or foreigners. For instance, in the interactive design team for multimedia products with a global diffusion, the more multinational the group is, the more integrated will be their members. In those work groups and with the latest breakthroughs in interactive technology (hardware and software) which cut down to the minimum the distance or feedback factor of audiovisual communication in few seconds, good results can be obtained in little time and on top of that saving costs. However, the only exceptions to that reality is that aimed at the educational policy where some European professionals have been 100% integrated to the work teams of Latin American private universities (religious) with the same working conditions as the local workers (a common denominator in almost the whole American continent, for instance). Now sometimes also are generated atypical examples of creativity or educational antimodels inside the set of the exceptions. An example are the agreements among Latin American and European universities. These anomalies inside the international educational context are due to the fact that the governing bodies of the universities are more concerned in signing the highest possible number of international covenants, instead of developing their own educational models or the programs of study according to the current and future demands of the labor market, eradicating endogamy from their classrooms, eliminating the use of the university facilities for private economic purposes of some students, professors, etc.

Fig. 6. Signature of a collaboration agreement between an elitist university of Paraguay (Our Lady of the Assumption Catholic University) and the University of Trento (Italy) –www.oics.it

In the signing of agreements for student and/or professor interchange can be seen not only how these are activities where politics prevail over the education and/or research. For instance, the in situ presence of a Paraguayan education minister in a European university to sign a few simple documents. This reality shows the existence of professors (as a rule, in private or religious universities) who foster parochialism inside and outside the borders of the country to which they belong. That is, while the new technologies offer a myriad means for the electronic and long distance signing in the 21st century, the taxpayers of nations like Paraguay still have to pay travels and stay fees for some signatures on pieces of paper. This example makes apparent to what extent an European dynamic persuader in the university context may negatively influence the future of a Latin American community which is located thousands of kilometers away from his own land, prompting technological backwardness outside the European borders, although locally they present themselves as promoters of technologies for the physically disabled, eradicators of the digital divide with the One Laptop per Child (OLPC), etc. Evidently, all these examples, where creativity is equal to zero because it is only about adding elements which already exist inside or outside Europe.

5   How Can Destructive Relationships of Creativity Be Detected?

Answering a rhetorical question always demands previous knowledge and/or experiences in formal and factual sciences. In the case of our question, we can resort to the flowchart of the logical programming. The notions of international design can also be used such as the traffic signaling for those people who do not belong to the group of programmers, computer scientists, etc., and the graphic information in the printed press with an analog support. A combination is ideal for the analysis of web attacks with the purpose of fostering the local and international business in the multimedia editorial sector. The attacks in the web generally are not carried out randomly but they respond to the guidelines of parochialism (figure 7). In the case of the study we can see how the origin may go back to the 90s, with an initial web attack in the spring of 2012 and a constant increase until the summer of 2012 (web attack "ubi et orbi" from Springer in Germany [16]). The dotted lines depict interrelations for the attacks that are maintained and/or activated on a systematic basis. The shaded rectangles indicate the places from which the attacks are continuous. Those which have the shading on the upper part signal the universities, organizations and/or publishers where the ethical limits of trade, the scientific editorial sector and the epistemological principles of the sciences have been left behind.

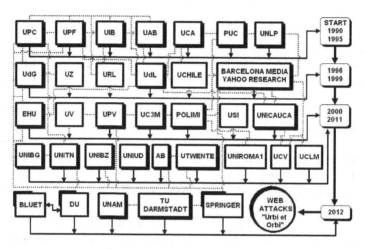

Fig. 7. Unidirectional and bidirectional relationships which stay across time (straight lines) and relationships which are activated in certain moments (dotted lines)

For privacy reasons in the diagram have been inserted the acronyms name (online website) of the public, private (or religious), hybrid educational institutions and private, public and hybrid firms: Autonomous University' of Barcelona (UAB, Spain), Bangladesh University of Engineering and Technology (BUET, Bangladesh), Dhaka University (DU, Bangladesh), Free University of Bozen-Bolzano (UNIBZ, Italy), Fundació Barcelona Media – Yahoo Research (BARCELONA-MEDIA, Spain), National University of La Plata (UNLP, Argentina), Our Lady of the Assumption Catholic University (UCA, Paraguay), Polytechnic University of Catalonia (UPC, Spain), Polytechnic University of Valencia (UPV, Spain), Pompeu Fabra University (UPF, Spain), Pontifical Catholic University of Rio de Janeiro (PUC, Brazil), Pontifical Catholic University of Valparaiso (UCV, Chile), Portuguese Open University – Universidade Aberta (AB, Portugal), Ramon Llull University (URL, Spain), National Autonomous University of Mexico (UNAM, Mexico), Springer (Germany), Technical University of Darmstadt (TU-DARMSTADT, Germany), Technical University (Politecnico) of Milan (POLIMI, Italy), University Castilla-La Mancha (UCLM, Spain), University of Twente (UTWENTE, the Netherlands), University of Bergamo (UNIBG, Italy), University of Carlos III (UC3M, Spain),

University of Cauca (UNICAUCA, Colombia), University of Chile (UCH, Chile), University of Gerona (UdG, Spain), University of Lérida (UdL, Spain), University of Lugano (USI, Swiss), University of Mallorca (UIB, Spain), University of the Basque Country (EHU, Spain), Sapienza – University of Rome (UNIROMA1, Italy), University of Trento (UNITN, Italy), University of Udine (UNIUD, Italy), University of Valencia (UV, Spain), and University of Zaragoza (UZ, Spain).

The directional and bidirectional interrelations in straight and dotted lines make apparent the existing conflict between secular and religious (or private) education and the profit purposes stemming from that education and/or interrelation with the working sector, under the neutral formula of knowledge transfer between the university and the industry, and vice versa. In other words, a set of destructive relationships for creativity in the development of the multimedia systems. The diachronic and synchronic analysis makes apparent how the parochialism of the educational sector is transferred to the business sector. The inverse sense is detected in the figure when a member of the university sector has switched to the business sector, and yet keeps online his false allegiance to the university sector. This dynamism in the constant changes of status of the destroyers in contrast to the creative constructors, leads us to the notions enounced by Piaget for the assimilation and accommodation to explain the adaptation of the organisms to permanently variable events. In Piaget's theories, the first step to face any event consists in assimilating said event to the knowledge one has, that is, trying to make fit in the best possible way the knowledge into what one knows. In our specific case they are true data stemming from experiences accumulated across time. Later on, according to Piaget, it is necessary to accommodate the answer to the novel aspects of the event (surprise attack in the Internet in the month of August of 2012) and study of the human interrelations of the attackers along time), thus bringing forth a new response which is adapted to the new situation (elaboration of a set o techniques and methods for the detection and eradication of the negative human and social factors in the ICT, prevention of the cyber destroyers from enjoying immunity with parochialism, and fostering of the cyber behavior control).

6   Conclusions

Although the m-commerce (multimedia mobile phones and the PC tablet) is edging out the e-commerce (personal computers), the original human and social factors in the educational sector and then taken to the industry and commerce seriously damage the quality of the goods and services in the south of Europe. Factors which directly and indirectly also affect the creativity of solutions in the face of the new challenges of software and hardware communicability for the multimedia mobile phones. The social factors make the best prepared people for the ICT sector be systematically excluded from the educational context, one of the main cornerstones of the developed societies, with consequences for the current and future generations of users of interactive systems such as the high unemployment rate and the exponential increase of the digital divide phenomenon. The parochialism implemented in the 90s is not only responsible for the unemployed figure 2 or the lack of creativity, although those societies are allegedly crammed with ICT innovators, but also for the lack of communicability in the software developed for the interactive systems. Besides, it has been established in the analyzed example how we are in the face of a global ballooning phenomenon of little transparent human interrelations between the university, the industry and/or the firms. All of this exists under the caption of the invisible excellence. These interrelations like the ballooning phenomenon are open lines for future research.

References

1. McFarland, D., Wolpaw, J.: Brain-Computer Interfaces for Communication and Control. Communications of the ACM 54(5), 60–66 (2011)
2. Billinghurst, M., Dünser, A.: Augmented Reality in the Classroom. IEEE Computer 45(7), 56–63 (2012)
3. Bolter, J., Engberg, M., MacIntyre, B.: Media Studies, Mobile Augmented Reality, and Interaction Design. Interactions 20(1), 36–45 (2013)
4. Schirmer, G., et al.: The Future of Human-in-the-Loop Cyber-Physical Systems. IEEE Computer 46(1), 36–45 (2013)
5. Pfeifer, R., Lungarella, M., Iida, F.: The Challenges Ahead for Bio-Inspired 'Soft' Robotics. Communications of ACM 55(11), 76–87 (2012)
6. Salvendy, G.: Handbook of Human Factors and Ergonomics. John Wiley, Hoboken (2012)
7. Weisberg, R.: Creativity, Genius and other Myths. Freeman and Company, New York (1986)
8. Ficarra, F.V.C., Ficarra, V.M., Ficarra, M.C.: New Technologies of the Information and Communication: Analysis of the Constructors and Destructors of the European Educational System. In: Cipolla-Ficarra, F., Veltman, K., Verber, D., Cipolla-Ficarra, M., Kammüller, F. (eds.) ADNTIIC 2011. LNCS, vol. 7547, pp. 71–84. Springer, Heidelberg (2012)
9. Nielsen, J., Mack, R.: Usability Inspection Methods. Willey, New York (1994)
10. Nielsen, J.: Let's Ask the Users. IEEE Software 3(14), 110–111 (1997)
11. Mehlenbacher, B.: Software Usability: Choosing Appropriate Methods for Evaluating On-line Systems and Documentation. In: Proc. SIGDOC 1993, pp. 209–222. ACM Press, New York (1993)
12. Wiklund, M.: Usability in Practice. Academic Press, London (1994)
13. Cipolla-Ficarra, F.: Eyes: A Virtual Assistant for Analysis of the Transparency and Accessibility in University Portal. In: CD Proc. Applied Human Factors and Ergonomics, Las Vegas (2008)
14. Cipolla-Ficarra, F., et al.: New Horizons in Creative Open Software, Multimedia, Human Factors and Software Engineering. Blue Herons Editions, Bergamo (2012)
15. Saussure, F.: Course in General Lingistics. McGraw-Hill, New York (1983)
16. Cipolla-Ficarra, F.: Advanced Research and Trends in New Technologies, Software, Human-Computer Interaction and Communicability. IGI Global, Hershey (2013)

Development of Smart Device-Based Thermostatic Control System Appling on Cooling Vests

Jing-Jing Fang[1], Tai-Hong Kuo[2], and Cheng-Ying Wu[1]

[1] Dept. of Mechanical Engineering, National Cheng Kung University, Tainan, Taiwan
[2] Medical Device Innovation Center, National Cheng Kung University, Tainan, Taiwan
tylerkuo@gmail.com

Abstract. This paper presents a smart device-based thermostatic control system for cooling vest application. The whole system consists of three parts: a pump-based circulating cooling system, a temperature sensing module, and an Android-based application software. The smart device uses Bluetooth technology to receive temperature sensor datum from the vest. The thermostatic control App determines whether to turn the pump motor on or off in order to transmit the motor signal to the vest. One smart device can control and record multiple cooling or heating vests at the same time in order to easily manipulate and save resources. A simple experiment was designed and implemented to verify the effect of thermostatic control to the vests. The results showed that this system helps to enhance the duration of the cooling or heating system and provides high efficiency and flexibility. The future work will focus on biomedical signal monitoring and web-based remote control.

Keywords: Smart device, cooling/heating vests, thermostatic control, Bluetooth.

1 Introduction

In equator or tropical areas, cooling is important necessity for labors working in open and harzard environment. A cooling vest is a piece of equipment worn to monitor temperature and to keep the user comfortable in fields where there are in extreme temperatures. Cooling vests are developed for industry workers, athletes, soldiers and for people with multiple sclerosis or Hypohidrotic Ectodermal Dysplasia. Most portable cooling vests use a highly specific heat coolant to cool down the temperature [1]. Due to lacking temperature control, users may feel cold and uncomfortable. Moreover, the temperature stability and cooling efficiency are weakened over time passing by, and re-cooling is necessary in an hour. Some cooling and heating vests [2] use highly specific heat mediums or filtered compressed air with vortex tube technology to work as thermostatic control system. A vortex tube which forces a simple heat exchange is connected to the vest and delivers continuous cooled or heated medium through its inner lining. The temperature is easily adjusted and stays on the setting temperature.

C. Stephanidis and M. Antona (Eds.): UAHCI/HCII 2013, Part III, LNCS 8011, pp. 603–610, 2013.
© Springer-Verlag Berlin Heidelberg 2013

The related literature [3-5] discussed different portable, wearable or implantable devices, using mobile or stationary devices such as sensors, actuators or other information and communication technology components embedded in everyday objects. Smart devices, including mobile phones or tablet PCs, can offer advanced capabilities with PC-like functionality, boasting powerful processors, abundant memory and large screens. Smart devices are able to run complete operating system software, which provides a standardized interface and platform for application developers. It is possible to develop new graphical interfaces that can be easily used to perform tasks such as clinical and sensor data management, smart sensor data exchange and alarm generation. More and more healthcare systems have been developed on smart device platforms because of their prevalence and convenience with regard to development [6-9]. Related studies have indicated that combining feedback techniques with the convenience of smart devices is promising, and people can perform desired feedback anytime and anywhere. Postolache [10] implemented a wireless Bluetooth-enabled sensing network for indoor air quality monitoring, including humidity, temperature, gases and vapors. The experimental results showed that using this smart phone-based distribution measurement system can reduce the risk of asthma or chronic obstructive pulmonary disease. Zhang [11] presented a breathing bio-feedback system based on smart phone and Bluetooth technology, and this system was capable of guiding the user to breathe slowly and deeply in an effortless manner, eventually resulting in beneficial effects on the cardiovascular system. Postolache [12] used an Android smart phone through a Bluetooth communication-linked smart wrist-worn device to confirm user health. A web-based health information system was implemented for long term monitoring of vital signs and daily activities in patients using pervasive sensing and pervasive computing. Furthermore, different web-based information system architectures have been reported in the literature on electronic health records [13].

In our study, the developed cooling vest has a circulating cooling system [14] and uses a special gel as a coolant. The circulating cooling system offers an effective way to provide convenient and controllable cold temperature to the body by circulating cool water throughout the vest. This paper describes a new design for a thermostatic control system based on a general platform – smart devices. This system helps to reduce weight and unnecessary space, as well as having more efficiency and better flexibility. The LCD screen of the smart devices is used for feedback, and a temperature sensor with Bluetooth built in is used to sense and transmit a temperature signal [15]. The smart device receives data to assure immediate processing, graphical user interface and data synchronization. The application software (App) in Android OS Smart devices is developed by combining the capabilities of Android SDK, Java, and SQLite for embedded database. The temperature of the user's skin and motor signals are presented and recorded in the App. According to the experimental data or the working environment information captured from the smart device, the App in these smart devices is able to control the cooling motor effectively. One smart device can additionally offer control and records for multi-cooling vests at the same time in order to easily manipulate resources.

2   Method and Materials

A block diagram of the implemented system is shown in Fig. 1, including Bluetooth protocols associated with data communication. The entire cooling vest with a thermostatic control system consists of a temperature sensing module, a pump based circulating cooling system, a Bluetooth module, and an Android OS smart device (smart phone or tablet PC) with a running application and audiovisual user interface. The Bluetooth connection is set up before connection. The temperature sensed from the user's skin by temperature sensor and a micro control unit, MCU 8051[16] with embedded software written in C language with low power consumption performed data acquisition, filtering and wireless transmission through a Bluetooth module. The thermostatic control application software determined whether to turn the pump motor on or off and transmitted the motor signal via Bluetooth to the cooling vest. When the temperature of the coolant is over a present temperature or the battery is running out, the App will automatically send a warning signal to alert the user.

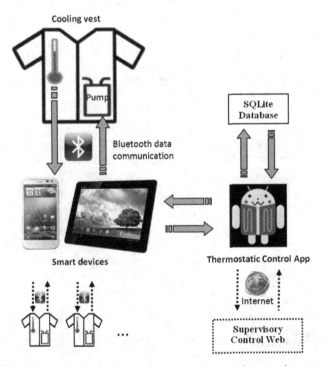

Fig. 1. Block diagram of the cooling vest thermostatic control system

As an extension of this concept, when one smart device is connected to several cooling vests at the same time, the thermostatic control App can do all the immediate controls and data representation for each of the cooling vests at the same time. If these data captured from vests and processed signals are also transmitted to a website through the Internet or a Wi-Fi Mobile Internet service, the users' temperature situation and the time to change the coolant can be monitored.

3   Thermostatic Control Application Software

The thermostatic control application software used in this study was developed in Java programming language (compiled by Eclipse IDE) with Android SDK 4.0.3 in order to implement the BT communication, thermostatic control, data management, and representation on the smart device display [17]. Important elements of the embedded software are the Activity Classes, which are mainly related to the implementation of the user interface. The presenting App implemented a set of activity classes:

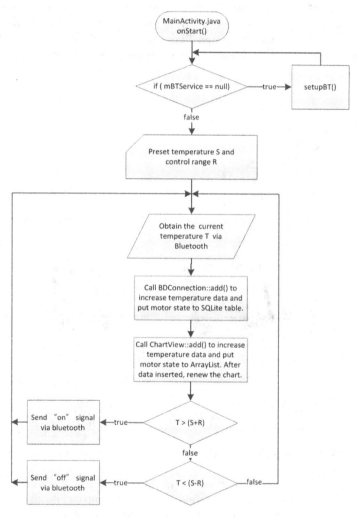

Fig. 2. The flowchart of the thermostatic control system in *MainActivity.java*

BluetoothService.java related with Bluetooth data communication which can identify the existing Bluetooth devices near the smart device and receive data in numerical format; *DeviceListActivity.java* displays a list of Bluetooth devices which are paired with the smart device. The selection of the Bluetooth-compatible module can be done manually or automatically using the information previously been stored in the smart device memory; *MainActivity.java* is the main program used to manage all the information. It also displays the data received from the Bluetooth device as well as providing graphical representation. Fig. 2 shows the thermostatic control part in the *MainActivity.java* activity class interaction with Bluetooth Service, list and chart drawing.

Additional activity classes used in the SQLite database engine are: *DBConnection.java* that sets up a SQLite table for data access, which is recorded by date to store information such as acquisition time, temperature, and the status of motor; *ListActivity.java* that inserts an Activity to display the data in the SQLite table; *ChartView.java* that draws line charts to show the temperature changes by using the charting library for Android- AChartEngine.

4   Results and Discussion

The smart devices used in this study are the HTC Sensation XL smart phone and the ASUS Eee Pad TF201, both of which run the Android 4.0.3 mobile OS. The user interface status and settings are shown at the right side of Fig. 3. The time axis (horizontal-axis) can be scaled and adjusted in order to get detailed information, and the status of the motor (on/off) is displayed in different colors. The life-expiration data on the chart is deleted automatically in order to save memory space. Fig. 4 shows the lists of SQLite data, including acquisition time, temperature, and the motor status. The list is built as a view that can be added to intent, and all the data is stored in the smart device and can be removed manually.

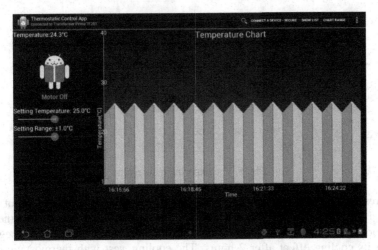

Fig. 3. The chart of recorded temperature data

A simple experiment was designed and implemented to verify the effect of thermostatic control of the cooling vests. Three pieces of circulating cooling vests were measured in the same situations (ambient: 32℃, skin: 35℃, coolant: -7℃, setting temperature: 24.5℃, control range: 0.5℃). One of the vests was without thermostatic control; the others were both monitored by the App. A lightweight type cooling vest had 250 mg of coolant gel and 210 mg of circulating water, and the other vests had 400 mg of coolant gel and 300 mg of circulating water. The results are shown in Fig. 5.

Thermostatic Control App			
Date	Time	Temperature	Motor Status
2012_08_14	16:11:24	24.7	ON
2012_08_19	16:11:25	24.6	ON
2012_08_26	16:11:26	24.5	ON
	16:11:27	24.4	ON
2012_08_27	16:11:28	24.3	ON
2012_08_31	16:11:29	24.2	ON
2012_09_03	16:11:30	24.1	ON
2012_09_04	16:11:31	24	ON
2012_09_05	16:11:32	23.9	OFF
	16:11:33	23.9	OFF

Fig. 4. The list of recorded temperature data

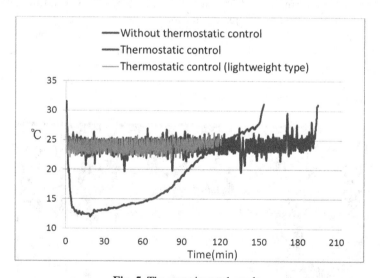

Fig. 5. The experimental results

The results showed that the cooling vest without thermostatic control is not able to provide a comfortable and stable temperature for the user. Even when using the circulating cooling system, it was still colder than the setting temperature in the beginning and lost its cooling effect after 2 hours. The cooling vest with thermostatic control gave the user a stable temperature for up to 3 hours, and the lightweight type stayed cold for almost 3 hours (170 minutes).

5 Conclusions

Smart device technology is getting more and more powerful in its specifications, and the adoption *rate* of *smart devices* is 10X faster than during the 80s PC revolution. It is an interesting idea that someday an embedded intelligence system in portable products might be superseded by smart devices, and we implemented this concept on a circulating cooling vest. In this paper we developed a novel thermostatic control App based on smart devices and Bluetooth technology, and a simple experiment was executed to verify the feasibility. This application platform receives temperature information from user's skin via Bluetooth and provides a corresponding reaction to the motor of a circulating cooling system. Using smart device, the heat exchange situation can be dynamically adjusted, and coolant waste can be reduced in order to enhance the duration of the cooling system. The interface also provides *real-time audible* and *visual feedback* for the *user*.

Future work will additionally involve simple biomedical signal monitor on the cooling or heating vest in order to provide the latest and complete information for workers/users in extreme temperature areas. We also plan to focus on remote control - a web based information system that can monitor and ensure whether individual cooling vests and smart devices are working or not. Furthermore, data backup and the planning of coolant replacement time could be done on the server-side. Base on the experiment in this study, this smart device-based application could be used on medical instruments or other embedded intelligence systems, especially for applications in the field of medical care.

Acknowledgement. The study is granted by National Science Council, Taiwan, under the project number of NSC 101-2815-C-006-042-E.

References

1. Cooling Vests - Body Cooling Vest - Cool Vest - Ice Vests - MS Cooling Vests - ARCTIC HEAT USA North America, http://www.arcticheatusa.com/ (accessed on August 30, 2012)
2. Vortec - Cooling and Heating Vests, http://www.vortec.com/products/vests/index.html (accessed on August 30, 2012)
3. Karlsson, J., Wiklund, U., Berglin, L., et al.: Wireless Monitoring of Heart Rate and Electromyographic Signals using a Smart T-shirt. In: Proc. of the IEEE Engineering in Medicine, http://www.phealth2008.com/Events/papers/p7.pdf
4. Okada, Y., Yoto, T.Y., Suzuki, T., Sakuragawa, S., Sugiura, T.: Development of a Wearable ECG Recorder for Measuring Daily Stress. In: Proceedings of Int. Conf of Information Science and Applications (ICISA), pp. 1–5 (2010)

610 J.-J. Fang, T.-H. Kuo, and C.-Y. Wu

5. Postolache, O., Postolache, G., Girão, P.: New Device for Assessment of Autonomous Nervous System Functioning in Psychophysiology. In: Proc. IEEE International Workshop on Medical Measurements and Applications, Warsaw, Poland, vol. I, pp. 95–99 (May 2007)
6. Cantor, J.C., Brownlee, S., Zukin, C., Boyle, J.M.: Implications of the growing use of wireless telephones for health care opinion polls. Health Serv. Res. 44(5 Pt. 1), 1762–1772 (2009)
7. Medvedev, O., Marshall, A., Antonov, A.: User-Friendly Interface for the Smartphone-based Self Management of Pulmonary Rehabilitation. In: International Conference on BioMedical Engineering and Informatics, China, Sanya, pp. 673–676 (May 2008)
8. Ryan, D., Cobern, W., Wheeler, J., et al.: Mobile phone technology in the management of asthma. Journal of Telemedicine and Telecare 11(suppl. 1), 43–46 (2005)
9. T+ Medical website, http://www.tplusmedical.com/ (accessed on August 30, 2012)
10. Postolache, O., Girao, P., Pereira, M.D., et al.: Indoor Monitoring of Respiratory Distress Triggering Factors Using a Wireless Sensing Network and a Smart Phone. In: Instrumentation and Measurement Technology Conference, Singapore, pp. 451–456 (2009)
11. Zhang, Z.B., Wu, H., Wang, W.D., Wang, B.Q.: A smartphone based respiratory biofeedback system. In: International Conference on Biomedical Engineering and Informatics, pp. 717–720 (2010)
12. Postolache, O., Girao, P.S., Ribeiro, M., et al.: Enabling telecare assessment with pervasive sensing and Android OS smartphone. In: Proc. IEEE International Workshop on Medical Measurements and Applications, Bari, Italy, pp. 288–293 (2011)
13. Patra, D., Ray, S., Mukhopadhyay, J., et al.: Achieving e-health care in a distributed EHR system. In: Proc. of IEEE Healthcom, pp. 101–107 (2009)
14. Luomala, M.J., Ksa, J.O., Salmi, J.A., et al.: Adding a cooling vest during cycling improves performance in warm and humid conditions. Journal of Thermal Biology 37, 47–55 (2012)
15. Bluetooth SIG, Bluetooth v4.0 with low energy technology paves the way for Bluetooth Smart devices, http://www.bluetooth.com/Pages/Low-Energy.aspx (accessed on August 30, 2012)
16. MacKenzie, I.S.: The 8051 Microcontroller, Merrill, New York (2006)
17. Meier, R.: Professional Android 4 Application Development. Wrox Ed. (2012)

Dead-Until-Touched: How Digital Icons Can Transform the Way We Interact with Information

Isabel Cristina G. Fróes

IT University of Copenhagen, Copenhagen, Denmark
icgf@itu.dk

Abstract. This paper challenges the way we currently use and interact with information through digital icons and static metaphors. The latest computer and mobile devices' graphical user interfaces need to be reevaluated in order to support the paradigm shift from static and local to mobile and cloud-based interactions. Furthermore this paper questions the lingering of static icons used in computers, mobile and tablet interfaces. The paper also presents concrete suggestions on how expanding the functionality of digital icons can better afford how users interact with information.

Keywords: GUI, UI, Icons, Metaphors, Interaction Design.

1 Introduction

Notwithstanding the vast literature on graphical user interfaces (GUI), including research and usability methods to test them from within and outside applications [5], [8], [12], [13], [15], [20], [21], little has been done to the core of the system in relation to the metaphors, iconography and their functionality. This paper approaches user interfaces by looking at icons, metaphors and their current use on computers and mobile devices, in order re-approach GUIs by discussing how to challenge the user interface metaphor, and how iconography can serve as an information hub instead of a static representation of an object. This topic is currently pertinent given the current diffusion of cloud based-computing, tablets and touch-based smartphones, as well as the number of applications being developed for such devices. Digital interfaces need to be re-examined in order to fulfill the various uses of technology and data, and augment the way information is consumed and manipulated.

The launch of graphical user interfaces (GUI) in 1973 at Xerox PARC has undoubtedly revolutionized the way we interact with digital devices [6], [11]. The shift from a command-line digital interface to digital icon metaphors represented a key point in facilitating a relationship between machine and user [18], [23]. Digital user interfaces predated 1973, but they became popularly known after the introduction of the personal computer and its graphical user interface [8]. GUI's history has been covered in the HCI field [14], [20], [24], with more recent authors concentrating their research efforts on specific points of user interface (UI) [22-25].

C. Stephanidis and M. Antona (Eds.): UAHCI/HCII 2013, Part III, LNCS 8011, pp. 611–619, 2013.
© Springer-Verlag Berlin Heidelberg 2013

The UI as a tangible artifact [14] and its application in design of personal computers was, among other things, due to the fact that GUI followed direct and overly literal metaphors from a known working environment: the office desktop [6], [18], [23], [27]. The clear recognition of the objects and devices from the users' workspace provided a direct understanding of the icons and their functionalities on the digital domain.

The user interface presents itself on a computer screen with desktop icons, which directly correlates to the desktop context as its metaphor [1-3], [11], [16-19], [23], [25]. The icons are graphical representation of existing physical objects, such as file folders. However, the icons can carry other objects within them, leading to a literal metaphor with mismatched functionality [6], [23] as not all objects have the same kind of functionality in the physical world. File folders in physical cabinets do not often store videos, documents or music in one folder, for example. Despite this distinction between the physical objects and their digital equivalent icon properties, such metaphors also perpetuate some of the limitations of the physical world [6], [23] about layout and interaction. For example, Hudson [11] presents the case of the Lotus organizer program for the Windows platform, which was an exact digital copy of its physical counterpart, with all its physical limitations translated to the digital format. The digital versions of such objects did not necessarily add to their physical functionality, but the physical resemblance was presented as a positive aspect allowing an intuitive interaction. However, such literal designs also limited the amount of other physical world possibilities to be used, such as the action of clearing the desktop with a hand swipe, which was possible in the physical world, but not transcoded to the digital desktop [23].

Despite its initial innovative approach, GUI design for desktops and laptops has to some extent stagnated over time, not following the growth curve in hardware developments. Attempts to challenge the basic levels of GUI and the windows, icons, menus, pointer (WIMP) and Post-WIMP interface standards [12], [22-23], [27], [29], which are represented by the desktop/folder/files structure, did not succeed in becoming mainstream; and very little has been implemented to update iconography and its functionality on computers. The idea of a blank canvas/space as presented by the desktop – either filled with icons of various types, or empty, containing just one or two icons such as the recycle bin, does not address current use of the device, nor does it facilitates an initial overview of the recently accessed files and programs.

1.1   The Interface at the Work, Social and Personal Setting

As computers became ubiquitous in the work space, computer users became more heterogeneous and more dependent on their computer tools. These same tools migrated into homes to fulfill some of the same tasks of the work environment, such as home budgets and personal communication (both offline as well as online with the advent of the Internet).

Upon entering the home environment, the computer also became an entertainment platform, and games and leisure activities attracted younger users. Furthermore, the computers were no longer only for work purposes, but with the advent of the Internet, they became a major communication platform, allowing their users to chat, write and talk to other computer users. Their role in the households and workplaces evolved along with the Internet's growth.

However, despite this dislocation from work to home, little happened to the interface metaphor. This metaphor continued to limit the ways the information was accessed through the desktop structure, despite the varied styles of communication and interactions taking place. Some of these limitations were identified and challenged by a number of authors, such as Raskin [22], who discussed why current GUIs are flawed and dives into a variety of interface aspects that needed to be taken in consideration for the success of later developments.

The home computer initially was the personal device, family-owned and used. This was followed by each family member owning their own desktop device, and later on with portable laptop computers becoming more competitive in the market price and replacing the desktop computers. Yet, very little modification occurred on computers digital interface metaphors; even with the advent of these rarely shared personal computers, with social and communication roles beyond the work.

1.2   The Interface Everywhere

The growth of the portable laptop computer market for personal and professional use brought a clear distinction from a fixed to a flexible location. In the late 1990's, laptops became also customizable in a variety of ways. Such settings as hardware case colors (e.g., first generation of iMacs), backgrounds, accounts, programs and shortcuts were used as personal identity statements, allowing users to customize their digital environment even further. With the spread of the Internet, the computer became an indispensable tool of communication, obliging a large number of the population to own at least one device for basic communication, such as emails [9]. Despite computers becoming ubiquitous machines, the interfaces they carried (and still carry) did not accommodate a larger revision, even as the single-user-per-device paradigm continued to grow. These machines were now being used everywhere and on the go by students, doctors, businessmen, musicians, to cite a few. Furthermore, the spaces where people interact with these machines have also become flexible due to software and hardware developments.

The paradigm shift started with home and portable computers was followed by a number of mobile devices and the cloud. The mobile phone interface continued the use of the metaphor approach, with different icons illustrating distinct programs or functions. Mobile phones became the most ubiquitous communication device with a global penetration of 86% as by the end of 2011[15]. The growth in numbers of regular phones into screen-based interaction with the advent of smartphones and, more recently, tablets, has brought the GUI metaphor to a different direction, however, not one that is necessarily innovative. With the dissemination of portable devices iconography functionality could have been challenged further. Still this did not happen widely and icons and workspace metaphors, such as folders, lingered and maintained their static role on the mobile platforms.

2   Beyond Icons

This ubiquitous presence of digital devices and the growth in information accessibility brings opportunities to evolve and transform interfaces. It is time we started advancing our designs for the interaction with information or the "interformation" [28]. The growth in research and developments of data visualization [4] with designs trying to illustrate and inform beyond a set of static data is one example in this direction. Data visualization augments one's capacity to understand and interact with such data by making the data malleable through visuals and allowing a tangible feel despite its digital content.

The digital interfaces of the majority of current smartphones differ very little from their predecessors (earlier phones or first generations of the Palm, beeper and digital agendas) in the sense of only having icons with button functionalities (or digital switches) that could only be tapped. The PalmPilot's interface, for example, was button-based, both in the physical and the digital sense, the user needed to press one of their physical buttons or tap a button on the screen in order to open/launch an application. These digital buttons did not provide much information, since, as in the physical world, they were not more than switches to "turn on" an application. Despite the button-orientation of the early mobile digital interface, other behaviors, such as swiping or pinching, have become an integrated part of current operating systems, though these additional behaviors are often accessible only from within applications (e.g., browsing music albums or looking at pictures and maps) or at the first layer of interaction (e.g., browsing apps).

2.1   Dead-Until-Touched

The Dead-Until-Touched paradigm refers to the static behavior typical to icons, which behave only as on-off buttons, and this paradigm needs to gain a larger focus in interface developments assessment.

The icons with static symbolic representation, without any additional information being displayed on them linger on current platforms. This brings two main questions:

- Why are users now still subjected to static icons (buttons) and folder interfaces, which have so little information on the "tip of the eye"?
- How digital icons can expand their functionality, gaining a larger role in user interface experience?

The weather icon that do not show current forecast on OS5 is an example of a Dead-Until-Touched icon. Despite the fact that Weather applications and others, as well as different operating systems such as Android and Windows, have tackled this issue, other applications' icons still carry the IOS5 weather example.

Fig. 1. Widgets informing visually the weather conditions on Windows and Android platforms. Next to them, on top right, the calendar appointment detail as it is currently available on Windows phones; and on bottom right, a mock-up illustration of another use of the same tile.

To better illustrate my point about how an icon could inform beyond a static button, the calendar icon on the Windows phone (left image, Fig. 1) could show, besides the next appointment in line (calendar detail, top right Fig. 1), maybe the next two appointments or even chosen appointments, small details that could be customized by the user (bottom right of Fig. 1).

The interface should support icons that inform instead of just being a static symbol; this could be defined as *infonography* or *iconformation*. Icons would work more as live avatars, always informing instead of just representing an unanimated object. They would need to be renamed as *licons* (live icons) or *iconars* (icon avatars) in order to distinguish themselves from their current static counterparts or from the gadgets, widgets or tiles, which have their own meanings and would not necessarily best describe this new type of icon functionality.

The latest Windows and Android devices have most certainly progressed with some of the considerations raised here. The Windows 8 platform has customized live tiles, although with limitations as illustrated in the previously mentioned calendar case. The live tiles on Windows 8 desktop platforms, as well as the gadgets of Windows 7, or the dashboard widgets on Apple computers, have similar functionalities to the mobile widgets and live tiles – extra programs or information areas one can attach to the computer desktop. However, none of the widgets or gadgets has extended its concept towards the larger scope of the digital interfaces, such as folders or files, which remain giving little or no information about their contents and remain "dead until touched" icons. Why should users be required to interact with information in a "dead icon conceptual model", while its digital nature, with its vast graphical possibilities could be explored to deliver a lot more?

2.2   Clouded Files

In the existing networked and cloud-based environments, "dead icons" become a greater issue. With the growth of cloud-based services, devices could regain their multi-user aspect, allowing user accounts to be linked to their equivalent cloud-based items, with devices themselves being only temporary hosts of a file. The cloud paradigm brings further considerations of interfaces, as cloud-based files afford distinct possibilities, such as easier co-sharing, which implies multi-user accessibility in distinct spaces and time zones. As files stored in the cloud are also detached from specific devices, detailed levels of information are particularly important. The context expectation, for example, the location where the file has been last accessed, by whom and even from which platform, can help users interact with files and devices in distinctive ways. Besides, with files stored remotely, they do not depend on the local device hardware to keep updating themselves. This facilitates the *live* information display, as it can be argued that some programs need to be constantly running in the background in order to keep updating their *licons*.

As a scenario, imagine users not carrying laptops, but logging on in distinct platforms to access their data from anywhere. As a user opens his/her cloud interface, its *licons* inform from which platform the document has been last accessed and, in the case of shared documents, who last accessed it or even if it had been simultaneously accessed (Fig. 3). Distinct and valuable information would be visible even before the document is clicked or opened. As an illustration, avatars could be linked to specific devices and/or locations, allowing the user to identify where it was last accessed. Furthermore the avatars shape, round or square in the examples given below, could inform if the file is shared or not (Fig. 2 and 3). The time stamp when the file was last saved could also be part of the *licon* with even a distinct color to differentiate itself visually from earlier versions (Fig. 2).

HCl home avatar   HCl home avatar

Fig. 2. Image on the left: A file with user's home avatar and time stamp indicating the last day file was saved; the red color on the time stamp also helps visualize that it is an older version of the file; the round shape of the avatar indicates the file is not shared. Image on the right: Its round home avatar shape indicates file is not shared, and the green color of the time stamp indicates it is the last saved version.

HCI revised   Course Plan

Fig. 3. Image on the left: Round shape of the avatar indicates the file is not shared and the time when the file was last saved. However the user's avatar is the one from the work place. Image on the right: Shows squared avatar indicating it is a shared file. It also indicates through the order of the avatars, which user has last accessed and saved the file with a time stamp. Also, the green border indicates the file being in use by the other user at that moment.

This kind of intervention is a way forward to facilitating the interaction with the file's information that is relevant for the user. These examples could also apply for any file type as well as folders. These considerations about Dead-Until-Touched icons and cloud-based interfaces could help inform and define some of the future scenarios towards more distinguishable and optimized graphical user interfaces.

3   Conclusion

Current digital interfaces, their icons and metaphors were discussed with the intent to reconsider some of the designed functionality attributed to them. This paper contribution lies on providing a distinguished view on user interfaces and helping elaborate on future iconography design and its role on UI developments.

The cloud-based paradigm and the growth in numbers of computers and portable devices bring a shift in how information is consumed. Consequently the approach of Dead-Until-Touched icons on digital interfaces should also come to an end soon. Data accessibility is gaining a distinct value as users of digital devices interact with different types of information, and it is time interfaces have addressed that with more care.

As when interacting with physical spaces, and despite all the direct metaphors used in graphical user interfaces, cues from the physical world are not yet reaching the same level of visual attributes on digital devices. This does not lie necessarily in lack of processing power, but due to a lingering concept from previously known interfaces. Questions such as "why do most computers and mobile devices have to host the same GUI for different age groups and uses?" and "why do static icons have to continue?" become appropriate.

As computers and portable devices change from a "lasting" good to something obsolete in few years, and as they need constant updates and upgrades, the UI design could fit different purposes and their different uses. From schools to work and personal environments, GUIs could comply with the diverse contexts of their uses in a single device, by, for example, recognizing the device location, and changing the configuration accordingly.

Other questions for consideration involve the growing number of files being stored on cloud-based services and how GUIs can better inform users about them. Physical spaces are constantly challenged, objects are moved around, and whole areas are redesigned and reorganized. This very tangible physical human behavior has not spread itself into GUIs yet. Mobility has gained new meanings as well as our relationship to technology and information. Therefore such changes need to be taken in consideration by interface designers in order to apply more creative and innovative approaches towards graphical user interface environments. And consequently *Interformation* should gain the center stage in UI by adding visual accessibility to digital communication through *licons*; and, by augmenting user experiences through challenging the current Dead-Until-Touched paradigm.

Acknowledgments. I would like to thank all my previous and current students, who have been asked to challenge current interfaces and who have answered this challenge with various creative approaches. I would also like to thank Nalini Kotamraju and Rilla Khaled, who read and provided helpful comments on previous versions of this document.

References

1. Agarawala, A., Balakrishnan, R.: Keepin' it real: pushing the desktop metaphor with physics, piles and the pen. In: CHI 2006, SIGCHI Conference on Human Factors in Computing Systems, pp. 1283–1292. ACM Press, New York (2006)
2. Kay, A.: User interface: A personal view. In: Laurel, B. (ed.) The Art of Human-Computer Interface Design. Addison-Wesley Publishing Company, New York (1990)
3. Barr, P.: User-Interface Metaphors in Theory and Practice. MSc. New Zealand, http://www.pippinbarr.com/academic/ Pippin_Barr_MSc_Thesis.pdf
4. Baudisch, P., Good, N., Stewart, P.: Focus plus context screens: Combining display technology with visualization techniques. In: Proc. UIST 2001 ACM Symposium on User Interface Software and Technology, CHI Letters, vol. 3(2), pp. 31–40. ACM Press, New York (2001)
5. Benbasat, I., Todd, P.: An Experimental Investigation of Interface Design Alternatives: Icon vs. Text and Direct Manipulation vs. Menus. International Journal of Man-Machine Studies 38(3), 369–402 (1993)
6. Brockerhoff, R.: User Interface Metaphors (2000), http://203.130.231.110/pub/books/Cultural-HCI/ Cultural-HCI/User-Interface-Metaphor.pdf
7. Buxton, B.: Sketching User Experience: Getting the Design Right and the Right Design. Morgan Kaufmann, San Francisco (2007)
8. Grudin, J.: The computer reaches out: the historical continuity of interface design. In: Proc. CHI 1990, SIGCHI Conference on Human Factors in Computing Systems, pp. 261–268. ACM Press, New York (1990)
9. http://www.itu.int/ITU-D/ict/statistics/

10. Holz, C., Baudisch, P.: Understanding touch. In: Proc. CHI 2011, SIGCHI Conference on Human Factors in Computing Systems, pp. 2501–2510. ACM Press, New York (2011)

11. Hudson, W.: Metaphor in User Interface Design: A view from the trenches, http://www.syntagm.co.uk/design/articles/muid01.pdf (retrieved June 2012)

12. Jacob, R.: What is the next generation of human-computer interaction? In: Proc. CHI 2006, Extended Abstracts on Human Factors in Computing Systems, pp. 1707–1710. ACM Press, New York (2006)

13. Jørgensen, A.K.: Taking stock of user interface history. In: NordiCHI 2008, Proc. of the 5th Nordic Conference on Human-Computer Interaction: Building Bridges, pp. 479–482. ACM Press, New York (2008)

14. Jørgensen, A.K., Myers, B.A.: User Interface History. In: Proc. CHI 2008, Extended Abstracts on Human Factors in Computing Systems, pp. 2415–2418. ACM Press, New York (2008)

15. Key statistical highlights: ITU data release (June 2012), http://www.itu.int/ITU-D/ict/statistics/material/pdf/2011%20Statistical%20highlights_June_2012.pdf

16. Krug, S.: Don't make me think. New Riders Press, Berkeley (2005)

17. Lanquetin, N.: Evaluation & Use of Metaphor in Advanced Interface Design (2007), http://psbase.com/studies/uad/wdd/ca1034a_report/ca1034a_report.pdf

18. Marcus, A.: Metaphor design in user interfaces: how to manage expectation, surprise, comprehension, and delight effectively. In: Proc. CHI EA 1997 Extended Abstracts on Human Factors in Computing Systems, pp. 172–173. ACM Press, New York (1997)

19. Marcus, A.: Metaphor design for user interfaces. In: Proc. CHI 1998 Conference Summary on Human Factors in Computing Systems, pp. 129–130. ACM Press, New York (1998)

20. Moggridge, B.: Designing Interactions. MIT Press (2007)

21. Nielsen, J., Molich, R.: Heuristic evaluation of user interfaces. In: Proc.CHI 1990 SIGCHI Conference on Human Factors in Computing Systems, pp. 249–256. ACM Press, New York (1990)

22. Raskin, J.: The Humane Interface: New Directions for Designing Interactive Systems. Addison-Wesley, Reading (2000)

23. Saffer, D.: The Role of Metaphor in Interaction Design. Master Thesis, http://www.odannyboy.com/portfolio/thesis/saffer_thesis_paper.pdf

24. Smith, D.C., Kimball, R., Harslem, E.: The Star User Interface: An Overview. In: Proc. of the AFIPS 1982 National Computer Conference, pp. 515–528. ACM Press, New York (1982)

25. Thomas, D.: Erickson. Working with interface metaphors. In: Laurel, B. (ed.) The Art of Human-Computer Interface Design, pp. 65–73. Addison-Wesley Publishing Company (1990)

26. Wiklund, M.: Usability in practice: How companies develop user-friendly products. Academic Press, Boston (1994)

27. Zigelbaum, et al.: Reality-based interaction: a framework for post-WIMP interfaces. In: CHI 2008, Proc. of the Twenty-Sixth Annual SIGCHI Conference on Human Factors in Computing Systems, pp. 201–210. ACM Press, New York (2008)

28. Froes, I.: New Perspectives on Interaction Design Lecture. Second Interaction South America (IXDA South America) Curitiba, PR, Brazil (2010)

29. Saffer, D.: Designing for Interaction: Creating Smart Applications and Clever Devices, pp. 238–240. New Riders, Berkeley (2009)

AwareCover: Interactive Cover of the Smartphone for Awareness Sharing

Ayumi Fukuchi[1], Koji Tsukada[2,3], and Itiro Siio[1]

[1] Ochanomizu University, 2-1-1 Ohtsuka, Bunkyo-ku, Tokyo 112-8610, Japan
[2] Future University Hakodate, Japan
[3] PRESTO, Japan Science and Technology Agency, Japan
ayumi.kawakami@is.ocha.ac.jp, {tsuka,siio}@acm.org

Abstract. Although there are many systems that support communication by sharing activities of people in separate locations, these systems still have problems to be used in daily environment. Smart phones are promising platform to solve these problems since many people always carry them. Therefore, we focus on the cover for the smart phones, and propose a cover-type system called AwareCover that supports users to share remote awareness by attaching the sensors/actuators in a cover of a smart phone. We also implement PadPet as a prototype based on this concept.

Keywords: Smartphone cover, tablet cover, awareness sharing, tangible.

1 Introduction

Although there are many systems that support communication by sharing activities of people in separate locations, these systems still have problems to be used in daily environment. For example, some systems installed in the environment (e.g., furniture or wall) can be used in only limited locations. Other systems carried by users have advantages in presenting personal information in almost any locations; however, the users often have difficulty to carry such systems all the time. Smartphones are promising platform to solve these problems since many people always carry them. However, we need to design the systems not to disturb main functions of the smartphones (e.g., phone, email, or web). Therefore, we focus on the cover for the smartphones and propose a cover-type system called AwareCover that supports users to share remote awareness by attaching the sensors/actuators in the smartphone cover.

2 AwareCover Concepts

The main concepts of the AwareCover are as follows:

- Sharing awareness by extending the smartphone.
- Cooperation between the cover and smartphone.
- Appropriate display methods suited for the cover material

C. Stephanidis and M. Antona (Eds.): UAHCI/HCII 2013, Part III, LNCS 8011, pp. 620–625, 2013.

First, smartphones are suited for the platform of awareness sharing system since many users already carry them. To avoid disturbing common use of smartphones, we designed the system as a smartphone cover.

Second, we install only small numbers of devices (e.g., actuators, sensors, and communication) in the cover since the smartphone itself has several sensors, enough computing power, and a battery.

Third, we need to select a proper display method that is suited for the shape and texture of the cover and avoid disturbing common use of smartphones.

Here, we focused on the soft texture and selected the fur material. Based on the above concepts, we implemented a prototype system called the PadPet that helps users share awareness using pet metaphor: the actions of the ears and a tail of a pet.

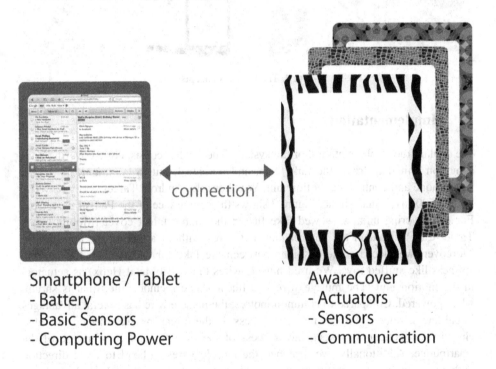

Fig. 1. The AwareCover concepts

2.1   PadPet Concepts

The PadPet presents suitable information of the human presence and emotion by moving its ears and tail based on the pet metaphor. Pet animals (e.g., dogs and cats) are important partners for many people. They have soft fur and body, and communicate with humans by physical gestures. The pet breeders are usually familiar with reading the pet emotion from these gestures. Here, we focused on the gestures with the ears and tail that are especially well-known among people: a dog shakes his tail quickly when he is happy and a cat shakes her tail slowly when she is in a good mood; both dogs and cats bend their ears when they are scared.

The PadPet applies these gestures to provide awareness information without disturbing the main functions of the smartphone.

Fig. 2. The PadPet concepts

3   Implementation

We explain the implementation of the system. The PadPet consists of a covering unit, a motion unit that drives the tail / ears, and a control unit to communicate with a smartphone and control the motion unit. We chose the Android Tablet (Acer ICONIA TAB A500) as a smartphone. Figure 3 shows the appearance of the PadPet prototype. For the covering unit, we sewed fake fur on the rubber tablet cover (Mobile Gears Tablet Case) to attach the control unit and wires without affecting the appearance. Moreover, we placed some cushions between the fake fur and devices to keep the softness like stuffed toys. We used muscle wires (Toki BioMetal Helix) as actuators in the motion unit. The muscle wire is a linear shape memory alloy that is shrunk when powered. Compared to common motors, the muscle wire has several advantages in calmness, smooth movement, and softness. In these reasons, we selected the muscle wires as actuators to keep the softness of the fake fur and comfort use of the smartphone. Additionally, we designed the muscle wires to bend to fixed direction without complicated mechanism: by adjusting supporting points, fabric shapes, and fabric materials (Figure 4). For example, we integrated different materials for the ear parts (thin/stretchy fabric on the front and thick fake fur on the back) to bend the ears to the front direction when the muscle wires are activated.

The control unit consists of the IOIO module and an original board to control muscle wires through transistors. The IOIO module can easily control sensors/actuators attached to the smartphone via USB using Android ADK (Accessory Development Kit).

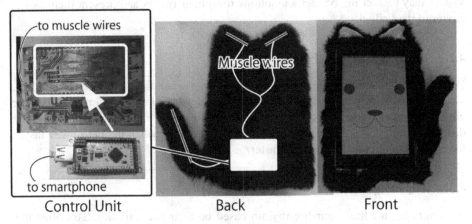

Fig. 3. The PadPet prototype

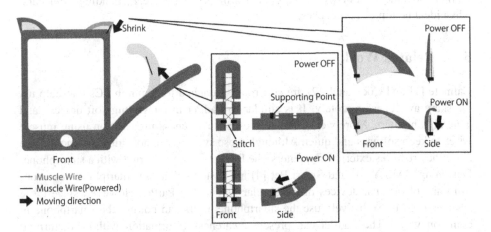

Fig. 4. Locations and movements of the muscle wires

4   Application

In this section, we propose several applications of the PadPet.

4.1   Sharing Remote Activities

When a pair of PadPet and smartphones is installed remotely, the system can estimate rough activities of the remote partner from the smartphone operations (e.g., touch control or physical movement) and present them as behavior of the PadPet. For example, when users apply this application along with text/video chats, they can also share surrounding information (e.g., posture or physical movement). Moreover, the system may extract the partner's emotions from their tweets and present them as behavior of the PadPet.

4.2   Presenting Remote Pet Status

Pet lovers often want to know their pet status even when they are away from home. When we install a pet sensing system that can detect pet status using a camera or wireless sensors, the PadPet can present pet status using the pet metaphor without disturbing common use of the smartphone. For example, when the pet moves faster, the movement of ears/tail becomes faster.

4.3   Adjusting Life Rhythm

Pet lovers often adjust their life rhythm based on their pet activities. To utilize this habit, the system might adjust their life rhythm by presenting ideal life rhythm using PadPet movements. For example, PadPet will act sleepy (e.g., bending both ears) when ideal bedtime[1] approaches.

5   Related Work

Calmate [1] and Coconatch [2] are soft robots attached to common PCs that help users share awareness remotely. It is similar to PadPet in integrating soft devices and general computers. Moreover, Calmate presents awareness information using muscle wires to keep softness and quiet. Although these systems are not suited for mobile use since they requires external computers, the PadPet is easily carried with a smartphone. Designing CALLY [3] and Smart Pet [4] are systems that use smartphones as   control units of original devices in the similar way of the PatPet. However, since these systems need to exclusively use the smartphone, users can not use the smartphone in common way.   The PadPet can present awareness information without disturbing common use of the smartphone using the cover-type implementation.

In Sensing Through Structure [5], soft shape sensor made of silicon polymer with built-in electrode is proposed. They also propose a cover-type input device for iPhone based on the same technology. Our device is designed mainly as output device with an exterior of soft cover for mobile devices. FuwaFuwa [6] proposes spherical sensing modules inside flexible cushion containing cotton, and turns it to an input device by detecting distance between the sensor and cotton surface. PINOKY [7] is a sensor and actuator device that can be attached to conventional stuffed toys, and move these toys with computers. PINOKY uses servo motors as actuators, on the other hand, we uses noise-less memory alloy wire to provide devices that is more acceptable in daily life.

---

[1] Ideal life rhythm can be set by users with the smartphone.

6   Conclusion

To provide awareness sharing, we proposed the AwareCover that is designed as a cover for mobile computers such as smartphones and tablets. Then, we have implemented a PadPet device that presents pet-like motion. We plan to deploy our cover device to smaller smartphones and to implement applications as mentioned in the application section. We will also implement the input methods and various appearances suited for users' taste.

Acknowledgements. This work was supported by Panasonic Corporation and JST PRESTO program.

References

1. Nakagawa, M., Tsukada, K., Siio, I.: Calmate: Communication support system for couples using a calm avatar. In: Adjunct Proceedings of Ubicomp 2012, pp. 604–605 (September 2012)
2. Coconuch, http://www.coconatch.com/
3. Yim, J.-D., Shaw, C.D.: Designing CALLY: a cell-phone robot. In: Proceedings of the 27th International Conference Extended Abstracts on Human Factors in Computing Systems, CHI EA 2009, pp. 2659–2662 (2009)
4. SmartPet: http://sp.asovision.com/
5. Slyper, R., Poupyrev, I., Hodgins, J.: Sensing through structure: designing soft silicone sensors. In: Proceedings of the Fifth International Conference on Tangible, Embedded, and Embodied Interaction, TEI 2011 (2011)
6. Sugiura, Y., Kakehi, G., Withana, A., Lee, C., Sakamoto, D., Sugimoto, M., Inami, M., Igarashi, T.: Detecting shape deformation of soft objects using directional photo reflectivity measurement. In: Proceedings of the 24th Annual ACM Symposium on User Interface Software and Technology, UIST 2011 (2011)
7. Sugiura, Y., Lee, C., Ogata, M., Withana, A., Makino, Y., Sakamoto, D., Inami, M., Igarashi, T.: PINOKY: a ring that animates your plush toys. In: Proceedings of the 2012 ACM Annual Conference on Human Factors in Computing Systems, CHI 2012 (2012)

Mobile Technology and E-Inclusion

John Isaacs[1,*], Santiago Martinez[2], Ken Scott-Brown[2], Allan Milne[1],
Aled Evans[1], and Daniel Gilmour[3]

[1] School of Engineering, Computing & Applied Mathematics,
University of Abertay Dundee, UK
[2] School of Social & Health Sciences, University of Abertay Dundee, UK
[3] School of Contemporary Sciences, University of Abertay Dundee, UK
{j.isaacs,a.milne}@abertay.ac.uk,
{s.martinez,k.scott-brown}@abertay.ac.uk,
d.gilmour@abertay.ac.uk

Abstract. This paper will describe work funded by the European Union (Intereg NSR) iAge project which attempts to address the issues surrounding accessibility to mobile devices and services. The project takes the approach of combining three approaches directed at allowing greater inclusion in mobile technologies for our increasingly aging population. Focus groups sessions are used to ascertain the real problems the older generation has with mobile devices. An iterative design process is then used to create assistive applications which not only assist the user but give them a purpose to interact with the technology. Workshops are then used to provide developers and service providers with an interactive experience of how the elderly feel when using mobile technology. Finally the paper describes how the combination of these approaches will create a transnational framework of best practice for future developers.

Keywords: E-inclusion, Mobile HCI, Assistied Living.

1 Introduction

There is a persistent belief within the technology industry that devoting time and effort to making products more accessible is impractical as it increases development time and cost for little or no tangible reward [1]. Designers and developers tend to build applications, whether consciously or not, with themselves in mind as the typical target user [2]. This results in any potential accessibility issues only being identified after the development process and any measures to address the accessibility being retrofitted to the original design.

The diverse literature on human aging and disability speaks directly to the core problem of accessible design. The combination of sensory and cognitive changes, together with loss of social and economic status apparent in both groups can work against the adoption and uptake of new technologies. This traditional approach is also based on the assumption that the physical and cognitive characteristics of users will

---

* Corresponding author.

C. Stephanidis and M. Antona (Eds.): UAHCI/HCII 2013, Part III, LNCS 8011, pp. 626–635, 2013.

not change with time and that the technology itself will also remain unchanged [3]. As this perpetuates, a vicious circle of exclusion can accrue, where successive generations of designers design for an increasingly young and able core market exclusively focused on latest generation.

With the development of industry standards and punitive legislation in support of accessibility, choosing not to cater for the abilities of users with functional impairments can result in peer reprimand and even prosecution under laws such as Section 508 in the US [4], the Equality Act in the UK [5] and the EU Equal Treatment Directive [6]. These legislations in simplest terms state that all users should have equal and unrestricted access to public and private services, regardless of any disability they may have. The implications of choosing to forgo accessibility when developing IT products can reach far beyond the threat of disciplinary action. Last year in Britain over ten million people were reported to have disabilities which affected their ability to perform everyday tasks [7]. This represents around 16% of the population, a sizable portion, to whom 'standard' technology may be inaccessible. In the European Union, the number of people over 65 years old, relative to those aged between 15 and 64 is expected to more than double by 2050 [8]. As the risk of acquiring a disability is known to rise with age, it is reasonable to predict that we will witness a dramatic increase in the percentage of this population who suffer from some form of functional impairment.

2 Rise of Mobile Technologies

Mobile technologies, such as smartphones and tablets, represent the most recent step in the evolution of portable information and communication technology. Essentially hand held computers, they not only offer the user portable access to standard internet based services such as banking and shopping, but through mobile applications (or Apps) can be used to perform a vast array of communication, entertainment and assistive functions. Take up of smart phones in the UK has risen from 27% in Q1 2011 to 39% in Q1 2012 [9]. This dramatic rise in use will not only increase the ubiquity of mobile devices but it will also change how society in general accesses services. Already 40% of the UK adults now view their phone as the most important device for accessing the internet [9] and as Fig 1 shows it is predicted that around 2014 the number of mobile internet users will overtake the number of users accessing the internet from desktop machines.

It is clear that mobile technologies are fundamentally changing the way we interact with the world; and whilst this rise in mobile device use is largely evident in the younger generation (<40), it is reasonable to assume that this generation will continue to use this technology in later life. Many, if not all, of the functional impairments faced by this new generation of older technology users will be same as those faced by today's older generation (55+). This does beg the question as to what happens when these users become unable to use the devices due to age related functional impairments.

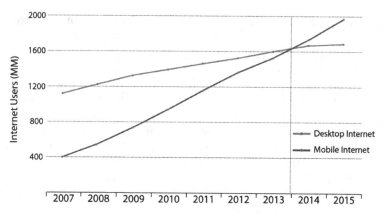

Fig. 1. Graph showing current & projected Mobile Internet use vs Desktop (fixed) internet use [10]

This paper will describe work funded by the European Union (Intereg NSR) iAge¹ project which attempts to address these issues by focusing on the following three main areas; identifying the user's real issues in using mobile technology, development of assistive applications through an iterative design process and finally educating developers and service providers.

3   Identifying the Users Real Issues in Using Mobile Technology

For true inclusive design approach to be taken, a full understanding of the target users needs, capabilities and limitations must be gained. The first stage uses a focus group approach to get an insight into what barriers the older user faces when dealing with mobile technologies. There are a variety of reasons why developing for the older generation presents problems: namely: disability, visual impairment, movement impairment, colloquial language and also some older people still find using the technology daunting [11,12] The Inclusive Design paradigm states that it is this variety of abilities that should inform the design of any solution to ensure the widest access to the services provided [13]. These problems are common across Europe to varying degrees, especially in countries where the older generations speak a distinct dialect and not the supposedly 'perfect', usually English, usually impersonal, language demonstrated on consumer devices. As such the focus groups include participants from Scotland, Norway, Denmark, Germany, Belgium and the Netherlands allowing the identification of ethnic differences and commonalities in technology use.

From the focus groups, Persona templates (first used in Marketing by [14]; and then in Software Interface Design by [15]) are made based on participant's characteristics, their problems and the stories behind them. These personas will be used to inform and remind the developers of the applications, described in the next section, of who their target users are and what range of capabilities and limitations they may have.

The input of the focus group participants will not stop with their initial input but will continue into an iterative design process where they will be inherently involved in the design of the applications themselves [16]. The final application development will not be finished until a sufficient number of cycles have been completed, to achieve the acceptance of the target users and achieve optimal functionality. This process of developing the applications with the target users will not only produce more usable systems with more appropriate interfaces [17] but will also give an insight into how applications can be developed to suit and solve these wide ranging problems. Transnationally this process can be repeated with target users in different countries and the results compiled into a framework defining a best practice in the development of applications for users 55+.

4   Development of Assistive Applications

Assistive technologies can be described "any device or system that allows an individual to perform a task that they would otherwise be unable to do, or increases the ease and safety with which the task can be performed" [18]. They tend to address the limitations caused by a particular functional impairment: for example, mobility problems (wheelchairs), loss of hearing (hearing aids) or loss of sight (screen-reading software). By specifically targeting the needs of users with a particular disability, assistive technologies are able to provide focused solutions that can offer great benefits to the intended users but they are often significantly more expensive and less practical than comparable mainstream devices. This high cost can prove to be a prohibitive factor for those who need the technology.

In contrast, appropriated technology is not intended for use as a disability aid, but can be re-purposed to perform assistive functions. For example, a pen and paper may be used by a person who is non-verbal to communicate by writing or drawing. While dedicated assistive devices exist that are specifically designed to facilitate non-verbal communication, a pen and paper may be appropriated to serve the same assistive purpose.

Dawe [19] describes how parents of disabled children often choose to appropriate popular consumer devices instead of buying dedicated assistive technology. Their reasons included the cheaper cost and wider availability of the mainstream devices, lower learning curves (assistive devices usually require a greater investment of time and effort to set up and use) and the reassurance that the technology would be easier and cheaper to replace if lost or broken.

This stage of the project investigates the possibilities of how mobile technology, through custom developed applications, could be used to provide similar assistive functionality. Smartphones are relatively inexpensive, widely available and would be well positioned for such appropriation [20]. The modern smart phone platform provides many features, such as touch screen interaction, location awareness, accelerometers and communication components that can be utilized by assistive applications.

A number of assistive applications are being developed to address issues that have come directly from the target users themselves. The participants from the focus groups in stage one are used heavily throughout this stage to provide feedback on the suitability of the app design, usability and accessibility. This ensures that the applications developed fulfill their actual requirements and not those requirements perceived by the developers. Two of the applications being developed are introduced below.

4.1   Prescription Medicine Identification App

A UK wide survey performed in 2009 by the RNIB, showed that 72% of the 600 respondents could not read the health information they were provided with [21,22]. This inability to understand the information being provided has in the past resulted in patients missing appointments, not understanding medical advice given about their health condition and more worryingly either under dosing or overdosing of their medication [23] The research also revealed that blind and partially sighted people who reported particular difficulty Identifying and using medication frequently relied on others to help both identify it and administer it. Clearly this could lead to situations where the patient – doctor confidentiality is broken and could be both embarrassing and distressing for the patient.

When a person is required to take medication, labeling on the prescription drug plays a vital role. A label provides the patient with the important information so that the correct dose of the medication within the container is taken. However, it has been argued that "medicines within these containers are becoming ever more diverse, complex and potent." [24]. These difficulties in using and identifying medication are particularly evident in the older generation due to deterioration of their cognitive and visual ability [25].   It is however this generation that will require the highest levels of medication, with 60% of all medicines prescribed in the UK going to those aged 60 and over [26]. Consequently, it can be stressed that there is a demand for an alternative method to not only identify their medication but also to understand the directions and precautions associated with it.

Based on these findings and feedback from the target user groups, an application is being developed that will utilize the mobile phone camera to identify the patients medication. Medical packets sold over the counter in the UK must have a printed barcode which will uniquely identify the product. Similarly prescription medicine will have a prescription label as described above, which could be extended to include an identifying barcode. This barcode can be read by the mobile phone camera allowing the medicine to be identified. The product can then be linked to the patient via a unique identifier on the phone. These two IDs can then be used to access a database stored online and accessible by the medical practitioner, where a voice recording of the prescription and any warnings about doses and drug combinations can be accessed (Fig 2).

Using this identification technique and the audio recording, which could be performed by the patient's own doctor, allows the patient to reduce their reliance on others and gain a higher level of independence in managing their own care. It has the added benefit of personalizing medicine, since the nuances of speech provided by a familiar person, in a friendly tone can effectively emphasize the correct dosage sequence and method far more effectively and naturally than can a piece of text in verbose prose.

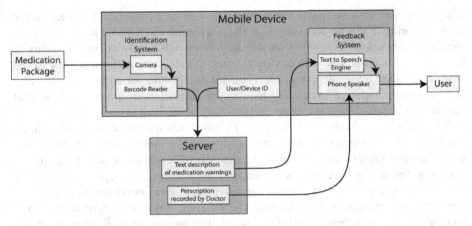

Fig. 2. Diagram showing the structure, main components and data flows of the medicine identification app

4.2   Text Communication App

The development of this application aims to assess if equivalency of access to text messaging can be achieved regardless of the functional ability of the user. This will be evaluated from an objective view-point to determine if the same functionality can be provided as well as subjectively evaluating how equivalent the overall experience is. There have been attempts to quantify how efficient methods of interaction are. There have been studies into the efficiency and appropriateness of mobile interaction techniques [27,28]. However these studies are not targeted specifically on the elderly.

There have also been numerous studies into the creation of assistive mobile applications for a particular disability [29-31], which could also be applied to age related functional impairments. These applications were evaluated to determine how effective they were at overcoming a particular disability but not how equivalent their operation or user experience was with a standard application performing the same function. Usually evaluation procedures include time of target acquisition for physical interaction, the general time taken to complete a task as well as error rates for measures of a method of interaction's suitability. These are valid both under laboratory and field conditions [32,33], but do not quite inform of the experience that the user has. Indeed more recently the use of touch screens has led to debate about the continued relevance of Fitts' law for post-GUI interaction metaphors such as pinch-zooming and scrubbing [34].

A text messaging application will be developed which attempt to allow the same level of user experience for a range of functionally impairments, including deafness or auditory impairment, blindness or vision impairment, physical disability relating to the arms or hands including dexterity issues and cognitive impairment. To address each of these functional impairments the specific needs of the users must be taken into account. For blind or visually impaired users it is important that any visual interfaces have an equivalent text to speech component and that the interfaces are easily navigable by touch without the requirement for a high degree of precision. Voice recognition may also be useful for dictation or issuing commands. For deaf or the hard of hearing it will be necessary that all information has a visual and non audible means of interaction. Depending on the disabilities which may affect the ability to hold a phone or for people with dexterity issues, the ability to perform actions should again not require a high degree of precision but also should not require a large range of movement. Cognitive issues will require that the functions are made clear what they do and help is always available, gestures may be difficult to understand.

To enable the creation of a high level of equivalency the application will utilize a full range of the interaction methods available on the mobile platform. The touch screen, accelerometers, audio IO and vibration feedback will all be used to attempt to overcome the user's impairments or range of impairments. The application will be tested with focus groups of target users at different stages of development to ascertain how well the application is addressing the different functional impairments. Even though this process is being applied to a simple text messaging application the results of this evaluation will inform how similar interaction techniques can be incorporated into any mobile application, to achieve a comparable level of interaction to a unimpaired user.

5   Educating Developers and Service Providers

A major driver in the creation of accessible apps will be to allow the developers to understand the impact legally, ethically, economically and socially of not ensuring their applications are inclusive. Part of the problem of inclusive design is the inspirational nature of the creative process where personal insights and experience often shape the genesis of ideas. James Dyson famously devised his dual-cyclone based on frustrations with conventional Hoovers [35]. For inclusive design, the problem is one of perspective taking. How can a population of typically young, technologically savvy IT developers imagine what the issues are for older user groups [36]. Participatory design and observational learning are only part of the solution. Until one has experienced problems directly, it can be difficult to visualize or empathize with the problems faced by diverse user.

Over several years, the team has developed a first-person perspective, immersive experience based workshop to create reflective practice in designers, service providers and developers. The 'Instant Aging' workshop participants see and feel the world as their clients experience it. Beginning with visual sight loss simulation spectacles (RNIB) further age-related sensory losses are progressively introduced to the group as they undertake simple everyday tasks, to gain an understanding of the isolation and frustration an older user actually experiences. The addition of arthritis simulating gloves and artificial hearing impairment with earplugs often surprises the participants, who may take far longer than anticipated to count change from a transaction, or try and send a text message on a phone. These exercises are used to provoke group and individual reflection through written responses and group discussions. The experiences are framed in the context of recent advances in the social and emotional consequences of making the transition from sightedness to blindness [22,23] and widely published issues relating to visual impairment (eg [37]). It is the emotional and the social connections possible that at once have the potential to exclude or include large sections of the population from the possible gains and benefits of mobile technology.

These sessions allow the developers and more importantly the potential service providers an understanding of the emotional experience elderly or disabled uses have with mobile technology. It is believed that through similar workshops and age related functional impairment simulation that the traditional egocentric perspective of application design can be shifted into an empathetic and allocentric one, based in seeing and feeling the world in the way the users experience it.

6   Conclusions

The physiological apparatus we are born with changes throughout life. The natural aging process can be supplemented by additional acquired or inherited conditions. Some of these conditions progress so slowly that people are unaware of the changes to their sensory input. Others can progress very quickly. These changes are difficult to perceive and to accept for those people who experience them; it is even more difficult for those who still have not experienced them. Despite extensive publicity of issues surrounding accessible design, most of us tend to assume that the world appears everyone in the same fidelity of sight, sound and touch as it does to us. As has been discussed this prevents real inclusion being incorporated into mobile application design.

This project describes a combination of three approaches directed at allowing greater inclusion in mobile technologies for our increasingly aging population. The focus groups sessions with the target users will inform the developers of the real issues they have and ensure the applications developed here will be fit for purpose. The applications developed will not only fulfill a specific purpose for the target users but will provide a much needed reason for them to use the technology in the first place. An older user who has never used a mobile device before is unlikely to start using it for a simple convenience application but would use a application they find enabling or empowering. Once they are using the device they will then gain the confidence to use it for other purposes.

The iterative design process with the focus groups session will provide a commentary of how the design of the application is evolving to match the user's requirements and feedback. This will give the researchers an unrivaled opportunity to document the effective measures both of the development but also of the communication and feedback process. This combined with the initial access problems identified by the target users and the current range of legislative material allows the researchers to produce a framework for best practice in the development of mobile applications. This framework will detail how mobile applications should be designed with inclusion in mind, both from a moral point of view but also detailing particular legislation that must be adhered to.

The impact of age related sensory changes is of great importance to a society interested in wellbeing and longevity, yet design, particularly electronic design is only slowly beginning to practice inclusive design from the start, this project is a transnational step towards making the e-inclusion agenda evidence-based and practically guided.

References

1. Keates, S., Clarkson, J.: Countering design exclusion: An introduction to inclusive design. Springer, London (2003)
2. Keates, S.: Pragmatic research issues confronting HCI practitioners when designing for universal access. Int. J. on Universal Access in the Information Society 5(3), 269–278 (2006)
3. Newell, A.: Technology is older people phobic, not vice versa. In: Mieczakowski, A., Clarkson, J. (eds.) Ageing, Adaption and Accessibility: Time for the Inclusive Revolution!, Engineering Design Centre University of Cambridge, vol. 70 (2012)
4. Section508 (2012), http://www.Section508.gov
5. Directive 2006/54/Ec of The European Parliament and of The Council of July 5, 2006 on the implementation of the principle of equal opportunities and equal treatment of men and women in matters of employment and occupation (2006)
6. Equality Act 2010. The Stationery Office, London (2010)
7. Disability facts and figures. Office for Disability Issues, http://odi.dwp.gov.uk/disability-statistics-and-research/
8. Carone, G., Costello, D.: Can Europe afford to grow old? Finance and Development 43(1) (2006)
9. Pieper, M., Morasch, H., Piéla, G.: Bridging the educational divide. Universal Access in the Information Society 2(3), 243–254 (2003)
10. Hargittai, E.: Digital Na(t)ives Variation in Internet skills and uses among members of the "Net Generation". Sociological Inquiry 80(1), 92–113 (2010)
11. Savidis, A., Stephanidis, C.: Unified user interface design: designing universally accessible interactions. Interaction with Computers 16(2), 243–270 (2004)
12. Cooper, A.: The inmates are running the asylum - why tech products drive us crazy and how to restore the sanity. SAMS, Indianapolis (1999)
13. Jenkinson, A.: Beyond Segmentation. Journal of Targeting, Measurement and Analysis of Marketing 1 (1994)
14. Nielsen, J.: Iterative User Interface Design. IEEE Computer 26(1), 32–41 (1993)
15. Potosnak, K., Hayes, P.J., Rosson, M.B., Schneider, M.L., Whiteside, J.A.: Classifying users: a hard look at some controversial issues. ACM SIGCHI Bulletin 17(4), 84–88 (1986)
16. Cowan, D., Turner-Smith, A.: The role of assistive technology in alternative models of care for older people. In: Royal Commission on Long Term Care, Research vol. 2, Appendix 4. The Stationery Office, London (1999) Volume 2,
17. Dawe, M.: Desperately seeking simplicity: how young adults with cognitive disabilities and their families adopt assistive technologies. In: Proceedings of the SIGCHI Conference on Human Factors in Computing Systems (CHI 2006), Montréal, Canada, April 22-27. ACM Press, New York (2006)
18. MacKenzie, I.S., Zhang, S.X., Soukoreff, R.W.: Text entry using soft keyboards. Behaviour & Information Technology 18(4), 235–244 (1999)
19. RNIB, Royal National Institute of Blind People, http://www.rnib.org.uk/
20. Thurston, M., Thurston, A.: The accessibility of health information for blind and partially sighted people. RNIB, Edinburgh (2010)
21. Thurston, M., Thurston, A., McLeod, J.: The socio-emotional effect of the transition from sight to blindness. The British Journal of Visual Impairment 28(2), 90–112 (2010)
22. A Spoonful of Sugar, Medicine Management in NHS Hospitals, Audit Commission Briefing, London (2001)

23. Cramer, J., Enhancing, A.: patient compliance in the elderly: role of packaging aids and monitoring. Drugs & Aging 12(1), 7–15 (1998)

24. Prescriptions Dispensed in the Community: England, Statistics for 2001 to 2011, HM Government (2012)

25. Chittaro, L.: Distinctive aspects of mobile interaction and their implications for the design of multimodal interfaces. Journal on Multimodal User Interfaces 3(3), 157–165 (2012)

26. Rukzio, E., Broll, G., Leichtenstern, K., Schmidt, A.: Mobile interaction with the real world: An evaluation and comparison of physical mobile interaction techniques. In: Schiele, B., Dey, A.K., Gellersen, H., de Ruyter, B., Tscheligi, M., Wichert, R., Aarts, E., Buchmann, A.P. (eds.) AmI 2007. LNCS, vol. 4794, pp. 1–18. Springer, Heidelberg (2007)

27. Chiti, S., Leporini, B.: Accessibility of android-based mobile devices: a prototype to investigate interaction with blind users. Computers Helping People with Special Needs, 607–614 (2012)

28. Kane, S.K., Bigham, J.P., Wobbrock, J.O.: Slide rule: making mobile touch screens accessible to blind people using multi-touch interaction techniques. In: Proceedings of the 10th International ACM SIGACCESS Conference on Computers and Accessibility, pp. 73–80. ACM (2008)

29. Guerreiro, T., Lagoá, P., Nicolau, H., Santana, P., Jorge, J.: Mobile text-entry models for people with disabilities. In: Proceedings of the 15th European Conference on Cognitive Ergonomics: the Ergonomics of Cool Interaction, p. 39. ACM (2008)

30. Duh, H.B.L., Tan, G.C., Chen, V.H.H.: Usability evaluation for mobile device: a comparison of laboratory and field tests. In: Proceedings of the 8th Conference on Human-Computer Interaction with Mobile Devices and Services, pp. 181–186. ACM (2006)

31. Kallio, T., Kaikkonen, A.: Usability testing of mobile applications: A comparison between laboratory and field testing. Journal of Usability Studies 1(4-16), 23–28 (2005)

32. Pavlus, J.: Does Gestural Computing Break Fitts' Law? Technology Review (2013)

33. Mahoney, P.G.: Design the Dyson Way. Machine Design 80(15), 58–64 (2008)

34. Martinez, S., Carrillo, A., Scott-Brown, K., Falgueras, J.: AGILE interface for 'No-Learning nor Experience required' interaction. In: Martín, E., Haya, P.A., Carro, R.M. (eds.) User Modeling and Adaptation for Daily Routines. Providing Assistance to People with Special Needs. ch. 5, pp. 119–151. Springer, London (2013)

35. McLannahan, H.: Visual impairment: a global view. Oxford University Press, London (2008)

How Unfamiliar Words in Smartphone Manuals Affect Senior Citizens

Tatsuya Ishihara, Masatomo Kobayashi, Hironobu Takagi, and Chieko Asakawa

IBM Research – Tokyo, NBF Toyosu Canal Front, Toyosu 5-6-52, Koto, Tokyo, Japan
{tisihara,mstm,takagih,chie}@jp.ibm.com

Abstract. Elderly people are motivated to continue working, but may have difficulties working in full-time jobs and need flexible working styles to compensate for their declining physical abilities. ICT can help support flexible working styles by enhancing communication between people in distant places. Smartphones offer various features for communication and information gathering, thus creating more opportunities to work. However, smartphone adoption has been slow for the elderly. One of the reasons is that elderly people have lower familiarity with computer terminology and therefore find the manuals difficult to understand. In this study, we investigated factors that make smartphone manuals hard to understand. We first asked elderly people about their familiarity with words found in smartphone manuals. Our second survey asked about sentences extracted from the smartphone manuals. By analyzing these results, we found that the comprehension was highly correlated with their familiarity with the specialized vocabulary.

Keywords: Word familiarity, text readability, ageing, smartphone.

1 Introduction

Elderly people want to work and contribute to their societies [1], but often have difficulties with full-time employment because of their declining physical abilities. They need more flexible work [2] where they can participate in part-time jobs or from remote offices. Flexible working styles can be supported by ICT (Information-Communication Technology). Smartphones are rapidly gaining popularity because they offer various useful functions for communication and information gathering such as e-mail, Web browsing, and GPS navigation. In addition to these functions, they offer various accessibility features such as zoom and screen reading functions. Many of these features were originally designed for computer-use by people with disabilities, but are also helpful for senior citizens whose physical abilities are gradually declining. If the elderly can fully utilize smartphones, they will find more opportunities to work and easily communicate with their friends and families and be more involved in their local communities.

However, smartphones are not yet popular among elderly people. In the US, 45% of all people over 18 years old own a smartphone, but only 12% of people over 65

C. Stephanidis and M. Antona (Eds.): UAHCI/HCII 2013, Part III, LNCS 8011, pp. 636–642, 2013.
© Springer-Verlag Berlin Heidelberg 2013

have one [3]. One of the reasons for their limited popularity is that elderly people who have weaker computer skills find it difficult to adopt new computer-like devices.

Nicholas et al. [4] showed that elderly people with less Internet experience had difficulties in using touch screen kiosks because of their lower literacy as regards computer-related terms. Leung et al. [5] found that elderly people preferred to study instruction manuals rather than learn by trial and error. Elderly people often felt frustration when the manuals were inadequate or difficult to understand [5]. Creating easy-to-understand manuals is essential to help them adopt the new technologies. Though many of elderly people experience declines in their cognitive skills and short-term working memory, it is known that the language skills of elderly people are good [6]. Therefore, we hypothesized that elderly people may have special difficulties with these manuals because they are unfamiliar with the computer-related terms.

In our two-part experiment, we first asked elderly people about their familiarity with various technical words extracted from smartphone manuals. We then asked about their comprehension of sentences extracted from smartphone manuals. By analyzing both of these results, we investigated factors that make smartphone manuals hard to understand for elderly people.

2   Related Work

Text readability research involves metrics to relate the reading difficulty to educational levels. In English, several metrics such as FOG, SMOG, and Flesch-Kincaid are used to estimate the appropriate educational level of a text [7]. All of these metrics uses sentence structures, such as the number of words per sentence, average number of syllables per word.

Collins-Thompson et al. [8] showed that a statistical language model can help assess text readability more accurately. They used a unigram language model to predict the grade level of text. Pitler et al. [9] showed a language model can help estimate the text readability for various purposes. They used a unigram language model that was calculated from newspaper articles, and estimated the text quality for educated adults. Kanungo et al. [10] assessed the text readability for the summaries of webpages that were created by search engines.

Although the Japanese language has a special problem in that the words are not separated by spaces, several methods have been devised to predict the readability of a text by analyzing the sentence at the character level [11, 12].

3   Word Familiarity and Sentence Difficulty

In contrast to the methods for calculating text readability, we focused on the vocabulary of the elderly to recognize the kinds of sentences that elderly people may find difficult. Word familiarity describes how familiar people are with specific words. In Japanese, there is a major database for word familiarity [13], but the participants were young people in their twenties, and only general vocabulary was tested. Because elderly people have higher language skills and are already familiar with this general vocabulary, we focused only on computer-related terms.

To assess the senior citizens' familiarity with computer terms, we used a similar approach to that used in [13]. To collect the computer terms, we analyzed five smart-phone manuals and extracted some frequently used terms. In our study, all of the participants were senior citizens over 60 years old. Each participant indicated how familiar they were with each of the words by selecting an answer from three candidate answers: "I know this word" (scored as 3 points), "I recognize this word" (2 points), and "I do not know the word" (1 point). In this paper, we defined word familiarity by averaging the numeric values for all of the participants, so each word had a familiarity value between 1 and 3.

We defined sentence difficulty in a similar way. We selected certain sentences from the smartphone manuals, where each sentence should contain more than one word included in the word familiarity survey. For some of the sentences, the words from the word familiarity survey were replaced with other words that have similar meanings. For each sentence, the participants answered by selecting from three candidate answers: "The sentence is clear" (scored as 3 points), "The sentence is partly unclear" (2 points), "I do not understand the sentence" (1 point). We defined sentence difficulty as the average value for all of the participants, so each sentence also had a difficulty value between 1 and 3.

4   Experiments

4.1   Experimental Settings

When collecting the word familiarity data, we prepared both paper and online versions of our surveys. A total of 341 words were studied. For the online survey, the questions appeared at the side of the top page of our SNS. Each question asked about the user's familiarity with one word. When participants answered one question, another question was automatically displayed. A total of 52 elderly people participated in this online survey. For the paper-based survey, 24 elderly people participated. All of the participants live near our lab, and all of them are over 60 years old (mean=68.8, SD=5.3, two people who did not provide their accurate age were excluded from the analysis). All of them were native Japanese speakers, and the experiment was conducted in Japanese. In total, 76 people participated and the average for the number of responses from each participant was 143.84 (SD=100.45). The most active participant responded to 341 words, while the least active participant answered for 1 word. The average number of participants for each word was 32.15 (SD=10.5).

For sentence difficulty, we used only an online survey with 105 experimental sentences. Each question asked about the sentence difficulty of one sentence. At least 30 participants answered one or more questions. All 30 of the sentence-level participants had also answered word familiarity questions. All of the sentence-level participants were over 60 years old (mean=66.0, SD=8.7). The experiment was conducted in Japanese. The average number of questions answered about sentences was 28.9

(SD=36.39). The most active participants evaluated 105 sentences, while the least active answered for only 1 sentence. The average number of responses for each sentence was 8.09 (SD=1.3).

4.2   Results for Word Familiarity

We categorized the words in the word familiarity survey into three categories: (A) Words that are specific to smartphones, cell phones, or touchscreen devices, (B) Words that are specific to a vendor or a product, and (C) Other computer-related terms. Table 1 shows the five most difficult and five easiest words for each category. The number of words classified in categories (A), (B), and (C) were 100, 29, and 211, respectively. The average word familiarity for the categories (A), (B), and (C) were 2.25, 1.86, and 2.5. Analysis of variance showed a significant main effect for the category (F_2=103.9, p<.001). A post-hoc analysis found that the word familiarity for all three categories was significantly different from each other (p<.001).

Table 1. Five most difficult and five easiest words in each category: (A) Words that are specific for smartphones, cell phones, or touchscreen devices, (B) Words that are specific to vendors or products, and (C) Other computer-related terms. The numeric value in parentheses for each word is the word familiarity. The Japanese word in brackets for each word is the word that was used in our questions. The words that do not have Japanese equivalents in parentheses were asked using English.

Category	Aver. Word Familiarity (SD)	Five most difficult words	Five easiest words
A	2.25 (0.87)	Pinch Open (1.15, ピンチオープン), Pinch Close (1.15, ピンチクローズ), Pinch Out (1.23, ピンチアウト), Scrub (1.24, スクラブ), Scrub Bar (1.29, スクラブバー)	Vibrator (2.95, バイブレータ), Redial (3, リダイヤル), Emoji (3, 絵文字), International Call (3, 国際電話), Received Calls (3, 着信履歴)
B	1.86 (0.91)	i-Concier (1.14, iコンシェル®), Siri® (1.15), mi-niUIM (1.16), VoiceOver (1.17), ToruCa (1.23, トルカ®)	YouTube™ (2.57), Google Maps™ (2.71, Googleマップ), iPad® (2.77), Twitter (2.85), iPhone® (2.93)
C	2.5 (0.79)	CalDav (1.03), DiXiM (1.16), Widget (1.21, ウィジェット), HDR Picture (1.27, HDR写真), WPA2 (1.27)	Reboot (3, 再起動), Device (3, 端末), Press and Hold (3, 長押し), Transfer (3, 転送), Junk Mail (3, 迷惑メール)

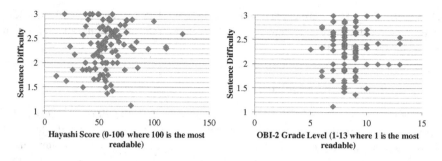

Fig. 1. Relationships of Japanese text readability and sentence difficulty for the elderly

4.3   Results for Sentence Difficulty

For this survey, we first evaluated the relationship between the sentence difficulty as reported by our participants and two text readability metrics for Japanese text, the Hayashi Score [11] and the OBI-2 Grade Level [12] rating. The cb's Japanese Text Analysis Tool[1] was used to calculate the text readability scores. The left-side scatterplot in Fig. 1 shows the relationship of sentence difficulty and Hayashi score for all of the tested sentences, while the right-side shows the relationship of sentence difficulty and OBI-2 Grade Level. The vertical axis shows the sentence difficulty and the horizontal axis shows the text readability score. Each dot shows the results for one of the tested sentences. The sentence difficulty and the Hayashi score are not highly correlated (R^2=.02). The correlation is even weaker for the OBI-2 Grade Level (R^2=1.0 $\times$ 10^{-4}).

We then evaluated the relationship between reported sentence difficulty and word familiarity. The left-side scatterplot in Fig. 2 shows the relationship of sentence difficulty and average word familiarity for each sentence. The average word familiarity for each sentence was calculated by averaging the word familiarity for the words that were tested in word familiarity survey. The right-side of Fig. 2 shows the relationship of sentence difficulty and the least familiar word of each sentence. By comparing this with the text readability, the sentence difficulty and the average word familiarity shows a meaningful correlation (R^2=.35), and the sentence difficulty and the smallest word familiarity is even more strongly correlated (R^2=.49).

From these results, it appears that the existing methods for measuring text readability are not appropriate for predicting the sentence difficulty for elderly people. It appears that it is more effective to estimate the sentence difficulty for elderly people based on the least familiar words in the sentences, which means that the key is their familiarity with the most difficult words.

---

[1] https://code.google.com/p/japanese-text-analysis-tool/

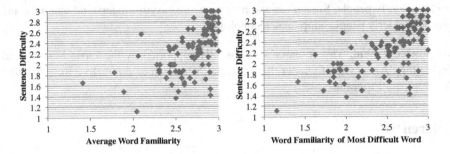

Fig. 2. Relationships of word familiarity and sentence difficulty for the elderly

5 Discussion

As shown in Table 1, the words that are specific for vendors or products are the least familiar words for senior citizens. The words that are specific for smartphones, cell phones, or touchscreen devices are more familiar, but less familiar compared with general computer-related terms. The writers of manuals should be careful when using these words. Additional explanations for these unfamiliar words may help to make the manuals easier to understand.

As shown in Fig. 1, the text readability has a weaker correlation with the sentence difficulty for elderly people, and the word familiarity for the most difficult words in each sentence has a stronger correlation. From these results, word familiarity appears to be a suitable metric for an automatic checking tool that will detect the sentences that elderly people will find hard to understand. To create such tools, we need to collect more data for statistical reliability and test more terms. One of the limitations of this study was that some of the same participants answered both in the word familiarity survey and the sentence difficulty survey. To evaluate the quality of an automatic checking tool, we need to test these two categories separately.

In this study, we focused on problems with manuals. Creating natural and intuitive menus is also important to improve usability. We are planning to investigate if word familiarity will also help to detect menu items that are difficult for senior citizens to understand and use.

6 Conclusion

In this study, we conducted a survey to investigate the word familiarity of computer-related terms that were extracted from smartphone manuals. Our second survey studied the difficulty of sentences that were also extracted from these smartphone manuals. Our results indicate that the word familiarity is the dominant factor when estimating the sentence difficulty, and showed that existing text readability metrics are not fully suitable for estimating the sentence difficulty for senior citizens who have good language skills but limited computer literacy. This research is part of our preliminary work for automatic checking tools that will help us assess manuals to be used by elderly people. Such tools will help to create easy-to-understand manuals, and thus help elderly people adopt new technologies.

Acknowledgement. This research was partially supported by the Japan Science and Technology Agency (JST) under the Strategic Promotion of Innovative Research and Development Program.

References

1. United Nations University, Active Ageing,
   http://wisdom.unu.edu/en/active-aging (accessed February 20, 2013)
2. Leibold, M., Voelpel, S.: Managing the Aging Workforce. John Wiley & Sons (2006)
3. Pew Internet: Mobile,
   http://pewinternet.org/Commentary/2012/February/
   Pew-Internet-Mobile.aspx (accessed February 20, 2013)
4. Nicholas, D., Huntington, P., Williams, P.: Delivering Consumer Health Information Digitally: A Comparison Between the Web and Touchscreen Kiosk. J. Med. Syst. 27(1), 13–34 (2003)
5. Leung, R., Tang, C., Haddad, S., McGrenere, J., Graf, P., Ingriany, V.: How Older Adults Learn to Use Mobile Devices: Survey and Field Investigations. TACCESS 4(3), 11 (2012)
6. Ouchi, Y., Akiyama, H. (eds.): Gerontology – Overview and Perspectives, 3rd edn. Univ. of Tokyo Press (2010) (in Japanese)
7. Feng, L., Jansche, M., Huenerfauth, M., Elhadad, N.: A comparison of features for automatic readability assessment. In: Proc. COLING, pp. 276–284 (2010)
8. Collins-Thompson, K., Callan, J.: A language modeling approach to predicting reading difficulty. In: Proc. HLT/NAACL (2004)
9. Pitler, E., Nenkova, A.: Revisiting readability: a unified framework for predicting text quality. In: Proc. EMNLP, pp. 186–195 (2008)
10. Kanungo, T., Orr, D.: Predicting the readability of short web summaries. In: Proc. WSDM, pp. 202–211 (2009)
11. Hayashi, Y.: A three level revision model for improving Japanese bad styled expressions. In: Proc. COLING, pp. 665–671 (1992)
12. Sato, S., Matsuyoshi, S., Kondoh, Y.: Automatic Assessment of Japanese Text Readability Based on a Textbook Corpus. In: Proc. LREC, pp. 28–30 (2008)
13. Amano, S., Kondo, T.: Nihongo no Goi tokusei (Lexical properties of Japanese), vol. 1-6, pp. 1–6. Sansei do, Tokyo (1999) (in Japanese)

The Relationship between Touchscreen Sizes of Smartphones and Hand Dimensions

Yu-Cheng Lin

Overseas Chinese University, Taichung City, Taiwan
yclin@ocu.edu.tw

Abstract. With the development of communication technology, mobile phone seems to become an important personnel device that everyone must have. As the introduction of 3rd-generation mobile telecommunication, the technology of touch screen was started to be applied on the mobile phones. A smartphone is a mobile phone built on a mobile operating system with advanced computing capability. Many functionality and application like digital cameras, GPS and web-browser, were combined on the smartphone to form a multi-use device. Most of modern smartphones include high-resolution touchscreens for display and control. As the development of smartphone, the size of touchscreen becomes larger and larger. However, the question is that a larger screen is convenient to every user? The aim of this study is to realize the relationship between touchscreen sizes of smartphones and user's relative hand dimensions based on the operation time, operation error rate and subjective thumb fatigue. Sixty subjects, including 30 males and 30 females were invited to attend the experiment. The experiment design includes 3 touchscreen sizes. The hand length and palm width were both divided into three categories respectively. The analyzed results indicates that the relationships between touchscreen size and category of hand length and between touchscreen size and category of palm width are both positive from the views of error rate and the subjective fatigue. Therefore, larger touchscreen size is more appropriate to larger hand and palm. Furthermore, longer operation time is needed for people who have small hand and palm because they spend more time to move their thumb and handle the smartphone stably.

Keywords: touchscreen, anthropometry, hand dimension, smartphone.

1   Introduction

With the development of science and communication technology, the innovation on mobile phone has never stopped. Nowadays the smartphone with powerful functions becomes more and more popular. One of the most important evolvement from previous mobile phone to smartphone is the application of touchscreen to remove the traditional keypad. Full touchscreen operation allows the use of smartphones more intuitive. Moreover, the request for screen size, color saturation and resolution of touchscreen is increasing with the development on smartphone. Two years ago, Samsung started to lunch the Galaxy Note series with 5.3 inch touchscreen so Apple also

C. Stephanidis and M. Antona (Eds.): UAHCI/HCII 2013, Part III, LNCS 8011, pp. 643–650, 2013.

lunched iPhone 5 with 4 inch touchscreen instead of iPhone 4S with 3.5 inch screen last year. However, what is the appropriate screen size for users? T observe users who using various sizes of smartphone, it is very common that the size of touchscreen is not suitable for the user's hand dimensions. It is difficult to operate with single hand if the touchscreen is too large. On the other hand, too small touchscreen is not suitable for large hands. Thus, the operation error and performance may be reduced since the size of touchscreen is not appropriate to user's hand. People cannot use hands to operate too small input devices [1]. The mobility convenience of mobile devices let users frequently bring them in dynamic mobile environment and users must use single hand to operate the mobile device in order to deal with other things with the other hand [2]. For example, it is common that consumers handle and use the smartphone with one hand and take goods with the other hand. In the field survey, most people use single hand to operate mobile phone. An experimental result conducted by Karlson [3] also confirmed that people prefer to use one-handed operation is better than a two-handed operation in the subjective rating.

Shneiderman [4] pointed out that the user's finger is the most direct control tools on the touchscreen. Parhi et al. [5] explored the target size on the small touchscreen and indicated that the icon size (target) from 9.2mm to 9.6mm was better for touch tasks. Colle and Hiszem [6] pointed out that users preferred the recognition touch area of 20mm × 20mm in public information kiosks.

The handheld device should match the characteristics of the hand shape [7]. Hand anthropometry would affect the preferred size and shape of the grip area and movement of fingers would also affect the size and the layout of the buttons [8]. In order to make the input operation more stable, the gripping stability of mobile phone must also be consideration as well as movement range of operating finger and posture of handhold [7]. Furthermore, most people use thumb to operate the smartphone when they take the smartphone with single hand. However, Wobbrock et al. [9] indicated that using forefinger to operate had better performance on input time and error rate compared with thumb after compare thumb operation and forefinger operation if people use one hand to hold phone and use the other hand to operate it. Thus, the relationship between operating performance and user's hands should be emphasized.

The purpose of this study was to try to investigate the relationship between the touchscreen size of smartphone and the dimension of hand based on the operation time, operation error rate and subjective evaluation about thumb fatigue. Since most people likes to user smartphone with single hand, only one hand operation was considered in tis study. That is, subjects must use dominant hand to handle the phone and user thumb to operate on the touchscreen.

2   Methodology

This study used three smartphones whose touchscreen sizes are different as experimental equipment. Table 1 lists their brief characteristics. Although the widths of the 3 smartphones are different due to their touchscreen sizes, the distances between edge of touchscreen and body for each smartphone are similar. All operation systems are Andriod. The Martin type anthropometer was employed to measure 6 hand dimensions, including hand length, palm length, forefinger length, palm width, thumb length and thumb width that is shown in Table 2.

In order to let the thumb touch every place on the screen, a click app game was developed. This app game can display a 4 mm x 4 mm block randomly for 250 times and subjects have to touch the block within 1.0 second. If the subject didn't touch the screen on the right bock within 1.0 second, he took one error count. After 250 times, the app game calculates the error rate and total operating time automatically. Each subject had to complete 5 rounds of test.

Table 1. Brief summary of the smartphones

	Touchscreen Size (inch)	OS	Phone Size (mm)
hTC Wildfire S	3.2	Andriod	101.3 x 59 x 12
SAMSUNG GALAXY W	3.7	Andriod	105.5 x 59.8 x 11.6
SAMSUNG GALAXY S II	4.27	Andriod	125.8 x 66.1 x 8.5

Table 2. Hand dimensions and definitions

Dimensions	Definition
hand length	The distance from top of middle finger to bottom of hand
palm length	The distance from bottom of middle finger to bottom of hand
forefinger length	The distance from top of forefinger to bottom of forefinger
palm width	The width of palm without thumb
thumb length	The distance from top of thumb to first dorsal interosseous
thumb width	The width of thumb

Sixty college students, including 30 males and 30 females, were invited to attend the experiment. Every subject had extensive experience in operating the Android smartphone. Before the experiment, subject was asked to handle the smartphone with comfortable sitting posture and put the arm on a table. Neither the holding method nor the posture could be changed during the experiment. After experiment, a subjective evaluation about the thumb fatigue that was numbered from 1 to 5 according to the degree feeling was conducted.

3   Results and Discussions

3.1   Statistical Summary and Test

Table 3 and Table 4 list the statistical summaries of gender and touchscreen size respectively. The t-test and ANOVA was conducted to test difference between gender and touchscreen size. There are significant differences on subjective thumb fatigue between genders. Thus, males have better subjective fatigue than females.

In operation time and error rate, no significant difference was found. Although there is no significant different between genders, the means are less for male's operation time and error rate.

Table 3. The statistical summary of gender (α =0.05)

	male		Female		total		Sig.
	Mean	Std.	Mean	Std.	Mean	Std.	
Operation time (sec.)	160.76	16.74	163.62	20.67	162.19	18.76	
Error rate	0.0423	0.0353	0.0488	0.0377	0.0456	0.0365	
Subjective fatigue	2.62	1.60	3.69	1.24	3.16	1.52	**
Hand length (mm)	18.80	1.04	17.03	0.76	17.91	1.27	**
Palm length (mm)	10.82	0.68	9.88	0.53	10.35	0.77	**
Forefinger length (mm)	7.44	0.60	6.69	0.46	7.06	0.66	**
Palm width (mm)	8.73	0.48	7.69	0.25	8.21	0.65	**
Thumb length (mm)	6.44	0.63	5.75	0.41	6.10	0.63	**
Thumb width (mm)	2.16	0.16	1.85	0.23	2.00	0.25	**

Table 4. The statistical summary of touchscreen size (α =0.05)

	3.2-inch		3.7-inch		4.27-inch		Sig.
	Mean	Std.	Mean	Std.	Mean	Std.	
Operation time (sec.)	162.10	21.00	162.17	17.39	162.30	18.34	
Error rate	0.0493	0.0449	0.0563	0.0303	0.0310	0.0283	*
Subjective fatigue	2.73	1.48	3.23	1.43	3.50	1.59	*
Subjective fatigue	2.73	1.48	3.23	1.43	3.50	1.59	

About the touchscreen size, there exist significant differences on error rate and subjective thumb fatigue. The Duncan post-hoc test for error rate shows that 3.2 inch and 3.7 inch belong the same subgroup. Also, the Duncan test for subjective thumb fatigue shows there are two subgroups, 3.2 / 3.7 inch and 3.7 / 4.27 inch. Thus, there is obvious distinction between 3.2 inch and 4.27 inch.

3.2   The Relation between Touchscreen Size and Hand Dimension

The data was divided into three groups according to the hand length, i.e. small (15.5-17.4 cm), medium (17.5-19.5 cm) and large (19.5-21.4 cm) hand length categories. The mean and standard deviation are listed in Table 5. The ANOVA test shows there are significant difference between hand length categories in the operation time and subjective thumb fatigue (α =0.05). It is obvious that small hand length (15.5-17.4 cm) has poorest operation time and relative poorer thumb fatigue using 3.7-inch and 4.27-inch screen than other hand length categories (Fig. 1). However, in the thumb fatigue illustrated in Fig. 1, the trend is increasing from 3.2-inch to 4.27-inch screen for both small and medium categories and the 4.27-inch screen for small hand length category is especially high than others. On the contrary, the trend becomes decreasing for large hand length category.

Table 5. Statistical data of touchscreen size based on the hand length category

		Hand length					
		15.5-17.4 cm		17.5-19.4 cm		19.5-21.4 cm	
		Mean	Std.	Mean	Std.	Mean	Std.
Operation time (sec.)	3.2-inch	168.77	26.17	157.27	15.91	155.00	0.00
	3.7-inch	169.54	15.14	155.67	18.02	158.00	11.31
	4.27-inch	167.69	17.27	158.33	19.47	159.00	14.14
Error rate	3.2-inch	0.0408	0.0508	0.0343	0.0230	0.0875	0.1096
	3.7-inch	0.0573	0.0379	0.0357	0.0246	0.0550	0.0283
	4.27-inch	0.0523	0.0251	0.0307	0.0319	0.0250	0.0354
Thumb fatigue	3.2-inch	3.08	1.66	2.33	1.35	3.50	0.71
	3.7-inch	3.77	1.30	2.67	1.40	3.00	1.41
	4.27-inch	4.38	0.96	2.87	1.77	2.50	0.71

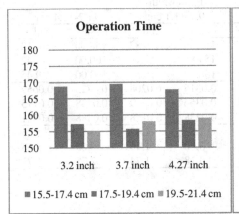
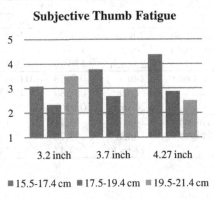

Fig. 1. The bar charts of touchscreen size divided by hang length category in the operation time and subjective thumb time respectively

Although no significant difference in the error rate was found, the change in trend is similar with the change trend of the subjective thumb fatigue. Moreover, the 3.2-inch screen for large hand length category is especially highest than others. Thus, in spite of the operation time, the touchscreen size and hand length have a positive relationship. In other words, larger touchscreen size is more appropriate to larger hand length. The long operation time for smaller hand length may indicate that the person who has smaller hand length must use more time to move his thumb and touch the screen.

The data of palm width was also divided into three categories, i.e. small (8.6-9.8 cm), medium (9.9-11.1 cm) and large (11.2-12.4 cm) palm width category and listed in Table 6. There are significant difference between palm width categories in the operation time and subjective thumb fatigue according to the ANOVA test ($\alpha = 0.05$). The small palm width (8.6-9.8 cm) has poorest operation time and relative poorer thumb fatigue in 3.7-inch and 4.27-inch screen than other categories (Fig. 2). Furthermore, the trend in the thumb fatigue is increasing from 3.2-inch to 4.27-inch screen for both small and medium palm width categories. Besides, the 4.27-inch screen for small palm width is especially high than others in the thumb fatigue. On the contrary, the trend becomes decreasing for large palm width category. Although there is no obvious difference in the error rate, the change in trend is similar with the trend in the subjective thumb fatigue and. the 3.2-inch screen for large palm width category is especially highest. Thus, in spite of the operation time, the touchscreen size and palm width have a positive relationship too. Therefore, larger touchscreen size is also more appropriate to larger palm width. The longer operation time for small palm width category imply that the person who has smaller palm width must spend more time to handle the smartphone in order to make the phone stable for operating.

Table 6. Statistical data of touchscreen size based on the palm width category

		Palm width					
		8.6-9.8 cm		9.9-11.1 cm		11.2-12.4 cm	
		Mean	Std.	Mean	Std.	Mean	Std.
Operation	3.2-inch	176.22	28.51	155.59	14.82	158.00	8.12
time (sec.)	3.7-inch	174.22	13.44	154.88	17.19	160.00	10.42
	4.27-inch	170.33	19.25	158.59	18.85	163.00	9.45
Error rate	3.2-inch	0.0528	0.0569	0.0315	0.0208	0.0725	0.0659
	3.7-inch	0.0589	0.0442	0.0356	0.0249	0.0538	0.0175
	4.27-inch	0.0567	0.0263	0.0238	0.0178	0.0488	0.0581
Thumb	3.2-inch	3.11	1.76	2.53	1.42	3.50	1.26
fatigue	3.7-inch	3.78	1.30	3.00	1.46	3.00	1.63
	4.27-inch	4.44	0.73	3.18	1.74	2.75	1.71

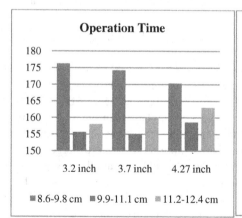 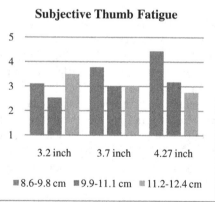

Fig. 2. The bar charts of touchscreen size divided by hang length category in the operation time and subjective thumb time respectively

4   Conclusion

In order to realize the relationship between touchscreen sizes and hand dimensions, this study recruited sixty subjects to attend the experiment. The operation time and error rate were calculated by the experimental app game. The subjective fatigue on thumb was asked after each game round. The statistical test shows there are obvious differences between touchscreen size, 3.2-inch, 3.7-inch and 4.27-inch, in both error rate and subjective thumb fatigue.

In order to analyze the data, the hand length and palm width were both divided into three categories respectively. For the part with regard to the hand length, there are significant difference between hand length categories in the operation time and subjective thumb fatigue at $\alpha = 0.05$. It is obvious that small hand length category has poorest operation time and relative poorer thumb fatigue using 3.7-inch and 4.27-inch screen than other hand length categories. In the thumb fatigue, the trend is increasing from 3.2-inch to 4.27-inch screen for both small and medium categories. On the contrary, the trend becomes decreasing for large hand length category. In spite of the operation time, the touchscreen size and hand length have a positive relationship. In other words, larger touchscreen size is more appropriate to larger hand length.

For the part with regard to the palm width, the analyzed result is similar. Small width category has poorest operation time. The trend in the thumb fatigue is increasing from 3.2-inch to 4.27-inch screen for both small and medium palm width categories but the trend becomes decreasing for large palm width category. The touchscreen size and palm width also have a positive relationship in spite of the operation time.

Hence, larger touchscreen size is more appropriate to larger hand and palm. Besides, longer operation time is needed for people who have small hand and palm because they spend more time to move their thumb and handle the smartphone stably.

Acknowledgment. The authors would like to acknowledge the National Science Council of the Republic of China for financially supporting this research.

References

1. Hare, C.B.: Redefining User Input on Handheld. 3G Mobile Communication Technologies, pp. 388-393 (2002)
2. Pascoe, J., Ryan, N., Morse, D.: Using while Moving: HCI Issues in Fieldwork Environments. ACM Trans. Computer-Human Interaction 7(3), 417–437 (2000)
3. Karlson, A.K., Bederson, B.B., Contreras-Vidal, J.L.: Understanding One Handed Use of Mobile Devices. In: Handbook of Research on User Interface Design and Evaluation for Mobile Technology. Idea Group Reference (2007)
4. Shneiderman, B., Plaisant, C.: Designing the User Interface: Strategies for Effective Human-Computer Interaction. Addison Wesley, USA (2005)
5. Parhi, P.K., Amy, K., Bederson, B.B.: Target Size Study for One-Handed Thumb Use on Small Touchscreen Devices. In: Proceedings of the 8th Conference on Human-Computer Interaction with Mobile Devices and Services, pp.12–15 (2006)

6. Colle, H.A., Hiszem, K.J.: Standing at a Kiosk: Effects of Key Size and Spacing on Touch Screen Numeric Keypad Performance and User Preference. Ergonomics 47(13), 1406–1423 (2004)
7. Hirotaka, N.: Reassessing Current Cell Phone Designs: Using Thumb Input Effectively. In: CHI 2003, New Horizons (2003)
8. Lee, M.W., Myung, H.Y., Jung, E.S., Freivalds, A.: High Touch: Ergonomics in a Conceptual Design Process - Case Studies of a Remote Controller and Personal Telephones. International Journal of Industrial Ergonomics 19(3), 239–248 (1997)
9. Wobbrock, J.O., Myers, B.A., Aung, H.H.: The Performance of Hand Postures in Front-and Back-of-Device Interaction for Mobile Computing. International Journal of Human-Computer Studies 66(12), 857–875 (2008)

Tilt-Based Support for Multimodal Text Entry on Touchscreen Smartphones: Using Pitch and Roll

Sandi Ljubic[1], Mihael Kukec[2], and Vlado Glavinic[3]

[1] Faculty of Engineering, University of Rijeka,
Vukovarska 58, 51000 Rijeka, Croatia
[2] Medimurje University of Applied Sciences in Cakovec,
Bana Josipa Jelacica 22a, 40000 Cakovec, Croatia
[3] Faculty of Electrical Engineering and Computing, University of Zagreb,
Unska 3, 10000 Zagreb, Croatia
sandi.ljubic@riteh.hr, mihael.kukec@mev.hr,
vlado.glavinic@fer.hr

Abstract. In this paper we propose a multimodal text entry method for touch-screen smartphones, where standard Tap modality can be used in combination with Pitch and Roll movements that change the orientation of the mobile device. Data from the built-in orientation sensors are used as a basis for commands that support character layout changing. Tilting the device in the appropriate direction will cause visual enlargement of the corresponding half of the current keyboard layout, thus enabling easier character selection, and solely sensor-based text entry. The prototype implementation of the proposed interaction method is analyzed and evaluated via usability testing experiments, with special focus on efficiency of text entry. As the proposed method is also applicable on touchscreen tablets, the form factor of mobile devices is reviewed with respect to text entry performance both of supported interaction modalities (tilt-only and tilt-and-tap) and of possible device orientations (portrait and landscape).

Keywords: text entry, multimodal interaction, accessibility, mobile device sensors, touchscreens.

1   Introduction

In the current mobile computing environment, the concept of quick message exchange has become a dominant phenomenon. Using standard messaging and social networks services "on the move" requires a convenient interaction with mobile devices and particularly efficient text methods. At the same time, touchscreens turned into the most popular platforms (including smartphones, tablets, and interactive tabletops) despite their chronic drawback: a generally slow, uncomfortable, and inaccurate typing [1]. On the other hand, touchscreen keyboards are software based, so they can support customization and automatic adaptation, as well as new interaction methods. The possibility of various soft keyboard implementations results with relevant

C. Stephanidis and M. Antona (Eds.): UAHCI/HCII 2013, Part III, LNCS 8011, pp. 651–660, 2013.
© Springer-Verlag Berlin Heidelberg 2013

HCI-based research and experimental testing, with the main goal being the introduction of trouble-free and more efficient text entry. Dealing with typical problems such as the "fat-finger syndrome", optimal character layout, and size of keys involves investigations in linguistics, ergonomics, and mathematical optimization, while concepts of universal access [2] and universal usability [3] motivate design solutions for all users, including those with special needs.

Contemporary touchscreen keyboards are usually provided with both full QWERTY layout and integrated dictionary support with related algorithms able to predict the next letter in the word, and/or next word in the sentence that is being typed. Advanced devices additionally support text entry via voice input, but this functionality largely depends on voice processing capabilities and language models availability. When it comes to interaction, the dominant technique used for text entry across the most of the available keyboards consists of direct touch (*Tap*) and of sliding gesture (*Swipe*). While conventional keyboards usually use *Tap* for character entry, and *Swipe* for control features (e.g. character layout change, keyboard settings dialog activation), more sophisticated implementations require combined *Tap-and-Swipe* interaction. This especially applies for zone-based keyboards, where less frequently used letters are entered after tapping into the appropriate zone and swiping in the proper direction.

While quite a number of soft keyboards has been researched so far, tilt interaction modality is hardly ever considered to be a part of the final text entry solution for touchscreen smartphones and/or tablets. Our goal is to provide tilt-based support by introducing a text entry method which (i) runs on contemporary mobile devices with embedded motion sensors, (ii) supports multimodal interaction by enabling typing both with finger touch and wrist motion, and (iii) works with a QWERTY-based layout, hence ensuring a higher level of learnability.

2   Tilt Interaction with Mobile Devices: Related Work

Tilt and orientation of a mobile device have already been examined as a prospective mobile interaction technique [4, 5]. Early implementations provided possibilities for scrolling, changing screen orientation, and navigation through lists and menus, while text entry was addressed by *Unigesture* [6], *TiltType* [7], and *TiltText* [8] prototypes. However, *Unigesture* system relies on specially developed hardware, *TiltType* was designed for small watch-like devices and requires two-hand interaction, while the *TiltText* prototype supports multitap-based keyboards only. Recent research on this topic includes human factors in wrist-based input [9], comparative analysis of tilt, touch, speech, and foot interaction [10], and accelerometer-based text entry systems [11, 12]. *GesText* [11] represents a text entry design that relies solely on tilt input, with the respective prototype being based on the Wiimote device and a remote 32" screen. *WalkType* [12] uses accelerometer data to improve typing on a standard QWERTY layout, by compensating extraneous movement while walking. The *Dasher* project [13] provides a novel text entry method which discards the traditional keyboard concept, and introduces zoom-and-point interaction for selecting "flying letters" in 2D space. Related implementations are freely available, including smartphone applications with pointing gestures supported by tilt movements.

3   Tilt-Based Multimodal Text Entry Method

We selected Android as the development platform and utilized *Pitch* and *Roll* movements (around device's lateral and longitudinal axes) as valid tilt actions (Fig. 1).

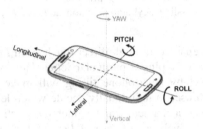

Fig. 1. Roll, *Pitch* and *Yaw* movements within orientation-based smartphone interaction. In our solution, tilting around the vertical axis is not interpreted for text entry support.

Altogether four tilt movements are mapped into the corresponding commands: twisting the smartphone up/down against the lateral axis generates *Pitch Down* and *Pitch Up*, while rotating left/right around the longitudinal axis results with *Roll Left* and *Roll Right* (see Fig. 2).

Fig. 2. Smartphone tilt movements used in our text entry method: *Pitch Down* (PD), *Pitch Up* (PU), *Roll Right* (RR), *Roll Left* (RL)

Fig. 3 shows the difference between a standard Android-based keyboard and our design, as well as a possible initial layout (*Level-1*) partition according to available tilt movements. It can be seen that the proposed keyboard configuration includes 15 interactive elements, each containing a set of four symbols for related characters and/or actions. While the QWERTY layout is available through the 8 upper left elements, the initial zone-based configuration additionally involves digits, punctuation marks, and supplementary symbols.

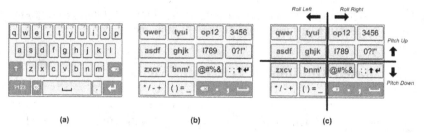

Fig. 3. Standard Android-based keyboard (a), proposed initial (*Level-1*) character layout for multimodal text entry (b), possible keyboard division at *Level-1* according to the available motion actions (c)

Character selection is enabled through direct touch from *Level-2* onwards, so two *Tap* actions are required for typing a particular letter. However, gradually reducing the available character set by smartphone tilting will make corresponding buttons larger, thus enabling each user to individually decide which level is most suitable for precise selection. Moreover, a character can be entered (or action fired) by using *Pitch* and *Roll* movements exclusively, as in case of *Level-5* final selection among maximum of four available options (Fig. 4).

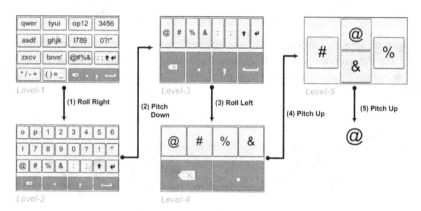

Fig. 4. Entering character "@" using *Pitch* and *Roll* only. User can also easily select "@" from *Level-2* onwards using *Tap*, with related key button dimensions being larger within each new level.

The largest interactive element in the initial layout contains symbols for frequently used characters/actions: backspace, full stop (period), comma, and space. Corresponding buttons are highlighted using different background color in order to notify the user on the possibility of shortcut activation. Namely, these four common options can be alternatively selected using tilt-and-hold, a special interaction case when *Pitch/Roll* is followed by retaining the device position for two seconds. Shortcut options can be selected regardless of the currently active character layout (*Level-1–Level-5*). Consequently, for our multimodal text entry method we define a set of available interactions *I*, with related events described in Table 1:

$$I = \{Tap, PD, PU, RL, RR, 2sPD, 2sPU, 2sRL, 2sRR\}.$$

Table 1. Interaction supported in proposed text entry method

Interaction	Triggered event
Tap [direct touch]	*Level-1*: displaying *Level-5* (4 symbols linked with corresponding button) *Level-2–Level-5*: character entry or action firing (uppercase, newline,…)
PD [*Pitch Down*]	*Level-1–Level-4*: reducing currently active character set to the bottom half *Level-5*: bottom-positioned character entry
PU [*Pitch Up*]	*Level-1–Level-4*: reducing currently active character set to the upper half *Level-5*: upper-positioned character entry
RL [*Roll Left*]	*Level-1–Level-4*: reducing currently active character set to the left half *Level-5*: left-positioned character entry
RR [*Roll Right*]	*Level-1–Level-4*: reducing currently active character set to the right half *Level-5*: right-positioned character entry
2sPD = PD + [2s hold]	*Level-1–Level-5*: comma character entry
2sPU = PU + [2s hold]	*Level-1–Level-5*: period character entry
2sRL = RL + [2s hold]	*Level-1–Level-5*: backspace (deleting last character)
2sRR = RR + [2s hold]	*Level-1–Level-5*: space (blank character entry)

4   Usability Evaluation

In order to evaluate the proposed method, we carried out usability testing. In the respective experiment, we wanted to analyze the effects on text entry performance (speed) and accuracy (rate of errors) of both device form factor and device orientation. In order to obtain qualitative results we focused on users' opinions regarding usability attributes and workload experienced with tilt-based interaction.

4.1   Materials, Methods, and Metrics

Participants. Twenty users were involved in our usability experiment (18 males, 2 females), their age ranging from 21 to 34 with an average of 25 years. While every user had previous experience working with touchscreen smartphones and tablets, 14 of them had already been interacting with tilt-based mobile applications (mainly games). The participants rated their text entry practice by approximation of the total number of text messages sent through various mobile messaging services on a daily basis. On average, this number appeared to be 10.

Apparatus. Four different mobile devices (D1–D4) were used by each participant during the experiment, two from the smartphone class, and two from the tablet one. All devices had a different form factor, according to the data presented in Table 2. In order to avoid a possible bias caused by devices' different technical specifications, the testing application was developed targeting minimal CPU and RAM requirements.

Table 2. Specifications of mobile device models used in usability testing experiment

Device	Model	Class	Display	Dimensions and Nominal Weight	CPU & RAM	OS
D1	*Samsung Galaxy Mini 2*	Smart-phone	**3.27"** 320x480 *TFT LCD capacitive*	W=58.6 mm H=109.4 mm D=11.6 mm **NW=105.3 g**	*ARM Cortex A5* 800 MHz 512 MB DDR	Android 2.3.6 *Gingerbread*
D2	*Samsung Galaxy S2*	Smart-phone	**4.3"** 480x800 *Amoled + capacitive*	W=66.1 mm H=125.3 mm D=8.5 mm **NW=116 g**	*DC ARM Cortex A9* 1.2 GHz 1 GB DDR	Android 2.3.4 *Gingerbread*
D3	*Huawei IDEOS S7 Slim*	Tablet	**7.0"** 480x800 *TFT LCD capacitive*	W=200 mm H=109.5 mm D=12.5 mm **NW=440 g**	*Scorpion* 1.0 GHz 512 MB DDR	Android 2.2 *Froyo*
D4	*Prestigio Multipad PMP7100C*	Tablet	**10.1"** 1024x600 *TFT LCD capacitive*	W=270 mm H=150 mm D=12 mm **NW=480 g**	*ARM Cortex A8* 1.0 GHz 256 MB DDR	Android 2.2 *Froyo*

Procedure. Before the actual experiment, we firstly collected participants' basic information about age, mobile devices' usage, and previous experience with tilt-based interaction. This initial survey was followed by a short individual practice session (approx. 30 minutes) for users to get familiar with both available devices and supported interaction techniques. Within the practice session, users were able to consider character layout changes and tilt angles used in the test application.

In the actual experiment, for each combination of available device (D1–D4) and device orientation (Portrait/Landscape), participants were instructed to enter three different text phrases using two interaction methods (tilt-only, tilt-and-tap). In landscape orientation, two-hand interaction with all devices was obligatory, while portrait orientation implied one-hand interaction only within the smartphone class. Each participant's 48 total phrases were randomly selected from a set of 500 phrases introduced in [14], all were in lowercase and without punctuation symbols. While users were instructed to input text "as quickly as possible, as accurately as possible", a single task was considered to be done when a particular phrase was fully and correctly transcribed. The input stream was analyzed "on the fly" with the test application itself, by monitoring phrase entry time and number of activated taps, tilts, and long tilts. To get around the possible learning effects in the experiment, we counterbalanced the sequence of experimental conditions using balanced Latin Squares. At the end of the experiment, users were asked to complete a post-study questionnaire, in order to get individual opinions about workload and usability attributes of the proposed method.

Metrics. Text entry speed was initially measured in characters per second, but is through a simple transformation here reported as words per minute (WPM). For accuracy metrics, we made use of the intensive work on text entry error rates provided in [15, 16, 17, 18]. Furthermore, we introduced a completely new metrics, which we devised specifically for our multimodal text entry method: *TiPC* (Tilts Per Character) and *TaPC* (Taps Per Character).

4.2   Results and Discussion

Participants entered 960 phrases in total: 480 for tilt-only tasks (where tapping was not allowed), and 480 for tilt-and-tap tasks (where interaction modality was the subject of free choice). The means and standard deviations for each condition and relevant metric are summarized in Table 3.

Table 3. Results: descriptive statistics summary

Modality	Device	Orient.	WPM		Total Error rate		TiPC		TaPC	
			Mean	SD	Mean	SD	Mean	SD	Mean	SD
Tilt-only	D1	P	1.600	0.526	0.052	0.069	4.974	0.726		
Tilt-only	D1	L	1.657	0.388	0.031	0.041	4.692	0.343		
Tilt-only	D2	P	1.442	0.422	0.058	0.060	5.028	0.646		
Tilt-only	D2	L	1.420	0.437	0.048	0.063	4.879	0.676	No tapping	
Tilt-only	D3	P	1.603	0.402	0.042	0.042	4.760	0.358	allowed	
Tilt-only	D3	L	1.627	0.293	0.030	0.024	4.677	0.317		
Tilt-only	D4	P	1.372	0.297	0.032	0.042	4.627	0.314		
Tilt-only	D4	L	1.187	0.291	0.057	0.056	4.846	0.498		
T-a-T	D1	P	6.202	1.402	0.027	0.041			2.098	0.180
T-a-T	D1	L	6.136	1.229	0.019	0.028	On the aver-		2.062	0.134
T-a-T	D2	P	6.185	1.367	0.018	0.024	age, the total		2.072	0.109
T-a-T	D2	L	6.360	1.272	0.011	0.025	number of tilts		2.047	0.109
T-a-T	D3	P	5.593	1.252	0.028	0.045	represents only		2.112	0.220
T-a-T	D3	L	5.536	0.809	0.024	0.032	0.29% of total		2.098	0.138
T-a-T	D4	P	5.656	1.320	0.022	0.038	taps count		2.073	0.189
T-a-T	D4	L	5.490	1.281	0.021	0.038			2.074	0.138

To analyze the obtained data, we ran a 4x2 repeated measures ANOVA on each metric, with Device (D1–D4) and Orientation (Portrait/Landscape) being the within-subjects factors. Interaction modality was not considered as a distinct factor, because there was no rationale for comparing completely different text entry strategies. In cases where significant effect was found, we utilized post-hoc pairwise comparisons with Bonferroni adjustment. The findings are presented in Table 4.

Device size/weight emerged as significant factor for both tilt-only and tilt-and-tap modality. Results showed that tilt-only text entry efficiency is higher when using smaller screens from both smartphone and tablet class. This can be explained by constraints of wrist movements (flexion, pronation, supination, ulnar and radial deviation) that are inherently higher when holding a larger mobile device. However, the source of no significant difference in performance between smaller smartphone (D1) and smaller tablet (D3) can be found in the nature of the interaction style: apparently, smaller smartphones are a better fit for one-hand tilt interaction, just as smaller tablets show to be a better choice for two-hand tilting.

Table 4. Significant effects and related post hoc analysis

Modality	Metric	Significant effect	Pairwise comparisons
Tilt-only	WPM	*Device* $F(3, 57)=17.049$ $p<0.001$ $\eta p^2=0.473$	Post hoc analysis revealed significantly higher text entry performance when using D1 (WPM=1.629±0.095) over D2 (WPM=1.431±0.081; $p=0.006$) and D4 (WPM=1.280±0.060; $p<0.001$). Similarly, efficiency with D3 (WPM=1.615±0.070) outperforms significantly both D2 ($p=0.006$) and D4 ($p<0.001$).
T-a-T	WPM	*Device* $F(3, 57)=6.833$ $p=0.001$ $\eta p^2=0.264$	Post hoc analysis revealed significantly higher text entry performance when using D1 (WPM=6.170±0.284) over D3 (WPM=5.565±0.212; $p=0.026$), as well as when using D2 (WPM=6.273±0.285) over both D3 ($p=0.015$) and D4 (WPM=5.573±0.284; $p=0.004$).

When it comes to tilt-and-tap, we must say that *Tap* was used as an arguably preferred option. In related tasks, tilts were used just occasionally for space or backspace actions. The reason for such phenomenon is rather obvious: there was no test user with any physical impairment, and given tasks requested from users to be as fast as possible. Since *Tap* is inherently faster than *Tilt*, all users decided to use it as the default input method. Results showed that tilt-and-tap (which came very closely to tap-only) text entry efficiency is significantly higher when using smartphones in relation to using tablets. Performance difference between smartphone D1 and tablet D4 however isn't statistically significant, but it is noteworthy nevertheless. Better tilt-and-tap efficiency with smartphones can be explained by a shorter hand/finger movement required for targeting each new character. Although tablet's keyboard presents larger buttons, its wider character layout does not help in improving speed of text entry, even in the case of two-hand interaction.

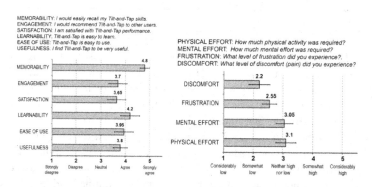

Fig. 5. Questionnaire response means: usability (left), and workload assessment (right)

No significant effects were found regarding *Total Error Rate*, *TiPC*, and *TaPC* metrics. *Total Error Rate* was reasonably low (maximum mean doesn't exceed 6%), while *TiPC* and *TaPC* mean values confirmed our expectations (close to 5, and slightly over 2, respectively). It is possible to predict *TiPC* and *TaPC* minimal values in advance, as they represent characteristics of related text entry techniques. In general, long (2s) tilts make 4.18% of tilt-only interaction, while wrong tilts (cases when wrong side of the keyboard was unintentionally activated) make only 1.4% of total tilts count. Wrong taps, cases when a wrong 4-key button was pressed at *Level-1* layout, make only 0.49% of total taps.

In the post-study questionnaire, usability attributes and workload were examined by 5-point Likert scale questions, with answers ranging from *Strongly disagree* (1) to *Strongly agree* (5) and *Considerably low* (1) to *Considerably high* (5), respectively. Users responded with encouraging outcomes (see Fig. 5).

5   Conclusion and Future Work

We have described a tilt-based multimodal text entry method for mobile devices that supports typing both with finger touch and wrist motion. Usability evaluation of both tilt-only and tilt-and-tap modality revealed smaller devices to be a better option when using the proposed method, and device orientation to be irrelevant for text entry performance. While the highest individual obtained WPM value for tilt-only was 2.63, even better performance could be expected after a longer period of usage, as users would eventually become more familiar with changing the keyboard layout. Enhancing the text entry speed with letter and/or word prediction algorithms was not the subject of our research, as we wanted to focus solely on functionality of multimodal interaction. In general, participants declared positive attitude towards method's usability, and considered physical and mental effort levels to be neither high nor low.

We believe that the proposed design could provide noteworthy in: (i) lowering the effect of the "fat-finger syndrome" thus improving text entry accuracy in mobile context, and (ii) assisting people who are unable to type conveniently on small screens. Although we were unable to recruit participants from the respective target group for usability testing, available results are promising and can validate our considerations.

Our future work plan includes providing alternative tilt-based methods where identical tilt actions will be used for shifting the cursor within a static keyboard layout, instead of constantly changing the character map. It would be very interesting to analyze a difference in text entry performance, as well as to find out whether users prefer a varying keyboard as presented in this paper, or the possibility to work with a consistent character layout when using the tilt-only entry method.

Acknowledgments. This paper describes the results of research being carried out within the project 036-0361994-1995 *Universal Middleware Platform for e-Learning Systems*, as well as within the program 036-1994 *Intelligent Support to Omnipresence of e-Learning Systems*, both funded by the Ministry of Science, Education and Sports of the Republic of Croatia.

References

1. Findlater, L., Wobbrock, J.O.: From Plastic to Pixels: In Search of Touch-Typing Touch-screen Keyboards. ACM Interactions XIX 3, 44–49 (2012)
2. Stephanidis, C.: Editorial. Universal Access in the Information Society 1(1), 1–3 (2001)
3. Shneiderman, B.: Universal Usability: Pushing Human-Computer Interaction Research to Empower Every Citizen. Communications ACM 43(5), 85–91 (2000)
4. Rekimoto, J.: Tilting Operations for Small Screen Interfaces. In: Proc. 9th ACM Symp. User Interface Software and Technology (UIST 1996), pp. 167–168. ACM Press, New York (1996)
5. Hinckley, K., Pierce, J., Sinclair, M., Horvitz, E.: Sensing Techniques for Mobile Interaction. In: Proc. 13th ACM Symp. User Interface Software and Technology (UIST 2000), pp. 91–100. ACM Press, New York (2000)
6. Sazawal, V., Want, R., Borriello, G.: The Unigesture Approach. In: Proc. 4th Int'l Symp. Mobile HCI (MobileHCI 2002), pp. 256–270. Springer, London (2002)
7. Partridge, K., Chatterjee, S., Sazawal, V., Borriello, G., Want, R.: TiltType: Accelerometer-Supported Text Entry for Very Small Devices. In: Proc. 15th ACM Symp. User Interface Software and Technology (UIST 2002), pp. 201–204. ACM Press, New York (2002)
8. Wigdor, D., Balakrishnan, R.: TiltText: Using Tilt for Text Input to Mobile Phones. In: Proc. 16th ACM Symp. User Interface Software and Technology (UIST 2003), pp. 81–90. ACM Press, New York (2003)
9. Rahman, M., Gustafson, S., Irani, P., Subramanian, S.: Tilt Techniques: Investigating the Dexterity of Wrist-based Input. In: Proc. 27th Int'l Conf. Human Factors in Computing Systems (CHI 2009), pp. 1943–1952. ACM Press, New York (2009)
10. Dearman, D., Karlson, A., Meyers, B., Bederson, B.: Multi-Modal Text Entry and Selection on a Mobile Device. In: Proc. Graphics Interface 2010 (GI 2010), pp. 19–26. Canadian Information Processing Society, Toronto (2010)
11. Jones, E., Alexander, J., Andreou, A., Irani, P., Subramanian, S.: GesText: Accelerometer-Based Gestural Text-Entry Systems. In: Proc. 28th Int'l Conf. Human Factors in Computing Systems (CHI 2010), pp. 2173–2182. ACM Press, New York (2010)
12. Goel, M., Findlater, L., Wobbrock, J.: WalkType: Using Accelerometer Data to Accommodate Situational Impairments in Mobile Touch Screen Text Entry. In: Proc. 2012 ACM Conf. Human Factors in Computing Systems (CHI 2012), pp. 2687–2696. ACM Press, New York (2012)
13. Inference Group: The Dasher Project,
    http://www.inference.phy.cam.ac.uk/dasher/
14. MacKenzie, I.S., Soukoreff, R.W.: Phrase Sets for Evaluating Text Entry Techniques. In: Proc. Extended Abstracts on Human Factors in Computing Systems (CHI EA 2003), pp. 754–755. ACM Press, New York (2003)
15. Soukoreff, R.W., MacKenzie, I.S.: Measuring Errors in Text Entry Tasks: An Application of the Levenshtein String Distance Statistic. In: Proc. Extended Abstracts on Human Factors in Computing Systems (CHI EA 2001), pp. 319–320. ACM Press, New York (2001)
16. MacKenzie, I.S.: KSPC (Keystrokes per Character) as a Characteristic of Text Entry Techniques. In: Proc. 4th Int'l Symp. Mobile HCI (MobileHCI 2002), pp. 195–210. Springer, London (2002)
17. Soukoreff, R.W., MacKenzie, I.S.: Metrics for Text Entry Research: An Evaluation of MSD and KSPC, and a New Unified Error Metric. In: Proc. SIGCHI Conf. Human Factors in Computing Systems (CHI 2003), pp. 113–120. ACM Press, New York (2003)
18. Soukoreff, R.W., MacKenzie, I.S.: Recent Developments in Text-Entry Error Rate Measurement. In: Proc. Extended Abstracts on Human Factors in Computing Systems (CHI EA 2004), pp. 1425–1428. ACM Press, New York (2004)

Audio Transportation System for Blind People

Jaime Sánchez[1] and Márcia de Borba Campos[2]

[1] Dept of Computer Science, Center for Advanced Research in Education (CARE)
University of Chile, Blanco Encalada 2120, Santiago, Chile
[2] Faculdade de Informática - FACIN
Pontifícia Universidade Católica do Rio Grande do Sul – PUCRS, Brazil
jsanchez@dcc.uchile.cl, marcia.campos@pucrs.br

Abstract. The purpose of this study was to design, develop and evaluate audio-based software to assist people who are blind in public bus transportation. The audio-based software for mobile devices Audiotransantiago was designed in order to provide information regarding authorized bus stops for the entire bus service in the city of Santiago de Chile (known as Transantiago). The study was designed to allow users who are blind to build up a mental map that is adjusted to their surroundings while traveling on the bus system. It was found that the use of the software improved information processing skills, tempo-spatial orientation and orientation and mobility skills (O&M), as users were able to navigate from one place to another without having to obtain information prior to their trip.

Keywords: People with visual disabilities, Audio-based interfaces, Orientation and Mobility, environmental perception and cognition.

1 Introduction

The varied and complex scenarios present in large cities have generated the need to implement urban policies designed to modernize transportation services, in order to facilitate movement between different areas within the city and seeking to eliminate the barriers that make traveling throughout the city more difficult [2]. As people who are blind lack a visual channel, they must orient themselves by recognizing their surroundings and establishing their position within their environment by using perceived information acquired through touch and hearing as a strategy [1][6]. In this way, visually disabled people obtain information from the environment and use it to be able to travel effectively and safely when navigating through the city [11], compensating for their lack of vision by obtaining information through other channels of perception as a source of knowledge for learning [1][9].

In taking the need to generate easy access for the use of public transportation by the disabled and elderly population into account [2], research has been carried out in many countries regarding the experiences of such users when using public transportation. Such research has been used in order to implement measures that favor the integration of these people into the system. Some examples are: Brazil (RIT: Red

C. Stephanidis and M. Antona (Eds.): UAHCI/HCII 2013, Part III, LNCS 8011, pp. 661–670, 2013.

Integrada de Transporte, BRT: Bus Rapid Transit) [3][15][16], Colombia (Transmilenio) [7][15], Venezuela (Transbarca) [12], Spain (TMB: Transport Metropolitans de Barcelona) [13], China (PTO: public transit oriented) [17], and Taiwan [18][19]. Based on this research, several state plans have been implemented that seek to facilitate the use of surface transportation by disabled or elderly people. These experiences have coincided in the need to generate a higher level of respect towards this population without distinction, guaranteeing their access to autonomous mobility through the city. One important aspect highlighted by these studies is the inclusion of an operational design that includes elements of accessibility capable of providing solutions to a number of needs, such as: spaces within buses for wheelchairs, tactile guides and signs, ramps, elevators, proper lighting, audio informational services, etc. These elements would provide general comfort and safety for the transportation of disabled and elderly populations.

In the city of Santiago de Chile it has been sought to implement policies and regulations regarding access to public transportation by people with disabilities [4], having established "Regulations on equality and the social inclusion of handicapped people" so that these individuals are able to utilize public transportation safely and independently. These regulations incorporate the concept of "easy access", accounting for and attending to the capabilities and the nature of each different mode of transportation based on its location and geography. In this way, changes in patterns of urbanization and the integration of the visually disabled into a variety of activities within society geared towards autonomous navigation with equal conditions among a wide variety of urban sectors and spaces, represents a special challenge and need for the population [5][8].

The purpose of this study was to design, develop and evaluate audio-based software to assist in public bus transportation for people who are blind. It is in this context that the Audiotransantiago [10] software has been developed. Audiotransantiago is an audio-based software program for mobile PocketPC devices. The purpose of the software is to provide information regarding authorized bus stops for the entire bus service in the city of Santiago de Chile (known as Transantiago), in addition to the streets around each stop and places of interest near to the scheduled routes. The idea is for the software to allow users who are blind to build up a mental map that is adjusted to their surroundings while traveling on the bus system. A synthetic voice, together with the commands available through the buttons on the PocketPC, allow a person who is blind to plan several different routes in an urban environment by establishing a point of departure and a destination point within the software.

2   Audiotransantiago Software

Regarding the interaction, the Audiotransantiago software provides sound-based information based on circular menus, with color contrast and the use of both synthesized voice and non-verbal audio cues. It makes use of a Text-To-Speech engine and an audio-based interface through which it conveys information to the user, complemented by non-verbal sounds that help to identify the navigational flow within the application menus. The software also utilizes a minimalist graphic interface, which includes only the name of the selection that is being used and the option that has been selected, using a strong color contrast that can be useful for those users with residual vision who can only distinguish shapes when displayed with highly contrasting colors.

To navigate between the various software functions, the user must utilize the buttons located on the inner part of the PocketPC (PPC), which allows the user to access the different functionalities of the software application. The software includes two main modes of interaction: (1) "Travel Planning", in which the user is able to plan a trip by using the various functions of the PPC keypad to select an area to navigate, the kind of transportation service to be used (bus), and then defining the direction in which the trip will be taken, establishing an initial bus stop and a final destination. Afterwards, the programmed trip remains stored in the "Execute Travel" option, in which the user is finally able to select the previously planned trip. The advantage of this option is that it allows the user to save multiple trips without having to reprogram the same trip every time it is taken. In selecting a pre-programmed trip, the user utilizes the PPC to anticipate the bus stops included on the planned route, and also has the option of requesting contextual information regarding streets and places of interest around each stop. This aids the user in creating a mental map of the environment through audio-based information, and in making decisions when faced with problems, which also implies reprogramming the initially planned route in real time. In this way, the user has a high degree of autonomy in navigating through different areas of the city by using the bus system, in order to arrive at his final destination.

In making comparisons, there are cities that provide interactive transportation guides for people. PoaTransporte [20] is an on-line system that allows users to access surface public transportation lines based on the direction of travel. Using the interactive map generated by the system, the user can also locate bus stops and taxi service locations. The user is also able to ask questions based on the specification of the names of each bus line. Despite the fact that PoaTransporte represents an efficient and practical information service, it does not possess the characteristics of digital accessibility that would make it beneficial for use by people with visual disability.

In allowing users with visual disability to be able to access information in a dynamic fashion, by constructing and generating questions regarding different routes, Audiotransantiago provides for a perception of the environment, mainly regarding collective public spaces. In this way, it seeks to appropriate space in the way that the user generates a symbolic identification with his surroundings, allowing the user to perform actions and change his plans during the bus ride. This implies a high degree of interaction with the environment and a mental (re)construction of the surrounding areas, providing for personal meaning in the user's interaction with the urban area.

3   Cognitive Evaluation

The experiment performed to evaluate Audiotransantiago was designed to determine whether an audio-based system favored autonomous navigation by people with visual disability on surface public transportation (buses).

3.1   Sample

The sample was made up of 14 individuals, including 10 men and 4 women, of whom 3 were totally blind and 11 had low-level vision. The sample selection was performed by using a non-probabilistic quota sampling method based on the following criteria: (a) being between 14 and 55 years old, (b) being blind or having low-level vision, (c) being registered in the National Registry of Disability, and (d) having previously been trained in orientation and mobility techniques. The sample was divided into 2 groups, one control group (CG) (Table 1) and one experimental (EG) (Table 2).

Table 1. Control Group (CG)

#	Genre	Age	Ophthalmological Diagnosis	Degree of Vision
1	F	20	Microphthalmia	Low Vision
2	M	20	Pigmentary retinitis	Low Vision
3	M	21	Pigmentary retinitis	Low Vision
4	F	22	Pigmentary retinitis	Low Vision
5	F	23	Retinopathy of prematurity	Low Vision
6	M	29	Glaucoma	Low Vision
7	M	33	Advance astigmatism	Low Vision

Table 2. Experimental Group (EG)

#	Genre	Age	Ophthalmological Diagnosis	Degree of Vision
1	M	14	Congenital Amaurosis	Totally Blind
2	M	16	Congenital retinopathy	Low Vision
3	M	26	Retinal damage - immature optic nerve	Low Vision
4	M	32	Retinal detachment	Low Vision
5	M	34	Retinopathy of prematurity	Low Vision
6	M	52	Pigmentary retinitis	Totally Blind
7	F	54	Myopic retinopathy	Totally Blind

The EG navigated the routes by using information provided by the software regarding which bus line to take, the initial bus stop, official bus stops between the point of departure and destination point, streets around the stops, and streets around the destination point. The users in the CG performed the same routes, by using only information regarding the point of departure and destination of the route. This latter group navigated the routes by using the navigational strategies that they utilize very effectively on a daily basis when using this mode of transportation.

3.2   Tasks

Three routes were developed between different geographic points in the city. The varying levels of difficulty were based on the number of stops and the distance (measured in meters) between the point of departure and the destination point. In order to provide for a higher degree of flexibility and to offer alternatives for navigation to the blind users, each route was designed in such a way that there are two possible bus routes to arrive at the destination. In addition, a third route incorporated changing from one bus to another in order to continue on the desired route.

3.3   Instruments

The evaluation of the tasks (routes) was carried out through the use of two different instruments: a "Route Evaluation Guideline" and a "Self-Performance Evaluation".

The Route evaluation guideline was used to collect information regarding the mobility, orientation and travel skills utilized on each of the scheduled routes. The guidelines were structured around the following dimensions: (a) Time, (b) Autonomy, (c) Spatial Orientation, (d) Navigational Efficacy, and (e) Problem Solving. In order to evaluate the items included in the guideline a 4-point scale was utilized, ranging from "always" to "never".

After having applied the Route Evaluation Guideline, which was carried out by a teacher-facilitator through direct observation, the "Self-Performance Evaluation" was administered to each user once the bus route had been successfully navigated. This instrument was designed to collect information on the effects of the user's experience during the bus rides, and the orientation and mobility strategies that had been used in order to face and solve the challenges that the users confronted. In the case of the EG, the application of this guideline allowed for the collection of information regarding the evaluation that the users themselves made of the software's effectiveness for aiding in autonomous and efficient navigation through the city by bus.

This latter instrument consisted of 9 questions, applied to each user once the route had been completed: "What did you think of the assigned route?", "Were you familiar with the starting and ending points of the route beforehand?", "Was this route familiar to you?", "What strategies did you use to take the trip?", "Did you experience any problematic situations during the trip? If so, what were they? What solution did you come up with for these difficulties?", "Were you able to anticipate situations or difficulties while you were taking the bus route?", "What information is useful in order to orient yourself and take a trip on the bus?", What kind of technologies would you use in order to help make better use of the transportation system? Why?", "On a scale of 1 to 7, how would you evaluate your performance?".

These questions point to issues related to concepts of perception and environmental cognition [21], regarding the way in which information on different places is organized, stored and remembered, including distances, the position of objects and spaces [22]. In this way, the instrument allows researchers to verify the users' arguments regarding how and what he learned during the interaction with Audiotransantiago.

3.4   Procedure

Initially, a facilitator provided the user with information on the route that was to be taken, informing the user of the starting point and the destination. Afterwards, the facilitator asked the user to interact with the buttons on the PPC, and by following the audio information through the use of headphones, to configure the "Travel Planning" mode by defining the bus to take, the starting bus stop, the direction of the trip, and the destination bus stop. This creates the trip file needed to initiate a bus travel route.

Fig. 1. User taking bus routes using Audiotransantiago

The second step consisted of recovering the trip file from the "Execute Trip" mode through the buttons on the PPC. After doing this and using the headphones in order to obtain the information, the user positioned himself at the bus stop, guided by the tactile patterns on the ground, in order to wait for the bus. Once the bus arrived, the user got on, aided by the facilitator, as the system does not provide information on the bus route prior to its stopping at the starting point.

Finally, the user entered the bus, executing navigational actions within the Audiotransantiago system through the buttons on the PPC, anticipating the bus stops that occur throughout the entire route. To complement their travel, many users consulted the system regarding streets or places of interest near the various bus stops. This was done in order to establish a mental map of the route navigated and to facilitate in the learning of information needed to reach their final destination (Figure 1). In this way, the users were able to better understand, structure, and learn about the environment through which they traveled.

During each route, the users were accompanied by a facilitator who supported them during any situations throughout the trip that they could not resolve, such as getting off the bus in the case that the bus was defective in this regard, setting another route in the case of excessive traffic, among other situations. In the same way, the facilitator collected information on the user's experience through direct evaluation, utilizing the Route Evaluation Guideline, and applied the Self-Performance Evaluation at the end of the route.

The implementation and development of the various activities lasted approximately 6 months, and was subject to the time availability of the participants. In this way, in several cases there were prolonged intermittent periods between the different stages of the experiment.

4   Results

All of the participants in both groups (CG and EG) were able to plan and execute the proposed routes using the Audiotransantiago software. However, in order to reach the destination the participants experienced difficulties that were unrelated to the use of the software, and were instead related to the bus transportation system itself. In this way, the evaluation was centered mainly on judging whether or not the user's interaction with the software favored autonomy, efficiency in travel, and the necessary problem-solving skills for selecting and managing the information needed to plan and execute a trip autonomously using the bus system in the city.

The results show the percentage of achievement for each route carried out by the users from each group, determined through the Route Evaluation Guideline. The EG obtained an average achievement rate of 81.7%, while the CG obtained an average rate of 71.8% (Table 3). These results show that the use of Audiotransantiago facilitates navigation through the city by bus for users with visual disabilities.

Table 3. Average percentage of achievement for sample routes

Group	Route 1	Route 2	Route 3	Avg.%
Experimental	84.6	84.7	75.9	81.7
Control	70.3	69.7	75.3	71.8

In the execution of the routes, the CG displayed lower execution results for all of the routes taken compared to the EG. Route 3 represented the highest level of complexity, and similar levels of performance were achieved between both groups. This is mainly due to the need to correctly reprogram the route by both groups, as all users were aided in this case by the help of the facilitators in order to continue with their trip. A T-test comparing the means between two independent samples was performed in order to compare the statistical relevance of the difference between the means of the CG and EG for each route. This test determined that the differences were not statistically significant.

Finally, although the results obtained were not statistically significant, the performance levels achieved for the 3 routes taken both by the Control Group and the Experimental Group represent an initial precedent in order to establish actions based on the use of audio-based technological tools that facilitate autonomous navigation by blind people through different areas of the city. Accordingly, obstacles can be at least partially eliminated, such as the need to depend on other people in order to move about and to actively utilize the public bus transportation system. In this way, Audiotransantiago has been determined to be an effective and useful tool for acquiring knowledge regarding the surroundings that the user has navigated, and at the same time providing necessary tools so that blind people themselves can make decisions regarding alternative routes towards different places in order to meet their travel needs.

5 Conclusions

The purpose of this study was to design, develop and evaluate audio-based software to assist in public bus transportation for people who are blind. As a result, Audiotransantiago allowed users to have access to and manage information on buses and their routes through a variety of urban areas, understand how the bus system works, learn the cost of tickets and, in many cases, to orient users in their spatial configuration of the areas within the bus (seats, sounds, doors). The use of the software improved information processing skills, tempo-spatial orientation and O&M skills, as users were able to navigate from one place to another without having to obtain information prior to their trip.

The main focus of this research was centered on evaluating whether or not an audio-based, technological tool favored autonomous navigation by people who are blind on surface bus transportation in order to travel between different points throughout the city. In this way, it is possible to conclude that the Audiotransantiago software provides information based on the bus service, its routes, bus stops, and streets around the various stops, including places that could be considered to be of cultural, social, economic or educational interest.

The results obtained allowed the researchers to conclude that the use of a mobile device makes putting navigational strategies into practice possible, supported by a system of contextual information in order for the user to be able to orient himself within the bus system, based on knowledge of bus stops, nearby streets and places of interest. As such, afterwards these places can be visited as many times as the user plans, in that the use of the software aids in the creation of a mental map of the environment through which the user travels, in addition to incorporating information that is able to take the surrounding environment into account, thus widening the user's overall knowledge of the city.

Audiotransantiago, as a sound feedback-based technological proposal, provides users who are blind with information that allows them to utilize surface, urban transportation independently. The proposed software supports these users' orientation and mobility skills, providing information on the physical surroundings with an emphasis on contextual information regarding bus stops, route change stations, as well as nearby places of interest surrounding the routes such as museums, public services, and others. Audiotransantiago can be seen as a tool that facilitates the inclusion of people with visual disabilities in interactions with the urban environment, as it allows for the development of strategies that seek improved cognition and environmental perception based on a direct experience with the surrounding environment at any given time. In this way, the recognition of spatial considerations is not the result of a passive process of receiving information, because it involves the interpretation and restructuring of information and actions by the visually impaired user.

Despite showing the effectiveness of using the Audiotransantiago software as a relevant tool for providing useful information for decision-making and problem solving, the public bus transportation system currently presents serious defects and complexities that emerge as variables that the software cannot control. This is the case regarding the frequency and circulation of the buses, the buses not stopping at each of the designated bus stops, and a lack of information on route changes or detours that can occur for various reasons. All of this is in addition to the high congestion during peak travel times, and the scarcity of Braille or audio-based traffic lights or information signs as integrated in the original design of the system, as well as the constant change of bus routes and the specific directions that they take. Often the general public, with or without visual impairment, is not informed of such changes in a timely manner, so that adequate planning measures can be taken to compensate for the diversions from normality.

Acknowledgments. This report was funded by the Chilean National Fund of Science and Technology, Fondecyt #1120330, and Project CIE-05 Program Center Education PBCT-Conicyt.

References

1. Arnaiz, P.: Deficiencias Visuales y Psicomotricidad: Teoría y Práctica. ONCE, Madrid (1994)
2. Blanco, R., Blanco, L., Luengo, S., Pastor, G., Rivero, M., Rodríguez, M., Vicente, M.: Accesibilidad para personas con ceguera y deficiencia visual. ONCE, Madrid (2003)
3. Ciudades para un Futuro Sostenible. Red Integrada de Transporte Easy Pass (Franca, Brasil) Buenas Prácticas - América Latina y el Caribe - Concurso Internacional (2004), http://habitat.aq.upm.es/bpal/onu04/bp2572.html (retrived January 26, 2012)
4. Diario Oficial De La República de Chile, Ley número 19.284 - Normas para la plena integración social de personas con discapacidad. Santiago, viernes 14 de enero de, núm. 34.764 año CXVI – n° 320.108 (1994)
5. Gazteis, V.: La aplicación de un programa de orientación y movilidad a personas ciegas y con discapacidad visual grave. In: Revista Psicodidáctica, vol. 15, pp. 155–169. Universidad del país Vasco, España (2003)
6. Lahav, O., Mioduser, D.: Blind Persons' Acquisition of Spatial Cognitive Mapping and Orientation Skills Supported by Virtual Environment. In: Proc. of the 5th International Conference on Disability, Virtual Reality and Associated Technologies, ICDVRAT, Oxford, UK, pp. 131–138 (2004)
7. Transmilenio, Población en situación de Discapacidad (2012), http://www.transmilenio.gov.co/WebSite/Contenido. aspx?ID=PoblacionEnSituacionDeDiscapacidad (Consulta 18 Enero 2012)
8. Sánchez, J., Aguayo, F., Hassler, T.: Independent Outdoor Mobility for the Blind. In: Proceedings of the IEEE Virtual Rehabilitation 2007 Conference, Venice, Italy, September 27-29, pp. 114–120 (2007)
9. Sánchez, J., De la Torre, N.: AHM, videojuego basado en audio y háptica para el desarrollo de la orientación y movilidad en estudiantes ciegos. In: Proc. VI Congreso Iberoamericano de Tecnologías de Apoyo a la Discapacidad (IBERDISCAP), pp. 118–124. Palma de Mallorca, Spain (June 2011) ISBN 978-84-8384-187-8
10. Sánchez, J., Oyarzún, C.: Mobile Audio Assistance in Bus Transportation for the Blind. In: Sharkey, P.M., Lopes-dos-Santos, P., Weiss, P.L., Brooks, A.L. (eds.) Proceedings of the 7th International Conference on Disability, Virtual Reality and Associated Technologies with Art Abilitation, Maia, Portugal, September 8-11, vol. (38), pp. 279–286 (2008)
11. Song, G., Lovie-kitchin, J., Brown, B.: Does Mobility Performance of Visually Impaired Adults Improve immediately After Orientation and Mobility Training Optometry & Vision Science, vol. 78(9), pp. 657–666 (September 2001)
12. Transbarca, http://www.transbarca.gob.ve/features/ (retrieved January 26, 2012)
13. Transport Metropolitan, http://www.tmb.cat/es/home (retrieved January 26, 2012)
14. Sampaio, B.R., Lima Neto, O., Sampaio, Y.: Efficiency analysis of public transport systems: Lessons for institutional planning. Transportation Research Part A: Policy and Practice 4(3), 445–454 (2008)

15. Rojas, F.: Aportes para a melhoria da gestão do transporte público por ônibus de Bogotá, a partir das experiencias de Belo Horizonte e Curitiba. Papel Político 11(2), 557–594 (2006)
16. Duarte, F., Rojas, F.: Intermodal Connectivity to BRT: A Comparative Analysis of Bogotá and Curitiba. Journal of Public Transportation 15, 1–18 (2012)
17. Shi, J., Wu, Z., Jin, J.: Reform Beijing to a public transit oriented city – from the view of transportation equity. J. Adv. Transp. 45, 96–106 (2011), doi:10.1002/atr.118
18. Kuo, C.-W., Tang, M.-L.: Relationships among service quality, corporate image, customer satisfaction, and behavioral intention for the elderly in high speed rail services. J. Adv. Transp. (2011), doi:10.1002/atr.179
19. Chang, H.-L., Wu, S.-C.: Applying the Rasch measurement to explore elderly passengers' abilities and difficulties when using buses in Taipei. J. Adv. Transp. 44, 134–149 (2010) doi:10.1002/atr.127
20. PoaTransporte: o guia de transportes de Porto Alegre, http://www.poatransporte.com.br/ (retrieved January 26, 2012)
21. Bassani, M.A.: Fatores psicológicos da percepção da qualidade ambiental. In: Maia, N.B., Martos, H.L., Barrella, W. (Org.) Indicadores Ambientais: conceitos e aplicações, pp. 47–57. EDUC, São Paulo (2001)
22. Paranhos, M.: Apropriação de espaço por adultos com deficiência visual: estudo de casos. Dissertação de Mestrado. PUC/SP, Brasil, p. 127 (2008)

Towards Mobile Embodied 3D Avatar as Telepresence Vehicle

Yutaka Tokuda[1], Atsushi Hiyama[2], Takahiro Miura[2],
Tomohiro Tanikawa[2], and Michitaka Hirose[2]

[1] Graduate School of Engineering, The University of Tokyo, 4-6-1,
Komaba, Meguro-ku, Tokyo 153-8904, Japan
[2] Graduate School of Information Science and Technology, The University of Tokyo,
7-3-1, Hongo, Bunkyo-ku, Tokyo 113-8656, Japan
{ytokuda,atsushi,miu,tani,hirose}@cyber.t.u-tokyo.ac.jp

Abstract. In this paper, we present mobile embodied 3D avatar to shift a rich experience of avatar from a virtual world to our real life with a new style of telepresence. Conventional telepresence research have focused on the exact re-creation of face-to-face communication at a fixed position in a specialized room, so there have been much less research on a life-sized mobile telepresence system despite many off-the-shelf mobile telepresence robots available. We propose various scalable holographic displays to visualize a life-sized avatar in an actual life. In addition, we introduce architecture to control embodied avatar according to user's intention by extending popular architecture for a multimodal virtual human, namely SAIBA. Our primitive prototype system was tested with 5 simple avatar animations to embody with a wheeled platform robot and a life-sized transparent holographic display and proved realistic avatar's movement complying user's intention and the situation at the remote location of avatar.

Keywords: interaction techniques, avatar, telepresence, telework, mobility, transparent display, platforms and metaphors, multimodal interaction, SAIBA.

1 Introduction

Thanks to the rapid advancement of core technologies for the telepresence, such as broadband internet, loss-less compression, high-resolution imaging/capturing, robotics, and computer vision, we are at the verge of transition from a classic video-based teleconference service to immersive tele-robotics exploration service in our daily life [1,2,3,4]; simply speaking, our projected body in a distant environment finally gained legs to move around from a fixed place. For instance, Double Robotics proposed iPad-based remote exploration robots at a reasonable cost of $1,999 [2]. iRobot introduced RP-VITA(Remote Presence Virtual + Independent and Telemedicine Assistant) as a "teledoctor" [3]. Willow Garage provided telepresence robot development kits and libraries [4]. Despite of many available resources of telepresence robots, their display size always settles for less than human-face size in order to just represent face expression and gaze direction of operators but not full body expression. Even if the

C. Stephanidis and M. Antona (Eds.): UAHCI/HCII 2013, Part III, LNCS 8011, pp. 671–680, 2013.
© Springer-Verlag Berlin Heidelberg 2013

robots deploy mechanical arms, torso, and head with motion capabilities, non-verbal expression from body gesture is limited by the DOF (Degree Of Freedom) of their corresponding movement, and thus likely become gawky: following the exact same problem as humanoid robots have. Studies about the impact of the human picture size on social telepresence have stated that the smaller the display size, the less realistic presence [5,6]. Furthermore, they warned a head only picture is more harmful to social telepresence. Even though many life-size telepresence display research have been done in a specialized immersive environment at a virtual reality laboratory, there is much less research on telepresence robot with a full-body human image because it is difficult to display such a large realistic image atop mobile robots. Especially, it is important and critical to reduce the occlusion of display itself on the background; otherwise, not only damages the social telepresence but also incites terror toward telepresence robots due to the bulk. Development of a mobile and immersive telepresence display is one of our goals to tackle in this paper. We present several solutions to this problem with a review of our previous research results along with currently available transparent displays and optical elements at the section 3 and introduce our prototype system at the section 4.

On the contrary to telepresence in an actual world, it is more popular and ordinary activity in the general public to beam their bodies to "avatars" in a virtual world, such as Second Life, MMORPG (Massively Multiplayer Online Role-Playing Game), SNS space at game consoles (e.g. Xbox Kinect Avatar, Nintendo's Mii space, PlayStation Home), and etc. Avatar can be any form of virtual creatures and virtual objects, so the potential diverseness and richness of expressions and activities are much beyond the ones realized by tele-robots in a conventional telepresence research. For example, a small boy can not only play a role of a matured dandy or an attractive woman to enjoy an adult life socializing with other people in a virtual space, but also gain a new experience with flying a sky with a form of a bird, swimming a deep sea with a form of a fish, or pretending his favorite animation characters. Such an endless possibility and creativity have inspired our goal to bring the avatar in a virtual world into our actual and physical world. To accomplish this goal, we propose a mobile embodied 3D avatar as a new telepresence style. Our research goal consists of the following three sub-themes (a) Mobile full-scale holographic display system, (b) Architecture to realize avatar's behavior with a dynamic robot display, and (c) Framework to map an operator's intention and trait onto embodied avatar.

It is essential and difficult part to re-create avatar's visual appearance and unique motion in a real world. Successfully embodied avatar should enable operators to explore in a building, a city, or even a sky and communicate with remote inhabitants without losing their chosen avatar's form and personalities. Thus, our research focus is not to reconstruct face-to-face communication as many existing telepresence research do but rather to bridge the gap between avatar in a virtual world and telepresence robot in a physical world to fuse respective advantages: e.g. rich expression and animation, mobility and sensory interface with the real world. It is quite important issue how remote inhabitants see and judge the appearance and behavior of telepresence robot in terms of creating "self" images [7]. If it shows poor appearance with a small display and miss-matched mechanical motion, there will arise a huge gap between operator's "self" image and reaction by remote inhabitants; for instance, tele-doctor and tele-teacher need friendly and faithful "self" image to work with remote patients and students smoothly. To avoid such a mismatch, we propose an architecture to grasp operator's intention, plan action based on the available animation of avatar, context of robot, and the remote situation, following a popular virtual agent's framework, so called SAIBA (Situation, Agent, Intention, Behavior, Animation)[8]. We review a SAIBA framework and present our extended version of SAIBA at the section 4 along with our primitive prototype system. It is predictable that if we embody many existing avatars from a game or a virtual space, people shift their favorite avatars from a virtual to a real world and enjoy limitless exploration and interaction with actual inhabitants through avatar's eyes. We can think this new telepresence as a novel vehicle to explore 2nd life in a real world.

At the next section, we review related research on a single full-body telepresence display and a mobile telepresence, and then discuss several methods with pros and cons analysis to develop scalable mobile telepresence display for a various form of full body avatar. After that, we introduce our primitive prototype system to pretest our architecture for avatar control according to user's intention and situation. In conclusion, we summarize our work and propose the next task to refine the system for more intuitive operation.

2   Related Research

Full-Body Telepresence. Whille most of conventional life-sized telepresence research have been studied at a large scale like a wall-screen or a specialized immersive shared space, there is a trend to develop a minimum-sized stereoscopic display to re-create a single-person in a life-size at a distant location. For example, Tachi et al. have developed TELEsarPHONE (Telesar II) to realize a mutual telexistence system for face-to-face telecommunication via slave robots [9]. In order to make a motion parallax image, they deployed retro-reflective materials atop of the robot's upper body and projected multi-view images of the pilot from multi angles; remote people can see a single-view of the pilot image projected from a corresponding projector close to their position because retro-reflective materials have very narrow range of reflection angle. Even though they successfully re-created precise 3D upper body image of a pilot in real time, it is designed for the fixed position and not scalable for mobile full-body telepresence. On the other hand, Michihiko et al. presented U-Tsu-Shi-O-Mi, which is an overlaid humanoid robot with virtual human (VH) in a video see through display [10]. U-Tsu-Shi-O-Mi nicely fuses advantage of rich expression of VH into a physical body of a humanoid to create embodied avatar; however, users can't see the augmented full-body telepresence image with their naked eyes and furthermore this system is not scalable to non-human avatar. Kim et al. proposed TeleHuman, a cylindrical 3D display portal for life-size human telepresence [11]. They deployed 6 kinects and a 3D projector to realize full-scale motion parallax image of a human in 360 degree-views with a correct gaze direction. The system can be applied to any avatar form as long as the size is within the cylinder, but likewise they have not considered the mobile telepresence at all but only static teleconference application.

Mobile Telepresence. As much as a display size is small, there have been many mobile telepresence robots at academia and markets as we described at Introduction. A robot of mobile telepresence with a display can fall into two principal types: blimps with a portable projector to move in mid air [12, 13] and wheeled carts with a flat panel display to move on the ground [2,3,4,12,]. Although it is possible to make full-body mobile telepresence in both ways, they have corresponding pros and cons. As Paulos et al. [12] pointed out, blimps have difficulty in controlling and staying at a point of space because of its lightweight body susceptible to air disturbance and require a constant maintenance for helium gas to float blimps. However, we can't ignore the fact that blimps can move anywhere in a space without complex calculation to avoid obstacles on the ground and can take any form. We can make use of the flexibility and scalability of blimps to realize flying avatars and a wide gamut of sizes, although we do not discuss a further detail in this paper. On the contrary, wheeled carts are the most popular style for mobile telepresence at the moment because of user-friendliness, high loading power, long lifespan, and accumulation of research and know-how. We chose this basic style for our primitive prototype system to test our concept and architecture because our laboratory owns a couple of wheeled platform robots and related research experience [14]. Nakanishi et al. verifies that a movable display imitating remote operator's movement along a depth direction can enhance a social telepresence more than a fixed display [15]. This result indicates such a possibility that corresponding movement of display for avatar's behavior is essential to actualize a realistic embodied avatar. Recently, Kuster et al. have suggested a concept of mobile telepresence system as the next generation teleconference [16]. They have shown currently available components to realize well immersive 3D telepresence system, such as semi-transparent holographic displays, free-view virtual cameras with kinect, transmission of 3D images with low latency, etc. Although they show a sketch of a mobile full-body telepresence platform, they have not constructed any prototype systems yet. Moreover, since their focus is how to re-create exact face-to-face communication but not how to actualize a life-sized avatar including non-humans, our research goal is different from them. To our best knowledge, there have been much less research to realize a mobile full-body telepresence display and no framework have been proposed to fuse a motion of robotic display, avatar's animation, and operator's intention.

At the next section, we discuss scalable and lightweight holographic display to actualize mobile embodied avatar, and finally introduce our architecture to realize a behavior of avatar with a robotic display according to user's intention based on SAIBA framework [8] at the section 4.

3   Scalable Mobile Telepresence Display

As we stated previous sections, there is less research on a mobile full-body telepresence display even though we can recognize the place to enjoy telepresence is shifting from a specialized laboratory to a public place in our daily life. In order to develop life-sized mobile displays, we have to solve two trade-offs: weight and display size, display size and feeling of oppression. Needless to say, when we install an immersive full-body display atop a mobile robot, we have to balance the weight of the display and a loading power of the mobile robot. In general, we need at least 80-inch display to display a full-scale human body. The weight of 80-inch is more than 50 kg. Taking an example of loading power of typical wheeled carts from Segway RMP 200 series [17], the average loading is 45 kg; thus, a human-sized display is over the loading power. It is true that the rapid advancement of flat displays like OLED displays are dramatically reducing the weight of displays; however, if we consider a scalability to deal with various forms and sizes of avatar, deployment of a projector is rather practical. Moreover, it is important to make a display frame and a background image as transparent as possible so that a life-sized display is less oppressive and more blended into a real world. There are couples of methods to make such transparent, scalable, lightweight, holographic displays: kinetic display, particle display, and transparent optical element (Fig.1 shows corresponding images).

Kinetic Display. As we know from principle of animation, our eyes have a persistence of vision to integrate all partial images we gained within a short time of human's temporal resolution (50-100ms in general). Thus, it is not always necessary to prepare as large screen as the size to show avatar; we only need a "part" of it to create large screen visible for our eyes. We have developed a scalable kinetic screen based on the persistence of vision (see Fig. 1-(a)) [18]. We called such display a kinetic display since it is not static but dynamically moving to scan a real space for a virtual display. Our propeller-shaped prototype system scans 4m-diameter circle with 6 rotating blade-screens at a speed of 1.5 rotations per a second; the total physical screen area is 4 % of the circle area. The transparency is about 93% with this rotation speed. In spite of the fact that we need a motor to rotate a propeller and a frame to support, the total weight is much less than expected from a large flat display. We can choose any material and size to create proper blades, although we have selected a regular reflective projection screen material with a frame made of light and tough bamboo. We verified the same holographic effect with a much smaller propeller display, whose size is 1/30 of the original. While it is not distant idea to deploy propeller-shaped kinetic displays for a terrestrial mobile telepresence robot due to the risk of injury, it is reasonable to build airborne avatar with kinetic display since they likely stay over human's hand reach: e.g. birds, dragons, angels, and so on. Nowadays, we can buy many remotely operable flying robots with a wifi camera installed as with AR Drone [19]. Besides, a size and a weight of portable projector is dramatically decreasing along with the cost, so it is practical to build mobile embodied avatar with a kinetic display. If we control multiple airborne robots of kinetic displays, it is even possible to create a dynamically deformable large avatar from combination of them.

Particle Display. We define a particle display as a screen consisting of many light diffusive particles such as fogs, mists, dusts, smokes, water droplets, and so forth. Since a particle display is scalable and easy to form a large transparent holographic display, it is popular and practical mid-air screen as with fog screens [20]. However, since fog screens are not originally intended for mobile application, current off-the-shelf fog screens are very susceptible to air disturbance while screens are in motion.

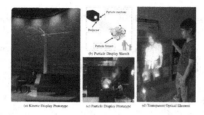

Fig. 1. (a) Kinetic Display Prototype showing a clock deploying 6 blade screens of 1.7m length rotating at the speed of 1.5 rotations per second [18] (b) Particle Display Sketch (c) Particle Display Prototype based on vortex ring fog screen, showing a flying dice more than 4.0 m at a constant speed [21] (d) Transparent Optical Element demo showing a full-scale human figure with a short range projector [22]

To break through such a low sustainability, we have proposed vortex ring based particle display [21]. Vortex ring (smoke ring) has attracted a lot of attention from fluid dynamics researchers because it has a high stability together with a great transportability to deliver any particles inside of it toward remote location at a constant speed. We have utilized vortex ring to build a stable particle display with a scalable depth range (see Fig.1 - (b) (c)). We verified vortex ring can function as a moving flat projection screen in a mid air and project avatar in a depth range for a short time (3 seconds per once). Current prototype has a quite low refresh rate (~ 0.5 Hz) to project mid-air image because currently available fog machines have small production capacity and also very slow are off-the-shelf piston-actuators to emit a vortex ring screen, so we are refining these bottle necks to enable 3D scanning of the space with high speed vortex ring screen in the same way as X-Ray scan. When we project a corresponding 2D sliced image with respect to a vertical position of a flying vortex ring at the speed faster than our temporal resolution, our eye should recognize full-body 3D image of avatar. In addition, vortex ring is expected to function as a multimodal display since it can transport odor and chemical particles together. We have not utilized a particle display for mobile telepresence yet, but we plan to do.

Transparent Optical Element. It is a beginning of a craze for a plat panel industry to produce a transparent flat panel display as the next trend. Especially, we can find many applications at digital signage and smart phone. On the other hand, there are more semi-transparent projection films obtainable at reasonable costs and with various optical properties: e.g. anisotropy, directional refraction, total internal reflection, and so on. We have selected highly diffusive semi-transparent film [22] for our prototype system because we can flexibly customize the shape and size of screen. This transparent film has well enough viewing angles (90 degrees in horizontal and vertical direction) and resolutions (50 lines/mm) to test the reality of mobile full-body avatar with our action framework without any display driven concerns (Fig.1 (d) shows sample full-body human image with the film). Microsoft research group proposed wedge shaped semi-transparent optical elements to guide projection image from the near side of the wedge screen to viewers in front of screen so that they can dramatically reduce the projection distance [23]. Inspired by such smart optical elements, at the next prototype system, we are going to investigate and develop more intelligent optical elements than now. At the first trial, we are currently experimenting with fast photochromic material [24] which responds to violet light instantly to change a color so that we can make contrast higher and as a result enhance visibility of avatar; though, it is not a topic to share further in this paper.

We have not discussed about a method of multi-view stereoscopy for all displays listed so far. If we can project multiple images with multi angles to a display without mixing each image, we can theoretically realize multi-view stereoscopy; this is possible, as long as we deploy directional refraction material as a screen component. Regarding kinetic displays and transparent optical elements, wedge shaped optical element is one of such solutions because it can work as a transparent directional lens. As for particle display, it is rather easy to realize direction refraction at particle screen, since small particles refract light in a quite narrow range because of Mie scattering property. Yagi et al. have developed a 360-degree fog display utilizing this advantage [25].

4   Prototype System and Architecture

We have developed our primitive prototype system for a proposed mobile telepresence system to embody avatar (see Fig.2). Our prototype system consists of three key components: transparent holographic display, wheeled platform robot, and architecture for action control of embodied avatar according to user's intention.

Transparent Holographic Display. As we stated at the section 3, we have deployed a highly diffusive transparent projection film [22] atop a 65-inch acryl panel to make immersive life-sized telepresence display. We have decided the size to make a total height of prototype system less than 1.9 m, which can range the height of most of people, especially in Japan. Furthermore, if we make the height too large, it is difficult to go through a standard door and exit and also more likely to be swung. We have deployed an ultra short-range projector, Epson EB-485W, which can project 80 -inch image from a 0.56m distance with 3100 lumens brightness. The net projection area is 1.136 m x 0.912m, which can include life-sized upper body together with an upper thigh for a height of 1.7m people. The projector and screen is fixed with an aluminum frame.

Wheeled Platform Robot. As we discussed at the section 2, we have decided to use a wheeled platform robot for our prototype because it is well studied and has great transportability with a high power. Since we own a Segway RMP 200 in our laboratory and have know-how to control, we used Segway for our experiment with a few modifications to reduce the weight and to mount holographic display on the top. Our wheel platform robot consists of a kinect to build virtual view similar to human's eyes' position and direction, two Hakuyo compact laser rangefinders, URG-04LX, at front end and back end of the robot, for a collision detection and 600w battery as a portable main power and a Maxon motor and a driver to rotate the upper body. All robot controls and graphics rendering are processed by one linux pc of 2.4 GHz Core-i7 CPU, 16 GB RAM, and Geforce GT650M 2GB GPU. The integrated mobile telepresence system can move about 1.5 hours without any external power supply.

We have chosen the left-handed coordinate system for our local coordinate, following the convention of ROS (Robot Operating System)[26].

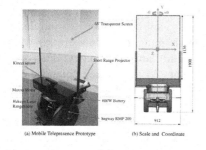

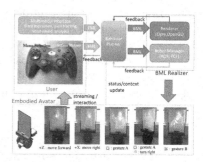

Fig. 2. (a) Mobile telepresence prototype system (b) Scale and coordinate of prototype system

Fig. 3. Architecture for embodied avatar control from user's intention

Architecture. To make an embodied avatar behave naturally, we need a simple architecture to intuitively handle user's intention, robot motion, and rendering of CG avatar at the same time. To build such systematic architecture, we have followed SAIBA[8] as a template since it is one of the most popular architectures to control multimodal behaviors of virtual humans and robots in the same manner. SAIBA simply consists of three components: intent planner, behavior planner, and behavior realizer. Intent planner basically describes user's intention and desire to do in an abstract format: e.g. want to go position A, want to grasp that fruit, etc. Behavior planner integrates all necessary information to make a schedule and logically design blue prints to realize the user's intention. Finally, behavior realizer makes a concrete action based on the blue prints given by behavior planner. All communication between each components are done by exchange of XML- based human readable languages: FML (Function Markup Language) and BML (Behavior Markup Language). You can find a specific form of these XML languages at the website of Mindmakers [27]. Following this framework, we have built our architecture as shown in Fig. 3. We have chosen a typical joystick game controller as an interface, since it is well designed to control avatar in a virtual reality. Left joystick controls avatar's directional movement in X and Z axis. Right joystick controls avatar's upper body motion. Left cross key buttons can select a menu to configure avatar and action parameters, although we have not utilized yet. User can choose action of avatar from 4 status buttons at the right. Each input into this joystick is translated to FML and passed to behavior planner. Even though we have not implemented yet, we intend to catch user's non-verbal cue from multimodal information such as gaze direction and face expression and pass those information as FML to the behavior planner too in a future. Behavior planner gathers environmental information from a kinect sensor and laser rangefinders to judge the user's intentional action is possible or not at the current status and position of the robot. The planner automatically translates the user's intention in BML format and pass to behavior realizers; that is, renderer to move avatar with animation and robot manager to control robots. If there is error during realization, realizer feedbacks the error to the planner and the user so that user can choose possible actions. When everything goes well, finally embodied avatar can move according to user's intention. After each action, the planner and user received update information of the new state of embodied avatar and interaction inputs by the remote inhabitants around the avatar.

We have tested our framework with simple 5 avatar animations (walk in Z and X direction, turn right, point the right bottom, point the right top) and found it reasonably create corresponding robot motion and synchronized animation according to user's intended action. We also verified the user can't select action which is judged impossible from the behavior planner based on the robot status; for instance, when people cross in front of the avatar, users received error feedback whenever they tried to move avatar forward, pushing a left joystick forward.

5   Conclusion

To shift avatar from virtual to real world, we proposed mobile embodied 3D avatar as a new telepresence style. People can explore a real world with appearance and ability from favorite avatar and also interact with real inhabitants at a remote location in a similar fashion as they do in a virtual world. Even though it is essential to build a scalable mobile telepresence display to actualize a life-sized avatar, we have found there is much less research on the development of such a mobile telepresence system. To break though the current situation, we have proposed 3 methods to make a lightweight and scalable holographic display as key components: kinetic display, particle display, and transparent optical elements. We have presented our primitive prototype system to test a life-sized avatar move realistically according to user's intention. To make a system organized and scalable, we built architecture inspired by a popular framework for a multimodal virtual human namely, SAIBA. We verified our architecture can deal with simple 5 avatar animations according to user's intention and the context and status of the avatar. As a next step, we are going to expand our architecture to handle user's intention from non-verbal cues such as gaze direction and face expression so that we can help senior workers can intuitively use our embodied avatar for their enforced telework.

Acknowledgments. This research is supported in part by S-innovation (Strategic Promotion of Innovative Research and Development) funding under Industry Academia Collaborative R&D Programs administered by Japan Science and Technology Agency (JST).

References

1. IEEE Spectrum,
   http://spectrum.ieee.org/automaton/robotics/
   robotics-hardware/robotics-trends-for-2012
2. Double Robotics, http://www.doublerobotics.com
3. iRobot, http://www.irobot.com
4. Willow Garage, http://www.willowgarage.com

5. Leigh, J., Rawlings, M., Girado, J., Dawe, G., Fang, R., Verlo, A., Khan, M.A., Cruz, A., Plepys, D., Sandin, D.J., DeFanti, T.A.: AccessBot: an Enabling Technology for Telepresence. In: INET 2000 (2000)
6. Nguyen, D.T., Canny, J.: More than Face-to-Face: Empathy Effects of Video Framing. In: Proc. ACM CHI 2009, pp. 423–432 (2009)
7. Canny, J., Paulos, E.: Tele-embodiment and shattered presence: Reconstructing the body for online interaction. In: The Robot in the Garden: Telerobotics and Telepistemology in the Age of the Internet, pp. 276–294 (2000)
8. Zwiers, J., van Welbergen, H., Reidsma, D.: Continuous Interaction within the SAIBA Framework. In: Vilhjálmsson, H.H., Kopp, S., Marsella, S., Thórisson, K.R. (eds.) IVA 2011. LNCS, vol. 6895, pp. 324–330. Springer, Heidelberg (2011)
9. Tachi, S., Kawashima, N., Nii, H., Watanabe, K., Minamizawa, K.: TELEsarPHONE: Mutual Telexistence Master-Slave Communication System Based on Retroreflective Projection Technology. SICE Journal of Control, Measurement, and System Integration 1, 335–344 (2011)
10. Shoji, M., Miura, K., Konno, A.: U-Tsu-Shi-O-Mi: the virtual humanoid you can reach. In: ACM SIGGRAPH 2006 Emerging Technologies, New York (2006)
11. Kim, K., Bolton, J., Girouard, A., Cooperstock, J., Vertegaal, R.: TeleHuman: effects of 3d perspective on gaze and pose estimation with a life-size cylindrical telepresence pod. In: Proc. ACM CHI 2012, pp. 2531–2540 (2012)
12. Paulosand, E., Canny, J.: PRoP: Personal Roving Presence. In: Proc. ACM CHI 1998, pp. 296–303 (1998)
13. Tobita, H., Maruyama, S., Kuzi, T.: Floating avatar: telepresence system using blimps for communication and entertainment. In: ACM CHI 2011 Extended Abstracts on Human Factors in Computing Systems, pp. 541–550 (2011)
14. Hiyama, A., Imai, T., Tanikawa, T., Hirose, M.: Remote Museum Guide using Augmented Reality Vehicle. In: 20th International Conference on Artificial Reality and Telexistence (ICAT 2010), Adelaide (2010)
15. Nakanishi, H., Kato, K., Ishiguro, H.: Zoom Cameras and Movable Displays Enhance Social Telepresence. In: Proc. ACM CHI 2011, Vancouver, pp. 63–72 (2011)
16. Kuster, C., Ranieri, N., Agustina, Z.H., Bazin, B.Z., Sun, C., Popa, T., Gross, M.: Towards Next Generation 3D Teleconferencing Systems. In: DTV Conference: The True Vision - Capture, Transmission and Display of 3D Video (2012)
17. SEGWAY, http://www.segway.com
18. Nishimura, K., Suzuki, Y., Tokuda, Y., Iida, T., Kajinami, T., Tanikawa, T., Hirose, M.: Tree-shaded screen: A Propeller type screen for Public Art. In: Proc. Joint Virtual Reality Conference of EGVE-ICAT-EuroVR, Lyon, pp. 101–104 (2009)
19. Parro, A.R.: DRONE2.0, http://ardrone2.parrot.com/
20. Fogscreen, http://www.fogscreen.com/
21. Tokuda, Y., Nishimura, K., Suzuki, Y., Tanikawa, T., Hirose, M.: Vortex Ring Based Display. In: Proc. IEEE VSMM 2010, Seoul, pp. 51–54 (2010)
22. TAGOS, http://www.tagos.jp/display/harumi.html
23. Travis, A.R.L., Large, T.A., Emerton, N., Bathiche, S.N.: Wedge Optics in Flat Panel Displays. In: Proc. of the IEEE 101(1), 45–60 (2013)
24. Kishimoto, Y., Abe, J.: A Fast Photochromic Molecule That Colors Only under UV Light. J. Am. Chem. Soc. 131(12), 4227–4229 (2009)
25. Yagi, A., Imura, M., Kuroda, Y., Oshiro, O.: 360-degree fog projection interactive display. In: ACM SIGGRAPH Asia 2011 Emerging Technologies, Hong Kong (2006)
26. ROS, http://www.ros.org/
27. Mindmaker, http://www.mindmakers.org/projects/bml-1-0/wiki/Wiki

One-Handed Gesture Design for Browsing on Touch Phone

Fong-Gong Wu and Jo-Yu Kuo

Department of Industrial Design, National Cheng Kung University, Tainan, Taiwan (R.O.C.)
fonggong@mail.ncku.edu.tw, sc1156@hotmail.com

Abstract. The goal of this research is to understand how dual-surface touch gesture helps user interact mobile phone with one hand from user experience perspective. Hence, we proposed a set of gestures and some design recommendations for enhancing the browsing usability. Finally we emulated the information seeking task on mobile phone. The results showed that, compare to traditional graphic user interface, browsing gestures eased the thumb fatigue, reduced the error rate and task completed time.

Keywords: one-handed interaction, dual-surface touch gesture, web browsing, touch phone.

1   Introduction

Smart phones have fulfilled the various multi-function needs of users, which require the showing of a large amount of information on limited screen space. 63% of the participants indicated that they are limited to two-handed operations due to the interface design, and that one-handed operation is preferred [1]. In the multi-mode research under a moving environment, it was found that users prefer to interact with phones using fingers or tilting plane motions [2]. Users tend to work with the convenience of different space using one-handed operation in order to leave the other hand free to hold other objects. Touch screens tend to have wilder displaying areas, but current touch interface designs of button space and positions have not put user experience into consideration. This often causes thumbs to operate back and forth when targets are too far away from the thumb, causing accumulated injury and fatigue. The single-thumb operation also eliminated the possibility and strength of multi-point touch screens, such as the intuitive motion of enlarging and zooming or rotating using two fingers.   From the research background and questions, we found that the habit of one-handed holding and browsing the net under limited thumb movement range, error rate, and fatigue has caused unhappy user experience. However, users needs for mobile phone and desktop systems are differentiating, applying fixed internet application sequences directly onto mobile phones is outdated. Therefore, mobile phone interface design standards should be in accordance with user habits, mobility, and small displaying screens. The top three browsing behaviors of mobile web pages are: fact finding, information gathering, and browsing [3]. Researches pointed out that when users

C. Stephanidis and M. Antona (Eds.): UAHCI/HCII 2013, Part III, LNCS 8011, pp. 681–690, 2013.
© Springer-Verlag Berlin Heidelberg 2013

click on a target on the center of the screen, the thumb joint does not need to be bent under a big range, but is presented in a comfortable slanting plane position [4].

However, during experiments, users are prepared and tend to focus more on aiming at the button on the edge of the screen. This may cause experimental inaccuracy in longer task times and lower error rates [5]. The index finger presented fine touch performance on either side of the mobile phone, with a better result in horizontal shift than vertical. The thumb presented a generally less satisfactory result on the front side of the phone with an user expectation of the see-through effect on the reverse side [6]. Gestures are meaningful in our daily lives. They can be categorized into the following according to different movement forms: symbolic, indicative, metaphoric, rhythmic, and controlling. Amongst which the controlling gestures indicate constructing a closer relationship with the controlled object using hand movements [7].

2   Methods

In order to improve user experience of single-handed browsing tasks, new cooperating relationships between the thumb and four fingers on different touch screen surfaces are brought up. A balance needs to be achieved between gesture interactions and the physical restrain of single-handed operation. A set of assistive gestures are designed specifically for browsing functions and evaluated according to usability and objective index.

2.1   Selection of Browsing Commands

Five participants were recruited for this stage. Participants were target users between 20 and 25 years old who have at least 6 months of smart-phone experience and habits of browsing web-pages using touch phones in order to avoid the effect of familiarity on experiment performance. Users should also maintain a habit of browsing non-mobile version of web pages at least twice a day. The participants were asked to fill in their basic information, personal experience on multi-point touch screen products, and motives, frequency, and occasions for non-mobile version of web browsing. The experiment procedures were explained and participants were asked to adjust to a comfortable sitting position before starting. Participants were required to hold the mobile phone single-handedly with no time limit. After the experiment, the videotapes were examined and function numbers and user descriptions were charted for questionnaire design. Gestures were designed with reference to frequencies each function is used and selecting appropriate browsing functions. The experiment devices used were the phones used by the participants on a daily basis. Therefore, the existing mobile browsing function arrangement differences do not affect the various browsing functions used with high frequencies. Referring to the observing statistics of the browsing function clicking frequency, the average answering time for four questions is 750 seconds for the 5 participants with no fatigue.

The tab function in the observing chart could be categorized in more details into "open new tab", "close tab", and "tab tour" to be more conformed to the present browsing interface. The functions were then made into questionnaires and distributed to 20 participants to select the functions keys used with the highest frequency.

Intergrading frequency and importance, 7±2 items of the 5 gestures were found to match the human short-term memories [8]. These were taken to the next design stage of "back/next", "zoom in/out", "open new tab", "close tab", and "search".

2.2   The Design of Browsing Hand-Gesture Samples

The size of the phone prototype is derived from the average size of the top 5 selling touch phones globally in 2011. The calculated average values were: 118.9mm x 62.1mm x10.4 mm, 138.4g in weight, and a 3.9 inch screen.

Six professionals with touch control hand gesture experience and more than 5 years of design experience were invited for a focus group discussion [9]. The host of the discussion was asked to avoid criticism and response directed towards concepts discussed. Related vocabulary was developed from the browsing functions selected in the first stage. Using the related adjectives, nouns, and verbs, the vocabulary was categorized into the portrait group, indication group, and the symbolizing group. The hand gesture design was then preceded. Six participants were invited to discuss using the Six-Three-Five thinking method, completing a design round every five minutes. Every five minutes, the participants pass the cards in their hands towards the right and so on, until their own cards are back in their hands. Participants can improve or use the design in their hands to produce various browsing hand gesture movement samples. This method is a combination of Brainstorming and the KJ card method. This ensures the communication of the completed design concept under limited language expression without being neglected during the verbal discussion of the focus group method. This also helps professionals to draw and present on the blank interface provided by the phone prototype using image mode, using speed to communicate design concepts and develop multi-interface design. Finally, according to the hand gesture design principles and finger movement restrictions mentioned in literature review, 5 hand gestures were selected from each function to enter the confusion matrix to evaluate hand gesture recognition level. During the selection of the final hand gesture samples, the cognitive confusion condition between various hand gestures and browsing commands were evaluated and improved. Considering the burden caused by the large sample during the matching of the conventional confusion matrix with the 25 hand gesture samples, Action Script 3.0 is used to write the experiment interface and the answers done on laptop computers. After the explaining of the experiment contents, participants were left to get used to the experiment application interface. Participants got to preview all the hand gesture images to ensure the understanding the meanings of all gestures, including clicking, sliding, pressing etc. Prototypes of the same ratio were given to participants for brainstorming. Thirty participants joined this stage of the experiment with only half of them experienced in touch-screen control. The experiment recorded the cognition time, error rate, and satisfaction rate of various hand gestures.

2.3   Browsing Gesture Usability Evaluation

The experiment system uses Arduino to control the touch panel and using Bluetooth to connect with Android phones as showing in diagram 3-8. The model web page interface was written by Flash ActionScript 3.0. The experiment phone was using the Android 4.0 system. The 2.8" TFT touch screen attached in the back was a 4-wire analog voltage control, allowing 4 GPIO to detect X and Y coordinates independently, used to identify gesture images or directions. According to the browsing hand gesture designed in the previous stage, the model web page browsing experiment procedure was planned. In the beginning of the experiment, participants were asked to sit comfortably to fill in their basic information and to listen to experiment details. Participants were also given enough time to familiarize the interface before starting. The experiment order of each group is random, with no time limit. Participants were asked to complete the objective questionnaire chart after all three groups are done.

The interface for the control group models the most popular Opera web browser [10]. Participants held the phone in two different ways (two-handed and single-handed) during operation. The browsing gesture interface for the control group does not include the assistive function tab, using single-handed touch control gestures to replace buttons. The browsing task and hand gesture performance under the three different models is compared. Twelve participants took part in this stage including 6 male and 6 female, all with touch phone internet browsing experiences, all right-handed with no hand injuries.

In order to model the finger movements of users during mobile phone browsing such as screen shifting and pointing-and-clicking links, participants were required to search on the screen to complete all valid target clicking. The target positions follow the Fitt's law to control the total shifting distance between targets. Fitt's law stated that the further the target distance the longer the shifting time, and the smaller the target, the longer the shifting time [11]. Upon selecting, the icons change color as feedback. There is no time limit for the experiment. The experiment tasks were designed with reference to the observation and calculation of the frequency of functions used during the first stage in order to be compatible with the actual browsing and hand gesture conditions. (1) The zoom in/out function: At the beginning, the icons were set to be 15 pixels. Participants were not able to recognize valid targets until they were zoomed in to the suitable size. The icons were able to be clicked on and the numbers accumulated anytime during the experiment. The error rate will be listed as part of the usability consideration as a reference for the browsing gesture system development and improvement. (2) The back/next function: Each tab represents a different icon, and each page shows 2 to 6 different targets randomly without repeating. Each tab includes 5 pages and 5 tabs include a total of 25 pages. Participants use the back/next gesture or click on the back/next function key to switch between pages. (3)The tab function: The system shows two random valid targets on the previous tab. Once more than three tabs are opened, participants need to close one tab before opening another one. (4) The search function: If users are lost or want to know their task progress, they are to click on the "search" button on the top right corner or use the "search" gesture. Therefore the participants will use the search function at least twice during the experiment. There are many ways to evaluate web browsing performances, such as recognition deduction, focus group, GOMS model, speed prototype, task analysis, interface investigation, and user tests [12, 13]. The index of learning possibility, recollection possibility, short-term memories, long-term memory load, and error and fatigue allowance were also objectively evaluated. Amongst which, task time and successful rate and user satisfaction are common interface design evaluation standards. These three indices have the same goal with the reaction time, error rate recognition, and confusion matrix in the laboratory regulations. Therefore the browsing gesture evaluation items for this experiment were set to be task time, error rate, NASA workload, and subjective assessment scales.

3   Results and Analysis

3.1   Browsing Gesture Sample Design

In this stage, six design professionals were invited for focus group discussions on the five functions derived from the observation and interview results from the first stage: back/next, zoom in/out, open new tab, close tab, and search. Adjective, noun, or verb association were done for the browsing functions and categorized into Table 1 for gesture design.

Table 1. Browsing function vocabulary association

	Portrait	Indicative	Metaphoric
Back/Next	cursor, back, skip	fork finger long/short (far/near), bottom left(back), top right(next), up(next), down(back), clicking frequency, arrow, direction	words, traffic lights
Zoom	magnifying class, balloon	distance between the index finger(far) and thumb(near), slanting angle, rotate, sound wave, forward and back dimensions, press/click, up to enlarge and down to shrink, compress	「+」 sign
New Tab	Homepage, home house, window	insert symbol, turn the page, flip up, divide, draw another circle, drag, pull page down, the feeling of paste, cut, check	plus sign, the number 2, N for new, H for home, A for add.
Close Tab	lock, seal, shut, close	trash can, throw, dump, cut, tear, completing a circle, period, shake, slide, invert, cover screen, outwards, flip away, eraser, cross out, paint	finish, 「×」 sign
Search	telescope, magnifying class	eye, fumble	S for search, Q for question, 「?」 sign

The 635 thinking method is used in stage 2 to design interface icon gestures. It is used to categorize a large amount of gesture interface in order to maintain the visibility of mobile phone reading. Movements require a big moving range such as those using arms will be excluded from the priority consideration list. Five feasible gestures were selected from each browsing function and redrawn on Table 2 using computers for the gesture recognition confusion matrix experiment in the following stage.

Table 2. Varies function gesture movement samples

Function	Gesture samples				
back/next	1 portrait	2 indicative	3b portrait	4 indicative	5 indicative
zoom	6 indicative	7 indicative	8 indicative	9 indicative	10 portrait
new tab	11 metaphoric	12 indicative	13 indicative	14 metaphoric	15 metaphoric
close tab	16 indicative	17 metaphoric	18 portrait	19 indicative	20 metaphoric
search	21 portrait	22 metaphoric	23 metaphoric	24 metaphoric	25 indicative

The results of confusion matrix refer to the confusion condition, recognition time, gesture satisfaction scores, and system recognition validity. The back/next gesture numbers 2 and 5 show no confusion, however, number 5 performed better in terms of time and satisfaction. The zoom gesture number 9 showed a lower confusion level than number 6 but similar user experience in terms of the zoom movement and touch-control in the back of the phone. Number 5 was chosen considering gripping stability of phone. The new tab gesture number 11 and the close tab gesture number 17 shared the same drawing shape in different angles (+ and ×). The finger angles in the touch-control from the back of the phone were not as horizontal or vertical as the front, therefore was deleted due to system recognition difficulties. The search gesture number 23 was revised subtly, simplifying the question mark image into a hook shape for easier gesture recognition input. Browsing gestures number 5, 6, 14, 17, and 23 were selected.

3.2   Browsing Gesture Feasibility Evaluation

The original zoom function operated by moving the thumb up and down on the side of the phone was improved to be moving the index finger on touch-screen on the back of the phone considering the high-frequency requirement of the thumb in the front, the hardware limitation of the model system, and the original gesture design concept (Fig. 1).

| back/next
indicative | zoom
indicative | new tab
metaphoric | close tab
metaphoric | search
metaphoric |

Fig. 1. Browsing gesture icon samples

The task completing time data of the three groups of operation models were analyzed using ANOVA. Under the condition of the test of homogeneity (p>0.05), this represents the reliability of the sample observation variance. A significant difference showed between the task completion time of the groups. In the post hoc analysis, a significant difference showed between the two-handed and the single-handed groups. There was no significant difference with either of the groups in gesture. The average task completion time for gesture was slightly lower than the single-handed group. Since the target size has an effect on the accuracy rate of the clicking, it was found from table 3 that there was no significant difference in size with any of the group during clicking. The main factor that affects the error rate should be the operation mode. The target clicking error data of the three operation modes were analyzed using ANOVA (Table 3) and significant difference shoed between the three gesture groups (p<0.05). In the post hoc analysis, there was a significant difference between the single-handed group and the gesture group. There was no significant difference between the two-handed group and either of the groups. The average error rate for the two-handed group was higher than the gesture group.

Table 3. ANOVA analysis result for the browsing gesture system

Item	S.S.	df	M.S.	F	Post Hoc
Task completion time	47256.72	2	23628.36	6.34*	Single-handed > two-handed, gesture
Target size	676.52	2	338.26	1.56	
Error rate	41.05	2	20.52	3.91*	Single-handed > gesture, two-handed

From the NASA workload scale ANOVA analysis results (Fig. 2), we found no significant difference in mental and physical strength used for task completion between the three groups (p>0.05). This shows no additional fatigue caused by gestures. The results match the analysis results for the operation mode subjective measurement scale. There was no significant difference in the wrist fatigue level between the three groups (p>0.05). From the average score we can see a lower level of haste and urgency when using two hands, with the highest time pressure felt by the gesture group. There was a positive relationship between the effort level, frustration, and gesture recognition rate. Integrating the above results, the browsing gesture input interface was less intuitive in operation performance than the conventional two-handed group, however showed a trend of better performance than the conventional single-handed group under situation simulation after learning. In terms of subjective evaluation, it scored better than the conventional groups, showing that the browsing gesture interface improves the operation feasibility of web page browsing.

The operation subjective scale ANOVA analysis results (Fig 3) showed significant difference between thumb fatigue, satisfaction, effort to use, effort to learn, and intuition. The post hoc analysis results show no significant difference between the usability of the single-handed and the gesture group. The gesture group showed a lower thumb fatigue level than the single-handed group.

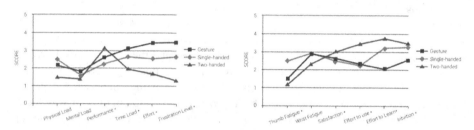

Fig. 2. NASA workload average score   **Fig. 3.** Operation mode subjective average

As a whole, the lack of sensitivity of the gesture recognition of the system has resulted in a higher effort level and frustration. However, in terms of the objective performance items such as task time and error rate, the gesture group performed better than the single-handed group. In the future, the system hardware recognition rate needs to be improved in order to elevate user subjective satisfaction as a whole.

4   Discussion

The metaphoric "search" function in the non-confusion number 21 and 23 gestures each represents the "S" and the "?" symbol. Considering users with different language backgrounds and recognitions, the "?" symbol is able to lower the usability difference even more. Users prefer reversing the words and images in the back. This matches the "see through" expectation in literature review [6, 14].

When constructing the browsing simulation system, it is important to pay attention to the confusion compatibility between gesture icons. For example the × symbol may result in users starting the movement from different starting points. The system needs to be able to recognize that these are the same command. Due to the gripping posture, movements from top to bottom are easier than from bottom to top; horizontal finger movements are easier than vertical; however, strokes moving in the back tend to slant. This matches the information from literature review [15]. During the experiment, the two-handed group took the shortest time to complete the tasks. The single-handed group and the gesture group were limited by physical strains and took a longer task time. Amongst which the gesture group was slightly faster than the single-handed group. The gesture group is affected by recognition sensitivity. Users need to be trained and maintain the feel of the operation. This causes more obvious individual differences. Users who learned better showed a completion time close to the two-handed group.

During single-handed operation, the average clicking target size was 7.6mm, which matches the literature review [16, 17]. In error rate evaluation, although the single-handed and the gesture group both hold the phone with one hand and clicks with the thumb in the front, significant difference showed between the two groups. It is speculated to be caused by the thumb bending phenomena pointed out in the literature review [4, 18]. Since the mobile browsing function keys are often at the bottom of the screen, the thumb in the single-handed group has a bigger moving range on the screen and higher frequency of joint movement. These factors increase user fatigue and error rate. Although the users express doubts in the gripping stability, there was no significant difference between the wrist fatigue levels of the three groups. This shows no increase in the wrist load of users using the new gesture system. Other than that, during the experiment we found that the gesture group does not need to click on the function key at the bottom of the screen. Therefore, to match the touch control gesture from the back, users changed the gripping posture, moving thumbs closer to the center of the screen. This decreased the thumb moving distance and hence improved operation performance. The high error rate of the two-handed group resulted from touching invalid targets. This represented the actual situation of operating the zoom gesture but often touching wrong links while browsing websites.

Finally, from the subjective scale we can see that users think that the gesture group lowers thumb fatigue. However, low scores showed in categories of effort to learn, frustration, time load, and effort. These indexes are affected by the system recognition sensitivity. Users need to spend more time learning the "correct" gesture icons in order to avoid system confusion. If gesture icons were designed to be too similar, the system may recognize them as the same gesture, creating a low recognition rate, increasing user frustration. Although practice could improve on the feel of the operation, hardware system support should still be improved to lower the icon error rate.

5   Conclusion

This research begins with user experience, aims at improving operation performance with single-handed gripping mobile phones, developing a series of gestures to compare to conventional icon interfaces in order to work out gesture design principles and ways for improvement. There is no most correct or the best icon for various innovative gesture designs. We aim at lowering individual subjective differences from the most objective angle. From the observing stage, gesture design procedures, and the interface analysis results, we found the following phenomena: (1) The browsing function selected by the gesture system is able to fulfill the mobile web needs of users. (2)

The function type affects the gesture design development direction. (3) Browsing gesture lowers thumb fatigue level, error rate, and task completion time.

References

1. Karlson, A.K., Bederson, B.B., Contreras-Vidal, J.L.: Understanding One-Handed Use of Mobile Devices. In: Handbook of Research on User Interface Design and Evaluation for Mobile Technology. ch. 6. Idea Group Reference, Hershey (2008)
2. Lemmelä, S., Vetek, A., Mäkelä, K., Trendafilov, D.: Designing and evaluating multimodal interaction for mobile contexts. In: Proceedings of the 10th International Conference on Multimodal Interfaces, pp. 265–272 (2008)
3. Kellar, M., Watters, C., Shepherd, M.: A goal-based classification of web information tasks. The American Society for Information Science and Technology 43(1), 1–22 (2006)
4. Park, Y.S., Han, S.H.: One-handed thumb interaction of mobile devices from the input accuracy perspective. International Journal of Industrial Ergonomics 40(6), 746–756 (2010)
5. Keith, B.P., Juan Pablo, H.: Evaluating one handed thumb tapping on mobile touchscreen devices. In: Proceedings of Graphics Interface 2008, pp. 57–64 (2008)
6. Wobbrock, J.O., Myers, B.A., Aung, H.: The performance of hand postures in front- and back-of-device interaction for mobile computing. International Journal of Human-Computer Studies 66(12), 857–875 (2008)
7. Karam, M.: A taxonomy of gestures in human computer interactions. Southampton, United Kingdom (2005)
8. Miller, G.A.: The magical number seven, plus or minus two: some limits on our capacity for processing information. Psychological Review 63(2), 81 (1956)
9. Nielsen, J.: Usability Engineering. Morgan Kaufmann, San Francisco (1993)
10. Top 9 mobile browsers (2012),
    http://gs.statcounter.com/#mobile_browser-ww-monthly-201101-201201
11. Fitts, P.M.: The information capacity of the human motor system in controlling the amplitude of movement. Journal of Experiental Psychology 47, 381–391 (1954)
12. Fu, L., Salvendy, G.: The contribution of apparent and inherent usability to a user's satisfaction in a searching and browsing task on the Web. Ergonomics 45(6), 415–424 (2002)
13. Nathan, R.J., Yeow, P.H.P.: Crucial web usability factors of 36 industries for students: a large-scale empirical study. Electronic Commerce Research 11(2), 151–180 (2011)
14. Wigdor, D., Forlines, C., Baudisch, P., Barnwell, J., Shen, C.: Lucid touch: a see-through mobile device. In: Proceedings of the 20th Annual ACM Symposium on User Interface Software and Technology, pp. 269–278 (2007)
15. Wobbrock, J.O., Chau, D.H., Myers, B.A.: An alternative to push, press, and tap-tap-tap: gesturing on an isometric joystick for mobile phone text entry. In: Proceedings of the SIGCHI Conference on Human Factors in Computing Systems, pp. 667–676 (2007)
16. Han, S.H., Park, Y.S.: Touch key design for one-handed thumb interaction with a mobile phone: Effects of touch key size and touch key location. International Journal of Industrial Ergonomics 40(1), 68–76 (2010)
17. Parhi, P., Karlson, A.K., Bederson, B.B.: Target size study for one-handed thumb use on small touchscreen devices. In: Proceedings of the 8th Conference on Human-Computer Interaction with Mobile Devices and Services, pp. 203–210 (2006)
18. Karlson, A.K., Bederson, B.B.: One-handed touchscreen input for legacy applications. In: Proceedings of the 26th Annual SIGCHI Conference on Human Factors in Computing Systems, pp. 1399–1408 (2008)

Author Index

694   Author Index